Remembered Childhoods

Remembered Childhoods

A Guide to Autobiography and Memoirs of Childhood and Youth

Jeffrey E. Long

LIBRARIES

UNLIMITED

OCM 85830722

A Member of the Greenwood Publishing Group

Westport, Connecticut • London

Library of Congress Cataloging-in-Publication Data

Long, Jeffrey E., 1953–
    Remembered childhoods : a guide to autobiography and memoirs of childhood and youth / Jeffrey E. Long.
      p. cm.
    Includes bibliographical references and indexes.
    ISBN 978–1–59158–174–1 (alk. paper)
    1. Autobiography—Bibliography. 2. Children—Biography—Bibliography.
    3. Youth—Biography—Bibliography. I. Title.
    Z5304.C5L66 2007
    [CT25]
    016.920—dc22   2007009011

British Library Cataloguing in Publication Data is available.

Library of Congress Catalog Card Number: 2007009011
ISBN-13: 978–1–59158–174–1

First published in 2007

Libraries Unlimited, 88 Post Road West, Westport, CT 06881
A Member of the Greenwood Publishing Group, Inc.
www.lu.com

Printed in the United States of America

♾™

The paper used in this book complies with the
Permanent Paper Standard issued by the National
Information Standards Organization (Z39.48–1984).

10 9 8 7 6 5 4 3 2 1

To Christine, who always encourages me

Contents

Acknowledgments

In this endeavor, I am indebted to a number of present and former library colleagues and friends. At the Lamar Soutter Library (University of Massachusetts Medical School), I am most grateful for the assistance and encouragement of Astrid Bergner, Nancy Boucher, Karen Cangello, Heather Chesna, Matthew Clark, Harvey Fenigsohn, Paul Julian, and David Pietrantoni.

Also, I would like to thank the following individuals with whom I worked in Colorado: Babette Hills, Robert Labaree, Trudy May, Elaine Weaver, and the late, great Frank Schmaus. (In his avuncular way, Frank could—and did—expertly advise Aurora [CO] Public Library patrons on everything from how to evaluate a mutual fund to how to build a Conestoga wagon.)

I am appreciative of Stan Haney, of the Holden (MA) Gale Free Library, for his generous sharing of reference materials.

I also want to thank my editors, Barbara Ittner and Sharon DeJohn. Their insights, patience, and tireless work with my manuscript deserve special recognition.

I extend my profound gratitude to my wife, Chris, whose loving counsel has sustained me and, perforce, this project, in ways too numerous to mention. Finally, although they did not live long enough to see this work to its completion, my parents are foremost in my thoughts as I send this manuscript to press. For they lovingly provided me with my own "remembered childhood"—one filled with memories I will forever treasure.

Of course, I alone am responsible for any errors of commission or omission in this book. I would appreciate these being brought to my attention, in care of the publisher.

Introduction: Autobiography, Memoir, and Biography

Usually told from a first-person perspective, prose writing said to be *autobiographical* is a narrative of someone's recollections, telling of his or her active or passive roles in one or more actual events or other experiences that occurred during his or her lifetime. Traditionally, these related occurrences are arranged in chronological order. Unlike *biographical* writing, it supplies a view of a life that is unmediated—not having been filtered through the eyes of another person.

The most articulate autobiographer is a sort of literary alchemist, who is able to transmute the inchoate and unvoiced dross of memory into a golden narrative that will both entertain and instruct. (At the other extreme, the driest of autobiographical writing may read like a ship's log or may seem to serve but as a catch basin for one person's regurgitated memories.)

Autobiography versus Memoir

Autobiographical prose writings fall into the subcategories of *autobiography* and *memoir*. An autobiography is a writer's recounting of the better part of a lifetime's worth of experiences that have most influenced the course of his or her life. It may possess some kind of thematic unity, or it may be little more than a shapeless gathering of events that spill across one page after another.

On the other hand, a memoir is an especially reflective type of autobiographical writing that usually covers a shorter time span. From the pages of a memoir we may glean the wisdom distilled from all manner of human experience—whether the experience be that of a holy pilgrimage or a prison sentence. In contrast, the plural of this term, *memoirs*, is synonymous with *autobiography*, because its focus can be as wide as its subject's lifetime.

In its concentrated re-creating of but a slice of life, a memoir may achieve greater coherence and unity through the use of a touchstone: a thematic link to a particular place, incident, person, or idea. Common touchstones that provide effective focus for a memoir include love affairs, college years, sibling relationships, battles with physical or emotional illness, or associations with a particular city or house. Using this book's subject index, examples of memoirs that embody these particular touchstones may be located. (See such index terms as "Sexuality," "College Life," "Brothers," "Mental Health," or "City Life.")

For many readers the term *autobiography* is apt to conjure thoughts of ponderous volumes containing exhaustive accounts of lives, their lengthy narratives' details having been laboriously corroborated for historical fidelity with pedantic rigor. As provenance of the scrupulousness of their factual accuracy, such autobiographies usually include many pages of endnotes and other accoutrements from academia. A memoir, on the other hand, is often thought of as a more impressionistic rendering of memory, and is therefore more likely to be forgiven for any laxity in its adherence to truth.

Although no doubt today's memoirs are often of the "dysfunctional family" or "kiss and tell" variety, produced from motives involving money, celebrity, or revenge, there have always been many additional reasons for people committing their reminiscences to paper.

The earliest memoirs were often confessional, with their authors admitting to lives of compromised virtue or sin.

Such works—at times written in the shadow of the gallows—sometimes culminated in proselytizing proclamations of their memoirists' having undergone religious conversion or other spiritual salvation. Other memoirs written under duress include battlefield and jailhouse journals, and writings chronicling painful times spent in hospitals, hospices, or asylums, battling the effects of alcoholism, emotional abuse, or other internal demons.

At the other end of the spectrum from memoirs by the wretched, the imprisoned, and the impoverished are those by heads of state and leaders of religions and businesses. These autobiographical works often trace "rags to riches" lives that began humbly and advanced to ones of great influence.

Memoirs of a less dramatic nature have been set down by elderly persons from all walks of life, who wished to leave behind an oral record of their lives for their immediate family members. Other individuals, seeking neither fame nor money for their recorded reminiscences, have simply tried to make sense of their lives by penning the memories of how they spent their years, while trying to place their actions and relationships into the context of the times. Still others have tried their hand at this genre primarily as a gratifying diversion during their retirement or convalescence from an illness.

Coming-of-Age Memoirs

What, then, is a *coming-of-age memoir*? It is a piece of autobiographical writing that usually relates a series of life experiences or widening cultural horizons that coincide with the emergence of a more mature worldview for the individual whose life is being examined. In the case of writings that tell of early years of brutality and abuse, it could be argued that the memoirist emerges from his or her recollections with little if anything more than physical survival. (Examples of such harrowing accounts include those by David Pelzer, Nicole Lea Helget, and Sue William Silverman.)

A coming-of-age memoir may be as brief as an essay or diary, or as lengthy as a multivolume autobiography (such as those by Maya Angelou, Ved Mehta, Leonard Woolf, or Osbert Sitwell). Some such memoirs focus on a particular era or part of the writer's life; others encompass an entire lifetime of experience.

Sometimes unexpected and unusual circumstances result in an adult's ability to recapture vivid recollections of his or her earliest years. W. H. Hudson famously wrote his 1918 memoir *Far Away and Long Ago* while recovering from an illness during his later years. Without warning one day, as though clouds in his mind had temporarily parted, his mind was able to view scenes of his childhood in South America with stunning clarity. Before they could fade, he put pen to paper.

In another instance, unexpectedly graphic recall of childhood was documented by professor of psychology A. R. Luria, in his 1972 book *The Man with a Shattered World*. Luria tells of a Russian soldier, Zasetsky, who, following a brain wound during World War II, found his memory was almost entirely limited to events, persons, and places of his childhood. As the soldier expressed it, his memories suddenly came from "the wrong end" of his life.

The Value of Memoirs

For a teacher, a specialized scholar, or a general reader, a well-written memoir is a uniquely valuable form of writing, differing from a short story or novel, in that it directly describes places, events, and persons that actually interacted with the author during his or her lifetime. Memoirs are perhaps the ultimate form of immersion journalism. Who better to describe the battle of Gettysburg than a soldier who fought there? Who can better describe the effects of juvenile diabetes than someone who suffered it? On the other hand, the human ego being what it is, an autobiography usually shows its human subject in a favorable light and includes events selectively, presenting them from perspectives that are most sympathetic to that person.

Rooted in reality, a memoir attempts to re-create this reality by employing imagery for both the inner eye and ear of the reader. The best memoirs achieve a balance between their amount of physical detail (such as descriptions of landscape and architecture) and dialogue (such as reconstituted conversations expressed as direct quotation). If a memoir relies too heavily on physical detail, its tone may approach that of a bloodless sociological study. On the other hand, if the pages of a memoir are overspread with little else but reconstructed conversations, the work will take on the contrived feel of a novel or the sensationalized tone of a tabloid.

Itinerant memoirs (of immigrants, pioneers, refugees) or those that are set in bucolic or exotic locales (jungles, summer resorts, mountains) tend to include more visually descriptive details than those that are set in uninspiring, cookie-cutter locales (despirited cities, strip mall suburbia), or that strongly focus on tidal forces of emotion between persons in the memoir. The autobiographical writings of John Muir, Elizabeth Hamilton, and George Woodcock exemplify the former of these, while the memoirs of Frank McCourt, June Jordan, and Patsy Klein illustrate the latter.

The Value of Coming-of-Age Memoirs

Coming-of-age memoirs are valuable and engaging resources for professionals and amateurs spanning all disciplines, as well as for the recreational reader. Librarians, teachers, psychologists, social workers, sociologists, genealogists and local history buffs will find these works to be a goldmine for their research. Extended first-person accounts are filled with background information on folkways and living conditions that may be difficult or impossible to access in standard history texts or elsewhere.

In addition, the beginnings of an individual's earliest (and often most vivid) senses of consciousness, identity, and loyalty (to communities involving family, religion, or nationality) are found in such writings. First articulations of personal philosophies and the first stirrings of a person's moral compass are discernible in early childhood memoirs, as well.

Using *Remembered Childhoods*, a teacher might motivate a reluctant reader by recommending a memoir by a celebrity (like an athlete or movie star) or a memoir dealing with a student's favorite sport or hobby. Teachers planning a unit on a foreign country, past or present, can quickly pull together a list of memoirs by men or women who grew up abroad or who are multiethnic Americans. Many students will find emotional connections between their own lives and those of the many cultural and ethnic minorities represented in this book's diverse selections.

As a reading therapy resource, this bibliography abounds with potential uses. Counselors, social workers, and therapists can refer victims of abuse to empowering memoirs by survivors of various physical, emotional, and sexual traumas. Similarly, to gain helpful perspectives from thoughtful writers, adoptees and adoptive parents can draw from the memoirs here that address pertinent issues in their lives.

A college student taking a history class can easily locate reminiscences by members of the "Baby Boom" generation or memoirs by persons subjected to racism in their youth. Professional and armchair historians will find memoirs by writers who, as civilians or soldiers, personally experienced the horror of war, or survived times of economic depression, or felt the chill of the Cold War. Local history buffs and genealogists will find telling accounts of the quotidian ways found in small country towns. General readers in the mood for a coming-of-age memoir in a lighter vein will be greeted with the writings of Jean Shepherd, Richard Armour, Catherine Gildiner, and other humorists.

As we read a memoir, in our gut we feel what it must have been like, decades or a century ago, to have been a Jew living in Nazi Germany, a girl working in a textile mill, an African American growing up on a plantation, or a teenage American soldier fighting in Vietnam. As we finish a memoir and return to our everyday realities, we are better able to understand the world we find ourselves in today. We are better able to understand the roots of the beliefs and lifestyles that divide or unite today's peoples by philosophy, religion, folkway, ethnicity, race, culture, or country.

The Need for and Purpose of This Book

Until now, little attention has been paid to the literary genres of autobiography and memoir. Recent writings (e.g., readers' advisory guides) have not provided assistance to those seeking memoirs for pleasure reading or research. This book attempts to remedy this gap in the reference literature, with its listing of more than 2,800 memoirs and autobiographies of youth, and organizes them by both broad and more narrow thematic content.

The Scope of This Book

Remembered Childhoods focuses on memoirs that detail the pre-adult years of their authors—that is, they cover some part of the first 21 years of the authors' lives. These most frequently consist of "coming-of-age" stories. A smaller number of the entries here are autobiographical works that focus on an even briefer period of the memoirist's life. For example, the works by Elizabeth Hamilton and Vladimir Soloukhin focus on only their first 7 years of life. The published recollections of Martin Booth, Lidiia Chukovskaia, Miles Franklin, Maurice Hayes, Frank Kendon, and Julian Maclaren-Ross cover only the first 10 years of their lives.

Some works target only a single year during a memoirist's youth. Farley Mowat's *The Dog Who Wouldn't Be* describes his life at age 8. A. E. Hotchner's reminiscence *Looking for Miracles* is limited to the summer when he was 16. Rosemary Mahoney writes only of her girlhood at 17, when she kept house for dramatist Lillian Hellman. Ralph Moody's *Shaking the Nickel Bush* concerns the author's life only when he was 19. Joseph Joffo re-creates 3 years of his boyhood in France during World War II, while Ernest Hillen describes conditions on Java during the 2 years that followed the war. Sterling North's classic memoir *Rascal* takes place entirely when the author was 11.

Among published diarists, Henry Shute tells of his boyhood in New Hampshire only while he was 11 years old. Anna Green Winslow's account is restricted to her girlhood from ages 12 to 14. That of Frances Wentworth Custer covers her life only during the days when she was between 15 and 16.

The memoirs included here are books that either were originally written in English or have been translated into English. Chronologically, the childhoods and periods of adolescence depicted in them span nearly 3 centuries, from the youthful exploits of Giacomo Casanova (born 1725) to memoirs published in 2007. (Casanova is but one of two dozen persons born in the 18th century whose early recollections have been included in this resource.)

Unusual parallels at times are evident among such a large body of literature that covers so many time periods. For example, a century apart, the first significant memories for Anna Clary and Jake Lamar were, respectively, reports of the deaths of Presidents Lincoln and Kennedy. Not surprisingly, a good number of the writings cited in this volume are set in New York City. What is surprising is that more than one memoir (those by Mark Salzman and Brenda Cullerton) is set in the small city of Ridgefield, Connecticut. One will occasionally encounter two or more memoirs by authors who share the same name (e.g., Henry James).

Although the majority of cited works are set in the U.S., hundreds of memoirs listed and described in this resource are set in other countries around the world. Likewise, memoirs written from all time periods have been collected within these covers. The user will encounter autobiographies by the famous, the infamous, and the obscure. Following the main body of the book, an appendix covering collective coming-of-age memoirs appears; this appendix has its own subject index.

Over the past 2 centuries, throughout the English-speaking world, thousands of publication houses and small presses have produced a staggering volume of autobiographical works. Many of these works were published in small or limited runs, received little if any critical notice or review, and today are out of print, at best to be found in but a few libraries around the world. Therefore, though this compilation aspires to be thorough in scope, it does not pretend to be exhaustive in its citations.

The publishing of coming-of-age memoirs enjoyed a noticeable upsurge in volume starting in the 1990s with the appearance of such works as *Girl, Interrupted*, by Susanna Kaysen (1993), and *Angela's Ashes*, by Frank McCourt (1996). Well-written as they are, these and similar recollections of abusive childhoods helped to spawn an avalanche of memoirs during the latter half of that decade—to such an extent that *New York Times* writer Michael Vincent Miller issued a public appeal for aspiring authors to produce accounts of refreshingly nondysfunctional childhoods. Examples of memoirs that answered Miller's plea include Marianne Gingher's *A Girl's Life* and Haven Kimmel's *A Girl Named Zippy*, both issued in 2001.

Another interesting subgenre concerns memoirs by relatives, lovers, friends, or other associates of celebrities. Arthur Miller, husband of Marilyn Monroe, offers a memoir, as does Marilyn's friend Susan Strasberg. British writers Christopher Milne and Richard Adams were acquaintances. J. D. Salinger is recalled by his lover Joyce Maynard; Joyce Johnson, intimate of Jack Kerouac, has also written a memoir.

For several decades, perhaps starting with Brooke Hayward's *Haywire* (1977) and Christina Crawford's *Mommie Dearest* (1978), a sizable portion of published memoirs has focused on an individual's formative years spent in the shadow of a celebrity parent. Not all such works paint negative or checkered portraits of parental figures, however. Some stand as loving tributes. In this volume are memoirs by sons or daughters of such notables as Archibald MacLeish, James Dickey, Joseph Conrad, Nathaniel Hawthorne, Robert Frost, Anne Sexton, Richard Brautigan, Martin Luther King Jr., Lafcadio Hearn (Kazuo Koizumi), Nat King Cole, Pat Boone, Judy Garland (Lorna Luft), Lucy Stone (Alice Blackwell), Brigham Young (Clarissa Spencer), Oscar Wilde (Vyvyan Holland), Thomas Mann, and Janet Flanner.

Grandchildren of celebrities have also occasionally produced autobiographical volumes of note. Some of these include those by Gwen Raverat (granddaughter of Charles Darwin), as well as the granddaughter of Ernest Hemingway and the grandson of John Philip Sousa. Ned Wynn tells of his childhood years in Hollywood as the son of actor Keenan Wynn and grandson of comic Ed Wynn.

Mothers and sons who have each contributed a memoir of their individual youths include Angela Thirkell—herself a cousin of Rudyard Kipling—and Graham McInnes. (Speaking of cousins, Elspeth Huxley, a cousin of Julian Huxley and Aldous Huxley, has contributed 3 memoirs to this volume.) Fathers and sons who have done likewise include Christopher and Alexander Milne, William Cooper Howells and William Dean Howells, Franklin and John Gould, and Evelyn and Auberon Waugh. Fathers and daughters who have done so include Richard Henry Dana Jr. and Henrietta Skinner, as well as Kornei Chukovsky and Lidiia Chukovskaia. Mothers and daughters who have done so include Mary and Emily Lutyens, as well as Charlotte and Madeleine Bingham.

In rare instances, memoirs have been coauthored by relatives. In this coming-of-age memoir compilation, such works may be found by consulting the subject index under the category "Collaborations Between Relatives."

Youthful recollections by siblings of the famed (and the infamous) include those by the brother or sister of President Eisenhower, William Faulkner, James Joyce, Hilaire Belloc (Bessie Lowndes), and executed killer Gary Gilmore. Siblings who have each penned a memoir of youth include Julian and Anne Green, Jon and Rumer Godden, Gypsy Rose Lee and June Havoc, Osbert and Sacheverell Sitwell, Alec and Evelyn Waugh, Golo and Klaus Mann, and Tobias and Geoffrey Wolff. A memoir will also be found here by activist Virginia Foster Durr, sister-in-law of Supreme Court Justice Hugo Black. Lylah Barber, wife of sportswriter "Red" Barber, has written a memoir of her early years, as well.

Memoirs by the nephew of a celebrity include those by the nephews of Lytton Strachey and Alec Waugh. Agnes De Mille, niece of Cecil B. De Mille, also has written a volume listed here. Spouses who have each written a memoir of youth include Peter and Ruth Gay, Gladys and Van Wyck Brooks, Marion and Arthur Schlesinger Jr., Anthony and (Lady) Violet Powell, and Charles and Anne Morrow Lindbergh. (Their daughter, Reeve, also produced a coming-of-age reminiscence.)

Selection Criteria

To bring some measure of meaningfulness to this enterprise, I have established several criteria for a given work's inclusion in this volume. I have cited only memoirs available in English or English translation that contain at least 50 pages on some or all of the authors' first 21 years. More than 80 percent of the memoirs by individuals that are listed here, however, devote many more than 50 pages to their authors' formative years. A sizeable number of autobiographical works cited here contain 100 pages or more on their authors' early years. Although the memoirist usually appears as an infant or young person in the opening pages of coming-of-age memoirs, such is not always the case. For example, Cornelia Otis Skinner is not seen in *Family Circle* until page 114.

Few works of autobiography can claim absolute fidelity to truth, for the human mind is imperfect in its retention of events. Furthermore, except for diaries and journals, the works cited in this volume were usually written a good many years after the events depicted in them, which occurred during the authors' formative years.

Also, when writing for the public eye about oneself, it is but human nature to equivocate, mention only in passing, or leave out discussion of unflattering acts one has committed. That said, generally, for a given work to be listed in this compilation as a coming-of-age memoir, it must appear to substantially succeed in faithfully and vividly evoking the feel and spirit of the personalities, events, and other significant forces that shaped the author's early years.

Moreover, one cannot always easily or clearly distinguish between a memoir, a semiautobiographical account, and an autobiographical novel. My aim has been to exclude autobiographical novels, such as Kenneth Rexroth's self-professed volume *An Autobiographical Novel* (1966) and Jan Myrdal's series *Childhood* (1982), *Another World* (1994), and *Twelve Going on Thirteen* (1995). (Myrdal explicitly informs his readers that his writings are to be regarded essentially as works of fiction rather than autobiography.)

As in most attempts to neatly define a category of genre literature, gray areas have arisen here. Ruling in or ruling out a given title has not always been easy. For example, in the writing of *A Vicarage Family: An Autobiographical Story* (1963), Noel Streatfeild admits to having altered some persons' names, including his own first name. There is no apparent reason to dismiss the work out of hand as a fabrication, however, so it has been included here.

Of course, the masking of principals' names within a memoir is most often done out of respect for the individuals or for the legal protection of the memoirist (as in the case of writer Gelsey Kirkland). In his moving autobiography, *Farther Off from Heaven* (1976), William Humphrey states, "The names of some of the people who figure in this account have been changed to spare them or their survivors pain or embarrassment." Stella Suberman, in her memoir *The Jew Store*, cloaks the identity of her Tennessee hometown under the fictitious name "Concordia."

Alternatively, autobiographers will sometimes provide some emotional—though not necessarily factual—distance between their memories of events and their recording of them by adopting a third-person perspective in their memoirs. Examples of this technique here include Bill Cullen's *It's a Long Way from Penny Apples* (2003) and Margaret Bailey's *Good-bye Proud World* (1945).

To enliven his or her written remembrances, a memoirist frequently will re-create dialogue between his or her recollected persona and that of others in the book. Usually such reconstructed dialogue is interwoven around both passages of physical description (of settings and events) and voicings of the memoirist's past or present thoughts and emotions (expressed through such devices as metaphor, emotive language, or direct asides to the reader).

In fashioning such dialogue, the memoirist runs the risk of unnecessarily embellishing his or her recollections with artfully contrived language that may significantly diverge from what actually was said during the period being evoked. It must be recognized, however, that an ostensibly autobiographical work's inclusion of dialogue (or other conventional elements of fiction, such as complicating incidents or climax) does not provide sufficient reason for it to be summarily cast out of the body of literature known as "memoir."

As attested to by the large number of memoirists' names found under "Novelists" and "Short Story Writers" in this volume, fiction writers are extraordinarily suited for the crafting of engaging memoir. To shape a memoir using some tools of the novelist is not necessarily to introduce inauthenticity of experience or falsity of fact into an autobiography. Such works as Edward Lodi's *Deep Meadow Bog: Memoirs of a Cape Cod Childhood* (1999) and Floyd Salas's *Buffalo Nickel: A Memoir* (1992) borrow novelistic technique while communicating to us, through the filter of their authors' memories, the essence of their remembered youth. Two other memoirs that appropriately employ novelistic trappings are those represented here by Eva Krutein and John Mullen. Perhaps this compilation's most imaginatively formatted memoir is John Gallant's compelling volume *Bannock, Beans and Black Tea* (2004), which effectively recounts the hardships of the author's Depression-era youth in the form of a graphic novel.

Better-written memoirs of youth maintain a viable balance between re-created dialogue, narrative description, and interior monologue. Without the bedrock of authentic persona, setting, and social context, a purported memoir whose structure is built of little else but re-created dialogue tends to wholly gravitate into the realm of fiction—which is to say, the realm of unreliable memoir.

Nevertheless, some allowance has been made to accommodate the lighthearted, chatty works of such humorists and family memoirists as Jean Shepherd, Cornelia Otis Skinner, Patrick McManus, Frank Gilbreth, and Daniel Pinkwater. (The "Humorists" and "Family Memoirs" entries in the subject index provide a complete listing of these lively memoirs of youth.) If, as Shakespeare claimed, "Many a truth there lies in jest," so it is that, in the shaping of a memoir, a gifted writer may be pardoned for occasionally using exaggeration or other comic contrivances to more aptly and vividly illuminate truths from his or her early years.

I have included caveats in the annotations of some entries, such as for the supposed memoir of cowboy Siringo, some of whose authenticity has been challenged by such scrupulous scholars as Ramon Adams. On the other hand, Gay Talese's fine semiautobiographical account, *Unto the Sons* (1992), is essentially a novelistic transmutation of his upbringing and family heritage, and therefore has been excluded.

Organization

This guide is organized thematically, or more specifically by the types of characters and lives covered in the works. Thus, there are chapters on "Travelers and Captive," "Thinkers and Believers," "Survivors and Victims," and "The Darker Side of Childhood." While the lives of the individual memoirists are generally the focal point in these writings, often a setting or cultural context plays an important role—as in "Homes and Haunts," "Connections with Nature," and "Multicultural Heritage." Obviously there is overlap in many of these themes, and many, if not most, books could fit into more than one category.

In such cases, categorization has been carried out according to my own best judgment, and cross-references in chapter introductions will, in some instances, lead users to related titles.

Users should refer to the subject index for further readings in any specific area. In particular, note that authors who have most prolifically contributed memoirs can be found in many chapters besides chapter 9, placed according to strong themes in their work. For example, the memoir of humorist writer Richard Armour is located in chapter 13, because much of his youth was spent in his father's pharmacy; the bookish recollection by fiction writer Heinrich Boll appears in chapter 8, listed among works by kindred intellectuals.

How to Use This Book

There are several means by which users can find those memoirs most useful to them. The table of contents and subject, settings, and author/title indexes allow the user quick thematic and bibliographic access to entries containing annotated descriptions for the thousands of coming-of-age memoirs contained in this book.

If one wishes to find out whether a certain person has written a coming-of-age memoir, simply consult the author/title index. One should also turn to this index to learn whether a known title has been cited in this book.

For broad subject access to the memoirs contained in this work, refer to the table of contents, which divides the bibliographies into 17 thematic chapters. If one is interested in perusing autobiographical writings according to their geographical focus, within or outside of the U.S., refer especially to the settings index and chapter 4, "Homes and Haunts," but do not overlook the subject index for works about some particular, general, or widespread locales (e.g., "Mississippi River," "Oil Fields," "Harvard University," "Jungle Life," "Island Life," "Mountain Life," "Lakes," "Resorts," "Worldwide Travel," "Voyages"). Memoirs that bear on blends of ethnic and national identity generally are largely found in chapter 5, "Multicultural Heritages," while personal recollections by immigrants and refugees are usually located in chapter 16, "The Darker Side of Childhood."

To locate a coming-of-age memoir according to its author's source of employment as an adult, consult chapters 8 through 15. These afford access to coming-of-age memoirs by persons engaged in such careers and fields as teaching, librarianship, historical scholarship, religion, social reform, children's authors, novelists, painters, fashion designers, architects, film stars, musicians, athletes, physicians, inventors, engineers, leaders (business, religion, politics), heads of state, and lawyers and judges.

To find additional memoirs that relate to vocation and to specific topics grouped by narrower subject categories, go to the comprehensive subject index. The subject index contains nearly 700 subject entries with extensive cross-indexing.

Subject entries direct the user to memoirs that focus on such important coming-of-age influences as setting, ethnicity, dysfunctional behavior, medical issues, sports, generations (e.g., "Baby Boomers," "Growing Up Between WWI and WWII," "Generation X") , family members and dynamics, religion, social reform, and modes of transportation (e.g., "Hitchhiking," "Railroad Travel," "Road Trips").

When a series of books or sequels/companion volumes by one author are listed, they are in publication date or chronological order, not alphabetical.

Elements of a Sample Entry

Sawamura, Sadako (1908–1996). Tr. from the Japanese by Norman E. Stafford and Yasuhiro Kawamura. *My Asakusa: Coming of Age in Pre-War Japan* (Tuttle, 2000) (First published in Japanese, 1976).
Entire memoir focuses on her first 21 years.
Motion Picture Actresses and Actors | Japan

This sample entry is from chapter 4, "Homes and Haunts." More specifically, this memoir is classified with other memoirs in the 9th section of chapter 4, which focuses on Asian cultures.

The name of the memoir's author ("Sawamura, Sadako") is given, followed by his or her year of birth (if known) and death (if the author is deceased and the date of death is known; if the author is not deceased, or is deceased but no date of death is known, there is a space after the dash: 1860–). A question mark (?) before or within a year denotes *less* uncertainty than "c." (circa). For example, "1931?–2003" suggests that it is very likely that the author was born no more than one year (1930 or 1932) removed from 1931. On the other hand, "c. 1931–2003" suggests that the author was born sometime in the late 1920s or early 1930s. If no date of birth or death appears, it is because such dates could not be determined or even estimated. If the author was known to be alive in a certain year or time period and no definite date of death is known, "living [year or decade]" is used: "1909–living 2003" or "1915–living 1990s." The name of the person(s) who translated the work into English (Norman E. Stafford and Yasuhiro Kawamura) follow(s). Next appear the memoir's title and subtitle (*My Asakusa: Coming of Age in Pre-War Japan*).

Next is the book's publication information, also in parentheses: the name of the publisher followed by its copyright year or first year of publication. If the work had earlier appeared in a language other than English, that fact is noted following the main publication information.

If a variant title of Sawamura's memoir had existed, it would be noted in parentheses following the publisher information. Such variants most often appear in this work in instances in which a British edition of a memoir has been given a title that differs from that given the same memoir's American counterpart.

For most entries a brief annotation of the memoir's scope or themes appears. In some citations, brief statements appear, such as "Pages 3–122" or "To 23 years." The first of these means that the first 21 years of the memoirist are focused on in pages 3 through 122. The second of these annotations means that the memoir covers the first 23 years of the author's life.

Some annotations include cross-references to other entries in the book; unless these specify the location of the related entry, readers should refer to the indexes to locate those entries.

Finally, entries provide subject and setting terms. In the instance of this citation, one gleans that the memoirist was involved with film acting and lived during most or all of her formative years in Japan. To find additional coming-of-age memoirs by actors or actresses, one could turn to this subject term ("Motion Picture Actresses and Actors") in the subject index.

Regarding subject entries that name a particular generation or other defined span of years, it should be noted that the intent is to point out memoirs set during periods of clearly identifiable cultural influence. For instance, the entry "Victoria Era British Memoirists" focuses on memoirs of persons born in the British empire from 1860 to 1895, despite the fact that Queen Victoria's reign began in 1837. Because neither the popularity nor the cultural influences of this ruler were significant until about 1870, a memoir chronicling, for example, an 1850s British childhood would more likely reflect vestigial cultural influences of the prior monarch, King William IV. Subject terms are separated by a diamond symbol. A question mark (?) after a subject term indicates that it is likely, but not certain, that the term is appropriate for that memoir. For some memoirs, no subjects could be determined.

A thin vertical line separates the subject terms from the following settings terms. The order of settings place-names is intended to approximate the chronological order of specific significant places at which the memoirist resided or otherwise spent time, according to the book being considered. Where a specific setting could not be identified, no settings terms are included. These sequences are not intended to provide an exhaustive itinerary of all places visited by the author throughout the pages of his or her memoir. In some instances, it is probable but not certain that a memoirist visited or resided in a given setting; in these cases that memoirist's bibliographical entry has a "(?)" next to the setting(s) in question.

In these strings of place-names, parentheses have been used to convey two types of information: either (1) a more modern place-name for the term that (accompanied by "i.e.") precedes the parentheses, or (2) the name of a smaller place (such as a city) that is located within a larger place (such as a Canadian province); in such an instance, the name of the larger place appears immediately preceding the place-name(s) in the parentheses.

Summary

In summary, coming-of-age memoirs and autobiographies open up and guide us through worlds of human experience in a visceral and immediate way that we could not know any way else. Like a time machine, memoirs take us back to the trappings of another era, a place that is best encountered, explored, and analyzed in its own terms, rather than in the terms familiar to us in the 21st century.

An effectively composed coming-of-age memoir represents one of the greatest challenges for a writer to produce, for it seeks to recapture the details and flavor of recollections that are among those that are the furthest removed, chronologically, from the writer's adult years. Its rewards to the reader are great, presenting the opportunity for us to consider which factors and rites of passages (as of family or school life) most critically aided or hindered the development of the mind and character of a fellow human being.

Such insights may assist us in our own development or in better understanding the development or personal histories of those around us. If, as Plato maintained, the unexamined life is not worth living, *Remembered Childhoods* is truly a lens through which a wide spectrum of human life may be examined, evaluated, and in many cases emulated.

Author's Note

As is true of any dynamically organic body of literature, there is no apparent end to the writing of new—or the discovery of older—memoirs of youth. The following titles became known to the author as this volume was being readied for publication. If fate and fortune (including sales levels for the present volume) are kind, these and other deserving titles will receive full bibliographic treatment in a second edition of *Remembered Childhoods*.

Memoirs by Individuals

Shalom Auslander's *Foreskin's Lament* (2007); Ishmael Beah's *A Long Way Gone: Memoirs of a Boy Soldier* (2007); Harry Bernstein's *The Invisible Wall: A Love Story That Broke Barriers* (2007); Helen Bonner's *The Laid Daughter: A True Story* (1995); Kristen Buckley's *Tramps Like Us: A New Jersey Tale* (2007); John Burnside's *A Lie About My Father* (2006); May-Lee Chai's *Hapa Girl* (2007); John Doyle's *A Great Feast of Light: Growing Up Irish in the Television Age* (2005); Dario Fo's *My First Seven Years (Plus a Few More)* (2005); Emily Fox Gordon's *Are You Happy?: A Childhood Remembered* (2006); Meredith Hall's *Without a Map* (2007); Patricia Hampl's *The Florist's Daughter* (2007); Marjorie Hart's *Summer at Tiffany* (2007); Monica Holloway's *Driving with Dead People* (2007); Madhur Jaffrey's *Climbing the Mango Trees: A Memoir of a Childhood in India* (2006); Mildred Armstrong Kalish's *Little Heathens: Hard Times and High Spirits on an Iowa Farm During the Great Depression* (2007); Wendy Kann's *Casting with a Fragile Thread: A Story of Sisters and Africa* (2006); Garrison Keillor's *Homegrown Democrat: A Few Plain Thoughts from the Heart of America* (2004); Sabine Kuegler's *Child of the Jungle: The True Story of a Girl Caught Between Two Worlds* (2007); Lucette Ladnado's *The Man in the White Sharkskin Suit: My Family's Exodus from Old Cairo to the New World* (2007); Caille Millner's *The Golden Road: Notes on My Gentrification* (2007); Bich Minh Nguyen's *Stealing Buddha's Dinner* (2007); Pati Navalta Poblete's *The Oracles: My Filipino Grandparents in America* (2006); Wade Rouse's *America's Boy* (2006); Tim Russert's *Big Russ and Me: Father and Son, Lessons of Life* (2004); Kevin Sessums's *Mississippi Sissy* (2007); Eric Severeid's *Canoeing with the Cree* (1935; rpt. 1968); Susan Richard Shreve's *Warm Springs: Traces of a Childhood at FDR's Polio Haven* (2007); Mary-Ann Tirone Smith's *Girls of Tender Age* (2006); and Sarah Thyre's *Dark at the Roots* (2007).

Collective Memoirs

Everything I Needed to Know About Being a Girl I Learned from Judy Blume, ed. by Jennifer O'Conell (2007); *Home: The Blueprints of Our Lives*, comp. by John Edwards (presidential aspirant) (2006); *Once Upon a Childhood: Stories and Memories of American Youth*, by Barbara H. Solomon and Eileen Panetta (2004); *Only Child: Writers on the Singular Joys and Solitary Sorrows of Growing Up Solo*, ed. by Deborah Siegel and Daphne Uviller (2006); *Uprooted Childhoods: Memoirs of Growing Up Global*, by Faith Eidse and Nina Sichel (2007); and *Wisdom of Our Fathers: Lessons and Letters from Daughters and Sons*, by Tim Russert (2006).

List of Abbreviations

AK	Alaska	MS	Mississippi
aka	also known as	MT	Montana
AL	Alabama	NC	North Carolina
anno.	annotated	ND	North Dakota
approx.	approximately	NE	Nebraska
AR	Arkansas	NH	New Hampshire
AZ	Arizona	NJ	New Jersey
b.	born	NM	New Mexico
BR COL	British Columbia (Canada)	NV	Nevada
c.	circa	NY	New York State
CA	California	NYC	New York City
ch.(s.)	chapter(s)	OH	Ohio
CO	Colorado	OK	Oklahoma
comp.	compiled	OR	Oregon
contr.	contributor	PA	Pennsylvania
CT	Connecticut	pbk.	paperback
DC	District of Columbia	pseud.	pseudonym
DE	Delaware	RI	Rhode Island
Ed., ed.	edited or edition	rpt.	reprint
incl.	including	SAS	Saskatchewan (Canada)
FL	Florida	SC	South Carolina
GA	Georgia	SD	South Dakota
HI	Hawaii	TN	Tennessee
IA	Iowa	TX	Texas
ID	Idaho	Tr., tr.	translated or translation
IL	Illinois	U.S.	United States
IN	Indiana	UT	Utah
KS	Kansas	VA	Virginia
KY	Kentucky	vol., vols.	volume, volumes
LA	Louisiana	VT	Vermont
MA	Massachusetts	WA	Washington
MD	Maryland	WI	Wisconsin
ME	Maine	WV	West Virginia
MI	Michigan	WWI	World War One
MN	Minnesota	WWII	World War Two
MO	Missouri	WY	Wyoming

Chapter 1

The Traveled and the Captive:
Adventurers, Explorers, and Warriors

This chapter focuses on memoirs of young persons who, willingly or not, have been displaced from their homes in times of either peace or war. The first section lists youthful reminiscences that center on air travel. The second section centers on memories of life aboard boats and other vessels. The lives of young sailors, whalers, and riverboaters come to life in these works. Finally, memoirs that describe the land-bound travels of young explorers, pioneers, and others comprise the chapter's third (and largest) section: war journals, accounts of railroad hopping, and tales of itinerant family life.

To find oneself far from home, left to one's own resources, can be both exhilarating and frightening. The nearly 100 memoirs in this chapter re-create such exotic accounts. The forces that can trigger such peripatetic lives are many. During their youth, some of these memoirists focused their energies on such diverse recreations as hitchhiking (see Michael C. Keith's *The Next Better Place*) or flying a small plane across the U.S. at age 15 (see Rinker Buck's *Flight of Passage*).

Others have suffered through times of civil unrest or outright war, as either the invader or the invaded. Some of these memoirists have unwillingly had to become familiar with a foreign culture from the inside, such as young persons kidnapped from early American pioneer families who were forced to grow up within Native American communities.

Still other authors included in this chapter have deliberately infiltrated a culture that had been alien to them, such as Sarah Emma Edmonds, who masqueraded as a male soldier in the Union Army during our nation's Civil War. (See her *Memoirs of a Soldier, Nurse, and Spy*.) And yet others, through no cause of their own, were born into and grew up in environments all but divorced from human contact. Harriet Vaughan Davies, for instance, spent her girlhood living on the ocean, on her father's squarerigger (see *Aboard the* Lizzie Ross).

Perhaps the traits most shared by these young writers are a boundless sense of curiosity and resourceful instincts—both of which can be essential for survival in unfamiliar and unfriendly environments. The ingenuity and tenacity exhibited by many of these individuals, caught in the midst of battlefield activity or other stressful circumstances, can inspire us and show us how to better cope with problems in our own lives.

Memoirs listed in this chapter include those by nonmilitary and military (enlisted and conscripted) individuals, as well as by medical and other emergency relief personnel.

1

In the Air

Fighter Pilots and Other Flyers

Buck, Rinker (1950–). *Flight of Passage* (Hyperion, 1997).
Focuses on the summer when he was 15 years old and flew a plane from New Jersey to California with his older brother.
Baby Boomers ✧ Brothers ✧ Flights ✧ Summer I U.S.

Gabel, Kurt (1923–). Ed. by William C. Mitchell. *The Making of a Paratrooper: Airborne Training and Combat in World War II* (University Press of Kansas, 1990).
Pages 3 to about 145 cover him from 19 to 21 years.
WWII I GA ✧ France ✧ Belgium

Hynes, Samuel Lynn (1924–). *Flights of Passage: Reflections of a WWII Aviator* (Naval Institute, 1988).
He also wrote a prequel (ch. 16).
College Teachers ✧ Critics (Literary) ✧ Fighter Pilots ✧ Growing Up Between WWI and WWII ✧ WWII I South Pacific Ocean ✧ Okinawa ✧ Uliti

Koger, Fred (1924–). *Countdown!* (Algonquin Books of Chapel Hill, 1990).
Fighter Pilots ✧ WWII I France ✧ Germany

Lindbergh, Charles A(ugustus) (1902–1974). *Boyhood on the Upper Mississippi: A Reminiscent Letter* (Minnesota Historical Society, 1972).
Memoir of 50 pages.
Letters ✧ Pilots I MN

Lindbergh, Charles A(ugustus) (1902–1974). *"We," by Charles A. Lindbergh: The Famous Flyer's Own Story of His Life and His Transatlantic Flight Together with His Views on the Future of Aviation* (Putnam, 1928).
The first 103 pages cover his first 22 years. See also "Lindbergh, Anne Morrow" (ch. 9) and "Lindbergh, Reeve" (ch. 9).
Pilots I U.S. (Midwest)

Wagstaff, Patty (1951–), with Ann L. Cooper. *Fire and Air: A Life on the Edge* (Chicago Review Press, 1997).
About page 12 to about page 70 (chs. 2–6).
Air Force, U.S. ✧ Baby Boomers ✧ Hippies ✧ Pilots I CA (Northern) ✧ Japan ✧ NY ✧ Switzerland ✧ England

On the Water

Military Duties and Engagements, Boating, and Ocean Voyages

Aebi, Tania, and Bernadette Brennan (1966–). *Maiden Voyage* (Simon and Schuster, 1989).
From 18 to 20 years. She endured a 36-month solo voyage around the world.
Generation X ✧ Sailing ✧ Voyages

Cloud, Enoch (1833?–). *Enoch's Voyage: Life on a Whaleship 1851–1854* (Moyer Bell, 1994).
  Pages 13–206 cover August 13, 1851 (when he was in his late teens) through December 31, 1852. Elizabeth McLean, his great, great granddaughter, wrote the introduction to this edition.
  Nineteenth-Century Pre-Industrial Age Memoirists ✧ Voyages ✧ Whaling | MA

Cogill, Burgess (1902?–). *When God Was an Atheist Sailor: Memories of a Childhood at Sea, 1902–1910* (W.W. Norton, 1990) (First issued privately in 1981).
  Entire memoir (pages 23–171) focuses on his first 8 years. For similar memoirs, see "Dana, Richard Henry, Jr.," "Tyng, Charles," and "Soucheray, Joe."
  Seafaring Life ✧ Voyages | CA (Northern)

Dana, Richard Henry, Jr. (1815–1882). *Two Years Before the Mast* (Harper, 1840).
  Covers his voyage, August 1834–September 1836. Henrietta Skinner was his daughter (see ch. 4 entry). For similar memoirs, see "Cogill, Burgess" and "Tyng, Charles."
  Nineteenth-Century Pre-Industrial Age Memoirists ✧ Seafaring Life ✧ Voyages

Davies, Harriet Vaughan (1879–1978). *Aboard the* Lizzie Ross (W.W. Norton, 1966).
  Entire memoir focuses on her girlhood years, spent on the sea. She grew up on her father's squarerigger.
  Voyages

Doane, Benjamin (1823–). *Following the Sea* (Nimbus, 1987).
  First published posthumously, shortly after the manuscript's discovery.
  Nineteenth-Century Pre-Industrial Age Memoirists ✧ Seafaring Life ✧ Voyages ✧ Whaling | Canada (Nova Scotia)

Graham, Robin Lee (1949–), with Derek L. T. Gill. *Dove* (Harper & Row, 1972).
  Baby Boomers ✧ Voyages

Kahn, Sy (1924–). *Between Tedium and Terror: A Soldier's World War II Diary, 1943–45* (University of Illinois, 1993).
  Diaries and Journals ✧ Military Life ✧ Poets ✧ WWII | Southwest Pacific Ocean

Kernan, Alvin (1923–). *Crossing the Line: A Bluejacket's World War II Odyssey* (Naval Institute, 1994).
  College Teachers ✧ Sailors ✧ WWII | South Pacific Ocean

Lince, George (1926–). *Too Young the Heroes: A World War II Marine's Account of Facing a Veteran Enemy at Guadalcanal, the Solomons and Okinawa* (McFarland, 1997).
  Memoir covers him from 12 to 19 years.
  Marines, U.S. | Pacific Theater of World War II

Loti, Pierre (pseud. of Louis-Marie-Julien Viaud) (1850–1923). Tr. by Caroline F. Smith. *The Story of a Child* (C.C. Birchard, 1901) (First French ed., 1890).
  This is a classic memoir.
  Family Memoirs ✧ Nineteenth-Century Pre-Industrial Age Memoirists ✧ Novelists ✧ Sailors ✧ Short Story Writers ✧ Travel Writers | France

Loti, Pierre (pseud. of Louis-Marie-Julien Viaud) (1850–1923). *Early Childhood* (Doubleday, Page, 1924) (Originally published c. 1919 as *Prime Jeunesse*; the unfinished first chapter of *Pierre Loti: Notes of My Youth: Fragments of a Diary Assembled by His Son Samuel Viaud*).

Was intended as a sequel to *Prime Jeunesse*; the first 24 pages of this latter work focus on Loti to age 21.

Family Memoirs ✧ Nineteenth-Century Pre-Industrial Age Memoirists ✧ Novelists ✧ Sailors ✧ Short Story Writers ✧ Travel Writers | France

Murray, Nina Chandler (1920–). *The Cruise of the* **Blue Dolphin***: A Family's Adventure at Sea* (Lyons, 2002).

She and her family traveled by boat from Nantucket Island to the Caribbean, through the Panama Canal, to the Galapagos Islands, and back again. She is a retired psychologist.

Boats ✧ Depressions (Economic) ✧ Eccentrics ✧ Family Memoirs ✧ Growing Up Between WWI and WWII ✧ Home Schooling ✧ Psychologists ✧ Voyages ✧ Wealth

Sherburne, Andrew (1765–1831). Ed. by Karen Zeinert. *The Memoirs of Andrew Sherburne, Patriot and Privateer of the American Revolution* (Linnet Books, 1993).

Covers him from 13 to 19 years.

Sailors ✧ War of Independence

Soucheray, Joe. *Waterline: Of Fathers, Sons, and Boats* (Harper & Row, 1989).

For a similar memoir, see "Cogill, Burgess."

Boats ✧ Fathers and Sons ✧ Journalists

Trelawny, Edward John (1792–1881). Ed. by William St. Clair. *Adventures of a Younger Son* (Oxford University, 1974).

Chapters 1–15 (pages 1–53) focus on about his first 18 years. This work was first published in 3 volumes in 1831, by H. Coburn and R. Bentley.

Adventurers ✧ Nineteenth-Century Pre-Industrial Age Memoirists ✧ Voyages | England

Tyng, Charles (1801–1879). Ed. by Susan Fels. *Before the Wind: The Memoir of an American Sea Captain, 1808–1833* (Viking, 1999).

About the first 100 pages focus on him from 13 to 15 years. He voyaged from MA to China, as a "sailor boy, on the ship *Cordelia*." For similar memoirs, see "Cogill, Burgess" and "Dana, Richard Henry, Jr."

Nineteenth-Century Pre-Industrial Age Memoirists ✧ Seafaring Life ✧ Voyages | MA

Weil, Dorothy (1929–). *The River Home: A Memoir* (Ohio University, 2002).

She tells of her formative years traveling around the U.S. on riverboats, up and down the Mississippi River.

Depressions (Economic) ✧ Growing Up Between WWI and WWII ✧ Motion Picture Producers and Directors ✧ Riverboats | Mississippi River

On the Land

Military Duties and Engagements, Expeditions, Wide Travels, and Tales of Indian Captivity

Allen, Catherine Ward (b. Catherine Blanche Ward) (1883–), and Harry E. Chrisman. *Chariot of the Sun* (Sage Books, 1964).

This book recounts her extensive travels, beginning at age 6, through frontier territory, partially along the Chisholm Trail.

Frontier and Pioneer Life ✧ Uncles | Oklahoma Territory

Applegate, Jesse A. (1835–1919). *Recollections of My Boyhood, by Jesse Applegate, Oregon Pioneer of 1843* (Press of Review, 1914).

This memoir also appears in his extended memoir, *A Day with the Cow Column in 1843, Recollections of My Boyhood* (1934).

Frontier and Pioneer Life ✧ Nineteenth-Century Pre-Industrial Age Memoirists I OR

Ball, Phil (194?–). *Ghosts and Shadows: A Marine in Vietnam, 1968–1969* (McFarland, 1998).

About 18 to 21 years. He was awarded the Purple Heart for his service in Vietnam.

Generation X ✧ Marines, U.S. ✧ Vietnam Conflict I Vietnam

Baring, Maurice (1874–1945). *Puppet-Show of Memory* (Little, Brown, 1922).

Pages 1 to about 153. As a youth, he acquired his education in Germany and Italy, as well as at private schools in England. He was fluent in 8 languages. During WWI, he was an officer in England's Royal Flying Corps.

Biographers ✧ Cambridge University ✧ Critics (Literary) ✧ Dramatists ✧ Essayists ✧ Eton College ✧ Foreign Correspondents ✧ High Society ✧ Novelists ✧ Poets ✧ Short Story Writers ✧ Victorian Era British Memoirists ✧ Wealth I England

Baring-Gould, Sabine (1834–1924). *Early Reminiscences, 1834–1864* (John Lane, Bodley Head, 1923).

Pages 3–255 (chs. 1–13). This memoir describes his travels to France, Germany, and elsewhere in Europe with his family, during his youth.

Biographers ✧ Children's Authors ✧ Folklorists ✧ Nineteenth-Century Pre-Industrial Age Memoirists ✧ Novelists ✧ Short Story Writers ✧ Theological Writers ✧ Travel Writers I England ✧ Europe

Barnes, James Strachey (1895?–). *Half a Life* (Coward McCann, 1934).

About the first 140–150 pages. He attended Eton and Cambridge University.

Cambridge University I India ✧ Italy ✧ England

Bashkirtseff, Marie (1859–1884). Tr. from the French by A(rthur) D. Hall. *The Journal of Marie Bashkirtseff* (Rand, McNally, 1890) (First French ed., 1888).

Entries begin when she was approx. 15. Her mother condensed Marie's 84-volume journal into 2 publishable volumes after her daughter's death. Born in the Ukraine, Marie grew up largely in France, studying art in Paris. She also toured Italy and visited her father in Russia. English Prime Minister William Gladstone hailed this as "a book without parallel."

Diaries and Journals ✧ Nineteenth-Century Pre-Industrial Age Memoirists ✧ Painters I Ukraine ✧ France

Bassett, John T. (1926?–). *War Journal of an Innocent Soldier* (Archon Books, 1989).

Focuses on him at age 19. As WWII ended, he was a soldier fighting Germans in the mountains of northern Italy.

Diaries and Journals ✧ WWII I Italy

Bidermann, Gottlob Herbert (1923–). Tr. from the German and ed. by Derek S. Zumbro. *In Deadly Combat: A German Soldier's Memoir of the Eastern Front* (University Press of Kansas, 2000).

Pages 11 to about 212 focus on him from 18 to 21 years.

WWII I Russia

Bode, E(mil) A(dolph) (1856–). Ed. by Thomas T. Smith. *A Dose of Frontier Soldiering: The Memoirs of Corporal E.A. Bode, Frontier Regular Infantry, 1877–1882* (University of Nebraska, 1882).

Approximately pages 15–74 focus on his first 21 or 22 years.

Frontier and Pioneer Life ✧ Military Life ✧ Nineteenth-Century Pre-Industrial Age Memoirists

Bonham Carter, (Lady) Violet (1887–1969). Ed. by Mark Bonham Carter and Mark Pottle. *Lantern Slides: The Diaries and Letters of Violet Bonham Carter, 1904–1914* (Weidenfeld & Nicholson, 1996).

She is an ancestor of actress Helen Bonham Carter and sister-in-law of Lady Cynthia Asquith (see entry in ch. 9). As daughter of British statesman H. H. Asquith, she traveled much in her youth.

Diaries and Journals ✧ High Society ✧ Letters ✧ Politicians ✧ Victorian Era British Memoirists ✧ Wealth | France ✧ England ✧ Italy ✧ Egypt ✧ U.S.

Bowley, F(reeman) S(parks) (1846–). *A Boy Lieutenant* (H. Altemus, 1906).

Covers him from 16 to 18 years.

African Americans ✧ Civil War (U.S.) ✧ Military Life ✧ Nineteenth-Century Pre-Industrial Age Memoirists | MA ✧ Washington, DC ✧ VA ✧ NC

Boyd, Maria Isabella ("Belle") (1843–1900). *Belle Boyd in Camp and Prison: Written by Herself: A New Edition Prepared from New Materials by Curtis Carroll Davis* (Saunders, Otley, 1968) (Originally published in 2 vols., 1865).

Pages 119 to about 346.

Civil War (U.S.) ✧ Military Life ✧ Nineteenth-Century Pre-Industrial Age Memoirists ✧ Spies | VA ✧ MD ✧ Washington, DC ✧ NYC ✧ MA ✧ Canada (Quebec, Ontario, Newfoundland) ✧ England ✧ PA ✧ DE

Braithwaite, Max (1911–1995). *Never Sleep Three in a Bed* (McClelland and Stewart, 1969).

He grew up in a large family that moved all over Canada.

Family Memoirs | Canada

Brookes, Tim (1953–). *"A Hell of a Place to Lose a Cow": An American Hitchhiking Odyssey* (National Geographic Society, 2000).

Memoir is set in 1973; Brookes recalls this trip while re-creating it in 1998.

Baby Boomers ✧ College Teachers ✧ Essayists ✧ Hitchhiking ✧ Summer | U.S.

Bryher (pseud. of Winifred Ellerman) (1894–1983). *The Heart to Artemis: A Writer's Memoirs* (Harcourt, Brace & World, 1962).

Pages 5 to about 165. In her youth she traveled throughout Europe, Egypt, and the Mediterranean.

Archaeologists ✧ Critics (Literary) ✧ Novelists ✧ Victorian Era British Memoirists ✧ Wealth | England

Calof, Rachel (1876–1952). Tr. from the Yiddish by Jacob Calof and Molly Shaw. *Rachel Calof's Story: Jewish Homesteader on the Northern Plains* (Indiana University, 1995).

Pages 1–61. (She began writing this in 1936.)

Frontier and Pioneer Life ✧ Jews | Ukraine (i.e., Russia) ✧ ND

Casanova, Giacomo (1725–1798). *History of My Life: Volumes 1 and 2* (Harcourt, Brace & World, 1966).
> In vol. 1, he is 18 or 19 on pages 44–321; in vol. 2, he turns 22 on page 235 (ch. ix).
>
> Adventurers ✧ Eighteenth-Century Memoirists ✧ Librarians | Italy

Conover, Ted (b. Frederick King Conover III) (1958–). *Rolling Nowhere* (Viking, 1981).
> Focuses on 1 year, at about age 20 or 21, when he traveled with hoboes.
>
> Anthropologists ✧ Baby Boomers ✧ Hitchhiking ✧ Hoboes | U.S. (Western)

Conroy, Frank (1936–2005). *Stop-Time* (Viking, 1967).
> This is a lively memoir built on an effective blend of exposition and re-created dialogue. It is widely considered a classic.
>
> College Teachers ✧ Musicians | Florida ✧ NYC ✧ Denmark ✧ PA

Cooke, Chauncey H(erbert) (1846–1919). *Soldier Boy's Letters to His Father and Mother, 1862–1865* (News-Office, 1915).
> Civil War (U.S.) ✧ Letters ✧ Military Life ✧ Nineteenth-Century Pre-Industrial Age Memoirists

Cropton, John (1897?–). *The Road to Nowhere* (Hurst & Blackett, 1936).
> About 190 pages (through about page 214).
>
> Gallipoli Campaign ✧ Military Life ✧ WWI | England ✧ Turkey

Davies, Eliza (1819–). *The Story of an Earnest Life: A Woman's Adventures in Australia and in Two Voyages Around the World* (Central Book Condern, 1881).
> She's 20 years old on page 140.
>
> Nineteenth-Century Pre-Industrial Age Memoirists ✧ Voyages | Australia

De Mist, Augusta (1783–1832). Tr. from the Dutch. *Diary of a Journey to the Cape of Good Hope and the Interior of Africa in 1802 and 1803* (A.A. Balkema, 1953).
> A memoir of 57 pages.
>
> Diaries and Journals ✧ Eighteenth-Century Memoirists ✧ Fathers and Daughters | South Africa

Dickson, Brenton (1903–). *Random Recollections* (Nobb Hill, 1977).
> About 135 scattered pages.
>
> MA ✧ NH ✧ VT ✧ NYC ✧ AZ ✧ RI

Edmonds, Sarah Emma (1841–1898). *Memoirs of a Soldier, Nurse, and Spy: A Woman's Adventures in the Union Army* (Northern Illinois University, 1865). (Originally published in 1864 as *Unsexed; or, the Female Soldier: The Thrilling Adventures, Experiences and Escapes of a Woman, as Nurse, Spy and Scout, in Hospitals, Camps and Battlefields*).
> About the first 200 pages of the 1999 ed. focus on her from 20 to 21 years.
>
> Nineteenth-Century Pre-Industrial Age Memoirists | VA ✧ Washington, DC

Ehrhart, W(illiam) D(aniel) (1948–). *Vietnam-Perkasie: A Combat Marine Memoir* (McFarland, 1983).
> Author is 18 years old through at least a large portion of this book.
>
> Baby Boomers ✧ Marines, U.S. ✧ Vietnam Conflict | Vietnam

Ettinger, Albert (1900–1984), and A. Churchill. *A Doughboy with the Fighting 69th: A Remembrance of World War I* (White Mane, 1992).

Collaborations by Relatives ✧ WWI I France

Greenman, Jeremiah (1758–1828). Ed. by Robert C. Bray and Paul E. Bushnell. *Diary of a Common Soldier in the American Revolution, 1775–1783: An Annotated Edition of the Military Journal of Jeremiah Greenman* (Northern Illinois University, 1978).

Pages 13–171 focus on him from 17 to 21 years.

Diaries and Journals ✧ Eighteenth-Century Memoirists ✧ Military Life ✧ War of Independence I North America (Northeast)

Hayes, Roger S. (1947?–). *On Point: A Rifleman's Year in the Boonies: Vietnam 1967–1968* (Presidio, 2000).

He was 20 years old when inducted in 1967.

Baby Boomers ✧ Vietnam Conflict I Vietnam

Hofvendahl, Russ (1921–). *A Land So Fair and Bright: The True Story of a Young Man's Adventures Across Depression America* (Sheridan House, 1991).

Depressions (Economic) ✧ Growing Up Between WWI and WWII ✧ Railroad Travel I CA ✧ Canada

Hunter, John Dunn (1798?–1827). *Memoirs of a Captivity Among the Indians of North America: From Childhood to the Age of Nineteen: With Anecdotes Descriptive of Their Manners and Customs* (Schocken Books, 1973) (Originally published as *Manners and Customs of Several Indian Tribes* [Philadelphia: J. Maxwell, 1823]).

In his youth, Hunter roamed successively with the Kickapoo Indians, the Kansas Indians, and the Osages. He traveled east of the Mississippi only as an adult.

Indian Captivity Tales ✧ Nineteenth-Century Pre-Industrial Age Memoirists I U.S. (Western)

Jewitt, John Rodgers (1783–1821). *The Captive of Nootka, Or, the Adventures of John R. Jewitt* (Ye Galleon, 1996) (Originally published in Edinburgh, Scotland in 1824; has appeared under variant titles, such as *The Adventures and Sufferings of John Rodgers Jewitt, Captive Among the Nootka, 1803–1805*).

About the first 240 pages of the 1996 ed. focus on him from 19 to 20 years.

Indian Captivity Tales ✧ Nineteenth-Century Pre-Industrial Age Memoirists I Canada (BR COL)

Johnston, Charles (1769?–1833). *A Narrative of the Incidents Attending the Capture, Detention, and Ransom of Charles Johnston* (J. & J. Harper, 1827).

Covers the 5 weeks up to his 21st birthday.

Eighteenth-Century Memoirists ✧ Indian Captivity Tales I VA (?)

Keith, Michael C. (1948–). *The Next Better Place: A Father and Son on the Road* (Algonquin Books of Chapel Hill, 2003).

Focuses on him at 11–12 years. This unusual memoir describes years hitchhiking across the U.S. with his father, after his parents had divorced.

Baby Boomers ✧ Children of Alcoholics ✧ College Teachers ✧ Divorce ✧ Fathers and Sons ✧ Hitchhiking I NY ✧ NYC ✧ PA ✧ IN ✧ KS ✧ CO ✧ CA (Southern) ✧ NV ✧ TX ✧ OH

Kelly, Fanny (1845–1904). *Narrative of My Captivity Among the Sioux Indians. With a Brief Account of General Sully's Indian Expedition in 1864, Bearing Upon Events Occurring in My Captivity* (Maclear, 1871) (1976 rpt., Garland).
She was 19 years old during her 5-month captivity.
Indian Captivity Tales ✧ Nineteenth-Century Pre-Industrial Age Memoirists | MT ✧ SD

Knef, Hildegard (1925–2002). Tr. by David Palastanga. *The Gift Horse: Report on a Life* (McGraw-Hill, 1971) (First German ed., 1970).
By page 117, she's 19–20 years.
Military Life ✧ Motion Picture Actors and Actresses | Germany

Knox, Cleone (1744–). Ed. by her KINSMAN [sic] Alexander Blacker Kerr. *The Diary of a Young Woman of Fashion in the Year 1764–1765* (D. Appleton and Company, 1926).
Largely a travel diary, this account covers this privileged Irish woman's life from 19 to 21 years.
Diaries and Journals ✧ Eighteenth-Century Memoirists ✧ High Society | Ireland ✧ England ✧ France ✧ Switzerland ✧ Italy

Kotlowitz, Robert (1924–). *Before Their Time: A Memoir* (Knopf, 1997).
He was an infantryman in Patton's Third Army.
Military Life ✧ WWII | France

Laurence, Mary Leefe (1872–1945). Ed. by Thomas T. Smith. *Daughter of the Regiment: Memoirs of a Childhood in the Frontier Army, 1878–1898* (University of Nebraska, 1996).
American Indian Wars | U.S. (West, from south TX to the Canadian border)

Lawrence, R(onald) D(ouglas) (1921–). *Green Trees Beyond: A Memoir* (H. Holt, 1994).
Pages 1–6, 11 through about page 114.
Civil War (Spanish) ✧ Growing Up Between WWI and WWII ✧ Natural History ✧ Wolves | Spain

Livermore, Thomas L(eonard) (1844–1918). *Days and Events, 1860–1866* (Houghton Mifflin, 1920).
He enlisted as a private at age 17 and rose to colonel at age 21.
Civil War (U.S.) ✧ Military Life ✧ Nineteenth-Century Pre-Industrial Age Memoirists

Longstreet, Stephen (1907–2002). *The Boy in the Model-T: A Journey in the Just Gone Past* (Simon and Schuster, 1956).
This is an account of a cross-country drive in 1919–1920 with his mother and grandfather. Illustrated with line drawings by Longstreet.
Critics (Art) ✧ Grandfathers ✧ Historians (Cultural) ✧ Mothers and Sons ✧ Novelists ✧ Painters ✧ Road Trips ✧ Screenwriters | U.S.

Mackin, Eltin (1898–1974). *Suddenly We Didn't Want to Die: Memoirs of a World War I Marine* (Presidio, 1993).
This memoir focuses on the 6 months that he served as a rifleman and runner in the Battle of Belleau Wood, at age 19.
Marines, U.S. ✧ WWI | France

Magoffin, Susan Shelby (1827–1855). Ed. by Stella M. Drumm. *Down the Santa Fe Trail and into Mexico: The Diary of Susan Shelby Magoffin, 1846–1847* (Yale University, 1926).

Diaries and Journals ✧ Frontier and Pioneer Life ✧ Nineteenth-Century Pre-Industrial Age Memoirists | U.S. (Southwest)

Mallonee, Richard C(arvel) (1923–). *Battle for Bataan: An Eyewitness Account from the Diary of Richard C. Mallonee* (Ibooks, 1980) (Variant title, *The Naked Flagpole: Battle for Bataan* [1980]).

Covers him from about 19 to about 21 years. This is the most authoritative diary that survived this South Pacific WWII battle.

Diaries and Journals ✧ Engineers ✧ WWII | Philippines

Masters, John (1914–1983). *Bugles and a Tiger: A Volume of Autobiography* (Viking, 1956).

Pages 3 to about 116 (chs. 1–9) focus on him from 19 to 21 years.

Growing Up Between WWI and WWII ✧ Military Life ✧ Novelists | India

Maurice, Edward Beauclerk (1914?–2003). *The Last Gentleman Adventurer: Coming of Age in the Arctic* (Houghton Mifflin, 2005).

Published posthumously, this author's only book recounts how, from 16 to 21 years of age, he apprenticed with the Hudson Bay Company in northern Canada.

Adventurers ✧ Booksellers ✧ Frontier and Pioneer Life ✧ Growing Up Between WWI and WWII ✧ Inuits ✧ Island Life ✧ Physicians | Canada (Baffin Island)

Peary, Marie (1893–1978). *The Snowbaby's Own Story* (Frederick A. Stokes, 1934).

Pages 1–266. Rear Admiral Robert Peary was her father. She writes much here about Eskimo culture.

Fathers and Daughters ✧ Peary, Robert | Greenland ✧ Europe

Pham, Andrew X. (1967–). *Catfish and Mandala: A Two-Wheeled Voyage Through the Landscape and Memory of Vietnam* (Farrar, Straus, and Giroux, 1999).

About 80 widely scattered pages. He and his family fled Vietnam when he was 10; as an adult, he bicycled through the western U.S., Mexico, Japan, and Vietnam.

Vietnamese Americans | Vietnam ✧ LA ✧ CA (Northern)

Randolph, Buckner (1871–1939). *Ten Years Old and Under; the Recollections of a Childhood Spent on a Farm Which Lay in the Battle Ground of the War Between the States, and Is Covered by the Period of 1873–1880* (Gardner Benson, 1935).

Farm Life ✧ Physicians | VA

Rawson, Kennett (1911–1992). *A Boy's-eye View of the Arctic* (Macmillan, 1926).

Explorers ✧ Seafaring Life | NYC ✧ Arctic

Richmond, (Sir) Arthur (1879–). *Twenty-Six Years, 1879–1905* (G. Bles, 1961).

Pages 12 to about 175 (chs. 1–6). He was the son, grandson, and great-grandson of noted painters. Through much of this memoir, he describes his extensive travels.

Education ✧ Painters ✧ Road Trips ✧ Victorian Era British Memoirists | England ✧ Scotland

Rubin, Hank (aka Trevor Rabin) (1916–living 2002). *Spain's Cause was Mine: A Memoir of an American Medic in the Spanish Civil War* (Southern Illinois University, 1997).
About the first 100 pages focus on him from 20 to 21 years.
Civil Wars (Spain) ✧ Growing Up Between WWI and WWII ✧ Jaundice ✧ Physicians | CA (Southern) ✧ France ✧ Spain

Russell, Marian Sloan (1845–1937). Ed. by Garnet M. Brayer. *Land of Enchantment: Memoirs of Marian Russell Along the Santa Fe Trail, as Dictated to Mrs. Hal Russell* (Branding Iron, 1954).
Pages 1 to about 120.
Frontier and Pioneer Life ✧ Nineteenth-Century Pre-Industrial Age Memoirists ✧ Road Trips ✧ Santa Fe Trail | MO ✧ NM ✧ KS

Schroeder, Walter (1928–). *Stars and Swastikas: The Boy Who Wore Two Uniforms* (Archon Books, 1992).
After coming to the U.S. with his parents from Germany, he returned to their native land, where he became active in the Hitler Youth movement; later, during WWII, he served with the U.S. Army
Cold War ✧ Depressions (Economic) ✧ Growing Up Between WWI and WWII ✧ Hitler Youth Movement ✧ Military Life ✧ WWII | NYC (Manhattan) ✧ Germany

Smith, James (1737–1814?). *An Account of the Remarkable Occurrences in the Life and Travels of Col. James Smith During His Captivity with the Indians, in the Years 1755, '56, '57, '58, and '59* (John Bradford, 1799) (1907 rpt. as "Number Five" in the Ohio Valley Historical Series, by The Robert Clarke Company, of Cincinnati, Ohio).
Pages 5–105 focus on him from 18 to 21 years.
Eighteenth-Century Memoirists ✧ Indian Captivity Tales | PA

Spiller, Harry (1945–). *Death Angel: A Vietnam Memoir of a Bearer of Death Messages to Families* (McFarland, 1992).
About the first 200 pages focus on him from 17 to 21 years.
College Teachers ✧ Marines, U.S. ✧ Vietnam Conflict | Vietnam ✧ MO ✧ IL

Standifer, Leon C. (b. 1924–1926). *Not in Vain: A Rifleman Remembers World War II* (Louisiana State University, 1992).
Focuses on him at 19 years, during the latter part of WWII.
Army ✧ College Teachers ✧ Horticulturalists ✧ WWII | France

Starkie, Walter (1894–1976). *Scholars and Gypsies* (University of California, 1963).
Pages 3–122 (chs. 1–5). The last 60 pages overlap with the first part of his memoir *Raggle-Taggle* (E.P. Dutton, 1933).
College Teachers ✧ Gypsies ✧ Historians (Cultural) ✧ Military Life ✧ Musicians ✧ Translators ✧ Victorian Era British Memoirists | Ireland

Stillwell, Leander (1843–1934). *The Story of a Common Soldier of Army Life in the Civil War, 1861–1865* (Press of the Erie Record, 1917).
Army ✧ Civil War (U.S.) ✧ Military Life ✧ Nineteenth-Century Pre-Industrial Age Memoirists | MS ✧ TN

Tanner, John (1780?–1847). *The Falcon: A Narrative of the Captivity and Adventures of John Tanner* (Penguin Books, 1994) (Originally published in 1830 by G. & C. & H.

Carvill as *A Narrative of the Captivity and Adventures of John Tanner*, by Dr. Edwin James).

Chs. 1–7 (pages 1–104) focus on his first 20 to 21 years.

Eighteenth-Century Memoirists ✧ Indian Captivity Tales | U.S. (Eastern) ✧ Canada

Trupin, Sophie (1902?–). *Dakota Diaspora: Memoirs of a Jewish Homesteader* (Alternative, 1984).

Pages 23–137 focus on her first 14–15 years.

Immigrants ✧ Jews | ND

Upson, Theodore F. (1845–1919). Ed. by Oscar O. Winther. *With Sherman to the Sea; the Civil War Letters, Diaries, & Reminiscences of Theodore F. Upson* (Louisiana State University, 1943).

As a soldier, he traveled with the MI infantry.

Civil War (U.S.) ✧ Diaries and Journals ✧ Letters ✧ Military Life ✧ Nineteenth-Century Pre-Industrial Age Memoirists | GA ✧ SC ✧ NC

Walls, Jeannette. *The Glass Castle* (Scribner, 2005).

Walls recounts the gritty tale of her impoverished and itinerant youth, during which she and her 3 siblings traveled with their alcoholic father and impractical mother—from CA and AZ across the country to the Appalachian Mountains of WV. A classic in the tradition of the hardscrabble memoirs by Frank McCourt and Mary Carr (see entries).

Abuse (Sexual) ✧ Alcoholism ✧ Children of Alcoholics ✧ Eccentrics ✧ Family Memoirs ✧ Generation X(?) ✧ Journalists ✧ Mountain Life ✧ Slums | U.S. ✧ WV ✧ NYC

Walter, Jakob (1788–1864). Ed. by Marc Raeff. *Diary of a Napoleonic Foot Soldier* (Doubleday, 1991).

Covers him from about 18 to about 25 years.

Eighteenth-Century Memoirists ✧ Military Life ✧ Napoleonic Wars | Russia

Wilson, Elijah Nicholas (1842–1915). *Among the Shoshones* (Skelton, 1910).

Focuses upon him from about 8 to 10 years.

Indian Captivity Tales ✧ Nineteenth-Century Pre-Industrial Age Memoirists | UT

Xie, Bingying (1906–2000). Tr. from the Chinese by Lily Chia Brissman and Barry Brissman. *A Woman Soldier's Own Story: The Autobiography of Xie Bingying* (Columbia University, 2001) (First published in China in 1946).

Covers her first 32 years; pages 1 to about 135 focus on her first 21 years.

Feminists ✧ Military Life | China

Chapter 2

Connections with Nature: On the Job, in the Field, at Home

Like a seismograph recording tremors within the earth, the writings in this chapter sensitively measure how human souls have been affected by interactions with the natural world.

The first part of this chapter focuses on memoirs in which animals occupy important roles. Here are recollections by a young falconer and other birders, as well as accounts by zoologists and other individuals who, in their youth, had memorable relationships with creatures both exotic (elephants, sharks) and domestic (dogs, cats, and such farm animals as horses). Sterling North's classic raccoon memoir, *Rascal*, is among the entries in this section.

The other part of this chapter contains some 3 dozen memoirs by persons who spent much of their early years in outdoor environments, whether at a summer camp or as an aspiring gardener, zoologist, or naturalist. For example, in *Trail of an Artist-Naturalist*, Ernest Thompson Seton (founder of the Boy Scouts of America) re-creates his youth in Ohio.

Baby Boomers Judy Blunt and Kim Barnes probe the effects men had on their lives as they grew up in the wilds of Montana and Idaho. The forests of Michigan and the lumber camps of Oregon are other settings that take center stage in other of these reminiscences. The cultures of the shepherd, the angler, and the hunter also come under review here.

Acquainting ourselves with these memoirs can, in an emotional sense, reconnect us with the natural bounty offered by our planet. Doing so also reminds us of our obligation to try to preserve as much of the natural world as possible for generations yet unborn.

Animal Life

Including Animal Lovers, Birders, and Zoologists

Agle, Nan Hayden (1905–). *My Animals and Me: An Autobiographical Story* (Seabury, 1970).

Her girlhood pets included dogs, cats, lambs, cows, donkeys, and roosters.

Animal Eccentrics ✧ Family Memoirs ✧ Teachers | MD

Durrell, Gerald (1925–1995). *My Family and Other Animals* (R. Hart-Davis, 1956).

Animal Eccentrics ✧ Growing Up Between WWI and WWII ✧ Natural History | England ✧ Greece

Ford, Emma (1962?–). *Fledgling Days: Memoir of a Falconer* (John Murray, 1996).
Covers her from 8 to about 18 years.

Baby Boomers ✧ Falconers | England

Kaufman, Kenn (1955?–). *Kingbird Highway: The Story of a Natural Obsession That Got a Little Out of Hand* (Houghton Mifflin, 1997).
Covers 1973–1974, when he was 18–19 years old and hitchhiked 69,000 miles.

Baby Boomers ✧ Birders ✧ Hitchhiking | North America

Maxwell, Gavin (1914–1969). *The House of Elrig* (E.P. Dutton, 1965).
Among his diversified accomplishments, he established a shark fishery. He was an intimate of Kathleen Raine (see ch. 9 entry).

Animal Eccentrics ✧ Children's Authors ✧ Growing Up Between WWI and WWII ✧ Homes and Haunts ✧ Journalists ✧ Natural History ✧ Novelists ✧ Painters ✧ Travel Writers | Scotland

Montagu, Ivor (1904–1984). *The Youngest Son: Autobiographical Sketches* (Lawrence & Wishart, 1970).
Covers his first 23 years.

Critics (Film) ✧ Journalists ✧ Motion Picture Producers and Directors ✧ Screenwriters ✧ Table Tennis ✧ Translators ✧ Zoologists | England

North, Sterling (1906–1974). *Rascal: A Memoir of a Better Era* (E.P. Dutton, 1963).
At age 11. This is a classic that won literary awards and was adapted into a Disney film, *Rascal,* in 1969.

Raccoons | WI

Patchett, Mary (1897–1989). *Ajax, Golden Dog of the Australian Bush* (Lutterworth, 1953) (British title, *Ajax the Warrior*).

Children's Authors ✧ Dogs | Australia

Pettingill, Olin Sewall, Jr. (1907–2001). *My Way to Ornithology* (University of Oklahoma, 1992).
Pages 6 to about 101 (chs. 1– 8).

Birders | ME

Poole, Joyce (1956–). *Coming of Age with Elephants: A Memoir* (Hodder & Stoughton, 1996).
She writes of being a single mother, working in Kenya.

Elephants | Kenya

Quarton, Marjorie (b. Marjorie Smithwick) (1930–). *Breakfast the Night Before: Recollections of an Irish Horse Dealer* (Lilliput, 2000).
About the first 80 pages. This ed. combines the text of the first ed. [Andre Deutsch, 1988] with the text of the sequel *Saturday's Child* [Andre Deutsch, 1993]; some material from these previous works has been deleted, and some has been updated or otherwise added.

Farm Life ✧ Growing Up Between WWI and WWII ✧ Horses ✧ Novelists | Ireland (North)

Sutton, George Miksch (1898–1982). *Bird Student: An Autobiography* (University of Texas, 1980).
Pages 4–86. In his youth he corresponded with naturalist Louis Agassiz Fuertes.

Birders | NE ✧ MN ✧ OR ✧ IL ✧ TX ✧ WV

Wilder, Harris Hawthorne (1864–1928). Ed. by Inez W. Wilder. *The Early Years of a Zoologist; the Story of a New England Boyhood* (Privately printed, 1930).
This is a 73-page memoir.
Zoologists | ME

Outdoor Living

Naturalists, Gardeners, Camping, and Sheepherding

Arthur, Elizabeth (1953–). *Looking for the Klondike Stone* (Knopf, 1993).
Covers her childhood and adolescence at summer camp in the early 1960s.
Baby Boomers ✧ Camps ✧ Natural History ✧ Summer | VT

Barnes, Kim (1958–). *In the Wilderness: Coming of Age in Unknown Country* (Doubleday, 1996).
Pages 28–256 cover her to age 18.
Baby Boomers ✧ Natural History ✧ Pentecostalism ✧ Poets | ID

Barnes, Kim (1958–). *Hungry for the World: A Memoir* (Villard, 2000).
The second half of this book covers her from 18 to 21 years. She tells of her break from fundamentalism and her self-destructive relationships with men.
Baby Boomers ✧ Poets | ID

Beard, Daniel Carter (1850–1941). *Hardly a Man Is Now Alive: The Autobiography of Dan Beard* (Doubleday, Doran, 1939).
Pages 12 to about 223. He cofounded the Boy Scouts of America. Among the book's many memorable passages is Beard's boyhood description of a tornado.
Boy Scouts of America ✧ Cartographers ✧ Children's Authors ✧ Engineers (Civil) ✧ Illustrators ✧ Natural History ✧ Nineteenth-Century Pre-Industrial Age Memoirists | OH

Blunt, Judy (1954–). *Breaking Clean* (Knopf, 2002).
She describes breaking free from the male-dominated ranch life of her childhood and young adulthood.
Baby Boomers ✧ Essayists ✧ Poets ✧ Ranch Life | MT

Brace, Gerald Warner (1901–1978). *Days That Were* (W.W. Norton, 1976).
To his 21st birthday. He tells of his idyllic youth, spent largely in such forms of recreation as fishing, canoeing, camping, and sailing in NYS and New England.
College Teachers ✧ Family Memoirs ✧ Lakes ✧ Outdoor Recreation ✧ Summer | NY ✧ ME ✧ MA

Burroughs, John (1837–1921). *My Boyhood* (Doubleday, Page, 1922).
Pages 1–132 are on his boyhood years. After being a bank examiner for 20 years, he devoted his life to the outdoors, writing dozens of books about nature.
Bankers ✧ Birders ✧ Catskill Mountains ✧ Essayists ✧ Farm Life ✧ Mountain Life ✧ Natural History ✧ Nineteenth-Century Pre-Industrial Age Memoirists ✧ Poets | NY

Churchill, Sam (1911–1991). *Big Sam* (Doubleday, 1965).
Businesspersons | OR

Churchill, Sam (1911–1991). *Don't Call Me Ma* (Doubleday, 1970).
Businesspersons ✧ Lumber Camps | OR

Creevey, Caroline (1843–1920). *A Daughter of the Puritans: An Autobiography* (Putnam, 1916).
Covers her first 23 years. As an adult she wrote on gardening.
Gardeners ✧ Nineteenth-Century ✧ Pre-Industrial Age Memoirists

Curwood, James Oliver (1878–1927). *Son of the Forests: An Autobiography* (Doubleday, Doran, 1930).
He wrote adventurous tales set in the outdoors. Unfinished at his death, this memoir was completed by Dorothea A. Bryant.
Natural History ✧ Novelists | MI

Eisner, Michael (1942–). *Camp* (Warner Books, 2005).
The former CEO of the Walt Disney Company focuses on his youth from 7 to 15 years as he re-creates life at Camp Keewaydin in northern Vermont. Includes a glossary of terms.
Businesspersons ✧ Camps ✧ Summer | VT

Foley, Winifred (1914–). *A Child in the Forest* (British Broadcasting Corporation, 1974) (1978 rpt., Taplinger, *As the Twig Is Bent*).
Forests ✧ Growing Up Between WWI and WWII | England

Homer, Art (1951–). *The Drownt Boy: An Ozark Tale* (University of Missouri, 1994).
Baby Boomers ✧ Ironworkers ✧ Mountain Life ✧ Outdoor Recreation ✧ Poets | MO

Irigaray, Louis (1930–), and Theodore Taylor. *A Shepherd Watches, a Shepherd Sings* (Doubleday, 1977).
He's only 17 on page 249.
Basque Americans ✧ Growing Up Between WWI and WWII ✧ Shepherds | CA (Northern)

Ledda, Gavino (1938–). Tr. by George Salmanazar. *Padre Padrone: The Education of a Shepherd* (Urizen Books, 1978) (First published in Spanish, 1975).
Pages 1–200.
Fathers and Sons ✧ Shepherds ✧ Teachers | Italy

McManus, Patrick F. (1933–). *The Night the Bear Ate Goombaw* (H. Holt, 1989).
For another memoir on his childhood, see the entry in chapter 11.
Humorists ✧ Outdoor Recreation | ID

Middleton, Harry (1950?–1994). *The Earth Is Enough: Growing up in a World of Trout and Old Men* (Simon and Schuster, 1989).
Tells of his childhood times with 2 elderly men, with whom he hunted, fished, and walked trails. Dialogue is effectively subordinated to narration throughout this work.
Baby Boomers ✧ Fishing ✧ Hunting ✧ Military Life | AR

Mills, Joe (1880–1935). *A Mountain Boyhood* (J.H. Sears, 1910, 1926).
Mountain Life ✧ Natural History | CO

Mowat, Farley (1921–). *Born Naked* (Key Porter Books, 1993).
Focuses on his first 16 years, with most of it covering him from about 12 to 16. In his works of nonfiction and fiction, he has drawn on decades of his own outdoor experiences (e.g., living for 2 years in the Arctic, his travels through Siberia, sailing many waters).
Children's Authors ✧ Growing Up Between WWI and WWII ✧ Historians (Cultural) ✧ Librarians ✧ Natural History ✧ Reformers | Canada (Ontario; SAS: Saskatoon)

Mowat, Farley (1921–). *The Dog Who Wouldn't Be* (Little, Brown, 1957).
Focuses on him at about age 8.
Animal Eccentrics ✧ Children's Authors ✧ Dogs ✧ Growing Up Between WWI and WWII ✧ Historians (Cultural) ✧ Librarians ✧ Natural History ✧ Reformers | Canada (SAS: Saskatoon)

Mowat, Farley (1921–). *Owls in the Family* (Little, Brown, 1961).
Part of his boyhood.
Animal Eccentrics ✧ Birds ✧ Children's Authors ✧ Historians (Cultural) ✧ Librarians ✧ Natural History ✧ Reformers | Canada (SAS: Saskatoon)

Muir, John (1838–1914). *Story of My Boyhood and Youth* (Houghton Mifflin, 1913).
Covers through his college graduation. Part of this also appeared in 1913 as *The Boyhood of a Naturalist*.
Forests ✧ Frontier and Pioneer Life ✧ Inventors ✧ Natural History ✧ Nineteenth-Century Pre-Industrial Age Memoirists | WI

Murrill, William (1869–1957). *Billy the Boy Naturalist: The True Story of a Naturalist's Boyhood in Virginia Just After the Civil War* (W.A. Murrill, 1918).
Civil War (U.S.) ✧ Natural History | VA

Pyle, Robert Michael (1947–). *The Thunder Tree: Lessons from an Urban Wildland* (Houghton Mifflin, 1993).
About 96 scattered pages
Baby Boomers ✧ Natural History | CO

Ray, Janisse (1962–). *Ecology of a Cracker Childhood* (Milkweed Editions, 1999).
About 146 scattered pages. (The author is a woman.)
Baby Boomers ✧ Natural History | GA

Rich, Louise Dickinson (1903–1991). *Innocence Under the Elms* (Lippincott, 1955).
Focuses on her years growing up in Bridgewater, MA. She was related to American poet Emily Dickinson.
Children's Authors ✧ Natural History ✧ Novelists ✧ Teachers | MA

Ross, Glen (1929–). *On Coon Mountain: Scenes from a Childhood in the Oklahoma Hills* (University of Oklahoma, 1992).
He grew up near the Ozarks.
College Teachers ✧ Country Life ✧ Growing Up Between WWI and WWII ✧ Mountain Life | OK

Sari, Riska Orpa (1969–), as told to Linda Spalding. *Riska: Memories of a Dayak Girlhood* (University of Georgia, 2000).
Headhunters ✧ Island Life ✧ Rain Forests | Indonesia

Servid, Carolyn (1953–). *Of Landscape and Longing: Finding a Home at the Water's Edge* (Milkweed Editions, 2000).
Nearly all of pages 6 through about 59, and pages 183–186. As a child, she lived among medical missionaries.
Essayists ✧ Natural History | India ✧ AK

Seton, Ernest Thompson (1860–1946). *Trail of an Artist-Naturalist: The Autobiography of Ernest Thompson Seton* (Scribner's Sons, 1940).

Pages 3–154 (chs. 1–19). This naturalist and prolific illustrator, who cofounded the Boy Scouts of America, was the 12th of 14 children.

Boy Scouts of America ✧ Illustrators ✧ Lecturers ✧ Malaria ✧ Natural History | Canada (Ontario)

Teale, Edwin Way (1899–1980). *Dune Boy: The Early Years of a Naturalist* (Dodd, Mead, 1943).

Covers his first 16 years.

Grandparents ✧ Lake Michigan ✧ Natural History | IN

Chapter 3

Rural and City Life: Living on the Land, Exotic Locales, Urban Living

Like the memoirs presented in the previous chapters, those contained here are arranged according to the environments in which they are set. In this case, however, the memoirists are more deeply rooted in these environments, and they provide less of a field of study than a backdrop upon which each memoirist's life unfolds.

More than 100 writers in the first section of this chapter recall youthful experiences growing up in such countrified areas as farmland, ranches, plantations, or mining country (as for ore or oil). Sonora Babb and Stephen Payne describe what it was like to grow up in the American West several generations ago, while Irving Bachellor evokes his early days in the Adirondacks, and Fred Archer reminisces about his boyhood on an English farm.

The conditions of life in such settings in some cases were anything but idyllic. Memoirs depicting challenging living conditions include Rebecca Caudill's *My Appalachia*, Henry Conklin's *Through "Poverty's Vale": A Hardscrabble Boyhood in Upstate New York . . .* , and Francis Bramlette Farris's *From Rattlesnakes to Road Agents: Rough Times on the Frio*.

The second part of this chapter gathers autobiographical writings set in such exotic locales as jungles and islands. The thick undergrowth of South America and Africa appear here. Among the nearly 2 dozen memoirs here are such memorable ones as Arnold Apple's *Son of Guyana*, which relates the author's formative years among African rain forests. Apple amazingly tells of an ingenious technique used by natives that allows boats to travel upriver against rushing waters that approach waterfall strength.

The island locales in this section include such far-flung places as islands in Texas and New England, Hawaii, the Philippines, and Okinawa, Barbados, Jamaica, and Martinique. Maurice O'Sullivan vividly re-creates for us his early life on the harsh Blasket Islands, off the coast of Ireland. His memoir ends as he comes of age and heads out across the waters to seek a life and living on the mainland.

More than 30 recollections of urban life complete this chapter. Most of the writers represented here, such as Hamilton Fish Armstrong, Julius Jacobs, and Nathalie Dana, have written accounts of life in New York City. Descriptions of what it was like to grow up in other U.S. metropolitan areas are also offered for Chicago (Rich Cohen); Washington, D.C. (Shawna Kenney); Detroit (Russell McLaughlin), Boston (Barbara Mullen), San Francisco (Naomi Wolf), and London (Ken Kimberley). (Note: memoirs by authors who rose to celebrity in various fields are often listed in chapters 8 through 16, organized by careers.)

Foreign metropolitan childhoods and years of adolescence are also delineated. Poet Joe Rosenblatt writes of growing up in Toronto during the 1930s and 1940s. Valerie Avery, Eileen Baillie, and Robert Barltrop have evoked youthful lives spent in London.

Working and Living on the Land

Country, Farm, Frontier and Pioneer, Ranch, Plantation, Mining, Mountain, and Oil

Archer, Fred (1915–1999). *The Distant Scene* (Hodder & Stoughton, 1967).
Country Life ✧ Farm Life I England

Archer, Fred (1915–). *Muddy Boots and Sunday Suits: Memories of a Country Childhood* (Hodder & Stoughton, 1973).
Country Life ✧ Farm Life ✧ Growing Up Between WWI and WWII I England

Babb, Sonora (1907–2005). *An Owl on Every Post* (McCall, 1970).
See also other rural Colorado memoirs: "Bennett, Edwin," "Borland, Hal," "Burroughs, John Rolfe," "Dempsey, Jack," "Moody, Ralph," "Payne, Stephen," and "Pyle, Robert Michael."
Farm Life ✧ Frontier and Pioneer Life ✧ Novelists I CO

Bacheller, Irving (1859–1950). *Coming Up the Road: Memories of a North Country Boyhood* (Bobbs-Merrill, 1928).
He grew up in the Adirondack Mountains.
Adirondack Mountains I NY

Baker, Pearl Biddlecome (1907–1992). *Robbers Roost Recollections* (Utah State University, 1976).
Pages 37–192.
Ranch Life I UT

Barnard, Ellsworth (1907–2003). *A Hill Farm Boyhood* (Dinosaur, 1983).
This is the first volume of his trilogy In Sunshine and in Shadow: A Teacher's Odyssey (Dinosaur, 1983–1987).
College Teachers ✧ Farm Life I MA

Beard, Carrie Hunt (1881–). Foreword by Lowell Thomas. *Colorado Gold Rush Days: Memories of a Childhood in the Eighties and Nineties* (Exposition, 1964).
Mountain Life I CO

Bennett, Edwin (1890–). *Boom Town Boy: In Old Creede, Colorado* (Sage Books, 1966).
As an adult, he was a ranger with the U.S. Forest Service.
Miners ✧ Mountain Life ✧ Rangers I CO

Bennett, Estelline (18??–1948). *Old Deadwood Days* (J.H. Sears, 1928).
Considered a classic.
Frontier and Pioneer Life I SD

Bernard, Connell (1922?–). *Now the Day Is Over* (Viking, 1985).
Takes place during 1938–1939. Author was a musical director for the BBC.
Aunts ✧ Country Life ✧ Musicians ✧ Summer ✧ Uncles I Wales/England (border area)

Bodwell, Dorothy (1905–). *Baked Potatoes in My Pocket* (Vantage, 1977).
Pages 1–80 (chs. 1–9).
Farm Life | NH

Bonebright, Mrs. Sarah (1837–). *Reminiscences of Newcastle, Iowa, 1848: A History of the Founding of Webster City, Iowa: Written by Her Daughter Harriet Bonebright-Closz* (Historical Department of Iowa, 1921).
This is an oral history that was recorded by Sarah's daughter. Set in the 1840s to early 1850s.
Collaborations by Relatives ✧ Farm Life ✧ Frontier and Pioneer Life ✧ Nineteenth-Century Pre-Industrial Age Memoirists | IA

Borland, Hal (pseud. of Harold Glen) (1900–1978). *High, Wide, and Lonesome* (Lippincott, 1956).
Focuses on his boyhood.
Frontier and Pioneer Life ✧ Journalists ✧ Natural History | CO

Borland, Hal (pseud. of Harold Glen) (1900–1978). *Country Editor's Boy* (Lippincott, 1970).
Focuses on his boyhood.
Frontier and Pioneer Life ✧ Journalists ✧ Natural History | CO

Britt, Albert (1874–1969). *An America That Was: What Life Was Like on an Illinois Farm Seventy Years Ago* (Barre, 1964).
Farm Life | IL

Brooks, E. Whitson. *A Place Called Bethel* (E.W. Brooks, 1991).
Set during 1910s–1920s.
Frontier and Pioneer Life | OK

Brown, Harriet (1872–). *Grandmother Brown's Hundred Years, 1827–1927* (Little, Brown, 1929).
About the first 80–90 pages contain a substantial amount of oral history that focuses on Maria D. Brown's first 21 years; her granddaughter, Harriet, transcribed these memories into this book.
Centenarians ✧ Collaborations by Relatives ✧ Farm Life ✧ Frontier and Pioneer Life | Northwest Territory (Ohio)

Carroll, J(ames) M(ilton) (1852–1931). *Just Such a Time: Recollections of Childhood on the Texas Frontier, 1858–1867* (Kairos, 1987).
Entire length of memoir is 65 pages (He is not to be confused with American physician James Carroll [1854–1907].).
Frontier and Pioneer Life ✧ Nineteenth-Century Pre-Industrial Age Memoirists | TX

Caudill, Rebecca (1899–1985). *My Appalachia: A Reminiscence* (Holt, Rinehart and Winston, 1966).
Includes many black-and-white photos.
Appalachian Mountains ✧ Mountain Life

Church, John L. (1925?–). *Pasadena Cowboy: Growing Up in Southern California and Montana, 1925 to 1947* (Conover-Patterson, 1996).
Growing Up Between WWI and WWII ✧ Ranch Life ✧ WWII | CA (Southern) ✧ MT

Collins, Hubert (1872–1932). *Warpath and Cattle Trail* (Morrow, 1928).

Native Americans ✧ Ranch Life | OK

Collins, Louisa. Ed. by Dale McClare. *Louisa's Diary: The Journal of a Farmer's Daughter* (Nimbus, 1989).

This is a memoir of about 54 pages, covering August 1815–January 1816.

Diaries and Journals ✧ Farm Life ✧ Nineteenth-Century Pre-Industrial Age Memoirists | Canada (Nova Scotia)

Conklin, Henry (1832–1915). Ed. by Wendell Tripages. *Through "Poverty's Vale": A Hardscrabble Boyhood in Upstate New York, 1832–1862* (Syracuse University, 1974).

Pages 17–157 (chs. 3–14). (Written 1891–1892).

Frontier and Pioneer Life ✧ Nineteenth-Century Pre-Industrial Age Memoirists | NY

Cook, Harold (1887–). *Tales of the 04 Ranch: Recollections of Harold J. Cook, 1887–1909* (University of Nebraska, 1968).

Except for pages 1–10, 28–36, and 42–50, nearly all of this memoir focuses on his first 21–22 years. This book, written in 1956, is an extension of *Fifty Years on the Old Frontier* (Yale University, 1923), by his father, Captain James H. Cook (see following entry).

Ranch Life | NE

Cook, James H(enry) (1857–1942). *Fifty Years on the Old Frontier, as Cowboy, Hunter, Guide, Scout, and Ranchman* (Yale University, 1923).

Pages 3 to about 132. (See previous entry by his son, Harold.)

Frontier and Pioneer Life ✧ Nineteenth-Century Pre-Industrial Age Memoirists | WY ✧ TX

Coursey, O(scar) W(illiam) (1873–). *Pioneering in Dakota* (Educator Supply, 1937).

About the first 140 pages. This is a vividly related account.

Frontier and Pioneer Life | South Dakota Territory

Cox, (Rev.) William Edward (1870?–). *Southern Sidelights: A Record of Personal Experience . . .* (Edwards & Broughton, 1942).

Pages 4–111. As an adult, he was a minister.

Clergy ✧ Plantation Life | NC

Coyle, Kathleen (1886–1952). *The Magical Realm* (E.P. Dutton, 1943).

Country Life ✧ Victorian Era British Memoirists | Ireland

Crowell, Evelyn (1899–). *Texas Childhood* (Kaleidograph, 1941).

Farm Life | TX

Croy, Homer (1883–1965). *Country Cured* (Harper & Brothers, 1943).

Set in 1880s.

Farm Life ✧ Humorists ✧ Journalists ✧ Novelists | MO

Croy, Homer (1883–1965). *Wonderful Neighbor* (Harper & Brothers, 1945).

Farm Life ✧ Humorists ✧ Journalists ✧ Novelists | MO

Dabney, Virginia Bell (1919–1997). *Once There Was a Farm . . . A Country Childhood Remembered* (Random House, 1990).

    Set in the 1920s. For a similar memoir, see "Baker, Russell" (ch. 8).

    Farm Life ✧ Growing Up Between WWI and WWII | VA

Davis, Donald (1944–). *Listening for the Crack of Dawn* (August House, 1990).

    He grew up in the western part of North Carolina, near Asheville.

    Mountain Life | NC

De Rosier, Linda Scott (1941–). *Creeker: A Woman's Journey* (University Press of Kentucky, 1999).

    From about page 4 to about page 156.

    Country Life | KY

DeLuca, Sara (1943–). *Dancing the Cows Home: A Wisconsin Girlhood* (Minnesota Historical Society, 1996).

    Farm Life | WI

Driscoll, Charles B(enedict) (1885–1951). *Kansas Irish* (Macmillan, 1943).

    This is the first volume of Driscoll's <u>Kansas Trilogy</u>.

    Farm Life ✧ Fathers and Sons | KS

Driscoll, Charles B(enedict) (1885–1951). *Country Jake* (Macmillan, 1946).

    This is the second volume of Driscoll's <u>Kansas Trilogy</u>.

    Farm Life ✧ Rheumatic Fever | KS

Eastman, E(dward) R(oe) (1885–1970). *Journey to Day Before Yesterday* (Prentice-Hall, 1963).

    See also "Ladd, Carl E(dwin)" (in this chapter).

    Farm Life | NY

Eddy, Roger (1920–). *The Bulls and the Bees* (Crowell, 1956).

    Growing Up Between WWI and WWII | CT

Eleazer, J(ames) M. (1895–1983). *A Dutch Fork Farm Boy* (University of South Carolina, 1952).

    Farm Life | SC

Engle, Paul E. (1908–1991), and Albert E. Stone. *A Lucky American Childhood* (University of Iowa, 1996).

    Farm Life ✧ Poets | IA

Erdman, Loula Grace (1905?–1976). *Life Was Simpler Then* (Dodd, Mead, 1963).

    Farm Life | MO

Esval, Orland. *Prairie Tales: Adventures of Growing Up on a Frontier* (Landmark House, 1979).

    Frontier and Pioneer Life | MT ✧ ND

Farris, Frances Bramlette (1865–1958). Ed. by C. L. Sonnichsen. *From Rattlesnakes to Road Agents: Rough Times on the Frio* (Texas Christian University, 1985).
About the first 100 pages cover her first 20 years.
Ranch Life | TX

Fish, Charles (1937–). *In Good Hands: The Keeping of a Family Farm* (Farrar, Straus, and Giroux, 1995).
Pages 3 to about 171.
Farm Life | VT

Fraser, Amy Stewart (1890?–). *The Hills of Home* (Routledge & Kegan Paul, 1973).
She was born and raised near Balmoral Castle. Her childhood is the focus from ch. 4 (page 27) through the rest of this 240-page book.
Castles ◇ Country Life | Scotland

Giscard, John (1928?–). *A Place of Stones* (Heinemann, 1958).
Covers his boyhood years; by page 186, he's only 9 years old. Focuses on him as a boy through the 1930s.
Country Life ◇ Depressions (Economic) ◇ Growing Up Between WWI and WWII | England

Good, Howard E. *Black Swamp Farm* (Ohio State University, 1967).
Farm Life | OH

Goodwin, Harry Samuel (1888?–). *The Clock Turned Back: Reminiscences of a Nineteenth Century Childhood* (Peter E. Randall, 1986).
Country Life | NH

Goodwyn, Frank (1911–2001). *Life on the King Ranch* (Crowell, 1951).
Ranch Life | TX

Goudge, Elizabeth (1900–1984). *The Joy of the Snow* (Coward, McCann & Geoghegan, 1974).
Pages 13 to about 220.
Country Life ◇ Novelists ◇ Spiritual Life | England

Gould, Franklin Farrar (1885–1966). *A Maine Man in the Making* (Harper, 1949).
About the first 200 pages. His son is John Gould (see entry in ch. 4).
Farm Life | ME

Gould, R(alph) E(rnest) (1870–). *Yankee Boyhood: My Adventures on a Maine Farm Seventy Years Ago* (W.W. Norton, 1950).
Farm Life | ME

Gray, John (1912–1985). *My New Friends Were Barefoot: A Story of Growing Up in the Upper Peninsula of Michigan During the 1920s* (Mid Peninsula Library Coop, 1994).
This is a volume of about 73 pages.
Country Life ◇ Growing Up Between WWI and WWII | MI

Greene, Clarence (1873–). *Life at Greene's Corners* (Meador, 1956).
Country Life | MI

Gresham, Douglas (1945–). *Lenten Lands: My Childhood with Joy Davidman and C. S. Lewis* (Macmillan, 1988).
Covers him from 7 to 18 years. His stepfather was C. S. Lewis.
Bereavement ✧ Country Life ✧ Lewis, C(live) S(taples) ✧ Stepfathers | England

Griffith, Llewelyn (1890–1977). *Spring of Youth* (E.P. Dutton, 1935).
Country Life | Wales

Groves, Theodore Francis (1907–). *Land of the Tamarack: Up-North Wisconsin* (North Atlantic Books, 1986).
Country Life | WI

Guerrant, Dick. *Growing Up in the Country* (Privately printed, 1994).
This is a volume of 50 pages.
Country Life | VA

Hacker, Shyrle (1910–). *A Gold Miner's Daughter: Memoirs of a Mountain Childhood* (Johnson Books, 1996).
Mountain Life | NV

Haley, Glen (1910?–). *Sparks Fly Upward: Growing Up in the Rockies* (Wayfinder, 1988).
Barber Shops ✧ Mountain Life ✧ Teachers | CO

Hall, Monty (1930–). *Growing Up Western* (Twodot, 1997).
Growing Up Between WWI and WWII ✧ Ranch Life | MT ✧ Canada (BR COL)

Hall, Sidney, Jr. (1951–). *Small Town Tales: A Brookline Boyhood* (Hobblebush Books, 1997).
Baby Boomers ✧ Country Life ✧ Journalists | NH

Hancock, George (1945–). *Go-Devils, Flies and Blackeyed Peas* (G. Hancock, 1985).
An 80-page memoir.
Farm Life ✧ Singers | TX

Hastings, Scott, Jr. (1924–). *Goodbye Highland Yankee: Stories of a North Country Boyhood* (Chelsea Green, 1988) (Variant title, *Goodbye Highland Yankee: Growing Up in the 1930's: A Memoir* [Chelsea Green, 1988]).
Country Life ✧ Growing Up Between WWI and WWII ✧ Teachers | NH

Hawley, Robert (1862–1945). *Skqee Mus, or Pioneer Days on the Nooksack: Being a Series of Personal Memoirs Published by the Author in His 83rd Year After 73 Years Residence* (Miller & Sutherlen, 1945).
According to this edition, he was from "the second white family to settle in the Lynden District on the Nooksack River, 1872."
Frontier and Pioneer Life ✧ Lumber Camps | WA

Hedrick, Ulysses (1870–1951). *Land of the Crooked Tree* (Oxford University, 1948).
Frontier and Pioneer Life | MI

Heiser, Ellinor. *Days Gone By* (Waverly, 1940).
Plantation Life | MD

Henderson, Brantley (1884–). *Only the Happy Memories: Reminiscences of a Virginia Boyhood* (Exposition, 1954).

Plantation Life I MA ✧ VA

Hill, Lewis (1924–). *Fetched-Up Yankee: A New England Boyhood Remembered* (Globe Pequot, 1990).

Country Life ✧ Growing Up Between WWI and WWII I VT

Hill, Margaret Hunt (1915–), with Burt Boyar and Jane Boyar. *H.L. and Lyda: Growing Up in the H.L. Hunt and Lyda Bunker Hunt Family as Remembered by Their Eldest Daughter* (August House, 1994).

Growing Up Between WWI and WWII ✧ Petroleum Industries I TX

Hufford, Georgia (1882–). *Then Came May* (Dorrance, 1950).

Frontier and Pioneer Life I MI

Huston, Paul Griswold. *Around an Old Homestead: A Book of Memories* (Jennings and Graham, 1906).

Set in about 1822.

Farm Life ✧ Natural History ✧ Nineteenth-Century Pre-Industrial Age Memoirists I OH

Jackson, Charles Tenney (1874–195?). *The Buffalo Wallow: A Prairie Boyhood* (Bobbs-Merrill, 1953).

Entire book is set during his first 21 years; much re-created and colloquial dialogue.

Frontier and Pioneer Life I NE

Jackson, Ralph Semmes. Introduction by J. Frank Dobie. *Home on the Double Bayou: Memories of an East Texas Ranch* (University of Texas, 1961).

Frontier and Pioneer Life ✧ Ranch Life I TX (East)

Jacobs, Harriet. *See* Brent, Linda

Jager, Ronald (1932–). Foreword by Donald Hall. *Eighty Acres: Elegy for a Family Farm* (Beacon, 1990).

See memoir by poet Hall (ch. 9).

Farm Life I MI

Jamison, Matthew (1840–). *Recollections of Pioneer and Army Life* (Hudson, 1911).

Civil War (U.S.) ✧ Frontier and Pioneer Life ✧ Military Life ✧ Mississippi River ✧ Nineteenth-Century Pre-Industrial Age Memoirists I IL

Johnson, Dorothy Marie (1905–1984). *When You and I Were Young, Whitefish* (Montana Historical Society, 1997).

Mountain Life I MT

Karr, Mary (1955–). *The Liar's Club: A Memoir* (Viking, 1995).

Of this memoir's 3 sections, the first 2 focus on her childhood and young adult years. See also her sequel (ch. 9).

Baby Boomers ✧ Children of Alcoholics ✧ College Teachers ✧ Eccentrics ✧ Essayists ✧ Family Violence ✧ Homes and Haunts ✧ Mental Health ✧ Oil Fields ✧ Poets I TX (East) ✧ CO

Kavanagh-Priest, Anne. *Memoirs of a Gothic American* (Macmillan, 1929).
Covers her life until she left the farm to attend college.
Farm Life | NH

Keys, Willis and Art Kidwell. *Growing Up at the Desert Queen Ranch* (Desert Moon, 1997).
Ranch Life | CA (Southern)

Kittredge, William (1932–). *Hole in the Sky: A Memoir* (Vintage Books, 1992).
About 101 scattered pages (pages 3–133).
Alcoholism ✧ College Teachers ✧ Divorce ✧ Farm Life ✧ Fighter Pilots ✧ Novelists ✧ Parents (Aging or Infirm) ✧ Ranch Life | OR

Knepper, Verna (1886?–). *My Papa's Daughter* (Naylor, 1971).
Frontier and Pioneer Life | Oklahoma Territory

Ladd, Carl E(dwin) (1888–1943), and E(dward) R(oe) Eastman (1885–1970). *Growing Up in the Horse and Buggy Days* (Nesterman, 1943).
Focuses on personal reminiscences of regional folkways in central and western NYS, during the approximate period 1880–1905; see also "Eastman, E(dward) R(oe)" (in this chapter).
Farm Life | NY

Lark, Fred A. (18??–). *The Lark's Nest* (Neale, 1918).
Farm Life | AR

Lee, Laurie (1914–1997). Introduction by T. S. Matthews. *The Edge of Day: A Boyhood in the West of England* (W. Morrow, 1960) (Variant title, *Cider with Rosie: A Boyhood in the West of England* [Hogarth, 1959]).
Civil War (Spanish) ✧ Country Life ✧ Growing Up Between WWI and WWII ✧ Poets ✧ Travel Writers | England

Lee, Laurie (1914–1997). *As I Walked Out One Midsummer Morning* (Atheneum, 1969).
This, the sequel to *The Edge of Day,* focuses on him at 19–20 years.
Civil War (Spanish) ✧ Country Life ✧ Growing Up Between WWI and WWII ✧ Poets ✧ Travel Writers | England

Lewis, Flannery (1913–). *Brooks Too Broad for Leaping, a Chronicle from Childhood* (Macmillan, 1938).
Country Life ✧ Growing Up Between WWI and WWII | U.S.

Lewis, William J. (1870–1960). *Tapadero: The Making of a Cowboy* (University of Texas, 1972).
Pages 3–182 focus on him from 15 to 21 years.
Ranch Life | TX

Lewis, Willie Newbury (1891–). *WILLIE, a Girl from a Town Called Dallas* (Texas A&M University, 1984).
The first 50–55 pages.
Ranch Life | TX (Dallas)

Lodi, Edward (1943–). *Deep Meadow Bog: Memoirs of a Cape Cod Childhood* (Rock Village, 1999).

This memoir is written in the form of a novel; Lodi also has written collections of ghost stories.

Bog Farming ✧ Civil Rights Workers ✧ College Teachers ✧ Short Story Writers | MA

Luibheid, Colm. *All the Green Gold: An Irish Boyhood* (Praeger, 1970).

Country Life | Ireland

Mabie, Janet (1893–1961). *Heaven on Earth* (Harper, 1951).

The daughter of a minister, she grew up in western MA.

Country Life ✧ Family Memoirs ✧ Summer | MA

MacConnell, C(harles) E(dward) (1890–). *XIT Buck: Personal Recollections of a Fast-Moving and Fascinating Boyhood* (University of Arizona, 1968).

Covering his first 21 years, this is a classic, entertaining account.

Ranch Life | KS ✧ IN ✧ MI ✧ CO ✧ AZ ✧ NM ✧ Mexico ✧ TX

Mason, Harry Morgan (1908–). *Life on the Dry Line: Working the Land, 1902–1944* (Fulcrum, 1992).

About 117 scattered pages (pages xix–162).

Automobiles ✧ Farm Life | KS

McInnis, Kathryn Cage (18??–). *Solid Lace and Tucks: Memories of a Girlhood in the Texas Hill Country, 1892–1918* (Vantage, 1983).

This is a 59-page memoir.

Country Life | TX

McLean, Evalyn Walsh (1886–), with Boyden Sparkes. *Father Struck It Rich* (Little, Brown, 1936).

Pages 4–145 (chs. 1–12).

Miners | CO ✧ Washington, DC

Mitchell, John (1794–1870) (pseud.: John Chester). *Derwent; or, Recollections of Young Life in the Country* (A.D.F. Randolph, 1872).

Country Life ✧ Homes and Haunts ✧ Nineteenth-Century Pre-Industrial Age Memoirists | CT

Mullen, Margaret (1909–). *An Arkansas Childhood: Growing Up in the Athens of the Ozarks* (M & M, 1989).

Mountain Life | AR

Mylar, Isaac (1847– or 1848–). *Early Days at the Mission San Juan Bautista: A Narrative of Incidents Connected with the Days When California Was Young* (Evening Pajaronian, 1929).

Except for pages 88–96 (ch. ix), the first 28 chapters (pages 12–156).

Frontier and Pioneer Life ✧ Nineteenth-Century Pre-Industrial Age Memoirists ✧ Ranch Life | CA

Nichols, Dave (1914–). *Cowman's Son: Boyhood on a Ranch* (Chilton, 1960).

Covers his first 16 years

Growing Up Between WWI and WWII ✧ Ranch Life | MT ✧ IL (Chicago)

Nordyke, Lewis (1905–). *Nubbin Ridge: My Boyhood on a Texas Farm* (Doubleday, 1960).

Farm Life | TX

North, Luther (1846–1935). Ed. by Donald Danker. Foreword by George Bird Grinnell. *Man of the Plains: Recollections of Luther North, 1856–1882* (University of Nebraska, 1961).

Pages 3–94 (chs. 1–4) cover his first 15 years.

Nineteenth-Century Pre-Industrial Age Memoirists ✧ Ranching Life | U.S. (Midwest)

Oaks, Hazel (?–1984). *Back There: Memories of a Girlhood on the Okanogan Frontier* (Omak Chronicle, 1984).

This is a 64-page memoir that was compiled from "Here & There," a series of columns that appeared in the *Omak-Okanogan Chronicle*.

Frontier and Pioneer Life | WA

O'Connor, Jack (1902–1978). *Horse and Buggy West: A Boyhood on the Last Frontier* (Knopf, 1968).

College Teachers ✧ Frontier and Pioneer Life ✧ Hunting ✧ Journalists ✧ Novelists | AZ

O'Flynn, Criostoir (1927–). *There Is an Isle: A Limerick Boyhood* (Mercier, 1998).

Country Life ✧ Dramatists ✧ Growing Up Between WWI and WWII ✧ Novelists ✧ Poets | Ireland

O'Kieffe, Charley (1879–). *Western Story: The Recollections of Charley O'Kieffe, 1884–1898* (University of Nebraska, 1960).

This is an unsentimentalized, realistic evocation of life in northwestern Nebraska.

Frontier and Pioneer Life | NE

Olson, Ted (1899–1981). *Ranch on the Laramie* (Little, Brown, 1973).

This reminiscence is very entertaining and informative; it does not rely on much re-created dialogue.

Foreign Correspondents ✧ Poets ✧ Ranch Life | WY

Orpen, Adela. *Memories of the Old Emigrant Days in Kansas, 1862–1865; Also, of a Visit to Paris in 1867* (Harper, 1926).

Frontier and Pioneer Life | KS ✧ France

Owens, William A. (1905–1990). *This Stubborn Soil* (Scribner, 1966) (Variant title, *This Stubborn Soil: A Frontier Boyhood* [Faber, 1967]).

Frontier and Pioneer Life | TX

Owens, William A. (1905–1990). *A Season of Weathering.* (Scribner, 1973) (Variant title, *This Stubborn Soil: A Frontier Boyhood* [Faber, 1967]).

About the first 130 pages focus on him from 18 or 19 to 21. Owens states (on page 120) that he was inspired to write about his early years after reading W. H. Hudson's classic memoir *Far Away and Long Ago* (see ch. 4 entry).

Frontier and Pioneer Life | TX

Patterson, Paul (1909–living 1990s). *Crazy Women in the Rafters: Memories of a Texas Boyhood* (University of Oklahoma, 1976).

Humorists ✧ Ranch Life | TX

Payne, Stephen (1888–1970). *Where the Rockies Ride Herd* (Sage Books, 1965).
Set in the area between Fort Collins (CO) and Laramie (WY).
Ranch Life ✧ Short Story Writers I CO ✧ WY

Percy, William Alexander (1885–1942). *Lanterns on the Levee: Recollections of a Planter's Son* (Knopf, 1941).
Pages 26 to about 100.
Mississippi River ✧ Plantation Life ✧ Poets I MS

Pitzer, Henry Littleton (1834–1903). *Three Frontiers: Memories, and a Portrait of Henry Littleton Pitzer As Recorded by His Son Robert Claiborne Pitzer* (Prairie Press, 1938).
About 57 pages.
Collaborations by Relatives ✧ Frontier and Pioneer Life ✧ Miners ✧ Nineteenth-Century Pre-Industrial Age Memoirists I IL ✧ IA

Porterfield, Bill (1933?–). *Diddy Waw Diddy: Passage of an American Son* (HarperCollins, 1994).
Pages 11 to about 338. He tells of a youth spent drifting around with his family.
Depressions (Economic) ✧ Eccentrics ✧ Grandfathers ✧ Journalists ✧ Oil Fields ✧ WWII I TX ✧ OK

Pryor, Mrs. Roger A. (1830–1912). *My Day: Reminiscences of Long Ago* (Macmillan, 1909).
Pages 4–83 focus on her childhood and youth.
Intellectual Life ✧ Nineteenth-Century Pre-Industrial Age Memoirists ✧ Plantation Life I VA

Reynolds, Ralph (1930–). *Growing Up Cowboy: Confessions of a Luna Kid* (Fulcrum, 1991).
Growing Up Between WWI and WWII ✧ Ranch Life I NM

Ripley, Thomas (1865–1956). *A Vermont Boyhood* (D. Appleton-Century, 1937).
Country Life I VT

Roberts, (Dean) Isaac Phillips (1833–1928). *Autobiography of a Farm Boy* (J.B. Lyon, 1916).
Farm Life ✧ Nineteenth-Century Pre-Industrial Age Memoirists I NY ✧ U.S. (Midwest)

Roberts, Jesse David (1882–). *Bears, Bibles and a Boy: Memories of the Adirondacks* (W.W. Norton, 1961).
Hunting ✧ Mountain Life I NY

Rose, Will(iam Palen) (1889–1977). *The Vanishing Village* (Citadel, 1963).
Covers him from about 7 to about 14 years.
Country Life I NY

Sanford, Mollie (1838?– 1915). *Mollie: The Journal of Mollie Dorsey Sanford in Nebraska and Colorado Territories, 1857–1866* (University of Nebraska, 1959).
About the first 150 pages.
Diaries and Journals ✧ Frontier and Pioneer Life ✧ Nineteenth-Century Pre-Industrial Age Memoirists I NE ✧ CO

Shatraw, Milton (1901–). *Thrashin' Time: Memories of a Montana Boyhood* (American West, 1970).

Farm Life | MT

Shears, Sarah. Introduction by R. F. Delderfield. *A Village Girl: Memoirs of a Kentish Childhood* (Curtis Books, 1971) (Original title, *Tapioca for Ten: Memories of a Kentish Childhood* [Elek, 1971]).

Country Life ✧ Growing Up Between WWI and WWII | England (Kent)

Siringo, Charles A(ngelo) (1855–1928). *A Texas Cowboy: Or, Fifteen Years on the Hurricane Deck of a Spanish Pony* (M. Umbdenstock, 1885) (2nd ed. [Siringo & Dobson, 1886] adds 30 pages of addendum, consisting of 7 parts).
The authenticity of some of his recounted anecdotes is suspect. Pages 7–96.

Civil War (U.S.) ✧ Fatherless Families ✧ Frontier and Pioneer Life ✧ Nineteenth-Century Pre-Industrial Age Memoirists ✧ Ranch Life | TX ✧ LA ✧ KS ✧ MO ✧ IL

Smith, Ethel Sabin (1887–). *Furrow Deep and True* (W.W. Norton, 1964).

Camps (Revivalist) ✧ Farm Life | WI

Smith, Sarah Bixby (1871–1935). *Adobe Days: Being the Truthful Narrative of the Events in the Life of a California Girl on a Sheep Ranch and in El Pueblo De Nuestra Senora de Los Angeles While It Was Yet a Small and Humble Town . . .* (Torch, 1925).

Frontier and Pioneer Life ✧ Ranch Life ✧ Sheep | CA (Southern)

Smithwick, Noah (1808–1899). *The Evolution of a State, or Recollections of Old Texas Days* (Steck-Vaughn, 1968).
Pages 10 to about 85 focus on him from 19 to 21 years. The author wrote this account when he was 89–91 years old.

Frontier and Pioneer Life ✧ Nineteenth-Century Pre-Industrial Age Memoirists | KY ✧ LA ✧ TX

Snyder, Grace (1882–1982), as told to Nellie Snyder Yost. *No Time on My Hands* (University of Nebraska, 1986) (Originally published Caxton [1963]).
Chapters 1–27 (pages 13 to about 308). The author's daughter contributed both the foreword and the epilogue to this edition. Includes 20 illustrations.

Centenarians ✧ Collaborations by Relatives ✧ Farm Life ✧ Frontier and Pioneer Life ✧ Quiltmakers | NE

Stahl, Frank (1841–1937). *One-Way Ticket to Kansas: The Autobiography of Frank M. Stahl as Told by Margaret Whittemore* (University of Kansas, 1959).
Pages 2 to about 82.

Frontier and Pioneer Life ✧ Nineteenth-Century Pre-Industrial Age Memoirists | OH

Stowe, Estha Briscoe (1916–). *Oil Field Child* (Texas Christian University, 1989).

Growing Up Between WWI and WWII ✧ Oil Fields | TX ✧ OK

Swan, Walter (1916–). *"me 'n Henry": A Story About Two Boys Growing Up on the Old Family Homestead in Cochise County When Arizona Was an Infant State* (Swan Enterprises, 1978).

Frontier and Pioneer Life ✧ Growing Up Between WWI and WWII | AZ

Taber, Gladys (1899–1980). *Especially Father* (MacRae-Smith, 1948).
Country Life ✧ Family Memoirs ✧ Journalists | CT

Taber, Gladys (1899–1980). *Harvest of Yesterdays* (Lippincott, 1976).
About the first 120 pages.
Country Life ✧ Family Memoirs ✧ Journalists | CT

Taylor, Alice (1938–). *An Irish Country Christmas* (St. Martin's, 1995).
This memoir is set when Taylor was 9.
Christmas ✧ Country Life | Ireland

Taylor, Alice (1938–). *To School Through the Fields: An Irish Country Childhood* (Brandon, 1988).
This recollection is set during Taylor's girlhood, preceding her adolescent years.
Country Life | Ireland

Taylor, Alice (1938–). *Quench the Lamp* (St. Martin's, 1991).
Focuses on her teenage years.
Country Life | Ireland

Thomas, Gwyn (1913–1981). *A Few Selected Exits: An Autobiography of* Sorts (Little, Brown, 1968).
College Teachers ✧ Depressions (Economic) ✧ Dramatists ✧ Growing Up Between WWI and WWII ✧ Miners ✧ Novelists | South Wales

Thompson, Flora (1877–1947). *Lark Rise to Candleford* (Oxford University, 1939).
Considered a classic memoir of a country childhood.
Country Life ✧ Postal Workers ✧ Victorian Era British Memoirists | England

Thompson, Flora (1877–1947). *Over to Candleford* (Oxford University, 1941).
Country Life ✧ Postal Workers ✧ Victorian Era British Memoirists | England

Tressler, Irving D. (1908–1944). *Horse and Buggy Daze* (Howell, Soskin, 1940).
In the course of writing a lighthearted biography of his clergyman father, Tressler reveals details of growing up in the heartland.
Clergy ✧ Farm Life ✧ Humorists | IN

Turner, Leigh Block. Comp. and augmented by William R. Turner. *Memoirs of a Happy Childhood* (Wrybolot, 1991).
This memoirist tells of growing up in the old mining town of Ouray, CO.
Collaborations by Relatives ✧ Mountain Life | CO

Turner, William H(enry) (1935–). *Chesapeake Boyhood: Memoirs of a Farm Boy* (Turner, 1995).
Farm Life ✧ Fishers ✧ Hunting | MD ✧ VA

Twedt, Jerry L. *Growing Up in the 40s: Rural Reminiscence* (Iowa State University, 1996).
See also other titles in this series (<u>Iowa Heritage Collection</u>) under "Harnack, Curtis" (ch. 16) and "Onerheim, Margaret Ott" (ch. 4).
Farm Life | IA

Utley, Minnie L. (1925–). *Yesterday and Tomorrow* (Carlton, 1968).
She was the daughter of a sharecropper.
African Americans ✧ Growing Up Between WWI and WWII ✧ Plantation Life | NC

Uttley, Alison (b. Alice Jane Uttley) (1884–1976). *Ambush of Young Days* (Faber & Faber, 1937).
The following entry by Uttley also focuses on her earliest years. C. F. Tunnicliffe illustrated this work; see also "Williamson, Henry" (ch. 9).
Children's Authors ✧ Country Life ✧ Teachers ✧ Victorian Era British Memoirists | England

Uttley, Alison (b. Alice Jane Uttley) (1884–1976). *Country World: Memories of Childhood* (Faber & Faber, 1984).
The previous entry by Uttley also focuses on her earliest years.
Children's Authors ✧ Country Life ✧ Teachers ✧ Victorian Era British Memoirists | England

Van Nuys, Laura Bower (1880–). *The Family Band: From the Missouri to the Black Hills, 1881–1900* (University of Nebraska, 1961).
Focuses on her first 19 years.
Family Memoirs ✧ Frontier and Pioneer Life | SD

Waldorf, John Taylor (1870–1932). *A Kid on the Comstock: Reminiscences of a Virginia City Childhood* (American West, 1970).
Covers him from about age 3 to about age 16. This is a lively account of growing up in a raucous mining town.
Frontier and Pioneer Life ✧ Miners | NV

Wallem, Irma (1908–). *Expect a Worm in Every Apple: An American Country Diary* (Mercury House, 1987).
At age 10 she moved with her family from San Diego, CA, to the Ozark Mountains in Oklahoma.
Diaries and Journals ✧ Mountain Life | OK

Walsh, Marrie (1929–). *An Irish Country Childhood: Memories of a Bygone Age* (Smith Gryphon, 1995).
Set in 1930s–1940s.
Country Life ✧ Growing Up Between WWI and WWII | Ireland

Warren, C(larence) Henry (1895–1966). *A Boy in Kent* (G. Bles, 1937).
Country Life ✧ Victorian Era British Memoirists | England (Kent)

Watson, Jo Anna Holt. *A Taste of the Sweet Apple: A Memoir* (Sarabande, 2004).
Watson tells of her childhood years growing up on a farm in 1940s Kentucky.
Farm Life | KY

Weitzman, David (1936–). *Thrashin' Time: Harvest Days in the Dakotas* (David R. Godine, 1991).
About 50 pages cover his youth.
Architectural Writers ✧ Children's Authors ✧ Farm Life ✧ Historians (Cultural) | ND ✧ SD

Winniford, Lee (1932–), and Carl Lindahl. *Following Old Fencelines: Tales from Rural Texas* (Texas A & M University, 1998).
Folklorists ✧ Ranch Life | TX

Wollaston, Percy (1904–1983), and Jonathan Raban. *Homesteading* (Lyons & Burford, 1997).

> Family Memoirs ✧ Farm Life ✧ Frontier and Pioneer Life | MT

Wysor, Rufus Johnston (1885–1967). *Boyhood Days in Southwest Virginia* (Vantage, 1961).

> Farm Life | VA

Exotic Locales

From Jungle to Island

Apple, Arnold (1932–). *Son of Guyana* (Oxford University, 1973).

> Pages 1–80. His account of jungle life includes a description of boats that seemingly climb waterfalls.
>
> Natural History ✧ Rain Forests | Guyana

Bishop, Sereno Edwards (1827–1909). *Reminiscences of Old Hawaii* (Hawaiian Gazette Co., 1916).

> The entire 64-page book focuses on his first 13 years. He was the son of a missionary.
>
> Island Life ✧ Missionaries ✧ Nineteenth-Century Pre-Industrial Age Memoirists | HI

Bridges, Doris A. (1900–1993). *Growing Up Way Downeast: A Memoir of Childhood on the Coast of Maine* (Windswept House, 1997).

> The second half of this book focuses on her youth, on Mount Desert Island, ME.
>
> Island Life | ME

Burke, Norah (1907–). *Jungle Child* (W.W. Norton, 1956).

> Includes 32 photos.
>
> India

Chamoiseau, Patrick (1953–). Tr. by Carol Volk. *Childhood* (University of Nebraska, 1999) (First French ed., 1993).

> See also his other memoir (ch 4).
>
> Baby Boomers ✧ Island Life | French West Indies (Martinique)

Clarke, Austin (1934–). *Growing Up Stupid Under the Union Jack: A Memoir* (McClelland and Stewart, 1980).

> His uncle was writer Edmund White. This is a companion volume to the following entry by Clarke.
>
> Island Life ✧ Novelists ✧ Short Story Writers | West Indies (Barbados)

Clarke, Austin (1934–). *Pig Tails 'N Breadfruit: A Culinary Memoir* (New Press, 1999).

> This is a companion volume to the preceding entry by Clarke.
>
> Cookery ✧ Novelists ✧ Short Story Writers ✧ Island Life | West Indies (Barbados)

Farnham, Joseph E(llis) C(offee) (1849–1933). *Brief Historical Data and Memories of My Boyhood Days in Nantucket* (Snow & Farnham, 1915).

> Pages 32–239 focus on his first 21 years, mostly his first 10–15 years.
>
> Island Life ✧ Nineteenth-Century Pre-Industrial Age Memoirists | MA

Gallant, John (1917–). *Bannock, Beans and Black Tea: Memories of a Prince Edward Island Childhood in the Great Depression* (Drawn & Quarterly, 2004).
This is a childhood memoir produced in the form of a graphic novel.
Depressions (Economic) ✧ Farm Life ✧ Graphic Novels ✧ Growing Up Between WWI and WWII ✧ Island Life | Canada (Prince Edward Island)

Hanna, James Scott, Sr. (1897–1972). *What Life Was Like When I Was a Kid* (Naylor, 1973).
Island Life | TX (Galveston Island)

Higa, Tomika (1938–). Tr. from the Japanese by Dorothy Britton. *The Girl with the White Flag* (Kodansha International, 1991).
Set in 1945.
Island Life ✧ WWII | South Pacific Ocean (Okinawa Island)

Hillen, Ernest (1934–). *The Way of a Boy: A Memoir of Java* (Viking, 1993).
Covers him from 8 to 11 years. See also his sequel (ch. 4).
Island Life ✧ WWII | Indonesia (Java)

Jocano, F. Landa. *Growing Up in a Philippine Barrio* (Holt, Rinehart and Winston, 1969).
Island Life ✧ Slums | Philippines

Leslie, Marjorie. *Girlhood in the Pacific: Samoa, Philippines, Spain* (MacDonald, 1943).
Her father was an American diplomat.
Island Life ✧ Samoa Islands | Philippines ✧ Spain

Low, Lema (c. 1915–1920–). *A Family in Fiji* (Pacific, 1962).
Covers 1928–1940.
Family Memoirs ✧ Growing Up Between WWI and WWII ✧ Island Life ✧ Plantation Life | Fiji

Lucie-Smith, Edward (1933–). *The Burnt Child: An Autobiography* (Gollancz, 1975).
Pages 9 to about 136. At age 9, after his father died, he moved with his mother to England.
Biographers ✧ Critics (Art) ✧ Fatherless Families ✧ Island Life ✧ Novelists ✧ Oxford University Poets | Jamaica ✧ England

Mahoney, Rosemary (1961?–). *A Likely Story: One Summer with Lillian Hellman* (Doubleday, 1998).
Set on Martha's Vineyard, this unusual memoir tells of the memoirist's challenges in serving as summer housekeeper, at age 17, for the famous playwright.
Baby Boomers ✧ Hellman, Lillian ✧ Island Life ✧ Seaside Resorts ✧ Summer | MA

Matane, Paulias (1931?–). *My Childhood in New Guinea* (Oxford University, 1972).
For a similar memoir, see "Tchernavin, Tatiana" (ch. 4).
Growing Up Between WWI and WWII ✧ Island Life | New Guinea

O'Sullivan, Maurice (1904–1950). Tr. from the Irish by Moya Davies and George Thomson. *Twenty Years A-Growing* (Viking, 1933).
More than the first 200 pages. He grew up on the Blasket Islands, off the coast of Ireland. He departs for Dublin, Ireland, at age 23.
Folklorists ✧ Island Life | Ireland

Payne, Nellie. *A Grenadian Childhood* (Women's Press, 1990).
> Covers her first 10 years, during the 1920s.
> Growing Up Between WWI and WWII ✧ Island Life | Grenada

Simpson, Dot (1905–1998). *The Island's True Child: A Memoir of Growing Up on Criehaven* (Down East Books, 2003).
> She describes the simple pleasures of growing up in a lobster-fishing village in ME during the early years of the 20th century.
> Island Life ✧ Stepchildren | ME

St. Aubin de Teran, Lisa (1953–). *The Hacienda: A Memoir* (Little, Brown, 1997).
> Focuses on her from 16 to 23 years. At 17 she married an abusive and unbalanced aristocrat.
> Family Violence ✧ Mental Health ✧ Mountain Life ✧ Novelists ✧ Plantation Life ✧ Poets | Venezuela

Starbuck, Mary (1856–1938). *My House and I; A Chronicle of Nantucket* (Houghton Mifflin, 1929).
> All but the final chapter (pages 287–293) focus on her childhood and youth. In her later years, she was a well-known socialite.
> Fishing ✧ High Society ✧ Island Life ✧ Nineteenth-Century Pre-Industrial Age Memoirists | MA ✧ Nantucket

Stryker, Charlotte. *Time for Tapioca* (Crowell, 1951).
> Family Memoirs ✧ Island Life | Java

Von Tempski, Armine (1892–1943). *Born in Paradise* (Duell, Sloan and Pearce, 1940).
> Some 200 pages focus on her youth.
> Island Life ✧ Novelists ✧ Ranch Life | HI

Williams, Alice Cary (1892–1983). *Thru the Turnstile: Tales of My Two Centuries* (Houghton Mifflin, 1976).
> As the daughter of the dean of Tufts Medical School, she met such notables as Julia Ward Howe, William James, and Oscar Wilde.
> Island Life ✧ Wealth | MA (Nantucket)

City Life

Including New York City, Chicago, Los Angeles, San Francisco, Washington, DC, Detroit, Toronto, and London

Armstrong, Hamilton Fish (1893–1973). *Those Days* (Harper & Row, 1963).
> Entire book is on his childhood. He created and edited the journal *Foreign Affairs*.
> City Life ✧ Editors ✧ High Society ✧ Wealth | NYC (Manhattan) ✧ NY ✧ Canada (Quebec) ✧ Europe

Armstrong, Maitland (1836–1918). Ed. by Margaret Armstrong. *Day Before Yesterday: Reminiscences of a Varied Life* (Scribner's Sons, 1920).
> Pages 14 to about 94.
> City Life ✧ Collaborations by Relatives ✧ Nineteenth-Century Pre-Industrial Age Memoirists | NY ✧ NYC ✧ SC

Avery, Valerie (1940–). *London Morning* (W. Kimber, 1964).
> Contains much re-created dialogue.
> City Life | England

Baillie, Eileen (1900?–). *The Shabby Paradise: The Autobiography of a Decade* (Hutchinson, 1958).

Turn-of-the-century childhood in an East End vicarage.

City Life ✧ Clergy | England (London)

Barltrop, Robert (1922–). *Growing Up in North East London Between the* Wars (London Borough of Waltham Forest, 1984).

This volume is composed of 2 parts that had been published separately: *My Mother's Calling Me* (London Borough of Waltham Forest, 1984) and *A Funny Age* (London Borough of Waltham Forest, 1985).

City Life ✧ Growing Up Between WWI and WWII | England

Bingham, Charlotte (1942–). *Coronet Among the Weeds* (Random House, 1963).

From 13 to 20 years. She is the daughter of Madeleine Bingham (see entry in ch. 14). Focuses on her youth in London.

City Life ✧ Novelists | England (London) ✧ France

Brooks, Gladys (1886–1984). *Gramercy Park: Memories of a New York Girlhood* (E.P. Dutton, 1958).

She was married to literary historian Van Wyck Brooks (see entry in ch. 9).

Biographers ✧ City Life | NYC

Cannell, Kathleen (1891–1974). *Jam Yesterday* (W. Morrow, 1945).

City Life | NYC ✧ Canada (Ontario)

Charyn, Jerome (1937–). *Bronx Boy: A Memoir* (St. Martin's, 2002).

This, the third volume of his memoirs, re-creates the colorful world of 1940s Bronx neighborhood life. He has written more than 30 books. For his previous memoirs, see chapter 6.

College Teachers ✧ Crime ✧ Jews ✧ Novelists | NYC (Bronx)

Clemens, Paul (1973–). *Made in Detroit: A South of 8 Mile Memoir* (Doubleday, 2005).

With occasional humor, Clemens describes his formative years growing up in an inner-city environment.

City Life ✧ Generation X ✧ Slums ✧ Working Class Whites | MI (Detroit)

Cohen, Rich (1968–). *The Lake Effect* (Knopf, 2002).

Cohen wistfully recalls his years growing up with his best friend.

City Life ✧ Fathers and Sons ✧ Friendships ✧ Generation X ✧ Jews ✧ Summer | IL (Chicago)

Dana, Nathalie (1878–). *Young in New York: A Memoir of a Victorian Girlhood* (Doubleday, 1963).

Her father was an Episcopal minister.

City Life ✧ Clergy ✧ Episcopalians | NYC

Halper, Albert (1904–1984). *On the Shore: Young Writer Remembering Chicago* (Viking, 1934).

About the first 170 pages focus on his first 21 years; a fair amount of re-created dialogue is sprinkled throughout this memoir.

City Life | IL (Chicago)

Jacobs, Julius. *Bronx Cheer: A Memoir* (Library Research Associates, 1976).
Set in the 1930s.
City Life ✧ Growing Up Between WWI and WWII I NYC (Bronx)

Jastrow, Marie (1897?–1991). *A Time to Remember: Growing Up in New York Before the Great War* (W.W. Norton, 1979).
Covers 1905–1917.
City Life ✧ Immigrants ✧ Jews I NYC

Jastrow, Marie (1897?–1991). *Looking Back: The American Dream Through Immigrant Eyes* (W.W. Norton, 1986).
Covers 1905–1918.
City Life ✧ Immigrants ✧ Jews I NYC

Jordan, June (1936–2002). *Soldier: A Poet's Childhood* (Basic Civitas Books, 2000).
Covers her first 12 years during the 1930s–1940s.
African Americans ✧ City Life ✧ Editors ✧ Essayists ✧ Family Violence ✧ Poets ✧ Reformers ✧ Teachers I NYC (Harlem, Brooklyn)

Jorgensen, Christine (1926–1989). *Christine Jorgensen: A Personal Autobiography* (Cleis, 1967).
From pages 15 to about 80.
City Life ✧ College Teachers ✧ Growing Up Between WWI and WWII ✧ Military Life ✧ Photographers ✧ Singers ✧ Transsexuals I NYC (Bronx) ✧ NJ ✧ NY ✧ CT

Kenney, Shawna (1973?–). *I Was a Teenage Dominatrix* (Retro Systems, 1999).
Pages 11 to about 114.
City Life ✧ Dominatrixes ✧ Generation X I MD ✧ Washington, DC

Kimberley, Ken (1925–). *Oi Jimmy Knacker! A Memoir of an East Ender's Childhood* (Silver Link, 1998).
This nostalgic memoir is set in London between WWI and WWII.
City Life ✧ Growing Up Between WWI and WWII I England (London)

Komroff, Manuel (1890–1974). *Big City, Little Boy* (A.A. Wyn, 1953).
City Life I NYC

Lamar, Jake (1961–). *Bourgeois Blues: An American Memoir* (Summit Books, 1991).
Pages 33–123. His earliest memory was of seeing his mother cry as they watched President Kennedy's funeral. See also "Clary, Anna" (ch. 4).
African Americans ✧ Baby Boomers ✧ City Life ✧ Fathers and Sons ✧ Journalists ✧ Novelists ✧ Racism I NYC (Bronx)

Lilienthal, Meta (1876–1949). *Dear Remembered World: Childhood Memories of an Old New Yorker* (R.R. Smith, 1947).
City Life I NYC

MacCracken, Henry (1880–1970). *The Family on Gramercy Park* (Scribner's Sons, 1949).
Entire memoir focuses on his childhood and adolescence; much light banter and other dialogue is re-created. Author was president of Vassar, 1945–1946.
City Life ✧ Education ✧ Family Memoirs I NYC

McLaughlin, Russell (1894–). *Alfred Street* (Conjure House, 1946).
Many of these essays first appeared in the *Detroit News.*
City Life | MI

Mullen, Barbara (1914–1979). *Life Is My Adventure* (Coward McCann, 1937).
She spent her formative years in Boston and NYC.
City Life ✧ Growing Up Between WWI and WWII ✧ Motion Picture Actors and Actresses | MA ✧ NYC

Pulsifer, Susan (1892?–). *A House in Time* (Citadel, 1958).
City Life ✧ Homes and Haunts | NYC

Roiphe, Anne (1935–). *1185 Park Avenue: A Memoir* (Free Press, 1999).
About the first 100 pages (chs. 1–19).
City Life ✧ Feminists ✧ Jews ✧ Novelists | NYC (Manhattan)

Rosenblatt, Joe (1933–). *Escape from the Glue Factory: A Memoir of a Paranormal Toronto Childhood in the Late Forties* (Exile Editions, 1985).
City Life ✧ Poets | Canada (Ontario: Toronto)

Roskolenko, Harry (1907–1980). *The Time That Was Then: The Lower East Side 1900–1914: An Intimate Chronicle* (Dial, 1971).
His memories are interspersed among many factual details of social history (mostly 1910–1920).
City Life ✧ Jews | NYC (Lower East Side)

Roskolenko, Harry (1907–1980). *When I Was Last on Cherry Street* (Stein and Day, 1965).
The first 8 chapters (pages 1–124). Chapter 8 recounts how, at age 21, he went on road adventures between NYC and Los Angeles.
City Life ✧ Hoboes ✧ Jews ✧ Lower East Side ✧ Road Trips | NYC (Lower East Side)

Ruskay, Sophie (1887–1980). *Horse Cars and Cobblestones* (Beechurst, 1948; A.S. Barnes, 1973).
Emigrating from Russia, her parents came to the U.S. and started a clothing factory.
City Life ✧ Immigrants ✧ Jews | NYC

Sandberg, Sara. *Mama Made Minks* (Doubleday, 1964).
Set in pre-Depression 1920s.
City Life ✧ Fur Trade ✧ Growing Up Between WWI and WWII ✧ Jews | NYC

Sandberg, Sara. *My Sister Goldie* (Doubleday, 1968).
Set in about 1932–1933.
Catskill Mountains ✧ City Life ✧ Depressions (Economic) ✧ Growing Up Between WWI and WWII ✧ Jews | NYC ✧ NY

Sanford, John (1904–2003) (pseud. of Julian L. Shapiro). *The View from Mt. Morris: A Harlem Boyhood* (Barricade Books, 1994).
All but the last chapter focus on his first 16 years.
City Life ✧ Historians (Cultural) ✧ Novelists | NYC (Harlem)

Savo, Jimmy (1895–1960). *I Bow to the Stones: Memories of a New York Childhood* (H. Frisch, 1963).

Actors ✧ City Life ✧ Comedians ✧ Italian Americans | NYC

Spewack, Bella (1899–1990). *Streets: A Memoir of the Lower East Side* (Feminist Press at the City University of New York, 1995).
Written in 1922. Covers her first 17–18 years. She was born in Transylvania.

City Life ✧ Dramatists ✧ Feminists ✧ Foreign Correspondents ✧ Immigrants ✧ Jews ✧ Journalists ✧ Screenwriters ✧ Short Story Writers ✧ Slums | NYC (Lower East Side)

Strong, George Templeton (1820–1875). Ed. by Allan Nevins and Milton Halsey Thomas. *The Diary of George Templeton Strong: Young Man in New York, 1835–1849* (Macmillan, 1952).
Pages 2 to about 172 are about him from 15 to about 21 years.

City Life ✧ Composers ✧ Diaries and Journals ✧ Nineteenth-Century Pre-Industrial Age Memoirists ✧ Painters | NYC

Thomas, Piri (1928–). *Down These Mean Streets* (Knopf, 1967).
The adaptation of this memoir into the 1973 film *Mean Streets* elevated director Martin Scorsese to fame.

City Life ✧ Crime ✧ Growing Up Between WWI and WWII ✧ Puerto Rican Americans | NYC (Harlem)

Witchel, Alex. *Girls Only* (Random House, 1996).
Covers about her first 30 years.

Journalists ✧ Mothers and Daughters | NYC

Woodward, Helen Rosen (1882–1969). *Three Flights Up* (Dodd, Mead, 1935).

Businesspersons ✧ Jews ✧ City Life | NYC

Chapter 4

Homes and Haunts: The Places and Cultures of Native Lands

Like the memoirs listed in the first 3 chapters of *Remembered Childhoods*, those included in this chapter are arranged by setting, within and outside of the U.S. But in contrast, here the arrangement is established according to types of institutions and by geographic location. Seventeen distinct parts comprise this chapter.

In the first 2 sections of this chapter, 3 dozen men and women tell of their youth spent in public and private schools, as well as in resorts, hotels, and similar environments of residence and study. Poet Jim Carroll writes about New York City high school life (*The Basketball Diaries*), while novelist Julian Green tells of his Virginia college days (*Love in America*), and Mary Wallace brings to life the summers of her youth at a resort in New England (*Summer Magic*). Other memoirs in these sections are set in such diverse locales as England, France, Scotland, the French West Indies, Manhattan, and Wisconsin.

Nearly 60 memoirs make up the third section. Their common element is that they relate the early years of lives spent in the northeastern and Mid-Atlantic U.S. From the Chesapeake Bay to the upper reaches of the rockbound coast of Maine, these works mainly recount countrified lives and folkways, as set down by such writers as Jennie Black (*I Remember. . .*), Charles Champlin (*Back There Where the Past Was*), and John Gould (*Last One In: Tales of a New England Boyhood*)—engaging writers all. Additional memoirs situated in this highly populated part of the U.S. may be found particularly in the first and third sections of chapter 3.

More than 130 titles, listed in this chapter's fourth through eighth sections, center on the formative years of persons who grew up in other parts of the U.S. The cultural essence of America's heartland has been captured by such coming-of-age memoirists as Marilyn Coffey (*Great Plains Patchwork*) and Beatrice Henshaw (*Backward, Turn Backward: Recollections of a Childhood in Northern Michigan*). Southern and Southwestern life of years gone by is evoked in the writings of such memoirists as Chalmers Archer Jr. (*Growing Up Black in Rural Mississippi*) and Edward Dale (*The Cross Timbers: Memories of a North Texas Boyhood*). Memoirs set in the Western U.S. include such works as Ralph William Macy's *Wooden Sidewalks: Growing Up in Western Oregon;* Fred Hatfield's *North of the Sun: A Memoir of the Alaskan Wilderness*; and J. Juan Reid's *Growing Up in Colorado Springs: The 1920's Remembered*.

More than 2 dozen autobiographical accounts by Native Americans of North America can be found in the ninth part of the chapter. A wide range of ethnic and cultural experience and history is covered by the titles here. About half of these memoirs (e.g., works by Althea Bass, Left Handed, and John Neihardt) describe Great Plains life during the 19th century.

The remainder of this chapter provides glimpses of life in other parts of the world, as recalled through the mind's eye of youth. Sixteen of these illuminate childhoods lived in Canada—our neighbor to the north, about whose culture so many of us in the U.S. know so little. We can find out what it was like to grow up in Canada during the early 20th century through the eyes of Pulitzer Prize winner Wallace Stegner (in southern Saskatchewan) or activist Dorothy Livesay (in Toronto).

More than 250 memoirs tell us what it was like growing up in other cultures around the world. A random sampling of places and some memoirs set there: South America (Wendy Ewald's *Magic Eyes: Scenes from an Andean Childhood*); Scotland (Christine Fraser's *Blue Above the Chimneys*), Iran (Shusha Guppy's *Blindfold Horse: Memories of a Persian Childhood*), India (W. D. Merchant's *Home on the Hill: A Bombay Girlhood*), Communist China (Sansan's *Eighth Moon*), Cold War Russia (Cathy Young's *Growing Up in Moscow*), Nigerian Africa (*Wole Soyinka's Ake: The Years of Childhood*), and Australia (Katherine McKell's *Old Days and Gold Days in Victoria*).

As the distances between cultures in our world continue to diminish, exposure to foreign cultures through memoirs cannot help but increase understanding, knowledge, and tolerance.

Note: For memoirs focusing on first or second generation immigrants' experiences in adjusting to life in the U.S., either moving toward assimilation into mainstream American culture or finding a viable balance between their native cultures and American culture, see chapter 5.

School Life

Brinsley-Richards, James (1846–1892). *Seven Years at Eton, 1857–1864* (Bentley, 1883).
   Among the memorable vignettes in this memoir is the author's claim that he saw a ghost.
   Eton College ✧ Nineteenth-Century Pre-Industrial Age Memoirists I England

Burton, Warren (1800–1866). Ed. by Clifton Johnson. *The District School As It Was, By One Who Went to It* (Crowell, 1928). (1969 rpt., Arno) (Originally published by Carter, Hendee, 1833).
   From 3 to 17 years. The text is followed by 17 pages reproduced from old-time spelling primers.
   Country Life ✧ Education ✧ Nineteenth-Century Pre-Industrial Age Memoirists I NH

Carroll, Jim (1950–). *The Basketball Diaries* (Tombouctou, 1978).
   From about 13 to 16 years.
   Baby Boomers ✧ Basketball ✧ Catholics ✧ City Life ✧ Crime ✧ Diaries and Journals ✧ Drug Abuse ✧ Musicians ✧ Poets I NYC

Cary, Lorene (1956–). *Black Ice* (Knopf, 1991).
   Focuses on her years at a New England boarding school.
   African Americans ✧ Baby Boomers ✧ Education ✧ Racism I NH

Chamoiseau, Patrick (1953–). Tr. by Linda Coverdale. *School Days* (University of Nebraska, 1997) (First French ed., 1994).
   See also his other memoir (ch. 3).
   Baby Boomers ✧ Education ✧ Island Life I French West Indies (Martinique)

Fleming, George Thornton (1855–1928). *My High School Days, Including a Brief History of the Pittsburgh Central High School from 1855 to 1871 and Addenda* (William G. Johnston, 1904).

High School Life ✧ Nineteenth-Century Pre-Industrial Age Memoirists | PA

Foster, Larimore (1905–1924). *Larry: Thoughts of Youth* (Association, 1930).
Includes letters and selections from his diary.

College Life ✧ Diaries and Journals ✧ Lafayette College | PA

Green, Julian (1900–1998). Tr. by Euan Cameron. *Love in America: Autobiography: Volume III (1919–1922)* (M. Boyars, 1994) (First published in French, 1966).
See also 2 memoirs by him elsewhere in this chapter and in chapter 6. His sister is Anne Green (see entry in ch. 17).

Bisexuals ✧ College Life ✧ Dramatists ✧ Essayists ✧ Novelists ✧ Translators | VA

Greene, Bob (1947–). *Be True to Your School: A Diary of 1964* (Atheneum, 1987).

Baby Boomers ✧ High School Life ✧ Journalists | OH

James, M(ontague) R(hodes) (1862–1936). *Eton and King's: Recollections, Mostly Trivial* (Williams & Norgate, 1926).
Pages 1–97, 106–112. He is best remembered as a writer of ghost stories.

Critics (Art) ✧ Eton College ✧ King's College ✧ Short Story Writers ✧ Translators | England

Jeune, Margaret (1818?–1891). *My School-Days in Paris* (Thomas Nelson and Sons, 1871) (Variant title, *School Days in Paris*).

Education ✧ Nineteenth-Century Pre-Industrial Age Memoirists | France

Laflin, Louis Ellsworth (1898–1976). *Anxious Bench; Or, Life at a Prep School* (R.F. Seymour, 1929).

Lawrenceville Academy | NJ

Land, Brad (c. 1975–1980–). *Goat: A Memoir* (Random House, 2004).
This memoir focuses on his experiences involving college hazing, when he was 19.

Clemson University ✧ College Life ✧ Generation X (?) ✧ Hazing | SC

Markham, Captain F. (1837–). *Recollections of a Town Boy at Westminster, 1849–1855* (Edward Arnold, 1903).

Nineteenth-Century Pre-Industrial Age Memoirists ✧ Westminster School | England

McCaskey, Townsend (1908–1991). *Bustin' into an Education: A New Boys "Log" of Life as It Is Lived at School* (D. McCaskey, 1926).

High School Life ✧ St. John's Military Academy | WI

Miller, Hugh (1802–1856). *My Schools and Schoolmasters: Or, the Story of My Education: An Autobiography* (W.P. Nimmo, Hay, & Mitchell, 1859).
Starting on page 19, at least 100 pages.

Education ✧ Nineteenth-Century Pre-Industrial Age Memoirists | Scotland

Southall, James Powell Cocke (1871–1962). *In the Days of My Youth: When I Was a Student at the University of Virginia, 1888–1893* (University of North Carolina, 1947).

College Life ✧ University of VA | VA

Stearns, Alfred (1871–1949). *An Amherst Boyhood* (The College, 1946).

He includes descriptions of his college years. Stearns's grandfather was president of Amherst College.

Amherst College ✧ College Life ✧ Grandfathers | MA

Toth, Susan Allen (1940–). *Ivy Days: Making My Way Out East* (Little, Brown, 1984).

Pages 3 to about 67 focus on her life as a Smith College student from about 18 to 21 years. Toth states that many names have been altered, but the incidents that she describes did occur. See also her prequel (this ch.).

College Life ✧ Smith College | MA

Watkins, Paul (1964–). *Stand Before Your God: A Boarding-School Memoir* (Random House, 1993).

Baby Boomers ✧ Novelists | England

Windom, Jane Hutcheson. *European School-days in the Eighteen Seventies* (Princeton University, 1931).

She was born in Ohio but moved to Europe at a young age.

Education | Europe

Resorts, Bars, Carnivals, Hotels, and Retirement Homes

Corbett, Elizabeth Frances (1887–1981). *Out at the Soldiers' Home: A Memory Book* (D. Appleton-Century, 1941).

She grew up in a Civil War veterans' rest home, and later wrote historical novels set during the U.S. Civil War.

Civil War (U.S.) ✧ Homes and Haunts ✧ Novelists ✧ Poets | WI

Fenton, Peter (1949–). *Eyeing the Flash: The Education of a Carnival Con Artist* (Simon and Schuster, 2004).

In this humorous memoir Fenton reveals the chicanery and other inner mechanisms of the traveling carnival circuit.

Baby Boomers ✧ Carnivals ✧ Children of Alcoholics ✧ Crime ✧ Football ✧ Gambling ✧ Journalists | MI

Grossinger, Tania (1937–). *Growing Up at Grossinger's* (D. McKay, 1975).

Catskills ✧ Resorts | NY

Harriman, Margaret (1904–1966). *Blessed Are the Debonair* (Rinehart, 1956).

About 94 scattered pages.

High Society ✧ Resorts | NYC

Lewis, Stephen (1929–). *Hotel Kid: A Times Square Childhood* (Paul Dry Books, 2002).

Lewis recounts what it was like to grow up in the famous Hotel Taft in midtown Manhattan during the 1930s–1940s. For another Depression-era city hotel memoir by a boy, see *King of the Hill* by A. E. Hotchner (ch. 16).

City Life ✧ College Teachers ✧ Depressions (Economic) ✧ Growing Up Between WWI and WWII ✧ Jews ✧ Resorts | NYC (Manhattan)

Moehringer, J. R. (1965–). *The Tender Bar: A Memoir* (Hyperion, 2005).
Without a father, the author grew up in a bar under the influences of male relatives and customers. About the first 250 pages.

Alcoholism ✧ Bars ✧ City Life ✧ College Life ✧ Fatherless Families ✧ Generation X ✧ Grandfathers ✧ Journalists ✧ Uncles ✧ Working Class Whites ✧ Yale University | NY (Long Island)

Saginor, Jennifer. *Playground: A Childhood Lost Inside the Playboy Mansion* (HarperEntertainment, 2005).
Focuses on her from 6 to 14 years, growing up at Hugh Hefner's fantasy estate.

Alcoholism ✧ Bisexuals ✧ Divorce ✧ Drug Abuse ✧ Playboy Mansion | IL (Chicago)

Wallace, Mary (1919–). *Summer Magic* (Doubleday, 1967).
Covers the summers between the world wars.

Grandfathers ✧ Growing Up Between WWI and WWII ✧ Seaside Resorts ✧ Summer | MA

Northeastern and Mid-Atlantic United States

Maine, Vermont, New Hampshire, Massachusetts, Connecticut, Rhode Island, New York State, Pennsylvania, and Washington, DC

Abbott, Eleanor Hallowell (1872–1958). *Being Little in Cambridge When Everyone Else Was Big* (D. Appleton-Century, 1936).
City Life | MA

Albee, John (1833–1915). *Confessions of Boyhood* (R.G. Badger, 1910).
Nineteenth-Century Pre-Industrial Age Memoirists | MA

Anderson, Hesper (1954?–). *South Mountain Road: A Daughter's Journey of Discovery* (Simon and Schuster, 2000).
Covers her from 19 to 20 years; her father was playwright Maxwell Anderson.

Anderson, Maxwell ✧ Baby Boomers ✧ Fathers and Daughters | NY

Baker, Adelaide (1894–1974). *Return to Arcady* (Lawrence Hill Books, 1973).
Pages 1 to about 138.

Country Life | CT ✧ MA

Beardsley, Levi. *See* Jones, Louis Clark, in appendix A, "Bibliography of Collective Works."

Black, Jennie (1868–1945). *I Remember; a Short and Intimate Sketch of the Dignified Seventies, the Elegant Eighties and the Gay Nineties in or Near the Hudson Valley in the Vicinity of Sunnyside, the Home of Washington Irving, in the Land of Sleepy Hollow. Also a Few Episodes in the Young Life of the Author* (Thomas Clayton, 1938).
Pages 2–96 cover her first 16 years.

Hudson River ✧ Irving, Washington | NY

Bolster, Alice. *True Adventures of a Little Country Girl: An Autobiographical Narrative* (Vantage, 1950).
She grew up on a farm with many pets.

Animal Eccentrics ✧ Country Life ✧ Family Memoirs ✧ Farm Life | VT

Borst, Ruth Wilson (1891–). *A Turn-of-the-Century Child* (Wendover, 1979).
 The first part of the book describes summer trips to the family cottage by the Atlantic Ocean; the second part describes, month by month, growing up in western CT.
 Connecticut River Valley ✧ Social Workers ✧ Summer I CT

Braddock, Ellsworth C. (1891–), as told to E. J. Snow. *Memories of North Carver Village* (Channing Books, 1977).
 Pages 12–113 focus on people and places he interacted with during his formative years.
 Country Life I MA

Brooks, Walter (1856–1933). *A Child and a Boy* (Brentano's, 1915).
 Nineteenth-Century Pre-Industrial Age Memoirists I New England (?)

Camp, Mortimer. *Life and Adventures of a New England Boy* (F.W. Cone, 1893).
 He grew up in the early 1800s and assisted whalers.
 Whaling I New England

Champlin, Charles (1926–). Introduction by Ray Bradbury. *Back There Where the Past Was: A Small-Town Boyhood* (Syracuse University, 1989).
 Country Life ✧ Growing Up Between WWI and WWII I NY

Coburn, Philip F. *Growing Up in Weston* (Copigraph, 1981).
 This is a memoir of about 56 pages.
 Country Life I MA

Cowles, Julia (1785–1803). Ed. by Laura Moseley. *The Diaries of Julia Cowles: A Connecticut Record, 1797–1803* (Yale University, 1931).
 Collaborations by Relatives ✧ Diaries and Journals ✧ Eighteenth-Century ✧ Memoirists I CT

Cutler, Frances Wentworth (1887–1973). Ed. and anno. by Charles H. Knickerbocker. *The Minister's Daughter: A Time-Exposure Photograph of the Years 1903–04* (Dorrance, 1974).
 The diary (pages 1–134) was written when Cutler was 15–16 years old.
 Diaries and Journals I ME

Danforth, Judge Keyes (1822–1897). *Boyhood Reminiscences: Pictures of New England Life in the Olden Times in Williamstown* (Gazlay Brothers, 1895).
 Nineteenth-Century Pre-Industrial Age Memoirists I MA

Davis, Ted. *Sittin' and Thinkin'* (Marshall Jones, 1953).
 Nearly 80 pages focus on his childhood and youth in Middleborough.
 Country Life I MA

Dodge, Ernest (1913–1980). *Morning Was Starlight: My Maine Boyhood* (Globe Pequot, 1980).
 Growing Up Between WWI and WWII I ME

Dunham, Austin (1834–1918). *Reminiscences of Austin C. Dunham* (Case, Lockwood & Brainard, 1914).
 Nineteenth-Century Pre-Industrial Age Memoirists I CT

Durstewitz, Jeff (1952–), and Ruth Williams (1952–). *Younger Than That Now: A Shared Passage from the Sixties* (Bantam Books, 2000).
Parts 1–4 (pages 3–199) focus on their first 21 years.
Baby Boomers ✧ Letters ǀ NY (Long Island)

Earle, Virginia (1922–). *Three Homes: Recollections of Childhood* (W.L. Bauhan, 1992).
Growing Up Between WWI and WWII ✧ Homes and Haunts ǀ NY

Edey, Marion (1879–1957). *Early in the Morning* (Harper, 1954).
Hudson River ǀ NY

Fricke, Aaron (1962–). *Reflections of a Rock Lobster: A Story About Growing Up Gay* (Alyson, 1981).
Pages 12–105.
Baby Boomers ✧ Gays ǀ RI

Gillespie, Janet (1913–). *A Joyful Noise* (Harper & Row, 1971).
Covers about the same period as the following entry (her first 20 years). Contains a substantial amount of re-created dialogue.
Growing Up Between WWI and WWII ✧ Summer ǀ MA

Gillespie, Janet (1913–). *With a Merry Heart* (Harper & Row, 1976).
Covers her first 20 years. This memoir contains less re-created dialogue than the previous entry.
Growing Up Between WWI and WWII ǀ MA ✧ NJ

Goff, Beth (1913–). *Understanding Backwards* (Robert Hasbrouck, 1998).
Pages 1–240. Although most of the memoir is set in Ossining, NY, Goff also describes a trip she took to Italy.
Growing Up Between WWI and WWII ✧ Hudson River ǀ NY ✧ Italy

Goodman, Philip (1885–1940). *Franklin Street* (Knopf, 1942).
He was a friend of journalist H. L. Mencken.
City Life ǀ PA (Philadelphia)

Gould, John (1908–2003). *And One to Grow On: Recollections of a Maine Boyhood* (W. Morrow, 1949).
Covers about the same period as the following entry. His father was Franklin Farrar Gould (see entry in ch. 3).
Country Life ✧ Folklorists ✧ Humorists ✧ Journalists ǀ ME

Gould, John (1908–2003). *Last One In: Tales of a New England Boyhood, a Gently Pleasing Dip into a Cool, Soothing Pool of the Not-So-Long-Ago, So to Speak* (Little, Brown, 1966).
Covers about the same period as the preceding entry.
Country Life ✧ Folklorists ✧ Humorists ✧ Journalists ǀ ME

Harris, Paul Percy (1868–1947). *My Road to Rotary: The Story of a Boy, a Vermont Community and Rotary* (A. Kroch, 1948).
About the first 200 pages cover his youth.
Organizations ǀ VT

Henry, Katharine (pseud. of Katharine Krebs) (1867–). *Back Home in Pennsylvania* (Dorrance, 1937).

Country Life I PA

Hird, Mary (1873–). *Threads of Memory: Being Bits of Color, Grave and Gay, That Woven Together Helped Make the Fabric of My Life* (Harbor, 1932).

PA ✧ MA

Hitchcock, Alfred M(arshall) (1868–1941). *A New England Boyhood* (Quinn & Boden, 1934).

(He is not to be confused with the British-born film director [1899–1980].)

NH ✧ CT

Holton, Edith (1881–). *Yankees Were Like This* (Harper & Brothers, 1944).

Covers her girlhood in Wellshaven.

Country Life I MA

Horton, Gertrude. *Old Delaware County: A Memoir* (Purple Mountain, 1993).

Country Life I NY

Howe, Charles Oliver (1822–1915). *What I Remember* (Privately printed, 1928).

Written in 1895.

Nineteenth-Century Pre-Industrial Age Memoirists I MA

Hoyt, Murray (1904–2001). *30 Miles for Ice Cream* (Stephen Greene, 1974).

Country Life ✧ Short Story Writers ✧ Summer I VT

Israel, Betsy (1958–). *Grown-up Fast: A True Story of Teenage Life in Suburban America* (Poseidon, 1988).

Pages 15–221 cover her first 21 years.

Baby Boomers I NY (Western, Long Island)

Janes, E(dward) C. (1908–). *I Remember Cape Cod* (Stephen Greene, 1974).

Set in Wellfleet, during the summers of 1913–1918. Janes is known most for his instructional books on outdoor recreational activities.

Children's Authors ✧ Family Memoirs ✧ Fishing ✧ Hunting ✧ Journalists ✧ Natural History ✧ Summer I MA

Johnston, William Andrew (1871–1929). *My Own Main Street* (Standard, 1921).

Country Life I PA

Johnston, William Graham (1828–1913). *Life and Reminiscences from Birth to Manhood* (Knickerbocker, 1901).

Covers his life to 1848.

Nineteenth-Century Pre-Industrial Age Memoirists I PA

Jones, Louis C(lark) (1908–1990). *Growing Up in the Cooper Country: Boyhood Recollections of the New York Frontier* (Syracuse University, 1968).

Country Life I NY

Knowlton, John (1903–). *A Letter for Johanna: Memories of a Massachusetts Boyhood* (Exposition, 1978).
Pages 28–270 cover his youth in West Upton and Concord.
Country Life | MA

Locke, Elizabeth (1897?–). *Turn of the Century* (Vantage, 1967).
Country Life | VT ✧ MA

Miller, Christopher (1885–1956). *Hudson Valley Squire* (Frederick A. Stokes, 1941).
Hudson River | NY

Mullen, John (1903–). *In a Year of Our Lord: A Memoir of American Innocence* (Arbor House, 1977).
Focuses on him at 9 years old. This memoir employs a novelized style, with much re-created dialogue.
Country Life | PA

Pearson, Haydn (1901–1967). *New England Flavor: Memories of a Country Boyhood* (W.W. Norton, 1961).
Covers about the same period as the following entry.
Country Life ✧ Natural History | NH

Pearson, Haydn (1901–1967). *The New England Year* (W.W. Norton, 1966).
Covers about the same period as the preceding entry.
Farm Life ✧ Natural History | NH

Phelps, Orra (1867–). *When I Was a Girl in the Martin Box* (Island, 1949).
Country Life | CT

Pitkin, Olive (1923–). *There and Then: A Vermont Childhood* (Fithian, 1997).
Pages 9–136.
Country Life ✧ Growing Up Between WWI and WWII | VT

Richmond, Allen. *The First Twenty Years of My Life* (American Sunday-School Union, 1859).
He tries to atone for sinful living in NYS by returning to New England to apprentice for a carpenter.
Nineteenth-Century Pre-Industrial Age Memoirists ✧ Spiritual Life | New England ✧ NY

Schurmacher, Emile (1903–1976). *Knee Pants* (Crowell, 1950).
Journalists | NY

Shute, Henry (1856–1943). *The Real Diary of a Real Boy* (Everett, 1902).
Focuses on him at 11 years old.
Diaries and Journals ✧ Nineteenth-Century Pre-Industrial Age Memoirists | NH

Skinner, Henrietta (1857–1928). *An Echo from Parnassus; Being Girlhood Memories of Longfellow and His Friends* (J.H. Sears, 1928).
She was a daughter of Richard Henry Dana Jr. (see ch. 1 entry).
Longfellow, Henry Wadsworth ✧ Nineteenth-Century Pre-Industrial Age Memoirists | New England

Smith, Francis McKelden (1887–). *South of Yesterday; the Memoirs of Francis McKelden Smith: Volume I* (Exposition, 1963).
Pages 21 to about 99.
City Life | Washington, DC

Smith, Robert Paul (1915–1977). *"Where Did You Go?" "Out." "What Did You Do?" "Nothing."* (W.W. Norton, 1957).
Growing Up Between WWI and WWII | NY (Westchester County)

Snow, Wilbert (1884–1977). *Codline's Child: The Autobiography of Wilbert Snow* (Wesleyan University, 1974).
Pages 3–98. He was a political activist, as well as a teacher.
College Teachers ✧ Poets ✧ Reformers | ME

Spence, Lewis (1920–1998). *A Mountain View: A Memoir of Childhood Summers on Upper Saranac Lake* (Syracuse University, 2002).
Growing Up Between WWI and WWII ✧ Journalists ✧ Lakes ✧ Mountain Life ✧ Outdoor Recreation ✧ Summer | NY

Stephens, C(harles) A(sbury) (1844–1931). *Stories of My Home Folks* (Perry Mason, 1926).
Country Life ✧ Nineteenth-Century Pre-Industrial Age Memoirists | ME

Stone, W. L(awrence) (1903–). *Village Memories* (W.L. Stone, 1981).
Country Life | ME

Taylor, Helen V. (?–early 1980s). *A Time to Recall: The Delights of a Maine Childhood* (W.W. Norton, 1963).
Covers the general period 1910–1920.
Country Life ✧ Summer | ME

Wickham, Robert (1877–). *A Saratoga Boyhood* (Orange, 1948).
Set in the 1880s.
Country Life | NY

Winslow, Anna Green (1759–1779). Ed. by Alice Morse Earle. *Diary of Anna Green Winslow: A Boston School Girl of 1771* (Houghton Mifflin, 1894).
Covers her from about 12 to about 14 years old.
Diaries and Journals ✧ Eighteenth-Century ✧ Memoirists | MA

Wright, Henry Clarke. *See* Jones, Louis Clark, in appendix A, "Bibliography of Collective Works."

Midwest United States

Illinois, Indiana, Iowa, Kansas, Michigan, Minnesota, Nebraska, Ohio, and Wisconsin

Anderson, Elizabeth Callaway (1917–). *Memories of a Nebraska Childhood* (Privately printed, 1984).
A 54-page memoir.
Growing Up Between WWI and WWII | NE

Benjamin, David (1949–). *The Life and Times of the Last Kid Picked* (Random House, 2002).

This humorous memoir covers about his first 13 years.

Baby Boomers ✧ Catholics ✧ Country Life ✧ Editors ✧ Fatherless Families ✧ Humorists ✧ Journalists | WI

Blumenfeld, Ralph David (1864–1948). *Home Town: Story of a Dream That Came True* (Hutchinson, 1944).

Pages 7–119 (chs. 1–35).

Journalists | WI

Boys, Samuel Evans (1871–). *My Boyhood in the Flint Hills of Kansas, 1873–1893* (Privately printed, 1958).

This is a 61-page memoir.

Frontier and Pioneer Life | KS

Brush, Daniel Harmon (1813–1890). Ed. by Milo Milton Quaife. *Growing Up with Southern Illinois, 1820–1861: From the Memoirs of Daniel Harmon Brush* (Lakeside, R.R. Donnelley & Sons, 1944).

Pages 9–96. He moved to IL with his family at age 8.

Nineteenth-Century Pre-Industrial Age Memoirists | VT ✧ IL

Bryson, Bill (1951–). *The Life and Times of the Thunderbolt Kid: A Memoir* (Broadway Books, 2006).

In the vein of Jean Shepherd (ch. 11), Bryson spins a lighthearted account of growing up in the heartland of middle class America.

Baby Boomers ✧ Humorists ✧ Travel Writers | IA (Des Moines)

Buttz, Rachel Q. (1847–). *A Hoosier Girlhood* (R.G. Badger, 1924).

Pages 15–180 (chs. 2–21).

Nineteenth-Century Pre-Industrial Age Memoirists | IN ✧ OH

Carlson, Avis (1896–1987). *Small World . . . Long Gone: A Family Record of an Era* (Schori, 1975).

To 21 years. This is a classic reminiscence of the American heartland set at the start of the 20th century.

Family Memoirs | KS

Church, Steven (1971–). *The Guinness Book of Me* (Simon and Schuster, 2005).

In this amusing memoir, the author recounts how the famous book of records influenced his childhood imagination.

Books and Reading ✧ College Teachers ✧ Generation X | KS

Clary, Anna (1859–). *Reminiscences of Anna Lathrop Clary Written for Her Children* (Adcraft, 1937).

Except for pages 54–64, pages 1–106 are on her first 20 years, the last 17 of which she lived in MN. She and her family moved to MN when she was 3. Her first significant memory was learning of President Lincoln's assassination. (See also entry for Jake Lamar in chapter 3.) She also provides vivid descriptions of such incidents as grasshopper infestations and farming accidents. A classic.

Nineteenth-Century Pre-Industrial Age Memoirists | WI ✧ MN

Cloman, Flora (1869–). *I'd Live It Over* (Farrar & Rinehart, 1941).
About the first 80 pages. (Pages 379–80 provide a glossary of persons mentioned in this memoir.)
Country Life | MN ✧ WI

Coffey, Marilyn (1937–). *Great Plains Patchwork: A Memoir* (Iowa State University, 1989).
About 71 scattered pages, including the last 40 pages of the book. The author blends oral and written history with memoir.
Farm Life | NE

Decker, Edward (1869–1956). Ed. by Winthrop Chamberlain. *Busy Years* (Lund, 1937).
MN (?)

Detzer, Karl (aka Michael Costello) (1891–1987). *Myself When Young* (Funk & Wagnalls, 1968).
Country Life | IN

Frank, Judy Mattier. *Time That Was* (Judy Mottier Frank, 1977).
Set around 1900.
Country Life | IL

Grayson, David (pseud. of Ray Stannard Baker) (1870–1946). *Native American, the Book of My Youth* (Scribner's Sons, 1941).
Pages 1–247 (chs. 1–28).
Biographers ✧ Journalists ✧ Novelists | MI ✧ WI

Hampl, Patricia (1946–). *A Romantic Education* (Houghton Mifflin, 1981).
Some 97 scattered pages (3–120).
College Teachers ✧ Poets | MN

Harju, Jerry (1933–). *Northern Reflections: Lighthearted Account of "Growing Up North"* (Avery Color Studios, 1992).
Humorists | MI

Henshaw, Beatrice (1911–). *Backward, Turn Backward: Recollections of a Childhood in Northern Michigan* (Historical Society of Michigan, 1986).
Country Life | MI

Holmes, Frank Lincoln Duane (1881–). *Covered Wagon Memories* (Vantage, 1971).
Focuses on his early childhood.
Bereavement ✧ Peddlers and Peddling | MN

Holmes, Marjorie (pseud. of Lynn Mighell) (1910–2002). *You and I and Yesterday* (W. Morrow, 1973).
Novelists | IA

Holt, Robert E. *Two Little Devils: A Memoir: A Nostalgic Portrayal of Two Friends Growing Up in Michigan* (Exposition, 1979).
Set in the 1920s.
Growing Up Between WWI and WWII | MI

Howells, William Cooper (1815–1894). *Recollections of Life in Ohio, 1813–1840* (Robert Clarke, 1895).

The first 22 chapters, through page 158. He was the father of literary critic, editor, and novelist William Dean Howells (see ch. 9 entry).

Nineteenth-Century Pre-Industrial Age Memoirists | OH

Hutchison, Nell. *When I Was a Child in Minnesota* (Privately printed, 1996).

Farm Life | MN

Imhoff, Edgar Allen (1901–), and Robert J. Hastings. *Always of Home: A Southern Illinois Childhood* (Southern Illinois University, 1993).

Country Life | IL

Jones, Bryan L. (1945–). *Mark Twain Made Me Do It & Other Plains Adventures* (University of Nebraska, 1997).

Farm Life ✧ Humorists ✧ Twain, Mark | NE

Kimmel, Haven (1965–). *A Girl Named Zippy: Growing Up Small in Mooreland, Indiana* (Doubleday, 2001).

The author evokes a small-town childhood refreshingly bereft of dysfunctions.

Country Life ✧ Generation X ✧ Spiritual Lives | IN

Kimmel, Haven (1965–). *She Got Up Off the Couch: And Other Heroic Acts from Mooreland, Indiana* (Simon and Schuster, 2005).

In this sequel to the previous entry, Kimmel focuses on her adolescence and her interactions with her mother.

Country Life ✧ Generation X ✧ Mothers and Daughters ✧ Spiritual Lives | IN

Layman, Carol S(purlock) (1937–). *Growing Up Rich in Vernon, Indiana: A Celebration of American Small-town Life in the 1940s and '50s* (Still Waters, 1992).

This memoir has dozens of black-and-white photos, interspersed throughout the text.

Historians (Cultural) | IN

Lutes, Della (pseud. of Della Thompson) (1872–1942). *The Country Kitchen* (Little, Brown, 1936).

Both this and the following entry focus on Lutes's childhood. An index of recipes from her early years appears in this volume.

Cookery ✧ Country Life | MI

Lutes, Della (pseud. of Della Thompson) (1872–1942). *Home Grown* (Little, Brown, 1937).

Both this and the previous entry focus on Lutes's childhood.

Cookery ✧ Country Life | MI

May, Jim (1947–). *Farm on Nippersink Creek: Stories from a Midwestern Childhood* (August House, 1994).

Baby Boomers ✧ Catholics ✧ Farm Life | IL

Molee, Elias (1845–). *Molee's Wandering, An Autobiography with Many Surprising Adventures and Doings . . .* (Elias Molee, 1919).

Nineteenth-Century Pre-Industrial Age Memoirists | U.S. (Midwest)

Onerheim, Margaret (1917–). *Threads of Memory: A Memoir of the 1920s* (Iowa State University, 1993).

Her first 12 years. See also titles in this series (Iowa Heritage Collection) under "Harnack, Curtis" (ch. 16) and "Twedt, Jerry L." (ch. 3).

Growing Up Between WWI and WWII I IA

Osborn, Vera. . . . *There Were Two of Us* (McGraw-Hill, 1944).

Her girlhood and youth are covered in this memoir.

MI

Plumb, Ralph G. (1881–1976). *Born in the Eighties* (Brandt, 1940).

U.S. (Midwest)

Reichmann, Edith Cheever (1875–). *Gratefully Remembered: Reminiscences of My Childhood and Youth* (Hill and Dale, 1964).

Probably set in or near IL.

IL (?)

Santmyer, Helen (1895–1986). *Ohio Town* (Ohio State University, 1962).

Some 182 scattered pages. Her quintessentially Midwestern perspective informs this memoir, as it does her fiction.

College Teachers ✧ Historians (Cultural) ✧ Novelists I OH

Shoolroy, R(oss) K. (1893–). *Boyhood Recollections: 60 Years After* (Wooster Print & Litho, 1975).

OH

Skwiot, Rick (1947–). *Winter at Long Lake: A Childhood Christmas Memoir* (Antaeus, 2005).

The author recounts how, at age 6, he tried to help his family save their lakeshore home when his father lost his job at the steel mill.

Baby Boomers ✧ Christmas ✧ Country Life ✧ Lakes ✧ Novelists I IL

Smith, Herman (1881–). *Stina, the Story of a Cook* (M. Barrows, 1942).

Includes some recipes.

Cookery I MI

Stanforth, Willa Bare (1915–). *Each Blade of Grass* (Privately printed, 1974).

Pages 12–96 focus on her girlhood years. There are no formal chapter divisions in this memoir.

Country Life ✧ Family Memoirs ✧ Growing Up Between WWI and WWII I OH

Stephens, Kate (1853–1938). *Life at Laurel Town in Anglo-Saxon Kansas* (Alumni Association of the University of Kansas, 1920).

Covers her girlhood and adolescence, focusing more on the general life of her hometown than on her.

Country Life ✧ Nineteenth-Century Pre-Industrial Age Memoirists I KS

Toth, Susan Allen (1940–). *Blooming: A Small-Town Girlhood* (Little, Brown, 1978).

Covers her first 17 years. See also her sequel (this ch.).

Country Life I IA

Wilson, William Edward (1906–1988). *On the Sunny Side of a One-way Street: Humorous Recollections of a Hoosier Boyhood* (W.W. Norton, 1958).
Covers his first 18 years.
College Teachers ✧ Humorists ✧ Journalists ✧ Novelists ✧ Short Story Writers | IN

Witherbee, Orville O. *The Beginning of Myself* (Shepherd, 1934).
His father was an old-time country doctor.
Country Life ✧ Physicians | WI

Southeast United States

Alabama, Arkansas, Florida, Georgia, Kentucky, Louisiana, Mississippi, Missouri, North Carolina, Oklahoma, South Carolina, Tennessee, and Virginia

Abbott, Shirley (1934–). *The Bookmaker's Daughter: A Memory Unbound* (Ticknor & Fields, 1991).
Her father was a professional gambler but encouraged her in her education. This volume focuses on her childhood and adolescent years.
Crime ✧ Fathers and Daughters | AR

Abbott, Shirley (1934–). *Love's Apprentice: Confessions from the School of Romance* (Houghton Mifflin, 1998).
Pages 3–94. This memoir focuses on her blossoming interest in the opposite sex, beginning in adolescence.
Sexuality | AR

Abbott, Shirley (1934–). *Womenfolks: Growing Up Down South* (Ticknor & Fields, 1983).
Covering the same general time periods as the 2 entries above, this memoir interweaves Abbott's ideas regarding historical and mythical aspects of Southern women.
Farm Life | AR

Andrews, Raymond (1934?–). *The Last Radio Baby: A Memoir* (Peachtree, 1990).
To 15 years. He grew up in the rural area of Plainview, GA.
African Americans ✧ Novelists | GA

Archer, Chalmers, Jr. (1928–). *Growing Up Black in Rural Mississippi: Memories of a Family, Heritage of a Place* (Walker, 1992).
Covers about his first 16 years.
African Americans ✧ College ✧ Teachers ✧ Family Memoirs ✧ Growing Up Between WWI and WWII ✧ Racism | MS

Arnow, Harriette (1908–1986). *Old Burnside* (University Press of Kentucky, 1977).
This is reminiscent of the writings of Laura Ingalls Wilder (see ch. 9 entry).
Homes and Haunts | KY

Attaway, Roy (1937–). *A Home in the Tall Marsh Grass* (Lyons & Burford, 1993).
Scattered throughout the first 13 pages, plus pages 15–121.
Editors ✧ Journalists | SC ✧ NC

Barber, Lylah (1906–). *Lylah: A Memoir by Lylah Barber* (Algonquin Books of Chapel Hill, 1985).

About 56 pages (between 3 and 65). She later married sportswriter "Red" Barber.

Sportswriters I FL

Bartel, Irene Brown. *No Drums or Thunder* (Naylor, 1970).

Farm Life I OK

Belvin, Ed (1923?–). *Growing Up in Williamsburg: From the Depression to Pearl Harbor* (Virginia Gazette, 1981).

Personal memories from 1929 to 1941 are interspersed among descriptions of community life.

Country Living ✧ Depressions (Economic) ✧ Growing Up Between WWI and WWII I VA

Blackman, Marion Cyrenus (1902?–). *Look Away! Dixie Land Remembered* (McCall, 1971).

Virtually entire book focuses on his youthful years; a pleasant memoir, with not too much re-created dialogue.

LA

Chamberlain, Hope (1870–1960). *This Was Home* (University of North Carolina, 1938).

NC

Clark, Dewey G. (1897–). *My South: Southern Sketches of Growing Up in South Carolina* (Carlton, 1970).

SC

Clinkscales, John (1855–1942). *On the Old Plantation: Reminiscences of His Childhood* (Band & White, 1916).

Nineteenth-Century Pre-Industrial Age Memoirists ✧ Plantation Life ✧ Slavery I SC

Davis, Clyde Brion (1894–1962). *The Age of Indiscretion* (Lippincott, 1950).

MO

Dunbar-Ortiz, Roxanne (1938–). *Red Dirt: Growing Up Okie* (Verso, 1997).

Pages 18, 23, to about 217 (chs. 2–13).

College Teachers I OK

Giles, Janice (1909–1979). *The Kinta Years: An Oklahoma Childhood* (Houghton Mifflin, 1973).

Novelists I OK

Gilman, Caroline (1794–1888). *Recollections of a Southern Matron and a New England Bride* (Harper & Brothers, 1838).

Covers her girlhood and youth; ends with her marriage.

Eighteenth-Century ✧ Memoirists I SC

Gingher, Marianne (1947–). *A Girl's Life: Horses, Boys, Weddings, and Luck* (Louisiana State University, 2001).

Gingher, director of the Creative Writing Program at the University of North Carolina, wrote this memoir in response to a plea for a memoir of a nondysfunctional childhood from Michael Vincent Miller of the *New York Times*.

Baby Boomers ✧ College Teachers ✧ Country Life I NC

Green, Ely (1893–1968). *Ely: An Autobiography* (Seabury, 1966).
Covers his first 18 years.
Country Life | TN

Greenhaw, Wayne (1940–). *Beyond the Night: A Remembrance* (Black Belt, 1999).
Journalists | AL

Hokett, Norene (1932–). *Main Street Was Two Blocks Long: Growing Up in the Forties and Fifties in Oklahoma* (Rutledge Hill, 1993).
Country Life ✧ WWII | OK

Johnson, Josephine Winslow (1910–1990). *Seven Houses: A Memoir of Time and Places* (Simon and Schuster, 1973).
Homes and Haunts | MO

Jordon, Nell Sutton (1905–). *The Doctor's Daughters* (Naylor, 1972).
Physicians | AR ✧ OK

Kercheval, Jesse Lee (1957–). *Space: A Memoir* (Algonquin Books of Chapel Hill, 1998).
Starting on page 8, about 300 pages focus on her from age 9 to about age 17.
Baby Boomers ✧ Outer Space | FL

Kirk, Mary Wallace (1889–1978). *Locust Hill* (University of Alabama, 1975).
About 99 scattered pages (between 11 and 134) focus on her childhood and adolescence.
Homes and Haunts ✧ Poets | AL

Koenig, Janie Ray Shofner (1925–). *Pine Trees and Cotton Fields: Reminiscences of a Childhood, NE Texas-NW Louisiana, 1925–1942* (Piney Woods, 1991).
Growing Up Between WWI and WWII | TX ✧ LA

Lee, Agnes (1841–1873). Ed. by Mary Curtis Lee deButts. *Growing Up in the 1850s: The Journal of Agnes Lee* (University of North Carolina, 1984).
Pages 3–105 cover her from 12 to 16 years. She was the daughter of General Robert E. Lee. This memoir shows slices of antebellum life; includes 26 illustrations. The editor is Agnes Lee's niece.
Civil War (U.S.) ✧ Collaborations by Relatives ✧ Confederate States of America ✧ Diaries and Journals ✧ Military Life ✧ Nineteenth-Century Pre-Industrial Age Memoirists | VA

Long, Augustus (1862–). *Son of Carolina* (Duke University, 1939).
From page 3 through (at least) 132. This memoir has a straightforward and unpretentious style; little if any dialogue is re-created.
College Teachers ✧ Intellectual Life | NC

Mathias, Frank F(urlong) (1925–). *The GI Generation: A Memoir* (University Press of Kentucky, 2000).
Entire memoir is on his first 18 years.
Depressions (Economic) ✧ Growing Up Between WWI and WWII ✧ WWII | KY

McBride, Mary Margaret (1899–1976). *How Dear to My Heart* (Macmillan, 1940).
Country Life | MO

McDowell, Deborah (1951–). *Leaving Pipe Shop: Memories of Kin* (Scribner, 1996).
Pages 51 to about 224.
African Americans ✧ Baby Boomers | AL

Meyer, Lewis (1913–). *Preposterous Papa* (World, 1959).
Growing Up Between WWI and WWII | OK

Meyer, Lewis (1913–). *Mostly Mama* (Doubleday, 1971).
Growing Up Between WWI and WWII | OK

Moorman, Fay (1887–). *My Heart Turns Back: Childhood Memories of Rural Virginia in the Nineties* (Exposition, 1964).
Country Life | VA

Mordecai, Ellen (1820–1916). *Gleanings from Long Ago* (Braid & Hutton, 1933).
Nineteenth-Century Pre-Industrial Age Memoirists | NC

Morrow, D(ecatur) F(ranklin) (1856–). *Then and Now; Reminiscences and Historical Romance, 1856–1865* (J.W. Burke, 1926).
Nineteenth-Century Pre-Industrial Age Memoirists | NC

Murray, Albert (1916–). *South to a Very Old Place* (McGraw-Hill, 1971).
African Americans ✧ College Teachers ✧ Cookery ✧ Critics (Music) ✧ Growing Up Between WWI and WWII ✧ Homes and Haunts ✧ Military Life ✧ Novelists ✧ Photographers | AL

Nordan, Lewis (1941?–). *Boy with Loaded Gun: A Memoir* (Algonquin Books of Chapel Hill, 2000).
About the first 125 pages (chs. 1–10).
MS

O'Hara, Lucy Hudgins (1893–). *Yorktown, As I Remember* (McClure, 1981).
Pages 3–72 focus on her girlhood and adolescent years. This reminiscence was originally written for her children and grandchildren.
Collaborations by Relatives ✧ Homes and Haunts | VA

Reid, Loren (1905–living 1990s). *Hurry Home Wednesday: Growing Up in a Small Missouri Town, 1905–1921* (University of Missouri, 1978).
Country Life ✧ Journalists | MO

Robertson, Ben (1905–1943). *Red Hills and Cotton: An Upcountry Memory* (Knopf, 1942).
Country Life | SC

Sartor, Margaret (1960–). *Miss American Pie: A Diary of Love, Secrets and Growing Up* (Bloomsbury, 2006).
Focuses on her from 12 to 17 years. To protect their privacy, Sartor has changed the names of her hometown and some persons.
Baby Boomers ✧ College Teachers ✧ Diaries and Journals ✧ Photographers | LA

Scott, Evelyn (1893–1963). *Background in Tennessee* (R.M. McBride, 1937).
Children's Authors ✧ Country Life ✧ Novelists | TN

Smith, Chesley T. (1910?–). *Childhood in Holly Springs: A Memoir* (Thomas Berryhill, 1996).

Country Life | MS

Topp, Mildred (1897–1963). *Smile Please* (Houghton Mifflin, 1948).

Her mother trained herself as a professional photographer, to save her family from poverty. Like the following entry, this memoir focuses on Topp's girlhood.

Family Memoirs ◆ Photographers | AL

Topp, Mildred (1897–1963). *In the Pink* (Houghton Mifflin, 1950).

Like the preceding entry, this memoir focuses on Topp's girlhood.

Family Memoirs ◆ Photographers | AL

Vance, Joel M. (1934–). *Down Home Missouri: When Girls Were Scary and Basketball Was King* (University of Missouri, 2000).

He moved to Missouri at age 13; the memoir focuses on his high school years.

Country Life ◆ Hunting ◆ Natural History ◆ Racism ◆ Resorts ◆ Sports Writers | MO

Williams, Rebecca Yancey (1899–1976). *Carry Me Back* (E.P. Dutton, 1942).

VA

Wilson, Marie Melton (1913–). *Nellie's Girl* (Apollo Books, 1985).

Set from 1917 to 1928.

Growing Up Between WWI and WWII | OK

Southwest United States

Arizona, Colorado, New Mexico, Texas, and Utah

Aldredge, J(oseph) D(avid) (1883–1923). *The Romance of Growing: A Boy in Texas; Autobiographical Sketches of His Early Life as a Boy, to Be Completed in Three Volumes* (Multigraph Print, Pastor's Office, and Banner and Progress, 1923).

As an adult, he was a clergyman. Volumes 2 and 3 of this intended trilogy were never published.

Clergy | TX (East)

Balcomb, Kenneth C. (1891–1979). *A Boy's Albuquerque, 1898–1912* (University of New Mexico, 1980).

NM

Beasley, Gertrude (1895?–). *My First Thirty Years* (Three Mountains, 1925).

H. L. Mencken was very impressed by the writing and candor of this memoir.

Ranch Life | TX (West)

Bosworth, Allan (pseud. of Allan Rucker) (1901–1986). *New Country* (Harper, 1962).

Frontier and Pioneer Life | TX ◆ New Mexico Territory

Burroughs, John Rolfe (1902–). *Headfirst in the Pickle Barrel* (Morrow, 1963).

To 15 years. Recounts many escapades of his youth, through evocative detail and re-created dialogue.

Country Life | CO

Caldwell, Gail (1951–). *A Strong West Wind: A Memoir* (Random House, 2006).
This *Boston Globe* book critic recollects her early life growing up in Amarillo, TX.
Baby Boomers ✧ Books and Reading ✧ Critics (Literary) ✧ Editors ✧ Family Memoirs ✧ Journalists I TX

Corder, Jim(my) W(ayne) (1929–1998). *Chronicle of a Small Town* (Texas A & M University, 1989).
Perusing old issues of his hometown newspaper catalyzed his childhood memories.
Growing Up Between WWI and WWII I TX

Dale, Edward Everett (1879–1972). *The Cross Timbers: Memories of a North Texas Boyhood* (University of Texas, 1966).
Focuses on 1882–1892.
Country Life I TX

Foster, Dora. *My Childhood Days in Colorado Sunshine* (Dentan-Berkeland, 1967).
CO

Geary, Edward A(cord) (1937–). *Goodbye to Poplarhaven: Recollections of a Utah Boyhood* (University of Utah, 1985).
College Teachers I UT

Hammock, Robert (1908–1980). Ed. by Martin S. Stanford. *Below the Llano Estacado—and Beyond* (Hunterdon, 1981).
Ranch Life I TX

Holland, Ellen Bowie. *Gay as a Grig: Memories of a North Texas Girlhood* (University of Texas, 1963).
TX

James, Henry (1900–). *Territorial Tales* (Walsworth, 1984).
Note: This is *not* by the famous novelist Henry James (see ch. 9 entry).
Frontier and Pioneer Life I AZ ✧ NM

McDougal, Virginia Hill. Footsteps Through Childhood with Jenny: An Autobiography (Privately printed, 1981).
This is a 79-page memoir.
TX

Reid, J. Juan (1908–1981). *Growing Up in Colorado Springs: The 1920's Remembered* (Century One, 1981).
Includes many photographs.
CO

Truett, Joe C(lyde) (1941–). *Circling Back: Chronicle of a Texas River Valley* (University of Iowa, 1996).
Natural History I TX

Walters, Arley (1928–). *East Texas Memories: Growing Up in the Big Thicket* (Larksdale, 1995).
Country Life ✧ Growing Up Between WWI and WWII I TX (East)

Northwest United States

Idaho, Montana, Oregon, and Washington State

Cayton, Horace R(oscoe) (1903–1970). *Long Old Road* (Trident, 1964).
About the first 145–160 pages.
African Americans | WA (Seattle)

Love, Marianne (1947–). *Pocket Girdles and Other Confessions of a Northwest Farm Girl* (Green Mountain, 1994).
Baby Boomers ✧ Catholics ✧ Farm Life ✧ Humorists | ID

Macy, Ralph William (1905–). *Wooden Sidewalks: Growing Up in Western Oregon* (Hapi, 1983).
For a similar OR memoir, see "Quick, John."
Country Life | OR

Maple, Maude. *Maudie: An Oregon Trail Childhood* (Lincoln Square, 1993).
Frontier and Pioneer Life | OR

Porter, Barton. *Listen to the Millrace* (M.J. Stone, 1978).
He grew up near the Cascades.
Cascade Mountains ✧ Mountain Life ✧ Railroad Travel | WA

Quick, John (1931–). *Fool's Hill: A Kid's Life in an Oregon Coastal Town* (Oregon State University, 1995).
For a similar OR memoir, see "Macy, Ralph William."
Country Life | OR

Tempe, Gertrude. Ed. by Carole Chelsea George. *The Right to Tell a Lie: Memories of a Montana Girlhood* (C.A. George, 1994).
The author's granddaughter edited this work. Set in the early 1900s.
Collaborations by Relatives ✧ Methodists | MT

Whiteman, Dave (1954–). *An Oregon Tale: The Memoirs of One Man's Failed Attempt to Escape Childhood* (1st Books, 1999).
In 65 chapters, Whiteman provides vignettes of the times and misadventures of his youth.
Baby Boomers ✧ Country Life ✧ Humorists | OR

Pacific Coast and General

Alaska, California, Hawaii, Composite Region, and Unidentified U.S. Settings

Erickson, Melody (195?–). *Growing Up Stubborn at Gold Creek* (Vanessapress, 1990).
This memoir is set in the 1960s in south-central AK, south of Denali National Park. The author's family moved there from San Francisco, CA when she was 10.
Baby Boomers | AK

Hatfield, Fred (1910–). *North of the Sun: A Memoir of the Alaskan Wilderness* (Carol Publishing Group, 1990).
About the first 140 pages cover him from 18 to 20 years.
Frontier and Pioneer Life | AK

Morris, Bonnie J. (1961–). *Girl Reel: A Lesbian Remembers Growing Up at the Movies: Memoir* (Coffee House, 2000).

Baby Boomers ✧ Lesbians ✧ Movies I CA (Southern) ✧ NC ✧ Washington, DC

Pinson, Elizabeth Bernhardt (1912–). *Alaska's Daughter: An Eskimo Memoir of the Early Twentieth Century* (Utah State University, 2004).

She tells of her interactions with other native Alaskans and such visitors as explorer Roald Amundsen. Pinson lost her legs to frostbite at age 6.

Amputees ✧ Diaries and Journals ✧ Eskimos ✧ Frostbite ✧ German Americans ✧ Grandparents ✧ Growing Up Between WWI and WWII ✧ Influenza I AK

Wray, Fay (1907–2004). *On the Other Hand: A Life Story* (St. Martin's, 1989).

About the first 100 pages cover her first 20 years. While a teenager she was sent from UT, by her mother, to live with a friend in Los Angeles. She achieved immortality in her performance in the film *King Kong* (1933).

Fatherless Families ✧ Motion Picture Actors and Actresses I UT ✧ CA (Southern, Hollywood)

Zuber, William Physick (1820–1913). Ed. by Janis Boyle Mayfield. *My Eighty Years in Texas* (University of Texas, 1971).

About pages 20 to about 112 (most of chapters 2–4).

Nineteenth-Century Pre-Industrial Age Memoirists I LA ✧ TX

Native Americans (U.S., Canada)

Alford, Thomas Wildcat (1860–1938), as told to Florence Drake. *Civilization* (University of Oklahoma, 1936).

About pages 10–110. He had to help support his family at age 11, when his father became ill and died.

Fatherless Families ✧ Native Americans I OK

Apess, William (1798–1839). Ed. by Barry O'Connell. *A Son of the Forest: The Experience of William Apes* [sic], *a Native of the Forest; Comprising a Notice of the Pequod Tribe of Indians* (Privately printed, 1829).

To 19 or 20 years old. This is one of the oldest surviving memoirs by a Native American; he converted to Christianity during his late adolescence and became a minister.

Christian Converts ✧ Native Americans ✧ Nineteenth-Century Pre-Industrial Age Memoirists I MA

Barnes, Jim (1933–). *On Native Ground: Memoirs and Impressions* (University of Oklahoma, 1997).

Pages 3–132.

Native Americans ✧ Poets I OK

Bass, Althea (1892–1988). *The Arapaho Way: A Memoir of an Indian Boyhood* (C. Potter, 1966).

He was one of the last full-blooded Arapaho Indians living on an OK reservation.

Native Americans I OK

Bennett, Kay (1922–). *Kaibah: Recollection of a Navajo Girlhood* (Westernlore, 1964).
Written from a third-person perspective, this memoir re-creates the world of Kaibah (Kay Bennett).

Depressions (Economic) ✧ Growing Up Between WWI and WWII ✧ Native Americans | NM

Bruchac, Joseph (1942–). *Bowman's Store: A Journey to Myself* (Dial, 1997).
Covers his first 28 years. He grew up in the Adirondack Mountains and describes working at his grandfather's general store and gas station.

Adirondack Mountains ✧ Folklorists ✧ Grandparents ✧ Mountain Life ✧ Native Americans | NY

Chisholm, Colin (1967–). *Through Yup'ik Eyes: An Adopted Son Explores the Landscape of Family* (Alaska Northwest, 2000).
Some 84 scattered pages.

Adoptees ✧ Eskimos ✧ Generation X | CA (Central) ✧ WA ✧ AK

Crow Dog, Mary (1953–), and Richard Erdoes. *Lakota Woman* (Grove Weidenfeld, 1990).

Baby Boomers ✧ Native Americans | SD

Denny, Emily Inez (1853–1918). *Blazing the Way; or, True Stories, Songs and Sketches of Puget Sound and Other Pioneers* (Rainier, 1909).
Her father was a founder of Seattle.

Artists ✧ Native Americans ✧ Nineteenth-Century Pre-Industrial Age Memoirists | WA

Eastman, Charles Alexander (b. Ohiyesa) (1858–1939). *Indian Boyhood* (McClure, Phillips, 1902).

Native Americans ✧ Nineteenth-Century Pre-Industrial Age Memoirists | Canada (Western Provinces) ✧ Dakota Territory

Freeman, Minnie Aodla (1936–). *Life Among the Qallunaat* (Hurtig, 1978).

Native Americans | Canada

Grinnell, George Bird (1849–1938). *When Buffalo Ran* (Yale University, 1920) (1996 rpt., University of Oklahoma).
Pages 11 to about 88 are about him from about age 5 to age 21.

Frontier and Pioneer Life ✧ Native Americans ✧ Natural History ✧ Nineteenth-Century Pre-Industrial Age Memoirists | U.S. (Great Plains)

Hale, Janet Campbell (1947–). *Bloodlines: Odyssey of a Native Daughter* (Random House, 1993).

Baby Boomers ✧ Essayists ✧ Native Americans ✧ Novelists | ID ✧ WA

Hifler, Joyce Sequichie. (1925–). *When the Night Bird Sings* (Council Oak Books, 1999).
Over 100 scattered pages.

Growing Up Between WWI and WWII ✧ Native Americans | OK

Hundley, Will (1860?–). *Squawtown: My Boyhood Among the Last Miami Indians* (Caxton, 1939).

Native Americans ✧ Nineteenth-Century Pre-Industrial Age Memoirists | IN

Iron Eye Dudley, Joseph (1940–). *Choteau Creek: A Sioux Reminiscence* (University of Nebraska, 1992).
Covers him from about 8 to 17 years.
Native Americans I SD

Johnston, Basil (1929–). *Indian School Days* (University of Oklahoma, 1989).
Growing Up Between WWI and WWII ✧ Native Americans I Canada (Ontario)

Left Handed (1868–). Introduction by Edward Sapir. *Son of Old Man Hat: A Navaho Autobiography Recorded by Walter Dyk* (Harcourt, Brace, 1938).
Although his age is not given, he seems to be under 22 well past the first 100 pages of this memoir.
Anthropologists ✧ Native Americans I U.S. (Southwest)

Momaday, N(avarre) Scott (1934–). *Names: A Memoir* (Harper & Row, 1976).
Covers up to about age 15. Includes a glossary of Native American terms.
Growing Up Between WWI and WWII ✧ Native Americans I OK ✧ NM ✧ AZ ✧ KY ✧ LA

Neihardt, John (aka Black Elk) (1881–1973). *All Is But a Beginning: Youth Remembered, 1881–1901* (Harcourt Brace Jovanovich, 1972).
He passed away while working on the second volume of his autobiography.
Critics (Literary) ✧ Dramatists ✧ Native Americans ✧ Novelists ✧ Poets ✧ Short Story Writers I KS ✧ NE

Nequatewa, Edmund (1880–1969), as told to Alfred F. Whiting. Ed. by P. David Seaman. *Born a Chief: The Nineteenth-Century Hopi Boyhood of Edmund Nequatewa* (University of Arizona, 1993).
This is one of a scarce number of Hopi memoirs. He was an only child and heir to his village's chief; he attended boarding school. Covers him into his early twenties.
Native Americans I Arizona Territory

Paquin, Ron, and Robert Doherty. *Not First in Nobody's Heart: The Life Story of a Chippewa* (Iowa State University, 1992).
Native Americans I MI

Rogers, John (Chief Snow Cloud) (1890–1977). *A Chippewa Speaks* (Snow Cloud, 1957) (Variant title, *Red World and White: Memories of a Chippewa Boyhood,* [University of Oklahoma, 1974]).
Native Americans I U.S. (Great Plains)

Sekaquaptewa, Helen (1898–1990), as told to Louise Udall. *Me and Mine: The Life Story of Helen Sekaquaptewa* (University of Arizona, 1969).
Pages 6–152 (chs. 1–13).
Native Americans I Arizona Territory/AZ

Standing Bear, Chief Luther (1868–1939?). *My Indian Boyhood* (Houghton Mifflin, 1931).
This memoir was written for a young audience.
Native Americans I U.S. (Great Plains)

Zitkala-Sa (aka Gertrude Simmons Bonnin) (1876–1938). *American Indian Legends* (Hayworth Publishing House, 1921) (1985 rpt., University of Nebraska, *American Indian Stories*).

About the first 100 pages. Helen Keller so enjoyed this book that she wrote her a fan letter.

Native Americans I SD ✧ IN

Canadian Cultures

Aitken, Kate (1891–1971). *Never a Day So Bright* (Longmans, 1956).

She was a well-known personality on Canadian television and radio.

Victorian Era British Memoirists I Canada (Ontario)

Allen, Robert Thomas (1911–1990). *My Childhood and Yours: Happy Memories of Growing Up* (Macmillan of Canada, 1977).

This memoir is set from about 1915 to about 1925. He provides details of the street games and other activities of his youth. Some material herein appeared in his book *When Toronto Was for Kids* (McClelland and Stewart, 1961).

Growing Up Between WWI and WWII ✧ Humorists I Canada (Ontario: Toronto)

Collins, Robert (1924–). *Butter Down the Well: Reflections of a Canadian Childhood* (Western Producer Prairie Books, 1980).

Growing Up Between WWI and WWII I Canada (SAS)

Craig, John (1921–1982). *How Far Back Can You Get?* (Doubleday Canada, 1974).

He worked for 20 years in market research. This is a light, entertaining memoir.

Businesspersons ✧ Children's Authors ✧ Depressions (Economic) ✧ Growing Up Between WWI and WWII I Canada (Ontario)

Dodge, Helen Carmichael. My Childhood in the Canadian Wilderness (Vantage, 1961).

A 77-page memoir.

Canada (New Brunswick)

Doucet, Clive (1946–). *My Grandfather's Cape Breton* (McGraw-Hill Ryerson, 1980).

Focuses on him at 12 years. Includes much re-created dialogue.

Grandfathers ✧ Novelists ✧ Summer I Canada (Nova Scotia)

Gray, James H(enry) (1906–1986). *The Boy from Winnipeg* (Macmillan of Canada, 1970).

Historians (Cultural) ✧ Journalists ✧ WWI I Canada (Manitoba)

Gutkin, Harry (1915–), and Mildred Gutkin (1915–). *The Worst of Times, the Best of Times: Growing Up in Winnipeg's North End* (Fitzhenry & Whiteside, 1987).

Depressions (Economic) ✧ Growing Up Between WWI and WWII ✧ Jews I Canada (Manitoba)

Hillen, Ernest (1934–) *Small Mercies: A Boy After War* (Viking, 1997).

Covers him from 11 to 13 years. See also his prequel (ch. 3).

Immigrants I Canada (Ontario: Toronto)

Johnston, Wayne (1958–). *Baltimore's Mansion: A Memoir* (Knopf, 1999).
Pages 45–194.

Baby Boomers ✧ Novelists | Canada (Newfoundland)

Livesay, Dorothy (1909–1996). *Beginnings: A Winnipeg Childhood* (New Press, 1975)
(Variant title, *Winnipeg Childhood* [Peguis, 1973]).

Memoir describes her youth in both Winnipeg and (after 10 years) in Toronto; as an adult, she
became known as a political poet and worked for women's rights and in social work.

College Teachers ✧ Poets ✧ Teachers | Canada (Manitoba: Winnipeg; Ontario: Toronto)

Maynard, Fredelle (1922–). *Raisins and Almonds* (Doubleday Canada, 1972).

Fathers and Daughters ✧ Growing Up Between WWI and WWII ✧ Jews | Canada (SAS)

Roy, Gabrielle (1909–1983). Tr. by Patricia Claxton. *Enchantment and Sorrow: The
Autobiography of Gabrielle Roy* (Lester & Orpen Dennys, 1987).

Covering about her first 30 years, this is an unfinished autobiography that was published
posthumously. Her book *Street of Riches* (Harcourt, Brace, 1957), despite containing
autobiographical elements, is intended as a novel.

Children's Authors ✧ Novelists ✧ Short Story Writers | Canada (Manitoba)

Salverson, Laura Goodman (1890–1970). *Confessions of an Immigrant's Daughter*
(University of Toronto, 1981) (First published by Faber & Faber, 1939).
Pages 9 to about 365.

Immigrants ✧ Novelists ✧ Poets ✧ Victorian Era British Memoirists | Canada (Manitoba: Winnipeg)

Stegner, Wallace (1909–1993). *Wolf Willow: A History, A Story, and a Memory of the
Last Plains Frontier* (Viking, 1962).

Covers him from about 5 to 11 years He won the Pulitzer Prize for his novel *Angle of Repose*
(Doubleday, 1971). For a more recent memoir set in this part of the U.S., see "Marquart, Debra" (ch.
11).

College Teachers ✧ Frontier and Pioneer Life ✧ Novelists | MT ✧ Canada (SAS)

Woodcock, George (1912–1995). *Letter to the Past* (Fitzhenry & Whiteside, 1982).
Pages 25–175.

Biographers ✧ College Teachers ✧ Critics (Literary) ✧ Editors ✧ Essayists ✧ Farm Life ✧ Growing Up
Between WWI and WWII ✧ Historians ✧ Poets ✧ Revolutionaries ✧ Travel Writers | Canada
(Manitoba [?])

Mexico; South and Central American Cultures

Chamberlain, Henriquetta. *Where the Sabia Sings: A Partial Autobiography*
(Macmillan, 1947).

About the first 200 pages appear to focus on her childhood and adolescence. Her parents were
Baptist missionaries.

Baptists ✧ Missionaries | Brazil

Ewald, Wendy (1951–). *Magic Eyes: Scenes from an Andean Childhood: From Stories
Told by Alicia and Maria Vasquez* (Bay, 1992).
Pages 11–171 focus on her girlhood and adolescence.

Mothers and Daughters ✧ Mountain Life | Colombia

Hudson, W(illiam) H(enry) (1841–1922). *Far Away and Long Ago: A History of Early Life* (E.P. Dutton, 1918).

For a similar memoir, see "Jaramillo, Cleofas" (ch. 9).

Family Memoirs ✧ Frontier and Pioneer Life ✧ Natural History ✧ Nineteenth-Century Pre-Industrial Age Memoirists ✧ Novelists | Argentina

Jamieson, Tulitas Wulff (1886–), as told to Evelyn Payne. *Tulitas of Torreon: Reminiscences of Life in Mexico* (Texas Western, 1969).

Pages 1–111 (chs. i–xiv).

Mexico

Morley, Helena (pseud. of Brant, Senhora Augusto Mario, Caldeira) (1881?–). Tr. from the Portuguese by Elizabeth Bishop. *Diary of "Helena Morley"* (Farrar, Straus, and Cudahy, 1957) (First published in Portuguese, 1942).

Covers her from 12 to 15 years.

Diaries and Journals | Brazil

Perera, Victor (1934–). *Rites: A Childhood in Guatemala* (Harcourt Brace Jovanovich, 1986) (Variant title, *A Guatemalan Boyhood* [1986]).

Pages 3–164.

College Teachers ✧ Essayists ✧ Jews ✧ Short Story Writers ✧ Translators | Guatemala

Romero, Jose (1890–1952). Tr. by John Mitchell and Ruth Mitchell. *Notes of a Villager: A Mexican Poet's Youth and Revolution* (Plover, 1988).

Poets | Mexico

Shields, Karena. The Changing Wind (Crowell, 1959).

This is an account of a happy, but not overly sentimentalized, childhood during the early 1900s.

Family Memoirs ✧ Plantation Life | Mexico

Western European Cultures

Including Great Britain, France, Spain, Austria, Scandinavia, Slavic Countries, Greece, and Italy

Adams, Gerry (1948–). *Falls Memories* (Rinehart, 1994).

A vivid evocation of growing up in working class Belfast.

Baby Boomers ✧ Catholics | Ireland (North)

Adams, Richard (1920–). *The Day Gone By: An Autobiography* (Knopf, 1991).

Pages 1–280. The author was a childhood friend of Christopher Milne (see entry in this chapter); as an adult, Adams wrote the popular fantasy novel *Watership Down* (Macmillan, 1972).

Growing Up Between WWI and WWII ✧ Novelists | England

Anonymous (attributed to Grete Lanier). Tr. by Eden Paul and Cedar Paul. *A Young Girl's Diary* (T. Seltzer, 1921).

Covers this Viennese girl's life from 11 to 14 years. Sigmund Freud contributed the preface to this volume.

Diaries and Journals | Austria

Baines, Frank (1915–1987). *Look Towards the Sea* (E.P. Dutton, 1958).
Covers his life to age 18 or 19.
Growing Up Between WWI and WWII | England

Baldwin, Michael (pseud. of Michael Jesse) (1930–). *Grandad with Snails* (Routledge & Kegan Paul, 1960).
Covers from 12 to 15 years. In the present tense, he recounts a series of scrapes he got into with a gang of other boys.
Grandfathers ✧ Growing Up Between WWI and WWII | England

Barea, Arturo (1897–1957). Tr. from the Spanish by Ilsa Barea. *The Forge* (Faber & Faber, 1941).
This classic memoir, the first volume of a trilogy, covers him to 16 or 17 years.
Biographers ✧ Broadcasters ✧ Critics (Literary) ✧ Novelists ✧ Short Story Writers | Spain

Barke, James (1905–1958). *The Green Hills Far Away: A Chapter in Autobiography* (Collins, 1940).
Covers his life from about age 2 to age 13.
Country Life | Scotland

Beevor, Kinta (1946–). *A Tuscan Childhood* (Viking, 1993).
Country Life | Italy

Brazdova, Amelie (1884–). Tr. from the Swedish by Grenville Grove. *In the Beginning Was the Light* (E.P. Dutton, 1942).
Country Life | Sweden

Burney, Frances (aka Fanny Burney) (1752–1840). Ed. by Annie Raine Ellis (1752–1840). *The Early Diary of Frances Burney, 1768–1778.* **2 vols.** (Bell, 1913).
Pages 1–316 of vol. 1 (first published by Bell in 1889).
Diaries and Journals ✧ Eighteenth-Century ✧ Memoirists | England

Byrne, Muriel (1895–1974). *Common or Garden Child: A Not Unfaithful Record* (Faber & Faber, 1942).
Victorian Era British Memoirists | England

Canetti, Elias (1905–1994). Tr. from the German by Joachim Neugroschel. *The Tongue Set Free: Remembrance of a European Childhood* (Seabury, 1979).
Covers Canetti's childhood and early adolescence. He was awarded the Nobel Prize for Literature in 1981.
Novelists | Bulgaria

Carbery, (Lady) Mary (1867–1949). *Happy World: The Story of a Victorian Childhood* (Longmans, Green, 1941).
Victorian Era British Memoirists | Ireland

Clements, Roy (1934–). *Memory of Memories of Derry* (Guildhall, 1994).
At least 53 scattered pages (between page 7 and page 104).
Ireland (North)

Cole, J(ohn) A(lfred) (1905–). *The View from the Peak* (Faber & Faber, 1979).
Entire work (pages 13–159) covers from about 2–24 years of age. As an adult, he served as an intelligence officer in Germany, and wrote for the British Broadcasting Corporation.
Broadcast Journalists | England

Cushman, Mary (1865?–). *She Wrote It All Down* (Scribner's Sons, 1936).
Covers 1876–1880.
Diaries and Journals | Europe

Dennis, Geoffrey (1892–1963). *Till Seven* (Eyre & Spottiswoode, 1957).
Victorian Era British Memoirists | England

Dewes, Simon (1909–). *A Suffolk Childhood* (Hutchinson, 1959).
Country Life | England

Elias, Eileen (pseud. of Eileen Winifred Davies) (1910–). *On Sundays We Wore White* (W.H. Allen, 1978).
Covers her to age 10.
England

Ellis, Alice Marie (1932–2005). *A Welsh Childhood* (M. Joseph, 1990).
Entire memoir is set in 1930s–1940s.
Novelists | Wales

Foakes, Grace (1901–). *Between High Walls: A London Childhood* (Shepheard-Walwyn, 1972).
This and the following entry detail Foakes's impoverished childhood in London's East End. She had 14 siblings.
City Life ✧ Slums | England (London)

Foakes, Grace (1901–). *My Part of the River* (Shepheard-Walwyn, 1974).
City Life ✧ Slums | England (London)

Forman, (Sir) John Denis (1917–). *Son of Adam* (Andre Deutsch, 1990).
This memoir is the basis of the 1999 film *My Life So Far.*
Arts Patrons ✧ Country Life ✧ Growing Up Between WWI and WWII | Scotland

Fraser, Christine (1946–). *Blue Above the Chimneys* (Hutchinson, 1980).
This memoir, continued by the following entry, focuses on her childhood. At this time, she contracted a rare muscular disease, which confined her to a wheelchair.
Novelists ✧ Paraplegia | Scotland

Fraser, Christine (1946–). *Roses Round the Door* (Fontana Books, 1986).
About the first two-thirds of this 221-page memoir focus on her from her later childhood until she is 21.
Novelists ✧ Paraplegia | Scotland

Gallagher, Charles. *Acorns and Oak Leaves: A Derry Childhood: Growing Up in Derry 1920–1945* (Dubh Regles Books, 1982).
Growing Up Between WWI and WWII | Ireland (North)

Goytisolo, Juan (1931–). Tr. from the Spanish by Peter Bush. *Forbidden Territory: The Memoirs of Juan Goytisolo, 1931–1956* (North Point, 1989) (First published in Spanish, 1985).
About the first 150 pages.
Abuse (Sexual) ◇ Catholics ◇ Novelists | Spain

Green, Julian (1900–1998). *Memories of Happy Days* (Harper & Brothers, 1942).
A companion to the following entry, this memoir covers about the first 20 years of Green's life.
Bisexuals ◇ Dramatists ◇ Essayists ◇ Novelists ◇ Translators | France

Green, Julian (1900–1998). Tr. by Julian Green and Anne Green. *The Green Paradise: Autobiography: Volume I (1900–1916)* (Marion Boyars, 1992) (Previously tr. by Julian Green and Anne Green as *To Leave Before Dawn* [Harcourt, Brace & World, 1967]) (First published in French, 1963).
Covers his first 16 years. (Note: His name has appeared variously as "Julian" and "Julien"; his sister is Anne [see ch. 17 entry].) See also his memoirs in this chapter and chapter 6.
Bisexuals ◇ Dramatists ◇ Essayists ◇ Novelists ◇ Translators | France

Hamilton, (Muriel) Elizabeth (1906–). *An Irish Childhood* (Chatto & Windus, 1963).
Covers her first 7 years. This memoir is continued by the following entry.
Country Life | Ireland

Hamilton, (Muriel) Elizabeth (1906–). *A River Full of Stars* (W.W. Norton, 1954).
Pages 9 to about 130 cover her first 21 years.
Country Life | Ireland ◇ England ◇ FL

Hamilton, Hugo (1953–). *The Speckled People: Memoir of a Half-Irish Childhood* (Fourth Estate, 2003).
Growing up as the son of a German mother and Irish father in Dublin, Hamilton's early years were a search for identity.
Baby Boomers ◇ Cold War ◇ Journalists ◇ Novelists | Germany ◇ Ireland (North)

Hamilton, (Sir) Ian (1853–1947). *When I Was a Boy* (Faber & Faber, 1939).
Covers his first 20 years. As an adult he was a British general.
Military Life ◇ Nineteenth-Century Pre-Industrial Age Memoirists | England ◇ Germany ◇ Ireland

Hayes, Maurice (1927–). *Sweet Killough, Let Go Your Anchor* (Blackstaff, 1994).
His first 10 years; this memoir is continued by the following entry.
Growing Up Between WWI and WWII | Ireland (North)

Hayes, Maurice (1927–). *Black Puddings with Slim: A Downpatrick Boyhood* (Blackstaff, 1996).
His boyhood, starting at age 10.
Growing Up Between WWI and WWII | Ireland (North)

Helias, Pierre-Jakez (1914–1995). Tr. and abridged by June Guicharnaud. *The Horse of Pride: Life in a Breton Village* (Yale University, 1978).
Adapted into a 1980 film of the same title.
Country Life ◇ Dramatists ◇ Folklorists ◇ Linguists ◇ Poets ◇ WWI | France

Henrey, Madeleine (pseud. of Mrs. Robert Henrey) (1906–2004). *The Little Madeleine: The Autobiography of a Young Girl in Montmartre* (E.P. Dutton, 1953).
The author wrote some 20 books of autobiographical stories in her <u>Madeleine</u> series, which this volume begins.
Journalists ✧ Manicurists | France (Paris)

Henrey, Madeleine (pseud. of Mrs. Robert Henrey) (1906–2004). *An Exile in Soho* (J.M. Dent, 1953).
This continues the preceding entry.
Journalists ✧ Manicurists | England

Higgins, Aidan (1927–). *Donkey's Years: Memories of a Life as Story Told* (Secker & Warburg, 1995).
The first 150–180 pages.
Growing Up Between WWI and WWII ✧ Novelists | Ireland

Holland, Vyvyan (1887–1967). *Son of Oscar Wilde* (E.P. Dutton, 1954).
Pages 26 to about 123 (chs. 1–4 and part of 5).
Dramatists | England ✧ Germany ✧ Italy

Hughes, Mary Vivian (1866–). *A London Child of the Seventies* (Oxford University, 1934).
This work and the following entry were later incorporated into her autobiography, *A Victorian Family, 1870–1900* (Guild Publishing, 1990).
Victorian Era British Memoirists | England

Hughes, Mary Vivian (1866–). *A London Girl of the Eighties* (Oxford University, 1936).
Victorian Era British Memoirists | England

Hulton, Edward (1906–1988). *When I Was a Child* (Cresset, 1952).
Covers him to age 16, with extraordinary details from his early life starting at age 2.
Harrow ✧ Lawyers | England

Hunt, Irmgard (1934–). *On Hitler's Mountain: Overcoming the Legacy of a Nazi Childhood* (W. Morrow, 2005).
Growing up in Bavaria during WWII, Hunt at 10 years old was a member of the Hitler Youth.
Hitler Youth Movement ✧ Nazis and Neo-Nazis ✧ WWII | Germany

Jackson, Annabel (1870–1944). *A Victorian Childhood* (Methuen, 1932).
Intellectual Life ✧ Victorian Era British Memoirists | England

Jannopoulo, Helen (1875–). *And Across Big Seas* (Caxton, 1949).
Immigrants | Romania ✧ U.S. (?)

Jolis, Alan (1953–1999). *Speak Sunlight: A Memoir* (St. Martin's, 1996).
Baby Boomers ✧ City Life ✧ Journalists ✧ Lawyers ✧ Novelists ✧ Summer | France (Paris) ✧ Spain

Jones, L(awrence) E(velyn) (1885–1969). *A Victorian Boyhood* (St. Martin's, 1955).
Covers his first 19 years. This memoir is continued by the following entry.
Eton College ✧ Victorian Era British Memoirists | England

Jones, L(awrence) E(velyn) (1885–1969). *An Edwardian Youth* (St. Martin's, 1956).
About the first 200 pages cover him from 19 to 21 years.
Oxford University | England

Joyce, Stanislaus (1884–1955). *My Brother's Keeper* (Viking, 1958).
Covers his first 19 years, including insights on his famous brother, novelist James Joyce.
Victorian Era British Memoirists | Ireland

Kavanagh, Patrick (1904–1967). *The Green Fool* (M. Joseph, 1938).
About the first 100 pages.
Poets | Ireland

Kazantzakis, Nikos (1885–1957). Tr. from the Greek by P.A. Bien. *Report to Greco*
(Simon and Schuster, 1965) (First published in Greek, 1961).
Pages 42 to about 140.
Dramatists ✧ Intellectual Life ✧ Novelists ✧ Poets ✧ Travel Writers | Greece

Kelly, Bill (1922–). *Me Darlin' Dublin's Dead and Gone* (Ward River Press, 1983).
Pages 1–59 (chs. 1–5).
Growing Up Between WWI and WWII ✧ Journalists | Ireland (North)

Kendon, Frank (1893–1955). *The Small Years* (University Press, 1930).
For examples of other memoirs focusing on a child's first 10 years, see "Maclaren-Ross, Julian" (ch. 4), "Booth, Martin" (ch. 4), and "Berners, (Lord) Gerald" (first entry, ch. 11).
Victorian Era British Memoirists | England

Keppel, Sonia (1900–1986). *Edwardian Daughter* (Hamilton, 1958).
Covers her first 20 years.
England

MacCarthy, Mary (1882–1953). Introduction by Sir John Betjeman. *A Nineteenth-Century Childhood* (Doubleday, Page, 1924).
Focuses on her girlhood at Eton, where her father was vice-provost.
Eton College ✧ Victorian Era British Memoirists | England

MacDonagh, Tom (1934–). *My Green Age* (Poolbeg, 1986).
About the first 80–100 pages.
Short Story Writers | Ireland (North) ✧ England

Maclaren-Ross, Julian (1912–1964). *The Weeping and the Laughter: A Chapter of Autobiography* (R. Hart-Davis, 1953).
See also "Kendon, Frank" (ch. 4), "Booth, Martin" (ch. 4), and "Berners, (Lord) Gerald" (ch. 11) for other memoirs that focus on only the author's first 10 years.
Growing Up Between WWI and WWII | England

Mahler-Werfel, Alma (b. Alma Maria Schindler) (1879–1964). Selected and tr. from the German by Antony Beaumont and Susanne Rode-Breymann. *Diaries, 1898–1902* (Cornell University, 1999).
The first 360–460 pages. She was married to composer Gustav Mahler, architect Walter Gropius, and writer Franz Werfel (*Song of Bernadette* [Viking, 1942]).
Artists ✧ Diaries and Journals ✧ Intellectual Life ✧ Musicians ✧ Werfel, Franz | Austria

Marokvia, Mirelle (1918–). *Immortelles: Memoir of a Will-o'-the-Wisp* (MacMurray and Beck, 1996).
This memoir depicts rural French life following World War I.
Children's Authors ✧ Decorative Arts ✧ Growing Up Between WWI and WWII ✧ Translators | France

McCullough, Elizabeth (1928–). *A Square Peg: An Ulster Childhood* (Marino Books, 1997).
Set in the 1930s and 1940s.
Growing Up Between WWI and WWII | Ireland (North)

McHugh, Mary. *Thalassa: A Story of Childhood by the Western Wave* (Macmillan, 1931).
Country Life | Ireland

Meyerstein, Edward Harry William (1889–1952). *Of My Early Life, 1889–1918* (Spearman, 1957).
Pages 17–78 (chs. 1–5).
Oxford University ✧ Victorian Era British Memoirists | England

Milne, Christopher (1920–1996). *Enchanted Places* (Eyre Methuen, 1974).
This memoir is continued by the following entry. Christopher was a childhood friend of Richard Adams (see entry in this chapter). See also "Milne, A(lan) A(lexander)" (ch. 9; his father, author of *Winnie-the-Pooh* [1926]).
Booksellers ✧ Country Life ✧ Fathers and Sons ✧ Growing Up Between WWI and WWII ✧ Milne, A. A. ✧ Natural History | England

Milne, Christopher (1920–1996). *The Path Through the Trees* (E.P. Dutton: 1979).
Pages 3 to about 80 focus on him from 19 to 21 years.
Booksellers ✧ Children's Authors ✧ Growing Up Between WWI and WWII ✧ Military Life ✧ Milne, A. A. ✧ Natural History | England ✧ Europe

Miss Read (pseud. of Dora Saint) (1913–living 2007). *A Fortunate Grandchild* (M. Joseph, 1982).
Covers her first 6 years.
Country Life ✧ Grandmothers ✧ Growing Up Between WWI and WWII | England

Miss Read (pseud. of Dora Saint) (1913–living 2007). *Time Remembered* (Houghton Mifflin, 1987).
Covers her from 7 to 10 years.
Country Life ✧ Growing Up Between WWI and WWII | England

Morris, Edita (1902–1988). *Straitjacket: Autobiography* (Crown, 1978).
Written in a novelistic style.
Novelists ✧ Royalty ✧ Short Story Writers | Sweden

Mortimer, Penelope (1918–1999). *About Time: An Aspect of Autobiography* (Doubleday, 1979).
Pages 53–215.
Anthroposophy ✧ Eccentrics ✧ Growing Up Between WWI and WWII | England

Neilson, Elisabeth (1882?–1968). *The House I Knew: Memories of Youth* (Houghton Mifflin, 1941).

At the end of this memoir, she departs for Boston, MA to begin her adult life.

Homes and Haunts | Germany ✧ Switzerland

Nemcova, Bozena (1820–1862). Tr. by Edith Pargeter. *Granny: Scenes from Country Life* (ARTIA, 1962).

Country Life ✧ Grandmothers ✧ Nineteenth-Century Pre-Industrial Age Memoirists | Czechoslovakia

Oakes, Philip (1928–2005). *From Middle England: A Memory of the 1930s* (St. Martin's, 1980).

Covers him from 8 to 11 years. Contains a significant amount of re-created dialogue. He attended a boarding school, starting at age 8, following his father's death and his mother's illness from a brain tumor.

Critics (Film) ✧ Fatherless Families ✧ Growing Up Between WWI and WWII ✧ Journalists ✧ Poets | England

Oakes, Philip (1928–2005). *Dwellers All in Time and Space: A Memory of the 1940s* (St. Martin's, 1981).

Covers him from 13 to 16 years. Contains a significant amount of re-created dialogue.

Child Institutional Care ✧ Critics (Film) ✧ Fatherless Families ✧ Growing Up Between WWI and WWII ✧ High School Life ✧ Journalists ✧ Novelists ✧ Poets | England

O'Brien, George (1945–). *The Village of Longing* (Lilliput, 1987).

Set in the 1950s.

Country Life | Ireland

O'Brien, George (1945–). *Dancehall Days* (Lilliput, 1988).

Covers him from about 17 to 19 years. In 1989 Viking published a volume containing his first 2 memoirs, this book and *The Village of Longing* (see previous entry).

Country Life | Ireland

O'Brien, George (1945–). *Out of Our Minds: London in the Sixties: Sex, Drugs and Rock'n'Roll, Politics and Pop* (Blackstaff, 1994).

About the first 4 chapters (pages 13–95) focus on him from 19 to 21 years, in England. He then departs for the U.S.

City Life | England

O'Driscoll, Herbert (1928–). *The Leap of the Deer: Memories of a Celtic Childhood: Cowley's Lent Book for 1994* (Cowley, 1994).

Clergy ✧ Growing Up Between WWI and WWII | Ireland

Owen, Maggie (1896–). *The Book of Maggie Owen* (Bobbs-Merrill, 1941).

Journal kept when Owen was age 12.

Diaries and Journals | Ireland

Palmer, Herbert E. (1880–1961). *The Mistletoe Child: An Autobiography of Childhood* (J.M. Dent, 1935).

Critics (Literary) ✧ Poets ✧ Teachers ✧ Victorian Era British Memoirists | England

Paul, Leslie Allen (1905–1985). *The Living Hedge* (Faber & Faber, 1946).
On his childhood. This memoir is continued by the following entry.
Country Life ✧ Journalists ✧ Poets ✧ Teachers | England

Paul, Leslie Allen (1905–1985). *Angry Young Man* (Faber & Faber, 1951).
Pages 11 to about 101 (chs. 1–5).
City Life ✧ Journalists ✧ Poets ✧ Teachers | England

Pekkanen, Toivo (1902–1957). Tr. by Alan Blair. *My Childhood* (University of Wisconsin, 1966) (First published in Finnish, 1953).
Covers him up to 16 years of age.
Finland

Pinti, Pietro (1927–), and Jenny Bawtree. *Pietro's Book: The Story of a Tuscan Peasant* (Arcade, 2004).
He and his family grew up as sharecroppers; he was his mother's 12th child. This memoir includes a glossary of terms familiar to Italian peasants during the 1930s–1940s.
Country Life ✧ Farm Life ✧ Growing Up Between WWI and WWII | Italy

Pollock, Alice Wykeham-Martin (1868–1970 or 1971). *Portrait of My Victorian Youth* (Johnson Books, 1971).
Pages 19 to about 102.
Centenarians ✧ Victorian Era British Memoirists | England

Potter, Stephen (1900–1969). *Steps to Immaturity* (R. Hart-Davis, 1959).
Covers him to about 18 years.
Humorists ✧ Oxford University ✧ Socialists ✧ Westminster School | England

Rees, Coronwy (1909–). *A Chapter of Accidents* (Library, 1972).
He's only 19 on page 99.
Oxford University | Wales

Salusbury, Hilda Ann. *Only My Dreams: An English Girlhood* (Academy Chicago, 1990).
England

Seaton, Grace Mary (1894–1979?). *A Double Life in the Kaiser's Capital* (Phoenix, 1973).
WWI | Germany

Sender, Ramon (Jose) (1902–1982). *Chronicle of Dawn* (Doubleday, Doran, 1944).
One of the finest memoirs of youth in Spain that is available in English.
Civil War (Spanish) ✧ College Teachers ✧ Critics (Literary) ✧ Editors ✧ Novelists | Spain

Shaw, Charles (1832–1906). *When I Was a Child* (Methuen, 1903).
This 256-page memoir focuses on his boyhood, except for the final 2 chapters (chs. 24 and 25), which focus on him at 20 or 21 years old.
Nineteenth-Century Pre-Industrial Age Memoirists ✧ Potters | England

Sibbald, Susan (1783–1866). Ed. by Francis Paget Hett. *The Memoirs of Susan Sibbald (1783–1812)* (John Lane, 1926).

Pages 4 to about 225 focus on her first 21 years; the remainder covers her to 29 years old.

Collaborations by Relatives ◇ Eighteenth-Century Memoirists | England ◇ Scotland

Sillar, Eleanor Hallard (1869–). *Edinburgh's Child: Some Memories of Ninety Years* (Oliver & Boyd, 1961).

Covers her first 18 years.

Aunts | Scotland

Spring, (Robert) Howard (1889–1965). *Heaven Lies About Us: A Fragment of Infancy* (Viking, 1939).

He was one of 9 children, whose father was a gardener.

Dramatists ◇ Journalists ◇ Novelists | Wales

Strachey, Richard (1902–). *A Strachey Child* (Simonette Strachey, 1979).

Pages 22–150 focus on his first 7 years. He was a nephew of Lytton Strachey.

City Life ◇ Strachey, Lytton | India ◇ England (London)

Sykes, John. *Slawit in the 'Sixties: Reminiscences of the Moral, Social, and Industrial Life of Slaithwaite and District in and About the Year 1860* (Schofield and Sims, 1926).

England

Undset, Sigrid (1882–1949). Tr. from the Norwegian by Arthur G. Chater. *The Longest Years* (Knopf, 1935) (First published in Norwegian, 1934).

Covers her first 11 years. She calls herself "Ingvild" in this memoir.

Catholics ◇ Novelists ◇ Secretaries ◇ Translators | Denmark

Varney, Joyce. *A Welsh Story* (Bobbs-Merrill, 1965).

WWII | Wales

Vaughan, Richard (pseud. of Ernest Lewys Thomas) (1904–1983). *There Is a River* (E.P. Dutton, 1961).

Journalists ◇ Screenwriters ◇ Teachers | Wales

Verschoyle, Moira (1904–). *Four to Fourteen by a Victorian Child* (R. Hale, 1939).

She grew up in a castle, on the banks of the River Shannon.

Castles ◇ Country Life | Ireland

Verschoyle, Moira (1904–). *So Long to Wait: An Irish Childhood* (G. Bles, 1960).

Castles ◇ Country Life | Ireland

Watkins, Bill (1950–). *A Celtic Childhood* (Hungry Mind, 1999).

This memoir covers Watkins's life to age 17.

Bereavement ◇ Catholics ◇ Musicians ◇ Slums | Ireland ◇ England

Watkins, Bill (1950–). *Scotland Is Not for the Squeamish* (Ruminator Books, 2000).

Covers him from 19 to 21 years.

Seafaring Life | Arctic ◇ Scotland

Welfare, Mary (1901–). *Growing Up at Haddo: A Scottish Childhood* (Weidenfeld & Nicolson, 1989).

Country Life ✧ Homes and Haunts | Scotland

Wynne, Elizabeth (1779–). Selected and ed. by Anne Fremantle. *The Wynne Diaries: 1789–1820.* **3 vols.** (Oxford University, 1935, 1937, and 1940).
Pages 1–307 (chs. 1–22).

Collaborations by Relatives ✧ Diaries and Journals ✧ Eighteenth-Century Memoirists | Europe

Russia and Eastern European Countries

Russia, Soviet Union, Hungary, Czechoslovakia, Poland, Ukraine, and Romania

Aksakoff, Sergei (1791–1859). Tr. by J. D. Duff. *A Russian Schoolboy* (Arnold, 1917).
This memoir is continued by the following entry.

Nineteenth-Century Pre-Industrial Age Memoirists | Russia

Aksakoff, Sergei (1791–1859). Tr. by J.D. Duff. *Years of Childhood* (Longmans, Green, 1916) (First published in Russian, 1858).
This is the second volume in Aksakoff's opus *Family Chronicle* (Routledge, 1924).

Nineteenth-Century Pre-Industrial Age Memoirists | Russia

Boldyreff, Tatiana W. (c. 1900–). *Russian Born: A Pageant of Childhood Memories* (Chapman & Grimes, 1935).
This classic memoir focuses only on her girlhood.

Russia (St. Petersburg)

Chukovskaia, Lidiia (1907–1996). Tr. from the Russian by Eliza Kellogg Klose. *To the Memory of Childhood* (Northwestern University, 1988) (Originally published in Russian, 1983).
To about age 10. Her father, Kornei Chukovsky, was a noted author and literary critic (see following entry).

Fathers and Daughters ✧ Novelists | Russia

Chukovsky, Kornei (pseud. of N. I. Korneichuk) (1882–1969). Tr. by Beatrice Stillman. *The Silver Crest: My Russian Boyhood* (Holt, Rinehart and Winston, 1976) (Originally published in Russian, 1961).
His daughter, Lidiia Chukovskaia, also wrote a coming-of-age memoir (see preceding entry).

Children's Authors ✧ Critics (Literary) ✧ Poets ✧ Translators | Russia

de Holstein, Alexandra (1850?–), and Dora B. Montefiore. *Serf Life in Russia: The Childhood of a Russian Grandmother* (Heinemann, 1906).
This memoir covers her life to 11 years old.

Nineteenth-Century Pre-Industrial Age Memoirists | Russia

Fraser, Eugenie (1905?–2002). *The House by the Dvina: A Russian Childhood* (Mainstream, 1984).

Russia (Northern)

Hautzig, Esther (1930–). *The Endless Steppe: Growing Up in Siberia* (Crowell, 1968). Covers 1941–1945.

Family Memoirs ✧ Growing Up Between WWI and WWII ✧ Immigrants | Poland ✧ Siberia

Hindus, Maurice (1891–1969). *Green Worlds: An Informal Chronicle* (Doubleday, Doran, 1938).

Historians (Cultural) | Russia

Hindus, Maurice (1891–1969). *A Traveler in Two Worlds* (Doubleday, 1971). Pages 25 to about 160.

Historians (Cultural) | Russia ✧ NY

Karadja, Kyra. Preface by Dr. Margaret Mead. *Kyra's Story: Reminiscences of a Girlhood in Revolutionary Russia* (W. Morrow, 1975).

Soviet Union

Kataev, Valentin (1897–1986). Tr. from the Russian by Moira Budberg and Gordon Latta. *A Mosaic of Life: Or, the Magic Horn of Oberon: Memoirs of a Russian Childhood* (Angus and Robertson, 1976).

Dramatists ✧ Humorists ✧ Novelists ✧ Short Story Writers | Russia

La Zebnik, Edith (1897–). *Such a Life* (W. Morrow, 1978). This is a memoir of prerevolutionary Russia.

Jews | Russia

Nikitenko, Aleksandr (1804–1877). Tr. by Helen S. Jacobson. *Up from Serfdom: My Childhood and Youth in Russia, 1804–1824* (Yale University, 2001). Nikitenko began writing his diaries, from which this memoir was drawn, in 1851.

Diaries and Journals ✧ Teachers | Russia

Patai, Joseph (1882–1953). Tr. from the Hungarian Raphael Patai. *The Middle Gate: A Hungarian Jewish Boyhood* (Jewish Publication Society, 1994) (First published in Hungarian, 1927).

Editors ✧ Jews ✧ Poets ✧ Spiritual Life ✧ Translators | Hungary

Paustovsky, Konstantin Georgevich (1892–1968). Tr. by Manya Harari and Michael Duncan. *Childhood and Schooldays* (Harvill, 1964). This is the first volume of his 6-volume memoir <u>Story of a Life</u> (Pantheon Books, 1946). It is continued by the following entry.

Novelists ✧ Short Story Writers | Ukraine

Paustovsky, Konstantin Georgevich (1892–1968). Tr. by Manya Hatari and Michael Duncan. *Slow Approach of Thunder* (Harvill, 1965). This sequel to the previous entry covers his life to age 21.

Novelists ✧ Short Story Writers | Ukraine

Peterkiewicz, Jerzy (1916–). *In the Scales of Fate: An Autobiography* (M. Boyars, 1993). This is the first volume of a projected 2-volume autobiography. Pages 12 to about 132 (Part One–Part Two).

Critics (Literary) ✧ Dramatists ✧ Editors ✧ Essayists ✧ Growing Up Between WWI and WWII ✧ Novelists ✧ Poets | Poland

Pilon, Juliana (1947–). *Notes from the Other Side of the Night* (Regnery Gateway, 1979). About 97 scattered pages.

Children of Holocaust Survivors ✧ Jews | Romania

Skariatina, Irina (1883–1962). *Little Eva in Old Russia* (Bobbs-Merrill, 1934).

Russia

Skvorecky, Josef (1924–). Tr. by Kaca P. Henley. *Headed for the Blues: A Memoir* (Ecco, 1996).

Communists ✧ Growing Up Between WWI and WWII | Czechoslovakia

Soloukhin, Vladimir (1924–1997). Tr. by David Martin. *Laughter Over the Left Shoulder* (Owen, 1991). Covers his first 7 years.

Beekeeping ✧ Country Life ✧ Grandfathers ✧ Growing Up Between WWI and WWII | Russia

Sudermann, Hermann (1857–1928). Tr. by Wyndham Harding. *The Book of My Youth* (Harper & Brothers, 1923).

Dramatists ✧ Nineteenth-Century Pre-Industrial Age Memoirists ✧ Novelists ✧ Short Story Writers | East Prussia (later part of Poland and Russia; now Lithuania)

Tchernavin, Tatiana. *My Childhood in Siberia* (Oxford University, 1972). For a similar memoir, see "Matane, Paulias" (ch. 3).

Russia (Siberia)

Tene, Benjamin (1914–). Tr. from the Hebrew by Reuben Ben-Joseph. *In the Shade of the Chestnut Tree* (Jewish Publication Society, 1981).

Growing Up Between WWI and WWII ✧ Jews | Poland

Vodovozova, Elizaveta (1844–1923). Tr. by Anthony Brode and Olga Lane. *A Russian Childhood* (Faber & Faber, 1961). This account was drawn from the first volume of a longer work.

Nineteenth-Century Pre- Industrial Age Memoirists | Russia

Young, Cathy (b. Ekaterina Jung) (1963–). *Growing Up in Moscow: Memories of a Soviet Girlhood* (Ticknor & Fields, 1989).

Immigrants ✧ Journalists ✧ Translators | Soviet Union (i.e., Russia)

Zhigalova, Olga. Tr. by Tatiana Balkoff Drowne. *Across the Green Past* (H. Regnery, 1952) (First published in French, 1948). Focuses on her girlhood, from about 1900 to 1917.

Country Life | Russia

Middle Eastern Cultures

Including Iran, Israel, Lebanon, Palestine, Syria, and Turkey

Accawi, Anwar (1943–). *The Boy from the Tower of the Moon* (Beacon, 1999).

Lebanon

Carhart, Alfreda. *It Happened in Syria* (F.H. Revell, 1940).

To age 15, when she moved to the U.S.; written from a third-person perspective. Her father was a missionary.

Missionaries | Syria

Diqs, Isaak (b. Al-Diqs, Isaak ibn-Abdulaziz) (1938–). *A Bedouin Boyhood* (Universe, 1967).

Bedouins | Palestine

Farmaian, Sattareh (1921–), with Dona Munker. *Daughter of Persia: A Woman's Journey from Her Father's Harem Through the Islamic Revolution* (Crown, 1992).
She grew up in a theatrical family. Pages 3 to about 133 (chs. 1–6).

Growing Up Between WWI and WWII ✧ Muslims | Iran

Guppy, Shusha (1938–). *Blindfold Horse: Memories of a Persian Childhood* (Beacon, 1988).

Contains 32 titled chapters.

Persia (i.e., Iran)

Jordan, Ruth (1926–1994). *Daughter of the Waves: Memories of Growing Up in Pre-War Palestine* (Harlequin, 1982).

Growing Up Between WWI and WWII ✧ Jews | Palestine (i.e., Israel)

Pamuk, Orhan (1952–). *Istanbul: Memories and the City* (Knopf, 2005).

This is a complex and melancholy memoir that interweaves Pamuk's emotions and analysis, regarding his childhood, his extended family, and the sociopolitical realities of life in Istanbul. Pamuk won the Nobel Prize for Literature in 2006.

City Life ✧ Family Memoirs ✧ Novelists | Turkey (Istanbul)

Schauffler, Adolphus (1845–1919). *Memories of a Happy Boyhood "Long Ago, and Far Away"* (F.H. Revell, 1919).

Nineteenth-Century Pre-Industrial Age Memoirists | Ottoman Empire (i.e., Turkey)

Asian Cultures

Including India, Pakistan, Thailand, Japan, and China

Addleton, Jonathan S. (1957–). *Some Far and Distant Place* (University of Georgia, 1997).

His parents were Baptist missionaries.

Baptists | Pakistan

Alter, Stephen (1956–). *All the Way to Heaven: An American Boyhood in the Himalayas* (H. Holt, 1998).

Baby Boomers | India

Booth, Martin (1945–2004). *Golden Boy: Memories of a Hong Kong Childhood* (St. Martin's, 2005).

This is a vividly evoked memoir of his first 10 years, which corresponded with the decade that followed WWII. Includes a glossary of more than 70 Cantonese words and phrases. Booth began writing this work shortly after learning he had a brain tumor. See also "Kendon, Frank,"

"Maclaren-Ross, Julian," and "Berners, (Lord) Gerald" for other memoirs that focus on only the author's first 10 years.

Children's Authors ✧ Novelists | China (Hong Kong)

Candlin, Enid Saunders (1909–1995). *The Breach in the Wall: A Memoir of Old China* (Macmillan, 1973).

Novelists ✧ Travel Writers | China

Cao, Guanlong (1945–). Tr. by Cao Guanlong and Nancy Moskin. *The Attic: Memoir of a Chinese Landlord's Son* (University of California, 1996).

China's Cultural Revolution | China (Shanghai)

Chandruang, Kumat (1914–). *My Boyhood in Siam* (Day, 1940).

From 7–18 years, until his departure to the U.S.

Siam (i.e., Thailand)

Chang, Jung (1952–). *Wild Swans: Three Daughters of China* (Simon and Schuster, 1991).

About page 191 to about page 474 (chs. 10–26).

China's Cultural Revolution ✧ Grandmothers ✧ Mothers and Daughters | China

Chiang, Yee (1903–1977). *A Chinese Childhood* (Methuen, 1940) (1952 rpt., Day).

Includes line drawings by the author.

Illustrators | China

Chow, Ching-li (1936–). Tr. from the French by Abby Israel. *Journey in Tears: Memory of a Girlhood in China* (McGraw-Hill, 1978).

China

Da Chen (1962–). *Colors of the Mountain* (Random House, 1999).

This memoir, continued by the following entry, was adapted as the companion volume *China's Son: Growing Up in the Cultural Revolution* (Delacorte, 2001).

China's Cultural Revolution | China

Da Chen (1962–). *Sounds of the River: A Memoir* (HarperCollins, 2002).

Covers him from 16 to 23 years.

China's Cultural Revolution ✧ College Life | China

Fritz, Jean (1915– living 2007). *Homesick: My Own Story* (Putnam, 1982).

This is a memoir in the form of a novel, as explained in her introductory essay. See also "Espey, John" (ch. 8) and "Patent, Gregory" (ch. 6) for similar memoirs with a Western perspective by authors who grew up in China.

Growing Up Between WWI and WWII | China

Ginsbourg, Sam (1914–). *My First Sixty Years in China* (New World Press, 1982).

Pages 7 to about 85.

Growing Up Between WWI and WWII | China

Heng, Liang (1954–), and Judith Shapiro. *Son of the Revolution* (Knopf, 1983).

Pages 3–242 (chs. 1–20).

China's Cultural Revolution | China (Shanghai, Peking)

Hong Ying (1962–). Tr. by Howard Goldblatt. *Daughter of the River* (Grove, 1998).
More than 100 scattered pages. Focuses on life in Communist China from the late 1970s to early 1980s.

Novelists ✧ Poets ✧ Short Story Writers ✧ Slums I China

Jiang, Ji-li (1954–). *Red Scarf Girl: A Memoir of the Cultural Revolution* (HarperCollins, 1997).

Revolutionaries I China (Shanghai)

Kawahara, Dawn (193?–). *Jackal's Wedding: A Memoir of a Childhood in British India* (1st Books, 2002).

India

Kaye, M(ary) M(argaret) (1911?–2004). *The Sun in the Morning: My Early Years in India and England* (St. Martin's, 1990).
This memoir is continued by the following entry.

Children's Authors ✧ Novelists I India ✧ England

Kaye, M(ary) M(argaret) (1911?–2004). *Golden Afternoon: Being the Second Part of Share of Summer, Her Autobiography, Volume 2* (Viking, 1997).
At least the first 300 pages focus on her from 19 to 21 years.

Children's Authors ✧ Novelists I India

Khaing, Mi Mi (1916–). *Burmese Family* (Indiana University, 1962).
Pages 43–161.

Family Memoirs ✧ Growing Up Between WWI and WWII I Burma

Koizumi, Kazuo (1893–). *Father and I: Memories of Lafcadio Hearn* (Houghton Mifflin, 1935).
Entire memoir focuses on his first 11 years; he was the son of writer Lafcadio Hearn.

City Life ✧ Hearn, Lafcadio I Japan

Lee, Yan Phou (1861–). *When I Was a Boy in China* (Lothrop, 1887).
The final 7 pages are set in the U.S.

Chinese Americans I China ✧ U.S.

May, Someth (1957–). Ed. by James Fenton. *Cambodian Witness: The Autobiography of Someth May* (Random House, 1986).
Pages 21 to about 193.

Family Memoirs ✧ Refugees I Cambodia

Merchant, W(habiz) D. (1946–). *Home on the Hill: A Bombay Girlhood* (Three Continents, 1991).
Pages 12–13, 17–126 focus on her girlhood years. She moved to the U.S. (MI) in 1967.

City Life I India

Moon, Vasant. Tr. by Gail Omvedt. *Growing Up Untouchable in India: A Dalit Autobiography* (Rowman & Littlefield, 2000).

Asian Americans I India

Moraes, (F.) Dom(inic) (1938–). *My Father's Son: A Poet's Autobiography* (Macmillan, 1968).
The first 111 pages cover his childhood. He moved to England at about age 16.
Poets | India

Nanchu (1953–). *Red Sorrow: A Memoir* (Arcade, 2001).
When her parents were jailed by the government when she was 13, she was forced to join a youth work camp.
China's Cultural Revolution | China

Ning Lao T'Ai-T'Ai (1867–living 1938), as told to Ida Pruitt. *A Daughter of Han: The Autobiography of a Chinese Working Woman* (Yale University, 1945).
Pages 20–73.
Victorian Era British Memoirists (?) | China

Niu-Niu (1966–). Tr. by Enne Amann and Peter Amann. *No Tears for Mao: Growing Up in the Cultural Revolution* (Academy Chicago, 1995) (First published in French, 1989).
China's Cultural Revolution ✧ Communists ✧ Grandparents | China

Onon, Urgunge (1919–). *My Childhood in Mongolia* (Oxford University, 1972).
Growing Up Between WWI and WWII | China

Ramakrishnan, Prema. *Growing Up at Grandpa's: Reminiscences of a Happy Childhood* (Writer's Workshop, 1991).
Children's Authors ✧ Grandfathers ✧ Poets ✧ Short Story Writers | India

Sansan (1938–), as told to Bette Lord. *Eighth Moon: The True Story of a Young Girl's Life in Communist China* (Harper & Row, 1964).
Focuses on her from 4 to 17 years.
Communists | China

Sawamura, Sadako (1908–1996). Tr. from the Japanese by Norman E. Stafford and Yasuhiro Kawamura. *My Asakusa: Coming of Age in Pre-War Japan* (Tuttle, 2000) (First published in Japanese, 1976).
Entire memoir focuses on her first 21 years.
Motion Picture Actresses and Actors | Japan

Su-Ling, Wong (1918–), and Earl Herbert Cressy. *Daughter of Confucius: A Personal History* (Farrar, Straus, and Young, 1952).
She is under 21 years old until about page 314.
Growing Up Between WWI and WWII | South China

Surayya, Kamala (1934–). Tr. by Gita Krishnankutty. *A Childhood in Malabar: A Memoir* (Penguin, 2003).
These are the recollections of a Malayalam and English author.
WWII | India

Taring, Rinchen Dolma (1910–2000). *Daughter of Tibet* (John Murray, 1970) (1986 rpt., Wisdom Publications).
Pages 43–101 (chs. 3–6).
China (Tibet)

Thwe, Pascal Khoo (1967–). *From the Land of Green Ghosts: A Burmese Odyssey* (HarperCollins, 2002).

He tells of his intellectual and political awakenings while living under a dictatorship, before fleeing to the U.S.

Burmese British ✧ Catholics ✧ College Life ✧ Generation X ✧ Intellectual Life ✧ Jungle Life ✧ Revolutionaries I Burma

Wei, Katherine (1930–), and Terry Quinn. *Second Daughter: Growing Up in China, 1930–1949* (Little, Brown, 1984).

Chinese Americans ✧ Growing Up Between WWI and WWII I China

Yang, Rae (1950–). *Spider Eaters: A Memoir* (University of California, 1997).

China's Cultural Revolution I China

African Cultures

Including Egypt, Ethiopia, Kenya, Nigeria, Rhodesia, Senegal, Sierra Leone, South Africa, and Southern Rhodesia

Abrahams, Peter (1919–). *Tell Freedom* (Knopf, 1954) (Variant title, *Tell Freedom: Memories of Africa* [Knopf, 1969]).

An abridged edition was published in 1970.

Africans ✧ Growing Up Between WWI and WWII ✧ Journalists ✧ Novelists ✧ Poets ✧ Short Story Writers ✧ Slums I South Africa

Aciman, André (1951–). *Out of Egypt: A Memoir* (Farrar, Straus, and Giroux, 1994).

Focuses on the 1950s to 1960s.

College Teachers ✧ Jews I Egypt

Aman (pseud.) (1952–), as told to Virginia Lee Barnes and Janice Boddy. *Aman: The Story of a Somali Girl* (Knopf Canada, 1994).

She is only 17 at book's end, when she fled to Kenya. As an adult, she started an import business.

Business Persons ✧ Family Violence ✧ Refugees I Somalia ✧ Kenya

Ammar, Hamid (1907?–1974). *Growing Up in an Egyptian Village* (Routledge & Kegan Paul, 1954).

Anthropologists ✧ Government Officials ✧ Labor Leaders and Unions I Egypt

Anderson, Daphne (1919–). *Toe-rags: The Story of a Strange Up-bringing in Southern Rhodesia* (Andre Deutsch, 1989).

Growing Up Between WWI and WWII ✧ Slums I Southern Rhodesia (i.e., Zimbabwe)

Bugal, Ken (pseud. of Marietou M'Baye) (1948–). Tr. from the French by Marjolijn de Jager. *The Abandoned Baobab: The Autobiography of a Senegalese Woman* (Lawrence Hill Books, 1991).

To about 20 years old.

Aunts I Senegal ✧ Belgium

Coetzee, J(ohn) M(ichael) (1940–). *Boyhood: Scenes from Provincial Life* (Viking, 1997).
Focuses on him from about 8 to about 13 years old.
Slums | South Africa

Cole, Robert Wellesley (1907–living 1995). *Kossoh Town Boy* (Cambridge University, 1960).
Pages 32–191 cover his first 16 years.
Sierra Leone

Diallo, Nafissatou (1941–1982). *A Dakar Childhood* (Longman, 1975).
Memoir ends with her marriage, her father's death, and her move to Paris.
Fathers and Daughters ◇ Grandmothers ◇ Muslims | Senegal

Forna, Aminatta (1964–). *The Devil That Danced on the Water: A Daughter's Memoir* (Atlantic Monthly, 2002).
She tells how her childhood was ripped apart, at age 10, by the political execution of her father.
Africans ◇ Political Executions | Sierra Leone ◇ Nigeria ◇ Scotland

Fugard, Athol (1932–). *Cousins: A Memoir* (Witwatersrand University, 1984).
Dramatists | South Africa

Fuller, Alexandra (1969–). *Don't Let's Go to the Dogs Tonight: An African Childhood* (Picador, 2002).
She tells of the loss of 3 siblings during her family's hard years farming in South Africa.
Bereavement ◇ Civil War ◇ Diaries and Journals ◇ Farm Life ◇ Generation X ◇ Jungle Life ◇ Malaria ◇ Racism | Rhodesia ◇ Southern Rhodesia (i.e., Zimbabwe) ◇ Zambia

Gatheru, R. Mugo (1925–). *Child of Two Worlds, a Kikuyu's Story* (Praeger, 1964).
The first 70 pages cover the author's first 21 years.
Africans ◇ Growing Up Between WWI and WWII | Kenya

Godwin, Peter (1957–). *Mukiwa: A White Boy in Africa* (Atlantic Monthly, 1996).
About the first 200 pages cover about his first 18 years.
Baby Boomers ◇ Journalists ◇ Police | Rhodesia ◇ Zimbabwe

Huxley, Elspeth (1907–1997). *The Flame Trees of Thika: Memories of an African Childhood* (Chatto & Windus, 1959).
Covers her girlhood in Africa from 1913 until WWI.
Natural History ◇ Novelists ◇ Travel Writers | England ◇ Kenya

Huxley, Elspeth (1907–1997). *On the Edge of the Rift: Memories of Kenya* (W. Morrow, 1962) (British title, *Mottled Lizard* [1962]).
Covers from about 1919 through about 1922. See also her sequel (ch. 9).
Natural History ◇ Novelists ◇ Travel Writers | Kenya

Juta, Jan (1895–1990). *Background in Sunshine: Memories of South Africa* (Scribner, 1972).
Painters ◇ Victorian Era British Memoirists | South Africa

Laye, Camara (1928–1980). Tr. by James Kirkup and Ernest Jones. *The Dark Child* (Farrar, Straus, and Giroux, 1954) (Variant title, *The African Child* [Collins, Fontana Books, 1954]) (First published in French, 1953).
He's only 15 years old on page 137.
Growing Up Between WWI and WWII ✧ Novelists | Guinea

Lessing, Doris (1919–). *Under My Skin: Volume One of My Autobiography, to 1949* (HarperCollins, 1994).
Pages 18 to about 224. Includes 16 pages of black-and-white plates of her family.
Essayists ✧ Growing Up Between WWI and WWII ✧ Novelists ✧ Short Story Writers | Persia (i.e., Iran) ✧ England ✧ Rhodesia ✧ England

Lively, Penelope (1933–). *Oleander, Jacaranda: A Childhood Perceived: A Memoir* (HarperCollins, 1994).
Covers her first 12 years, at which time she moved to England (to boarding school). This memoir contains vivid descriptions of Cairo and the beaches of Alexandria. There is little re-created dialogue.
Novelists ✧ Short Story Writers ✧ WWII | Egypt

Mezlekia, Nega (1958–). *Notes from the Hyena's Belly: An Ethiopian Boyhood* (Picador USA, 2001).
He describes participating in guerrilla warfare at age 18, during his homeland's civil war, resulting in his imprisonment.
Africans ✧ Engineers (Civil) ✧ Folklorists ✧ Prisoners ✧ Revolutionaries | Ethiopia

Mphahlele, Ezekiel (1919–1983). *Down Second Avenue* (Faber & Faber, 1959).
Africans ✧ College Teachers ✧ Critics (Literary) ✧ Essayists ✧ Growing Up Between WWI and WWII ✧ Intellectual Life ✧ Journalists ✧ Short Story Writers | South Africa

Plomer, William (1903–1973). *Double Lives: An Autobiography* (Jonathan Cape, 1943).
Covers his first 25–26 years.
Librettists ✧ Novelists ✧ Poets ✧ Short Story Writers ✧ Teachers | South Africa ✧ England

Rossant, Colette (1932–). *Memories of a Lost Egypt: A Memoir with Recipes* (C. Potter, 1999).
Pages 18–148 cover her first 21 years.
Cookery ✧ Journalists | Egypt

Segun, Mabel (1930–). *My Father's Daughter* (East African Publishing House, 1965).
About 80 pages. This memoir was written for children. For 2 other Nigerian memoirs, see "Soyinka, Wole" (following entries).
Africans ✧ Children's Authors ✧ Fatherless Families ✧ Fathers and Daughters ✧ Poets ✧ Translators | Nigeria

Soyinka, Wole (1934–). *Ake: The Years of Childhood* (Collings, 1981).
This and the following entry both focus on Soyinka's childhood years. For another Nigerian memoir, see "Segun, Mabel" (preceding entry).
Africans ✧ Dramatists ✧ Novelists ✧ Poets | Nigeria

Soyinka, Wole (1934–). *Isara: A Voyage Round "Essay"* (Random House, 1989).
Africans ✧ Dramatists ✧ Novelists ✧ Poets | Nigeria

Van Wyck, Chris (1957–). *Shirley, Goodness & Mercy: A Childhood Memoir* (Pan Macmillan, 2004).
   Prolific writer Van Wyck recounts his brutalized childhood, growing up black in South Africa during the 1960s–1970s. He has won awards for his poetry and fiction.
   Africans ✧ Biographers ✧ Children's Authors ✧ Editors ✧ Poets ✧ Racism ✧ Short Story Writers ✧ Slums | South Africa

Waciuma, Charity (1936–). *Daughter of Mumbi* (East African Publishing House, 1969).
   Describes 7 years during her adolescence, living among the Kikuyu people.
   Africans ✧ Children's Authors ✧ Grandfathers ✧ Novelists ✧ Teachers | Kenya

Australian and New Zealand Cultures

Adam-Smith, Patsy (1924–). *Hear the Train Blow* (Ure Smith, 1964).
   Growing Up Between WWI and WWII | Australia

Arney, Ivy V. *Twenties Child: A Childhood Recollection* (Collins Dove, 1987).
   Australia

Banks, Mary MacLeod (?–1914). *Memories of Pioneer Days in Queensland* (Heath Cranton, 1931).
   About 80 pages cover her youth.
   Australia

Brown, Margaret Emily (1849–). *A Port Fairy Childhood, 1849/60: The Memoirs of Margaret Emily Brown (Youngman)* (Port Fairy Historical Society, 1990).
   This is a 71-page memoir.
   Governesses ✧ Nineteenth-Century Pre-Industrial Age Memoirists | Australia (Victoria)

Campbell, Ellen. *An Australian Childhood* (Blackie, 1892).
   Set in 1850s in New South Wales, Australia.
   Australia

Colebrook, Joan (1913?–1991). *A House of Trees: Memoirs of an Australian Girlhood* (Farrar, Straus, and Giroux, 1987).
   She's about 20 years old on page 200. This is a lyrically written memoir with little re-created dialogue.
   Growing Up Between WWI and WWII | Australia

Conigrave, Sarah. *My Reminiscences of the Early Days: Personal Incidents on a Sheep and Cattle Run in South Australia; Where the Writer, Mrs. J. Fairfax Conigrave (a Daughter of One of Australia's Well Remembered Pioneers, Mr. Charles Price of Hindmarsh Island), Spent Her Childhood* (Brokensha & Shaw, 1938).
   A scarce 1914 ed. may also exist.
   Australia

Drake, Mary (1912–). *The Trees Were Green: Memories of Growing Up After the Great War* (Hale & Iremonger, 1984).
   Growing Up Between WWI and WWII ✧ Wealth | Australia

Drewe, Robert (1943–). *The Shark Net: Memories and Murder* (Viking, 2000).
Focuses on a period of his adolescence.
Murder ✧ Novelists | Australia

Fitzpatrick, Kathleen (1905–). *Solid Bluestone Foundations and Other Memories of a Melbourne Girlhood, 1908–1928* (Macmillan, 1983).
Historians | Australia

Franklin, (Stella Maria Sarah) Miles (1879–1954). *Childhood at Brindabella: My First Ten Years* (Angus and Robertson, 1963).
Country Life ✧ Victorian Era British Memoirists | Australia

Hughes, Mrs. F. *My Childhood in Australia: A Story for My Children* (Digby, Long, 1891).
Australia

Inglis, Amirah (1926–). *Amirah: An Un-Australian Childhood* (Heinemann, 1983).
Growing Up Between WWI and WWII ✧ Jews | Belgium ✧ Australia

James, Clive (1939–). *Unreliable Memoirs* (J. Cape, 1980).
Pages 13–156 (chs. 1–15).
Critics (Literary) ✧ Critics (Television) ✧ Novelists ✧ Poets | Australia

Keneally, Thomas (1935–). *Homebush Boy: A Memoir* (William Heinemann Australia, 1995).
Focuses on him in 1952; author also wrote *Schindler's Ark*, later adapted as the 1993 film *Schindler's List*.
Catholics | Australia

Lindsay, Jack (pseuds.: Peter Meadows, Richard Preston) (1900–1990). *Life Rarely Tells: An Autobiographical Account Ending in the Year 1921 and Situated Mostly in Brisbane, Australia* (Bodley Head, 1958).
Covers his first 20–21 years. He was a prolific writer of both nonfiction and fiction.
Novelists ✧ Poets | Australia

Lindsay, Rose (1885–1978). *Ma and Pa; My Childhood Memories* (Ure Smith, 1963).
Victorian Era British Memoirists | Australia

Liverani, Mary Rose (1939–). *The Winter Sparrows: Growing Up in Scotland and Australia* (Thomas Nelson and Sons, 1975).
Journalists ✧ Librarians ✧ Teachers | Scotland ✧ Australia

Lloyd, Rosemary. *Out of the Valley: Memoirs of an Australian Childhood* (1st Books, 2002).
Country Life | Australia

Mangan, Kathleen (1906–). *Daisy Chains, War, Then Jazz* (Hutchinson of Australia, 1984).
She was the youngest child of Heidelberg School artist Frederick McCubbin; the memoir tells of her first 19 years in Melbourne.
McCubbin, Frederick | Australia

McGuire, Frances (1900–). *Bright Morning* (Rigby, 1975).
Australia

McInnes, Graham (1912–1970). *The Road to Gundagai* (Hamilton, 1965).
Covers this novelist's childhood before and after he left England for Australia at age 8; continues to about age 18. See also "Thirkell, Angela" (ch. 9; his novelist mother).
City Life ✧ Critics (Art) ✧ Growing Up Between WWI and WWII ✧ Novelists ✧ Thirkell, Angela | England ✧ Australia

McInnes, Graham (1912–1970). *Humping My Bluey* (Hamilton, 1966).
Focuses on him from 16 to 21 years.
Critics (Art) ✧ Growing Up Between WWI and WWII ✧ Novelists | Australia

McInnes, Graham (1912–1970). *Goodbye Melbourne Town* (Hamilton, 1968).
Focuses on him at his transition from youth to manhood.
Critics (Art) ✧ Growing Up Between WWI and WWII ✧ Novelists | Australia

McKell, Katherine (1851–). *Old Days and Gold Days in Victoria (1851–1873): Being Memories of a Pioneer Family* (Edward A. Vidler, 1924).
Miners ✧ Nineteenth-Century Pre-Industrial Age Memoirists | Australia

McManus, Mary A. (1844–). *Reminiscences of the Early Settlement of the Maranoa District in the Late Fifties and Early Sixties* (Howard, 1913).
Nineteenth-Century Pre-Industrial Age Memoirists | Australia

Morgan, Sally (1951–). *My Place: An Aborigine's Stubborn Quest for Her Truth, Heritage, and Origins* (Seaver, 1987).
Australian Aboriginal People ✧ Baby Boomers ✧ Racism | Australia

Porter, Hal (1911–1984). *The Watcher on the Cast-Iron Balcony: An Australian Autobiography* (Faber & Faber, 1963).
His prose is very ornate.
Dramatists ✧ Growing Up Between WWI and WWII ✧ Novelists ✧ Short Story Writers | Australia

Praed, Rosa (1851–1935). *My Australian Girlhood: Sketches and Impressions of Bush Life, By Mrs. Campbell Praed* (T.F. Unwin, 1902).
Australian Aboriginal People ✧ Country Life ✧ Nineteenth-Century Pre-Industrial Age Memoirists | Australia

Ruhen, Olaf (1911–1989). *Tangaroa's Godchild* (Little, Brown, 1962).
On page 112 he is 22 years old.
Fishing ✧ Island Life ✧ Journalists ✧ Teachers | New Zealand

Stirling, Amie (1880–1945). *Memories of an Australian Childhood 1880–1900* (Schwartz, 1980).
Victorian Era British Memoirists | Australia

Tucker, Margaret (1904–). *If Everyone Cared: Autobiography of Margaret Tucker* (Ure Smith, 1977).
She worked as a domestic servant.
Australian Aboriginal People ✧ Servants | Australia

Wallace, Judith (1932–). *Memories of a Country Childhood* (University of Queensland, 1977).

Country Life | Australia

Chapter 5

Multicultural Heritages: Lives and Cultures in Transition

The theme uniting the memoirs listed in this chapter is that of young lives adapting to the ways of a culture that is different from their roots as individuals or families. These works describe lives of first- or second-generation transplants. Often these are immigrants or children of immigrants—people who have pulled up their roots elsewhere in order to seek a better life in the U.S. (Several dozen additional memoirs concerning these issues are found in chapter 16, which focuses on the related subjects of poverty and other forms of marginalization outside the cultural mainstream.)

As the "melting pot" that it is, the U.S. has always accepted people of richly diverse racial, ethnic, religious, and cultural heritages. Although many of the authors represented in this chapter came from modest backgrounds, a number of these recollections trace the life paths of individuals who, over time, became empowered to achieve goals that they had once thought impossible. For instance, consider the arc of Patrice Gaines's life, as described in *Laughing in the Dark: From Colored Girl to Woman of Color—A Journey from Prison to Power.*

As in most of the previous chapter, entries are arranged geographically. African ancestral heritages are illuminated first, through the listings of some 2 dozen memoirs. (Note that other memoirs relating to the subjugation of African Americans are found in chapter 6.) Established works, such as Claude Brown's *Manchild in the Promised Land*, stand shoulder-to-shoulder here with such modern classics as Yvonne S. Thornton's *Ditchdigger's Daughter.*

These are followed by reminiscences from writers with Middle Eastern origins. This section includes memoirs by Armenian Americans, whose ancestors faced the prospect of genocide. Today their plight is known by relatively few Americans, who are aware of the Holocaust that a generation later meant suffering and death for millions of Jews.

Having previously written about his mother and his Armenian heritage in general, David Kherdian's contributions, *Root River Run* and *I Called It Home*, tell of his early years growing up in Wisconsin. Another pair of memorable accounts are offered by the well-known and prolific writer William Saroyan. He recounts tales of his early years in Fresno, California, where his family life was affected by Armenian culture.

The next 2 sections are devoted to writings by persons whose forebears lived in Europe. The first of these contains memoirs by authors whose ancestors hailed from Western Europe, with a large number covering lives affected by Scandinavian cultural influences. The hardships of 19th-century Swedish American pioneers are chronicled here by Ellen Glaum (*On Creaking Wheels*). Dennis Smith, noted historian of American firefighting, contributes a memorable coming-of-age account set in the Irish American community of New York City. The rich experience of Italian Americans comes alive in the writing of Luigi Barzini.

Memoirs by Greek Americans and Russian Americans make up the fourth part of this chapter. Works by such authors as Nicholas Gage, Joseph Berger, and Dorothy Gallagher appear here, as well as a masterful coming-of-age account by accomplished novelist Harry Petrakis.

The subsequent section contains works mirroring diverse Asian ethnic heritages. Born nearly a half century apart, Indian women writers Carmit Delman and Nayantara Sahgal share their perceptions. Other memoirists included in this section tell of roots in China, Japan, Vietnam, Korea, and the Philippines.

Coming-of-age recollections by individuals whose lineage derives from the Caribbean or Central America are found in the sixth and seventh sections of the chapter. Cuban American authors have furnished a half-dozen memoirs, such as those by Emilio Bejel and Carlos Eire, who left Cuba shortly after Fidel Castro assumed control of that island. Memoirs produced by Puerto Rican Americans Judith Ortiz Cofer, Edward Rivera, and Esmeralda Santiago (who offers 2 volumes) can be found here as well.

Noted poet Derek Walcott, Maryse Conde, and Latoya Hunter (in her popular journal, written when in junior high school) describe West Indian culture. Hispanic family life in New York City is evoked by writers Gil Alicia and Dalton Conley, while Mary Ponce writes of her early years in southern California, in *Hoyt Street: Memories of a Chicana Childhood*.

The final section of this chapter offers 3 memoirs whose authors claim 3 or more ethnic or racial heritages. Among these is Michael Ondaatje's celebrated memoir *Running in the Family*, which explores his Dutch, Sinhalese, and Tamil roots. The other authors represented in this section are African American Jews Rebecca Walker and James McBride.

African Americans

Arnett, Marvin V. (1928–). *Pieces from Life's Crazy Quilt* (University of Nebraska, 2003).

African Americans ✧ Depressions (Economic) ✧ Growing Up Between WWI and WWII ✧ Lecturers ✧ Racism ✧ WWII I MI

Blue, Carroll Parrott (1943–). *The Dawn at My Back: Memoir of a Black Texas Upbringing* (University of Texas, 2003).

African Americans ✧ Mothers and Daughters ✧ Photographers ✧ Racism I TX

Bolton, Ruthie (pseud.) (1961–). *Gal: A True Life* (Harcourt, Brace, 1994).
More than the first 100 pages.

African Americans ✧ Baby Boomers I SC

Brooks, Sara (1911–). Ed. by Thordis Simonsen. *You May Plow Here: The Narrative of Sara Brooks* (Simon and Schuster, 1986).
Pages 19–160.

African Americans ✧ Farm Life I AL

Brown, Cecil (1943–). *Coming Up Down Home: A Memoir of a Southern Childhood* (Ecco, 1993).
Except for final four pages, this book covers his first 18 years. He attended college in NYC and Chicago before teaching at the University of California.

African Americans ✧ College Teachers ✧ Family Memoirs ✧ Farm Life ✧ Magicians ✧ Musicians ✧ Racism | NC

Brown, Claude (1937–2002). *Manchild in the Promised Land* (Macmillan, 1965).

African Americans ✧ Racism | NYC (Harlem)

Brown, Elaine (1943–). *A Taste of Power: A Black Woman's Story* (Pantheon Books, 1992).
Pages 17–73. She was a member of the Black Panther Party.

African Americans ✧ Black Panthers ✧ Immigrants ✧ Revolutionaries | PA

Datcher, Michael (1967–). *Raising Fences: A Black Man's Love Story* (Riverhead Books, 2001).
He grew up without a father in inner-city Los Angeles.

Adoptees ✧ African Americans ✧ Crime ✧ Editors ✧ Fatherless Families ✧ Generation X ✧ Poets ✧ Stuttering | CA (Southern: Los Angeles)

Dickerson, Debra J. (1959–). *An American Story* (Pantheon Books, 2000).
Pages 10 to about 98.

Abuse (Sexual) ✧ African Americans ✧ Baby Boomers ✧ Books and Reading ✧ Journalists ✧ Racism | MO

Fairbanks, Evelyn (1928–). *The Days of Rondo* (Minnesota Historical Society, 1990).

African Americans ✧ Growing Up Between WWI and WWII | MN

Fields, Mamie (1888–). *Lemon Swamp and Other Places: A Carolina Memoir* (Free Press, 1983).
Pages 1–110.

African Americans ✧ Collaborations by Relatives ✧ Farm Life | SC

Gaines, Patrice (1949–). *Laughing in the Dark: From Colored Girl to Woman of Color—A Journey from Prison to Power* (Crown, 1994).
Pages 7–101.

African Americans ✧ Baby Boomers ✧ Crime ✧ Journalists | VA ✧ SC ✧ MD ✧ NC

Gates, Henry Louis, Jr. (1950–). *Colored People: A Memoir* (Knopf, 1994).

African Americans ✧ Baby Boomers ✧ Critics (Literary) ✧ Historians (Cultural) | WV

Goodwin, Ruby Berkley (1903–1961). *It's Good to Be Black* (Doubleday, 1953) (1976 rpt., Southern Illinois University).

African Americans | IL

Greenfield, Eloise (1929–), and Lessie Jones Little (1906–1986), with Material by Pattie Ridley Jones. *Childtimes: A Three-Generation Memoir* (Crowell, 1979).
Covers 3 generations of women's youths between the 1880s and 1950s.

African Americans ✧ Grandmothers ✧ Growing Up Between WWI and WWII ✧ Mothers and Daughters | NC ✧ Washington, DC

Heath, Gordon (1918–1991). *Deep Are the Roots: Memoirs of a Black Expatriate* (University of Massachusetts, 1992).

Actors ✧ African Americans ✧ Gays ✧ Growing Up Between WWI and WWII I NYC

hooks, bell (1952–). *Bone Black: Memories of Girlhood* (H. Holt, 1996).

African Americans ✧ Baby Boomers ✧ College Teachers ✧ Critics (Social) ✧ Feminists I KY

hooks, bell (1952–). *Wounds of Passion: A Writing Life* (H. Holt, 1997).

About the first 100 pages are on her from 19 to 21 years.

African Americans ✧ Baby Boomers ✧ College Teachers ✧ Critics (Social) ✧ Feminists ✧ Stanford University I CA (Southern)

Mabry, Marcus (1967–). *White Bucks and Black-Eyed Peas: Coming of Age Black in White America* (Scribner, 1995).

African Americans ✧ Generation X ✧ Grandmothers ✧ Journalism ✧ Lawrenceville Academy ✧ Racism I NJ

Majozo, Estella Conwill (1949–). *Come Out the Wilderness: Memoir of a Black Woman Artist* (Feminist Press at the City University of New York, 1998).

About the first 120 pages.

African Americans ✧ Baby Boomers ✧ Catholics ✧ College ✧ Teachers ✧ Poets ✧ Racism I KY

Staples, Brent (1951–). *Parallel Time: Growing Up in Black and White* (Pantheon Books, 1994).

He has written for the *Chicago Sun-Times* and the *New York Times*.

African Americans ✧ Baby Boomers ✧ Children of Alcoholics ✧ Editors ✧ Journalists I PA

Taulbert, Clifton (1945–). *Once Upon a Time When We Were Colored* (Council Oak Books, 1989).

Covers his first 16 years.

African Americans ✧ Air Force, U.S. ✧ Bankers ✧ Family Memoirs ✧ Journalists ✧ Racism I MS

Taulbert, Clifton (1945–). *The Last Train North* (Council Oak Books, 1992).

Continues his reminiscences from age 17. See the sequel to this memoir in chapter 14.

African Americans ✧ Air Force, U.S. ✧ Bankers ✧ Journalists ✧ Racism I MO ✧ ME

Thornton., Yvonne S. (1947–), as told to Jo Coudert. *The Ditchdigger's Daughter: A Black Family's Astonishing Success Story* (Carol Publishing Group, 1995).

Pages 14 to about 150 (chs. 1–9, plus the first few pages of ch. 10).

African Americans ✧ Baby Boomers ✧ Family Memoirs ✧ Fathers and Daughters ✧ Musicians ✧ Physicians I NJ

Tillage, Leon Walter (1936–). *Leon's Story* (Farrar, Straus, and Giroux, 1997).

African Americans ✧ Racism I NC

Ugwu-Oju, Dympna (1956–). *What Will My Mother Say: A Tribal African Girl Comes of Age in America* (Bonus Books, 1995).

College Teachers ✧ Feminists ✧ Immigrants ✧ Mothers and Daughters I Nigeria ✧ CA (?)

Upchurch, Carl (1950–). *Convicted in the Womb: One Man's Journey from Prison to Peacemaker* (Bantam Books, 1996).
Pages 4–72.
African Americans ✧ Baby Boomers ✧ Crime ✧ Journalists ✧ Poets ✧ Prisoners ✧ Slums I PA

Watkins, Mel (1940–), and Roz Targ. *Dancing with Strangers: A Memoir* (Simon and Schuster, 1998).
Pages 11 to about 287.
African Americans ✧ Basketball ✧ Editors I OH

Williams, Rita (b. early 1950s). *If the Creek Don't Rise: My Life Out West with the Last Black Widow of the Civil War* (Harcourt, 2006).
In this unique memoir, the author recounts the years she spent with an elderly war widow, in the Steamboat Springs area of Colorado's Western Slope.
Actors ✧ African Americans ✧ Aunts ✧ Baby Boomers ✧ Bereavement ✧ Civil War (U.S.) ✧ College Teachers ✧ Counselors ✧ Fatherless Families ✧ Musicians ✧ Orphans ✧ Radio Broadcasters I CO

Middle Eastern Americans

From Armenia, Iran, Iraq, and Turkey

Avakian, Arlene Voski (1939–). *Lion Woman's Legacy: An Armenian-American Memoir* (Feminist Press at the City University of New York, 1992).
Pages 1 to about 82 (chs. 1–7). This memoir covers her first 35 years.
Armenian Americans I NYC ✧ NY (Western)

Balakian, Peter (1951–). *Black Dog of Fate: A Memoir* (Basic Books, 1997).
Armenian Americans ✧ Baby Boomers ✧ Grandmothers ✧ Poets I NJ

Dumas, Firoozeh (1964?–). *Funny in Farsi: A Memoir of Growing Up Iranian in America* (Villard, 2003).
She moved to the U.S. from Iran at age 7.
Humorists ✧ Immigrants ✧ Iranian Americans I CA (Southern)

Hakakian, Roya (1966–). *Journey from the Land of No: A Girlhood Caught in Revolutionary Iran* (Crown, 2004).
The author recounts her turbulent years growing up in Iran at a time of repression against women and Jews. She emigrated from her native land with her family in 1984.
Anti-Semitism ✧ City Life ✧ Generation X ✧ Iranian Americans ✧ Jews ✧ Refugees I Iran (Tehran)

Kherdian, David (1931–). *Root River Run* (Carol Rhoda Books, 1984).
Covers him from about 9 to 16 years. It is the third volume of a trilogy, whose first 2 volumes focus on his mother and his family's Armenian heritage in general. The following entry covers a similar period of Kherdian's youth, growing up in Racine, WI.
Armenian Americans I WI

Kherdian, David (1931–). *I Called It Home* (Blue Crane Books, 1997).
Armenian Americans I WI

Latifi, Afschineh (1969?–). *Even After All This Time: A Story of Love, Revolution, and Leaving Iran* (HarperCollins, 2005).

The author, a NYC attorney, tells of growing up during and after the Iranian revolution of 1979, a social upheaval that resulted in her father's execution.

Fatherless Families ✧ Generation X ✧ Iranian Americans ✧ Lawyers ✧ Murder ✧ Refugees | Iran ✧ Austria ✧ VA

Salbi, Zainab (c. 1972–), and Laurie Becklund. *Between Two Worlds: Escaping from Tyranny; Growing Up in the Shadow of Saddam* (Penguin, 2005).

She fled Iraq at age 19, moving to the U.S. in 1991. She is founder and president of Women for Women International.

Generation X ✧ Iraqi Americans ✧ Journalists ✧ Reformers ✧ Refugees | Iraq ✧ U.S.

Saroyan, William (1908–1981). *Here Comes, There Goes, You Know Who* (Simon and Schuster, 1961).

This volume contains more than 100 pages on his first 21 years; it is considered the first volume in his autobiography. See also the entry for his wife, Carol Matthau (ch. 14).

Dramatists ✧ Essayists ✧ Immigrants ✧ Novelists ✧ Short Story Writers | CA (Central)

Saroyan, William (1908–1981). *Places Where I've Done Time* (Praeger, 1972).

Some 83 scattered pages focus on his pre-adult years.

Dramatists ✧ Essayists ✧ Immigrants ✧ Novelists ✧ Short Story Writers | CA (Central)

Sciaky, Leon (1893–). *Farewell to Salonica: Portrait of an Era* (Current Books, A.A. Wyn, 1946) (2000 rpt., Isis, *Farewell to Ottoman Salonica*).

Aside from "Epilogue" (pages 227–235), the entire book (pages 3–226) focuses on about his first 20 years. He came to the U.S. with his family during WWI.

Immigrants ✧ Turkish Americans | Turkey

Surmelian, Leon (pseud.: Cyril Vandour) (1905–1995). Introduction by William Saroyan. *I Ask You, Ladies and Gentlemen* (E.P. Dutton, 1945).

Pages 13–304.

Armenian Americans ✧ College Teachers ✧ Editors ✧ Government Officials ✧ Orphans ✧ Probation Officers ✧ Screenwriters ✧ Short Story Writers ✧ Translators | Armenia ✧ Turkey ✧ Russia ✧ Greece ✧ NYC ✧ KS

Western European Americans

From Great Britain, Denmark, the Netherlands, Finland, Italy, Norway, Sweden, and Germany

Barzini, Luigi (1908–1984). *O America, When You and I Were Young* (Harper & Row, 1977).

Pages 19 to about 123. Barzini is a masterful chronicler of American social history of the early 20th century.

Italian Americans ✧ Journalists | NYC

Cascone, Gina (1956?–). *Life al Dente: Laughter and Love in an Italian-American Family* (Atria Books, 2003).

Her father was a lawyer whose clients included organized crime figures. See entry for her other memoir in chapter 8.

Baby Boomers ✧ Catholics ✧ Children's Authors ✧ Crime ✧ Family Memoirs ✧ Italian Americans | NJ

De Caro, Frank (1962–). *A Boy Named Phyllis: A Suburban Memoir* (Viking, 1996).

Baby Boomers ✧ Catholics ✧ Gays ✧ Italian Americans | NJ

De Salvo, Louise (1942–). *Vertigo: A Memoir* (E.P. Dutton, 1996).

College Teachers ✧ Critics (Literary) ✧ Italian Americans | NJ

Engelmann, Ruth (1919–). *Leaf House: Days of Remembering: A Memoir* (Harper & Row, 1982).

Covers her first 18 years; verso page states: "Though I have changed the names of all persons and most places, *Leaf House* is a faithful recounting of the life I knew as I grew up."

Finnish Americans ✧ Growing Up Between WWI and WWII | WI

Favrholdt, Visti (1920?–). *Junction City to Denmark: A Boyhood Journey* (Danish American Heritage Society, 1996).

Danish Americans ✧ Growing Up Between WWI and WWII | OR ✧ Denmark

Forbes, Kathryn (pseud. of Kathryn Anderson McLean) (1909–1966). *Mama's Bank Account* (Harcourt, Brace, 1943).

This memoir inspired a play and movie (each titled *I Remember Mama*), as well as a long-running television program (*Mama*). This work consists of 17 chapters, each of whose title begins with "Mama" or "Mama's." See also "Van Druten, John" (ch. 9).

Norwegian Americans | CA (Northern)

Glaum, Ellen (1866–). *On Creaking Wheels: The Memoirs of Ellen Brant Glaum, As Told to Eloise Wade Hackett* (Privately printed, 1940).

Some 147 pages.

Frontier and Pioneer Life ✧ Swedish Americans | MN ✧ Dakota Territory ✧ MT

Hamlin, Huybertie (1873– or 1878–1964). Ed. by Alice Kenney. *An Albany Girlhood* (Washington Park, 1990).

Dutch Americans ✧ Hudson River | NY

Manley, Seon (1921–). *My Heart's in the Heather* (Funk & Wagnalls, 1968).

She edited several anthologies with her sister, Gogo Lewis.

Children's Authors ✧ Editors ✧ Growing Up Between WWI and WWII ✧ Scottish Americans | NY

Murphy, Maureen (1914–1991). *A Child of Two Continents* (RSB Design , 1995).

Growing Up Between WWI and WWII | Ireland ✧ India

Ronning, N(ils) N(ilsen) (1870–1962). *The Boy from Telemark* (Friend, 1933).

Norwegian Americans | Norway

Skoyles, John (1949–). *Secret Frequencies: A New York Education* (University of Nebraska, 2003).

Skoyles engagingly relates the circumstances of his life growing up in NYC during the 1960s–1970s, surrounded by a galaxy of colorful relatives and friends.

Aunts ✧ Baby Boomers ✧ Books and Reading ✧ City Life ✧ College Teachers ✧ Eccentrics ✧ Fatherless Families ✧ Humorists ✧ Italian Americans ✧ Poets ✧ Summer ✧ Uncles I NYC (Queens, Manhattan)

Smith, Dennis (1940–). *A Song for Mary: An Irish-American Memory* (Warner Books, 1999).

Catholics ✧ Fatherless Families ✧ Firefighters ✧ Irish Americans I NYC (Manhattan)

Xan, Erna Oleson (1898–). *Home for Good* (I. Washburn, 1952).

This is Thurine Oleson's memoir as told to her daughter, and covers Erna from about 10–12 years.

Farm Life ✧ Norwegian Americans I WI

Russian, Greek, and Jewish Americans

Berger, Joseph (1944–). *Displaced Persons: Growing Up American After the Holocaust* (Scribner, 2001).

He came to the U.S. at age 5. This charming memoir evokes the magic of life in a new country.

Children of Holocaust Survivors ✧ Children of Immigrants ✧ Jews ✧ Russian Americans I NYC

Gage, Nicholas (1939–). *A Place for Us* (Houghton Mifflin, 1989).

The first 315 pages cover him from 10 to 21 years.

Family Memoirs ✧ Greek Americans ✧ Journalists I MA

Gallagher, Dorothy (1935–). *How I Came into My Inheritance: And Other True Stories* (Random House , 2001).

With a rich mixture of affection and humor, Gallagher describes life in 1940s NYC in a family of Russian immigrants. About 80 pages (pages 37–117).

Aunts ✧ City Life ✧ Communists ✧ Eccentrics ✧ Family Memoirs ✧ Humorists ✧ Immigrants ✧ Journalists ✧ Russian Jews I NYC (Washington Heights, Harlem)

Petrakis, Harry (1923–). *Stelmark: A Family Recollection* (D. McKay, 1970).

Some 92 scattered pages.

Depressions (Economic) ✧ Greek Americans ✧ Growing Up Between WWI and WWII I IL (Chicago)

Thompson, Ariadne (1910–). *Octagonal Heart* (Bobbs-Merrill, 1956).

Greek Americans ✧ Wealth I MO

Asian Americans

From India, China, Philippines, Japan, Korea, Vietnam, and Cambodia

Chen Chen (1939–), and Ted King. *Come Watch the Sun Go Home* (Marlowe, 1998).

Chinese Americans I China ✧ CA (Southern)

Delman, Carmit (1975–). *Burnt Bread and Chutney: Growing Up Between Cultures: A Memoir of an Indian Jewish Girl* (One World/Ballantine Books, 2002).
Her father was a Jewish American; her mother was a Jew from India.
Generation X ✧ Indian Americans ✧ Jews | Israel ✧ U.S.

Fong-Torres, Ben (1945–). *The Rice Room: Growing Up Chinese-American—From Number Two Son to Rock'n'Roll* (Hyperion, 1994).
Pages 7–144 (chs. 1–15).
Chinese Americans ✧ Critics (Music) | CA (Northern)

Huynh, Jade Ngoc Quang (1957–). *South Wind Changing: A Memoir* (Graywolf, 1994).
Covers him from about 18 to 27 years; he's only 19 on page 111.
Boat People ✧ Refugees ✧ Vietnamese Americans | Vietnam ✧ VT

Huynh, Quang Nhuong (1946–). *The Land I Lost: Adventures of a Boy in Vietnam* (Harper & Row, 1982).
See also following entry.
Vietnamese Americans | Vietnam

Huynh, Quang Nhuong (1946–). *Water Buffalo Days: Growing Up in Vietnam* (HarperCollins, 1997).
This is a children's version of *The Land I Lost* (see previous entry).
Vietnamese Americans ✧ Water Buffalo | Vietnam

Kim, Elizabeth (c. 1947–). *Ten Thousand Sorrows: The Extraordinary Journey of a Korean War Orphan* (Doubleday, 2000).
About the first 150 pages.
Bereavement ✧ Fundamentalism (Christian) ✧ Korean Americans ✧ Murder ✧ Orphans ✧ Racially Mixed Children | Korea ✧ CA (Southern)

Kim, Richard E. (1932–). *Lost Names: Scenes from a Korean Boyhood* (Praeger, 1970).
Korean Americans ✧ Novelists | Korea

Kingston, Maxine Hong (1940–). *The Woman Warrior: Memoirs of a Girlhood Among Ghosts* (Knopf, 1976).
Chinese Americans ✧ College Teachers ✧ Mothers and Daughters | CA (Northern)

Lee, Li-Young (1957–). *The Winged Seed: A Remembrance* (Simon and Schuster, 1995).
Chinese Americans ✧ Island Life ✧ Poets | Indonesia

Lim, Sing (born c.1915–1920). *West Coast Chinese Boy* (Tundra Books, 1979).
Memoir of 64 pages.
Chinese Canadians ✧ Growing Up Between WWI and WWII | Canada (BR COL)

Lin, Alice (1943?–). *Grandmother Had No Name* (China Books & Periodicals: 1988).
About 54 scattered pages.
Chinese Americans ✧ Grandmothers ✧ Mental Health ✧ Personnel | China

Mar, M. Elaine (1966–). *Paper Daughter* (HarperCollins, 1999).
Chinese Americans ✧ Generation X | China (Hong Kong) ✧ CO

Min, Anchee (1957–). *Red Azalea* (Pantheon Books, 1994).
Covers 1966–1969. She has lived in the U.S. since 1984.

Bisexuals ✧ China's Cultural Revolution ✧ Chinese Americans ✧ Communists ✧ Painters ✧ Photographers ✧ Revolutionaries I China

Nguyen, Kien (1967–). *The Unwanted: A Memoir* (Little, Brown, 2001).
Focuses on his life from 8 to 18 years, from the time of the U.S. pullout from Vietnam until the author's immigration to the U.S. with his family. He is now a dentist in NYC.

Dentists ✧ Generation X ✧ Immigrants ✧ Racism ✧ Vietnam Conflict ✧ Vietnamese Americans I Vietnam ✧ U.S.

Reyes, Norman (1922–1999). *Child of Two Worlds: An Autobiography of a Filipino-American—Or Vice Versa* (Three Continents, 1995).
Pages 36 to about 285 (chs. 7–23) focus on his first 20 years.

Filipino Americans ✧ Growing Up Between WWI and WWII ✧ Radio Broadcasters I Philippines

Sahgal, Nayantara (1927–). *Prison and Chocolate Cake* (Knopf, 1954).
She was a political analyst who attended college in India and Wellesley College in the U.S. Indira Gandhi was her cousin.

Ambassadors ✧ College Teachers ✧ Growing Up Between WWI and WWII ✧ Journalists ✧ Novelists I India

Sugimoto, Etsu (1873–1950). *A Daughter of the Samurai: How a Daughter of Feudal Japan, Living Hundreds of Years in One Generation, Became a Modern American* (Tuttle, 1966) (First published in Japanese, 1926).
She's under 21 for about the first 200 pages.

Japanese Americans ✧ Samurai I Japan

Trenka, Jane Jeong (1972–). *The Language of Blood: A Memoir* (Borealis Books, 2003).
The author, a native Korean, was adopted and raised by a conservative white couple in MN.

Adoptees ✧ Farm Life ✧ Generation X ✧ Korean Americans I MN

Wong, Jade Snow (1922–). *Fifth Chinese Daughter* (Harper, 1950).
About the first 160 pages (ch. 1–part of ch. 19) of this third-person memoir. She grew up in San Francisco.

Chinese Americans ✧ Growing Up Between WWI and WWII ✧ Potters I CA (Northern)

Caribbean Americans

From Cuba, Dominica, West Indies, and Puerto Rico

Alvarez, Julia (1950–). *Something to Declare* (Algonquin Books of Chapel Hill, 1998).
This is a collection of essays.

Baby Boomers ✧ City Life ✧ Dominican Americans ✧ Essayists ✧ Island Life ✧ Novelists ✧ Poets ✧ Refugees I Dominican Republic ✧ NYC

Anders, Gigi (c. 1958–). *Jubana ! The Awkwardly True and Dazzling Adventures of a Jewish Cuban Goddess* (HarperCollins , 2005).
This lighthearted memoir focuses on her relationship with her mother.

Cuban Americans ✧ Immigrants ✧ Jews ✧ Mothers and Daughters I FL (Miami)

Bejel, Emilio (1944?–). Tr. by Stephen J. Clark. *The Write Way Home: A Cuban American Story* (Versal Books , 2003).
He immigrated to Florida from Cuba at age 18.

Anti-Communist Movements ✧ Catholics ✧ Cold War ✧ College Teachers ✧ Critics (Literary) ✧ Cuban Americans ✧ Fatherless Families ✧ Gays ✧ Grandfathers ✧ Immigrants I Cuba ✧ FL

Conde, Maryse (b. Maryse Boucolon) (1937–). Tr. by Richard Philcox. *Tales from the Heart: True Stories from My Childhood* (Soho , 2001).
She tells of her privileged childhood in Guadeloupe and Paris.

Dramatists ✧ High Society ✧ Novelists ✧ West Indian Americans I West Indies ✧ France (Paris)

Eire, Carlos (1951–). *Waiting for Snow in Havana: Confessions of a Cuban Boy* (Free Press , 2003).
Focuses on him from 8 to 11 years; he was air-lifted to the U.S. after Fidel Castro rose to power.

Baby Boomers ✧ Eccentrics ✧ Immigrants I Cuba ✧ FL

Fernandez Barrios, Flor (1955–). *Blessed by Thunder: Memoir of a Cuban Girlhood* (Seal, 1999).

Baby Boomers ✧ Cuban Americans ✧ Refugees I Cuba

Hunter, Latoya (1978?–). *The Diary of Latoya Hunter: My First Year in Junior High* (Crown, 1992).

Diaries and Journals ✧ Generation X ✧ West Indian Americans I NYC (Bronx)

Medina, Pablo (1948–). *Exiled Memories: A Cuban Childhood* (University of Texas, 1990).
Focuses on his first 12 years.

Baby Boomers ✧ Cuban Americans ✧ Essayists ✧ Immigrants ✧ Poets I Cuba

Ortiz Cofer, Judith (1952–). *Silent Dancing: A Partial Remembrance of a Puerto Rican Childhood* (Arte Publico, 1990).
She left Puerto Rico in 1956. This is a series of autobiographical essays.

Baby Boomers ✧ College Teachers ✧ Essayists ✧ Immigrants ✧ Novelists ✧ Poets ✧ Puerto Rican Americans I Puerto Rico ✧ NJ

Rivera, Edward (1939–2001). *Family Installments: Memories of Growing Up Hispanic* (W. Morrow, 1982).
Starting with ch. 2 (page 33), this memoir covers him to about 20 years. He attended public and parochial schools in NYC.

City Life ✧ College Teachers ✧ Hispanic Americans I Puerto Rico ✧ NYC (Spanish Harlem)

Santiago, Esmeralda (1948–). *When I Was Puerto Rican* (Addison-Wesley, 1993).
She was the eldest of 11 children.

Baby Boomers ✧ City Life ✧ Family Memoirs ✧ Journalists ✧ Novelists ✧ Puerto Rican Americans ✧ Slums I Puerto Rico ✧ NYC (Brooklyn)

Santiago, Esmeralda (1948–). *Almost a Woman* (Perseus Books, 1998).

Baby Boomers ✧ City Life ✧ Family Memoirs ✧ Journalists ✧ Novelists ✧ Puerto Rican Americans ✧ Slums I NYC

Suarez, Virgil (1962–). *Spared Angola: Memories from a Cuban-American Childhood, 1962–1996* (Arte Publico, 1997).
Includes essays, as well as stories and poems, on his childhood.
Baby Boomers ✧ Cuban Americans | Cuba ✧ Spain ✧ CA

Walcott, Derek (1930–). *Another Life* (Farrar, Straus, and Giroux, 1973).
Dramatists ✧ Growing Up Between WWI and WWII ✧ Poets ✧ West Indian Americans | West Indies

Mexican Americans, Central Americans, and Other Latino Americans

Alicea, Gil C. (1979–), Carmine Desena, and Carmine Desano (contr.). *The Air Down Here: True Tales from a South Bronx Boyhood* (Chronicle Books, 1995).
Consists of 115 short autobiographical essays.
City Life ✧ Generation X ✧ Hispanic Americans | NYC (Bronx)

Conley, Dalton (1969–). *Honky* (University of California, 2000).
Pages 1–12, 43 to about 223.
Generation X ✧ Hispanic Americans ✧ Slums | NYC (Lower East Side)

Galarza, Ernesto (1905–1984). *Barrio Boy* (University of Notre Dame, 1971).
Covers about his first 14 years.
Mexican Americans ✧ Slums | Mexico ✧ CA

Garcia, Lionel G. (1935–). *I Can Hear the Cowbells Ring* (Arte Publico, 1994).
Mexican Americans ✧ Novelists | TX

Ponce, Mary (1938–). *Hoyt Street: Memories of a Chicana Childhood* (University of New Mexico, 1993).
Mexican Americans ✧ Novelists ✧ Racism | CA (Southern)

Rodriguez, Richard (1944–). *Hunger of Memory: An Autobiography: The Education of Richard Rodriguez* (David R. Godine, 1982).
He is the son of Mexican immigrants.
Baby Boomers ✧ Education ✧ Essayists ✧ Mexican Americans ✧ Journalists | CA (Northern)

Soto, Gary (1952–). *Living Up the Street: Narrative Recollections* (Strawberry Hill, 1985).
This and the following 4 entries by Soto cover his childhood and adolescent years, in no particular chronological sequence.
Baby Boomers ✧ Catholics ✧ Children's Authors ✧ College Teachers ✧ Mexican Americans ✧ Poets ✧ Slums | CA (Northern)

Soto, Gary (1952–). *Small Faces* (Arte Publico, 1986).
He grew up in a poor section of Fresno, CA, and records his memories in the form of poignant essays.
Baby Boomers ✧ Catholics ✧ Children's Authors ✧ College Teachers ✧ Mexican Americans ✧ Poets ✧ Slums | CA (Northern)

Soto, Gary (1952–). *Lesser Evils: Ten Quartets* (Arte Publico, 1988).

Baby Boomers ✧ Catholics ✧ Children's Authors ✧ College Teachers ✧ Mexican Americans ✧ Poets ✧ Slums I CA (Northern)

Soto, Gary (1952–). *A Summer Life* (University Press of New England, 1990).

Focuses on him from 5 to 12 years.

Baby Boomers ✧ Catholics ✧ Children's Authors ✧ College Teachers ✧ Mexican Americans ✧ Poets ✧ Slums I CA (Northern)

Soto, Gary (1952–). *Effects of Knut Hamsun on a Fresno Boy* (Persea Books, 2000).

Reprints all of *Small Faces* and much of *Lesser Evils*, and collects 5 new essays.

Baby Boomers ✧ Catholics ✧ Children's Authors ✧ College Teachers ✧ Mexican Americans ✧ Poets ✧ Slums I CA (Northern)

Taylor, Sheila Ortiz (1939–), and Sandra O. Taylor. *Imaginary Parents* (University of New Mexico, 1996).

Mexican Americans ✧ Vaudevillians ✧ WWII I CA (Southern)

Urrea, Luis Alberto (1955–). *Nobody's Son: Notes from an American Life* (University of Arizona, 1998).

The other 2 titles in his Border Trilogy are not memoirs (*Across the Wire: Life and Hard Times on the Mexican Border* [Anchor Books, 1993] and *By the Lake of Sleeping Children: The Secret Life of the Mexican Border* [Anchor Books, 1996]).

Baby Boomers ✧ College Teachers ✧ Immigrants ✧ Mexican Americans I CA (Southern)

Mixed Heritages

Lives and Cultures in Transition

McBride, James (1957–). *The Color of Water: A Black Man's Tribute to His White Mother* (Riverhead Books, 1996).

Baby Boomers ✧ Jews ✧ Mothers and Sons ✧ Musicians ✧ Racially Mixed Children ✧ Slums I NYC

Ondaatje, Michael (1943–). *Running in the Family* (W.W. Norton, 1982).

His ethnicity derives from mixed Dutch, Sinhalese, and Tamil ancestry. He left Ceylon at age 11, when his parents divorced. He later wrote the novel *The English Patient* (Bloomsbury, 1992).

Critics (Literary) ✧ Ceylonese Canadians ✧ Divorce ✧ Eccentrics ✧ High Society ✧ Immigrants ✧ Letters ✧ Novelists ✧ Poets I Ceylon (i.e., Sri Lanka) ✧ Canada

Rekdal, Paisley (1971–). *The Night My Mother Met Bruce Lee: Observations on Not Fitting In* (Pantheon Books, 2000).

About 77 scattered pages.

Chinese Americans ✧ Family Memoirs ✧ Generation X ✧ Norwegian Americans ✧ Poets ✧ Racially Mixed Children ✧ Teachers I WA

Walker, Rebecca (1969–). *Black, White, and Jewish: Autobiography of a Shifting Self* (Riverhead Books, 2001).

Covering her first 17 years, this memoir describes growing up as the daughter of a black mother (Alice Walker) and a white Jewish father.

African Americans ✧ Divorce ✧ Generation X ✧ Jews ✧ Mothers and Daughters ✧ Novelists ✧ Racially Mixed Children ✧ Racism ✧ Walker, Alice ✧ Wealth I MS ✧ NYC (Brooklyn, Bronx) ✧ CA (Northern) ✧ Washington, DC

Chapter 6

Survivors and Victims: Slavery, Racism, Holocaust, and Other Traumas of War

Among the most poignant within the genre of coming-of-age memoirs are those covered in this chapter, because they are filled with descriptions of some of the greatest sufferings known to humanity.

Supplementing the general recollections of African Americans contained in chapter 5, this chapter's opening section describes 17 memoirs by African Americans who endured the indignities and pains of slavery and other forms of racial oppression. Although the journals of Frederick Douglass (listed in the section of chapter 8 that focuses on reformers) are familiar to many Americans, the writings of such 19th-century African Americans as Harriet Jacobs (whose pen name was Linda Brent), Mattie Griffith, and Charlotte are not. Their memoirs provide further indictment of the "peculiar institution" of slavery.

More than 50 Holocaust memoirs make up the second portion of this chapter. (Additional accounts by Holocaust victims are found in chapters 5, 8, and 16, which respectively list recollections by immigrants, Jews, and prisoners.) Although the vast majority of these works are by persons who survived the Holocaust, some are the sad and eloquent legacy of memoirists whose lives ended tragically, such as Anne Frank. These memoirs are set in the countries and regions that defined the Europe of the mid-20th century: Germany, France, Poland, Austria, Romania, Hungary, Czechoslovakia, and the Ukraine.

The balance of the chapter is composed of recollections by individuals who, in their formative years, were caught up in everything from the violence of open combat, to the horrors of genocide, to the harsh living conditions attendant on civilian internment—as befell many Asian Americans living in the U.S. during World War II. Elizabeth Randolph Allan provides us with a firsthand glimpse of life in Virginia during the American Civil War. Joel Agee re-creates what life was like for him, an American boy, in what became East Germany, during and immediately after World War II.

The thematic range of this section (encompassing more than 60 works) is wide. For example, included here is a volume by prolific British author Anthony Bailey, who writes of being sent from England to the U.S. by his parents, who feared the approach of Nazi terror to their homeland. Elizabeth Morgan tells us what life was like as a child growing up in Florida during World War II. The chilling effects of the Cold War on one family are forcefully written of by Sally Belfrage, whose parents were the target of anticommunist fervor during the 1950s.

Slavery and Racism

Including Memoirs of Attempted Integration

See entries in the section "Reformers, Activists, Abolitionists, Civil Rights Workers, and Counterculture Society" in chapter 8 for memoirs involving civil rights workers; see entries in the section "Crime, Criminals, and Prisoners" in chapter 9 for memoirs involving general crimes.

Adams, Elizabeth (1909–). *Dark Symphony* (Sheed & Ward, 1942).
> Pages 7 to about 176.
>
> African Americans ✧ Catholics ✧ Fatherless Families ✧ Racism I CA (Southern)

Bates, Daisy (1914–1999). *The Long Shadow of Little Rock: A Memoir* (D. McKay, 1962).
> She mentored the "Little Rock Nine," a group of black high school students who, in 1957, unsuccessfully tried to enroll in an all-white high school in that city.
>
> African Americans ✧ Civil Rights Workers ✧ Growing Up Between WWI and WWII ✧ Publishers ✧ School Integration I AR

Beals, Melba Pattillo (1941–). *Warriors Don't Cry: A Searing Memoir of the Battle to Integrate Little Rock's Central High* (Pocket Books, 1994).
> Focuses on her at age 15.
>
> School Integration I AR

Bok, Francis (1979–), and Edward Tivnan. *Escape from Slavery: The True Story of My Ten Years in Captivity—and My Journey to Freedom in America* (St. Martin's, 2003).
> Focuses on his captivity as a farm slave in Africa from 7 to 17 years. Following 3 more years of captivity in a prison, he escaped to the U.S.
>
> Abolitionists ✧ Blacks ✧ Generation X ✧ Prisoners ✧ Refugees ✧ Slavery I Sudan

Brent, Linda (pseud. of Harriet Jacobs) (1818?–1896?). Ed. by L(ydia) Maria Child. *Incidents in the Life of a Slave Girl* (Harcourt Brace Jovanovich, 1973).
> About the first 100 pages. This work was originally privately printed in 1861. Jacobs felt compelled to provide fictitious names for significant persons in this memoir.
>
> Abuse (Sexual) ✧ African Americans ✧ Nineteenth-Century Pre-Industrial Age Memoirists ✧ Orphans ✧ Runaways ✧ Slavery I NC

Briggs, Wallace (1915–). *Riverside Remembered* (University Press of Kentucky, 1992).
> Of its 5 chapters, the first 4 focus on him from about 5 to 12 years. Includes much re-created dialogue. The author tells of being a white boy from IN who vacationed at his grandparents' home in the South during summers and Christmases. There he became friends with a black boy and learned about racism.
>
> Christmas ✧ Grandparents ✧ Growing Up Between WWI and WWII ✧ Homes and Haunts ✧ Racism ✧ Summer I MS

Douglass, Frederick (1817–1895). Ed. by Michael McCurdy. *Escape from Slavery: The Boyhood of Frederick Douglass in His Own Hands* (Knopf, 1994).
> A 63-page book. (See further memoirs by Douglass in ch. 8.)
>
> Abolitionists ✧ African Americans ✧ Nineteenth-Century Pre-Industrial Age Memoirists ✧ Racism ✧ Reformers ✧ Slavery I MD

Forten, Charlotte L(ottie) (1838?–1914). Ed. by Ray Allen Billington. *The Journal of Charlotte L. Forten: A Free Negro in the Slave Era* (W.W. Norton, 1953).
Pages 43–126.
African Americans ✧ Diaries and Journals ✧ Nineteenth-Century Pre-Industrial Age Memoirists ✧ Slavery I SC

Griffith, Mattie (aka Martha Griffith Browne) (1826?–1906). *Autobiography of a Female Slave* (Redfield, 1857) (1998 rpt., Banner Books).
More than the first 100 pages (in reprint ed.).
African Americans ✧ Nineteenth-Century Pre- Industrial Age Memoirists ✧ Slavery I KY

Hughes, Louis (1832–). *Thirty Years a Slave: From Bondage to Freedom* (Southside, 1897) (1969 rpt., Negro Universities Press).
Pages 5 to about 90.
African Americans ✧ Nineteenth-Century Pre-Industrial Age Memoirists ✧ Slavery I VA

McLaurin, Melton (1941–). *Separate Pasts: Growing Up White in the Segregated South* (University of Georgia, 1987).
Historians (Cultural) ✧ Racism I NC

Moss, Thylias (1954–). *Tale of a Sky-Blue Dress* (Bard, 1998).
African Americans ✧ Baby Boomers ✧ Children's Authors ✧ Poets I OH

Navarrette, Ruben, Jr. (1967?–). *A Darker Shade of Crimson: Odyssey of a Harvard Chicano* (Bantam Books, 1993).
Pages 2 to about 200 focus on him from 17 to 20 years. He is a nationally syndicated columnist.
College Life ✧ Generation X ✧ Harvard University ✧ Journalists ✧ Mexican Americans ✧ Racism I CA (Northern) ✧ MA

Oliver, Kitty (1947–). *Multicolored Memories of a Black Southern Girl* (University Press of Kentucky, 2001).
Pages 24 to about 92. In 1965 she was one of the first African American women to attend classes at the University of Florida.
African Americans ✧ Baby Boomers ✧ College Life ✧ Journalists ✧ Racism ✧ University of Florida I FL

Robinson, Sharon (1950–). *Stealing Home: An Intimate Family Portrait by the Daughter of Jackie Robinson* (HarperCollins, 1996).
Her father was the first African American to play major league baseball in the U.S.
African Americans ✧ Baby Boomers ✧ Racism ✧ Robinson, Jackie

Roper, Moses (1815–). *Narrative of the Adventures and Escape of Moses Roper, from American Slavery* (Merrihew & Gunn, 1838).
Memoir of about 63 pages. At age 18 he fled from SC.
African Americans ✧ Slavery ✧ Nineteenth-Century Pre-Industrial Age Memoirists ✧ Slavery I SC ✧ New England

Washington, Booker T. (1858?–1915). *Up from Slavery: An Autobiography* (A.L. Burt, 1901).
About the first 8 chapters focus on his first 21 years.
African Americans ✧ College Presidents ✧ Miners ✧ Nineteenth-Century Pre-Industrial Age Memoirists ✧ Slavery ✧ Teachers I VA

Webber, Thomas L. (1949–). *Flying Over 96th Street: Memoir of an East Harlem White Boy* (Scribner, 2004).
> The author tells of the many adjustments he made in his boyhood when his father, a minister, moved their family from an affluent part of NYC to East Harlem, in order to be closer to his congregation.
>
> Baby Boomers ✧ City Life ✧ Racism I NYC (Harlem)

Williams, Gregory Howard (1943–). *Life on the Color Line: The True Story of a White Boy Who Discovered He Was Black* (E.P. Dutton, 1995).
> Except for the last several pages, this memoir focuses entirely on his first 21 years.
>
> Children of Alcoholics ✧ Racially Mixed Children ✧ Racism I IN

Wright, Richard (1908–1960). *Black Boy: A Record of Childhood and Youth* (Harper & Brothers, 1937).
> African Americans ✧ Racism ✧ Slums I MS

Holocaust Victims

See entries in the section "Slavery and Racism" in chapter 6 and the section "Crime, Criminals, and prisoners" in chapter 15 for other memoirs involving crime and imprisonment; see entries in the section "Outcasts" in chapter 16 for other memoirs involving immigrants.

Appleman-Jurman, Alicia. *Alicia: My Story* (Bantam Books, 1988).
> A contemporary of Anne Frank (see entry, this section), this memoirist was bold in her efforts to save others from the Holocaust.
>
> Holocaust Survivors ✧ Jews I Ukraine

Auerbacher, Inge (1934–). *I Am a Star: Child of the Holocaust* (Prentice-Hall Books for Young Readers, 1986).
> Holocaust Survivors ✧ Jews I Germany

Birenbaum, Halina (1929–). Tr. from the Polish by David Welsh. *Hope Is the Last to Die: A Coming of Age Under Nazi Terror* (M.E. Sharpe, 1996) (First published in Polish, 1992).
> Holocaust Survivors ✧ Jews I Poland

Bitton-Jackson, Livia (1931–). *I Have Lived a Thousand Years: Growing Up in the Holocaust* (Simon and Schuster, 1997).
> Focuses on her at age 13. See also "Jackson, Livia" (ch. 6).
>
> Auschwitz ✧ Holocaust Survivors ✧ Jews I Hungary ✧ Poland

Bitton-Jackson, Livia (1931–). *My Bridges of Hope: Six Long Years to Freedom After Auschwitz* (Simon and Schuster Books for Young Readers, 1999).
> Focuses on her subsequent teenage years. See also "Jackson, Livia" (ch. 6).
>
> Holocaust Survivors ✧ Jews I Czechoslovakia ✧ Austria ✧ Germany

Blatt, Thomas Toivi (1927–). *From the Ashes of Sobibor: A Story of Survival* (Northwestern University, 1997).
> Pages 6–225 are on his first 17 years. This is a classic Holocaust memoir.
>
> Holocaust Survivors ✧ Jews I Poland

Breznitz, Shlomo (1936–). *Memory Fields* (Knopf, 1993).

He was hidden from Nazis in an orphanage and in a hospital.

Auschwitz ✧ Catholics ✧ Holocaust Survivors ✧ Immigrants ✧ Jews | Czechoslovakia ✧ Poland

Darvas, Miriam (1926–). *Farewell to Prague: A Memoir* (MacAdam/Cage, 2001).

Covers her from 6 to 21 years. At age 12, to escape the Nazis, she traveled alone from Czechoslovakia to England.

Activists ✧ Historians ✧ Holocaust Survivors ✧ Immigrants ✧ Jews | Germany ✧ Czechoslovakia ✧ Poland ✧ England

De Gaulle-Anthonioz, Genevieve. Tr. from the French by Richard Seaver. *The Dawn of Hope: A Memoir of Ravensbruck* (Arcade, 1999).

Holocaust Survivors ✧ Humanitarians ✧ Prisoners ✧ WWII | France ✧ Germany

Defonseca, Misha (1934?–). *Misha: A Memoire [sic] of the Holocaust Years* (Mt. Ivy, 1997).

Holocaust Survivors ✧ Jews | Belgium

Deutschkron, Inge (1922–). Tr. from the German by Jean Steinberg. *Outcast: A Jewish Girl in Wartime Berlin* (Fromm International, 1989) (First published in German, 1978).

About the first 200 pages cover her from 10 to 21 years.

Holocaust Survivors ✧ Jews | Germany

Edvardson, Cordelia (1929–). *Burned Child Seeks the Fire: A Memoir* (Beacon, 1984).

Catholics ✧ Holocaust Survivors ✧ Journalists | Germany ✧ Poland

Eisenstein, Bernice (1949–). *I Was a Child of Holocaust Survivors* (Riverhead Books, 2006).

The author describes what it was like to grow up in Canada as the daughter of Polish survivors of Auschwitz. It is in the graphic novel format.

Aunts ✧ Baby Boomers ✧ Books and Reading ✧ Children of Immigrants ✧ Graphic Novels ✧ Holocaust Survivors ✧ Jews ✧ Movies ✧ Uncles | Canada (Ontario: Toronto)

Fleuk, Toby (1926–). *Memories of My Life in a Polish Village, 1930–1949* (Knopf, 1990).

The author illustrated this memoir with 94 paintings and drawings; entire work is on his boyhood and adolescence.

Holocaust ✧ Jews | Poland (now part of Ukraine)

Frank, Anne (comp. by Otto H.) (1929–1945). Tr. from the Dutch in 1952 by B. M. Mooyaart-Doubleday. *The Diary of a Young Girl* (Doubleday, 1952; definitive ed., ed. by Otto Frank and Mirjam Pressler, Viking, 1997).

See also "Kent, Evelyn" (this section) and "Schildkraut, Joseph" (ch. 11); for a similar memoir from a different culture, see "Ung, Loung" (ch. 16).

Diaries and Journals ✧ Jews ✧ WWII | Netherlands

Friedlander, Saul (1932–). Tr. from the French by Helen R. Lane. *When Memory Comes* (Farrar, Straus, and Giroux, 1979).

Focuses on his first 16 years.

Holocaust Survivors ✧ Jews | Czechoslovakia ✧ France

Geve, Thomas (1929–). *Guns and Barbed Wire: A Child Survives the Holocaust* (Academy Chicago, 1987) (Rev. ed. of *Youth in Chains* [R. Mass, 1958]). Covers 1939–1945.

Auschwitz ✧ Holocaust Survivors ✧ Jews | Poland

Gold, Ruth (1930–). *Ruth's Journey: A Survivor's Memoir* (University Press of Florida, 1996). Pages 14 to about 219 (chs. 1–13).

Holocaust Survivors ✧ Jews | Romania

Gotfryd, Bernard (1924–). *Anton the Dove Fancier and Other Tales of the Holocaust* (Andre Deutsch, 1990).

Jews | Poland ✧ Germany

Graf, Malvina (1920?–). *The Krakow Ghetto and the Plaszow Camp Remembered* (Florida State University, 1989). Pages 3 to about 70 focus on her from about 19 to 21 years.

Holocaust Survivors ✧ Jews | Poland

Heller, Fanya. *Strange and Unexpected Love: A Teenage Girl's Holocaust Memoirs* (KTAV Publishing House, 1993). Covers 5 years.

Holocaust Survivors ✧ Immigrants ✧ Jews ✧ Mental Health | Poland (now part of Ukraine)

Horn, Joseph (1926–). *Mark It with a Stone: A Moving Account of a Young Boy's Struggle to Survive the Nazi Death Camps* (Barricade Books, 1996).

Auschwitz ✧ Bergen-Belsen ✧ Holocaust Survivors ✧ Jews | Poland ✧ Germany

Isaacson, Judith (1925–). *Seed of Sarah: Memoirs of a Girlhood* (University of Illinois, 1990). Focuses on her at age 19.

Auschwitz ✧ Holocaust Survivors ✧ Jews | Hungary ✧ Germany ✧ Poland

Isacovici, Salomon (1924–1998), with Juan Manuel Rodriguez. *Man of Ashes* (University of Nebraska, 1999). Pages 1–126 (about chs. 1–10) focus on him from about 15 to 21 years.

Auschwitz ✧ Birkenau ✧ Holocaust Survivors ✧ Jews | Romania ✧ Poland

Jackson, Livia (1931–). *Elli: Coming of Age in the Holocaust* (Times Books, 1980). Set in 1944–1945; description is effectively mixed with re-created dialogue. See also "Bitton-Jackson, Livia" (ch. 6).

Holocaust Survivors ✧ Jews | Hungary

Joffo, Joseph (1931–). Tr. from the French by Martin Sokolinsky. *A Bag of Marbles* (Houghton Mifflin, 1974). Covers him from 10 to 13 years.

Holocaust Survivors ✧ Jews | France

Kalib, Goldie (1931–) with Sylvan Kalib and Ken Wachsberger. *The Last Selection: A Child's Journey Through the Holocaust* (University of Massachusetts, 1991).

Auschwitz ✧ Bergen-Belsen ✧ Holocaust Survivors ✧ Jews | Poland ✧ Germany

Kent, Evelyn Julia. *Eva's Story: A Survivor's Tale by the Step-Sister of Anne Frank* (St. Martin's, 1988).

She was a Dutch Jewish survivor of the Holocaust. See also "Frank, Anne" (this section).

Holocaust Survivors ✧ Jews ✧ WWII | Netherlands

Kimmelman, Mira (1923–). *Echoes from the Holocaust: A Memoir* (University of Tennessee, 1997).

Auschwitz ✧ Holocaust Survivors ✧ Jews | Poland

Kluger, Ruth (1931–). *Still Alive: A Holocaust Girlhood Remembered* (Feminist Press at the City University of New York, 2001) (British title, *Landscapes of Memory: A Holocaust Girlhood Remembered* [Bloomsbury, 2003]).

Kluger provides an unvarnished look at concentration camp life.

Auschwitz ✧ Birkenau ✧ Camps (Internment) ✧ Christianstadt ✧ Gross-Rosen ✧ Holocaust Survivors ✧ Jews ✧ Slums ✧ Theresienstadt | Austria ✧ Czechoslovakia ✧ Poland

Korn, Abram (1923–1972). Ed. by Joseph Korn, anno. by Richard Voyles. *Abe's Story: A Holocaust Memoir* (Longstreet, 1995).

At least the first 11 chs. (pages 1–103).

Buchenwald ✧ Holocaust Survivors ✧ Jews | Poland ✧ Germany

Kroh, Aleksandra (1932–). Tr. by Austryn Wainhouse. *Lucien's Story* (Marlboro Press/Northwestern University, 1996).

Memoir of 67 pages, covering 18 months of his boyhood in concentration camps.

Camps (Internment) ✧ Holocaust Survivors ✧ Jews | Germany

Lauer, Betty (1926–). *Hiding in Plain Sight: The Incredible True Story of a German-Jewish Teenager's Struggle to Survive in Nazi-Occupied Poland* (Smith & Kraus, 2004).

A classic account of a girl's survival against incalculable odds.

Holocaust Survivors ✧ Jews ✧ WWII | Germany ✧ Poland

Leitner, Isabella (1924–). Ed. and with an epilogue by Irving A. Leitner. *Fragments of Isabella: A Memoir of Auschwitz* (Crowell, 1978).

In a 1983 Dell paperback edition, pages 13 to about 100 focus on her at about 19 to 20 years. Note: This title, combined with both its sequel, which focuses on her adult years (*Saving the Fragments: From Auschwitz to New York* [New American Library, 1985]), and additional material, make up *Isabella: From Auschwitz to Freedom* (Anchor Books, 1994).

Auschwitz ✧ Holocaust Survivors ✧ Jews ✧ Prisoners | Hungary ✧ Poland ✧ Germany

Leitner, Isabella (1924–). *The Big Lie: A True Story* (Scholastic, 1992).

Pages 12–79 focus on her adolescence. This book is intended for an audience of children.

Auschwitz ✧ Camps (Internment) ✧ Holocaust Survivors ✧ Jews | Hungary ✧ Poland

Levi, Trude (1924–). *A Cat Called Adolf* (Vallentine Mitchell, 1995).

Pages 1 to about 78.

Auschwitz ✧ Camps (Internment) ✧ Holocaust Survivors ✧ Jews | Hungary ✧ Poland ✧ Germany

Ligocka, Roma (1938–), with Iris Von Finckenstein. Tr. by Margot Bettauer Dembo. *The Girl in the Red Coat: A Memoir* (St. Martin's, 2002).

Chapters 1–9 (pages 1–217). One of the best Holocaust memoirs produced in recent years, this volume chronicles Ligocka's survival against great odds. She was the basis of the red-coated figure seen in the film *Schindler's List* (1993).

Actresses ✧ Holocaust Survivors ✧ Jews | Poland

Morhange-Begue, Claude (19??–). *Chamberet: Recollections from an Ordinary Childhood* (Marlboro, 1987).

Set during the Holocaust.

Holocaust Survivors ✧ Jews | France

Nir, Yehuda (1930–). *The Lost Childhood: A Memoir* (Harcourt Brace Jovanovich, 1989).

Covers him from 9 to 15 years.

Growing Up Between WWI and WWII ✧ Holocaust Survivors ✧ Jews | Poland

Opdyke, Irene (1921–), and Jennifer Armstrong. *In My Hands: Memories of a Holocaust Rescuer* (Knopf, 1999).

Focuses on her at age 17. A classic.

Abuse (Sexual) ✧ Holocaust Survivors ✧ Jews ✧ Nurses ✧ Waitresses ✧ WWII | Poland

Perel, Shlomo (aka Solomon Perel) (1925–). Tr. from the German by Margot Dembo. *Europa, Europa: A True Story of World War II* (Wiley, 1997).

Holocaust Survivors ✧ Jews ✧ Military Life ✧ Translators ✧ WWII | Germany ✧ Poland ✧ Russia

Reiss, Johanna (1932–). *The Upstairs Room* (Crowell, 1972).

Holocaust Survivors ✧ Jews | Holland

Rosen, Sara (1925?–). *My Lost World: A Survivor's Tale* (Valentine Mitchell, 1993).

Pages 3 to about 286 (chs. 1–33).

Growing Up Between WWI and WWII ✧ Holocaust Survivors ✧ Jews | Poland ✧ Hungary ✧ Romania

Schulman, Faye (b. c. 1920–1922). *A Partisan's Memoir: Woman of the Holocaust* (Second Story, 1995).

Growing Up Between WWI and WWII ✧ Holocaust Survivors | Jews ✧ Poland

Sender, Ruth (1926–). *The Cage* (Macmillan, 1986).

Written for younger readers, this memoir is largely set at Auschwitz and at a Russian labor camp.

Auschwitz ✧ Camps (Internment) ✧ Holocaust Survivors ✧ Jews | Poland ✧ Germany

Sendyk, Helen. *The End of Days* (St. Martin's, 1992).

Covers her childhood and adolescence during the 1930s and 1940s. Contains much re-created dialogue.

Camps (Internment) ✧ Family Memoirs ✧ Holocaust Survivors ✧ Jews | Poland

Siegal, Aranka (1930–). *Upon the Head of a Goat: A Childhood in Hungary 1939–1944* (Farrar, Straus, and Giroux, 1981).

Holocaust Survivors ✧ Jews | Hungary

Sierakowiak, David (1924?–1943). Ed. by Alan Adelson. Tr. by Kamil Turowski. *The Diary of David Sierakowiak: Five Notebooks from the Lodz Ghetto* (Oxford University, 1996).
Entries cover him from 14 to 19 years.
Diaries and Journals ✧ Holocaust Survivors ✧ Jews ✧ Slums | Poland

Steinberg, Paul (1926–). Tr. by Bill Ford and Linda Coverdale. *Speak You Also: A Survivor's Reckoning* (Metropolitan Books/H. Holt, 2000) (First published in French, 1996).
Focuses on him from 16 to 18 years.
Auschwitz ✧ Camps (Internment) ✧ Holocaust Survivors ✧ Jews ✧ Prisoners | France ✧ Poland ✧ Germany ✧ Italy ✧ Spain

Stern, Edgar (1927–). *The Peppermint Train: Journey to a German-Jewish Childhood* (University Press of Florida, 1992).
His childhood reminiscences are inextricably woven into his trip from the U.S. back to his homeland, when he was in his mid-fifties.
Holocaust Survivors ✧ Jews | Germany

Toll, Nelly S. *Behind the Secret Window: A Memoir of a Hidden Childhood During World War Two* (Dial Books, 1993).
Holocaust Survivors ✧ Jews | Poland (now part of Ukraine)

Trahan, Elizabeth (1924–). *Walking with Ghosts: A Jewish Childhood in Wartime Vienna* (Peter Trahan, 1998).
Focuses on her from 15 to 21 years.
Holocaust Survivors ✧ Jews ✧ WWII | Czechoslovakia ✧ Austria

Turgel, Gena (1923–), with Veronica Groocock. *I Light a Candle* (Valentine Mitchell, 1995) (First published in England, Grafton, 1987).
Pages 11 to about 95.
Holocaust Survivors ✧ Jews ✧ Prisoners ✧ WWII | Poland

Velmas, Edith (1925–). *Edith's Story* (Soho, 1999) (Originally published as *Edith's Book* [Viking, 1998]).
Holocaust Survivors ✧ Jews | Netherlands

Weisman, Murray (1930–). *The Burning Generation: Memoirs of a Holocaust Childhood* (AmErica House, 2001).
Weisman was incarcerated in 7 camps, including Auschwitz. He emigrated to the U.S. in 1950.
Auschwitz ✧ Holocaust Survivors ✧ Jews ✧ Lawyers | Poland

Wieck, Michael. Tr. from the German by Penny Milbouer. *A Childhood Under Hitler and Stalin: Memoirs of a "Certified Jew"* (University of Wisconsin, 2003).
The son of a Jewish mother and a Gentile father, Wieck was persecuted in turn by the Nazis and by the Russian occupiers of his fire-bombed homeland. This work was a best seller in Germany.
Holocaust Survivors ✧ Jews | Germany

Wiesel, Elie (1928–). *All Rivers Run to the Sea: Memoirs* (Knopf Canada, 1995) (First published in French, 1994).
Pages 4–197. He is an eloquent spokesman on the evils of anti-Semitism, having himself survived the Holocaust.

    College Teachers ✧ Fatherless Families ✧ Holocaust Survivors ✧ Jews ✧ Journalists ✧ Lecturers ✧ Novelists ✧ Orphans ✧ Reformers I Romania ✧ Germany ✧ France

Winter, Miriam (1933–). *Trains: A Memoir of a Hidden Childhood During and After World War II* (Kelton, 1997).

    Holocaust Survivors ✧ Jews ✧ WWII I Poland

Zamoyska-Panek, Christine (1923–), with Fred Benton Holmberg. *Have You Forgotten? A Memoir of Poland, 1939–1945* (Doubleday, 1989).
Covers her life from 16 to 22 years. She moved to the U.S. in 1947.

    High Society ✧ Holocaust Survivors ✧ WWII I Poland

Other Wartime Traumas of Civilians and Fighting Forces

On American Soil

Indian Wars; War of Independence (1775–1783); Civil War (1861–1865); World War I (1914–1918); Domestic WWII Internment of Asian Americans (1942–1945); Cold War (Including Joseph McCarthy Era, 1945–1991); Home Front (During Any War Abroad); and Military Families in the U.S.

Allan, Elizabeth Randolph (1848–1933). Ed. by Janet Allan Bryan. *A March Past: Reminiscences of Elizabeth Randolph Preston Allan* (Dietz, 1938).
About the first 200 pages. At the repeated request of her children, the author wrote this in her seventies; her daughter edited it. Little re-created dialogue intervenes in this excellent work.

    Civil War (U.S.) ✧ Collaborations by Relatives ✧ Family Memoirs ✧ Nineteenth-Century Pre-Industrial Age Memoirists I VA

Bailey, Anthony (1933–). *America, Lost & Found* (Random House, 1980).
To age 11. This work focuses on the 4 years he spent in the U.S., where his British parents sent him for his safety when WWII threatened Great Britain.

    Critics (Art) ✧ Historians ✧ Travel Writers ✧ WWII I OH

Bailey, Anthony (1933–). *England, First & Last* (Viking, 1985).
Focuses on his return to England (from age 11 into young manhood). (This memoirist should not be confused with Paul Bailey; see next section.) Bill Bryson (ch. 4) is another writer whose sensibilities are divided between England and the U.S.

    Critics (Art) ✧ Historians ✧ Sailing ✧ Travel Writers ✧ WWII I England

Barringer, [Dr.] Paul B. (1857–1941). *The Natural Bent: The Story of a Confederate Childhood, A Reconstruction Boyhood, and the Education of . . .* (University of North Carolina, 1949).
Pages 3–232 (chs. I–XXXI).

    Confederate States of America ✧ Nineteenth-Century Pre-Industrial Age Memoirists ✧ Physicians I NC

Beers, David (1957?–). *Blue Sky Dream: A Memoir of America's Fall from Grace* (Doubleday, 1996).
About 84 scattered pages
Aerospace Industries ✧ Baby Boomers ✧ Cold War | CA (Northern)

Belfrage, Sally (1936–1994). *Un-American Activities: A Memoir of the Fifties* (HarperCollins, 1994).
For a similar memoir, see "Kimmage, Ann" (ch. 8).
Anti-Communist Movements ✧ Cold War | NYC (Bronx)

Bernstein, Carl (1944–). *Loyalties: A Son's Memoir* (Simon and Schuster, 1989).
The coauthor of *All the President's Men* (Simon and Schuster, 1974) recollects the persecution of his parents during the McCarthy era.
Cold War ✧ Communists ✧ Family Memoirs ✧ Journalists | Washington, DC

Birmingham, Frederic (1911–1982). *It Was Fun While It Lasted* (Lippincott, 1960).
Growing Up Between WWI and WWII ✧ WWI | NYC (Harlem)

Charyn, Jerome (1937–). *The Dark Lady from Belorusse* (St. Martin's, 1997).
This memoir focuses on Charyn's childhood during WWII; it is continued by the following entry.
City Life ✧ College Teachers ✧ Crime ✧ Jews ✧ Novelists ✧ WWII | NYC (Bronx)

Charyn, Jerome (1937–). *The Black Swan: A Memoir* (Thomas Dunne/St. Martin's, 2000).
Focuses on him at age 11. See also his third memoir (ch. 3).
City Life ✧ Cold War ✧ College Teachers ✧ Crime ✧ Jews ✧ Movies ✧ Novelists ✧ NYC (Bronx)

Ford, William Wallace (1898–). *Wagon Soldier* (Privately Printed, 1980).
Pages 1–about 62.
Military Life ✧ West Point ✧ WWI | VA ✧ NY

Grierson, Francis (1848–1927). *The Valley of Shadows: Recollections of the Lincoln Country, 1858–1863* (Houghton Mifflin, 1909).
Civil War (U.S.) ✧ Nineteenth-Century Pre-Industrial Age Memoirists ✧ Essayists ✧ Musicians ✧ Spiritual Life | IL ✧ MO

Harrison, Mrs. Burton (1843–1920). *Recollections, Grave and Gay* (Scribner's Sons, 1911).
About page 10 to about page 130 focus on her first 20 years.
Confederate States of America ✧ Nineteenth-Century Pre-Industrial Age Memoirists | VA

Houston, Jeanne Wakatsuki (1934–), and James D. Houston. *Farewell to Manzanar: A True Story* (Bantam Books, 1973).
Covers her from 7 to 11 years.
Camps (Internment) ✧ Collaborations by Relatives ✧ Japanese Americans ✧ WWII | CA (Central)

Johnston, David E. (1845–1917). *The Story of a Confederate Boy in the Civil War* (Glass & Prudhomme, 1914) (Originally published as *Four Years a Soldier* [Privately printed, 1887]).
Civil War (U.S.) ✧ Nineteenth-Century Pre-Industrial Age Memoirists | VA

Macon, Emma (1847–). *Reminiscences of the Civil War* (Torch, 1911).

    Civil War (U.S.) ✧ Nineteenth-Century Pre-Industrial Age Memoirists I VA

Martin, Joseph Plumb (1760–1850). Ed. by George Scheer. *Private Yankee Doodle: Being a Narrative of Some of the Adventures, Dangers and Sufferings of a Revolutionary Soldier* (Little, Brown, 1962) (1968 rpt., New York Times) (First published [Privately printed], 1830).

    About the first 200 pages. He spent time at Valley Forge with George Washington's men and was in the Yorktown military campaign.

    Eighteenth-Century Memoirists ✧ Military Life ✧ War of Independence I PA ✧ VA

Morgan, Elizabeth (1938–). *Uncertain Seasons* (University of Alabama, 1994).

    Covers her from about 3 to about 6 years.

    Farm Life ✧ Military Life ✧ WWII I FL

Nagel, Charles (1849–1940). *A Boy's Civil War Story* (Eden Publishing House, 1934).

    He was Secretary of Commerce under President Taft.

    Civil War (U.S.) ✧ Government Officials ✧ Nineteenth-Century Pre-Industrial Age Memoirists ✧ Pacifists I TX ✧ MO

Nakagara, George (1932?–). *The Cross on Castle Rock: A Childhood Memoir* (Universe, 2004).

    This work focuses on the author from 10 to 13 years, during which he was incarcerated in internment camps in the U.S.

    Camps (Internment) ✧ Japanese Americans ✧ Racism ✧ WWII I CA

Pasquarello, Tony (1933–). *The Altar Boy Chronicles* (Gustav Broukal, 1999).

    Set during WWII on the home front, in the "Little Italy" section of Philadelphia.

    Catholics ✧ Italian Americans ✧ WWII I PA (Philadelphia)

Richards, Caroline Cowles (1842–1913). *Diary of Caroline Cowles Richards, 1852–1872* (Privately printed, 1908) (Later published as *Village Life in America, 1852–1872, Including the Period of the American Civil War, As Told in the Diary of a Schoolgirl* [Unwin, 1912]).

    Civil War (U.S.) ✧ Diaries and Journals ✧ Nineteenth-Century Pre-Industrial Age Memoirists I NY

Robertson, George F. (1853–). *A Small Boy's Recollections of the Civil War (War Between the States . . .)* (Privately printed, 1932).

    Civil War (U.S.) ✧ Nineteenth-Century Pre-Industrial Age Memoirists I TN

Schickel, Richard (1933–). *Good Morning Mr. Zip Zip Zip: Movies, Memories, and World War II* (Ivan R. Dee, 2003).

    From the perspective of his youth (1941–1945), this well-known film critic (*Time* magazine) traces the way movies conditioned the consciousness of Americans during WWII.

    Critics (Movie) ✧ Intellectual Life ✧ Journalists ✧ Movies ✧ Novelists ✧ Screenwriters ✧ WWII I WI

Shaw, John Robert (1761–1813). Ed. by Oressa M. Teagarden. *John Robert Shaw: An Autobiography of Thirty Years, 1777–1807* (Ohio University, 1992) (Originally published by Daniel Bradford, 1807).

    Pages 9 to about 72 focus on him from 16 to 21 years. He was a British soldier captured by American colonial forces.

    Eighteenth-Century Memoirists ✧ Military Life ✧ War of Independence I RI

Smith, William Jay (1918–). *Army Brat: A Memoir* (Persea Books, 1980).

Army, U.S. ✧ Growing Up Between WWI and WWII I MO

Steel, Samuel Augustus (1849–1934). *The Sunny Road: Home Life in Dixie During the War* (Latsch & Arnold, 1925).

Confederate States of America ✧ Farm Life ✧ Military Life ✧ Nineteenth-Century Pre-Industrial Age Memoirists I TN

Uchida, Yoshiko (1921–1992). *Desert Exile: The Uprooting of a Japanese-American Family* (University of Washington, 1982).

Set in 1942.

Camps (Internment) ✧ Children's Authors ✧ Family Memoirs ✧ Japanese Americans ✧ WWII I CA (Northern) ✧ UT

Uchida, Yoshiko (1921–1992). *The Invisible Thread: An Autobiography* (Beech Tree Books, 1995).

This is a children's book version of *Desert Exile* (previous entry).

Camps (Internment) ✧ Children's Authors ✧ Family Memoirs ✧ Japanese Americans ✧ WWII I CA (Northern) ✧ UT

Wakeman, Sarah Rosetta (1843–1864). Ed. by Lauren Cook Burgess. An *Uncommon Soldier: The Civil War Letters of Sarah Rosetta Wakeman, Alias Private Lyons Wakeman, 153rd Regiment, New York State Volunteers* (Minerva Center, 1994).

She is 18 to 21 years old in her letters that appear on pages 18–72.

Civil War (U.S.) ✧ Farm Life ✧ Letters ✧ Military Life ✧ Nineteenth-Century Pre-Industrial Age Memoirists I VA ✧ Washington, DC ✧ MS ✧ LA

Winfrey, Carey (1941–). *Starts and Finishes: Coming of Age in the Fifties* (Saturday Review, 1975).

His father trained horses.

Editors ✧ Horses ✧ Journalists ✧ Marines, U.S. I NY ✧ FL ✧ CA

Wister, Sarah (Sally) (1761–1804). Ed. by Albert Cook Myers. *Sally Wister's Journal: A True Narrative: Being a Quaker Maiden's Account of Her Experiences with Officers of the Continental Army, 1777–1778* (Ferris & Leach, 1902) (First published: Privately Printed, 1830).

Pages 65–185 cover her from about 16 to 17 years. She describes her interactions with troops who were encamped near her family's house.

Diaries and Journals ✧ Eighteenth-Century Memoirists ✧ Military Life ✧ Quakers ✧ War of Independence I PA

Beyond American Shores

Napoleonic Wars; Crimean War (1853–1856); Sino-Japanese War (1894–1895); World War I (1914–1918); Russian Purges (1930s–1950s); Spanish Civil War (1936–1939); World War II (1939–1945); Cold War (Including Joseph McCarthy Era, 1945–1991); Korean War (1950–1953); Vietnam Conflict (1960–1975); China's Cultural Revolution (1966–1977); Iran-Iraq War (1980–1990); First Persian Gulf War (1991); Bosnian War (1992–1993); Second Persian Gulf War (2003); and Military Families Abroad

See entries in the section "Reformers and Activists" in chapter 8 for memoirs involving draft resisters.

Abish, Walter (1932–). *Double Vision: A Self-Portrait* (Knopf, 2004).

He complements his childhood memories with those from a book tour in Germany during the 1980s.

High Society ✧ Immigrants ✧ Jews ✧ Librarians ✧ Refugees ✧ Wealth ✧ WWII I Austria ✧ France ✧ China (Shanghai) ✧ Israel

Accomando, Claire Hsu (1937–). *Love and Rutabaga: A Remembrance of the War Years* (St. Martin's, 1993).

Fatherless Families ✧ Grandparents ✧ WWII I France

Agee, Joel (1940–). *Twelve Years: An American Boyhood in East Germany* (Farrar, Straus, and Giroux, 1981).

Focuses on him from 8 to 20 years.

Anti-Communist Movements ✧ Cold War ✧ WWII I East Germany

Alvarez, Manuel (1927–). *The Tall Soldier: My 40-Year Search for the Man Who Saved My Life* (Virgo, 1980).

Pages 1–148 (chs. 1–12).

At 11 years old, the author's life was saved during the Spanish Civil War by a Canadian soldier.

Civil War (Spanish) I Spain

Bailey, Paul (1937–). *An Immaculate Mistake: Scenes from Childhood and Beyond* (E.P. Dutton, 1992).

His first 18 years. He grew up in a working-class part of London. (This memoirist should not be confused with Anthony Bailey; see previous section.).

Actors ✧ City Life ✧ Gays ✧ Novelists ✧ Working Class Whites ✧ WWII I England

Bernhard, Thomas (1931–1989). Tr. from the German by David McClintock. *Gathering Evidence: A Memoir* (Vintage Books, 1993).

Gathers his 5 autobiographical works, which together cover his first 19 years.

WWII I Austria

Carlisle, Olga (1930–). *Island in Time: A Memoir in Childhood* (Holt, Rinehart and Winston, 1980).

See "Green, Julian" (this section) for a comparable memoir.

Growing Up Between WWI and WWII ✧ Poets ✧ WWII I France

Couterie, Sylvia (1928?–). *No Tears in Ireland: A Memoir* (Free Press, 2001).

Focuses on her from 11 to 15 years. She and her younger sister were marooned in Ireland apart from their parents, while on holiday away from their aristocratic home in France.

Country Life ✧ High Society ✧ Orphans ✧ Radio Journalists ✧ Wealth ✧ WWII I Ireland

David, Janina (pseud. of Janina Davidowicz) (1930–). *A Touch of Earth: A Wartime Childhood* (Hutchinson, 1966).

Jews ✧ WWII I Poland

David, Janina (pseud. of Janina Davidowicz) (1930–). *A Square of Sky: Recollections of My Childhood* (New Authors Ltd., 1964).

Jews ✧ WWII I Poland

Durlacher, Gerhard (1928–1996). *Drowning: Growing Up in the Third Reich* (Serpent's Tale, 1993).

Hitler Youth Movement | Germany (Baden-Baden)

Figes, Eva (1932–). *Little Eden: A Child at War* (Persea Books, 1978).
Covers 1940–1941.

Jews ✧ Novelists ✧ Refugees | Germany ✧ England

Filipovic, Zlata (1980–). Tr. from the Serbo-Croatian by Christina Pribichevich-Zoric. *Zlata's Diary* (Viking, 1994).
Covers her from 10 to 13 years.

Bosnian War ✧ Diaries and Journals ✧ Generation X | Yugoslavia (i.e., Bosnia and Herzegovina)

Foreman, Michael (1938–). *War Boy: A Country Childhood* (Arcade, 1989).

Country Life ✧ WWII | England

Graves, Robert (1895–1985). *Goodbye to All That: An Autobiography* (J. Cape, 1929).
Pages 13–136 (chs. 1–11 and part of ch. 12).

Critics (Literary) ✧ Editors ✧ Novelists ✧ Poets ✧ Translators ✧ Victorian Era British Memoirists ✧ WWI | England

Green, Julian (1900–1998). Tr. by Euan Cameron. *The War at Sixteen: Autobiography: Volume II (1916–1919)* (M. Boyars, 1993) (First published in French, 1964).
See also his 3 memoirs in chapter 4. His sister is Anne Green (see ch. 17 entry).

Bisexuals ✧ Dramatists ✧ Essayists ✧ Novelists ✧ Translators ✧ WWI | Europe

Hatsumi, Reiko. *Rain and the Feast of the Stars* (Houghton Mifflin, 1959).
Covers her to 9 or 10 years, during WWII.

Family Memoirs | Japan

Idrac, Armand (1928–). *Memoirs from Normandy: Childhood, War & Life's Adventures* (Peach Lloyd, 2004).
Focuses on his teenage years during WWII.

Country Life ✧ WWII | France (Normandy)

Kelly, Clara Olink (1938?–). *The Flamboya Tree: Memories of a Mother's Wartime Courage* (Random House, 2002).
Kelly recounts her life from 4 to 8 years, during which she and her family were held in a concentration camp in Java.

Camps (Internment) ✧ Fatherless Families ✧ Mothers and Daughters ✧ WWII | Indonesia

Kosterina, Nina (1921–1941). Tr. from the German by Mirra Ginsburg. *The Diary of Nina Kosterina* (Crown, 1968).
Covers her from 15 to about 20 or 21 years.

Diaries and Journals ✧ Growing Up Between WWI and WWII ✧ Russian Purges | Russia

Kwan, Michael David (1934–2001). *Things That Must Not Be Forgotten: A Childhood in Wartime China* (Soho, 2001).
He lived his first 12 years in China. His ethnic roots are in Japan, Switzerland, and China.

Fathers and Sons ✧ High Society ✧ Racially Mixed Children ✧ Sino-Japanese Conflict ✧ Translators ✧ WWII | China

Lambert, Derek (1929–2001). *The Sheltered Days; Growing Up in the War* (Andre Deutsch, 1965).

WWII | England

Liebster, Simone Arnold. *Facing the Lion: Memoirs of a Young Girl in Nazi Europe* (Grammaton, 2000).

Includes account of her forced attendance (when 13–15 years old) at a "reform school," for denouncing the Nazis, who had sent her parents to concentration camps.

Jehovah's Witnesses ✧ Nazis and Neo-Nazis ✧ Orphans ✧ WWII | France ✧ Germany

Loy, Rosetta (1931–). Tr. by Gregory Conti. *First Words: A Childhood in Fascist Italy* (Metropolitan Books/ H. Holt, 2000).

Covers 1936–1943. She grew up in a privileged family under Mussolini's Fascist regime.

Catholics ✧ Fascism ✧ Holocaust Survivors ✧ Jews ✧ Journalists ✧ Novelists ✧ Wealth | Italy

Lynch, Jessica (1984–), as told to Rick Bragg. *I Am a Soldier, Too: The Jessica Lynch Story* (Knopf, 2003).

Focuses on her ambush and capture on March 23, 2003, while a U.S. soldier in Iraq.

Generation Y ✧ Military Life ✧ Persian Gulf War (2003) | WV ✧ Iraq

Manea, Norman (1936–). Tr. by Angela Jianu. *Hooligan's Return: A Memoir* (Farrar, Straus, and Giroux, 2003).

Having immigrated to the U.S. as an adult, while on a trip to Europe, Manea reflects on his WWII childhood in Romania. A former Fulbright scholar, Manea has also been honored as a recipient of a Guggenheim fellowship, a MacArthur Foundation fellowship, and a National Book Award.

Camps (Internment) ✧ College Teachers ✧ Engineers ✧ Essayists ✧ Jews ✧ Short Story Writers ✧ WWII | Romania

Markovna, Nina (1921?–). *Nina's Journey: A Memoir of Stalin's Russia and the Second World War* (Regnery Gateway, 1989).

More than 100 pages.

Growing Up Between WWI and WWII ✧ WWII | Russia

Massaquoi, Hans J. (1926?–). *Destined to Witness: Growing Up Black in Nazi Germany* (W. Morrow, 1999).

Blacks ✧ Growing Up Between WWI and WWII ✧ Racism | Germany

Ogden, Richard E. (1945–). *Green Knight, Red Mourning* (Zebra Books, 1985).

Focuses on him at 17–18 years. Much re-created dialogue permeates this memoir.

Marines, U.S. ✧ Stuntmen ✧ Vietnam Conflict | Vietnam

Patent, Gregory (1939–). *Shanghai Passage* (Clarion Books, 1990).

Focuses on him to 11 years. For other accounts of growing up in China from a Western perspective, see "Espey, John" (ch. 8) and "Fritz, Jean" (ch. 4).

Jews ✧ WWII | China

Phathanothai, Sirin (1948–), with James Peck. *The Dragon's Pearl* (Simon and Schuster, 1994).

Pages 15 to about 290.

China's Cultural Revolution ✧ Cold War | Thailand ✧ China

Post, Gaines, Jr. (1937–). *Memoirs of a Cold War Son* (University of Iowa, 2000).
About 80 pages (between pages 1 and 104). As an adult, he served in Berlin during the Cold War crisis there.

Cold War ✧ Cornell University | France ✧ WI ✧ TX ✧ NY

Samuel, Wolfgang W. E. Foreword by Stephen E. Ambrose. *German Boy: A Refugee's Story* (University Press of Mississippi, 2000).
Author recounts living in battle-scarred Germany during WWII's final phases, and his imprisonment in refugee camps.

Air Force, U.S. ✧ Camps (Internment) ✧ Refugees | Germany

Sandulescu, Jacques. *Donbas* (D. McKay, 1968).
Focuses on him from 15 to about 18 years, during WWII. He tells how he escaped from a Russian labor camp in his native Romania.

Camps (Internment) ✧ Slavery | Romania

Skriabina, Elana (1906–). Tr. and ed. by Norman Luxenburg. *Coming of Age in the Russian Revolution: The Soviet Union at War, Volume 4* (Transaction, 1985).
Pages 6–73.

WWII | Russia

Snider, Hideko (1934–). *One Sunny Day: A Child's Memories of Hiroshima* (Open Court, 1996).

Atomic Bomb Victims | Japan

Sun-Childers, Jaia (1964–), and Douglas Childers. *The White-Haired Girl: Bittersweet Adventures of a Little Red Soldier* (Picador USA, 1996).

China's Cultural Revolution | China (Beijing)

Swofford, Anthony (1970–). *Jarhead: A Marine's Chronicle of the Gulf War and Other Battles* (Scribner, 2003).
Most of this memoir is a flashback from fields of battle to his childhood and adolescence. This was adapted as a movie in 2005.

Generation X ✧ Marines, U.S. ✧ Military Life ✧ Persian Gulf War (1991) | CA (Northern)

Triplet, William S. (1900–). *Youth in the Meuse-Argonne: A Memoir, 1917–1918* (University of Missouri, 2000).

Army, U.S. ✧ Military Life ✧ WWI | France

Van Den Berghe, Pierre (1933–). *Stranger in Their Midst* (University Press of Colorado, 1989).

College Teachers ✧ Ethnologists ✧ Intellectual Life ✧ Nazis ✧ WWII | Belgian Congo ✧ Belgium ✧ U.S.

Von Staden, Wendegard (1925–). Tr. by Mollie Comerford Peters. *Darkness Over the Valley: Growing Up in Nazi Germany* (Ticknor & Fields, 1981) (First published in German, 1979).
More than 100 pages focus on her childhood and young adult years.

Family Memoirs ✧ Government Officials ✧ Growing Up Between WWI and WWII ✧ Hitler Youth Movement ✧ Nazis and Neo-Nazis ✧ WWII | West Germany

West, Paul (1930–). *My Mother's Music* (Viking, 1996).
> Chronicles his adolescence, during WWII.
>
> Biographers ✧ Critics (Literary) ✧ Essayists ✧ Mothers and Sons ✧ Novelists ✧ Poets ✧ WWII | England

Wheal, Donald James. *World's End: A Memoir of a Blitz Childhood* (Arrow, 2006).
> This best-selling author evokes a childhood during the WWII bombing of London.
>
> City Life ✧ Slums ✧ WWII | England (London)

Zhu, Xiao Di (1958–). *Thirty Years in a Red House: A Memoir of Childhood and Youth in Communist China* (University of Massachusetts, 1998).
> China's Cultural Revolution | China

Chapter 7

Coping with Challenges of Body and Mind: Diseases, Disabilities, and Conditions

The 70 memoirs surveyed in this chapter were written by individuals who have faced various physical, mental, or emotional diseases or other afflictions that affected the quality—and sometimes threatened the length—of their lives. Ten sections arrange these memoirs alphabetically by malady. Few individuals have had the courage to write memoirs regarding physical deformity, within a society that places a premium on physical beauty. The reminiscences here by Debbie Fox, Lucy Grealy, Natalie Kusz, and Heather Mills are unforgettable.

More than a half dozen manifestations of psychological disturbance or weakness are found in the seventh part of this chapter, devoted to "Mental Illness" issues. Among the memoirs catalogued here are Janet Frame's *To the Is-land*, which documents her years of torturous treatment for a disease, schizophrenia, that she never had. Volumes that recall girlhoods afflicted by eating disorders are also included in this chapter.

Neurological afflictions are catalogued both under the fourth section ("Cerebral Palsy") and the eighth ("Paralysis and Motor Dysfunctions"). Among these, perhaps Christy Brown's *My Left Foot* is the best known, having been experienced by countless readers as well as moviegoers who have watched its eponymous film version. Leonard Kriegel's *The Long Walk Home* is another classic in this genre.

Memoirs involving sensory impairment or deprivation are located in the sixth ("Hearing Impairment") and ninth ("Sight Impairment") sections. For example, Ved Mehta's extraordinary *Continents of Exile* series consists of about a dozen volumes that focus on the intellectual development of a blind man. Charlotte Abrams's reminiscence *The Silents* tells the remarkable story of the author's early years growing up with 2 deaf parents, one of whom also lost her sight.

Other sections have been set aside for accounts focusing on such diseases as AIDS, tuberculosis, and diabetes. It should be mentioned that the eloquent memoir by AIDS victim David Brudnoy, *Life Is Not a Rehearsal*, is listed in chapter 11, due to its late author's celebrity as a radio talk show host for many years. The memoirs by persons having diabetes that appear in this chapter are by Andie Dominick and Lisa Roney.

(See chapter 13 for memoirs involving health professionals; see entries in the fourth section of chapter 16 for memoirs involving substance abuse.)

AIDS and Other Sexually Transmitted Diseases

Cooper, Bernard (1951–). *Truth Serum: Memoirs* (Houghton Mifflin, 1996).
Pages 3 to about 103.
AIDS Virus ✧ Baby Boomers ✧ Gays | CA (Southern) ✧ NYC (Brooklyn)

Monette, Paul (1945–1995). *Becoming a Man: Half a Life Story* (Harcourt Brace Jovanovich, 1992).
Pages 1–156. A modern classic.
AIDS Virus ✧ Gays ✧ Novelists | MA ✧ CT

White, Ryan (1971–1990), and Ann Marie Cunningham. *Ryan White: My Own Story* (Dial, 1991).
AIDS Virus ✧ Generation X | IN

Amputation and Physical Deformity

Baker, Louise (1909–). *Out on a Limb* (McGraw-Hill, 1946).
Pages 1 to about 76. With much re-created dialogue, Baker describes how her life changed when she was struck by a car while bicycling at age 8.
Amputees | CA (Northern)

Fox, Debbie (1955–), with Jean Libman Block. *A Face for Me* (Simon and Schuster, 1978).
Baby Boomers ✧ Facial Abnormalities | TN

Fries, Kenny (1960–). *Body, Remember: A Memoir* (E.P. Dutton, 1997).
Pages 4 to about 60.
Critics (Literary) ✧ Dramatists ✧ Essayists ✧ Leg Abnormalities ✧ Poets | NYC (Brooklyn)

Grealy, Lucy (1963–2002). *Autobiography of a Face* (Houghton Mifflin, 1994).
Baby Boomers ✧ Cancer ✧ Facial Abnormalities ✧ Poets | NYS

Kusz, Natalie (1962–). *Road Song* (Farrar, Straus, and Giroux, 1990).
Baby Boomers ✧ Facial Abnormalities | AK

Mills, Heather (1968–), with Pamela Cockerill. *Out on a Limb* (Little, Brown, 1995).
About chs. 1–12 (pages 7–185). She is an ex-wife of former Beatle Paul McCartney.
Amputees ✧ Generation X ✧ Models | England ✧ France

Moore, Judith (1940–2006). *Fat Girl: A True Story* (Hudson Street Press, 2005).
The author, without self-pity, describes a bleak childhood in which an eating addiction further compounded her problems. She died of colon cancer.
Abuse (Sexual) ✧ Cancer ✧ Divorce ✧ Editors ✧ Family Violence ✧ Grandmothers ✧ Obesity ✧ School Bullying ✧ Uncles | OK

Rapp, Emily. *Poster Child* (Bloomsbury, 2007).

Because of a congenital leg deformity, Rapp endured dozens of surgeries that culminated, at age 8, in the amputation of her left leg below the knee. She is a former recipient of a Fulbright Scholarship.

Amputees ✧ College Teachers ✧ Generation X (?) I NE ✧ WY ✧ CO

Cancer

Including Hodgkin's Disease

Barry, Dan (1958–). *Pull Me Up: A Memoir* (W.W. Norton, 2004).

A writer for the *New York Times*, Barry tells of growing up during the 1960s, during which he lost his mother to cancer and fought it himself, as well.

Baby Boomers ✧ Bereavement ✧ Cancer ✧ Catholics ✧ Irish Americans ✧ Journalists I NY (Long Island)

Blount, Roy, Jr. (1941–). *Be Sweet: A Conditional Love Story* (Knopf, 1998).

About 85 scattered pages. His mother lost an eye to cancer when he was a boy.

Cancer ✧ Humorists ✧ Mothers and Sons ✧ Sports ✧ Writers I GA ✧ TX

Lidz, Franz (1952–). *Unstrung Heroes: My Improbable Life With Four Impossible Uncles* (Random House, 1991).

Pages 3–178. In this memoir, Lidz seeks solace in the companionship of his eccentric uncles, as his mother's health fails from cancer. This work was adapted into an Oscar-nominated 1995 film of the same title. For a similar memoir, see "Crystal, Billy" (ch. 11).

Baby Boomers ✧ Cancer ✧ Eccentrics ✧ Jews ✧ Mothers and Sons ✧ Sports Writers ✧ Uncles I NY (Long Island) ✧ PA

Malcolm, Andrew (1943–). *Someday* (Knopf, 1991).

Almost all of pages 3–160 focus on his first 21 years. See also his companion memoir, *Huddle* (ch. 17).

Cancer ✧ Historians (Cultural) ✧ Journalists ✧ Mothers and Sons ✧ Right to Die I OH

Sawyer, Scott. *Earthly Fathers: A Memoir: A Coming-of-Age Story About Faith and the Search for a Father's Love* (Zondervan Publishing House, 2001).

Sawyer describes how his family tried to cope with his 16-year-old brother's death from cancer. He also reveals his spiritual links to his biological father and stepfather.

Bereavement ✧ Cancer ✧ Fathers and Sons ✧ Spiritual Life ✧ Stepfathers I TX

Shapiro, Dan (1966–). *Mom's Marijuana: Insights About Living* (Harmony Books, 2000).

Widely scattered pages (54; pages 5–224), especially almost all of pages 5–45.

Generation X ✧ Hodgkin's Disease ✧ Psychologists ✧ Vassar College I CT ✧ MA ✧ NY ✧ NYC

Wilson, Barbara (1950–). *Blue Windows: A Christian Science Childhood* (Picador USA, 1997).

Her mother, suffering from cancer, attempted suicide.

Baby Boomers ✧ Cancer ✧ Christian Scientists ✧ Mothers and Daughters ✧ Suicide and Suicide Victims I CA

Cerebral Palsy

Berger, Clyde (1917?–). Ed. by Elaine Waterhouse. *Grandpa's Boy and What Became of Him: An Autobiography* (Institute of Logopedics, 1981).
> Cerebral Palsy ✧ Growing Up Between WWI and WWII I KS

Brown, Christy (1932–1981). *My Left Foot* (Secker & Warburg, 1954).
> To about 18–21 years. Afflicted with cerebral palsy, he wrote this book with his foot.
> Cerebral Palsy I Ireland

Gallego, Ruben (1968–). Tr. by Marian Schwartz. *White on Black* (Harcourt, 2006) (First published in Russian, 2004).
More than 100 pages focus on his first 21 years. Separated from his mother at age 9 and abandoned by his grandfather, Gallego was raised in a series of Soviet state institutions. This remarkable story of survival won the 2003 Russian Booker Prize.
> Cerebral Palsy ✧ Child Institutional Care ✧ Generation X ✧ Grandfathers I Russia (Soviet Union: Moscow)

Smith, Mark (1971–). *Growing Up with Cerebral Palsy* (WRS, 1995).
> Cerebral Palsy ✧ Generation X I CA (Northern)

Diabetes and Juvenile Diabetes

Covelli, Pat(rick) (1954–). *Borrowing Time: Growing Up with Juvenile Diabetes* (Crowell, 1979).
> About 74 pages (between pages 17 and 123).
> Baby Boomers ✧ Diabetes I NYC ✧ MA

Dominick, Andie (1971–). *Needles: A Memoir of Growing Up with Diabetes* (Scribner, 1998).
> Diabetes ✧ Generation X I IA

Roney, Lisa (1960–). *Sweet Invisible Body: Reflections on a Life with Diabetes* (H. Holt, 1999).
> Pages 5 to about 134. She has coped with diabetes since age 11.
> Baby Boomers ✧ Diabetes I TN ✧ MN

Hearing Impairment

Abrams, Charlotte (1929–). *The Silents* (Gallaudet University, 1996).
> Pages 3 to about 143 (chs. 1–16). Both of her parents were deaf, and her mother's sight fails during the course of this memoir.
> Deafness ✧ Depressions (Economic) ✧ Growing Up Between WWI and WWII I IL (Chicago)

Carstens, Grace (?–1989). *Born a Yankee* (Macmillan, 1954).
> About 60–70 pages seem to be on her first 21 years.
> Artists ✧ Deafness ✧ Novelists I NJ and/or MA

Davis, Lennard (1949–). *My Sense of Silence: Memoirs of a Childhood with Deafness* (University of Illinois, 2000).
Both of his parents were deaf.
Baby Boomers ✧ Children of Immigrants ✧ Deafness ✧ Jews ✧ Working Class Whites I NYC (Bronx)

Golan, Lew (1933–). *Reading Between the Lips: A Totally Deaf Man Makes It in the Mainstream* (Bonus Books, 1995).
Pages 15–95, 112–23.
Deafness I IL

Heppner, Cheryl M. (1951–). *Seeds of Disquiet: One Deaf Woman's Experience* (Gallaudet University, 1992).
Pages 5–61 (chs. 1–9).
Baby Boomers ✧ Deafness ✧ Meningitis I ME ✧ PA

Keller, Helen (1880–1968). *The Story of My Life: With Her Letters (1887–1901) and a Supplementary Account of Her Education, Including Passages from the Reports and Letters of Her Teacher, Anne Mansfield Sullivan, by John Albert Macy . . .* (Doubleday, Page, 1903).
Blindness ✧ Deafness ✧ Education ✧ Letters I AL

Kisor, Henry (1940–). *What's That Pig Outdoors: A Memoir of Deafness* (Hill and Wang, 1990).
Deafness ✧ Editors I NJ

Laborit, Emmanuelle (1972–). Tr. by Constantina Mitchell and Paul R. Cote. *The Cry of the Gull* (Gallaudet University, 1998).
She has become a major advocate for the rights of the deaf.
Activists ✧ Actresses ✧ Deafness ✧ Generation X ✧ Motion Picture Actors and Actresses I France

Miller, R(obert) H(enry) (1938–). *Deaf Hearing Boy: A Memoir* (Gallaudet University, 2004).
Written by a retired English professor, this Midwestern memoir describes what it was like to grow up as a hearing person raised by deaf parents.
College Teachers ✧ Deafness ✧ Farm Life ✧ Grandparents ✧ WWII I OH

Sidransky, Ruth (1929–). *In Silence: Growing Up in a Hearing World* (St. Martin's, 1990).
Pages 3 to about 297.
Deafness ✧ Growing Up Between WWI and WWII I NYC (Bronx, Brooklyn)

Walker, Lou Ann (1952–). *A Loss for Words: The Story of Deafness in a Family* (Harper & Row, 1986).
Pages 7–14, 55 to about 144.
Baby Boomers ✧ Deafness ✧ Harvard University I IN ✧ MA

Whitestone, Heather (1973–), and Angela Elwell Hunt. *Listening with My Heart* (Doubleday, 1997).
Pages 4–82 (chs. 1–2). She was the first woman with a disability to be crowned "Miss America."
Deafness ✧ Generation X ✧ Spiritual Life I AL ✧ MO

Wright, David (1920–1994). *Deafness* (Stein and Day, 1969).
>
> Pages 5 to about 114 focus on his first 21 years.
>
> Deafness ✧ Growing Up Between WWI and WWII ✧ Journalists ✧ Poets ✧ Translators I South Africa

Mental Illnesses and Diseases

Including Alzheimer's Disease, Anorexia Nervosa/Bulimia, Attention Deficit Disorder, Autism, Borderline Personality, Depression, Learning Disabilities, and Schizophrenia

Apostolides, Marianne. *Inner Hunger: A Young Woman's Struggle Through Anorexia and Bulimia* (W.W. Norton, 1998).
>
> Pages 10 to about 67.
>
> Anorexia Nervosa/Bulimia ✧ Princeton University I NY ✧ NJ

Ardell, Maureen (1966–), and Corry-Ann. *Portrait of an Anorexic: A Mother and Daughter's Story* (Flight, 1985).
>
> Pages 28–128 cover her from 16 to about 18 years. The perspective shifts from daughter to mother, in alternating chapters.
>
> Collaborations by Relatives ✧ Generation X ✧ Mothers and Daughters I Canada (BR COL)

Barron, Judy (1939–), and Sean Barron (1961–). *There's a Boy in Here* (Simon and Schuster, 1992).
>
> About 134 scattered pages. This is a collaboration between mother and son.
>
> Autism ✧ Baby Boomers ✧ Collaborations by Relatives ✧ Mothers and Sons I OH

Daniels, Lucy (1934?–). *With a Woman's Voice: A Writer's Struggle for Emotional Freedom* (Madison Books, 2001).
>
> A practicing psychotherapist since 1977, Daniels tells of her traumatic childhood, which included electroconvulsive shock therapy.
>
> Anorexia Nervosa/Bulimia ✧ Child Institutional Care ✧ Mental Health ✧ Psychologists I NC

Foster, Patricia (1948–). *All the Lost Girls: Confessions of a Southern Daughter* (University of Alabama, 2000).
>
> Pages 9–246 (Parts One–Two).
>
> Baby Boomers ✧ College Teachers ✧ Mental Health I AL ✧ TN ✧ MA

Frame, Janet (1924–2004). *To the Is-land* (G. Braziller, 1982) (G. Braziller, 1991).
>
> More than 100 pages. This memoir, and the memoirs on her adult years, *An Angel at My Table* (G. Braziller, 1984) and *The Envoy from Mirror City* (G. Braziller, 1985), have been collected as *Autobiography* (G. Braziller, 1991). These memoirs were adapted into the 1990 award-winning film *An Angel at My Table*, directed by Jane Campion.
>
> Growing Up Between WWI and WWII ✧ Novelists ✧ Schizophrenia I New Zealand

Gordon, Emily Fox (1948–). *Mockingbird Years: A Life In and Out of Therapy* (Basic Books, 2000).
>
> About the first 170 pages.
>
> Baby Boomers ✧ Mental Health ✧ Suicide and Suicide Victims I MA ✧ NYC (Manhattan) ✧ Washington, DC

Gregory, Julie. *Sickened: The Memoir of a Munchausen by Proxy Childhood* (Bantam Books, 2003).

In this memoir, the author details abuse that included the forced, inappropriate use of medical treatments.

Family Violence ✧ Munchausen Syndrome by Proxy | OH

Holley, Tara (1951–), and Joe Holley. *My Mother's Keeper: A Daughter's Memoir of Growing Up in the Shadow of Schizophrenia* (W. Morrow, 1997).

Abuse (Sexual) ✧ Baby Boomers ✧ Christian Scientists ✧ Family Violence ✧ Grandparents ✧ Schizophrenia | TX

Holman, Virginia (1966–). *Rescuing Patty Hearst: Memories from a Decade Gone Mad* (Simon and Schuster, 2003).

The author traces the effect that her mother's schizophrenia had on their family, focusing on when she was 9–12 years old. See also "Hearst, Patricia" (ch. 15).

Family Memoirs ✧ Generation X ✧ Mothers and Daughters ✧ Schizophrenia | VA

Hornbacher, Marya (1974–). *Wasted: A Memoir of Anorexia and Bulimia* (HarperCollins, 1998) (Variant title, *Wasted: A Life of Anorexia and Bulimia* [HarperFlamingo, 1998]).

She was bulimic by age 9 and anorexic by age 15.

Anorexia Nervosa/Bulimia ✧ Generation X ✧ Journalists | CA (Central)

Karasik, Paul, and Judy Karasik. *The Ride Together: A Brother and Sister's Memoir of Autism in the Family* (Washington Square, 2003).

About 100 pages. Through chapters that alternately employ comic book illustrations and conventional narration, authors Paul (a cartoonist) and Judy (a former editor) describe growing up with an autistic brother. Written in the form of a graphic novel.

Autism ✧ Baby Boomers ✧ Brothers ✧ Collaborations by Relatives ✧ Graphic Novels | MD

Kaysen, Susanna (1948–). *Girl, Interrupted* (Turtle Bay Books, 1993).

Covers her from 18 to 20 years. The same-titled 1999 film adaptation of this memoir won an Academy Award (Best Supporting Actress).

Baby Boomers ✧ MacLean Hospital ✧ Mental Health | MA

Kirkland, Gelsey (1952–), with Greg Lawrence. *Dancing on My Grave: An Autobiography* (Doubleday, 1986).

Pages 13 to about 120.

Anorexia Nervosa/Bulimia ✧ Baby Boomers ✧ City Life ✧ Dancers | PA ✧ NYC

Miranda, James. *Wasting My Life: An Autobiography* (Chester House, 1993).

Learning Disabilities | NYC

Moorman, Margaret (1949–). *My Sister's Keeper: Learning to Cope with a Sibling's Mental Illness* (W.W. Norton, 1992).

Pages 19–87. The author had to come to grips with her sister's manic-depression following the death of their mother. See also ch. 16 for her companion memoir.

Baby Boomers ✧ Bereavement ✧ Journalists ✧ Manic-Depression ✧ Sisters | VA

O'Neill, Cherry Boone (1954–). *Starving for Attention* (Continuum, 1982).
> More than the first 100 pages. She is the daughter of singer Pat Boone.
>
> Anorexia Nervosa/Bulimia ✧ Baby Boomers ✧ Boone, Pat ✧ Singers ✧ Wealth | CA (Southern: Beverly Hills)

Rozelle, Ron (1952–). *Into That Good Night* (Farrar, Straus, and Giroux, 1998).
> Alzheimer's Disease ✧ Baby Boomers ✧ School Superintendents ✧ Teachers | TX (East)

Schiller, Lori (1959?–), and Amanda Bennett. *The Quiet Room: A Journey Out of the Torment of Madness* (Warner Books, 1994).
> Covers her from 15 to 23 years.
>
> Baby Boomers ✧ Schizophrenia | NYC

Sechehaye, Marguerite (pseud: Renee) (1887–). Tr. by Grace Rubin-Rabson. *Autobiography of a Schizophrenic Girl: Reality Lost and Regained* (New American Library, 1951).
> Schizophrenia

Simon, Clea (1961–). *Mad House: Growing Up in the Shadows of Mentally Ill Siblings* (Doubleday, 1997).
> Pages 1–110.
>
> Baby Boomers ✧ Family Memoirs ✧ Schizophrenia ✧ Suicide and Suicide Victims | NY (Long Island)

Vilar, Irene (1969–). Tr. from the Spanish by Gregory Rabassa. *A Message from God in the Atomic Age: A Memoir* (Pantheon Books, 1996).
> More than 200 scattered pages (between pages 4 and 260).
>
> Bereavement ✧ Children of the Mentally Ill ✧ Generation X ✧ Mental Health ✧ Prisoners ✧ Puerto Rican Americans ✧ Suicide and Suicide Victims | NY ✧ Puerto Rico ✧ NH

Williams, Donna (1963–). *Nobody Nowhere: The Extraordinary Autobiography of an Autistic* (Times Books, 1992).
> Pages 3–132.
>
> Autism ✧ Family Violence ✧ Teachers | Australia

Paralysis and Motor Dysfunctions

Including Multiple Sclerosis, Paraplegia, Quadriplegia, Polio, and Parkinson's Disease

Eareckson, Joni (1960–), with Joe Musser. *Joni* (Zondervan Publishing House, 1976).
> Baby Boomers ✧ Quadriplegia ✧ Spiritual Life | MD

Hockenberry, John (1956–). *Moving Violations: War Zones, Wheelchairs, and Declarations of Independence* (Hyperion, 1995).
> About 100 pages, scattered throughout pages 15–149.
>
> Baby Boomers ✧ Journalists ✧ Paraplegia | PA

Kriegel, Leonard (1933–). *The Long Walk Home* (Appleton-Century, 1964).
> But for a few pages, this entire memoir focuses on Kriegel from 11 to 21 years.
>
> Camps ✧ City Life ✧ College Teachers ✧ Polio | NYC (Bronx)

Kriegel, Leonard (1933–). *Falling into Life* (North Point, 1991).
Pages 3–60 and 14 subsequent scattered pages focus on his pre-adult years, especially when he was 10–11.

Camps ✧ City Life ✧ College Teachers ✧ Polio | NYC (Bronx)

Kriegel, Leonard (1933–). *Flying Solo: Reimagining Manhood, Courage, and Loss* (Beacon, 1998).
About 65 scattered pages focus on his early years.

Child Institutional Care ✧ City Life ✧ College ✧ Teachers ✧ Polio | NYC (Bronx)

Mairs, Nancy (1943–). *Remembering the Bone House: An Erotics of Place and Space* (Harper & Row, 1989).
Pages 16 to about 174.

Island Life ✧ Mental Health ✧ Multiple Sclerosis ✧ Sexuality | CA ✧ South Pacific ✧ ME ✧ MA ✧ AZ

Marshall, Alan (1902–1984). *I Can Jump Puddles* (Cheshire, 1955).
At age 5 he was a victim of paralysis.

Humorists ✧ Journalists ✧ Polio ✧ Short Story Writers | Australia

Martin, Carolyn (1946–). *I Can't Walk—So I'll Learn to Dance* (Zondervan Publishing House, 1994).
Pages 16 to about 129.

Abuse (Sexual) ✧ Cerebral Palsy | CA (Central) ✧ WA

Mee, Charles L. (1939–). *A Nearly Normal Life: A Memoir* (Little, Brown, 1999).
Mee has written an incisive and highly readable memoir that focuses on how he has coped with polio, which he contracted at age 14, in 1953. A modern classic.

Cold War ✧ Dramatists ✧ Historians ✧ Intellectual Life ✧ Polio | IL

Ototake, Hirotada (1976–). Tr. by Gerry Harcourt. *No One's Perfect* (Kodansha International, 2000) (First published in Japan, 1998).

Generation X ✧ Tetra-amelia | Japan

Roy, Travis (1975–), with E(dward) M(cKelvy). *Eleven Seconds: A Story of Tragedy, Courage and Triumph* (Warner Books, 1998).
Fewer than the first 40 pages are on his first 19–20 years; more than the last 180 pages are on him from 20 to 21 years.

Boston University ✧ Generation X ✧ Hockey ✧ Quadriplegia | ME ✧ MA ✧ GA

Rush, William L. (1955–). *Journey Out of Silence* (Media Productions & Marketing, 1986).
There are more than 80 pages on his first 21 years.

Baby Boomers ✧ Quadriplegia | NE

Sight Impairment

Alexander, Sally Hobart (1943–). *Taking Hold: My Journey into Blindness* (Macmillan, 1994).
Blindness

Arms, Mrs. Mary L. (Day) (1836–). *Incidents in the Life of a Blind Girl: Mary L. Day, A Graduate of the Maryland Institution for the Blind* (J. Young, 1859).

Blindness ✧ Maryland Institution for the Blind ✧ Nineteenth-Century Pre-Industrial Age Memoirists I MD

Bjarnhof, Karl (1898–1980). Tr. from the Danish by Naomi Walford. *The Stars Grow Pale* (Knopf, 1958).

This memoir recounts his failing eyesight during his youth.

Blindness ✧ Intellectual Life I Denmark

Flavel, Doreen E., with Donald S. McDonald. *The Promise and the Challenge* (Privately printed, 1986).

Blindness I Australia

Husayn, Taha (1889–1973). Tr. 1932 by E. H. Paxton. *An Egyptian Childhood* (Routledge, 1929).

Covers his first 13 years. This memoir is continued by the following entry.

Blindness ✧ High School Life ✧ Novelists ✧ Short Story Writers ✧ Victorian Era British Memoirists I Egypt

Husayn, Taha (1889–1973). Tr. 1948 by Hilary Wayment. *The Stream of Days: A Student at the Azhar* (al-Maaref, 1943).

Covers him from 13 to 21 years. *An Egyptian Childhood* and *The Stream of Days* were reprinted in *The Days: His Autobiography in Three Parts* (following entry).

Blindness ✧ Novelists ✧ Short Story Writers ✧ Victorian Era British Memoirists I Egypt

Husayn, Taha (1889–1973). *The Days: His Autobiography in Three Parts* (American University of Cairo, 1997).

Contains the preceding 2 entries, as well as *A Passage to France* (tr. by Kenneth Cragg [E.J. Brill, 1976]), which focuses on him from 21 to 33 years at the Sorbonne. Pages 9 to about 257 of this composite volume focus on his first 21 years. (Only about the first 13 pages of *A Passage to France* focus on him before he turned 22.)

Blindness ✧ Novelists ✧ Short Story Writers ✧ Victorian Era British Memoirists I Egypt ✧ France

Kuusisto, Stephen (1955–). *Planet of the Blind* (Dial, 1998).

Pages 8 to about 72.

Baby Boomers ✧ Blindness ✧ Poets ✧ Teachers I NC (?)

Mehta, Ved (1934–). *Face to Face: An Autobiography* (Little, Brown, 1957).

This volume provides a compact overview of his childhood and youth, which he later expanded into his <u>Continents of Exile</u> series, which begins with the following entry.

Asian Americans ✧ Blindness ✧ Education ✧ Essayists I India ✧ AR

Mehta, Ved (1934–). *Daddyji* (Farrar, Straus, and Giroux, 1972).

This is the first in Mehta's <u>Continents of Exile</u> series of memoirs. Here he focuses on his early relationship with his father.

Asian Americans ✧ Blindness ✧ Essayists ✧ Fathers and Sons ✧ Physicians I India

Mehta, Ved (1934–). *Mamaji* (Oxford University, 1979).

Here he focuses on his early relationship with his mother.

Asian Americans ✧ Blindness ✧ Essayists ✧ Mothers and Sons ✧ Physicians I India

Mehta, Ved (1934–). *Vedi* (Oxford University, 1982).
Focuses on him from 5 to 9 years.
Asian Americans ✧ Blindness ✧ Education ✧ Essayists | India

Mehta, Ved (1934–). *Ledge Between the Streams* (W.W. Norton, 1984).
Focuses on him from 9 to 15 years.
Asian Americans ✧ Blindness ✧ Education ✧ Essayists | India

Mehta, Ved (1934–). *Sound-Shadows of the New World* (W.W. Norton, 1985).
Focuses on him from 15 to 18 years.
Asian Americans ✧ Blindness ✧ Education ✧ Essayists | AR

Mehta, Ved (1934–). *The Stolen Light* (W.W. Norton, 1989).
About the first 400 pages focus on him from 18 to 22 years.
Asian Americans ✧ Blindness ✧ College Life ✧ Essayists | CA (Southern)

Milsap, Ronnie (1943–), with Tom Carter. *Almost Like a Song* (McGraw-Hill, 1990).
First 100 pages (chs. 1–11) focus on his first 20 years. He lost his sight to an illness, when he was very young. Includes a 4-page discography.
Blindness ✧ Singers | NC

Sullivan, Tom (1947–) and Derek Gill. *If You Could See What I Hear* (Harper & Row, 1975).
Pages 6–133 (chs. 2–11).
Actors ✧ Baby Boomers ✧ Blindness ✧ Singers | MA

Thurber, James (1894–1961). *My Life and Hard Times* (Harper & Brothers, 1933).
Blindness ✧ Cartoonists ✧ Dramatists ✧ Humorists ✧ Illustrators | OH

Tuberculosis

Bottome, Phyllis (pseud. of Mrs. Ernan Forbes-Dennis) (1882–1963). *Challenge* (Harcourt, 1953) (First published by Faber & Faber, 1952).
Pages 13–64 focus on her from 18 to 21 years. See also entry in chapter 8.
Clergy ✧ Feminists ✧ Novelists ✧ Tuberculosis | KY ✧ NY

McDougal, Gwynn (1928?–). *The Last Camilles: The Rutland Years, 1949–1953* (Acropolis South, 1995).
Pages 6–82.
Growing Up Between WWI and WWII ✧ Tuberculosis | MA

Meyers, Kent (b. during 1960s). *The Witness of Combines* (University of Minnesota, 1998).
Bereavement ✧ College Teachers ✧ Farm Life ✧ Tuberculosis | MN

Rice, Clyde (1903–1997?). *A Heaven in the Eye* (Breitenbush Books, 1990).
About 100 pages. Memoir covers 1918–1934.
Tuberculosis | OR ✧ CA (Northern)

Swan, Madonna (1928–), as told through Mark St. Pierre. *Madonna Swan: A Lakota Woman's Story* (University of Oklahoma, 1991).

Pages 3–96. St. Pierre conducted a series of interviews with Swan, who was confined for years in a sanitarium due to tuberculosis.

Grandmothers ✧ Growing Up Between WWI and WWII ✧ Native Americans ✧ Teachers ✧ Tuberculosis I SD

West, Jessamyn (1902–1984). *Hide and Seek: A Continuing Journey* (Harcourt Brace Jovanovich, 1973).

About 154 scattered pages. She was related to Richard Nixon through her mother's family. West wrote many of her works while confined in a sanatorium with tuberculosis.

College Teachers ✧ Dramatists ✧ Librettists ✧ Novelists ✧ Poets ✧ Quakers ✧ Screenwriters ✧ Short Story Writers ✧ Tuberculosis I IN ✧ CA

Chapter 8

Thinkers and Believers: Intellectuals, Historians, Journalists, and Reformers

This chapter shares with us early memoirs of individuals who, as adults, became committed to ideas and ideals that have rocked civilizations. As their minds blossomed, these writers progressively displayed the qualities of deep intellect, eloquent thought, and impassioned emotion that are on display in their autobiographical works.

The first section describes the reminiscences of more than 2 dozen philosophers, intellectuals, and lecturers. Among male writers, such penetrating minds as those of Jean-Paul Sartre, Nirad Chaudhuri, and Edward Dahlberg are represented here. Jill Ker Conway, Mary Ellen Chase, and Harriet Martineau are among the gifted women whose recollections are cited here.

The second, third, and fourth sections of this chapter focus on lives of individuals touched by a wide variety of religious faiths and spiritual beliefs. The most extended of these sections, the second, lists memoirs by adherents of some religions that have helped to define Western civilization. In the this section, "Religious Cultures and Leaders," entries are arranged alphabetically, according to denomination, with nearly 2 dozen such represented. For instance, Juanita Brooks tells her story (in *Quicksand and Cactus*) of growing up as a young Mormon in Nevada at the start of the 20th century.

Works by Baptists, Catholics, Methodists, and Presbyterians may be found here. Less populous sects and denominations are also found here, however, such as the Dutch Reformed Church, Jehovah's Witnesses, and Christian Scientists. Memoirs by exponents of Eastern religions are also found here, such as Buddhists and Lamas.

Individuals who, as adults, became religious leaders are found in the third section. (However, family memoirs centering on church family life are also listed in the fifth section of chapter 17.) Cult followers and persons whose lives are generally marked by spiritual orientations are also profiled by their memoirs in the fourth section of this chapter.

The memoirists covered in the fifth and sixth sections have found vocation as historians and journalists—fields of endeavor that survey the sweep of events, past and present, and study how their comingling affects the world. Dee Brown, best known for his stirring history *Bury My Heart at Wounded Knee*, tells his story of what it was like to grow up as a Native American in Arkansas in the opening decades of the 20th century. We see what life was like growing up a generation later on the plains of South Dakota in broadcast journalist Tom Brokaw's memoir, *A Long Way from Home*. (Other professional writers' memoirs are showcased in chapter 9.)

The final 2 parts of chapter 8 concern the formative years of reformers, activists, and teachers. The recollections of protest singer Joan Baez and Soviet dissident Elena Bonner are included here, as are those by Kentucky educator Jesse Stuart and English teacher Anne Treneer.

Philosophers, Intellectuals, and Lecturers

Acton, Harold (1904–1994). *Memoirs of an Aesthete* (Methuen, 1948).
Pages 1–142 (chs. 1–6). He was an acquaintance of Osbert Sitwell (see entry in this chapter). He lectured on English literature at China's Peking University.

Arts Patrons ✧ High Society ✧ Intellectual Life ✧ Lecturers ✧ Wealth | Italy ✧ England

Altick, Richard D. (1915–living 2007). *Of a Place and a Time: Remembering Lancaster* (Archon Books, 1991).
From 2 to 26 years. He wrote the classic *The Art of Literary Research* (W.W. Norton, 1963).

Critics (Literary) ✧ Growing Up Between WWI and WWII ✧ Historians (Cultural) ✧ Intellectual Life ✧ Lecturers | PA

Benjamin, Walter (1892–1940). Tr. from the German by Howard Eiland. *Berlin Childhood Around 1900* (Belknap Press, 2006) (First published in German, 1950).
Written in the 1930s.

City Life ✧ Critics (Art) ✧ Critics (Literary) ✧ Critics (Social) ✧ Historians (Cultural) ✧ Intellectual Life ✧ Wealth | Germany (West Berlin)

Boll, Heinrich (1917–1985). Tr. from the German by Leila Vennewitz. *What's to Become of the Boy? Or: Something to Do with Books* (Knopf, 1984).
About 80 pages on his adolescence.

Books and Reading ✧ Dramatists ✧ Essayists ✧ Growing Up Between WWI and WWII ✧ Intellectual Life ✧ Lecturers ✧ Novelists ✧ Pacifists ✧ Philosophers ✧ Poets ✧ Short Story Writers | Germany

Bose, Pradip (1928–). *Growing Up in India* (Minerva Associates, 1972).
Pages 3 to about 89 focus on his intellectual development up to 21 years.

Growing Up Between WWI and WWII ✧ Intellectual Life | India

Bottome, Phyllis (pseud. of Mrs. Ernan Forbes-Dennis) (1882–1963). *Search for a Soul (Fragment of an Autobiography)* (Reynal & Hitchcock, 1948) (First published by Faber & Faber, 1947).
Covers her to age 18. The first 6 chapters are set in England; then she and her family move to Yonkers, NY, when she is 7 years old. Her novel *The Mortal Storm* (Faber & Faber, 1937) warned of the growing Nazi menace. See also entry in chapter 7.

Clergy ✧ Feminists ✧ Lecturers ✧ Novelists ✧ Short Story Writers ✧ Victorian Era British Memoirists | England ✧ NYC ✧ NY

Bowles, Paul (1910–1999). *Without Stopping: An Autobiography* (Putnam, 1972).
Pages 9 to about 136.

Composers ✧ Fathers and Sons ✧ Gays ✧ Intellectual Life ✧ Poets ✧ Translators | NYC ✧ NY ✧ MA ✧ VA ✧ France ✧ Germany ✧ Morocco

Buscaglia, Leo (1924–1998). *Papa, My Father: A Celebration of Dads* (SLACK, 1989).
Some 50 scattered pages.

College Teachers ✧ Education ✧ Growing Up Between WWI and WWII ✧ Lecturers ✧ Speech Pathologists | CA (Southern)

Chace, James (1931–2004). *What We Had: A Memoir* (Summit Books, 1990).
The first half of the book covers his first 21 years. He was a noted foreign affairs scholar.

College Teachers ✧ Editors ✧ Historians ✧ Journalists ✧ Lecturers ✧ Novelists | MA

Chase, Mary Ellen (1887–1973). *The White Gate: Adventures in the Imagination of a Child* (W.W. Norton, 1954).
Focuses on her from 9 to 12 years.

Birders ✧ College Teachers ✧ Country Life ✧ Gardeners ✧ Intellectual Life ✧ Lecturers ✧ Novelists | ME

Chase, Mary Ellen (1887–1973). *A Goodly Heritage* (H. Holt, 1932).
Covers from her childhood into her first year in college.

Birders ✧ College Life ✧ College Teachers ✧ Country Life ✧ Gardeners ✧ Intellectual Life ✧ Lecturers ✧ Novelists | ME

Chaudhuri, Nirad (1897–1999). *The Autobiography of an Unknown Indian* (Macmillan, 1951).
More than 165 scattered pages (between pages 127 and 317). This work skillfully blends ethnography with autobiography. Winston Churchill stated that this was one of the best books he ever read.

Broadcasters ✧ Centenarians ✧ Children's Authors ✧ Editors ✧ Intellectual Life | India

Cole, Margaret (1893–1980). *Growing Up into Revolution: Reminiscences of Margaret Cole* (Longmans, Green, 1949).
Pages 2–57.

Cambridge University ✧ Editors ✧ Education ✧ Lecturers ✧ Novelists ✧ Socialists ✧ Teachers ✧ Victorian Era British Memoirists | England

Conway, Jill Ker (1934–). *Road from Coorain* (Knopf, 1989).
Pages 28 to about 172. In 1975 she became Smith College's first woman president.

College Presidents ✧ College Teachers ✧ Feminists ✧ Historians ✧ Intellectual Life ✧ Lecturers ✧ Shepherds ✧ Smith College | Australia

Dahlberg, Edward (1900–1977). *Because I Was Flesh: The Autobiography of Edward Dahlberg* (New Directions, 1959).
Pages 11 to about 145. Often considered a classic.

Critics (Literary) ✧ Essayists ✧ Novelists ✧ Orphans | MA ✧ MO ✧ OH ✧ CA (Southern)

Fitzgerald, Robert (1910–1985). Ed. by Penelope Laurans Fitzgerald. *The Third Kind of Knowledge: Memoirs & Selected Writings* (New Directions, 1993).
Pages 3–57 cover 5 memoirs on his youth.

Classical Scholars ✧ Editors ✧ Education ✧ Intellectual Life ✧ Journalists ✧ Poets ✧ Translators | IL ✧ England ✧ NYC

Goethe, Johann Wolfgang von (1749–1832). Ed. by Thomas Saine and Jeffrey Sammons. Tr. by Robert R. Heitner. *From My Life: Poetry and Truth: Parts One to Three* (Suhrkamp, 1987).
Pages 21 to about 196 (Book One–Book Six).

Dramatists ✧ Eighteenth-Century Memoirists ✧ Intellectual Life ✧ Lawyers ✧ Novelists ✧ Poets ✧ Scientists I Germany

Gough, John B. (1817–1886). *Autobiography and Personal Recollections of John B. Gough, with Twenty-Six Years as a Public Speaker* (Bill, Nichols & Co., 1870).
Pages 19–86.

Lecturers ✧ Nineteenth-Century Pre-Industrial Age Memoirists ✧ Temperance I England ✧ NY ✧ MA

Guerard, Albert Leon (1880–1959). *Personal Equation* (W.W. Norton, 1948).
Pages 19 to about 162 focus on his intellectual development through his first 21 years.

College Teachers ✧ Intellectual Life I France ✧ England

Hamilton, Iain (1920–1986). *Half a Highlander: An Autobiography of a Scottish Youth* (E.P. Dutton, 1957).

Critics (Art) ✧ Critics (Film) ✧ Critics (Literature) ✧ Critics (Theater) ✧ Growing Up Between WWI and WWII I Scotland

Kato, Shuichi (1919–). Tr. and anno. by Chia-ning Chang. *A Sheep's Song: A Writer's Reminiscences of Japan and the World* (University of California, 1999) (First published in Japan, 1968).
Pages 4 to about 157 focus on him from 4 to 21 years.

Critics (Literary) ✧ Essayists ✧ Growing Up Between WWI and WWII ✧ Intellectual Life I Japan

Koestler, Arthur (1905–1983). *Arrow in the Blue: The First Volume of an Autobiography, 1905–31* (Macmillan, 1952).

Anti-Communist Movements ✧ Foreign Correspondents ✧ Intellectual Life ✧ Philosophers I Hungary

Martineau, Harriet (1802–1876). Ed. by Maria Weston Chapman. *Harriet Martineau's Autobiography*. 2 vols. (J.R. Osgood, 1877).
Despite the early onset of deafness (at age 12) and other maladies in her life, Martineau distinguished herself as the author of hundreds of forceful and articulate works.

Abolitionists ✧ Children's Authors ✧ Deafness ✧ Economists ✧ Feminists ✧ Historians ✧ Intellectual Life ✧ Novelists ✧ Short Story Writers ✧ Travel Writers I England

Maurois, André (born Emile Herzog) (1885–1967). Tr. by Denver Lindley and Jane Lindley. *I Remember, I Remember* (Harper & Brothers, 1942) (Rev. by the author and tr. by Denver Lindley as *Memoirs, 1885–1967* [1970]).
About 67 pages are on his childhood.

Biographers ✧ Businesspersons ✧ Children's Authors ✧ College Teachers ✧ Critics (Literary) ✧ Historians ✧ Intellectual Life ✧ Lecturers ✧ Military Life ✧ Novelists ✧ Short Story Writers ✧ Translators I France

Partridge, Frances (1900–2004). *Love in Bloomsbury: Memories* (Little, Brown, 1981) (British title, *Memories* [Gollancz, 1983]).
Pages 11 to about 70 (chs. 1–5). She is generally regarded as the final member of Virginia Woolf's "Bloomsbury Group."

Bloomsbury Group ✧ Booksellers ✧ Centenarians ✧ Intellectual Life ✧ Pacifists ✧ Translators I England

Perlman, Helen (1905–2004). *The Dancing Clock and Other Childhood Memories* (Cambridge University, 1987).
Sections 2–3 (pages 21–158).
College Teachers ✧ Intellectual Life ✧ Social Workers | MN

Phillips, Margaret Mann (1906–1987). *Within the City Wall: A Memoir of Childhood* (Cambridge University, 1943).
City Life ✧ Classical Scholars ✧ College Teachers ✧ Critics (Literary) ✧ Editors ✧ Intellectual Life ✧ Translators | England

Polk, Noel (1943–). *Outside the Southern Myth* (University Press of Mississippi: 1997).
About 75 scattered pages.
College Teachers ✧ Critics (Literary) ✧ Intellectual Life | MS

Ruskin, John (1819–1900). *Praeterita: Outlines of Scenes and Thoughts, Perhaps Worthy of Memory, in My Past Life, 1885–1889.* **3 vols.** (R. Hart-Davis, 1949) (1978 rpt., Oxford University).
This is an unfinished autobiography that was serialized. Pages 5–184 (Vol. I) focus on his first 19 years; pages 187–200 (ch. 1 of Vol. II) focus on him from 20 to 21 years.
Critics (Architecture) ✧ Critics (Art) ✧ Critics (Social) ✧ Natural History ✧ Nineteenth-Century Pre-Industrial Age Memoirists ✧ Oxford University | England

Russell, (Sir) Bertrand (1872–1970). *Autobiography of Bertrand Russell: Volume I* (Little, Brown, 1967).
About the first 67 pages cover up to his entrance into Cambridge University.
College Teachers ✧ Lecturers ✧ Mathematicians ✧ Philosophers ✧ Politicians ✧ Reformers ✧ Victorian Era British Memoirists | England

Said, Edward (1935–2003). *Out of Place: A Memoir* (Knopf, 1999).
Nearly the first 150 pages. He was a well-known Arab American intellectual who grew up in Jerusalem. He wrote this memoir in his declining years, while battling leukemia. This memoir was loosely adapted as the 2006 film *Out of Place: Memories of Edward Said.*
College Teachers ✧ Historians (Cultural) ✧ Immigrants ✧ Intellectual Life | Israel ✧ U.S.

Santayana, George (1863–1952). *Persons and Places: The Background of My Life* (Scribner, 1944).
Pages 56–180. Includes his years as a Harvard undergraduate.
Harvard University ✧ Philosophers | Spain ✧ MA

Sarraute, Nathalie (1900–1999). Tr. by Barbara Wright. *Childhood* (G. Braziller, 1984) (First published in French, 1983).
Covers her first 12 years.
Critics (Literary) ✧ Dramatists ✧ Essayists ✧ Intellectual Life ✧ Lawyers ✧ Novelists ✧ Stepmothers | Russia

Sartre, Jean-Paul (1905–1980). Tr. from the French by Bernard Frechtman. *The Words* (G. Braziller, 1964).
Covers his first 12 years.
Books and Reading ✧ Critics (Literary) ✧ Dramatists ✧ Fatherless Families ✧ Grandparents ✧ Intellectual Life ✧ Novelists ✧ Philosophers | France

Sitwell, (Sir) Osbert (1892–1969). *Left Hand, Right Hand* (Little, Brown, 1944).

Covers him to about 7 years. See also "Holroyd, Michael" (ch. 9), whose life and family background bear marked similarities; see "Mitford, Jessica" (ch. 17) for a memoir of another British family having similarly gifted and eccentric members. For another 5-volume memoir by a British writer, see "Woolf, Leonard Sidney" (ch. 9). Sitwell was an acquaintance of Harold Acton (see entry in this chapter).

Arts Patrons ✧ Eccentrics ✧ Essayists ✧ Eton College ✧ High Society ✧ Intellectual Life ✧ Military Life ✧ Novelists ✧ Poets ✧ Short Story Writers ✧ Travel Writers ✧ Victorian Era Memoirists ✧ Wealth | England

Sitwell, (Sir) Osbert (1892–1969). *The Scarlet Tree* (Little, Brown, 1946).

Covers him from about 7 to 17 years.

Arts Patrons ✧ Eccentrics ✧ Essayists ✧ Intellectual Life ✧ Eton College ✧ High Society ✧ Military Life ✧ Novelists ✧ Poets ✧ Short Story Writers ✧ Travel Writers ✧ Victorian Era Memoirists ✧ Wealth | England

Sitwell, Sacheverell (1897–1988). *All Summer in a Day: An Autobiographical Fantasia* (George H. Doran, 1926).

Pages 15 to about 111. Osbert Sitwell was his brother (see previous entries).

Arts Patrons ✧ Baronets ✧ Biographers ✧ Critics (Architectural) ✧ Critics (Art) ✧ Historians (Cultural) ✧ Intellectual Life ✧ Journalists ✧ Oxford University ✧ Poets ✧ Publishers ✧ Travel Writers | England

Tagore, Rabindranath (1861–1941). Tr. by Surendranath Tagore. *My Reminiscences* (Macmillan, 1917).

Pages 3 to about 186 (chs. 1–5) cover his first 21 years. He was the first person from India to win a Nobel Prize for Literature, which was for poetry. His artistic ventures gave way to political activism during his adult years. He was knighted, but rejected the title.

Dramatists ✧ Education ✧ Lecturers ✧ Musicians ✧ Novelists ✧ Painters ✧ Philosophers ✧ Poets ✧ Reformers ✧ Short Story Writers | India

Tagore, Rabindranath (1861–1941). Tr. by Marjorie Sykes. *My Boyhood Days* (Visva-Bharati, 1941).

Covers his first 17 years.

Dramatists ✧ Education ✧ Lecturers ✧ Musicians ✧ Novelists ✧ Painters ✧ Philosophers ✧ Poets ✧ Reformers ✧ Short Story Writers | India

Wolf, Naomi (1962–). *Promiscuities: The Secret Struggle for Womanhood* (Random House, 1997).

She grew up in San Francisco.

Baby Boomers ✧ Feminists ✧ Hippies | CA (Northern)

Wollheim, Richard (1923–2003). *Germs: A Memoir of Childhood* (Waywiser, 2005).

He meticulously evokes a childhood spent in hotels, cared for by nannies, while his parents traveled. (This memoir's title derives from his mother's obsessive-compulsive fixation on cleanliness.)

Books and Reading ✧ College Teachers ✧ Eccentrics ✧ Growing Up Between WWI and WWII ✧ Jews ✧ Painters ✧ Philosophers ✧ Resorts | England

Religious Cultures and Leaders

Including Baptists, Buddhists, Catholics (Including Nuns), Christian Converts, Christian Scientists, Dutch Reformed Church, Fundamentalists, Jehovah's Witnesses, Jews, Lamas, Methodists, Missionaries, Mormons, Muslims, Pentacostalists, Presbyterians, Quakers, Shakers, Televangelists, True Believers, Unitarians; Includes Also Memoirists Who Studied to Be Part of the Clergy or Who, as Adults, Became Part of the Clergy

Adams, John Quincy (1849–1940). *An Old Boy Remembers* (Ruth Hill, 1935).
About 65 pages. Adams was a Presbyterian minister from Rochester, NY.
Clergy ✧ Nineteenth-Century Pre-Industrial Age Memoirists I NY

Adlerblum, Nima H. (1882–1974). Ed. by Els Benheim. *Memoirs of Childhood: An Approach to Jewish Philosophy* (Jason Aronson, 1999).
Jews ✧ Spiritual Life I Palestine (i.e., Israel)

Agosin, Marjorie (1955–). Tr. by Celeste Kostopulos-Cooperman. *A Cross and a Star: Memoirs of a Jewish Girl in Chile* (University of New Mexico, 1995).
She moved to Maryland in 1969.
Chilean Americans ✧ College Teachers ✧ Critics (Literary) ✧ Immigrants ✧ Jews I Chile

Agosin, Marjorie (1955–). Tr. by Nancy Abraham Hall. *The Alphabet in My Hands: A Writing Life* (Rutgers University, 2000).
College Teachers ✧ Critics (Literary) ✧ Immigrants ✧ Poets I Chile

Ahmed, Leila (1940–). *A Border Passage: A Woman's Journey* (Farrar, Straus, and Giroux, 1999).
From about pages 47 to 194.
Cambridge University ✧ College Teachers ✧ Feminists ✧ Mothers and Daughters ✧ Muslims I Egypt ✧ England

Armstrong, Karen (1944–). *Through the Narrow Gate* (St. Martin's, 1981).
From 17 to 24 years. Seven years after entering a Roman Catholic convent she left it, due to a nervous breakdown.
Nuns I England

Bakker, Jay (1975–), with Linden Gross. *The Son of a Preacher Man: My Search for Grace in the Shadows* (HarperSanFrancisco, 2001).
Pages 4 to about 173. The author's parents are televangelists Jim Bakker and Tammy Faye Bakker.
Alcoholism ✧ Children of Drug Abusers ✧ Fathers and Sons ✧ Generation X ✧ Sexual Scandals ✧ Televangelism I NC

Baldwin, James (pseud.: Robert Dudley) (1841–1925). *In My Youth: From the Posthumous Papers of Robert Dudley* (Bobbs-Merrill, 1914) (Variant title, *In the Days of My Youth: An Intimate Personal Record of Life and Manners in the Middle Ages of the Middle West* [Bobbs-Merrill, 1923]).
He is not to be confused with the novelist James Baldwin (1924–1987).
Nineteenth-Century Pre-Industrial Age Memoirists ✧ Quakers I IN

Boyle, Harry (1915–). *Mostly in Clover* (E.P. Dutton, 1961).
Covers his boyhood and youth, generally, as does the following entry. He became vice-chairman of the Canadian Radio-Television Commission.

Catholics ✧ Farm Life ✧ Growing Up Between WWI and WWII I Canada (Ontario)

Boyle, Harry (1915–). *With a Pinch of Sin* (Doubleday, 1966).
Covers his boyhood and youth, generally.

Catholics ✧ Farm Life ✧ Growing Up Between WWI and WWII I Canada (Ontario)

Boyle, Harry (1915–). *Memories of a Catholic Boyhood* (Doubleday, 1973).
Covers through his first year of college.

Catholics ✧ Farm Life ✧ Growing Up Between WWI and WWII I Canada (Ontario)

Brooks, Juanita (1898–). *Quicksand and Cactus: A Memoir of the Southern Mormon Frontier* (Howe Brothers, 1982).
Pages 11 to about 220 (Part I, ch. 2–Part II, ch. 4).

Frontier and Pioneer Life ✧ Historians ✧ Mormons I NV

Buechner, Frederick (1926–). *The Sacred Journey* (Harper & Row, 1982).
Pages 9 to about 94. Religious and ethical themes run through his fiction and nonfiction writings.

Essayists ✧ Growing Up Between WWI and WWII ✧ Lawrenceville Academy ✧ Novelists ✧ Presbyterians ✧ Short Story Writers I NYC ✧ Bermuda ✧ NC ✧ NJ

Byrnes, Thomas (1911–). *My Angel's Name Is Fred: Tales of Growing Up Catholic* (Harper & Row, 1987).
This work is set in the 1930s–1940s. He was a frequent contributor to *Catholic Digest*.

Catholics ✧ City Life ✧ Dramatists ✧ Humorists ✧ Journalists ✧ Poets I IL (Chicago)

Cascone, Gina (1956?–). *Pagan Babies and Other Catholic Memories* (St. Martin's, 1982).
See entry for her other memoir in ch. 5.

Baby Boomers ✧ Catholics ✧ Children's Authors ✧ Italian Americans I NJ

Cornwell, John (1940–). *Seminary Boy* (Doubleday, 2006).

Abuse (Sexual) ✧ Catholics ✧ Country Life ✧ Crime ✧ Seminaries ✧ Spiritual Life ✧ WWII I England (West Midlands)

Espey, John (1913–2000). *Tales Out of School: More Delightful, Humorous Stories of Boyhood in China* (Knopf, 1947).
Despite its subtitle, this is the first of 4 volumes (see following entries) on Espey's early years. See also "Fritz, Jean" (ch. 4) and "Patent, Gregory" (ch. 6).

Critics (Literary) ✧ Growing Up Between WWI and WWII ✧ Missionaries ✧ Novelists I China (Shanghai)

Espey, John (1913–2000). *Minor Heresies, Major Departures: A China Mission Boyhood* (University of California, 1949).
This memoir continues *Tales Out of School*.

Critics (Literary) ✧ Growing Up Between WWI and WWII ✧ Missionaries ✧ Novelists I China (Shanghai)

Espey, John (1913–2000). *The Other City* (Knopf, 1949).

Focusing on his years at the Shanghai American School, this volume continues *Minor Heresies, Major Departures.*

Critics (Literary) ✧ Growing Up Between WWI and WWII ✧ Missionaries ✧ Novelists ✧ Shanghai American School | China (Shanghai)

Espey, John (1913–2000). *Strong Drink, Strong Language* (J. Daniel, 1990).

Espey's final volume of memoirs takes place during the 1920s–1930s.

Critics (Literary) ✧ Growing Up Between WWI and WWII ✧ Missionaries ✧ Novelists | China (Shanghai)

Feeney, Leonard (1897–1978). *Survival Till Seventeen* (St. Bede, 1980) (Originally appeared in *The Leonard Feeney Omnibus* [Sheed & Ward, 1943]).

He was a Jesuit priest.

Catholics | MA

Fitzgerald, John D(ennis) (1907–1988). *Papa Married a Mormon* (Prentice-Hall, 1955).

This reminiscence is continued by the following entry.

Mormons | UT

Fitzgerald, John D(ennis) (1907–1988). *Mama's Boarding House* (Prentice-Hall, 1958).

This concluding volume is set at the turn of the century, in Adenville, Utah.

Mormons | UT

Flexner, Helen (1871–1956). *A Quaker Childhood* (Yale University, 1940).

To about 17–18 years.

Quakers | MD

Gold, Michael (born Irving Granich) (1894–1967). *Jews Without Money* (Liveright, 1930). (1984 rpt., Carroll & Graf).

City Life ✧ Jews | NYC (East Side)

Greene, Graham (1904–1991). *A Sort of Life* (Simon and Schuster, 1971).

Pages 12 to about 160 (chs. 2 to about 8).

Catholics ✧ Children's Authors ✧ Christian Converts ✧ Novelists ✧ Short Story Writers | England

Hagen, Lois (1881–living 1966). *Parish in the Pines* (Caxton, 1938).

Family Memoirs ✧ Frontier and Pioneer Life ✧ Missionaries | MN

Hale, Edward Everett (1822–1909). *A New England Boyhood and Other Bits of Autobiography* (Cassell, 1893; Little, Brown, 1900 [enlarged ed.]).

His granddaughter was Nancy Hale; see ch. 9 entry. See also "Dall, Caroline" (ch. 8).

Children's Authors ✧ Clergy ✧ Nineteenth-Century Pre-Industrial Age Memoirists ✧ Short Story Writers ✧ Unitarians | MA

Hannam, Charles (1925–). *A Boy in That Situation: An Autobiography* (Andre Deutsch, 1977) (Variant title, *A Boy in Your Situation* [Harper & Row, 1978]).

Verso page states: "The events described in this book are as true as the author's memory allows, but a number of names have been changed." The main character is named "Karl." By page 210, "Karl" is only about 17.

Growing Up Between WWI and WWII ✧ Jews | Germany ✧ England

Hayward, Helen Harry (1898?–). *The Other Foot* (Vantage, 1951).

Methodists I U.S. (Southeast)

Heller, Michael (1937–). *Living Root: A Memoir* (State University of New York, 2000).

Jews ✧ Poets I NYC (Brooklyn) ✧ FL

Hill, James Langdon (1848–1931). *My First Years as a Boy* (Andover, 1927).

He should not be confused with James Jerome Hill (1838–1916), the MN railroad magnate.

Clergy ✧ Farm Life ✧ Nineteenth-Century Pre-Industrial Age Memoirists I IA

Hoffman, William (1914–). *Those Were the Days* (T.S. Denison, 1957).

Growing Up Between WWI and WWII ✧ Jews I MN

Horowitz, Irving (1929–). *Daydreams and Nightmares: Reflections on a Harlem Childhood* (University Press of Mississippi, 1990).

African Americans ✧ Growing Up Between WWI and WWII ✧ Jews I NYC (Harlem)

Hunter, Rodello (pseud. of Rodello Calkins) (1920–). *A House of Many Rooms: A Family Memoir* (Knopf, 1965).

Growing Up Between WWI and WWII ✧ Mormons I UT

Jones, Rufus Matthew (1863–1948). *A Small-Town Boy* (Macmillan, 1941).

Quakers I ME

Kaufman, Alan (1952–). *Jew Boy: A Memoir* (Fromm International, 2000).

At least pages 3–345 (the book's first 3 sections); he may be over 21 in the section set in Israel.

Baby Boomers ✧ Jews ✧ Poets I NYC (Bronx) ✧ CO ✧ NE ✧ NYC (Lower East Side) ✧ Israel

Kingdon, Frank (1894–1972). *Jacob's Ladder: The Days of My Youth* (L.B. Fischer, 1943).

Clergy ✧ Educators ✧ Historians ✧ Journalists ✧ Victorian Era British Memoirists I England

Koehn, Ilse (1929–1991). *Mischling, Second Degree: My Childhood in Nazi Germany* (Greenwillow Books, 1977).

A substantial part of this memoir consists of re-created dialogue.

Growing Up Between WWI and WWII ✧ Hitler Youth Movement ✧ Jews I Germany

Lamont, Thomas (1870–1948). *My Boyhood in a Parsonage: Some Brief Sketches of American Life Toward the Close of the Last Century* (Harper & Brothers, 1946) (British edition published by Heinemann, 1945).

Pages 6 to about 186.

Clergy ✧ Harvard University ✧ Hudson River ✧ Phillips-Exeter Academy I NY ✧ NH ✧ MA

Levin, Shmarya (1867–1935). Tr. by Maurice Samuel. *Childhood in Exile* (Harcourt, Brace, 1929).

Covers his first 14 years.

Jews I Russia

Levin, Shmarya (1867–1935). Tr. by Maurice Samuel. *Youth in Revolt* (Harcourt, Brace, 1930).

Pages 3–185 (chs. 1–13) cover him from his teenage years to age 21.

Jews I Russia ✧ Germany

Levy, Harriet Lane (1867–1950). *920 O'Farrell Street: A Jewish Girlhood in Old San Francisco* (Doubleday, 1947).

City Life ✧ Jews | CA (Northern)

Lewis, C(live) S(taples) (1898–1963). *Surprised by Joy: The Shape of My Early Life* (Harcourt, Brace, 1955).

Christian Converts ✧ Critics (Literary) ✧ Novelists ✧ Poets ✧ Theological Writers | England

Maynard, Isabelle (1929–). *China Dreams: Growing Up Jewish in Tientsin* (University of Iowa, 1996).

Growing Up Between WWI and WWII ✧ Jews | China

Meyers, Odette (1934–). *Doors to Madame Marie* (University of Washington, 1997).

Aided by a concierge during the Holocaust, Meyers tells also of her affinity with Catholicism, though raised as a secular Jew.

Catholics ✧ Holocaust Survivors ✧ Jews | France

Moss, James (1875–1962). *Jimmy Moss* (Deseret Book, 1963).

Basketball ✧ Coaches (Athletic) ✧ Mormons | UT (?)

Newton, Louie DeVotie (1892–1986). *Why I Am a Baptist* (Thomas Nelson and Sons, 1957).

Pages 4 to about 75. He found his calling as a minister in Atlanta, GA.

Clergy ✧ Journalists | GA

Repplier, Agnes (1855?–1950). *In Our Convent Days* (Houghton Mifflin, 1905).

Catholics ✧ Nineteenth-Century Pre-Industrial Age Memoirists ✧ Nuns | PA

Rosen, Christine. *My Fundamentalist Education: A Memoir of a Divine Girlhood* (Public Affairs, 2005).

Set in St. Petersburg, Florida during the 1980s, this memoir traces the author's religious upbringing.

Fundamentalism (Christian) ✧ Generation X | FL

Salsitz, Norman (1920–), with Richard Skolnik. *A Jewish Boyhood in Poland: Remembering Kolbuszowa* (Syracuse University, 1992).

Captures life in Poland leading up to the Nazi invasion.

Growing Up Between WWI and WWII ✧ Immigrants ✧ Jews | Poland

Scheeres, Julia. *Jesus Land: A Memoir* (Counterpoint, 2005).

Scheeres and her 2 adopted brothers grew up in a Fundamentalist Christian community; they coped with various forms of abuse, including racism (she is white; her adopted brothers are black).

Abuse (Sexual) ✧ African Americans ✧ Brothers ✧ Family Violence ✧ Farm Life ✧ Fundamentalism (Christian) ✧ Generation X ✧ Racism | IN

Shapiro, Malkah (1895–). Tr. by Nehemia Polen. *The Rebbe's Daughter: Memoir of a Hasidic Childhood* (Jewish Publication Society, 2002).

Clergy ✧ Jews | Poland

Simmons, Thomas (1956–). *The Unseen Shore: Memories of a Christian Science Childhood* (Beacon, 1991).

Baby Boomers ✧ Christian Scientists ✧ Pilots ✧ Poets | PA

Smith, Charles Henry (1875–1948). *Mennonite Country Boy: The Early Years of C. Henry Smith* (Faith and Life, 1962).

Country Life ✧ Mennonites ✧ Spiritual Life | OH (?)

Smith, Hannah. *For Heaven's Sake* (Little, Brown, 1949).

This unusual memoir tells of her travels to revivalist camp meetings that she attended with her father, a minister.

Camps (Revivalist) ✧ True Believers | NE ✧ AZ ✧ CO ✧ CA

Sorensen, Virginia (1912–1991). *Where Nothing Is Long Ago: Memories of a Mormon Childhood* (Harcourt, Brace & World, 1963).

Growing Up Between WWI and WWII ✧ Mormons | UT

Spencer, Clarissa (1860–). *One Who Was Valiant* (Caxton, 1940).

She was a daughter of Brigham Young.

Mormons ✧ Young, Brigham | UT

Stivender, Ed (1946–). *Raised Catholic: Can You Tell?* (August House, 1992).

Focuses on his childhood; the following entry is its sequel.

Catholics ✧ Humorists | PA (Philadelphia)

Stivender, Ed (1946–). *Still Catholic After All These Fears* (August House, 1995).

Focuses on his adolescence.

Catholics ✧ Humorists | PA (Philadelphia)

Suberman, Stella (1922–). *The Jew Store: A Family Memoir* (Algonquin Books of Chapel Hill, 1998).

Covers 1922–1933. "Concordia" is a made-up name for her hometown.

Businesspersons ✧ Growing Up Between WWI and WWII ✧ Immigrants ✧ Jews ✧ Racism | TN

Tate, Sonsyrea. *Little X: Growing Up in the Nation of Islam* (HarperSanFrancisco, 1997).

She has been a journalist for the *Washington Post* and *Chicago Tribune*.

Generation X (?) ✧ Journalists ✧ Muslims | Washington, DC

Ten Boom, Corrie (1892–1983), with Carole C. Carlson. *In My Father's House: The Years Before "The Hiding Place"* (F.H. Revell, 1976).

Pages 23–95.

Clockmakers ✧ Holocaust Survivors ✧ Religious Leaders | Holland

Trobisch, Ingrid Hult (1926–). *On Our Way Rejoicing!* (Harper & Row, 1964).

Growing Up Between WWI and WWII ✧ Missionaries | Tanzania

Tulman, Victor David (c. 1900–), with Marcelle Routier. Tr. from the French by Eileen Finletter. *Going Home* (Times Books, 1977).

Jews | Hungary

Venable, William Henry (1836–1920). *A Buckeye Boyhood* (Robert Clarke, 1911).

Historians (Cultural) ✧ Intellectual Life ✧ Nineteenth-Century Pre-Industrial Age Memoirists ✧ Poets ✧ Quakers ✧ Teachers | OH

Vining, Elizabeth Gray (1902–1999). *Quiet Pilgrimage* (Lippincott, 1970).

Pages 16 to about 70.

Bryn Mawr ✧ Children's Authors ✧ Novelists ✧ Quakers ✧ Royalty ✧ Short Story Writers | PA

Williams, Elizabeth Whitney (1923–1984). *A Child of the Sea; and Life Among the Mormons* (Privately printed, 1905).

Growing Up Between WWI and WWII ✧ Mormons | MI

Willis, Janice Dean (1948–). *Dreaming Me: An African American Woman's Spiritual Journey* (Riverhead Books, 2001),

Except for 12 scattered pages, pages 6 to about 114 all focus on her first 21 years. She and her family marched with Martin Luther King Jr. in Birmingham, AL. She found spiritual strength in Buddhism.

African Americans ✧ Baby Boomers ✧ Baptists ✧ Buddhists ✧ Civil Rights Workers ✧ Cornell University ✧ Racism ✧ Spiritual Life | AL ✧ NY ✧ India ✧ Tibet

Spiritual Lives

Including the Psychically Gifted

Anonymous. *The Boy Who Saw True* (Neville Spearman, 1953) (1961 rpt., C.W. Daniel).

This boyhood diary's entries span January 1, 1885–October 20, 1887 (pages 11–203).

Diaries and Journals ✧ Spiritual Life | England

Asbury, Herbert (1891–1963). *Up from Methodism . . .* (Knopf, 1926).

The first 167 pages cover his first 16 years. This book tells of his breaking away from Methodism during his youth.

Spiritual Life | MO

Eby, Kermit (1903–1962). *For Brethren Only* (Brethren Press, 1958).

About 77 pages (between 29 and 219).

Mennonites ✧ Spiritual Life | IN

Eliade, Mircea (1907–1986). Tr. from the Romanian by Mac Linscott Ricketts. *Autobiography: Volume I, 1907–1937: Journey East, Journey West* (University of Chicago, 1981).

Pages 5 to about 154.

Historians (Religious) ✧ Novelists ✧ Philosophers ✧ Spiritual Life | Romania

Iacuzzo, Terry (1948–). *Small Mediums at Large: The True Tale of a Family of Psychics* (Putnam, 2004).

Cosmo Girl! columnist Iacuzzo, in this highly entertaining memoir, tells of growing up in a family of psychics in Buffalo, NY from the 1950s to the 1970s.

Baby Boomers ✧ Brothers ✧ Drug Abuse ✧ Family Memoirs ✧ Hippies ✧ Italian Americans ✧ Journalists ✧ Occult ✧ Spiritual Life | NY ✧ NYC

Masson, Jeffrey Moussaieff (1941–). *My Father's Guru: A Journey Through Spirituality and Disillusion* (Addison-Wesley, 1993).

His father, Paul Brunton (1898–1961), was a journalist who wrote books on metaphysics regarding yoga and Eastern religions.

Spiritual Life | India ✧ Uruguay

McGahern, John (1934–2006). *All Will Be Well: A Memoir* (Knopf, 2006) (Originally published as *Memoir* [Faber & Faber, 2005]).

The eldest of 7 children, the author grew up in rural Ireland, in a household torn by his father's violence. McGahern's mother died of cancer when he was 9. This memoir traces his intent to become a priest, before he turned to writing as a vocation.

Bereavement ✧ Books and Reading ✧ Cancer ✧ Catholics ✧ Country Life ✧ Family Violence ✧ Novelists ✧ Short Story Writers ✧ Spiritual Life | Ireland

Reid, Forrest (1876–1947). *Apostate* (Constable, 1926).

Critics (Literary) ✧ Novelists ✧ Spiritual Life ✧ Victorian Era British Memoirists | England

Schimmels, Cliff. *Lessons from the Good Old Days* (Victor Books, 1994).

Spiritual Life | OK

Scholem, Gershom (1897–1982). Tr. from the German by Harry Zohn. *From Berlin to Jerusalem: Memories of My Youth* (Schocken Books, 1980).

Intellectual Life ✧ Jews ✧ Spiritual Life | Germany

Sprigg, June (1953–). *Simple Gifts: A Memoir of a Shaker Village* (Knopf, 1998).

She describes how the summer of 1972, which she spent as a museum tour guide in the Shaker community of Canterbury, NH, changed her life.

Baby Boomers ✧ Shakers ✧ Summer ✧ Spiritual Life | NH

Trungpa, Chogyam (1939–1987), as told to Esmé Cramer Roberts. *Born in Tibet* (Harcourt, Brace & World, 1966).

This memoir describes his years of religious training. He was the first Tibetan monk to teach English in the West; also, he founded the Naropa Institute.

Buddhists ✧ Lamas ✧ Spiritual Life ✧ Teachers | Tibet

Wakefield, Dan (1932–). *Returning: A Spiritual Journey* (Doubleday, 1988).

About 85 pages (mostly from 31 to about 111).

Columbia College ✧ Editors ✧ Journalists ✧ Novelists ✧ Screenwriters ✧ Spiritual Life | IN ✧ NYC

Cult Followers and Groupies

Des Barres, Pamela (1948–). *I'm with the Band: Confessions of a Groupie* (Beech Tree Books, 1987).

Covers her first 22 years.

Baby Boomers ✧ Groupies ✧ Musicians | CA (Southern)

Noyes, Pierrepont (1870–1959). *My Father's House: An Oneida Boyhood* (Farrar & Rinehart, 1937).

Pages 21–308 cover his first 16 years. He details life during the final years of the Oneida Community, a communal religious sect founded by his father, John Humphrey (1811–1886).

Cults ✧ Homes and Haunts | NY

Sullivan, Caroline (1958–). *Bye Bye Baby: My Tragic Love Affair with the Bay City Rollers* (Bloomsbury, 1999).

Baby Boomers ✧ Groupies | NJ

Historians

See entries in chapter 9 in the sections "Biographers" for memoirs by biographers and "Folklorists and Storytellers" for memoirs by folklorists.

Brown, Dee (1908–2002). *When the Century Was Young: A Writer's Notebook* (August House, 1993).

He is best known for his history *Bury My Heart at Wounded Knee: An Indian History of the American West* (Holt, Rinehart and Winston, 1970). The fiction and nonfiction of this writer focus on the American West.

Children's Authors ✧ Folklorists ✧ Historians ✧ Librarians ✧ Novelists | AR

Carroll, Gladys Hasty (1904–1999). *Only Fifty Years Ago* (Little, Brown, 1962).

She wrote regional fiction and works of history associated with ME.

Bates College ✧ Historians ✧ Novelists | NH

Carroll, Gladys Hasty (1904–1999). *To Remember Forever: The Journal of a College Girl 1922–1923* (Little, Brown, 1963).

Bates College ✧ College Life ✧ Diaries and Journals ✧ Historians ✧ Novelists | ME

Catton, (Charles) Bruce (1899–1978). *Waiting for the Morning Train: An American Boyhood* (Doubleday, 1972).

He wrote many histories of the Civil War. For a similar memoir, see "Dunbar, Willis F(rederick)" (this ch.).

Historians (Military) | MI

Cobb, Richard (1917–1996). *Still Life: Sketches from a Tunbridge Wells Childhood* (Chatto & Windus, 1983).

He grew up in a mostly middle class community.

Growing Up Between WWI and WWII ✧ Historians | England

Corke, Helen (1882–1978). *In Our Infancy: An Autobiography* (Cambridge University, 1975).

Historians ✧ Victorian Era British Memoirists | England

Dunbar, Willis F(rederick) (1902–1970). *How It Was in Hartford: An Affectionate Account of a Michigan Small Town in the Early Years of the Twentieth Century* (Eerdmans, 1968).

For a similar memoir, see "Catton, Bruce" (this ch.).

Historians | MI

Fraser, Ronald (1930–). *In Search of a Past: The Rearing of an English Gentleman: 1933–1945* (Atheneum, 1984) (British title, *In Search of a Past: The Manor House, Amnersfeld, 1933–1945* [Verso, 1984]).

From 50 to 70 scattered pages (between 9 and 85) focus on his youth.

Civil War (Spanish) ✧ Growing Up Between WWI and WWII ✧ Historians ✧ Homes and Haunts ✧ Journalists | Germany

Friesel, Evyatar (1930–). *The Days and the Seasons: Memoirs* (Wayne State University, 1996).

Historians (Religious) ✧ Holocaust Survivors ✧ Jews ✧ Refugees | Germany ✧ Brazil ✧ Israel

Furnas, J(oseph) C(hamberlain) (1905–2001). *My Life in Writing: Memoirs of a Maverick* (W. Morrow, 1989).
Pages 21 to about 142.
Biographers ✧ Historians (Cultural) | IN ✧ MA

Gay, Peter (Jack) (born Peter Froehlich) (1923–). *My German Question: Growing Up in Nazi Berlin* (Yale University, 1998).
His spouse is Ruth Gay (see following entry).
Growing Up Between WWI and WWII ✧ Historians (Cultural) | Germany ✧ NYC (?)

Gay, Ruth (1922–). *Unfinished People: Eastern European Jews* (W.W. Norton, 1996).
Her spouse is Peter Gay (see preceding entry). About 193 scattered pages (43–268).
City Life ✧ Growing Up Between WWI and WWII ✧ Historians (Cultural) ✧ Jews | NYC (Bronx)

Gilbert, Felix (1905–1991). *A European Past* (W.W. Norton, 1988).
Pages 3–78 (scattered pages).
College Teachers ✧ Historians | Germany

Goodwin, Doris Kearns (1943–). *Wait till Next Year: Recollections of a '50s Girlhood* (Simon and Schuster, 1997).
Baseball ✧ Historians | NY (Long Island)

Halivni, David Weiss (1928–). *The Book and the Sword: A Life of Learning in the Throes of Destruction* (Farrar, Straus, and Giroux, 1996).
About the first 80 pages, starting on page 5.
Historians (Religious) ✧ Holocaust Survivors ✧ Jews | Romania ✧ Hungary

Kaplan, Alice (1954–). *French Lessons: A Memoir* (University of Chicago, 1993).
About pages 3–103.
Baby Boomers ✧ College Teachers ✧ French (Language) ✧ Historians (Cultural) ✧ Intellectual Life | MN ✧ Switzerland ✧ France

Love, Edmund G. (1912–1990). *The Situation in Flushing* (Harper & Row, 1965).
Set in about 1920. See following entry for the sequel.
Education ✧ Growing Up Between WWI and WWII ✧ Historians (Military) ✧ Journalists ✧ Railroad Travel | MI

Love, Edmund G. (1912–1990). *Hanging On; Or, How to Get Through a Depression and Enjoy Life* (W. Morrow, 1972).
Covers him from 17–22 years (up to about page 178).
Depressions (Economic) ✧ Education ✧ Growing Up Between WWI and WWII ✧ Historians (Military) ✧ Journalists | MI ✧ MO

Mangione, Jerre (Geraldo) (1909–1998). *Mount Allegro* (Houghton Mifflin, 1942).
Written in novelistic style, this memoir of growing up in Rochester, NY, is by the author of the unique study *The Dream and the Deal: The Federal Writers' Project, 1935–1943* (Little, Brown, 1972) .
Family Memoirs ✧ Historians (Cultural) ✧ Italian Americans | NY

Mann, Golo (1909–1994). Tr. by Krishna Winston. *Reminiscences and Reflections: A Youth in Germany* (Faber & Faber, 1990).

He was the third of 6 sons of novelist Thomas Mann, nephew of novelist Heinrich Mann, and brother of Klaus Mann (see ch. 16 entry).

Historians ✧ Mann, Heinrich ✧ Mann, Thomas I Germany

Morison, Samuel Eliot (1887–1976). *One Boy's Boston, 1887–1901* (Houghton Mifflin, 1962).

Biographers ✧ College Teachers ✧ High Society ✧ Historians ✧ Seafaring Life I MA

Sante, Luc (1954–). *The Factory of Facts* (Granta, 1998).

About 105 scattered pages.

Historians (Cultural) I Belgium ✧ NJ

Schlesinger, Arthur, Jr. (1917–2007). *A Life in the 20th Century: Innocent Beginnings, 1917–1950* (Houghton Mifflin, 2000).

Pages 24–217. He was married to Marian Schlesinger (see ch. 10 entry).

Growing Up Between WWI and WWII ✧ Historians I MA

Van Loon, Hendrik Willem (1882–1944). *Report to Saint Peter: Upon the Kind of World in Which Hendrik Van Loon Spent the First Years of His Life* (Simon and Schuster, 1947).

Unfinished at the time of his death, this memoir covers only the author's Rotterdam boyhood.

College Teachers ✧ Foreign Correspondents ✧ Historians ✧ Illustrators ✧ Journalists I Netherlands

Journalists

Including Radio and Television Journalists

See entries in the section "Talk Shows Hosts and Broadcast Media Commentators and Interviewers," in chapter 11 for memoirs involving those media figures.

Alexander, Shana (1925–2005). *Happy Days: My Mother, My Father, My Sister & Me* (Doubleday, 1995).

Some 110 scattered pages (8–209). In 1951 she became the first female staff member for *Life* magazine. Also as an adult, she appeared on the "Point/Counterpoint" segment of the television program *60 Minutes*.

Camps ✧ City Life ✧ Family Memoirs ✧ Feminists ✧ Growing Up Between WWI and WWII ✧ Journalists I NYC

Baker, Russell (1925–). *Growing Up* (Congdon & Weed, 1982).

Pages 1 to about 234. This book was awarded the 1982 Pulitzer Prize for Biography/Autobiography. For a similar memoir, see "Dabney, Virginia Bell" (ch. 3).

Growing Up Between WWI and WWII ✧ Journalists I VA ✧ NJ ✧ MD

Brokaw, Tom (1940–). *A Long Way from Home: Growing Up in the American Heartland* (Pimlico, 2002).

Covers his first 22 years. This former (1982–2004) anchor of *NBC Nightly News* paints a vivid and honest portrait of growing up on the northern plains.

Broadcast Journalists ✧ Racism I SD

Canby, Henry Seidel (1878–1961). *Alma Mater; the Gothic Age of the American College* (Farrar & Rinehart, 1936).

About 75 pages. He was a prolific writer on American literary history. See ch. 9 for the prequel.

College Teachers ✧ Critics (Literary) ✧ Editors ✧ Education ✧ Episcopalians ✧ Essayists ✧ Intellectual Life ✧ Journalists ✧ Quakers ✧ Teachers ✧ Yale University | DE ✧ CT

Collier, Richard (1924–). *A House Called Memory* (E.P. Dutton, 1961).

He edited *Town and Country* magazine.

Editors ✧ Foreign Correspondents ✧ Growing Up Between WWI and WWII ✧ Historians (Military) ✧ Homes and Haunts ✧ Journalists | England

Connor, Lawrence S(tanton) (1925–). *Hampton Court: Growing Up Catholic in Indianapolis Between the Wars* (Guild Press of Indiana, 1995).

Catholics ✧ Editors ✧ Growing Up Between WWI and WWII ✧ Journalists | IN

Cronkite, Walter (1916–). *A Reporter's Life* (Knopf, 1996).

Pages 9 to about 76 (most of chs. 1–3).

Broadcast Journalists ✧ Foreign Correspondents ✧ Growing Up Between WWI and WWII | MO ✧ TX ✧ OK

Crume, Paul (1912–1975). *A Texan at Bay* (McGraw-Hill, 1961).

As an adult, he was a newspaper columnist.

Growing Up Between WWI and WWII ✧ Journalists | TX (West)

Cummings, Florence (pseud. of Florence Bonime) (1907–). *Yesterday* (Marshall Jones, 1936).

Editors | New England

Davis, Paxton (1925–1994). *Being a Boy* (J.F. Blair, 1988).

Growing Up Between WWI and WWII ✧ Journalists | NC

Davis, Paxton (1925–1994). *A Boy's War* (J.F. Blair, 1990).

Army, U.S. ✧ Journalists ✧ Military Life | VA ✧ Mexico ✧ India

Dovlatov, Sergei (1941–1990). Tr. from the Russian by Anne Frydman. *Ours: A Russian Family Album* (Weidenfeld & Nicolson, 1989) (Originally published in Russian, 1983).

He emigrated to the U.S. in 1978.

Journalists ✧ Novelists | Soviet Union (i.e., Russia)

Duffus, R(obert) L(uther) (1888–1972). *Nostalgia USA; or, If You Don't Like the 1960's, Why Don't You Go Back to Where You Came From?* (W.W. Norton, 1963).

Life in Vermont in 1900, through the eyes of a boy of 12.

Country Life ✧ Journalists | VT

Duffus, R(obert) L(uther) (1888–1972). *The Innocents at Cedro; A Memoir of Thorstein Veblen and Some Others* (Macmillan, 1944).

Set in 1907–1908, when he was 19.

Intellectual Life ✧ Journalists ✧ Stanford University | CA (Northern)

Duffus, R(obert) L(uther) (1888–1972). *Williamstown Branch: Impersonal Memories of a Vermont Boyhood* (W.W. Norton, 1958).

Set in 1898. For a similar autobiographical series, see "Paul, Elliot" (this ch.).

Country Life ✧ Journalists I VT

Duffus, R(obert) L(uther) (1888–1972). *Waterbury Record: More Vermont Memories* (W.W. Norton, 1959).

Set in 1906, the year between his high school graduation and his first year of college.

Country Life ✧ Journalists I VT

Fowler, Gene (pseud. of Eugene Devlan) (1890–1960). *A Solo in Tom Toms: The Story of a Rocky Mountain Boyhood and the Quest for a Father* (Viking, 1946).

Pages 35 to about 265 (chs. 5–20). (His 1931 memoir of the same title, published by Covici, Friede, contains only 30 pages.)

Fatherless Families ✧ Journalists I CO

Gilder, Jeanette (1849–1916). *The Autobiography of a Tomboy* (Doubleday, Page, 1901).

Journalists ✧ Nineteenth-Century Pre-Industrial Age Memoirists I NY (Long Island)

Hentoff, Nat(han) (1925–). *Boston Boy* (Knopf, 1986).

About the first 145 pages.

Critics (Music) ✧ Growing Up Between WWI and WWII ✧ Journalists I MA

Hunter-Gault, Charlayne (1942–). *In My Place* (Farrar, Straus, and Giroux, 1992).

Pages 3–246 (ch. 19).

African Americans ✧ Broadcast Journalists ✧ College Teachers I SC ✧ AK ✧ GA

Huntley, Chet (1911–1974). *The Generous Years: Remembrances of a Frontier Boyhood* (Random House, 1968).

Broadcast Journalists ✧ Ranch Life I MT

Johnston, Jill (1929–). *Mother Bound: Autobiography in Search of a Father: Vol. 1* (Knopf, 1983).

About 50–59 pages.

Critics (Art) ✧ Critics (Dance) ✧ Feminists ✧ Growing Up Between WWI and WWII ✧ Journalists ✧ Lesbians ✧ Schizophrenia I England

Kern, Janet (1924–1998). *Yesterday's Child* (Lippincott, 1962).

Broadcasters ✧ Growing Up Between WWI and WWII ✧ Radio Journalists I IL

Lancaster, Bob (1943–). *Going Down for Gum Wrappers* (August House, 1986).

This is a light memoir, unlike the more widely publicized book he wrote with B.C. Hall, *Judgment Day* (Seaview/Putnam, 1983), which chronicles the reign of terror waged on Skidmore, MO, by Ken Rex McElroy, whose own murder was never solved.

College Teachers ✧ Journalists I AR

Lehrer, Jim (1934–). *A Bus of My Own* (Putnam, 1992).

Only about pages 11–61 focus on his first 21 years. He is PBS's veteran evening news anchor.

Broadcast Journalists ✧ Buses ✧ Editors ✧ Novelists I KS

Lehrer, Jim (1934–). *We Were Dreamers* (Atheneum, 1975).

This is a companion volume to *A Bus of My Own* (previous entry). This book covers a year (July, 1946–July, 1947) in the author's life, as he accompanied his father on his bus routes. (Mr. Lehrer's father ran his own independent bus company.) This is a lighthearted memoir with much re-created dialogue.

Broadcast Journalists ✧ Buses ✧ Editors ✧ Novelists I KS

Lyden, Jacki (1954–). *Daughter of the Queen of Sheba* (Houghton Mifflin, 1997).

Pages 1 to about 150. (She is not to be confused with the journalist and memoirist Susan Gordon Lydon [1943–2005].)

Baby Boomers ✧ Children of the Mentally Ill ✧ Foreign Correspondents ✧ Radio Journalists I WI (?) ✧ IN

MacNeil, Robert (1931–). *Wordstruck: A Memoir* (Viking, 1989).

Nearly all of the first 7 chapters (pages 1–205).

Books and Reading ✧ Broadcast Journalists ✧ Philologists I Canada (Nova Scotia)

May, Lee. *In My Father's Garden* (Longstreet, 1995).

Pages 7–70.

Fathers and Sons ✧ Gardeners ✧ Journalists

Maynard, Joyce (1953–). *Looking Back: A Chronicle of Growing Up Old in the Sixties* (Doubleday, 1973).

Covers her from about 9 to about 20 years.

Baby Boomers ✧ Journalists I NH

Maynard, Joyce (1953–). *At Home in the World: A Memoir* (Picador USA/St. Martin's, 1998).

A sequel to the preceding entry, this memoir chronicles her love affair with the reclusive fiction writer J. D. Salinger.

Baby Boomers ✧ Journalists ✧ Salinger, J .D. I NH

Mencken, H(enry) L(ouis) (1880–1956). *Happy Days* (Knopf, 1940).

Journalists I MD

Miller, Max (1899–1967). *The Beginning of a Mortal* (E.P. Dutton, 1933).

This and the following memoir cover Miller's boyhood years.

Country Life ✧ Journalists ✧ Travel Writers I WA ✧ MT

Miller, Max (1899–1967). *Shinny On Your Side: And Other Memories of Growing Up* (Doubleday, 1958).

Covers about his first 18 years. He is best known for his memoir on his adult years, *I Cover the Waterfront* (E.P. Dutton, 1932).

Country Life ✧ Journalists ✧ Travel Writers I WA ✧ MT

Morris, Willie (1934–1999). *North Toward Home* (Houghton Mifflin, 1967).

More than the first 3rd of this 438-page work focuses on his youth.

Editors ✧ Journalists I MS ✧ TX (?)

Morris, Willie (1934–1999). *Good Old Boy: A Delta Boyhood* (Harper & Row, 1971).

This memoir has the light flavor and themes of Richard Bissell's (mainly adult) memoir *My Life on the Mississippi: Or, Why I Am Not Mark Twain* (Little, Brown, 1973), as well as the youthful memoirs of Jean Shepherd (ch. 11) and Mark Twain (ch. 11). This book was adapted as a film in 1988. Morris was editor of *Harpers* magazine.

> Editors ✧ Humorists ✧ Journalists ✧ Mississippi River | MS

Morris, Willie (1934–1999). *My Dog Skip* (Random House, 1995).

> Pages 3–120. This memoir focuses on his boyhood relationship with his pet. It was adapted as a 2000 film.

> Dogs ✧ Editors ✧ Journalists | MS

Muggeridge, Malcolm (1903–1990). *Chronicles of Wasted Time: Chronicle 1: The Green Stick* (W. Morrow, 1972).

> Covers his first 30 years.

> Clergy ✧ Editors ✧ Journalists ✧ Novelists | England

Murray, William (1926–). *Janet, My Mother, and Me: A Memoir of Growing Up with Janet Flanner and Natalia Danesi Murray* (Simon and Schuster, 2000).

> About 107 scattered pages (23–147).

> Danesi, Natalia ✧ Editors ✧ Flanner, Janet ✧ Foreign Correspondents ✧ Growing Up Between WWI and WWII ✧ Harvard University ✧ Mothers and Sons ✧ Novelists ✧ Singers | Italy ✧ NYC ✧ CA (Southern: Hollywood) ✧ MA

O'Faolain, Nuala (1945–). *Are You Somebody: The Accidental Memoir of a Dublin Woman* (H. Holt, 1996).

> About 72 pages between 14 and 92.

> Books and Reading ✧ Intellectual Life ✧ Journalists | Ireland (North)

Paul, Elliot (1891–1958). *Linden on the Saugus Branch* (Random House, 1947).

> This nostalgic reminiscence covers his boyhood, growing up outside Boston. It is the 1st volume in Paul's autobiographical series Items on the Grand Account. For a similar sequence, see the entries by R(obert) L(uther) Duffus (this ch.).

> Civil War (Spanish) ✧ Foreign Correspondents ✧ Journalists ✧ Novelists ✧ Screenwriters ✧ Travel Writers | MA

Paul, Elliot (1891–1958). *Ghost Town on the Yellowstone* (Random House, 1948).

> Focuses on him at about 16–17 years.

> Civil War (Spanish) ✧ Foreign Correspondents ✧ Journalists ✧ Novelists ✧ Screenwriters ✧ Travel Writers | MT

Paul, Elliot (1891–1958). *My Old Kentucky Home* (Random House, 1949).

> Focuses on him at about age 19.

> Civil War (Spanish) ✧ Foreign Correspondents ✧ Journalists Novelists ✧ Screenwriters | KY

Paul, Elliot (1891–1958). *Desperate Scenery* (Random House, 1954).

> Focuses on him at about age 19. This volume concludes the series.

> Civil War (Spanish) ✧ Foreign Correspondents ✧ Journalists ✧ Novelists ✧ Screenwriters ✧ Travel Writers | WY ✧ ID

Prescott, Peter S. (1935–2004). *A Darkening Green: Notes from the Silent Generation* (Coward, McCann & Geoghegan, 1974).

> Diary entries are linked by narrative passages.

> Books and Reading ✧ College Life ✧ Critics (Literary) ✧ Diaries and Journals ✧ Journalists ✧ Teachers | MA

Rather, Dan (1931–), with Peter Wyden. *I Remember* (Little, Brown, 1991).
Rather anchored the *CBS Evening News* (1981–2006).
Broadcast Journalists ✧ Oil Fields ✧ Ranch Life | TX

Roberts, Steven (1943–). *My Fathers' Houses: Memoir of a Family* (W. Morrow, 2005).
Husband of political analyst Cokie Roberts, the author tells of his youth growing up in NJ during the 1940s–1950s.
Divorce ✧ Family Memoirs ✧ Fathers and Sons ✧ Grandfathers ✧ Jews ✧ Journalists ✧ Polio | NJ

Sangster, Margaret (1838–1912). *An Autobiography: From My Youth Up: Personal Reminiscences* (F.H. Revell, 1909) (1980 rpt., Arno, *From My Youth Up*).
The first 12 chapters (through page 163). She grew up as the daughter of a Methodist minister.
Clergy ✧ Editors ✧ Essayists ✧ Journalists ✧ Nineteenth-Century Pre-Industrial Age Memoirists | NJ

Shirer, William L. (1904–1993). *The Start, 1904–30* (Bantam Books, 1992).
Foreign Correspondents ✧ Journalists ✧ Novelists | IL (Chicago) (?) ✧ IA

Simpson, John (1944–). *Days from a Different World: A Memoir of Childhood* (Macmillan, 2005).
Broadcast Journalists ✧ Foreign Correspondents | England

Sobol, Louis (1896–1986). *Some Days Were Happy* (Random House, 1947).
He was a noted Broadway columnist.
Editors ✧ Journalists | CT

St. Johns, Adela Rogers (1894–1988). *Final Verdict* (Doubleday, 1962).
St. Johns, who idealized her lawyer father, describes her early years tagging along with him, from courtrooms to whorehouses. As an adult, she received the Medal of Freedom for her lifelong journalistic contributions. Besides this account, she wrote 2 other autobiographies: *The Honeycomb* (Doubleday, 1969) and *Love, Laughter, and Tears: My Hollywood Story* (Doubleday, 1978).
Biographers ✧ College Teachers ✧ Divorce ✧ Dramatists ✧ Fathers and Daughters ✧ Journalists ✧ Novelists ✧ Short Story Writers ✧ Spiritual Life | CA (Southern: Hollywood)

Toomer, "Buffalo" George (1942?–). *Before I Forget: '50s Reflections Through a Jaded Eye* (Little, Brown, 1991).
Contains much social history minutiae about 1950s middle class life.
Humorists ✧ Journalists | TX

Wright, Lawrence (1947–). *In the New World; Growing Up with America, 1960–1984* (Knopf, 1984).
Pages 8 to about 89; much of this subordinates details of his personal life to discussion of the country's political climate.
Baby Boomers ✧ Journalists | TX

Ybarra, T(homas) R(ussell) (1880–1971). *Young Man of Caracas* (I. Washburn, 1941).
Journalists | Venezuela (?)

Reformers and Activists

Including Abolitionists, Civil Rights Workers, Counterculture Society, Anarchists, Beat Generation, Communists, Draft Resisters, Feminists, Hate Groups, Hippies and Other Pacifists, Labor Unions and Leaders, and Social Workers

Adler, Margot (1946–). *Heretic's Heart: A Journey Through Spirit and Revolution* (Beacon, 1997).
Pages 27 to about 158. She was a 1960s antiwar activist and is the daughter of psychiatrist Alfred Adler.
Radio Journalists ✧ Spiritual Life I NYC (?)

Alpert, Jane (1947–). *Growing Up Underground* (W. Morrow, 1981).
About the first 100 pages.
Baby Boomers ✧ City Life ✧ Revolutionaries I NYC

Baez, Joan (1941–). *Daybreak* (Dial, 1968).
She was involved in nonviolent Vietnam era protests.
Reformers ✧ Singers ✧ Vietnam Conflict I NYC (Staten Island) ✧ MA

Bamford, Samuel (1788–1872). *Early Days: The Autobiography of Samuel Bamford* (Simpkin, Marshall, 1849).
More than the first 200 pages.
Eighteenth-Century Memoirists ✧ Poets ✧ Reformers I England

Bell, Susan Groag (1928?–). *Between Worlds in Czechoslovakia, England, and America* (E.P. Dutton, 1991).
College Teachers ✧ Feminists ✧ Gardeners ✧ Growing Up Between WWI and WWII ✧ Historians ✧ Immigrants I Czechoslovakia ✧ England

Binns, Archie (1899?–1971). *The Roaring Land* (R.M. McBride, 1942).
Some 70 scattered pages.
College Teachers ✧ Farm Life ✧ Historians ✧ Journalists ✧ Novelists I WA

Blackwell, Alice (1857–1950). Ed. by Marlene Deahl Merrill. *Growing Up in Boston's Gilded Age: The Journal of Alice Stone Blackwell, 1872–1874* (Yale University, 1990).
From 14 to 16 years. Her mother was suffragist lecturer Lucy Stone. She edited *Woman's Journal* for 35 years.
Diaries and Journals ✧ Editors ✧ Feminists ✧ Nineteenth-Century Pre-Industrial Age Memoirists ✧ Reformers I MA

Bonner, Elena (1923–). Tr. by Antonina W. Bouis. *Mothers and Daughters* (Knopf, 1992).
This work focuses mostly on her at age 14, with some of the memoir on her childhood and some up to age 19. As an adult, she was married to Nobel Prize winner Andrei Sakharov and advocated democratic reform of the Soviet Union.
Anti-Communist Movements ✧ Government Officials ✧ Growing Up Between WWI and WWII ✧ High Society ✧ Mothers and Daughters ✧ Reformers ✧ Wealth I Soviet Union (i.e., Russia)

Brittain, Vera (1893–1970). *Testament of Youth: An Autobiographical Study of the Years 1900–1925* (Macmillan, 1933).

More than 100 pages. As an adult, she was very active in trying to prevent England from entering WWII.

Feminists ✧ Lecturers ✧ Novelists ✧ Nurses ✧ Oxford University ✧ Pacifists ✧ Victorian Era British Memoirists ✧ WWI | England

Brody, Leslie (1952–). Red Star Sister: Between Madness and Utopia (Hungry Mind, 1998).

A 20th-century activist, she grew up on Long Island and later traveled throughout the U.S. and Europe, protesting U.S. involvement in Vietnam.

Baby Boomers ✧ Pacifists ✧ Vietnam Conflict | NY (Long Island) ✧ U.S. ✧ Europe

Brown, Rachel Manija (c. 1975–). *All the Fishes Come Home to Roost: A Memoir* (Rodale, 2005).

When very young, she moved from Los Angeles to India with her parents, who were followers of Meher Baba (sometimes said to be the coiner of the phrase, "Don't worry—Be happy!"). As an adult, she is a screenwriter.

Dramatists ✧ Generation X ✧ Hippies | India

Brown, Rita Mae (1944–). *Rita Will: Memoir of a Literary Rabble-Rouser* (Bantam Books, 1997).

Pages 1 to about 200.

Dramatists ✧ Feminists ✧ Lesbians ✧ Novelists | PA ✧ FL (?)

Bullock, Jim (1903–). *Bowers Row: Recollections of a Mining Village* (E.P. Pub., 1976).

He was a trade union leader.

Miners | England

Calisher, Hortense (1911–living 2007). *Herself* (Arbor House, 1972).

Probably no more than 50–70 scattered pages focus on her first 21 years; the following entry is a companion volume.

City Life ✧ College Teachers ✧ Jews ✧ Novelists ✧ Short Story Writers ✧ Social Workers | NYC

Calisher, Hortense (1911–living 2007). *Kissing Cousins* (Weidenfeld & Nicolson, 1988).

Pages 3–52 and a few pages after page 93 focus on her first 21 years.

City Life ✧ College Teachers ✧ Jews ✧ Novelists ✧ Short Story Writers ✧ Social Workers | NYC

Cooper, Aimee. *Coloring Outside the Lines: A Punk Rock Memoir* (Rowdy's, 2003).

She describes life within the punk rock culture of the early 1980s.

Generation X (?) ✧ Punk Rock | CA (Southern: Los Angeles)

Dall, Caroline (1822–1912). *"Alongside": Being Notes Suggested by "A New England Boyhood" of Doctor Edward Everett Hale* (Thomas Dodd, 1900).

She wrote or edited more than 12 books. See also "Hale, Nancy" (ch. 9).

Editors ✧ Essayists ✧ Feminists ✧ Hale, Edward Everett ✧ Lecturers ✧ Nineteenth-Century Pre-Industrial Age Memoirists ✧ Teachers ✧ Wealth | MA

De Beauvoir, Simone (1908–1986). Tr. from the French by James Kirkup. *Memoirs of a Dutiful Daughter* (World, 1959) (First published in French, 1958).

Feminists | France

Devlin, Bernadette (1947–). *The Price of My Soul* (Pan Books, 1969).

Baby Boomers ✧ Catholics ✧ Revolutionaries | Ireland (North)

Djilas, Milovan (1911–1995). *Land Without Justice* (Harcourt Brace Jovanovich, 1958).
As an adult, he helped to organize the Yugoslav Communist Party.

Communists ✧ Novelists ✧ Short Story Writers ✧ Translators | Yugoslavia

Douglass, Frederick (1817–1895). *Life and Times of Frederick Douglass* (C.K. Paul, 1881).
Pages 27 to about 214 are on his first 21 years; this represents all 21 chapters of the "First Part" and some or all of the first 2 chapters of the 19 chapters that constitute the "Second Part." In addition to the following 2 entries, see memoir by Douglass in chapter 6.

African Americans ✧ Nineteenth-Century Pre-Industrial Age Memoirists ✧ Racism ✧ Reformers ✧ Slavery | MD

Douglass, Frederick (1817–1895). *My Bondage and My Freedom* (Miller, Orton & Mulligan, 1855).
More than 100 pages focus on his first 21 years.

African Americans ✧ Nineteenth-Century Pre-Industrial Age Memoirists ✧ Racism ✧ Reformers ✧ Slavery | MD

Douglass, Frederick (1817–1895). *Narrative of the Life of Frederick Douglass, an American Slave* (Anti-slavery Office, 1845).
In the Library of America 1994 ed., pages 15 to about 96 focus on his first 21 years.

African Americans ✧ Nineteenth-Century Pre-Industrial Age Memoirists ✧ Racism ✧ Reformers ✧ Slavery | MD

Durr, Virginia Foster (1903–1999). Ed. by Hollinger F. Barnard. *Outside the Magic Circle: The Autobiography of Virginia Foster Durr* (University of Alabama, 1985).
About 60 pages. She was sister-in-law of U.S. Supreme Court Justice Hugo Black.

African Americans ✧ Civil Rights Workers ✧ Wealth | AL ✧ NYC ✧ MA

El Saadawi, Nawal. Tr. by Sherif Hetata. *A Daughter of Isis: The Autobiography of Nawal El Saadawi* (Zed Books, 1999).

Feminists ✧ Muslims | Egypt

Faderman, Lillian (1940–). *Naked in the Promised Land* (University of Wisconsin, 2003).

Children of Immigrants ✧ College Teachers ✧ Feminists ✧ Jews ✧ Lesbians ✧ Strippers | CA (Southern: Los Angeles) ✧ CA (Northern)

Farnham, Eliza (1815–1864). *My Early Days* (Thatcher & Hutchinson, 1859) (Variant title, *Eliza Woodson; or, The Early Days of the World's Workers* [A.J. Davis, 1864]).
Pages 13–121 are about her from 7 to 10 years; she seems to be only finishing high school at memoir's end.

Adoptees ✧ Nineteenth-Century Pre-Industrial Age Memoirists ✧ Reformers ✧ Uncles | England

Flynn, Elizabeth Gurley (1890–1964). *The Rebel Girl: An Autobiography: My First Life (1906–1926)* (International, 1973) (Variant title, *I Speak My Own Piece: Autobiography of "The Rebel Girl"* [Masses & Mainstream, 1955]).
Pages 33–126.

Communists ✧ Labor Leaders and Unions | NH ✧ OH ✧ NYC

Fraser, Joelle (1966–). *Territory of Men: A Memoir* (Villard, 2002).
She tells of her rootless childhood, growing up with a mother involved with one man after another.

Children of Alcoholics ✧ Fatherless Families ✧ Generation X ✧ Hippies | CA (Northern) ✧ HI ✧ OR

Golden, Harry (b. Harry Goldhurst) (1902–1981). *For 2 Cents Plain* (World, 1959).
Some 55 scattered pages focus on his first 21 years.

Activists ✧ City Life ✧ Civil Rights Workers ✧ Editors ✧ Humorists ✧ Jews ✧ Journalists ✧ Labor Leaders and Unions | NYC (Lower East Side)

Golden, Harry (b. Harry Goldhurst) (1902–1981). *The Right Time: An Autobiography* (Golden, 1969).
Pages 20–93, 97–103 focus on his first 21 years.

Activists ✧ City Life ✧ Civil Rights Workers ✧ Editors ✧ Humorists ✧ Jews ✧ Journalists ✧ Labor Leaders and Unions | NYC (Lower East Side)

Goldman, Emma (1869–1940). *Living My Life.* 2 vols. (Knopf, 1931).
Pages 3–82 (chs. 1–7). (Penguin Classics released a 1-volume ed. of this work in 2006.)

Anarchists ✧ Feminists | Lithuania ✧ Russia ✧ U.S. (Northeast) ✧ NYC

Gornick, Vivian (1935–). *Fierce Attachments* (Farrar, Straus, and Giroux, 1987).
Pages 3, 10 to about 128.

City Life ✧ Feminists ✧ Jews | NYC (Bronx)

Hasselbach, Ingo (1967–), with Tom Reiss. *Fuhrer-ex: Memoirs of a Former Neo-Nazi* (Random House, 1996).
Pages 3 to about 76.

Generation X ✧ Nazis and Neo-Nazis | East Germany

Herrick, William (1915–2004). *Jumping the Line: The Adventures and Misadventures of an American Radical* (University of Wisconsin, 1998).
Pages 4 to about 94 (chs. 1–12).

Bereavement ✧ Bisexuals ✧ Civil War (Spanish) ✧ Communists ✧ Family Violence ✧ Growing Up Between WWI and WWII ✧ Hoboes ✧ Jews ✧ Novelists ✧ Strikes and Lockouts | NJ ✧ NYC (Bronx, Manhattan) ✧ MI ✧ FL

Jerome, Judson (1927–1991). *Flight from Innocence: A Memoir, 1927–1947* (University of Arkansas, 1990).
Covers his first 20 years.

Growing Up Between WWI and WWII ✧ Poets | TX

Johnson, Joyce (1935–). *Minor Characters: A Young Woman's Coming-of-Age in the Beat Orbit of Jack Kerouac* (Houghton Mifflin, 1983).
Pages 1–125 (chs. 1–7 and part of ch. 8).

Beat Generation ✧ City Life ✧ Groupies | NYC

Jones, G(reen) C. (1913–). *Growing Up Hard in Harlem County* (University Press of Kentucky, 1985).
About the first 105–120 pages.

Depressions (Economic) ✧ Growing Up Between WWI and WWII ✧ Labor Leaders and Unions ✧ Miners | KY

Kimmage, Ann (1942–). *An Un-American Childhood* (University of Georgia, 1996).
All but about the book's final 10 pages. For a similar memoir, see "Belfrage, Sally" (ch. 6).
Anti-Communist Movements I NYC (Queens) ✧ Mexico ✧ Czechoslovakia ✧ China

King, Dexter Scott (1961–), with Ralph Wiley. *Growing Up King: An Intimate Memoir* (IPM, 2003).
About the first 100 pages. King describes what it was like to grow up as a son of the famous civil rights leader.
African Americans ✧ Attention Deficit Disorder ✧ Baby Boomers ✧ Civil Rights Workers ✧ Fatherless Families ✧ Fathers and Sons ✧ King, Martin Luther, Jr. ✧ Murder ✧ Pacifists ✧ Racism I GA

Kopelev, Lev (1912–1997). Tr. from the Russian by Gary Kern. *The Education of a True Believer* (Harper & Row, 1980).
Tells how he was imprisoned for 10 days at age 16, for distributing Trotskyite propaganda. Focuses on about his first 20 years.
Anti-Communist Movements ✧ Civil Rights ✧ Growing Up Between WWI and WWII ✧ Translators I Russia

Kovic, Ron (1946–). *Born on the Fourth of July* (McGraw-Hill, 1976).
He went to fight in Vietnam at age 17.
Pacifists ✧ Paraplegia ✧ Vietnamese Conflict I WI ✧ NY (Long Island) ✧ Vietnam

Kropotkin, Peter (born Pyotr) (1842–1921). *Memoirs of a Revolutionist* (Horizon, 1930).
"Part First" (pages 6–70) covers his first 15 years; "Part Second" (pages 71–153) covers him from 15 to 20; pages 154 to about 207 of "Part Third" cover him from 20 to about 21.
Bereavement ✧ Civil Rights ✧ Communists ✧ Crimean War ✧ Geographers ✧ High Society ✧ Intellectual Life ✧ Journalists ✧ Military Life ✧ Nineteenth-Century Pre-Industrial Age Memoirists ✧ Philosophers ✧ Revolutionaries ✧ Typhoid Fever I Russia

Lewis, John (1940–), with Michael D'Orso. *Walking with the Wind: A Memoir of the Movement* (Simon and Schuster, 1998).
Nearly all of pages 17 to about 187.
African Americans ✧ Civil Rights Workers ✧ Politicians I AL ✧ TN

Lucas, Maria (1941–). Ed. by Fran Buss. *Forged Under the Sun/Forjada bajo el sol: The Life of Maria Elena Lucas* (University of Michigan, 1993).
Pages 53 to about 142.
Labor Leaders and Unions ✧ Mexican Americans I Mexico ✧ TX

Lutyens, Emily (1874–1964). *A Blessed Girl: Memoirs of a Victorian Girlhood Chronicled in an Exchange of Letters, 1887–1896* (R. Hart-Davis, 1953).
She married eminent British architect Sir Edwin Lutyens; also, she was the granddaughter of novelist Edward Bulwer-Lytton and mother of Mary Lutyens (see ch. 9 entry).
Feminists ✧ Letters ✧ Lutyens, Sir Edwin ✧ Victorian Era British Memoirists I England

Malcolm X (b. Malcolm Little) (1925–1965), as told to Alex Haley. *The Autobiography of Malcolm X* (Ballentine Books, 1964).
Pages 3 to about 110.
African Americans ✧ Black Muslims ✧ Murder ✧ Racism I MI ✧ MA ✧ NYC

Mattera, Don (1935–). *Sophiatown: Coming of Age in South Africa* (Beacon, 1989) (Published in England as *Gone with the Twilight: A Story of Sophiatown* [Zed Books, 1987]).
Pages 27–124.

Africans ✧ Journalists ✧ Poets ✧ Racism | South Africa

McCarthy, Mary (1912–1989). *Memories of a Catholic Girlhood* (Harcourt Brace Jovanovich, 1957).
Both of her parents died when she was young. She married literary critic Edmund Wilson. (See also memoir by Wilson's daughter, Rosalind Baker Wilson, in chapter 17.)

Bereavement ✧ Catholics ✧ Critics (Art) ✧ Critics (Literary) ✧ Feminists ✧ Growing Up Between WWI and WWII ✧ Intellectual Life ✧ Journalists ✧ Novelists ✧ Orphans ✧ Short Story Writers | WA ✧ MN

McCarthy, Mary (1912–1989). *How I Grew* (Harcourt Brace Jovanovich, 1987).
Covers her from 13 to 21 years. Memoir is followed by Carol Brightman's 10-page biographical glossary of 30 "lesser-known" figures.

Bereavement ✧ Catholics ✧ Critics (Art) ✧ Critics (Literary) ✧ Feminists ✧ Growing Up Between WWI and WWII ✧ Intellectual Life ✧ Journalists ✧ Novelists ✧ Orphans ✧ Short Story Writers ✧ Vassar College | MN ✧ WA ✧ NY

McNaron, Toni (1937–). *I Dwell in Possibility: A Memoir* (Feminist Press at the City University of New York, 1992).
Pages xiii–xiv, 3 to about 109 (first ed.). A revised and expanded second ed. was published by the Feminist Press in 2001, adding 104 pages to the overall text.

Alcoholism ✧ College Teachers ✧ Feminists ✧ Lesbians ✧ Racism | AL

Meeropol, Robert (1947–). *An Execution in the Family: One Son's Journey* (St. Martin's, 2003).
Pages 1–94. He writes of his coming of age as the son of Julius and Ethel Rosenberg, a couple who were convicted of espionage and executed in 1953.

Activists ✧ Adoptees ✧ Bereavement ✧ City Life ✧ Grandmothers ✧ Jews ✧ Political Executions ✧ Stepchildren | NYC (Manhattan) ✧ NJ ✧ NYC (Brooklyn) ✧ NY ✧ IN ✧ MI

Michaels, Lisa (1966–). *Split: A Counterculture Childhood* (Houghton Mifflin, 1998).

Generation X ✧ Hippies | NYC ✧ CA (Northern)

Modisane, Bloke (born William Modisane) (1923–1986). *Blame Me on History* (E.P. Dutton, 1963).
Pages 16 to about 85.

Actors ✧ Africans ✧ Dramatists ✧ Growing Up Between WWI and WWII ✧ Intellectual Life ✧ Journalists ✧ Poets ✧ Racism | South Africa

Moody, Anne (1940–). *Coming of Age in Mississippi* (Dial, 1968).
Covers her first 24 years.

African Americans ✧ Civil Rights Workers | MS

Naughton, Bill (1910–1992). *On the Pig's Back: An Autobiographical Excursion* (Oxford University, 1987).
Focuses on his early childhood. He is best known as the author of the novel *Alfie* (MacGibbon & Kee, 1966).

Catholics ✧ Dramatists ✧ Miners Novelists ✧ Pacifists | England

Naughton, Bill (1910–1992). *Saintly Billy: A Catholic Boyhood* (Oxford University, 1988).
Covers him from 10 to 13 years.
Catholics ✧ Dramatists ✧ Miners ✧ Novelists ✧ Pacifists | England

Naughton, Bill (1910–1992). *Neither Use Nor Ornament: A Memoir of Bolton, 1924* (Bloodaxe Books, 1995).
Focuses on him during the month of June 1924. (Published posthumously.)
Catholics ✧ Dramatists ✧ Novelists ✧ Pacifists ✧ Summer | England

Naughton, Bill (1910–1992). *A Roof Over Your Head* (Pilot, 1945; Blackie, 1967 [rev. ed., ed. by Vincent Whitcombe]).
Semiautobiographical account, set during the 1920s.
Catholics ✧ Dramatists ✧ Miners ✧ Novelists ✧ Pacifists | England

Neill, A(lexander) S(utherland) (1883–1973). *"Neill! Neill! Orange Peel!": An Autobiography* (Hart Publishing Company, 1972).
Some 83 pages.
Education ✧ Reformers ✧ Teachers ✧ Victorian Era British Memoirists | Scotland

Noble, Christina (1944–), with Robert Coram. *Nobody's Child: A Woman's Abusive Past and Inspiring Dream That Led Her to Rescue the Street Children of Saigon* (Grove, 1994).
Pages 43 to about 162.
Abuse (Sexual) ✧ Bereavement ✧ Children of Alcoholics ✧ Depressions (Economic) ✧ Family Violence ✧ Mental Health ✧ Reformers ✧ Slums ✧ Vietnam Conflict | Ireland (North) ✧ England

O'Callaghan, Sean. *Down by the Glenside: Memoirs of an Irish Boyhood* (Mercier, 1992).
The author grew up during the 1920s–1930s. He was a member of the Irish Republican Army and wrote for the London *Daily Mirror*.
Farm Life ✧ Journalists | Ireland

Perks, Micah (1963–). *Pagan Time: An American Childhood* (Counterpoint, 2001).
Micah evokes the counterculture society created by his father, who started a commune school removed from mainstream society.
Adirondack Mountains ✧ Baby Boomers ✧ Counterculture Childhoods ✧ Teachers | NY

Radosh, Ronald (1937–). *Commies: A Journey Through the Old Left, the New Left and the Leftover Left* (Encounter Books, 2001).
Pages 7 to about 60.
Communists ✧ University of Wisconsin | NYC (Queens) ✧ NY ✧ WI

Ratushinskaya, Irina (1954–). Tr. by Alyona Kojevjikov. *In the Beginning* (Knopf, 1991).
Pages 9–101 (about chs. 1–16).
Poets ✧ Prisoners ✧ Reformers | Soviet Union (now Ukraine)

Register, Cheri (1945–). *Packinghouse Daughter: A Memoir* (Minnesota Historical Society, 2000).
Labor Leaders and Unions ✧ Strikes and Lockouts | MN

Ross, Marie (1864–). *Child of Icaria* (City Printing Company, 1938).
She grew up in a commune.

Cults ✧ Reformers

Schrank, Robert (1917–). *Wasn't That a Time? Growing Up Red and Radical in America* (MIT, 1998).
Focuses on 1920s–1940s.

Bereavement ✧ City Life ✧ Communists ✧ Growing Up Between WWI and WWII ✧ Immigrants ✧ Labor Leaders and Unions ✧ Mental Health | NYC (Bronx)

Schumann, Willy (1927–). *Being Present: Growing Up in Hitler's Germany* (Kent State University, 1991).
Pages 1–188 (chs. 1–14).

College Teachers ✧ Critics (Literary) ✧ Essayists ✧ Growing Up Between WWI and WWII ✧ Hitler Youth Movement ✧ WWII | Germany

Shen, Tong (1968–), with Marianne Yen. *Almost a Revolution* (Houghton Mifflin, 1990).
Covers about his first 20 years.

Anti-Communist Movements ✧ Tiananmen Square Incident | China

Sinclair, Upton (1878–1968). *Candid Reminiscences: My First Thirty Years* (T.W. Laurie, 1932).
About 80 pages. He is best known as the author of *The Jungle* (Doubleday, Page, 1906), the classic exposé of the American meat packing industry. Like (Joseph) Lincoln Steffens (see entry this chapter), Sinclair was an early 20th-century reformer.

Children's Authors ✧ City Life ✧ Dramatists ✧ Novelists ✧ Reformers ✧ Socialists | MD ✧ NYC (Manhattan)

Smith, Lillian (1897–1966). *Memory of a Large Christmas* (W.W. Norton, 1962).
She lived in Florida for her first 17 or 18 years before moving to GA. Pages 11–78 focus on her childhood.

Cancer ✧ Christmas ✧ Civil Rights Workers ✧ Feminists ✧ Lesbians ✧ Novelists | FL

Souljah, Sister (b. Lisa Williamson) (1964–). *No Disrespect* (Times Books, 1994).
Pages 5 to at least 100.

African Americans ✧ Baby Boomers ✧ City Life ✧ Reformers ✧ Singers | NYC (Bronx)

Steffens, (Joseph) Lincoln (1866–1936). *Autobiography of Lincoln Steffens* (Harcourt, Brace, 1931).
The first quarter of this work appeared under separate cover as *Boy on Horseback* (Harcourt, Brace, 1935). Like Upton Sinclair (see entry this chapter), he was an early 20th-century reformer.

Editors ✧ Journalists ✧ Reformers ✧ Socialists | CA (Northern)

Tarry, Ellen (1906–living 2007). *The Third Door: The Autobiography of an American Negro Woman* (D. McKay, 1955).
In the 1966 Guild Press edition, pages 3–78.

African Americans ✧ Biographers ✧ Catholics ✧ Centenarians ✧ Children's Authors ✧ Civil Rights Workers ✧ Journalists ✧ Social Workers ✧ Teachers | AL

Tompkins, Ptolemy (Christian) (1962?–). *Paradise Fever: Growing Up in the Shadow of the New Age* (Avon Books, 1997) (Variant title, *Paradise Fever: Despatches from the Dawn of the New Age* [Bloomsbury, 1997]).

His father was a New Age guru who wrote *The Secret Life of Plants* (Harper & Row, 1972) and studied the subject of Atlantis.

Baby Boomers (?) ✧ Fathers and Sons ✧ New Age | New England ✧ Bahamas ✧ VA (?)

Von der Grun, Max (1926–). Tr. by Jan van Heurck. *How I Like the Wolves: Growing Up in Nazi Germany* (W. Morrow, 1980) (First published in German, 1979).

Some 66 scattered pages.

Growing Up Between WWI and WWII ✧ Hitler Youth Movement ✧ Nazis and Neo-Nazis ✧ WWII | Germany

Webb, Beatrice (1859–1947). *My Apprenticeship* (Longmans, Green, 1926).

Based on diaries she kept between 15 and 34 years; 50–65 pages.

Diaries and Journals ✧ Nineteenth-Century Pre-Industrial Age Memoirists ✧ Reformers | England

Teachers and Other Educators

See entries in the section "Books, Reading, Librarians, and Booksellers" in chapter 9 for memoirs by librarians and booksellers.

Anderson, George K(umler) (1901–1980). *Schoolboy with Satchel* (Carlton, 1979).

Pages 9, 21–350 cover his first 16 years. His father, with whom he traveled, was a U.S. diplomat.

College Teachers ✧ Worldwide Travel | IL

Bresee, Clyde (1916–). *Sea Island Yankee* (Algonquin Books of Chapel Hill, 1986).

Pages 6–264 are on his childhood and adolescence. As an adult, he was a school guidance counselor and lecturer.

Guidance Counselors ✧ Lecturers | PA

Demas, Corinne (1947–). *Eleven Stories High: Growing Up in Stuyvesant Town, 1948–1968* (State University of New York, 2000).

Baby Boomers ✧ Children's Authors ✧ City Life ✧ College Teachers | NYC

Doud, Guy Rice (1953–). *Molder of Dreams* (Focus on the Family, 1990).

He was named National Teacher of the Year in 1986. Text includes many biblical scriptural allusions; as an adult, he was pastor in a MN church.

Baby Boomers ✧ Children of Alcoholics ✧ Clergy ✧ Teachers | MN

Edmundson, Mark (1952–). *Teacher: The One Who Made the Difference* (Random House, 2002).

Memoir focuses on the effect a free-thinking teacher had on him, during his high school years in a blue collar community. Edmundson is a college professor and literary critic.

Baby Boomers ✧ College Teachers ✧ Critics (Literary) ✧ Teachers | MA

Fairey, Wendy W. (1942?–). *One of the Family* (W.W. Norton, 1992).

Some 60–80 pages (scattered between 39 and 147). Movie columnist Sheilah Graham and philosopher A. J. Ayer were her parents.

College Teachers | CA (Southern: Hollywood)

Harris, Trudier (1948–). *Summer Snow: Reflections from a Black Daughter of the South* (Beacon Press, 2003).

Through a series of essays, Harris details her experiences growing up in the South after WWII.

African Americans ✧ Baby Boomers ✧ College Teachers ✧ Essayists ✧ Racism | AL

Jennings, Kevin (1963?–). *Mama's Boy, Preacher's Son: A Memoir of Becoming a Man* (Beacon, 2006).

Jennings recalls his difficulties growing up gay in a fatherless family in the 1970s. His father died when he was 8 years old.

Baby Boomers ✧ Bereavement ✧ Fatherless Families ✧ Gays ✧ Sexuality ✧ Teachers ✧ Working Class Whites | NC

Johnson, Henry (1867–). *The Other Side of Main Street; A History Teacher from Sauk Centre* (Columbia University, 1943).

Pages 4 to about 64 (the first 5½ chapters).

College Teachers ✧ Intellectual Life | MN

Lancaster, Robert S. (1909–). *The Better Parts of a Life: An Autobiography* (Proctor's Hall, 1990).

Pages 3–60. He taught at the Sewanee Military Academy for 46 years.

College Teachers ✧ Dogs ✧ Family Memoirs ✧ Farm Life ✧ Lawyers | VA

Larcom, Lucy (1824–1893). *A New England Girlhood, Outlined from Memory* (Houghton Mifflin, 1889).

Pages 21–259 of the 1973 Peter Smith reprint.

Nineteenth-Century Pre-Industrial Age Memoirists ✧ Poets ✧ Teachers | MA

Masters, Hilary (pseud.: P. J. Coyne) (1928–). *Last Stands: Notes from Memory* (David R. Godine, 1982).

Poet Edgar Lee Masters was his father. This memoir is a classic.

College Teachers ✧ Grandparents ✧ Growing Up Between WWI and WWII ✧ Masters, Edgar Lee ✧ Photographers | MO ✧ NYC ✧ Washington, DC

Parnell, Mary Davies (1936–). *Block Salt and Candles: A Rhondda Childhood* (Dufour Editions, 1991).

This memoir is continued by the following entry.

Teachers | Wales

Parnell, Mary Davies (1936–). *Snobs and Sardines: Rhondda Schooldays* (Seren Books, 1993).

Set during the 1940s, this memoir is continued by the following entry.

Teachers | Wales

Parnell, Mary Davies (1936–). *Plateaux, Gateaux, Chateaux* (Seren Books, 1997).

This is the final memoir in Parnell's autobiographical trilogy.

Teachers | Wales

Pattee, Fred Lewis (1863–1950). *Penn State Yankee: The Autobiography of Fred Lewis Pattee* (Pennsylvania State College, 1953).

College Teachers ✧ Critics (Literary) ✧ Farm Life | NH

Reese, Lizette Woodworth (1856–1935). *The York Road* (Farrar & Rinehart, 1931).
Essayists ✧ Poets ✧ Nineteenth-Century Pre-Industrial Age Memoirists ✧ Teachers | MD

Rivers, Caryl (1937–). *Aphrodite at Mid-Century: Growing Up Catholic and Female in Post-War America* (Doubleday, 1973).
Catholics ✧ College Teachers ✧ Journalists ✧ Novelists | MD

Rodaway, Angela (1918–). *A London Childhood* (Batsford, 1960).
Growing Up Between WWI and WWII ✧ Teachers | England

Sears, James T. (1951–). *Growing Up Gay in the South: Race, Gender, and Journeys of the Spirit* (Haworth, 1991).
African Americans ✧ Baby Boomers ✧ College Teachers ✧ Gays ✧ Sexuality | U.S (Southeast)

Sneller, Anne Gertrude (1883–). *A Vanished World* (Syracuse University, 1964).
Farm Life ✧ Teachers | NY

Stuart, Jesse (1907–1984). *Beyond Dark Hills: A Personal Story* (E.P. Dutton, 1938).
Children's Authors ✧ Essayists ✧ Poets ✧ School Superintendents ✧ Short Story Writers ✧ Teachers | KY

Stuart, Jesse (1907–1984). *To Teach, to Love* (World, 1960).
Pages 11–132 (chs. 1–most of 4).
Children's Authors ✧ Essayists ✧ Poets ✧ School Superintendents ✧ Short Story Writers ✧ Teachers | KY

Sturt, George (aka George Bourne) (1863–1927). *A Small Boy in the Sixties* (Cambridge University, 1927).
He was descended from a line of wheelwrights.
Teachers | England

Theroux, Phyllis (1939–). *California and Other States of Grace: A Memoir* (W. Morrow, 1980).
About the first 200 pages (chs. 1–10) cover her pre-college years.
Teachers | CA (Northern)

Treneer, Anne (1891–1966). *School House in the Wind* (J. Cape, 1944).
Covers her first 15 years. This memoir was later included with the 2 memoirs of her adult years in *School House in the Wind: A Trilogy by Anne Treneer* (University of Exeter, 1998).
Biographers ✧ Country Life ✧ Intellectual Life ✧ Poets ✧ Teachers ✧ Victorian Era British Memoirists | England

Wade-Gayles, Gloria (1938–). *Pushed Back to Strength: A Black Woman's Journey Home* (Beacon, 1993).
African Americans ✧ College Teachers ✧ Poets ✧ Racism | TN

Wakefield, Tom (1935–1996). *Forties' Child* (Routledge & Kegan Paul, 1980).
His father was a coal miner; as an adult, the author was a special education teacher.
Country Life ✧ Gays ✧ Miners ✧ Novelists ✧ Teachers | England

Chapter 9

Men and Women of Words: Writers, Publishers, Poets, and Other Book People

The coming-of-age memoirs of this chapter are the products of wordsmiths of various callings. Writers of popular works and of scholarly works, and those who analyze and parse language and literature for a living can be found here. It should come as no surprise that this is the longest chapter, in that writers are more likely to set down their lives in print than those in other professions. In fact, this chapter does not contain all of the writers in this collection; many appear in other chapters as well. (Check the subject index under "Writers" to find more.) Unlike the leaders of movements and molders of young minds surveyed in the previous chapter, most of the more than 250 writers in this chapter have led more private lives, preferring to let the written page be their emissary to the world. Often writers will produce work in more than one genre or format—e.g., poetry, novels, and essays—so if desired, check the subject index for further references in a given category.

The better-known authors in chapter 9 include many writers of fiction profiled in its third and fourth sections. Anthony Burgess, Colette, Daphne DuMaurier, Tony Hillerman, and Rosemary Sutcliff are but a handful of the nearly 70 novelists whose recollections are listed here, while some of the well-known short story writers included here are Sherwood Anderson, Isaac Bashevis Singer, and Frederik Pohl. Memoirs by writers of children's fiction are also catalogued here (e.g., Laura Ingalls Wilder, Paul Zindel).

Famous writers of plays and essays also appear in this chapter, in the sixth and seventh sections, respectively. Among the nearly 2 dozen dramatists who tell of their early years are Neil Simon, Arthur Miller, and Ben Hecht. Autobiographical volumes by essayists include those by Annie Dillard, Gore Vidal, and Faye Moskowitz.

Those who mold words in the oral tradition of storytellers and folklorists are also represented in this chapter (e.g., J. Frank Dobie and Selma Lagerlof). So are those who record, select, define, or interpret the words of countless past generations of other writers. In this chapter, one may find a memoir by a lexicographer (Frederic Mistral), biographer (Catherine Drinker Bowen), or translator (Juliet M. Soskice).

Those whose livelihood depends on reviewing and critiquing such elements of our culture as movies, sports, architecture, and food are covered in the ninth section. A few of the some 50 memoirists included here are contemporary book reviewer Michael Dirda, the late critiquer of fine cuisine M. F. K. Fisher, and the monumental 20th-century sportswriter A. J. Liebling.

Turn to this chapter to find memoirs by a librarian (Lawrence Clark Powell), publisher (Felice Picano), or bookseller (Bentz Plagemann)—persons responsible for preserving and dispersing humanity's written words.

Because these individuals have made their livelihoods as writers, these memoirs are among the most articulate and stylistically polished of those collected in this volume. On the other hand, one might anticipate that a memoir penned by a novelist is more likely to include elements of fiction—either intentionally or unintentionally—than a memoir written by nearly anyone else.

Children's Authors

Bagnold, Enid (1889–1981). *Enid Bagnold's Autobiography (from 1889)* (Heinemann, 1969).
Pages 3 to about 60.
Children's Authors ✧ Dramatists ✧ Novelists ✧ Translators ✧ Victorian Era British Memoirists ✧ Wealth | England

Bemelmans, Ludwig (1898–1962). *My War with the United States* (Viking, 1937).
Includes illustrations by the author. Covers Bemelmans's teenage years, starting at age 16. He is best remembered as the author of the popular Madeleine series of children's books. For similar memoirs, see "Enters, Angna" (ch. 10) and "Lang, George" (this ch.).
Children's Authors ✧ Humorists ✧ Illustrators ✧ Painters ✧ Restaurateurs ✧ Travel Writers ✧ WWI | NY

Boston, L(ucy) M(aria) (1892–1990). *Perverse and Foolish: A Memoir of Childhood and Youth* (Bodley Head, 1979).
Pages 9 to about 96. This memoir possesses a smooth style, with little re-created dialogue. It includes about 10 black-and-white photos. She wrote a series of children's books based on the manor house she restored after her divorce.
Children's Authors ✧ Nurses ✧ Painters ✧ Victorian Era British Memoirists | England

Burgess, Thornton (1874–1965). *Now I Remember: Autobiography of an Amateur Naturalist* (Little, Brown, 1960).
Pages 3–72. He created the character "Peter Rabbit."
Children's Authors ✧ Journalists ✧ Natural History ✧ Radio Broadcasters | MA

Burnett, Frances Hodgson (1849–1924). *The One I Knew Best of All: A Memory of the Mind of a Child* (Scribner's Sons, 1893).
Written in the third person. She and her family immigrated to the U.S. when she was 16. Burnett is famous as the author of *The Secret Garden* (Frederick A. Stokes, 1911).
Children's Authors ✧ Immigrants ✧ Nineteenth-Century Pre-Industrial Age Memoirists ✧ Novelists | England ✧ TN

Cleary, Beverly (1916–living 2007). *Girl from Yamhill: A Memoir* (W. Morrow, 1988).
To the start of her college years; continued by the following entry.
Children's Authors ✧ Depressions (Economic) ✧ Growing Up Between WWI and WWII ✧ Intellectual Life | OR

Cleary, Beverly (1916–living 2007). *My Own Two Feet* (HarperCollins Children's Book Group, 1995).

About the first 100 pages are on her freshman, sophomore, and junior years in college.

Booksellers ✧ Children's Authors ✧ Growing Up Between WWI and WWII ✧ Intellectual Life ✧ Librarians | CA (Southern)

Cross, John Keir (1914–1967). *Aspect of Life: An Autobiography of Youth* (Selwyn & Blount, 1937).

Children's Authors ✧ Growing Up Between WWI and WWII | Scotland

Dahl, Roald (1916–1990). *Boy: Tales of Childhood* (Jonathan Cape, 1984).

Author of the children's books *James and the Giant Peach* (Knopf, 1961) and *Charlie and the Chocolate Factory* (Knopf, 1964), Dahl is also known for horror stories.

Bereavement ✧ Children's Authors ✧ Fatherless Families ✧ Growing Up Between WWI and WWII ✧ Novelists ✧ Short Story Writers ✧ South Wales | Norway ✧ England

De Paola, Tomie (1934–). *26 Fairmount Avenue* (Putnam, 1999).

In this memoir of about 56 pages, the focus is on the author at age 5.

Children's Authors ✧ Illustrators | CT

Garis, Roger (1901–1967). *My Father Was Uncle Wiggily* (McGraw-Hill, 1966).

About 97 scattered pages. His father wrote the "Uncle Wiggily" books and was a friend of Robert Frost.

Children's Authors ✧ Frost, Robert | CT

Glynne-Jones, William (1907–1977). *The Childhood Land* (Batsford, 1960).

Children's Authors ✧ Novelists | Wales

Jackson, Jacqueline Dougan (1928–). *Stories from the Round Barn* (TriQuarterly Books/Northwestern University, 1997).

Children's Authors ✧ Farm Life ✧ Growing Up Between WWI and WWII | WI

Kastner, Erich (1899–1974). Tr. by Isabel McHugh and Florence McHugh. *When I Was a Boy* (F. Watts, 1961) (Variant title, *When I Was a Little Boy* [Jonathan Cape, 1959]) (First published in German, 1957).

Pages 56–181 (chs. 5–16) cover his first 15 years, until the outbreak of WWI. This memoir was awarded the Hans Christian Andersen Medal, a children's book award.

Children's Authors ✧ Novelists ✧ Poets | Germany

Kent, Louise (1886–1969). *Mrs. Appleyard and I* (Houghton Mifflin, 1968).

Pages 1–112 (chs. 1–12).

Children's Authors | MA

Kerr, M. E. (pseud. of Marijane [Agnes] Meaker) (1927–). *Me, Me, Me, Me, Me: Not a Novel* (Harper & Row, 1983).

Children's Authors ✧ Growing Up Between WWI and WWII ✧ Novelists | NY

Lawson, Robert (1892–1957). *At That Time: With Decorations by the Author* (Viking, 1947).

Focuses on his childhood.

Children's Authors ✧ Illustrators | NJ ✧ MA

Lindbergh, Reeve (1945–). *Under a Wing: A Memoir* (Simon and Schuster, 1998).

She was the daughter of Charles and Anne Morrow Lindbergh. See also "Lindbergh, Charles A(ugustus)" (ch. 1) and "Lindbergh, Anne Morrow"(this ch.).

Children's Authors ✧ Lindbergh, Charles A(ugustus) ✧ Novelists ✧ Pilots ✧ Teachers I CT

Meltzer, Milton (1915–living 2007). *Starting from Home: A Writer's Beginnings* (Viking Kestrel, 1988).

He has written dozens of books on U.S. history, primarily on social history for young readers.

Children's Authors ✧ Growing Up Between WWI and WWII ✧ Historians (Cultural) I MA

Milne, A(lan) A(lexander) (1882–1956). *It's Too Late Now: The Autobiography of a Writer* (Methuen, 1939) (Variant title, *Autobiography* [E.P. Dutton, 1939]).

Pages 1–141 (chs. 1–9). This memoir, which originally ran in serial form (entitled "What Luck," in *The Atlantic Monthly*), is largely on his childhood. See also "Milne, Christopher" (his son; ch. 4).

Cambridge University ✧ Children's Authors ✧ Victorian Era British Memoirists ✧ Westminster School I England

Moody, Ralph (1898–1982). *Little Britches: Father and I Were Ranchers* (W.W. Norton, 1950).

Set in 1906–1910, this memoir is continued by the following entries. It was adapted as the 1971 film *The Wild Country.* For similar memoirs, see "Wilder, Laura Ingalls" (this section).

Accountants ✧ Children's Authors ✧ Ranch Life I CO

Moody, Ralph (1898–1982). *Man of the Family* (W.W. Norton, 1951).

This memoir is set in 1910 in Littleton, CO.

Accountants ✧ Children's Authors ✧ Ranch Life I CO

Moody, Ralph (1898–1982). *Mary Emma & Company* (W.W. Norton, 1961).

Continuing the previous entry, this memoir is set in Medford, MA after Moody's father died.

Accountants ✧ Children's Authors ✧ Country Life ✧ Family Memoirs ✧ Farm Life ✧ Fatherless Families I MA

Moody, Ralph (1898–1982). *Home Ranch* (W.W. Norton, 1962).

Set on a cattle ranch one summer during his youth.

Accountants ✧ Children's Authors ✧ Country Life ✧ Farm Life ✧ Ranch Life ✧ Summer

Moody, Ralph (1898–1982). *Fields of Home* (W.W. Norton, 1962).

Tells of efforts by his grandfather and him, in his teenage years, to restore an old farm.

Accountants ✧ Children's Authors ✧ Country Life ✧ Farm Life ✧ Grandfathers I ME

Moody, Ralph (1898–1982). *Shaking the Nickel Bush* (W.W. Norton, 1962).

Focuses on him at age 19, when he was erroneously told he had only 6 months to live.

Accountants ✧ Children's Authors ✧ Country Life ✧ Farm Life

Nesbit, Edith (1858–1924). *Long Ago When I Was Young* (Whiting & Wheaton, 1966).

Children's Authors ✧ Dramatists ✧ Editors ✧ Nineteenth-Century Pre-Industrial Age Memoirists ✧ Novelists ✧ Poets ✧ Short Story Writers I England

Paulsen, Gary (1939–). *Eastern Sun, Winter Moon: An Autobiographical Odyssey* (Harcourt Brace Jovanovich, 1993).

Covers him to 9 years.

Children's Authors ✧ Military Life ✧ WWII I MN ✧ IL ✧ HI ✧ Philippines

Paulsen, Gary (1939–). *The Beet Fields: Memories of a Sixteenth Summer* (Delacorte, 2000).

Children's Authors ✧ Military Life ✧ Summer ✧ WWII I ND

Perl, Lila, and Marion Lazan. *Four Perfect Pebbles: A Holocaust Story* (Greenwillow Books, 1996).

Children's Authors ✧ Holocaust Survivors ✧ Jews I Germany

Petry, Ann (1911–1997). *When I Was a Child* (Children's Literature Association, 1992).
Memoir of 54 pages.

African Americans ✧ Children's Authors ✧ Journalists ✧ Novelists I CT

Pinkwater, Daniel (1941–). *Fish Whistle: Commentaries, Uncommentaries and Vulgar Excesses* (Addison-Wesley, 1989).
About 50 scattered pages.

Children's Authors ✧ Humorists ✧ Radio Broadcasters ✧ Sculptors I TN and/or IL (Chicago)

Spinelli, Jerry (1941–). *Knots in My Yo-Yo String: The Autobiography of a Kid* (Knopf, 1998).

Children's Authors I PA

Trevino, Elizabeth Borton de (1904–living 1990s). *The Hearthstone of My Heart* (Doubleday, 1977).

Children's Authors ✧ Journalists ✧ Musicians ✧ Novelists I CA (Southern)

Whipple, Dorothy (1893–1966). *The Other Day: An Autobiography* (M. Joseph, 1936). (Later published as *The Other Day: The World of a Child* [Macmillan, 1950]).
Covers her first 12 years.

Children's Authors ✧ Novelists ✧ Victorian Era British Memoirists I England

Wiggin, Kate Douglas (1856–1923). *My Garden of Memory: An Autobiography* (Houghton Mifflin, 1923).
Pages 4 to about 99. She organized the first free kindergarten in the U.S., in San Francisco. She also wrote *Rebecca of Sunnybrook Farm* (Houghton Mifflin, 1903). Includes a detailed 17-page subject index.

Children's Authors ✧ Education ✧ Nineteenth-Century Pre-Industrial Age Memoirists I ME

Wilder, Laura Ingalls (1867–1957). *Little House in the Big Woods* (Harper & Brothers, 1932).
Focuses on her at age 5. The following entries continue this memoir. For similar memoirs, see series entries for Ralph Moody (this section) and Harriette Arnow (ch. 4).

Children's Authors ✧ Family Memoirs ✧ Frontier and Pioneer Life ✧ Teachers I WI

Wilder, Laura Ingalls (1867–1957). *The Little House on the Prairie* (Harper & Brothers, 1935).
This third-person account tells of Wilder and her family traveling out of WI in a covered wagon.

Children's Authors ✧ Family Memoirs ✧ Frontier and Pioneer Life ✧ Teachers I WI ✧ MN

Wilder, Laura Ingalls (1867–1957). *On the Banks of Plum Creek* (Harper & Brothers, 1937).
   The family settles in MN.
   Children's Authors ✧ Family Memoirs ✧ Frontier and Pioneer Life ✧ Teachers | MN

Wilder, Laura Ingalls (1867–1957). *By the Shores of Silver Lake* (Harper & Brothers, 1939).
   The Ingalls family relocates once more.
   Children's Authors ✧ Family Memoirs ✧ Frontier and Pioneer Life ✧ Teachers | Dakota Territory

Wilder, Laura Ingalls (1867–1957). *The Long Winter* (Harper & Brothers, 1940).
   Laura's family survives a brutal winter in a small town.
   Children's Authors ✧ Family Memoirs ✧ Frontier and Pioneer Life ✧ Teachers

Wilder, Laura Ingalls (1867–1957). *Little Town on the Prairie* (Harper & Brothers, 1941).
   Focuses on her at age 15 and her initial efforts as a teacher.
   Children's Authors ✧ Family Memoirs ✧ Frontier and Pioneer Life ✧ Teachers

Wilder, Laura Ingalls (1867–1957). *These Happy Golden Years* (Harper & Brothers, 1943).
   This, the concluding volume of the series, includes her marriage to Almanzo Wilder.
   Children's Authors ✧ Family Memoirs ✧ Frontier and Pioneer Life ✧ Teachers

Zindel, Paul (1936–). *The Pigman and Me* (HarperCollins, 1992).
   He wrote popular young adult novels in the 1970s.
   Children's Authors | NYC (Staten Island)

Folklorists and Storytellers

Andersen, Hans Christian (1805–1875). Tr. by Mary Howitt. *The True Story of My Life* (J. Munroe, 1847; [rev. ed.], Hurd & Houghton, 1871) (Variant title, *Fairy Tale of My Life* [Nyt Nordisk Forlag, 1955]).
   Depending on the edition, at least 80 pages are on his first 21 years.
   Folklorists ✧ Nineteenth-Century Pre-Industrial Age Memoirists | Denmark

Dobie, J(ames) Frank (1888–1964). *Some Part of Myself* (Little, Brown, 1967).
   Pages 12 to about 165. He was an authority on the history and folklore of the Old West.
   College Teachers ✧ Folklorists ✧ Ranch Life | TX

Howard, Dorothy Gray (pseud.: Dorothy Mills) (1902–1996). *Dorothy's World: Childhood in Sabine Bottom, 1902–1910* (Prentice-Hall, 1977).
   Folklorists ✧ Ranch Life | TX (East)

Jaramillo, Cleofas M. (1878–1956). *Shadows of the Past* (Seton Village Press, 1941).
   Memories of her childhood and youth are interspersed between her cultural and sociological observations, pages 27–116. For a similar memoir, see "Hudson, W. H." (ch. 4).
   Catholics ✧ Country Life ✧ Folklorists ✧ Food Writers ✧ Politicians | NM

Lagerlof, Selma (1858–1940). Tr. from the Swedish by Velma Swanston Howard. *Marbacka* (Doubleday, Page, 1924) (First published in Swedish, 1922).
Told in the third person, this memoir refers to the author as "Selma" or "the girl"; focus is on her first 8–10 years. This memoir is continued by the following entries.
Folklorists ✧ Nineteenth-Century Pre-Industrial Age Memoirists ✧ Novelists ✧ Paraplegia | Sweden

Lagerlof, Selma (1858–1940). Tr. from the Swedish by Velma Swanston Howard. *Memories of My Childhood: Further Memories at Marbacka* (Doubleday, Doran, 1934) (First published in Swedish, 1930).
Focuses on her at age 10.
Folklorists ✧ Nineteenth-Century Pre-Industrial Age Memoirists ✧ Novelists ✧ Paraplegia | Sweden

Lagerlof, Selma (1858–1940). Tr. from the Swedish by Velma Swanston Howard. *Diary of Selma Lagerlof* (Doubleday, Doran, 1936) (First published in Swedish, 1932).
Entire diary focuses on her at 14 years.
Diaries and Journals ✧ Folklorists ✧ Nineteenth-Century Pre-Industrial Age Memoirists ✧ Novelists | Sweden

Lagerlof, Selma (1858–1940). Tr. from Doubleday. Compilation and notes by Greta Anderson. *Memories of Marbacka* (Penfield, 1996).
This is a selective compilation from her nonfiction and fiction; pages 10–136 focus on her first 21 years.
Folklorists ✧ Nineteenth-Century Pre-Industrial Age Memoirists ✧ Novelists ✧ Paraplegia | Sweden

Lynch, Patricia (1898–1972). *A Storyteller's Childhood* (J.M. Dent, 1947).
Storytellers | Ireland

Machen, Arthur (b. Arthur Llewellyn Jones) (1863–1947). *Far Off Things* (Knopf, 1923).
Pages 34 to about 185. This is a pleasantly meditative memoir by one of the finest writers of fantasy tales.
Folklorists ✧ Novelists ✧ Short Story Writers ✧ Victorian Era British Memoirists | Wales ✧ England (London)

Van Gorden, John H. *Country Tradition* (Homes Guild of Wyoming Conference, United Methodist Church, 1975).
The author combines boyhood memories with folklore involving the tools and machines rural people used at the start of the 20th century.
Country Life ✧ Folklorists | WY (?)

Wagstaff, Henry McGilbert (1876–1945). *Wiley Buck and Other Stories of the Concord Community* (University of North Carolina, 1953).
Folklorists | NC

Worcester, Donald (1915–). *A Visit from Father and Other Tales from the Mojave* (Texas A&M University, 1990).
He wrote many books on the history and legends of the American West.
Children's Authors ✧ College Teachers ✧ Folklorists ✧ Growing Up Between WWI and WWII ✧ Historians (Cultural) ✧ Horses ✧ Native Americans | CA (Southern)

Novelists

Alvarez, A(lfred) (1929–). *Where Did It All Go Right? A Memoir* (W. Morrow, 1999).
About 80 pages (about 19 scattered pages in the sequence of pages 3–49, and the continuous run of pages 55–115).

College Teachers ✧ Critics (Literary) ✧ Essayists ✧ Growing Up Between WWI and WWII ✧ Lecturers ✧ Novelists ✧ Poets | England

Bates, H(erbert) E(rnest) (1905–1974). *The Vanished World* (University of Missouri, 1969).
Pages 5–189 are on his first 20 years. He authored more than 50 books; he is known for his realistic novel *The Poacher* (Macmillan, 1935).

Novelists ✧ Short Story Writers | England

Boyce, Neith (1872–1951). Ed. by Carol DeBoer-Langworthy. *The Modern World of Neith Boyce: Autobiography and Diaries* (University of New Mexico, 2003).
About the first 110 pages. She refers to herself as "Iras."

Diaries and Journals ✧ Dramatists ✧ Novelists ✧ Journalists | WI ✧ IL ✧ CA (Southern) ✧ MA ✧ NYC

Burgess, Anthony (1917–1993) (pseud. of John Anthony Burgess Wilson; he also used the pseud. Joseph Kell). *Little Wilson and Big God* (Heinemann, 1987).
Pages 17 to about 193. He wrote the novel *A Clockwork Orange* (Heinemann, 1962).

College Teachers ✧ Critics (Literary) ✧ Growing Up Between WWI and WWII ✧ Novelists ✧ Teachers | England

Caldwell, Taylor (1900–1985). *On Growing Up Tough* (Devin-Adair, 1971).
About the first 90–100 pages.

Novelists | England

Cloete, Stuart (born Edward Fairly Stuart Graham Cloete) (1897–1976). *A Victorian Son: An Autobiography, 1897–1922* (Collins, 1972).

Biographers ✧ Essayists ✧ Novelists ✧ Poets ✧ Short Story Writers ✧ WWI | France

Colette (pseud. of Sidonie Gabrielle Colette) (1873–1954). *My Mother's House/Sido* (Farrar, Straus, and Giroux, 1953) (*My Mother's House* tr. 1953 by Una Vicenzo Troubridge and Enid McLeod; originally published in French, 1922) (*Sido* tr. by Enid McLeod; originally published in French, 1929).

Bisexuals ✧ Dramatists ✧ Novelists ✧ Short Story Writers | France

Conrad, (Alfred) Borys (1898–1979). *My Father: Joseph Conrad* (Coward-McCann, 1970).

Conrad, Joseph | England

Cowper, Richard (1926–). *One Hand Clapping: A Memoir of Childhood* (Gollancz, 1975).

Growing Up Between WWI and WWII ✧ Novelists | England

Crews, Harry (1935–). *Childhood: The Biography of a Place* (Harper & Row, 1978).

Children of Alcoholics ✧ Farm Life ✧ Homes and Haunts ✧ Novelists ✧ Polio | GA

De Blasis, Celeste (1946–). *Graveyard Peaches: A California Memoir* (St. Martin's, 1991).
About pages 35–295. She is known for her historical novels.
Novelists ✧ Ranch Life | CA (Southern)

Deland, Margaret (1857–1945). *If This Be I, As I Suppose It Be* (D. Appleton-Century, 1935).
Covers her childhood; continued by the following entry.
Nineteenth-Century Pre-Industrial Age Memoirists ✧ Novelists | PA ✧ NYC (?)

Deland, Margaret (1857–1945). *Golden Yesterdays* (Harper, 1941).
About the first 80–85 pages focus on her from 13 to 21 years.
Nineteenth-Century Pre-Industrial Age Memoirists ✧ Novelists | PA ✧ VT ✧ NY ✧ NYC

Delderfield, R(onald) F(rederick) (1912–1972). *For My Own Amusement* (Hodder & Stoughton, 1968).
Parts One and Two are on his first 21 years.
Growing Up Between WWI and WWII ✧ Novelists | England

Doig, Ivan (1939–). *Heart Earth: A Memoir* (Atheneum, 1993).
This reminiscence focuses on Doig's childhood in the 1940s; it is continued by the following entry.
Novelists ✧ Ranch Life | MT ✧ AZ

Doig, Ivan (1939–). *This House of Sky: Landscapes of a Western Mind* (Harcourt Brace Jovanovich, 1978).
Although published before *Heart Earth*, this volume continues Doig's autobiography.
Novelists ✧ Ranch Life | MT

Douglas, Lloyd C(assel) (1897–1951). *Time to Remember* (Houghton Mifflin, 1951).
First volume of a projected trilogy. Before becoming a novelist, he was a clergyman in two Protestant faiths.
Clergy ✧ Novelists ✧ Spiritual Life | IN ✧ OH

Dreiser, Theodore (1871–1945). *Dawn: A History of Myself* (Liveright, 1931).
Covers his first 19 years.
Novelists ✧ Slums ✧ Spiritual Life | IN

DuMaurier, Daphne (1907–1989). *Myself When Young: The Shaping of a Writer* (Doubleday, 1977) (Variant title, *Myself When Young: Growing Pains: The Shaping of a Writer* [Gollancz, 1977]).
Dramatists ✧ Novelists | England

Duncan, Lois (1934–). *Chapters: My Growth as a Writer* (Little, Brown, 1982).
About the first 130 pages.
Novelists | FL

Ernaux, Annie (1940–). Tr. from the French by Tanya Leslie. *Shame* (Seven Stories, 1998) (First published in French, 1997).
Novelists | France

Falkner, Murry C. (1899–1975). *The Falkners of Mississippi: A Memoir* (Louisiana State University, 1967).
Pages 3 to about 106. See also "Faulkner, William" (following entry).
Faulkner, William I MS

Faulkner, William (1897–1962). Ed. by James G. Watson. *Thinking of Home: William Faulkner's Letters to His Mother and Father, 1918–1925* (W.W. Norton, 1992).
Pages 17–117. See also "Falkner, Murry C." (previous entry).
Letters ✧ Novelists ✧ Short Story Writers I CT (?)

Ferber, Edna (1887–1968). *A Peculiar Treasure: Autobiography* (Doubleday, Doran, 1939).
About the first 102 pages (chs. 1–7) are on her first 18 years.
Dramatists ✧ Jews ✧ Journalists ✧ Novelists ✧ Short Story Writers I MI ✧ WI

Fergusson, Harvey (1890–1971). *Home in the West: An Inquiry into My Origins* (Duell, Sloan and Pearce, 1944).
Grandfathers ✧ Novelists ✧ Ranch Life I NM

Forester, C(ecil) S(cott) (1899–1966). *Long Before Forty* (M. Joseph, 1967).
About 75 pages.
Biographers ✧ Foreign Correspondents ✧ Novelists ✧ Screenwriters ✧ Short Story Writers I Egypt (?) ✧ England

France, Anatole (pseud. of Jacques Anatole Francois Thibault) (1844–1924). Tr. by J. Lewis May. *My Friend's Book* (John Lane, 1913) (First published in French, 1885).
This is the first volume of France's trilogy of memoirs on his childhood.
Catholics ✧ City Life ✧ Intellectual Life ✧ Nineteenth-Century Pre-Industrial Age Memoirists ✧ Novelists ✧ Publishers I France

France, Anatole (pseud. of Jacques Anatole Francois Thibault) (1844–1924). Tr. by J. Lewis May. *Little Pierre* (John Lane, 1920) (First published in French, 1918).
This memoir continues the previous entry.
Catholics ✧ City Life ✧ Intellectual Life ✧ Nineteenth-Century Pre-Industrial Age Memoirists ✧ Novelists I France

France, Anatole (pseud. of Jacques Anatole Francois Thibault) (1844–1924). Tr. by J. Lewis May. *The Bloom of Life* (John Lane, 1923) (First published in French, 1922).
This is the concluding volume of France's trilogy on his childhood.
Catholics ✧ City Life ✧ Intellectual Life ✧ Nineteenth-Century Pre-Industrial Age Memoirists ✧ Novelists I France

Franzen, Jonathan (1959–). *The Discomfort Zone: A Personal History* (Farrar, Straus, and Giroux, 2006).
The author of *The Corrections* (the 2001 National Book Award winner for fiction), Franzen here writes of his awkward adolescence in suburban St. Louis.
Baby Boomers ✧ Birders ✧ Books and Reading ✧ Novelists I MO

Gale, Zona (1874–1938). *When I Was a Little Girl* (Macmillan, 1925).
Novelists I WI

García Márquez, Gabriel (1927–). Tr. by Edith Grossman. *Living to Tell the Tale* (Knopf, 2003).
Covering about his first 30 years, this is the first volume of a projected trilogy. He was the eldest of 11 siblings. Marquez writes here in his characteristic poetic style.

Books and Reading ✧ Eccentrics ✧ Family Memoirs ✧ Grandfathers ✧ Growing Up Between WWI and WWII ✧ Journalists ✧ Novelists ✧ Short Story Writers | Colombia

Garland, Hamlin (1860–1940). *Boy Life on the Prairie* (Macmillan, 1899).
This is a companion volume to the following entry.

Critics (Literary) ✧ Novelists | IA

Garland, Hamlin (1860–1940). *A Son of the Middle Border* (Macmillan, 1917).

Critics (Literary) ✧ Novelists | WI ✧ IA

Gorky, Maxim (1868–1936). *My Childhood* (Century, 1915).

Dramatists ✧ Novelists ✧ Socialists | Russia

Green, Henry (pseud. of Henry Vincent Yorke) (1905–1974). *Pack My Bag: A Self-Portrait* (Hogarth, 1940).
Pages 1–213.

Essayists ✧ Eton College ✧ Novelists ✧ Oxford University ✧ Short Story Writers | England

Harris, E. Lynn (1955–). *What Becomes of the Brokenhearted: A Memoir* (Doubleday, 2003).
This best-selling novelist tells of his coming of age in Arkansas, including his interactions with his abusive stepfather and the emergence of his gay gender identity.

African Americans ✧ Baby Boomers ✧ Depressions (Mental) ✧ Family Violence ✧ Gays ✧ Novelists ✧ Stepchildren ✧ Suicide and Suicide Victims | AR

Hawthorne, Julian (1846–1934). *The Memoirs of Julian Hawthorne* (Memoir, 1938).
Nearly all of pages 17 to about 196. Nathaniel Hawthorne was his father.

Children's Authors ✧ College Life ✧ Essayists ✧ Historians ✧ Nineteenth-Century Pre-Industrial Age Memoirists ✧ Novelists ✧ Short Story Writers | MA

Haymon, S(ylvia) T(heresa) (1918?–1995). *Opposite the Cross Keys: An East Anglican Childhood* (Constable, 1988).

Biographers ✧ Novelists | England

Haymon, S(ylvia) T(heresa) (1918?–1995). *The Quivering Tree: An East Anglican Childhood* (St. Martin's, 1990).
Memoir begins in 1930 when she is 12 years old and concludes while she is entering puberty.

Biographers ✧ Novelists | England

Heller, Joseph (1923–1999). *Now and Then: From Coney Island to Here* (Knopf, 1998).
About 75 scattered pages.

City Life ✧ College Teachers ✧ Dramatists ✧ Growing Up Between WWI and WWII ✧ Military Life ✧ Novelists ✧ Screenwriters | NYC (Brooklyn)

Hillerman, Tony (1925–). *Seldom Disappointed: A Memoir* (HarperCollins, 2001).

Pages 3 to about 177. A writer of mysteries involving Native Americans, Hillerman shares his memories of growing up in the heartland.

College Teachers ✧ Depressions (Economic) ✧ Farm Life ✧ Growing Up Between WWI and WWII ✧ Journalists ✧ Military Life ✧ Native Americans ✧ Novelists ✧ WWII I OK ✧ GA ✧ TX ✧ NJ ✧ NYC ✧ France ✧ Germany

Isherwood, Christopher (1904–1986). *Lions and Shadows: An Education in the Twenties* (New Directions, 1977).

He admits in text to having altered the names of certain persons and places in this memoir.

Cambridge University ✧ Dramatists ✧ Gays ✧ Intellectual Life ✧ Novelists ✧ Screenwriters ✧ Short Story Writers ✧ Spiritual Life ✧ Translators I England

James, Henry (1843–1916). *A Small Boy and Others* (Scribner's Sons, 1913).

Covers his life to 1855.

City Life ✧ Critics (Literary) ✧ Nineteenth-Century Pre-Industrial Age Memoirists ✧ Novelists ✧ Short Story Writers ✧ Travel Writers I NYC

James, Henry (1843–1916). *Notes of a Son and Brother* (Scribner, 1914).

Covers 1855–1870.

City Life ✧ Critics (Literary) ✧ Nineteenth-Century Pre-Industrial Age Memoirists ✧ Novelists ✧ Short Story Writers ✧ Travel Writers I MA ✧ Europe ✧ U.S. (Northeast)

Kantor, MacKinlay (1904–1977). *But Look, the Morn: The Story of a Childhood* (Coward McCann, 1947).

Novelists ✧ Short Story Writers I IA

Kipling, Rudyard (1865–1936). *Something of Myself; for My Friends Known and Unknown* (Doubleday, Doran, 1937).

Pages 3–74. See also "Thirkell, Angela" (ch. 9).

Children's Authors ✧ Editors ✧ Essayists ✧ Family Violence ✧ Foreign Correspondents ✧ Journalists ✧ Mental Health ✧ Novelists ✧ Poets ✧ Short Story Writers ✧ Travel Writers I India ✧ England

Lawrence, Kathleen Rockwell (1945–). *The Boys I Didn't Kiss and Other Essays* (British American, 1990).

About 75 pages focus on her first 21 years.

Humorists ✧ Novelists I NY

Leduc, Violette (1907–1972). Tr. by Derek Coltman. Foreword by Simone de Beauvoir. *La Batarde* (Farrar, Straus, and Giroux, 1965).

Pages 14 to about 125. She was praised as a major writer by Camus, Sartre, Cocteau, and Genet.

Lesbians ✧ Novelists ✧ Poets I France

Lindbergh, Anne Morrow (1906–2001). *Bring Me a Unicorn* (Harcourt, 1962).

Her letters and diary written from 1922 to 1928; she was married to pilot Charles Lindbergh; see also "Lindbergh, Charles A(ugustus)" (ch. 1) and "Lindbergh, Reeve"(this ch.).

Diaries and Journals ✧ Essayists ✧ Kidnappings ✧ Letters ✧ Lindbergh, Charles A(ugustus) ✧ Novelists ✧ Pilots ✧ Travel Writers I NJ (?)

London, Jack (1876–1916). *The Road* (Macmillan, 1907).

Covers him from 16 to about 18 years. Some of the North American cities he refers to in his travels are Reno, Nevada; Omaha, Nebraska; Baltimore, Maryland; and Montreal, Canada.

Hoboes ✧ Novelists ✧ Railroad Travel ✧ Short Story Writers I Canada ✧ U.S.

Lowndes, Bessie Belloc (aka Marie Belloc Lowndes) (1868–1947). *I Too Have Lived in Arcadia: A Record of Love and of Childhood* (Dodd, Mead, 1941).

Her girlhood travels throughout Europe furnished her with exotic settings for her novels of crime, mystery, and romance. Writer Hilaire Belloc was her brother.

Dramatists ✧ Novelists ✧ Short Story Writers | France ✧ Europe

Lutyens, Mary (pseud.: Esther Wyndham) (1908–1999). *To Be Young: Some Chapters in Autobiography* (R. Hart-Davis, 1959).

She was the daughter of Emily Lutyens (ch. 8). Primarily known for her romance novels, she also edited writings of the Indian philosopher-teacher Krishnamurti.

Biographers ✧ Novelists | England

Lynch, Hannah (1862–1904). *Autobiography of a Child* (Dodd, Mead, 1899).

Novelists | U.S.

MacKenzie, Compton (1883–1972). *My Life and Times: Octave One, 1883–1891* (Chatto & Windus, 1963).

Covers him to age 8. This is the first volume of a 10-volume indexed autobiography.

Biographers ✧ Children's Authors ✧ Dramatists ✧ Novelists ✧ Victorian Era British Memoirists | England

MacKenzie, Compton (1883–1972). *My Life and Times: Octave Two, 1891–1900* (Chatto & Windus, 1963).

Covers him from 8 to 17 years.

Biographers ✧ Children's Authors ✧ Dramatists ✧ Novelists ✧ Victorian Era British Memoirists | England

MacKenzie, Compton (1883–1972). *My Life and Times: Octave Three, 1900–1907* (Chatto & Windus, 1964).

Covers him from 17 to 21 years.

Biographers ✧ Children's Authors ✧ Dramatists ✧ Novelists ✧ Victorian Era British Memoirists | England

Márquez, Gabriel García. *See* García Márquez, Gabriel

Marsh, Ngaio (1895 or 1899–1982). *Black Beech and Honeydew: An Autobiography* (Little, Brown, 1965).

More than 100 pages.

Dramatists ✧ Novelists ✧ Painters ✧ Theatrical Producers and Directors ✧ Victorian Era British Memoirists | New Zealand

Moates, Marianne (1942–). *A Bridge of Childhood; Truman Capote's Southern Years* (H. Holt, 1989).

As narrated to Capote by his cousin, Jennings Faulk Carter, this is a collection of anecdotes on the childhoods of Carter, Capote, and Harper Lee. The 1996 film *Grass Harp* is loosely based on these anecdotal materials.

Capote, Truman ✧ Lee, Harper ✧ Novelists | AL

Nabokov, Vladimir (1899–1977). *Speak, Memory: An Autobiography Revisited* (Putnam, 1966) (Rev. ed. of *Speak, Memory* [Grosset & Dunlap, 1960]; which was originally published as *Conclusive Evidence* [Gollancz, 1951]).

Covering him from 4 to 41 years, this memoir is widely considered a classic. It includes a 6-page index.

Butterflies ✧ College Teachers ✧ Critics (Literary) ✧ Dramatists ✧ Essayists ✧ Novelists ✧ Poets ✧ Short Story Writers ✧ Translators I Russia ✧ England (?) ✧ France

Nathan, Daniel (pseuds.: Ellery Queen, Frederic Dannay) (1905–1982). *The Golden Summer* (Little, Brown, 1953).

Focuses on his 10th summer. He collaborated with Manfred Lee on many works of mystery fiction.

Advertising Copywriters ✧ College Teachers ✧ Novelists ✧ Short Story Writers ✧ Summer I NY

O'Brien, Edna (1936–). *Mother Ireland* (Harcourt Brace Jovanovich, 1976) (1978 rpt., Penguin).

About 67 pages focus on her first 21 years, with considerable blending in of general cultural and mythological observations.

Catholics ✧ Children's Authors ✧ Country Life ✧ Dramatists ✧ Feminists ✧ Novelists ✧ Screenwriters ✧ Short Story Writers I Ireland

O'Brien, Tim (1946–). *If I Die in a Combat Zone, Box Me Up and Send Me Home* (Delta/Seymour Lawrence, 1969).

Although some names have been changed, this is essentially nonfiction; it is a journal he kept at age 20.

Novelists ✧ Vietnam Conflict I Vietnam

Piercy, Marge (1936–). *Sleeping with Cats: A Memoir* (W. Morrow, 2002).

About 78 scattered pages (1–101).

Cats ✧ College Teachers ✧ Feminists ✧ Novelists ✧ Poets ✧ Revolutionaries I MI

Price, Reynolds (1933–). *Clear Pictures: First Loves, First Guides* (Atheneum, 1989).

Covers his first 21 years.

College Teachers ✧ Dramatists ✧ Essayists ✧ Novelists ✧ Poets ✧ Short Story Writers I NC

Prouty, Olive Higgins (1882–1974). *Pencil Shavings: Memoirs* (Riverside, 1961).

Pages 21–108 (chs. 3–most of 13). She is best remembered for her novel *Stella Dallas* (Houghton Mifflin, 1923), which she then helped to adapt to stage and screen.

Novelists I MA

Raymond, Ernest (1888–1974). *The Story of My Days: An Autobiography 1888–1922* (Cassell, 1968).

Pages 3–104 (Part I) focus on his first 15 years; Parts II and III focus on his adult years.

Catholics ✧ City Life ✧ Clergy ✧ Essayists ✧ Military Life ✧ Novelists ✧ Victorian Era British Memoirists ✧ WWI I England

Richardson, H(enry) H(andel) (b. Ethel Florence Lindesay) (1870–1946). *Myself When Young: Together with an Essay on the Art of Henry Handel Richardson by J.G. Robertson* (W.W. Norton, 1948).

Pages 6–120. (The author is a woman.)

Novelists ✧ Victorian Era British Memoirists I England

Richler, Mordecai (1931–2001). *The Street* (McClelland and Stewart, 1969).
He was best known as the author of *The Apprenticeship of Duddy Kravitz* (Little, Brown, 1959), in 1974 adapted into film starring Richard Dreyfuss.
Essayists ✧ Jews ✧ Novelists ✧ Screenwriters ✧ Short Story Writers | Canada (Quebec: Montreal)

Roberts, Cecil (1892–1976). *The Growing Boy: Being the First Book of an Autobiography, 1892–1908* (Hodder & Stoughton, 1967).
Pages 21–254 focus on his first 16 years.
Novelists ✧ Victorian Era British Memoirists | England

Roberts, Cecil (1892–1976). *The Years of Promise: Being the Second Book of an Autobiography, 1908–1919* (Hodder & Stoughton, 1968).
Pages 13 to about 218 focus on him from 16 to 21 years.
Novelists ✧ Victorian Era British Memoirists | England

Salzman, Mark (1959–). *Lost in Place: Growing Up Absurd in Suburbia* (Random House, 1995).
Covers him from about 14 to 22 years. Growing up in affluent Ridgefield, CT, the author tells of his time spent with Zen, cello lessons, and recreational drugs. For another memoir set in Ridgefield, CT, see "Cullerton, Brenda" (ch. 17).
Actors ✧ Baby Boomers ✧ College Teachers ✧ Novelists ✧ Screenwriters ✧ Sinologists | CT

Sand, George (pseud. of Amantine-Lucile-Aurore Dupin) (1804–1876). Ed. by Thelma Jurgrau. *Story of My Life: The Autobiography of George Sand: A Group Translation* (State University Press of New York, 1991).
Pages 418 (Part II, Ch. XI) to about 850 (Part IV, Ch. X).
Feminists ✧ Nineteenth-Century Pre-Industrial Age Memoirists ✧ Novelists ✧ Socialists | France

Scannell, Dorothy (b. Dolly Chegwidden) (1910–). *Mother Knew Best: Memoir of a London Girlhood* (Pantheon, 1974) (Variant title, *Mother Knew Best: An East End Childhood* [Macmillan, 1974]).
Covers her first 21 years.
Novelists ✧ Slums | England

Singer, I(srael) J(oshua) (1893–1944). Tr. by Joseph Singer. *Of a World That Is No More* (Vanguard, 1970).
His brother was Isaac Bashevis Singer (see entries in this ch.).
Dramatists ✧ Jews ✧ Novelists ✧ Short Story Writers | Poland

Spark, Muriel (1918–2006). *Curriculum Vitae* (Houghton Mifflin, 1993).
Easily more than 100 pages. She wrote *The Prime of Miss Jean Brodie* (Macmillan, 1961), a novel adapted as a film (1969).
Catholics ✧ Critics (Literary) ✧ Growing Up Between WWI and WWII ✧ Novelists ✧ Poets | Scotland

Sutcliff, Rosemary (1920–1992). *Blue Remembered Hills* (Bodley Head, 1983).
About the first 100 pages.
Arthritis ✧ Children's Authors ✧ Growing Up Between WWI and WWII ✧ Novelists | England

Tanizaki, Jun'ichiro (1886–1965). Tr. by Paul McCarthy. *Childhood Years: A Memoir* (Kodansha International, 1988).
Novelists | Japan

Thirkell, Angela (1890–1961). *Three Houses* (Oxford University, 1931).
She was the mother of memoirist Graham McInnes (see ch. 4) and was a cousin of Rudyard Kipling (see entry in this ch.).
Homes and Haunts ✧ Victorian Era British Memoirists ✧ Novelists | England

Tolstoy, (Count) Aleksei (1882–1945). Tr. by Violet Lansbury Dutt. *Nikita's Childhood* (Hutchinson International Authors, 1940) (First published in Russian, 1922).
He was a distant relative of Leo Tolstoy.
Dramatists ✧ Foreign Correspondents ✧ Immigrants ✧ Novelists ✧ Poets ✧ Short Story Writers | Russia

Tolstoy, (Count) Leo (1828–1910). Tr. by Isabel F. Hapgood. *Childhood, Boyhood, Youth* (Crowell, 1886).
This was originally published in Russian in 3 installments, under the titles *Childhood* (1852), *Boyhood* (1854), and *Youth* [or *Adolescence*] (1857).
Children's Authors ✧ Essayists ✧ Immigrants ✧ Novelists ✧ Philosophers ✧ Short Story Writers ✧ Spiritual Life | Russia

Warren, Robert Penn (1905–1989). *Portrait of a Father* (University Press of Kentucky, 1988).
Childhood memories are interspersed throughout this 79-page memoir.
College Teachers ✧ Critics (Literary) ✧ Dramatists ✧ Editors ✧ Essayists ✧ Fathers and Sons ✧ Novelists ✧ Poets | KY

Waugh, Evelyn (Arthur St. John) (1903–1966). *A Little Learning: The First Volume of an Autobiography* (Little, Brown, 1964) (Variant title, *A Little Learning: An Autobiography of Evelyn Waugh: The Early Years* [Chapman & Hall, 1964]).
See also "Waugh, Auberon" (his son; ch. 17) and "Waugh, Alec" (his brother; this ch.).
Biographers ✧ Critics (Literary) ✧ Essayists ✧ Novelists ✧ Oxford University ✧ Travel Writers | England

Wells, H(erbert) G(eorge) (1866–1946). *Experiment in Autobiography: Discoveries and Conclusions of a Very Ordinary Brain (Since 1866)* (Macmillan, 1934).
Pages 21–188.
Biographers ✧ Critics (Literary) ✧ Essayists ✧ Historians ✧ Journalists ✧ Novelists ✧ Short Story Writers ✧ Victorian Era British Memoirists | England

Welty, Eudora (1909–2001). *One Writer's Beginnings* (Harvard University, 1984).
Essayists ✧ Novelists ✧ Short Story Writers | MS

White, Patrick (1912–1990). *Flaws in the Glass: A Self-Portrait* (Viking, 1981).
About 60–65 pages.
Dramatists ✧ Growing Up Between WWI and WWII ✧ Novelists ✧ Poets ✧ Short Story Writers ✧ Spiritual Life | Australia

Short Story Writers

Anderson, Sherwood (1876–1941). *A Story Teller's Story* (B.W. Huebsch, 1924).
More than the first 100 pages focus on his first 21 years. The following entry is a companion volume. He was best known for his cycle of stories *Winesburg, Ohio* (1919).
Businesspersons ✧ Country Life ✧ Short Story Writers | OH

Anderson, Sherwood (1876–1941). *Sherwood Anderson's Memoirs* (Harcourt, Brace, 1942).

The first 4 chapters (pages 13–135) focus on his first 21 years. Nearly completed at the time of Anderson's untimely death, this volume was cast into its final form by Anderson's widow and others.

Businesspersons ✧ Country Life ✧ Short Story Writers | OH

Armstrong, Martin Donisthorpe (1882–1974). *Victorian Peep-Show* (M. Joseph, 1938).

To about 12 years. As an adult, he was a friend of writer Conrad Aiken for 20 years.

Children's Authors ✧ Editors ✧ Family Memoirs ✧ Journalists ✧ Novelists ✧ Poets ✧ Short Story Writers ✧ Translators ✧ Victorian Era British Memoirists ✧ Wealth | England

Auchincloss, Louis (1917–living 2007). *A Writer's Capital* (University of Minnesota, 1974).

Pages 29–88. The writer is known for his fiction, which examines the lives of the wealthy.

City Life ✧ Growing Up Between WWI and WWII ✧ Novelists ✧ Short Story Writers | NYC

Blackwood, Algernon (1869–1951). *Episodes Before Thirty* (Cassell, 1923).

About the first 100 pages focus on him from about 20 to 21 years. Blackwood was the author of dozens of short stories and about 20 novels, whose themes involve dark fantasy and horror.

Journalists ✧ Novelists ✧ Short Story Writers ✧ Spiritual Life | Canada (Ontario: Toronto) ✧ NYC

Butts, Mary (1892–1937). *The Crystal Cabinet: My Childhood at Salterns* (Methuen, 1937).

Her interest in natural and occult forces is evident in her fiction. She died in middle age of a burst appendix.

Country Life ✧ Critics (Literary) ✧ Novelists ✧ Occult ✧ Poets ✧ Short Story Writers ✧ Victorian Era British Memoirists | England

Davis, Rebecca Harding (1831–1910). *Bits of Gossip* (Constable, 1904).

She was one of the first American writers of realistic fiction. Some of her youth was spent in AL and WV.

Novelists ✧ Short Story Writers | PA ✧ U.S. (Southeast)

Dawson, Fielding (1930–). *Tiger Lilies: An American Childhood* (Duke University, 1984).

As an adult he taught writing to inmates in several prisons.

Country Life ✧ Essayists ✧ Growing Up Between WWI and WWII ✧ Illustrators ✧ Painters ✧ Short Story Writers ✧ Teachers | MO

Hurst, Fannie (1889–1968). *Anatomy of Me: A Wonderer in Search of Herself* (Jonathan Cape, 1959).

About the first 100 pages.

Novelists ✧ Short Story Writers | OH

Mortimer, John (1923–). *Clinging to the Wreckage* (Ticknor & Fields, 1982).

About 60–70 pages. He is best known as the creator of the fictitious detective Rumpole, who first appeared in the short story collection *Rumpole of the Bailey* (1978).

Dramatists ✧ Growing Up Between WWI and WWII ✧ Lawyers ✧ Novelists ✧ Oxford University ✧ Screenwriters ✧ Short Story Writers | England

Olmstead, Robert (1954–). *Stay Here with Me: A Memoir* (Metropolitan Books, 1996).
About 151 pages, scattered among pages 48–206. He grew up on his grandfather's dairy farm. This memoir, which contains much re-created dialogue, focuses on him at age 18.

Baby Boomers ✧ Farm Life ✧ Grandfathers ✧ Novelists ✧ Short Story Writers ✧ Summer I NH

Pohl, Frederik (pseud.: James McCreigh) (1919–living 2007). *The Early Pohl* (Doubleday, 1976).
About the first 84 pages. He is a noted science fiction writer.

Growing Up Between WWI and WWII ✧ Novelists ✧ Short Story Writers I NYC

Rhys, Jean (1894–1979). *Smile Please: An Unfinished Autobiography* (Andre Deutsch, 1979).
About the first 100 pages. She lived on Dominica during her first 17 years.

Island Life ✧ Novelists ✧ Short Story Writers I Dominica ✧ England

Singer, Isaac Bashevis (1904–1991). Tr. by Curt Leviant. *In My Father's Court* (Farrar, Straus, and Giroux, 1966) (Variant title, *A Day of Pleasure: Stories of a Boy Growing Up in Warsaw* [Farrar, Straus, and Giroux, 1969]).
His brother was I(srael) J(oseph) Singer (see entry this ch.). The following 2 entries are companion volumes.

Children's Authors ✧ Dramatists ✧ Jews ✧ Novelists ✧ Short Story Writers ✧ Translators I Poland

Singer, Isaac Bashevis (1904–1991). *A Little Boy in Search of God: Mysticism in a Personal Light* (Doubleday, 1976).
By page 97, he is only 13 years old. This book covers the same period of childhood as the previous and following entries, examining them from a theological perspective.

Children's Authors ✧ Dramatists ✧ Jews ✧ Novelists ✧ Short Story Writers ✧ Translators I Poland

Singer, Isaac Bashevis (1904–1991), and Ira Moskowitz. Tr. by Curt Leviant. *More Stories from My Father's Court* (Farrar, Straus, and Giroux, 2000).

Children's Authors ✧ Dramatists ✧ Jews ✧ Novelists ✧ Short Story Writers ✧ Translators I Poland

Suckow, Ruth (1892–1960). *A Memoir* (Rinehart, 1952).

Essayists ✧ Novelists ✧ Short Story Writers I IA

Trevor (Cox), William (1928–). *Excursions in the Real World: Memoirs* (Knopf, 1993).
About 66 scattered pages.

Advertising Copywriters ✧ Growing Up Between WWI and WWII ✧ Novelists ✧ Sculptors ✧ Short Story Writers I Ireland

Warner, Sylvia Townsend (1893–1978). *Scenes of Childhood* (Chatto & Windus, 1981).
Her novel *Lolly Willowes* (Viking, 1926) was the first selection offered by the Book of the Month Club.

Biographers ✧ Feminists ✧ Lesbians ✧ Musicologists ✧ Novelists ✧ Poets ✧ Short Story Writers ✧ Translators ✧ Victorian Era British Memoirists I England

Williamson, Henry (1895–1977). *The Children of Shallowford* (Faber & Faber, 1939; [rev. ed.], Macdonald and Jane's, 1978).

Children's Authors ✧ Country Life ✧ Essayists ✧ Natural History ✧ Novelists ✧ Short Story Writers I England

Williamson, Henry (1895–1977). *The Lone Swallow and Other Essays of Boyhood and Youth* (Alan Sutton, 1933) (Rev. ed. of *The Lone Swallows* [Collins, 1922]).

The illustrated ed. contains wood engravings by C(harles) F(rederick) Tunnicliffe. See also "Uttley, Alison" (ch. 3).

Children's Authors ✧ Country Life ✧ Essayists ✧ Natural History ✧ Novelists ✧ Short Story Writers I England

Woolson, Constance (pseud.: Ann March) (1840–1894). *The Old Stone House* (Lothrop, 1873).

Her mother was a niece of James Fenimore Cooper.

Critics (Literary) ✧ Nineteenth-Century Pre-Industrial Age Memoirists ✧ Poets ✧ Short Story Writers ✧ Travel Writers ✧ Wealth I OH

Poets

Alberti, Rafael (1902–1984). Tr. and ed. by Gabriel Berns. *The Lost Grove: Autobiography of a Spanish Poet in Exile* (University of California, 1976).

At least the first 3 chapters focus on his first 21 years; he is only 17 on page 127. Book I (covering 1902–1917) was first published in Mexico in 1942; the completed book, with the addition of Book II (covering 1917–1931), was published in Buenos Aires in 1959.

Catholics ✧ Dramatists ✧ Family Memoirs ✧ Painters ✧ Poets ✧ Uncles I Spain

Angelou, Maya (1928–). *I Know Why the Caged Bird Sings* (Random House, 1969).

This volume covers Angelou's first 16 years and is continued by the following entry.

Abuse (Sexual) ✧ African Americans ✧ Growing Up Between WWI and WWII ✧ Poets I MO ✧ AR

Angelou, Maya (1928–). *Gather Together in My Name* (Random House, 1974).

This memoir focuses on the popular poet from about 16 to 21 years.

Abuse (Sexual) ✧ African Americans ✧ Growing Up Between WWI and WWII ✧ Poets I CA (Northern)

Buckley, Christopher (1948–). *Cruising State: Growing Up in Southern California* (University of Nevada, 1994).

Pages 3 to about 158. This is a collection of essays.

Baby Boomers ✧ Essayists ✧ Poets I CA (Southern)

Church, Richard (1893–1972). *Over the Bridge: An Essay in Autobiography* (Heinemann, 1955).

Covers him to about 18 years. Both this volume and its sequel (following entry) won the *Times* Gold Medal award.

Children's Authors ✧ City Life ✧ Essayists ✧ Intellectual Life ✧ Novelists ✧ Poets ✧ Victorian Era British Memoirists I England

Church, Richard (1893–1972). *The Golden Sovereign: A Conclusion to Over the Bridge* (E.P. Dutton, 1957).

Covers him from about 18 to about 21 years, through page 221.

Bereavement ✧ Children's Authors ✧ City Life ✧ Essayists ✧ Intellectual Life ✧ Novelists ✧ Poets ✧ Victorian Era British Memoirists I England

Clark, (Sir) Leonard (1905–1981). *Green Wood: A Gloucestershire Childhood* (Max Parrish, 1962).

He produced more than 60 books, many of which were collections of verse for children. The following entry is a companion volume.

Children's Authors ✧ Editors ✧ Poets ✧ Spiritual Life ✧ Teachers I England

Clark, (Sir) Leonard (1905–1981). *A Fool in the Forest* (Dobson, 1965).

Children's Authors ✧ Editors ✧ Poets ✧ Spiritual Life ✧ Teachers I England

Coffin, Robert (1892–1955). *Lost Paradise: A Boyhood on a Maine Coast Farm* (Macmillan, 1934).

This is a third-person account. He was so acclimated to farm life that he operated 2 farms as an adult, despite his success as a teacher and writer.

College Teachers ✧ Editors ✧ Essayists ✧ Farm Life ✧ Lecturers ✧ Poets I ME

Corbett, William (1942–). *Furthering My Education: A Memoir* (Zoland Books, 1997).

Pages 19–84.

Fathers and Sons ✧ Poets I CT

Davison, Peter (1928–2004). *Half Remembered: A Personal History* (Harper & Row, 1973).

Before he was 16, he had climbed a dozen peaks higher than 13,000 feet.

Editors ✧ Growing Up Between WWI and WWII ✧ Lecturers ✧ Outdoor Recreation ✧ Poets I NY ✧ CO ✧ Washington, DC ✧ MA

Day-Lewis, C(ecil) (pseud.: Nicholas Blake) (1904–1972). *The Buried Day* (Harper, 1960).

Pages 16 to about 168. He was Poet Laureate of Great Britain, succeeding John Masefield (see entry, this ch.).

Children's Authors ✧ Critics (Literary) ✧ Dramatists ✧ Intellectual Life ✧ Lecturers ✧ Novelists ✧ Oxford University ✧ Poets ✧ Translators I Ireland

De Angeli, Marguerite (1889–1987). *Butter at the Old Price: The Autobiography of Marguerite de Angeli* (Doubleday, 1971).

Pages 1–54.

Children's Authors ✧ Illustrators ✧ Singers I MI ✧ PA

Digges, Deborah (1950–). *Fugitive Spring: A Memoir* (Knopf, 1992).

Pages 3 to about 140.

Baby Boomers ✧ College Teachers ✧ Dutch Reformed Church ✧ Poets I MO ✧ CA

Doolittle, Hilda (pseud.: H.D.) (1886–1961). *The Gift* (New Directions, 1982) (Written 1941–1943).

Bisexuals ✧ Essayists ✧ Grandmothers ✧ Movies ✧ Novelists ✧ Poets ✧ Short Story Writers ✧ Translators | PA

Doty, Mark (1953–). *Firebird: A Memoir* (HarperCollins, 1999).

Pages 11 to about 181.

Baby Boomers ✧ Poets | TN

Dyment, Clifford (1914–1971). *The Railway Game: An Early Autobiography* (J.M. Dent, 1963).

Critics (Literary) ✧ Growing Up Between WWI and WWII ✧ Journalists ✧ Motion Picture Producers and Directors ✧ Poets ✧ Screenwriters | England

Ellison, Edith Nicholl Bradley (1851– or 1858–). *A Child's Recollections of Tennyson* (E.P. Dutton, 1906).

Covers her from 3 to about 19 years. (She also wrote under the name Edith Nicholl Lewis; see entry, this ch.)

Nineteenth-Century Pre-Industrial Age Memoirists ✧ Tennyson, (Lord) Alfred | England

Follain, Jean (1903–1971). Tr. in 1981 from the French by Louise Guiney. *Canisy* (Gallimard, 1942).

Entire 64-page memoir focuses on his childhood. Includes an extended essay, "The Kingdom of Childhood," by Robert Morgan.

Lawyers ✧ Poets | France

Frost, Lesley (1899–1983). *New Hampshire's Child: The Derry Journals of Lesley Frost* (State University of New York, 1969).

She was Robert Frost's daughter; covers 1905–1909.

Diaries and Journals ✧ Frost, Robert | NH

Giovanni, Nikki (1943–). *Gemini: An Extended Autobiographical Statement on My First Twenty-Five Years of Being a Black Poet* (Bobbs-Merrill, 1971).

Pages 3 to about 70 (chs. 1–5).

African Americans ✧ Civil Rights Workers ✧ Grandmothers ✧ Lecturers ✧ Poets ✧ Racism | TN

Gonzalez, Ray (1952–). *Memory Fever: A Journey Beyond El Paso del Norte* (Broken Moon Press, 1993).

About 61 scattered pages.

Baby Boomers ✧ Editors ✧ Education ✧ Mexican Americans ✧ Poets | TX (West)

Hall, Donald (1928–). *String Too Short to Be Saved: Childhood Reminiscences* (Viking, 1961).

The author was named Poet Laureate of the U.S. in 2006. See also "Jager, Ronald" (ch. 3).

Children's Authors ✧ Country Life ✧ Critics (Literary) ✧ Depressions (Economic) ✧ Editors ✧ Essayists ✧ Farm Life ✧ Grandfathers ✧ Growing Up Between WWI and WWII ✧ Poets ✧ Short Story Writers | NH

Holden, Jonathan (1941–). *Guns and Boyhood in America: A Memoir of Growing Up in the 50s* (University of Michigan, 1997).

Poets | NJ

Horne, Donald (1921–2005). *The Education of Young Donald* (Angus and Robertson, 1967; [rev. ed.], Penguin, 1988).
Growing Up Between WWI and WWII ✧ Poets | Australia

Kashner, Sam (1957?–). *When I Was Cool* (HarperCollins, 2004).
Focus is on him from 19 to 21 years, during 1976–1978, at the "Jack Kerouac School of Disembodied Poetics" in Boulder, Colorado.
Baby Boomers ✧ Beat Generation ✧ Ginsberg, Allen ✧ Poets | CO

Kavanagh, P(atrick) J(oseph)(1931–). *The Perfect Stranger* (Graywolf, 1988).
Pages 10 to about 150.
Korean War ✧ Novelists ✧ Poets | England ✧ Korea

Kloefkorn, William (1932?–). *This Death by Drowning* (University of Nebraska, 1997).
Pages 1–63 (chs. 1–3). The author's earliest childhood years are focused on in this memoir, which is continued by the following entry. He has held the position of State Poet of Nebraska.
Country Life ✧ Depressions (Economic) ✧ Poets | KS

Kloefkorn, William (1932?–). *Restoring the Burnt Child: A Primer* (University of Nebraska, 2003).
The sequel to *This Death by Drowning*, this memoir covers him from 9 to 13 years.
Country Life ✧ Depressions (Economic) ✧ Paperboys ✧ Poets ✧ WWII | KS

Kloefkorn, William (1932?–). *At Home on This Moveable Earth* (University of Nebraska, 2006).
This is the third of a projected 4-volume autobiographical series.
Country Life ✧ Depressions (Economic) ✧ Paperboys ✧ Poets ✧ WWII | KS

Kreymborg, Alfred (1883–1966). *Troubadour: An Autobiography* (Boni and Liveright, 1925).
About page 31 to about page 84 (chs. 3–9).
Catholics ✧ City Life ✧ College ✧ Teachers ✧ Critics (Literary) ✧ Dramatists ✧ Editors ✧ Poets | NYC (Bronx)

Lewis, Edith Nicholl (1851 or 1858–). *As Youth Sees It; Personal Recollections of Great Victorians* (Meador, 1935).
All but the last chapter are on her childhood and youth. (She also wrote under the name Edith Nicholl Bradley Ellison; see entry, this ch.)
Nineteenth-Century Pre-Industrial Age Memoirists ✧ Tennyson, (Lord) Alfred | England ✧ MA

Lorde, Audre (1934–1992). *Zami: A New Spelling of My Name* (Persephone, 1982).
Pages 10 to about 210.
African Americans ✧ College Teachers ✧ Lesbians ✧ Librarians ✧ Poets ✧ Quakers | NYC (Harlem) ✧ CT ✧ Mexico

MacLean, Alasdair (1926–). *Field of Sighing: A Highland Childhood* (Berlinn, 2002).
This title is not to be confused with Donald Angus Cameron's *Field of Sighing: A Highland Boyhood* (see entry, this ch.).
Growing Up Between WWI and WWII ✧ Poets | Scotland

Masefield, John (1878–1967). *Grace Before Ploughing; Fragments of Autobiography* (Macmillan, 1966).

Focuses on him at about age 8. This modern classic is lyrically evocative and relies on no re-created dialogue. He was Poet Laureate of Great Britain, and was succeeded by C(ecil) Day-Lewis (see entry, this ch.).

Children's Authors ✧ Dramatists ✧ Editors ✧ Essayists ✧ Novelists ✧ Poets ✧ Seafaring Life ✧ Short Story Writers ✧ Translators | England

Masefield, John (1878–1967). *New Chum* (Macmillan, 1944).

Focuses on him at age 13. Set aboard the H.M.S. *Conway.*

Children's Authors ✧ Dramatists ✧ Editors ✧ Essayists ✧ Novelists ✧ Poets ✧ Seafaring Life ✧ Short Story Writers ✧ Translators ✧ Voyages

Masefield, John (1878–1967). *So Long to Learn: Chapters of an Autobiography* (Heinemann, 1952).

Pages 4–69 cover his first 18 years.

Bakers ✧ Children's Authors ✧ Dramatists ✧ Editors ✧ Essayists ✧ Novelists ✧ Poets ✧ Seafaring Life ✧ Short Story Writers ✧ Translators | England

Masefield, John (1878–1967). *In the Mill* (Macmillan, 1941).

Focuses on him from about 17 to about 19 years.

Children's Authors ✧ Dramatists ✧ Editors ✧ Essayists ✧ Novelists ✧ Poets ✧ Seafaring Life ✧ Short Story Writers ✧ Translators | U.S.

McCloskey, Eunice (1906–). *So Dear to My Heart* (Bruce Humphries, 1964).

Artists ✧ Poets | PA

Merrill, James (1926–1995). *A Different Person: A Memoir* (Knopf, 1993).

About 50–55 scattered pages.

Amherst College ✧ Dramatists ✧ Growing Up Between WWI and WWII ✧ Poets | NYC ✧ MA

Merwin, W(illiam) S(tanley) (1927–). *Unframed Originals: Recollections* (Atheneum, 1982).

Growing Up Between WWI and WWII ✧ Poets | PA

Peters, Robert (1924–). *Crunching Gravel: Growing Up in the Thirties* (Mercury House, 1988).

This memoir is continued by the following entry.

Depressions (Economic) ✧ Farm Life ✧ Gays ✧ Growing Up Between WWI and WWII ✧ Poets | WI

Peters, Robert (1924–). *For You, Lili Marlene: A Memoir of World War II* (University of Wisconsin, 1995).

Gays ✧ Military Life ✧ Poets ✧ WWII

Raine, Kathleen (1908–2003). *Farewell Happy Fields; Memories of Childhood* (Hamilton, 1973).

She was an intimate of Gavin Maxwell (see ch. 2).

Critics (Literary) ✧ Poets ✧ Translators | England

Raine, Kathleen (1908–2003). *The Land Unknown* (Hamilton, 1975).

Autobiographies (Skoob, 1991) collects both of these titles plus *The Lion's Mouth: Concluding Chapters of Autobiography* (Hamilton, 1977), which focuses on her adult years.

Critics (Literary) ✧ Poets ✧ Translators | England

Read, (Sir) Herbert (1893–1968). *The Innocent Eye* (Faber & Faber, 1933).

This memoir, continued by the following entry, was incorporated with 3 subsequent memoirs of his into *The Contrary Experience: Autobiographies* (Horizon, 1963).

Critics (Art) ✧ Journalists ✧ Poets ✧ Publishers ✧ Victorian Era British Memoirists | England

Read, (Sir) Herbert (1893–1968). *Annals of Innocence and Experience* (Faber & Faber, 1940).

Critics (Art) ✧ Journalists ✧ Poets ✧ Publishers ✧ Victorian Era British Memoirists | England

Rickel, Boyer (1951–). *Taboo* (University of Wisconsin, 1999).

At least 80 scattered pages.

Baby Boomers ✧ Gays ✧ Poets | AZ

Sandburg, Carl (1878–1967). *Always the Young Strangers* (Harcourt, Brace, 1952).

See also the following 2 entries.

Poets ✧ Socialists ✧ Swedish Americans | IL

Sandburg, Carl (1878–1967). *Prairie-Town Boy: Taken from Always the Young Strangers* (Harcourt, Brace, 1952).

This is adapted from part of *Always the Young Strangers* (previous entry). On page 164 he is 20.

Poets ✧ Socialists ✧ Swedish Americans | IL

Sandburg, Carl (1878–1967). Ed. by M. Sandburg and George Hendrick. *Ever the Winds of Chance* (University of Illinois, 1983) (First produced in 1953).

Covering up to age 20, this is the unfinished sequel to *Always the Young Strangers*. *New York Times* critic Robert E. Sherwood called this the best autobiography ever written by an American.

Poets ✧ Socialists ✧ Swedish Americans | IL

Sarton, May (1912–1995). *I Knew a Phoenix: Sketches for an Autobiography* (Rinehart, 1959).

Covers her first 26 years. The journals she kept focused on her adult years. She survived a stroke in 1986, and published her poems through 1994.

Diaries and Journals ✧ Growing Up Between WWI and WWII ✧ Novelists ✧ Poets ✧ Teachers | MA

Sassoon, Siegfried (1886–1967). *The Old Century and Seven More Years* (Faber & Faber, 1938).

Covers his first 21 years.

Poets ✧ Victorian Era British Memoirists | England

Simic, Charles (1938–). *A Fly in the Soup: Memoirs* (University of Michigan, 2000),

Pages 7 to about 109.

Poets | Yugoslavia ✧ France (Paris) ✧ NYC ✧ IL

Simpson, Louis (1923–). *North of Jamaica* (Harper & Row, 1972).

Pages 9 to about 100. He is a Pulitzer Prize winner in poetry.

Army, U.S. ✧ College Teachers ✧ Columbia University ✧ Growing Up Between WWI and WWII ✧ Island Life ✧ Poets | Jamaica ✧ NYC ✧ TX (Fort Hood)

Thomas, (Philip) Edward (1878–1917). *The Childhood of Edward Thomas: A Fragment of Autobiography* (Faber & Faber, 1938).

Poets | England

Verlaine, Paul (1844–1896). Tr. by Joanna Richardson. *Confessions of a Poet* (Philosophical Library, 1950) (First published in French, 1895).
  Starting with page 21, his first 21 years are focused on for well more than the next 80 pages.

  Nineteenth-Century Pre-Industrial Age Memoirists ✧ Poets | France

Webb, Ruth Cameron (1923–). *Journey into Personhood* (University of Iowa, 1994).
  Pages 4–76. A classic.

  Cerebral Palsy ✧ Education ✧ Growing Up Between WWI and WWII ✧ Poets | MA ✧ MD ✧ PA

Wingfield, Sheila (1906–1992). *Real People* (Cresset, 1952).
  Focuses on her adolescence.

  Poets | England ✧ Ireland

Yeats, William Butler (1865–1939). *Reveries Over Childhood and Youth* (Cuala, 1915).

  Dramatists ✧ Novelists ✧ Poets ✧ Short Story Writers ✧ Victorian Era British Memoirists | Ireland

Dramatists and Screenwriters

For others involved in the theater and film industries, see chapter 11.

Behan, Brendan (1923–1964). *Borstal Boy* (Hutchinson, 1958).
  This memoir is continued by the following entry.

  Dramatists ✧ Growing Up Between WWI and WWII | Ireland (North)

Behan, Brendan (1923–1964). *Confessions of an Irish Rebel* (B. Geis Associates, 1965).
  Over 100 pages.

  Dramatists ✧ Growing Up Between WWI and WWII ✧ Revolutionaries | Ireland (North)

Behrman, S(amuel) N(athaniel) (1893–1973). *The Worcester Account* (Random House, 1954).

  Dramatists ✧ Jews | MA

Berg, Gertrude (1899–1966). *Molly and Me* (McGraw-Hill, 1961).
  About the first half of book is on her childhood; she spent time in the Catskills, but attended public school in NYC. She created the popular radio (and later television) show *The Goldbergs*, based on her recollections of growing up with her parents and immigrant grandparents. She later adapted these into a stage production, *Me and Molly*, and then collaborated with N. Richard Nash on the writing of a film version, *Molly*.

  Actresses ✧ City Life ✧ Dramatists ✧ Family Memoirs ✧ Grandparents ✧ Immigrants ✧ Jews ✧ Mountain Life | NY ✧ NYC

Caspary, Vera (1899–1987). *Secrets of Grown-ups* (Macmillan, 1979).
  About 65–70 pages.

  Advertising Copywriters ✧ Dramatists ✧ Novelists ✧ Screenwriters | IL (?)

Cunningham, Laura (1947–). *A Place in the Country* (Riverhead Books, 2000).
  Pages 9 to about 80. See also the prequel, *Sleeping Arrangements* (ch. 17).

  Baby Boomers ✧ City Life ✧ Country Life ✧ Dramatists ✧ Novelists | NYC (Bronx)

Davis-Goff, Annabel (1942–). *Walled Gardens: Scenes from an Anglo-Irish Childhood* (Knopf, 1989).

  Bereavement ✧ Grandparents ✧ Screenwriters | Ireland

Foote, Horton (1916–living 2007). *Farewell: A Memoir of a Texas Childhood* (Scribner, 1999).
Covers his first 17 years, until he moves to CA. He wrote screenplays for the films *To Kill a Mockingbird* (1962) and *Terms of Endearment* (1983). He is not to be confused with the historian Shelby Foote (1916–2005).
Depressions (Economic) ✧ Dramatists ✧ Growing Up Between WWI and WWII ✧ Screenwriters I TX (East)

Gide, Andre (1869–1951). Tr. by Dorothy Bussy. *If It Die—* (Secker & Warburg, 1950).
Covers his first 25 years.
City Life ✧ Critics (Literary) ✧ Dramatists ✧ Essayists ✧ Intellectual Life ✧ Novelists ✧ Poets ✧ Short Story Writers ✧ Translators I France

Hart, Moss (1904–1961). *Act One* (Random House, 1959).
Pages 7–200 (Part One) cover him from about 12 to 21 years.
Dramatists I NY

Healy, Dermot (1947–). *The Bend for Home* (Harcourt, Brace, 1998).
Baby Boomers ✧ Country Life ✧ Dramatists ✧ Novelists I Ireland

Hecht, Ben (1894–1964). *A Child of the Century* (Simon and Schuster, 1954).
Pages 37 to about 178 (Book Two and more than the first half of Book Three) focus on his first 21 years, interspersing many intellectual musings.
Dramatists ✧ Journalists ✧ Novelists I WI ✧ IL (Chicago)

Hecht, Ben (1894–1964). *Gaily, Gaily* (Doubleday, 1963).
Covers him from 16 to 21 years.
Dramatists ✧ Journalists ✧ Novelists I IL (Chicago)

Kimbrough, Emily (1899–1989). *How Dear to My Heart* (Dodd, Mead, 1944).
Covers her first 11 years.
Fashion Editors ✧ Humorists ✧ Radio Broadcasters ✧ Screenwriters I IN

Kimbrough, Emily (1899–1989). *The Innocents from Indiana* (Harper & Brothers, 1950).
Focuses on her early adolescence after moving to Chicago.
Fashion Editors ✧ Humorists ✧ Radio Broadcasters ✧ Screenwriters I IL

Kunen, James (1948–). *The Strawberry Statement: Notes of a College Revolutionary* (Random House, 1969).
Baby Boomers ✧ City Life ✧ Diaries and Journals ✧ Revolutionaries ✧ Vietnam Conflict I NYC

Leonard, Hugh (pseud. of John Keyes Byrne) (1926–). *Home Before Night* (Andre Deutsch, 1979).
This memoir and the following entry, its companion, are set in the 1930s–1940s in Leonard's hometown, a village a few miles from Dublin.
Dramatists ✧ Essayists ✧ Growing Up Between WWI and WWII ✧ Screenwriters I Ireland

Leonard, Hugh (pseud. of John Keyes Byrne) (1926–). *Out After Dark* (Andre Deutsch, 1991).
Dramatists ✧ Essayists ✧ Growing Up Between WWI and WWII ✧ Screenwriters I Ireland

Loos, Anita (1888–1981) (claimed to have been b. as late as 1894). *A Girl Like I* (Viking, 1966).

About pages 22–90. She began writing film scripts at age 15.

Actresses ✧ Dramatists ✧ Humorists ✧ Novelists ✧ Librettists ✧ Screenwriters | CA (Southern)

Mayer, Edwin (1896–1960). *A Preface to Life* (Boni and Liveright, 1923).

Screenwriters | NYC (?)

Miller, Arthur (1915–2005). *Timebends: A Life* (Franklin Library, 1987).

About 80 pages.

City Life ✧ Dramatists ✧ Family Memoirs ✧ Growing Up Between WWI and WWII ✧ Jews | NYC (Harlem)

O'Casey, Sean (1880–1964). *I Knock at the Door: Swift Glances Back at Things That Made Me* (Macmillan, 1939).

This memoir covers O'Casey's earliest childhood. His 6 volumes of autobiography (published 1939–1956) were collected in 2 volumes as *Mirror in My House: The Autobiographies of Sean O'Casey* (Macmillan, 1956) in the U.S. and in Great Britain in 2 volumes as *Autobiographies* (Carroll & Graf, 1963).

Dramatists | Ireland

O'Casey, Sean (1880–1964). *Pictures in the Hallway* (Macmillan, 1942).

Covers him from about 11 to 18 years.

Dramatists | Ireland

Osborne, John (1929–1994). *A Better Class of Person: An Autobiography* (Faber & Faber, 1981).

Pages 16 to about 162. He wrote the play *Look Back in Anger* (1957) and became known as the first "Angry Young Man."

Actors ✧ City Life ✧ Dramatists ✧ Growing Up Between WWI and WWII | England

Semprun, Jorge (pseuds.: Federico Sanchez and Gerald Sorel) (1923–). Tr. from the French by Linda Coverdale. *Literature or Life* (Viking, 1997).

Nearly all of pages 4–310 focus on him from 18 to 21 years. While part of WWII's French Resistance, he was arrested and deported to the camp at Buchenwald.

Buchenwald ✧ Camps (Internment) ✧ Civil War (Spanish) ✧ Communists ✧ Holocaust Survivors ✧ Novelists ✧ Screenwriters | Spain ✧ France

Sheridan, Peter (1952–). *44, Dublin Made Me* (Macmillan, 1999).

Baby Boomers ✧ Dramatists ✧ Theatrical Producers and Directors | Ireland (North)

Simon, Neil (1927–). *Rewrites: A Memoir* (Simon and Schuster, 1996).

Pages 13–94.

City Life ✧ Dramatists ✧ Growing Up Between WWI and WWII | NYC (Bronx)

Spragg, Mark (1952–). *Where Rivers Change Direction* (University of Utah, 1999).

Baby Boomers ✧ Essayists ✧ Ranch Life ✧ Screenwriters | WY

Strindberg, August (1849–1912). Tr. by Evert Sprinchorn. *The Son of a Servant* (Anchor Books, 1966) (Originally part of 4-vol. work published in Swedish in 1886; *Son of a Servant* first tr. into English by Claud Field [Putnam, 1913]).

Pages 28–243 focus on first 21 years. He writes here in third person, referring to himself as "John."

Dramatists ✧ Nineteenth-Century Pre-Industrial Age Memoirists ✧ Painters I Sweden

Van Druten, John (pseud.: John Harewood) (1901–1957). *The Widening Circle* (Scribner, 1957).

He adapted Forbes's *Mama's Bank Account* (ch. 5) into the 1948 film *I Remember Mama*.

Dramatists ✧ Essayists ✧ Novelists ✧ Screenwriters I England

Williams, (George) Emlyn (1905–1987). *George: An Early Autobiography* (H. Hamilton, 1961).

He adapted this into a play, which was adapted into the film *The Corn Is Green* (1945).

Actors ✧ Dramatists I Wales

Essayists

Beard, Jo Ann (1955–). *The Boys of My Youth* (Little, Brown, 1998).

Over 100 scattered pages. This is a collection of essays.

Baby Boomers ✧ Children of Alcoholics ✧ Divorce ✧ Editors ✧ Essayists I IA ✧ IL

Chamson, André (1900–1983). Tr. from the French by John Rodker. *A Mountain Boyhood* (J. Lehmann, 1947).

He was curator of the National Museum in Paris (1933–1959).

Critics (Art) ✧ Curators ✧ Essayists ✧ Mountain Life ✧ Novelists I France

Chamson, Andre (1900–1983). Tr. from the French by Erik de Mauny. *A Time to Keep* (Faber & Faber, 1957).

From 5 to 14 years.

Bereavement ✧ Critics (Art) ✧ Curators ✧ Essayists ✧ Mountain Life ✧ Novelists I France

De Quincey, Thomas (1785–1859). Ed. by Edward Sackville-West. *Confessions of an English Opium-Eater: Together With Selections from the Autobiography of Thomas De Quincey* (Chanticleer, 1950).

Starting on about page 13, more than the first 200 pages. This work first appeared in the October/November 1821 *London Magazine*.

City Life ✧ Critics (Literary) ✧ Drug Abuse ✧ Editors ✧ Eighteenth-Century Memoirists ✧ Essayists Journalists I England ✧ Ireland ✧ Wales

Dillard, Annie (1945–). *An American Childhood* (Harper & Row, 1987).

From 5 to about 18 years.

Books and Reading ✧ Essayists ✧ Summer I PA

Ginzburg, Natalia (1916–1991). Tr. from the Italian by D.M. Low. *Family Sayings* (E.P. Dutton, 1967) (First published in Italian, 1963; reissued under title *The Things We Used to Say,* tr. by Judith Woolf [Arcade, 1991]).

About the first 100 pages.

Dramatists ✧ Essayists ✧ Growing Up Between WWI and WWII ✧ Novelists ✧ Translators I Italy

Karr, Mary (1955–). *Cherry: A Memoir* (Viking, 2000).

Covers her from about 12 to about 18 years. See also her prequel (ch. 3).

Baby Boomers ✧ Children of Alcoholics ✧ College Teachers ✧ Eccentrics ✧ Essayists ✧ Family Violence ✧ Homes and Haunts ✧ Mental Health ✧ Oil Fields ✧ Poets | TX (East)

Lopate, Phillip (1943–). *Getting Personal: Selected Writings* (Basic Books, 2003).

Pages 3–81 (the first 5 essays).

City Life ✧ College Teachers ✧ Critics (Film) ✧ Essayists ✧ Intellectual Life | NYC (Brooklyn)

Morris, Wright (1910–1998). *Will's Boy: A Memoir* (Harper & Row, 1981).

College Teachers ✧ Essayists ✧ Novelists ✧ Photographers ✧ Short Story Writers | NE ✧ IL (Chicago) ✧ TX

Moskowitz, Faye (1930–). *A Leak in the Heart: Tales from a Woman's Life* (David R. Godine, 1985).

About 82 scattered pages focus on her first 21 years, growing up in Jackson, MI. The following entry is a companion volume.

Bereavement ✧ College Teachers ✧ Depressions (Economic) ✧ Essayists ✧ Growing Up Between WWI and WWII ✧ Jews ✧ Poets ✧ Short Story Writers | MI

Moskowitz, Faye (1930–). *And the Bridge Is Love: Life Stories* (Beacon, 1991).

About 66 scattered pages.

Abuse (Sexual) ✧ Bereavement ✧ College Teachers ✧ Depressions (Economic) ✧ Essayists ✧ Growing Up Between WWI and WWII ✧ Jews ✧ Poets ✧ Short Story Writers | MI

Priestley, J(oseph) B(oynton) (1894–1984). *Margin Released: A Writer's Reminiscences and Reflections* (Harper & Row, 1962).

Pages 3–102 (Part One and the first quarter of Part Two) cover him from 16 to 21 years.

Critics (Literary) ✧ Dramatists ✧ Essayists ✧ Novelists ✧ Socialists ✧ Travel Writers ✧ Victorian Era British Memoirists | England

Quiller-Couch, (Sir) Arthur (1863–1944). *Memories and Opinions: An Unfinished Autobiography* (Macmillan, 1945).

Covers him to 24 years. His fiction writing included historical and adventure novels and ghost stories.

College Teachers ✧ Critics (Literary) ✧ Essayists ✧ Intellectual Life ✧ Journalists ✧ Novelists ✧ Poets ✧ Short Story Writers ✧ Victorian Era British Memoirists | England

Sedaris, David (1957–). *Me Talk Pretty One Day* (Little, Brown, 2000).

Except for about a half-dozen pages, about the first 75 pages (chs. 1–6). See also the companion memoir, *Naked* (ch. 11).

Baby Boomers ✧ Essayists ✧ Gays ✧ Humorists ✧ Radio Broadcasters ✧ Short Story Writers | NY ✧ NC

Vidal, Gore (1925–). *Screening History* (Harvard University, 1992).

The majority of text from pages 5 to 94 focuses on his first 21 years, intermingled with some social, artistic, and political commentary.

Essayists ✧ Exeter Academy ✧ Grandfathers ✧ Growing Up Between WWI and WWII ✧ Journalists ✧ Movies ✧ Novelists | Washington, DC ✧ NH

Warner, Charles Dudley (1829–1900). *Being a Boy: With a Biographical Sketch* (Houghton Mifflin, 1877).
He is best remembered as Mark Twain's collaborator on the novel *The Gilded Age* (1873).
Critics (Literary) ✧ Editors ✧ Essayists ✧ Farm Life ✧ Journalists ✧ Lawyers ✧ Nineteenth-Century Pre-Industrial Age Memoirists ✧ Novelists ✧ Surveyors ✧ Travel Writers | MA

Biographers

Benson, E(dward) F(rederic) (1899–1971). *As We Were* (Longmans, Green, 1930).
About 74 scattered pages. This is the first volume of a trilogy.
Biographers ✧ Dramatists ✧ Family Memoirs ✧ Novelists ✧ Short Story Writers | England

Bowen, Catherine Drinker (1897–1973). *Family Portrait* (Little, Brown, 1970).
Biographers ✧ Family Memoirs ✧ Lecturers | PA

Calder-Marshall, Arthur (1908–1992). *The Magic of My Youth* (R. Hart-Davis, 1951).
Set in the 1920s.
Biographers ✧ Critics (Literary) ✧ Crowley, Aleister ✧ Novelists ✧ Occult | England

Flexner, James Thomas (1908–). *Maverick's Progress: An Autobiography* (Fordham University, 1996).
Pages 13–104 (chs. 2–11).
Biographers ✧ City Life | NYC

Garnett, David (1892–1981). *The Golden Echo: Volume I* (Chatto & Windus, 1953).
Covers him to about 22 years.
Biographers ✧ Booksellers ✧ Novelists ✧ Publishers ✧ Victorian Era British Memoirists | England

Gordon, Lyndall (1941–). *Shared Lives: A Memoir* (W.W. Norton, 1992).
Pages 1–146.
Biographers ✧ Jews | South Africa

Hackett, Francis (1883–1962). *American Rainbow: Early Reminiscences* (Liveright, 1970).
Pages 3 to about 123 (the first 13 unnumbered chs.) cover him from 18 to 21 years. (Hackett finished writing the manuscript of this memoir in about 1952 or 1953.)
Biographers ✧ City Life ✧ Critics (Literary) ✧ Historians ✧ Immigrants ✧ Intellectual Life ✧ Novelists | NYC

Holroyd, Michael (1935–). *Basil Street Blues: A Memoir* (W.W. Norton, 2000).
Pages 101 to about 230. See also "Sitwell, (Sir) Osbert" (ch. 8); his life and family background bear marked similarities.
Biographers ✧ Eccentrics | England

James, Marquis (1891–1955). *The Cherokee Strip: A Tale of an Oklahoma Boyhood* (Viking, 1945).
Biographers ✧ Historians (Cultural) | OK

Lehmann, (Rudolph) John (Frederick) (1907–1987). *The Whispering Gallery: Autobiography I* (Harcourt, Brace, 1955).
The companion volume, *In My Own Time: Memoirs of a Literary Life* (Little, Brown, 1969), is a revision and condensation of this work and its sequels (*I Am My Brother: Autobiography II*

[Longmans, Green, 1960] and *The Ample Proposition: Autobiography III* [Eyre & Spottiswoode, 1966]).

Biographers ✧ Critics (Literary) ✧ Editors ✧ Poets | England

Origo, Iris (1902–1988). *Images and Shadows: Part of a Life* (John Murray, 1970).
Pages 13–171 focus on her youthful years.

Berenson, Bernard ✧ Biographers ✧ Classical Scholars ✧ Grandparents ✧ Intellectual Life | England ✧ Ireland ✧ NYC ✧ Italy

Powell, (Lady) Violet (1912–2002). *Five Out of Six: An Autobiography* (Heinemann, 1960).
Covers her to 18 years. She was married to Anthony Powell (see entry, this ch.).

Biographers ✧ Critics (Literary) ✧ Growing Up Between WWI and WWII | England

Powell, (Lady) Violet (1912–2002). *Within the Family Circle: An Autobiography* (Heinemann, 1976).
Covers her from 18 to 22 years.

Biographers ✧ Critics (Literary) ✧ Growing Up Between WWI and WWII | England ✧ Europe

Reid, B(enjamin) L(awrence) (1918–1990). *First Acts: A Memoir* (University of Georgia, 1988).
He won the 1969 Pulitzer Prize in Biography for *Man from New York: John Quinn and His Friends* (Oxford University, 1968).

Biographers ✧ College Teachers ✧ Critics (Literary) ✧ Depressions (Economic) ✧ Growing Up Between WWI and WWII ✧ Pacifists | KY

Richards, Laura E. (1850–1943). *When I Was Your Age* (Estes and Lauriat, 1894).
She was the daughter of Julia Ward Howe, the feminist who wrote the war poem "The Battle Hymn of the Republic" (1862). Laura and her sister won the 1917 Pulitzer Prize in Biography for *Julia Ward Howe* (Houghton Mifflin, 1916).

Biographers ✧ Children's Authors ✧ Nineteenth-Century Pre-Industrial Age Memoirists ✧ Poets | MA

Richards, Laura E. (1850–1943). *Stepping Westward* (D. Appleton and Company, 1931).
Pages 1–138, which make up nearly all of "Part I: Massachusetts, with Excursions," focus on her first 21 years.

Biographers ✧ Books and Reading ✧ Children's Authors ✧ Nineteenth-Century Pre-Industrial Age Memoirists ✧ Poets | MA ✧ RI ✧ England ✧ France ✧ Italy ✧ Greece ✧ Belgium ✧ NYC

Sutin, Lawrence (1951–). *A Postcard Memoir* (Graywolf, 2000).
About 50 scattered pages.

Baby Boomers ✧ Biographers ✧ Essayists ✧ Postcards ✧ Short Story Writers | MN ✧ OH ✧ Israel

Van Doren, Carl (1885–1950). *Three Worlds* (Harper & Brothers, 1936).
Pages 1–87. A professor of literature at Columbia University, he was a prolific writer whose biography *Benjamin Franklin* (Viking, 1938) won the 1939 Pulitzer Prize.

Biographers ✧ Critics (Literary) ✧ Editors ✧ Historians | IL

Wagenknecht, Edward (pseud.: Julian Forrest) (1900–2004). *As Far as Yesterday: Memories and Reflections* (University of Oklahoma, 1968).
Pages 3 to about 85. He produced some 2 dozen biographies, mostly on 19th-century American authors.

Biographers ✧ Centenarians ✧ Clergy ✧ College Teachers ✧ Critics (Literary) ✧ Editors | IL (Chicago)

Zweig, Stefan (1881–1942). *The World of Yesterday: An Autobiography* (Viking, 1943).
Pages 28–124. He was adept at writing psychological biographies.

Biographers ✧ Critics (Literary) ✧ Dramatists ✧ Librettists ✧ Novelists ✧ Pacifists ✧ Poets ✧ Short Story Writers | Austria

The Media

Writers on Architecture, Art, Books, Business, Dance, Film, Food, Literature, Music, Sports, Theatre, Theology, and Travel

Angell, Roger (1920–). *Let Me Finish* (Harcourt, Inc., 2006).
Stepson of *New Yorker* essayist E. B. White, Angell himself is a much-honored sportswriter who here tells of his roots in Prohibition-era New York City.

Baseball ✧ Divorce ✧ Editors ✧ Growing Up Between WWI and WWII ✧ Humorists ✧ Movies ✧ Short Story Writers ✧ Sportswriters | NYC

Brombert, Victor (1923–). *Trains of Thought: Memories of a Stateless Youth* (W.W. Norton, 2002).
Having fled from Europe at age 18, Brombert returned to his native land as an American soldier.

College Teachers ✧ Critics (Literary) ✧ Jews ✧ Refugees ✧ WWII | France ✧ Spain ✧ NYC ✧ Europe

Brooks, Van Wyck (1886–1963). *Scenes and Portraits: Memories of Childhood and Youth* (E.P. Dutton, 1954).
Except for "Chapter IV/My Forebears," pages 1 to about 141. This memoir and its 2 sequels were collected as *An Autobiography* (E.P. Dutton, 1965). He was married to Gladys Brooks (see ch. 3). Brooks was best known for his 5-volume history of American literature, *Makers and Finders: A History of the Writer in America, 1800–1915* (E.P. Dutton, 1936–1952).

Critics (Literary) ✧ Translators | NJ ✧ NYC ✧ MA ✧ Europe

Broun, Heywood Hale (1918–2001). *Whose Little Boy Are You? A Memoir of the Broun Family* (St. Martin's/Marek, 1983).

Actors ✧ Critics (Social) ✧ Growing Up Between WWI and WWII ✧ Journalists ✧ Sportswriters | NYC ✧ CT

Browning, Wilt (1937–). *Linthead: Growing Up in a Carolina Cotton Mill Village* (Down Home, 1990).

Public Relations ✧ Sportswriters ✧ Textile Mills | SC

Cameron, Donald Angus (pseud. of Robin Harbinson Bryans) (1928–2005). *Field of Sighing: A Highland Boyhood* (Longmans, 1966).
Bryans also adopted "Robert Harbinson Bryans" and "Robert Harbinson" (this ch.) as pseudonyms. This title is not to be confused with Alasdair MacLean's *Field of Sighing: A Highland Childhood* (in this chapter).

Dramatists ✧ Lecturers ✧ Shepherds ✧ Short Story Writers ✧ Travel Writers | Scotland

Canby, Henry Seidel (1878–1961). *The Age of Confidence: Life in the Nineties* (Farrar & Rinehart, 1934).
About the first 200 pages in this composite work focus on his first 21 years. See the sequel to this memoir (ch. 8). This work and *Alma Mater* (Farrar & Rinehart, 1936) (see ch. 8) were included

in his 1947 autobiography *American Memoir* (Houghton Mifflin, 1947), along with a final section on his adult years.

College Teachers ✧ Critics (Literary) ✧ Editors ✧ Episcopalians ✧ Essayists ✧ Intellectual Life ✧ Journalists ✧ Teachers | DE

Cardus, (Sir) Neville (1899?–). *Autobiography* (Collins, 1947).

About 53 pages. He was a self-educated, eclectic writer.

Critics (Music) ✧ Journalists ✧ Sportswriters | England

Clark, (Sir) Kenneth (1903–1983). *Another Part of the Wood: A Self-Portrait* (John Murray, 1974).

About pages 1–95. He was appointed director of the National Art Gallery when he was only 30.

City Life ✧ Critics (Art) ✧ Oxford University | England

Connolly, Cyril (1903–1974). "A Georgian Boyhood." In *Enemies of Promise* (Routledge, 1938).

Pages 183–335 are on his boyhood.

Critics (Literary) ✧ Eton College | England

Daiches, David (1912–2005). *Two Worlds: An Edinburgh Jewish Childhood* (Harcourt, Brace, 1956).

Critics (Literary) ✧ Growing Up Between WWI and WWII ✧ Jews | Scotland

Davenport, Marcia (1903–1996). *Too Strong for Fantasy* (Scribner, 1967).

Pages 11–117.

Biographers ✧ Radio Broadcasters ✧ Critics (Music) ✧ Editors ✧ Musicians ✧ Novelists | NYC

Dirda, Michael (1948–). *An Open Book: Coming of Age in the Heartland* (W.W. Norton, 2003).

Baby Boomers ✧ Books and Reading ✧ Critics (Literary) ✧ Intellectual Life | OH

Donoghue, Denis (1928–). *Warrenpoint* (Knopf, 1990).

About 122 scattered pages.

Critics (Literary) ✧ Growing Up Between WWI and WWII | Ireland (North)

Eisenberg, John (1956–). *Cotton Bowl Days: Growing Up with Dallas and the Cowboys in the 1960s* (Simon and Schuster, 1997).

Baby Boomers ✧ Football ✧ Sportswriters | TX

Elliott, George P(aul) (1918–1980). *A Piece of Lettuce: Personal Essays on Books, Beliefs, American Places, and Growing Up in a Strange Country* (Random House, 1964).

About 54 scattered pages focus on his first 21 years' intellectual development.

Books and Reading ✧ College Teachers ✧ Critics (Literary) ✧ Essayists ✧ Growing Up Between WWI and WWII ✧ Intellectual Life ✧ Novelists ✧ Poets | IN

Fermor, (Sir) Patrick Leigh (1915–living 2007). *A Time of Gifts: On Foot to Constantinople: from the Hook of Holland to the Middle Danube* (Harper & Row, 1977).

Growing Up Between WWI and WWII ✧ Translators ✧ Travel Writers | Europe

Fermor, (Sir) Patrick Leigh (1915–living 2007). *Between the Woods and the Water: On Foot to Constantinople from the Hook of Holland: The Middle Danube to the Iron Gates* (Viking, 1986).
Fermor was knighted in February 2004.
Growing Up Between WWI and WWII ✧ Translators ✧ Travel Writers I Europe

Fisher, M(ary) F(rances) K(ennedy) (pseuds.: Mary Frances Kennedy and Mary Frances Parrish) (1908–1992). *Among Friends* (Knopf, 1971).
This is a companion volume to *To Begin Again* and a prequel to *Long Ago in France* (see next 2 entries).
Food Writers I MI ✧ CA

Fisher, M(ary) F(rances) K(ennedy) (pseuds.: Mary Frances Kennedy and Mary Frances Parrish) (1908–1992). *To Begin Again: Stories and Memoirs, 1908–1929* (Pantheon Books, 1992).
This is a companion volume to *Among Friends* and a prequel to *Long Ago in France.*
Food Writers I MI ✧ CA

Fisher, M(ary) F(rances) K(ennedy) (pseuds.: Mary Frances Kennedy and Mary Frances Parrish) (1908–1992). *Long Ago in France: The Years in Dijon* (Prentice-Hall, 1991).
This is a sequel to *Among Friends* and *To Begin Again.*
Food Writers I France

Fussell, Paul (1924–). *Doing Battle: The Making of a Skeptic* (Little, Brown, 1996).
Pages 8 to about 175.
College Teachers ✧ Critics (Literary) ✧ Growing Up Between WWI and WWII ✧ Pomona College ✧ Travel Writers ✧ WWII I CA (Southern) ✧ Germany (?)

Gilbert, Fabiola Cabeza de Baca (1898–1991). *We Fed Them Cactus* (University of New Mexico, 1954).
About 72 scattered pages.
Food Writers ✧ Hispanic Americans ✧ Ranch Life I NM

Harbinson, Robert (pseud. of Robert Harbinson Bryans) (1928–2005). *No Surrender: An Ulster Childhood* (Faber & Faber, 1960)
Bryans also adopted "Robert Harbinson" and "Donald Angus Cameron" (this ch.) as pseudonyms.
Dramatists ✧ Growing Up Between WWI and WWII ✧ Lecturers ✧ Shepherds ✧ Short Story Writers ✧ Teachers ✧ Travel Writers I Ireland (North)

Hardy, Barbara (1924–). *Swansea Girl: A Memoir* (Owen, 1994).
Critics (Literary) ✧ Growing Up Between WWI and WWII I England ✧ Wales

Hare, Augustus John (1834–1903). Ed. by Malcolm Barnes. *The Story of My Life.* **2 vols.** (Allen & Unwin, 1952).
Pages 52 to about 409 of the first volume. This is a 2-volume distillation of the original 6-volume work (published by Dodd, Mead), whose first half appeared in 1896 and whose second half was published in 1900. A 1-volume abridgement of the entire work was later edited by Anita Miller and James Papp: *Peculiar People: The Story of My Life* (Academy Chicago, 1995); about 89

pages of it focus on Hare's first 21 years. An abridgement of the first 3 volumes of the entire work was also published, as *The Years with Mother* (Allen & Unwin, 1952).

Aunts ✧ Biographers ✧ Eccentrics ✧ Family Violence ✧ Nineteenth-Century Pre-Industrial Age Memoirists ✧ Oxford University ✧ Travel Writers | England ✧ Europe

Hazelton, Nika Standen (1912?–1992). *Ups and Downs: Memoirs of Another Time* (Harper & Row, 1989).

Pages 1–146 (chs. 1–5). According to various sources, she may have been born as early as 1908.

Food Writers ✧ Growing Up Between WWI and WWII | Italy ✧ Germany ✧ England ✧ Switzerland

Holloway, John (1920–). *A London Childhood* (Scribner, 1968).

Covers his first 9 years.

Critics (Literary) ✧ Growing Up Between WWI and WWII ✧ Poets | England

Howard, Maureen (1930–). *Facts of Life* (Little, Brown, 1978).

About the first 50 pages.

Critics (Literary) ✧ Editors ✧ Growing Up Between WWI and WWII ✧ Novelists | CT

Howells, William Dean (1837–1920). *A Boy's Town, Described for "Harper's Young People"* (Harper & Brothers, 1890).

Covers him from 3–11 years. See also "Howells, William Cooper" (his father).

Critics (Literary) ✧ Editors ✧ Nineteenth-Century Pre-Industrial Age Memoirists ✧ Novelists | OH

Huxley, Elspeth (1907–1997). *Love Among the Daughters: Memories of the Twenties in England and America* (W. Morrow, 1968).

See also her prequels (ch. 4).

Novelists ✧ Travel Writers | England ✧ U.S. (?)

Jaramillo, Cleofas M. (1878–1956). *Romance of a Little Village Girl* (Naylor, 1955).

Pages 10 to about 106 (chs. 3–16).

Aunts ✧ Bereavement ✧ Catholics ✧ Country Life ✧ Family Memoirs ✧ Folklorists ✧ Food Writers ✧ Politicians | NM

Kazin, Alfred (1915–1998). *A Walker in the City* (Harcourt, Brace, 1951).

City Life ✧ Critics (Literary) ✧ Editors ✧ Growing Up Between WWI and WWII | NYC (Brooklyn)

Kendall, Elizabeth (1947–). *American Daughter: Discovering My Mother* (Random House, 2000).

About page 25 to about page 185.

Baby Boomers ✧ Bereavement ✧ Critics (Dance) ✧ Mothers and Daughters ✧ Teachers | MO ✧ MA

Kidder, Rushworth (1944–). *In the Backyards of Our Lives: And Other Essays* (Yankee Books, 1992).

Some 78 scattered pages focus on his childhood and adolescence.

College Teachers ✧ Critics (Literary) | MA

Lancaster, (Sir) Osbert (1908–1986). *All Done from Memory* (Butler & Tanner, 1963).

Architectural Writers ✧ Cartoonists ✧ City Life ✧ Illustrators | England

Lancaster, (Sir) Osbert (1908–1986). *With an Eye to the Future* (Houghton Mifflin, 1967).

Pages 3 to about 92 focus on him from 9 to 21 years.

Architectural Writers ✧ Cartoonists ✧ City Life ✧ Eton College ✧ Illustrators | England

Lang, George (1924–). *Nobody Knows the Truffles I've Seen* (Knopf, 1998).
About 90 pages. He is a legendary restaurateur and raconteur.

Camps (Internment) ✧ Holocaust Survivors ✧ Immigrants ✧ Jews ✧ Musicians ✧ Prisoners ✧ Restaurateurs I Hungary

Langseth-Christensen, Lillian (1908–c. 1995). *A Design for Living* (Viking, 1987).
Covers the period of her tutelage under art teacher Josef Hoffman, from 14 to 17 years. In later years she became known for her cookbooks.

Cookery ✧ Decorative Arts ✧ Intellectual Life I Austria

Liebling, A(bbott) J(oseph) (1904–1963). *Back Where I Come From* (Sheridan House, 1938).

Boxing ✧ City Life ✧ Food Writers ✧ Journalists ✧ Military Life ✧ Sportswriters I NYC

Lubbock, Percy (1879–1965). *Earlham: Reminiscences of the Author's Early Life at Earlham Hall* (Scribner's Sons, 1922).
He was a friend of Henry James and Edith Wharton. This memoir is continued by the following entry.

Biographers ✧ Critics (Literary) ✧ Homes and Haunts ✧ Librarians I England

Lubbock, Percy (1879–1965). *Shades of Eton* (Jonathan Cape, 1929).

Biographers ✧ Critics (Literary) ✧ Eton College ✧ Librarians I England

Mendelsohn, Daniel (1960–). *The Elusive Embrace: Desire and the Riddle of Identity* (Knopf, 1999).
About 94 scattered pages.

Baby Boomers ✧ College Teachers ✧ Critics (Literary) ✧ Gays ✧ Journalists ✧ Translators I NY ✧ VA

Munro, Eleanor (1928–). *Memoir of a Modernist's Daughter* (Viking, 1988).
About 69 scattered pages.

Critics (Art) ✧ Growing Up Between WWI and WWII ✧ Mothers and Daughters I OH

O'Neill, Molly (194?–). *Mostly True: A Memoir of Family, Food, and Baseball* (Scribner, 2006).
More than 100 pages cover her first 21 years. The author, a former restaurant cook, tells of growing up with 5 younger brothers, including ex-New York Yankees star Paul O'Neill. She also has been a food writer for the *New York Times*.

Baby Boomers (?) ✧ Baseball ✧ Brothers ✧ Cookery ✧ Family Memoirs ✧ Food Writers I OH

Pasternak, Alexander (1893–1982). Ed. and tr. by Ann Pasternak Slater. *A Vanished Present: The Memoirs of Alexander Pasternak* (Oxford University, 1984).
Pages 2 to about 188. He was the brother of novelist Boris Pasternak.

Architectural Writers ✧ Pasternak, Boris I Russia

Powell, Anthony (1905–2000). *Infants of the Spring: The Memoirs of Anthony Powell* (Holt, Rinehart and Winston, 1976).
This is vol. 1 in his autobiographical tetralogy, <u>To Keep the Ball Rolling</u> (Heinemann, 1976–1982). He wrote the longest acclaimed work of fiction in the English language: *A Dance to the Music of Time* (Scribner; Little, Brown, 1951–1976); also, he was married to (Lady) Violet Powell (see entry, this ch.).

Critics (Literary) ✧ Novelists I England

Pritchett, (Sir) V(ictor) S(awdon) (1900–1997). *A Cab at the Door: An Autobiography; Early Years* (Chatto & Windus, 1968).

Biographers ✧ College Teachers ✧ Critics (Literary) ✧ Foreign Correspondents ✧ Novelists ✧ Short Story Writers | England

Quennell, (Sir) Peter (1905–1993). *The Marble Foot: An Autobiography, 1905–1938* (Collins, 1976).

About the first 130 pages. Overall, this memoir covers his first 30 years.

Biographers ✧ Essayists ✧ Historians ✧ Oxford University ✧ Poets | England

Raphael, Frederic (1931–). *A Spoilt Boy: A Memoir of Childhood* (Orion, 2003).

Prolific scholar Raphael traces his first 18 years, particularly those spent in England from the time he was 6.

Dramatists ✧ Education ✧ Essayists ✧ Jews ✧ Translators ✧ Travel Writers | England

Reichl, Ruth (1948–). *Tender at the Bone: Growing Up at the Table* (Random House, 1998).

Baby Boomers ✧ Cookery | NYC (Manhattan) ✧ CT ✧ Canada (Quebec: Montreal) ✧ MI

Rich, Frank (1949–). *Ghost Light: A Memoir* (Random House, 2000).

Focuses on his first 19 years.

Baby Boomers ✧ Critics (Film) ✧ Critics (Theater) | MD ✧ Washington, DC

Rittenhouse, Isabella Maud (1864–). Ed. and arranged for publication by Richard Lee Strout. *Maud* (Macmillan, 1939).

She grew up in a hardscrabble steamboating town on the Mississippi River. This is a 593-page abridgment from her journal.

Diaries and Journals ✧ Mississippi River | IL

Rosenbaum, Jonathan (1943–). *Moving Places: A Life at the Movies* (Harper & Row, 1980).

About page 15 to about page 146 of the 1995 ed. (University of California).

Critics (Film) ✧ Movies | AL

Rowse, A(lfred) L(eslie) (1903–1997). *A Cornish Childhood* (Jonathan Cape, 1942).

Covers up to October 11, 1922. This memoir is continued by the following entry. He was an eminent scholar of the Elizabethan Age.

Biographers ✧ College Teachers ✧ Critics (Literary) ✧ Historians (Cultural) ✧ Novelists ✧ Poets ✧ Short Story Writers | England

Rowse, A(lfred) L(eslie) (1903–1997). *A Cornishman at Oxford* (Jonathan Cape, 1965).

More than the first 100 pages cover him from 19 to 21 years.

Biographers ✧ College Life ✧ College Teachers ✧ Critics (Literary) ✧ Historians ✧ Novelists ✧ Oxford University ✧ Poets ✧ Short Story Writers | England

Runyon, Damon, Jr. (1918–1968). *Father's Footsteps* (Random House, 1953).

Pages 21 to about 97.

City Life ✧ Fathers and Sons ✧ Growing Up Between WWI and WWII ✧ Journalists ✧ Sportswriters | NYC

Sage, Lorna (1943–2001). *Bad Blood: A Memoir* (W. Morrow, 2000).
A winner of England's Whitbread Biography Award, this reminiscence recounts her early life growing up with her dysfunctional grandparents.

Books and Reading ✧ Clergy ✧ Critics (Literary) ✧ Grandparents ✧ Pregnancy (Teen) | England

Sheed, Wilfrid (1930–). *Frank & Maisie: A Memoir with Parents* (Simon and Schuster, 1985).

Catholics ✧ College Teachers ✧ Critics (Literary) ✧ Essayists ✧ Fathers and Sons ✧ Growing Up Between WWI and WWII ✧ Mothers and Sons ✧ Novelists ✧ Publishers ✧ Sportswriters | England ✧ U.S.

Simon, Kate (1912–1990). *Bronx Primitive: Portraits in a Childhood* (Viking, 1982).
This memoir is continued by the following entry.

City Life ✧ Fathers and Daughters ✧ Growing Up Between WWI and WWII ✧ Jews ✧ Travel Writers | NYC (Bronx)

Simon, Kate (1912–1990). *A Wider World: Portraits in an Adolescence* (Harper & Row, 1986).

City Life ✧ Fathers and Daughters ✧ Growing Up Between WWI and WWII ✧ Jews ✧ Travel Writers | NYC (Bronx)

Taylor, Suzanne. *Young and Hungry: A Cookbook in the Form of a Memoir* (Houghton Mifflin, 1970).

Cookery ✧ Summer | Norway

Thomas, Lowell (1892–1981). *Good Evening Everybody: From Cripple Creek to Samarkand* (W. Morrow, 1976).
About 60 pages.

Adventurers ✧ Editors ✧ Lecturers ✧ Radio Journalists ✧ Travel Writers | CO

Tobias, Andrew (pseud: John Reid). (1947–). *The Best Little Boy in the World* (Putnam, 1973).
Pages 1 to about 65.

Baby Boomers ✧ Business Writers ✧ Gays ✧ Yale University | NY ✧ CT

Toperoff, Sam (1933?–). *All the Advantages* (Little, Brown, 1966).
His father ran a chain of candy stores.

College Teachers ✧ Jews ✧ Novelists ✧ Sportswriters | NYC (Brooklyn, Queens, Manhattan)

Waugh, Alec (b. Alexander Raban Waugh) (1898–1981). *The Early Years of Alec Waugh* (Farrar, Straus and Company, 1962).
See also "Waugh, Evelyn" (his brother; this ch.) and "Waugh, Auberon" (his nephew; ch. 17).

Novelists ✧ Travel Writers ✧ WWI | England

Wechsberg, Joseph (1907–1983). *The Vienna I Knew: Memories of a European Childhood* (Doubleday, 1979).

Food Writers ✧ Foreign Correspondents ✧ Journalists ✧ Lawyers ✧ Musicians ✧ Novelists ✧ Photographers ✧ Travel Writers | Moravia (i.e., part of Austria and Czechoslovakia)

Wechsberg, Joseph (1907–1983). *Sweet and Sour* (Houghton Mifflin, 1948).

Food Writers ✧ Foreign Correspondents ✧ Journalists ✧ Lawyers ✧ Musicians ✧ Novelists ✧ Photographers ✧ Travel Writers | Czechoslovakia ✧ France

Windham, Kathryn Tucker (1918–). *A Serigamy of Stories* (University Press of Mississippi, 1988).
Set in the 1920s–1930s.

Editors ✧ Food Writers ✧ Growing Up Between WWI and WWII ✧ Journalists | AL

Young, Stark (1881–1963). *The Pavilion: Of People and Times Remembered, of Stories and Places* (Scribner's Sons, 1951).
He was an eminent theater critic.

College Teachers ✧ Critics (Theater) ✧ Dramatists ✧ Essayists ✧ Novelists ✧ Painters ✧ Translators | MS

Books, Reading, Librarians, and Booksellers

Birkerts, Sven (1951–). *My Sky Blue Trades: Growing Up Counter in a Contrary Time* (Viking, 2002).
Son of Latvian immigrants, he grew up in Detroit. He is the author of such books as *The Gutenberg Elegies* (Faber & Faber, 1994).

Baby Boomers ✧ Books and Reading ✧ Booksellers ✧ Children of Immigrants ✧ College Teachers ✧ Critics (Literary) ✧ Essayists ✧ Grandparents ✧ Hippies ✧ Immigrants ✧ Latvian Americans | MI

Croft-Cooke, Rupert (pseud.: Leo Bruce) (1903–1979). *The Gardens of Camelot* (Putnam, 1958).
This prolific author wrote more than 100 books. This volume, focusing on his childhood, is the first of more than 20 autobiographical volumes.

Booksellers ✧ Dramatists ✧ Editors ✧ Novelists ✧ Poets | England

Croft-Cooke, Rupert (1903–1979). *The Altar in the Loft* (Putnam, 1960).
Covers 11–14 years.

Booksellers ✧ Dramatists ✧ Editors ✧ Novelists ✧ Poets | England

Croft-Cooke, Rupert (1903–1979). *The Drums of Morning* (Putnam, 1961).
Covers 14–18 years.

Booksellers ✧ Dramatists ✧ Editors ✧ Novelists ✧ Poets | England

Greene, A(lvin) C(arl) (1923–2002). *A Personal Country* (Knopf, 1969).

Booksellers ✧ Growing Up Between WWI and WWII ✧ Historians ✧ Journalists ✧ Ranch Life | TX

Hailey, (Elizabeth) Kendall (1966–). *The Day I Became an Autodidact: And the Advice, Adventures, and Acrimonies That Befell Me Thereafter* (Delacorte, 1988).

Generation X ✧ Intellectual Life | CA ✧ England

Hutton, Laurence (1843–1904). *A Boy I Knew: Four Dogs, and Some More Dogs* (Harper & Brothers, 1900).
Among his many acquaintances was Helen Keller.

Books and Reading ✧ Dogs ✧ Editors ✧ Nineteenth-Century Pre-Industrial Age Memoirists | NYC

Picano, Felice (1944–). *Ambidextrous: The Secret Lives of Children: A Memoir in the Form of a Novel* (Gay Presses of New York, 1985).
Covers 11–13 years.

Booksellers ✧ City Life ✧ Gays ✧ Intellectual Life ✧ Novelists ✧ Poets ✧ Publishers ✧ Sexuality | NYC (Suburbia)

Plagemann, Bentz (1913–1991). *An American Past: An Early Autobiography* (W. Morrow, 1990).
Pages 15–100. As an adult, he was afflicted with polio.
Booksellers ✧ Children's Authors ✧ Growing Up Between WWI and WWII ✧ Novelists ✧ Polio | MA ✧ MI ✧ NYC ✧ OH

Powell, Lawrence Clark (1906–2001). *An Orange Grove Boyhood: Growing Up in Southern California, 1910–1928* (Capra, 1988).
Memoir of 80 pages.
Books and Reading ✧ Critics (Literary) ✧ Librarians | CA (Southern)

Spufford, Francis (1964–). *The Child That Books Built: A Life in Reading* (Metropolitan Books, 2002).
He tells of finding spiritual sustenance through reading fiction, during his sad childhood with his ill sister.
Baby Boomers ✧ Books and Reading ✧ Critics (Literary) ✧ Historians (Cultural) ✧ Intellectual Life ✧ Journalists ✧ Sisters | England

Winterich, John Tracy (1891–1970). *Another Day, Another Dollar* (Lippincott, 1947).
Covers his first 21 years.
Book Collectors ✧ Editors | RI

Wright, Louis (1899–1984). *Barefoot in Arcadia: Memories of a More Innocent Era* (University of South Carolina, 1974).
College Teachers ✧ Historians (Cultural) ✧ Journalists ✧ Librarians ✧ Shakespeare, William | SC

Lexicographers and Philologists

Mistral, Frederic (1830–1914). Tr. from the French by George Wickes. *The Memoirs of Frederic Mistral* (New Directions, 1986) (First published in French, 1906; abridged and paraphrased English translation published in 1907).
Pages 1 to about 136. This is a most engaging and evocative portrait of mid-19th-century life in rural France.
Country Life ✧ Lexicographers ✧ Nineteenth-Century Pre-Industrial Age Memoirists ✧ Poets | France

Renan, Ernest (1823–1892). Tr. from the French by C. B. Pitman. *Recollections of My Youth* (Routledge, 1929) (First published in French, 1883).
Archaeologists ✧ Nineteenth-Century Pre-Industrial Age Memoirists ✧ Philologists ✧ Spiritual Life | France

Publishing Industry

Publishers, Editors, and Printers

Asquith, (Lady) Cynthia (1887–1960). *Haply I May Remember* (J. Barrie, 1950).
About 180 pages. She compiled collections and anthologies of ghost stories written by herself and by such acquaintances as Algernon Blackwood (see entry, this ch.), Arthur Machen (see entry, this ch.), and Hugh Walpole. She was a sister-in-law of (Lady) Violet Bonham Carter (see ch. 1).
Biographers ✧ Children's Authors ✧ Country Life ✧ Editors ✧ High Society ✧ Novelists ✧ Victorian Era British Memoirists ✧ Wealth | England

Davis, Robert Hobart (1869–1942). *Tree Toad: The Autobiography of a Small Boy* (Frederick A. Stokes, 1935).
As an editor, he helped writer O. Henry.
Editors ✧ Essayists ✧ Journalists | CA (Northern) (?)

Dickson, (Horatio) Lovat (1902–1987). *The Ante-Room* (Macmillan, 1959).
Pages 1–213 (chs. 1–9).
Biographers ✧ Publishers | Australia ✧ South Africa ✧ England ✧ Canada

Girodias, Maurice (1919–1990). *The Frog Prince: An Autobiography* (Crown, 1980).
Covers his first 20 years.
City Life ✧ Growing Up Between WWI and WWII ✧ Publishers | France

Gollancz, (Sir) Victor (1893–1967). *My Dear Timothy: An Autobiographical Letter to His Grandson* (Simon and Schuster, 1952).
About 200–225 scattered pages.
Editors ✧ Grandfathers ✧ Humanitarians ✧ Jews ✧ Publishers ✧ Socialists ✧ Victorian Era British Memoirists | England

Hale, Judson (1933–). *Education of a Yankee: An American Memoir* (Harper & Row, 1987).
Editors ✧ Intellectual Life ✧ Journalists | MA

Hale, Nancy (1908–1988). *The Life in the Studio* (Little, Brown, 1969).
About 103 scattered pages. Her grandfather was Edward Everett Hale (see ch. 8).
Debutantes ✧ Editors High Society ✧ Journalists ✧ Novelists | MA

Israeloff, Roberta (1952–). *Lost and Found: A Woman Revisits Eighth Grade* (Simon and Schuster, 1996).
Baby Boomers ✧ Diaries and Journals ✧ Editors | NY (Long Island)

Kennedy, Richard (1910–1989). *A Boy at the Hogarth Press* (Whittington, 1972).
Focuses on him at age 16; he worked for Leonard Woolf and Virginia Woolf (see, respectively, entry in this ch. and in ch. 16).
Bloomsbury Group ✧ Growing Up Between WWI and WWII ✧ Printers | England

Krock, Arthur (1886–1974). *Myself When Young, Growing Up in the 1890's* (Little, Brown, 1973).
Editors ✧ Journalists | KY

Lindemeyer, Nancy. *Jenny Walton's Packing for a Woman's Journey* (Crown, 1998).
In 1987 she started the magazine *Victoria*, which was published until 2003.
Country Life ✧ Publishers | CT

May, James Lewis (1873–1961). *The Path Through the Wood* (G. Bles, 1930).
His childhood was spent first in Devon and then in London.
City Life ✧ Country Life ✧ Publishers ✧ Victorian Era British Memoirists | England

McClure, S(amuel) S(idney) (1857–1949). *My Autobiography* (Frederick A. Stokes, 1914).
About the first 100 pages. At age 9 he left Ireland to sail to the U.S. As an adult he established one of the earliest newspaper syndicates in the U.S.

College Life ✧ Editors ✧ Immigrants ✧ Knox College ✧ Nineteenth-Century Pre-Industrial Age Memoirists ✧ Publishers | Ireland ✧ IN ✧ IL

Paul, C(harles) Kegan (1828–1902). *Memoirs* (Routledge & Kegan Paul, 1971) (First published, Kegan Paul, Trench, Trubner, 1899).
Pages 12 to about 160.

Biographers ✧ Eton College ✧ Nineteenth-Century Pre-Industrial Age Memoirists ✧ Oxford University ✧ Publishers | England

Putnam, George Haven (1844–1930). *Memories of My Youth, 1844–1865* (Putnam, 1914).
He served in the Union Army.

Civil War (U.S.) ✧ Military Life Nineteenth-Century Pre-Industrial Age Memoirists ✧ Publishers | NY

Sullivan, Mark (1874–1952). *The Education of an American* (Doubleday, Doran, 1938).
Pages 12 to about 131.

Editors ✧ Foreign Correspondents ✧ Journalists ✧ Publishers | PA

Weeks, Edward (1898–1989). *My Green Age* (Little, Brown, 1973).
About 100 pages. He edited *Atlantic Monthly.*

Editors | NJ ✧ MA

White, William Allen (1868–1944). *The Autobiography of William Allen White* (Macmillan, 1946).
Pages 23 to about 177 (chs. 3–25).

Editors ✧ Journalists | KS

Woolf, Leonard Sidney (1880–1969). *Sowing: An Autobiography of the Years 1880 to 1904* (Harcourt, Brace, 1960).
He was married to Virginia Woolf (see ch. 16). For a similar 5-volume memoir, see "Sitwell, Osbert" (ch. 8). See also "Kennedy, Richard" (this ch.); he worked for the Woolfs.

Bloomsbury Group ✧ Critics (Literary) ✧ Essayists ✧ Jews ✧ Publishers ✧ Translators ✧ Victorian Era British Memoirists | England

Wright, J(acob) W(illiam) (1871–). *The Long Ago* (Press in the Forest, 1916).
Pages 9–61.

Printers | CA (Southern) (?)

Translators

De Rachewiltz, Mary (1925–). *Discretions* (Little, Brown, 1971).
About pages 3–270. She was the daughter of poet Ezra Pound. Her childhood with 2 families was divided between the Austrian countryside and the high society of Venice.

Adoptees ✧ Growing Up Between WWI and WWII ✧ Linguists ✧ Pound, Ezra ✧ Translators | Austria (Western, Tyrol) ✧ Italy (Northern, Tyrol)

Muir, Edwin (pseud: Edward Moore) (1887–1959). *The Story and the Fable: An Autobiography* (G.G. Harrap, 1940) (Later rev. as first part of *An Autobiography* [W. Sloane Associates, 1954]).
This is a classic memoir.
Bereavement ✧ College Teachers ✧ Critics (Literary) ✧ Farm Life ✧ Intellectual Life ✧ Island Life ✧ Novelists ✧ Poets ✧ Politicians ✧ Slums ✧ Translators ✧ Victorian Era British Memoirists | Scotland (Orkney Islands, Glasgow)

Soskice, Juliet M. *Chapters from Childhood: Reminiscences of an Artist's Granddaughter* (Selwyn & Blount, 1921).
Born in the 19th century, Soskice was related to painter Ford Madox Brown, as well as painter Dante Gabriel Rossetti and the poet Christina Rossetti. She earned fame with her translations of works by various Russian writers.
Grandfathers ✧ Painters ✧ Poets ✧ Translators | England

White, Claire Nicolas (1925–). *Fragments of Stained Glass* (Mercury House, 1989).
Pages 4–138.
Dramatists ✧ Editors ✧ Growing Up Between WWI and WWII ✧ Poets ✧ Teachers ✧ Translators | Netherlands ✧ CT ✧ MA

Chapter 10

Capturing the World in Color and Form: Artists, Architects, Designers, and Friends of the Arts

When our eyes face a movie, a museum, or an entire metropolis, we take in the visual art forms of cinema, of sculpture, of architecture. Some of the artists who have created these art forms have written well-drawn memoirs of their youth, some 2 dozen of which are collected in this chapter. In their careers as adults, they have brightened, livened up, or otherwise enhanced the surfaces and spaces of our visual environments.

Three coming-of-age memoirs by architects and interior designers make up the first section of this chapter. Whether their medium is the outside of a public building or the inside of a small studio apartment, these gifted artists, through their work, have produced satisfying and dynamic visual statements. Memoirs by such city planners and architects as Lewis Mumford, Louise Kehoe, and Louis Henry Sullivan bring the sensibilities of architects to us through their autobiographical writings.

Memoirs by those whose creations grace and enliven the interiors of both museums and magazines are contained in the second and third sections. These are recollections by those whose visual artistry ranges from paintings to political cartoons. The memoir of sculptor and costume designer Angna Enters is referenced here, as are the volumes of recollections by portrait artist Celia Beaux, illustrator Ernest Shepard, photographer Julia Scully, and cartoonist Bill Peet. (Set designer Ludwig Bemelmans, better known as the author of the book series Madeleine, appears in the children's author section of chapter 9.)

Note: The memoirs by potters Charles Shaw and Jade Snow Wong are entered, respectively, in chapters 4 (in the "European Cultures" section) and 5 (in the "Asian Americans" section). A memoir by wood engraver Gwen Raverat has been placed in chapter 17 (in the "Extended Families" section).

Those who create or wear clothing (both for purposes of artistic effect and commerce) are represented in the fourth and fifth sections of this chapter. Examples of persons in these fields whose memoirs are included are fashion designer Gloria Vanderbilt and model Irina Pantaeva. The chapter is rounded out by memoirs of 5 notable patrons of the arts: (Sir) Cecil Beaton, Mabel Dodge Luhan, Cornelia Lunt, Ben Sonnenberg, and Edith Wharton.

Architects

Kehoe, Louise (1949–). *In This Dark House* (Schocken Books, 1995).
Architects ✧ Baby Boomers ✧ Mental Health I England

Mumford, Lewis (1895–1990). *Sketches from Life: The Autobiography of Lewis Mumford: The Early Years* (Dial, 1982).
Pages 57–141 (chs. 5–11).
City Planners ✧ College Teachers ✧ Critics (Architectural) ✧ Critics (Literary) ✧ Editors ✧ Historians (Cultural) ✧ Intellectual Life ✧ Reformers I NYC ✧ VT

Sullivan, Louis Henry (1856–1924). *The Autobiography of an Idea* (Press of the American Institute of Architects, 1924).
Pages 10, 16, to about 250.
Architects ✧ Nineteenth-Century Pre-Industrial Age Memoirists I MA ✧ NY ✧ France

Fine Artists

Painters and Sculptors

Andrews, Marietta Minnigerode (1869–1931). *Memoirs of a Poor Relation . . .* (E.P. Dutton, 1927).
This reminiscence covers her first 25 years.
Painters I VA

Beaux, Cecilia (1863–1942). *Background with Figures: Autobiography of Cecilia Beaux* (Houghton Mifflin, 1930).
About the first 100 pages. Beaux was a largely self-taught portrait artist.
Painters I PA

Carr, Emily (1871–1945). *The Book of Small* (Oxford University, 1942).
On her early childhood.
Essayists ✧ Painters ✧ Victorian Era British Memoirists I Canada (Vancouver Island)

French, Mrs. Daniel Chester (1865?–). *Memories of a Sculptor's Wife* (Houghton Mifflin, 1928).
About 78 pages.
French, Daniel Chester I New England (?)

Hunt, Una (1876–). *Una May: The Inner Life of a Child* (Scribner's Sons, 1914).
Covers her to 14 years; this memoir is continued by the next entry.
Artists I OH ✧ Washington, DC

Hunt, Una (1876–). *Young in the "Nineties"* (Scribner's Sons, 1927).
Overlaps above memoir by a few months, starting when she was 13.
Artists I Washington, DC

Markino, Yoshio (1874–1942). *When I Was a Child* (Houghton Mifflin, 1912).
Painters I Japan

Rothenstein, (Sir) William (1872–1945). *Men and Memories: A History of the Arts 1872–1922: Recollections, 1872–1900* (Faber & Faber, 1932).

About the first 150–175 pages. He was a portraitist who, while serving with the English and Canadian armies during both world wars, produced renderings of his contemporaries.

Painters ✧ Victorian Era British Memoirists | England

Commercial Artists

Cartoonists, Illustrators, and Photographers

Artley, Bob. Ed. by Paul Gruchow. *A Book of Chores: As Remembered by a Former Kid* (The Printers, 1986).

Entire book covers his early 20th-century childhood, from the point of view of farm folkways, customs, tools, etc. Illustrated by Artley. The following entry is a companion memoir, focusing on Artley's childhood memories of Christmas.

Cartoonists | IA

Artley, Bob. *Country Christmas: As Remembered by a Former Kid* (Iowa State University, 1994).

Illustrated by Artley.

Cartoonists ✧ Christmas ✧ Farm Life | IA

Bechdel, Alison (1960–). *Fun Home: A Family Tragicomic* (Houghton Mifflin: 2006).

This is a memoir in the form of a graphic novel, which focuses on the bittersweet relationship between the author (a non-mainstream comic book artist) and her gay father.

Artists ✧ Baby Boomers ✧ Family Memoirs ✧ Fathers and Daughters ✧ Gays ✧ Graphic Novels ✧ Humorists ✧ Lesbians ✧ Mental Health ✧ Sexuality ✧ Suicide and Suicide Victims | PA

Bewick, Thomas (1753–1828). *Memoir of Thomas Bewick: Written by Himself: 1822–1828* (Southern Illinois University, 1961) (First published in England, 1862).

Chapters 1–5 (pages 5–69).

Eighteenth-Century Memoirists ✧ Engravers (Wood) ✧ Illustrators | England ✧ Scotland

Brainard, Joe (1942–1994). *I Remember* (Full Court Press, 1975).

This unusual book is a collection of sentences that each begins, "I remember." His companion volumes *I Remember More* (Angel Hair Books, 1972) and *I Remember Christmas* (Museum of Modern Art, 1973) are too short for formal inclusion in this bibliography.

Illustrators ✧ Painters | AR

Davenport, Homer (1867–1912). *The Country Boy: The Story of His Own Early Life* (G.W. Dillingham, 1910).

Cartoonists | OR

Gag, Wanda (1893–1946). *Growing Pains: Diaries and Drawings for the Years 1908–1917* (Coward McCann, 1940).

About the first 200 pages cover her from 15 to 21 years.

Artists ✧ Diaries and Journals ✧ Illustrators | MN

Mauldin, Bill (1921–2003). *A Sort of a Saga* (W.W. Norton, 1949).

Focuses only on his childhood.

Cartoonists ✧ Growing Up Between WWI and WWII ✧ Humorists ✧ Military Life | NM ✧ AZ

Mauldin, Bill (1921–2003). *The Brass Ring* (W.W. Norton, 1971).

About the first 100 pages focus on him from his high school years through age 20.

Cartoonists ✧ Growing Up Between WWI and WWII ✧ Humorists ✧ Military Life | NM ✧ AZ

McCall, Bruce (c. 1935–). *Thin Ice: Coming of Age in Canada* (Random House, 1997).

Covers his first 27 years, presenting a somewhat embittered view of his youth.

Advertising Copywriters ✧ Cartoonists ✧ Children of Alcoholics ✧ Family Violence ✧ Humorists ✧ Illustrators | Canada (Ontario)

Peet, Bill (1915–2002). *Bill Peet: An Autobiography* (Houghton Mifflin, 1989).

Nearly the first 90 pages. Contains entertaining drawings by the author. Peet was an illustrator for Walt Disney Studios.

Cartoonists ✧ Children's Authors ✧ Growing Up Between WWI and WWII | IN

Schlesinger, Marian (1912–living 2007). *Snatched from Oblivion: A Cambridge Memoir* (Little, Brown, 1979).

She was married to Arthur Schlesinger Jr. (see ch. 8 entry). She grew up near Harvard Yard; her father taught physiology at Harvard.

Growing Up Between WWI and WWII ✧ Illustrators ✧ Painters | MA

Scully, Julia (1929–). *Outside Passage: A Memoir of an Alaskan Childhood* (Random House, 1998).

Depressions (Economic) ✧ Growing Up Between WWI and WWII ✧ Miners ✧ Orphans ✧ Photographers ✧ Suicide and Suicide Victims ✧ WWII | CA (Northern) ✧ AK

Shepard, Ernest (1879–1976). *Drawn from Memory* (Lippincott, 1957).

He is best recalled as the original illustrator of *Wind in the Willows* (Scribner, 1907) and *Winnie-the-Pooh* (E.P. Dutton, 1926).

Cartoonists ✧ Children's Authors ✧ Illustrators ✧ Victorian Era British Memoirists | England

Villiard, Paul (pseud.: J. H. de Gros) (1910–1974). *Growing Pains: The Autobiography of a Young Boy* (Funk & Wagnalls, 1970).

Children's Authors ✧ Illustrators ✧ Photographers | WA

Wicks, Ben (1926–). *No Time to Wave Goodbye* (Bloomsbury, 1989).

Cartoonists ✧ Foreign Correspondents ✧ Growing Up Between WWI and WWII ✧ Journalists ✧ Radio Journalists ✧ WWII | England

Fashion and Costume Designers and Buyers; Models

Enters, Angna (1907–1989). *Silly Girl: A Portrait of Personal Remembrance* (Houghton Mifflin, 1944).

About the first 250 pages (Parts 1 and 2). Illustrated by the author, this memoir is told from a third-person perspective. For a similar memoir, see "Bemelmans, Ludwig" (ch. 9).

Artists ✧ Composers ✧ Dancers ✧ Designers (Costume) ✧ Mime ✧ Painters ✧ Sculptors | NYC ✧ England ✧ France

Gould, Lois (pseud.: Lois Benjamin) (1938–2002). *Mommy Dressing: A Love Story, After a Fashion* (Anchor Books, 1998).

Pages 7–10, 47, to about 209.

Editors ✧ Fashion Designers ✧ Journalists ✧ Novelists ✧ Wellesley College | NYC ✧ MA

Helms, Alan (1937–). *Young Man from the Provinces: A Gay Life Before Stonewall* (Faber & Faber, 1995).
Pages 4 to about 73.

Actors ✧ College Teachers ✧ Drug Abuse ✧ Gays ✧ Intellectual Life ✧ Mental Health ✧ Models | IN ✧ NYC

Lear, Frances (1923–). *The Second Seduction* (Knopf, 1992).
Most of pages 8–95. She is married to Norman Lear, who created the TV sitcom *All in the Family*.

Businesspersons ✧ College Teachers ✧ Editors ✧ Fashion Buyers ✧ Feminists ✧ Growing Up Between WWI and WWII | NY

Pantaeva, Irina (1974–). *Siberian Dream* (Avon Books, 1998).
About the first 300 pages.

Generation X ✧ Models ✧ Motion Picture Actors and Actresses | Soviet Union ✧ China ✧ France ✧ NYC (Manhattan)

Vanderbilt, Gloria (1924–). *Once Upon a Time: A True Story* (Chatto & Windus, 1985).
Covers up to 17 years.

Businesspersons ✧ City Life ✧ Fashion Designers ✧ Growing Up Between WWI and WWII ✧ High Society ✧ Novelists ✧ Wealth | NYC (Manhattan)

Vanderbilt, Gloria (1924–). *Black Knight, White Knight* (Knopf, 1987).
About the first 200 pages focus on her from 17 to 21 years.

Businesspersons ✧ City Life ✧ Fashion Designers ✧ Growing Up Between WWI and WWII ✧ High Society ✧ Novelists ✧ Wealth | NYC (Manhattan)

Patrons of the Arts

Beaton, (Sir) Cecil (1904–1980). *The Wandering Years: Diaries 1922–1939* (Little, Brown, 1961).
About 60–70 pages.

Designers (Costume) ✧ Designers (Set) ✧ Diaries and Journals ✧ Photographers ✧ Wealth | England

Luhan, Mabel Dodge (1879–1962). *Background* (Harcourt, Brace, 1933).
Covers her first 18–19 years. This is vol. 1 of the 4-volume autobiography Intimate Memories (Harcourt, Brace, 1933–1937).

Arts Patrons ✧ Intellectual Life | NY

Lunt, Cornelia (1843–1934). *Sketches of Childhood and Girlhood: Chicago, 1847–64* (Privately printed, 1925).
She served as first president of the University Guild of Northwestern University (1892–1895).

Arts Patrons ✧ Nineteenth-Century Pre-Industrial Age Memoirists | New England ✧ IL

Sonnenberg, Ben (1936–). *Lost Property: Memoirs & Confessions of a Bad Boy* (Simon and Schuster, 1991).
Pages 13–74.

Arts Patrons ✧ City Life ✧ Dramatists ✧ Editors ✧ Jews ✧ Lecturers ✧ Multiple Sclerosis ✧ Poets ✧ Translators ✧ Wealth | NYC

Wharton, Edith (1862–1937). *A Backward Glance* (D. Appleton-Century, 1934) (1988 rpt., Scribner's Sons).
Pages 21 to about 95.

Architectural Writers ✧ Arts Patrons ✧ Critics (Literary) ✧ Interior Designers ✧ Novelists ✧ Poets ✧ Short Story Writers ✧ Travel Writers ✧ Wealth | NYC ✧ Europe

Chapter 11

Let Us Entertain You: Actors, Musicians, Dancers, and Comedians

This chapter exposes us to reminiscences by persons who delight and inform us—whether through film, on the stage or dance floor, or before a microphone. (It should be noted that the ninth section of chapter 9 dovetails with this chapter, inasmuch as that section lists memoirs by individuals who have critiqued the performances of such entertainers.)

The first 2 sections involve memoirs by individuals active in movies and the theater. Represented in the first section are nearly four dozen coming-of-age memoirs by such actors as B-movie star Bruce Campbell, *Leave It to Beaver* character actor Frank Bank, action film star Jackie Chan, and *Our Gang* regular Tommy "Butch" Bond. The second part of chapter 11 contains autobiographical works by motion picture directors and producers. The volumes by Ingmar Bergman, Milos Forman, and Dore Schary are examples.

Titles and other information on more than 40 recollections make up the third section of this chapter. These are memoirs by persons involved in the worlds of music and dance, including those by such diverse talents as Louis Armstrong, Woody Guthrie, Martha Reeves, Gypsy Rose Lee, and Peter Duchin. Dancers Li Cunxin and comedian Carol Burnett offer their recollections of their formative years.

The final 2 parts of this chapter cover memoirs on the early lives of comedians and those who entertain through the interviews and commentaries they broadcast over the air. The fourth section includes memoirs by standup comic David Brenner, as well as by the late political satirist Art Buchwald and television personality Carol Burnett. The chapter concludes with listings of volumes by one television talk show host (Larry King), one radio talk show host (David Brudnoy), and one radio commentator (Scott Simon).

Actors and Actresses of Stage and Screen

Astor, Mary (1906–1987). *My Story: An Autobiography* (Doubleday, 1959).
Pages 32–126. She was a movie star before she turned 20.
Motion Picture Actors and Actresses I IL ✧ CA (Southern: Hollywood)

Bank, Frank (1941–), with Gib Jwyman. *Call Me Lumpy: My* Leave It to Beaver *Days and Other Wild Hollywood Life* (Addax Publishing Group, 1997).
Pages 14–39, 43, 46–143.
Actors ✧ Businesspersons I CA (Southern: Hollywood)

Barrymore, Drew (1975–), with Todd Gold. *Little Girl Lost* (Pocket Books, 1990).

> Generation X ✧ High Society ✧ Motion Picture Actors and Actresses ✧ Wealth | CA (Southern: Beverly Hills)

Bergen, Candice (1946–). *Knock Wood* (Linden, 1984).

> Pages 11–13, 17–18, 45 to about 176 (about chs. 2–8). Best known as the star of the 1980s television situation comedy *Murphy Brown*, Bergen is the daughter of ventriloquist Edgar Bergen (1903–1978). She also actively protested U.S. involvement in Vietnam during the 1960s.
>
> Actresses ✧ Fathers and Daughters ✧ Pacifists ✧ Photojournalists ✧ Wealth | CA (Southern: Beverly Hills)

Bernstein, Mrs. Aline (1881–1955). *An Actor's Daughter* (Knopf, 1941).

> She grew up in NYC's theater district.
>
> City Life ✧ Jews | NYC

Bogarde, Dirk (pseud. of Derek Jules Gaspard Ulric Niven Van de Bogarde) (1921–1999). *A Postillion Struck by Lightning* (Holt, Rinehart and Winston, 1977).

> Country Life ✧ Growing Up Between WWI and WWII ✧ Motion Picture Actors and Actresses | England

Bond, Tommy "Butch" (1927–), with Ron Genini. *Darn Right It's Butch: Memories of Our Gang, the Little Rascals* (Morgin, 1994).

> Growing Up Between WWI and WWII ✧ Motion Picture Actors and Actresses | CA (Southern: Hollywood)

Brando, Marlon (1924–2004), with Robert Lindsey. *Brando: Songs My Mother Taught Me* (Random House, 1994).

> Pages 3–106 (chs. 1–14) are on his first 21 or 22 years. Tells of his parents' separation, living with his mother and grandmother, attending a military academy, and moving to NYC to start his career as an actor.
>
> Divorce ✧ Grandmothers ✧ Growing Up Between WWI and WWII ✧ Mothers and Sons ✧ Motion Picture Actors and Actresses | NE ✧ IL ✧ CA (Southern) ✧ MN ✧ NYC

Buloff, Joseph (1899–1985). Tr. by Joseph Singer. *From the Old Marketplace* (Harvard University, 1991).

> From about 6 to 18 years, in Vilnus.
>
> Actors ✧ Jews | Lithuania

Campbell, Bruce (1958–). *If Chins Could Kill: Confessions of a B Movie Actor* (LA Weekly Books for Thomas Dunne Books, 2001).

> About the first 18 chapters (pages 1–117). He has appeared in such cult films as *Evil Dead* (1983) and *Bubba Ho-tep* (2002).
>
> Baby Boomers ✧ Motion Picture Actors and Actresses | MI

Cary, Diana (pseud. of Peggy-Jean Montgomery Cary) (1918–living 2007). *Whatever Happened to Baby Peggy? The Autobiography of Hollywood's Pioneer Child Star* (St. Martin's, 1996).

> She appeared in more than 50 films, from 1921 to 1938.
>
> Growing Up Between WWI and WWII ✧ Motion Picture Actors and Actresses | CA (Southern)

Chan, Jackie (b. Chan Kong-sang) (1954–), with Jeff Yang. *I Am Jackie Chan: My Life in Action* (Ballantine Books, 1998).
About the first 200 pages.
Motion Picture Actors and Actresses | China (Hong Kong) ✧ Australia

Chapin, Lauren (1945–), with Andrew Collins. *Father Does Know Best* (Thomas Nelson and Sons, 1989).
Actresses ✧ Drug Abuse | CA (Southern)

Coghlin, Frank "Junior" (1916–living 2007). *They Still Call Me Junior: Autobiography of a Child Star; with a Filmography* (McFarland, 1993).
Pages 4–126. As a child, he worked with Shirley Temple (see "Black, Shirley Temple, chs. 11 and 14), Charlie Chaplin (see entry, this ch.), Mickey Rooney (see entry, this section), and Jackie Cooper (see entry in this section). As an adult, he headed the Naval film cooperation program.
Growing Up Between WWI and WWII ✧ Motion Picture Actors and Actresses ✧ Movies | CA (Southern: Hollywood)

Cooper, Jackie (1921–). *Please Don't Shoot My Dog: The Autobiography of Jackie Cooper* (W. Morrow, 1981).
About pages 3–110. He is not to be confused with actor Jackie Coogan (1914–1984).
Actors ✧ Growing Up Between WWI and WWII | CA (Southern: Hollywood)

Crane, Cheryl (1943–), with Cliff Jahr. *Detour: A Hollywood Story* (Arbor House/W. Morrow, 1988).
At age 14 she killed Johnny Stompanato, the boyfriend of her mother, movie star Lana Turner.
Motion Picture Actors and Actresses ✧ Murder | CA (Southern: Hollywood)

Crawford, Christina (1939–). *Mommie Dearest* (W. Morrow, 1978).
See similar memoirs (in ch. 16) for "Hayward, Brooke" and "Hyman, B. D."
Family Violence ✧ Motion Picture Actors and Actresses | CA (Southern: Hollywood)

Duke, Patty (1946–), with Kenneth Duran. *Call Me Anna: The Autobiography of Patty Duke* (Bantam Books, 1987).
Pages 5 to about 91 (chs. 1–part of 11).
Actresses ✧ Children of Alcoholics ✧ Children of the Mentally Ill ✧ Mental Health | NYC

Fairbanks, Douglas, Jr. (1909–2000). *The Salad Days* (Doubleday, 1988).
Pages 19 to about 179.
Motion Picture Actors and Actresses | NYC ✧ CA (Southern: Hollywood)

Farrow, Mia (1945–). *What Falls Away: A Memoir* (Nan A. Talese, 1997).
Except for pages 18–23, pages 1 to about 126.
Motion Picture Actors and Actresses ✧ Polio | CA (Southern: Hollywood) ✧ England ✧ NYC (Manhattan)

Fonda, Peter (1940–). *Don't Tell Dad: A Memoir* (Hyperion, 1998).
About 150 pages.
Bereavement ✧ Motion Picture Actors and Actresses ✧ Suicide and Suicide Victims | NY (?)

Fontaine, Joan (1917– living 2007). *No Bed of Roses* (W. Morrow, 1978).
Pages 18–116. (Actress Olivia de Havilland is the older sister of this actress.)
Growing Up Between WWI and WWII ✧ Motion Picture Actors and Actresses | Japan ✧ CA (Northern)

Gielgud, (Sir) John (1904–2000). *Early Stages* (Mercury House, 1989).

Pages 1–73. His career was so lengthy that he was acquainted with such varied figures as Noel Coward, Helen Hayes, Sarah Bernhardt, George Bernard Shaw, Somerset Maugham, and Alfred Hitchcock.

Actors ✧ Gays ✧ Motion Picture Actors and Actresses ✧ Motion Picture Producers and Directors I England

Gish, Lillian (1896?–1993), as told to Selma Lanes. *An Actor's Life for Me!* (Viking Kestrel, 1987).

This is a memoir of about 73 pages, which tells of her youthful experiences with traveling theater companies, following her earliest years in OH.

Actresses ✧ Motion Picture Actors and Actresses I OH ✧ U.S.

Grammer, Kelsey (1955–). *So Far . . .* (E.P. Dutton, 1995).

Pages 22 to about 100.

Actors ✧ Alcoholism ✧ Baby Boomers ✧ Bereavement ✧ Drug Abuse I NJ ✧ FL

Henner, Marilu (1952–), with Jim Jerome. *By All Means Keep on Moving* (Pocket Books, 1994).

About 81 pages.

Actresses ✧ Baby Boomers I IL (Chicago area)

Jackson, Anne (1926–). *Early Stages* (Little, Brown, 1979).

Actresses ✧ Growing Up Between WWI and WWII ✧ Mental Health ✧ Movies I PA ✧ NYC

Kemble, Fanny (b. Frances Anne Kemble; aka Frances Butler) (1809–1893). *Records of a Girlhood* (H. Holt, 1879).

Actresses ✧ Dramatists ✧ Nineteenth-Century Pre-Industrial Age Memoirists I England

Lady Chablis (1957–). *Hiding My Candy: The Autobiography of the Grand Empress of Savannah* (Pocket Books, 1996).

About 50 pages.

Baby Boomers ✧ Entertainers ✧ Transvestites I FL

Leguizamo, John (1965–), with David Bar Katz. *Freak: A Semi-Demi-Quasi-Pseudo Autobiography* (Riverhead Books, 1997).

About the first 100 pages.

City Life ✧ Comedians ✧ Dramatists ✧ Generation X ✧ Hispanic Americans ✧ Motion Picture Actors and Actresses I NYC (Queens)

Madame Judith (b. Jule Bernat Judith) (1827–1912). Ed. by Paul G'Sell. Tr. from the French by Mrs. Arthur Bell. *Madame Judith: My Autobiography* (Eveleigh Nash, 1912).

About the first 115 pages (chs. 1–10); she belonged to the Comédie Française.

Actresses ✧ City Life ✧ Nineteenth-Century Pre-Industrial Age Memoirists ✧ France (Paris)

Marshall, Audrey. *Fishbones into Butterflies: A Kind of Remembering* (Chatto & Windus, 1964).

She grew up in a theatrical family.

Actresses ✧ Family Memoirs I England (?)

Massey, Raymond (1896–1983). *When I Was Young* (Little, Brown, 1976).
Pages 7–196.

Actors ✧ Military Life ✧ Princeton University ✧ Wealth ✧ WWI ✧ Yale University | Canada (Toronto, Quebec) ✧ England ✧ France ✧ CT ✧ NJ

Mathers, Jerry (1948–). *. . . And Jerry Mathers as "The Beaver"* (Berkley Boulevard, 1998).
About 140 pages, mostly from page 20 to about 148.

Actors ✧ Baby Boomers | CA (Southern)

McCowen, Alec (1925–). *Young Gemini* (Atheneum, 1979).
Set in the 1930s.

Actors ✧ Growing Up Between WWI and WWII | England

Moore, Dick (pseud. of John Richard Moore Jr.; aka "Dickie Moore" of *Our Gang* **comedy shorts) (1925–living 2007).** *Twinkle, Twinkle, Little Star, But Don't Have Sex or Take the Car* (Harper & Row, 1984).
Entire memoir focuses on his childhood years.

Growing Up Between WWI and WWII ✧ Motion Picture Actors and Actresses | CA (Southern)

O'Brien, Margaret (1937–). Foreword by Lionel Barrymore. *My Diary* (Lippincott, 1947).
Entries focus on her at about age 9.

Diaries and Journals ✧ Motion Picture Actors and Actresses | CA (Southern)

O'Toole, Peter (1932–). *Loitering with Intent: The Child* (Hyperion, 1992).
Covers his first 21 years.

Hitler, Adolf ✧ Motion Picture Actors and Actresses | England

Powell, Jane (b. Suzanne Burce) (c. 1929–). *The Girl Next Door . . . and How She Grew* (W. Morrow, 1988).
Pages 13–126 (chs. 1–8).

Growing Up Between WWI and WWII ✧ Motion Picture Actors and Actresses ✧ Singers | OR ✧ CA (Northern) ✧ CA (Southern)

Rooney, Mickey (b. Joe Yule Jr.) (1920–living 2007). *Life Is Too Short* (Villard, 1991).
Pages 7 to about 189 (chs. 1–23). Includes a 27-page filmography.

City Life ✧ Growing Up Between WWI and WWII ✧ Motion Picture Actors and Actresses | NYC (Brooklyn) ✧ U.S (Northeast and Midwest) ✧ Canada

Schildkraut, Joseph (1895–1964), as told to Leo Lania. *My Father and I* (Viking, 1959).
Pages 44–148. He gained fame portraying the father of Anne Frank (see ch. 6 entry). This memoirist's father, Rudolph Schildkraut, was also a well-known actor.

City Life ✧ Fathers and Sons ✧ Immigrants ✧ Motion Picture Actors and Actresses | Europe ✧ NYC (Manhattan)

Shepherd, Cybill (1950–), with Aimee Lee Ball. *Cybill Disobedience: How I Survived Beauty Pageants, Elvis, Sex, Bruce Willis, Lies, Marriage, Motherhood, and the Irrepressible Urge to Say What I Think* (HarperCollins, 2000).
About the first 100 pages (chs. 1–5).

Actresses ✧ Baby Boomers ✧ Motion Picture Actors and Actresses | TN ✧ NYC ✧ CA (Southern: Hollywood)

Skinner, Cornelia Otis (1901–1979). *Family Circle* (Houghton Mifflin, 1948).
Pages 114 to about 300. This is a most unusual memoir, in that the author does not appear until page 114. She was in the classic horror film *The Uninvited* (1944).

Actresses ✧ Dramatists ✧ Family Memoirs | PA

Skinner, Cornelia Otis (1901–1979), and Emily Kimbrough (1899–1989). *Our Hearts Were Young and Gay* (Dodd, Mead, 1942).
Focuses on their teenage years.

Actresses ✧ Dramatists | France ✧ Europe

Slezak, Walter (1902–1983), as Told to Smith-Corona Model 88E. *What Time's the Next Swan?* (Doubleday, 1962).
Pages 1 to about 130.

Bankers ✧ Family Memoirs ✧ Motion Picture Actors and Actresses | Austria

Smith, Bob (1941–). *Hamlet's Dresser: A Memoir* (Scribner, 2002).
Smith tells how his love of Shakespeare magically transformed his life, as he grew up with a profoundly retarded sister.

Actors ✧ Books and Reading ✧ Intellectual Life ✧ Mental Health ✧ Painters ✧ Shakespeare, William ✧ Sisters ✧ Theater | CT

Strasberg, Susan (1938–1999). *Bittersweet* (Putnam, 1980).
About the first 100 pages focus on her first 21 years in general; the following entry examines her relationship during that period with Marilyn Monroe. She was the daughter of actor and acting coach Lee Strasberg.

Actors ✧ Actresses ✧ City Life ✧ Strasberg, Lee ✧ Teachers ✧ Theatrical Producers and Directors | NYC (Manhattan)

Strasberg, Susan (1938–1999). *Marilyn and Me: Sisters, Rivals, Friends* (Warner Books, 1992).
Pages 1 to about 200.

Actors ✧ Actresses ✧ City Life ✧ Monroe, Marilyn ✧ Strasberg, Lee | CA (Southern: Hollywood) ✧ NYC (Manhattan)

Taylor, Jackie Lynn (1928–). *The Turned On Hollywood 7; Jackie Remembers Our Gang, by Jackie Lynn Taylor and in a Supporting Role Her Husband Jack Fries* (Pacifica House, 1970).
This 76-page work is of limited value; as indicated by film scholar Leonard Maltin (1992 letter to author), this is "more of a scrapbook than autobiography."

Growing Up Between WWI and WWII ✧ Motion Picture Actors and Actresses | CA (Southern: Hollywood)

Temple, Shirley (1928–), and the Editors of *Look*. *My Young Life* (Garden City Publishing, 1945).
See also "Black, Shirley Temple" (ch. 14).

Ambassadors and Diplomats ✧ Government Officials ✧ Growing Up Between WWI and WWII ✧ Motion Picture Actors and Actresses | CA (Southern: Hollywood)

Tierney, Gene (1920–1991), with Mickey Herskowitz. *Self-Portrait* (Wyden Books, 1978).
Pages 10–76.

Growing Up Between WWI and WWII ✧ Mental Health ✧ Motion Picture Actors and Actresses | NYC (Brooklyn) (?) ✧ Switzerland (?) ✧ CT (?)

Watson, Hildegarde Lasell (1888?–1976). *The Edge of the Woods* (Privately printed, 1979).
Pages 1 to about 74.
Motion Picture Actors and Actresses ✧ Wealth | MA ✧ Europe

Weir, Molly (1920–). *Shoes Were for Sunday* (Hutchinson, 1970).
Covers her first 12 years.
Grandmothers ✧ Growing Up Between WWI and WWII | Scotland

Weir, Molly (1920–). *Best Foot Forward* (Hutchinson, 1972).
Covers her from 12 to 18 years.
Actresses ✧ Growing Up Between WWI and WWII | Scotland

Weir, Molly (1920–). *A Toe on the Ladder* (Hutchinson, 1973).
Molly Weir's Trilogy of Scottish Childhood (Grafton, 1988) collects *Shoes Were for Sunday*, *Best Foot Forward*, and *A Toe on the Ladder*.
Actresses ✧ Growing Up Between WWI and WWII | Scotland

Williams, Barry (1954–), with Chris Kreski. *Growing Up Brady: I Was a Teenage Greg* (HarperPerennial, 1992).
Well over 100 pages.
Actors ✧ Baby Boomers | CA (Southern)

Winters, Shelley (b. Shirley Schrift) (1922–2006). *Shelley: Also Known as Shirley* (W. Morrow, 1980).
About the first 100 pages focus on her childhood.
Growing Up Between WWI and WWII ✧ Motion Picture Actors and Actresses | NYC (Brooklyn, Manhattan)

Wynn, Ned (1941–). *We Will Always Live in Beverly Hills: Growing Up Crazy in Hollywood* (W. Morrow, 1990).
Pages 9 to about 182. He is a grandson of Ed Wynn and son of Keenan Wynn. Wynn also is the stepson of actor Van Johnson. In his early years he earned money as an extra in Hollywood surfing movies.
Motion Picture Actors and Actresses ✧ Screenwriters ✧ Wynn, Ed ✧ Wynn, Keenan | CA (Southern) ✧ PA

York, Michael (aka Michael York-Johnson) (1942–). *Accidentally on Purpose: An Autobiography* (Simon and Schuster, 1991) (Published in England as *Travelling Player: An Autobiography* [Headline, 1991]).
Pages 17–111 (chs. 1–7).
Actors ✧ Motion Picture Actors and Actresses | England ✧ U.S.

Young, Loretta (1913–2000), as told to Helen Ferguson. *The Things I Had to Learn* (Bobbs-Merrill, 1961).
About 70 pages. See also "Lewis, Judy" (ch. 13).
Actresses ✧ Growing Up Between WWI and WWII ✧ Motion Picture Actors and Actresses | CA (Southern: Hollywood)

Motion Picture Directors and Producers

Bergman, Ingmar (1918–). Tr. from the Swedish by Joan Tate. *The Magic Lantern:
An Autobiography* (Viking, 1988).
About 101 scattered pages. He directed such films as *Seventh Seal* (1957) and *Whispers* (1972).
Growing Up Between WWI and WWII ✧ Motion Picture Producers and Directors | Sweden

Forman, Milos (1932–), and Jan Novak. *Turnaround: A Memoir* (Villard, 1993).
Pages 4–88.
Motion Picture Producers and Directors | Czechoslovakia

Guitry, Sacha (1885–1957). Tr. from the French by Lewis Galantiere. *If Memory
Serves: Memoirs of Sacha Guitry* (Doubleday, Doran, 1935) (First published in
French, 1934).
Pages 11 to about 175.
Actors ✧ Motion Picture Producers and Directors | Russia

House, Ray. *A Handful of Stars!* (Touchstone, 1970).
Motion Picture Producers and Directors ✧ Mountain Life | WV

Kurosawa, Akira (1910–1998). *Something Like an Autobiography* (Vintage Books,
1982).
Pages 3–78.
Motion Picture Producers and Directors ✧ Screenwriters | Japan

Mamet, David (1947–). *The Cabin: Reminiscence and Diversions* (Turtle Bay Books,
1992).
Some 71 scattered pages.
Baby Boomers ✧ Dramatists ✧ Motion Picture Producers and Directors ✧ Novelists ✧ Screenwriters |
IL (Chicago) ✧ NYC ✧ VT (?)

Pagnol, Marcel (1895–1974). Tr. from the French by Rita Barisse. *The Days Were Too
Short* (Doubleday, 1960) (1986 rpt., North Point, *My Father's Glory; and, My
Mother's Castle*).
Adapted as 2 films (1990). The setting is idyllic Provence.
Country Life ✧ Dramatists ✧ Motion Picture Producers and Directors ✧ Mountain Life ✧ Novelists ✧
Screenwriters ✧ Teachers | France

Parrish, Robert (1916–1995). *Growing Up in Hollywood* (Harcourt Brace Jovanovich,
1976).
Pages 3–111 (chs. 1–15).
Growing Up Between WWI and WWII ✧ Motion Picture Producers and Directors | GA ✧ CA (Southern:
Hollywood)

Salter, James (1925–). *Burning the Days: Recollection* (Random House, 1997).
Pages 7 to about 111.
City Life ✧ Fighter Pilots ✧ Military Life ✧ Motion Picture Producers and Directors ✧ Novelists ✧
Screenwriters ✧ Short Story Writers | NYC (Manhattan)

Schary, Dore (1905–1980). *For Special Occasions* (Random House, 1962).
During his childhood, his father ran a catering business. See also "Zimmer, Jill" (ch. 14; his daughter).
Dramatists ✧ Motion Picture Producers and Directors ✧ Screenwriters | NJ

Music

Composers and Performers of Song, Burlesque, and Dance; Includes Choreographers

Armstrong, Louis (1900–1971). *Satchmo: My Life in New Orleans* (Prentice-Hall, 1954).
Pages 7–222 (chs. 1–most of 13).
African Americans ✧ Singers | LA

Asher, Don (1926–). *Notes from a Battered Grand: A Memoir* (Harcourt Brace Jovanovich, 1992).
Some 70–80 pages. Asher deftly re-creates the jazz scene of the 1940s and 1950s.
Growing Up Between WWI and WWII ✧ Musicians | MA

Barber, Phyllis (1943–). *How I Got Cultured: A Nevada Memoir* (University of Georgia, 1992).
As an adult, she became a professional pianist and teacher of writing.
College Teachers ✧ Mormons ✧ Musicians | NV

Berlioz, Hector (1803–1869). Tr. by Rachel Holmes. *Memoirs of Hector Berlioz, from 1803 to 1865, Comprising His Travels in Germany, Italy, Russia, and England (Volume 1 of 2 vols.)* (n.p., 1884; second English translation [Tudor, 1932]) (First published in French, 1881).
About the first 90–95 pages. One of the most important of musical autobiographies.
Composers ✧ Nineteenth-Century Pre-Industrial Age Memoirists | France ✧ Europe

Berners, (Lord) Gerald (1883–1950). *First Childhood* (Farrar & Rinehart, 1934).
See "Kendon, Frank" (ch. 4) for another memoir focusing on a child's first 10 years.
Ambassadors and Diplomats ✧ Composers ✧ Novelists | England

Berners, (Lord) Gerald (1883–1950). *A Distant Prospect* (Constable, 1945).
Covers him from 14 to about 22 years.
Ambassadors and Diplomats ✧ Composers ✧ Novelists | England

Clooney, Rosemary (1928–2002), with Joan Barthel. *Girl Singer: An Autobiography* (Doubleday, 1999).
Pages 4 to about 54. Contains a 12-page index.
Catholics ✧ Children of Alcoholics ✧ Growing Up Between WWI and WWII ✧ Singers | KY ✧ OH ✧ IN ✧ NYC (Manhattan) ✧ CA (Southern: Hollywood)

Cole, Natalie (1950–), with Digby Diehl. *Angel on My Shoulder: An Autobiography* (Warner Books, 2000).
Pages 11–16, 18–80. She's the daughter of Nat King Cole.
Baby Boomers ✧ Cole, Nat King ✧ Drug Abuse ✧ Singers | CA (Southern: Hollywood) ✧ MA

Crosby, Gary (1933–1995), and Ross Firestone. *Going My Own Way* (Doubleday, 1983).

Fathers and Sons ✧ Singers | CA (Southern: Hollywood)

Davis, Skeeter (b. Mary Francis Penick) (1931–2004). *Bus Fare to Kentucky: The Autobiography of Skeeter Davis* (Carol Publishing Group, 1993).

Pages 7 to about 135.

Singers | KY

De Mille, Agnes (1905–1993). *Dance to the Piper* (Little, Brown, 1952).

Pages 9–80 (ch. 1–11). She was a niece of Cecil B. De Mille and granddaughter of political economist Henry George.

Dancers | NYC ✧ CA (Southern: Hollywood)

De Mille, Agnes (1905–1993). *Where the Wings Grow: A Memoir of Childhood* (Doubleday, 1978).

Dancers ✧ Summer | NYC

Dressler, Marie (b. Leila Marie von Koerber) (1869–1934), as told to Mildred Harrington. *My Own Story* (Little, Brown, 1934).

About 68 pages. During her itinerant childhood, Dressler lived in dozens of small Canadian towns.

Actresses ✧ Comedians ✧ Motion Picture Actors and Actresses ✧ Vaudevillians | Canada (Ontario)

Duchin, Peter (1937–), with Charles Michener. *Ghost of a Chance: A Memoir* (Random House, 1996).

About 158 scattered pages to about page 201.

Musicians | NY ✧ MA ✧ CT ✧ France

Dunham, Katherine (1909–2006). *Touch of Innocence* (Harcourt, Brace, 1959).

Third-person memoir of her first 20 years.

African Americans ✧ Anthropologists ✧ Dancers | IA (?) ✧ IL

Farrell, Suzanne (1945–), with Toni Bentley. *Holding On to the Air: An Autobiography* (Summit Books, 1990).

Pages 19–170.

Dancers | OH ✧ NYC

Guthrie, Woody (1912–1967). *Bound for Glory* (E.P. Dutton, 1943).

Pages 35–232 (chs. 2–11) focus on about the first 20 years of this influential folksinger. (His son, Arlo Guthrie, wrote the popular 1960s song "Alice's Restaurant.")

Musicians | OK

Haggard, Merle (1937–), with Peggy Russell. *Sing Me Back Home: My Story* (Times Books, 1981).

Pages 18 to about 170.

Singers | CA (Southern: Bakersfield) ✧ CA (Central: San Quentin)

Hamlisch, Marvin (1944–), with Gerald Gardner. *The Way I Was* (Scribner's Sons, 1992).

About the first 75 pages.

City Life ✧ Composers | NYC

Jackson, La Toya (1966–), with Patricia Romanowski. *La Toya: Growing Up in the Jackson Family* (E.P. Dutton, 1991).
About 70 pages.
African Americans ✧ Drug Abuse ✧ Family Violence ✧ Generation X ✧ Jehovah's Witnesses ✧ Singers | IN ✧ CA

Karmen, Steve (1935– or 1936–). *Me and Bobby D.: A Memoir* (Quality Books, 2003).
The author focuses on the dual rise to fame of his teenage friend (Bobby Darin) and himself. (Karmen is best known for writing jingles for products, such as Budweiser beer.)
Crime ✧ Musicians | NYC (Bronx) ✧ MI (Detroit)

Karsavina, Tamara (1885–1978). Foreword by J. M. Barrie. *Theatre Street: The Reminiscences of Tamara Karsavina* (E.P. Dutton, 1931).
Pages 3 to about 208.
Dancers | Russia

Kelly, Michael (1762?–1816). Ed. by Roger Fiske. *Reminiscences of Michael Kelly, of the King's Theatre, and Theatre Royal Drury Lane, Including a Period of Nearly Half a Century; with Original Anecdotes of Many Distinguished Persons, Political, Literary, and Musical* (Oxford University, 1975) (First published by J. & J. Harper, 1826).
Pages 1 to about 118 (chs. 1–9). He is credited with having written the only firsthand account of Mozart in English.
Dramatists ✧ Eighteenth-Century Memoirists ✧ Musicians ✧ Singers | England ✧ Europe

Kent, Allegra (b. Iris Margo Cohen) (1937–). *Once a Dancer—* (St. Martin's, 1997).
Pages 7–104.
Dancers ✧ Divorce | TX ✧ CA (Southern)

Kirstein, Lincoln (1907–1996). Ed. by Nicholas Jenkins. *By With To & From: A Lincoln Kirstein Reader* (Farrar, Straus, and Giroux, 1991).
About 60–65 scattered pages. He co-founded the School of American Ballet with George Balanchine (whom Kirstein brought to the U.S.).
Arts Patrons ✧ Critics (Art) ✧ Critics (Dance) ✧ Harvard University (?) ✧ Poets ✧ Wealth | NY ✧ Europe (?) ✧ MA

Kirstein, Lincoln (1907–1996). *Mosaic: Memoirs* (Farrar, Straus, and Giroux, 1994).
Pages 3 to about 175 (the first 11 sections).
Ballet Directors ✧ Dancers | NY ✧ MA ✧ Maine ✧ NH ✧ England ✧ Germany

Knight, Gladys (1944–). *Between Each Line of Pain and Glory: My Life Story* (Hyperion, 1997).
A section of this memoir (pages 23–173) follows her through her early concert tours throughout the U.S.
Singers | GA

Lankford, Mike (1951–). *Life in Double Time: Confessions of an American Drummer* (Chronicle Books, 1997).
About the first 180 pages
Baby Boomers ✧ Musicians | OK

Lee, Brenda (b. Brenda Mae Tarpley) (1944–), Robert K. Oermann, and Julie Clay. *Little Miss Dynamite: The Life and Times of Brenda Lee* (Hyperion, 2002).

Pages 7–183. She tells of her rise from poverty to early fame, including exposure on national television while still a teenager. This memoir follows Lee through her early singing venues.

Singers | GA ✧ NYC

Lee, Gypsy Rose (1914–1970) (b. Rose Louise Hovick). *Gypsy: A Memoir* (Harper, 1957).

Her sister was June Havoc (see entry in this chapter).

Burlesque ✧ Growing Up Between WWI and WWII ✧ Talk Show Hosts | WA (?) ✧ NYC (?)

Li Cunxin (1961–). *Mao's Last Dancer* (Putnam, 2003).

This inspiring memoir details the author's escape from a life of poverty by developing his balletic gifts, culminating in his defection to the U.S. in 1981.

China's Cultural Revolution ✧ Dancers ✧ Slums | China

Lisicky, Paul (1959–). *Famous Builder* (Graywolf, 2002).

This reminiscence tells of Lisicky's change of career focus: from architect of suburban communities to composer of liturgical music.

Architects ✧ Baby Boomers ✧ Composers ✧ Gays ✧ Novelists | PA ✧ NJ

Luft, Lorna (1952–). *Me and My Shadows: A Family Memoir* (Pocket Books, 1998).

Pages 68 to about 267. Her mother was Judy Garland and her half-sister is Liza Minnelli.

Actresses ✧ Baby Boomers ✧ City Life ✧ Family Memoirs ✧ Garland, Judy ✧ Minnelli, Liza ✧ Singers ✧ Suicide and Suicide Victims | CA (Southern)

Lynn, Loretta (1935–), with George Vecsey. *Loretta Lynn: Coal Miner's Daughter* (H. Regnery, 1976).

About the first 100 pages.

Abuse (Spousal) ✧ Mountain Life ✧ Singers | KY

Lynne, Gloria (1931–), with Karen Chilton. *I Wish You Love: A Memoir* (Forge, 2000).

Pages 21 to about 80. She won first prize at the Apollo Theater's Amateur Night at age 15.

Singers | NYC (Harlem)

Marquart, Debra (1956–). *Horizontal World: Growing Up Wild in the Middle of Nowhere: A Memoir* (Counterpoint, 2006).

This memoir is in the vein of the Western memoirs of Wallace Stegner (see ch. 4 entry) and Kathleen Norris; the author sang with heavy metal bands during the 1970s.

Baby Boomers ✧ Farm Life ✧ Poets ✧ Teachers | ND

Mingus, Charles (1922–1979). *Beneath the Underdog* (Knopf, 1971).

Pages 2 to about 90. He was a bass player, pianist, and jazz composer.

African Americans ✧ Composers ✧ Growing Up Between WWI and WWII ✧ Musicians | AZ ✧ CA

Montiel, Dito (1970–). *A Guide to Recognizing Your Saints: A Memoir* (Thunder's Mouth, 2003).

Son of a Nicaraguan immigrant and an Irish mother, Montiel recounts gritty tales from his youth, growing up on the streets of Queens, becoming a Calvin Klein model, and being lead singer of the punk rock band Gutterboy. This memoir was adapted as a film in 2006.

Children of Immigrants ✧ City Life ✧ Drug Abuse ✧ Generation X ✧ Ginsberg, Allen ✧ Models ✧ Musicians ✧ Punk Rock ✧ Racially Mixed Children | NYC (Queens, East Village)

Namu, Yang Erche (196?–), and Christine Mathieu. *Leaving Mother Lake* (Abacus, 2003).

Focuses on the late 1960s and early 1970s. She grew up in a matriarchal society, then ran away at age 16 and found fame as a singer.

Mothers and Daughters ✧ Mountain Life ✧ Singers | China

Nelson, Ozzie (b. Oswald Nelson) (1906–1975). *Ozzie* (Prentice-Hall, 1973).

Pages 9–62. Creator of long-running radio (1944–1954) and television (1952–1966) sitcoms on his family life, Ozzie may have been the first Boy Scout to attain the rank of Eagle Scout as young as age 13.

Actors ✧ Boy Scouts ✧ Football ✧ Musicians ✧ Orchestra Leaders | NJ ✧ England ✧ France

Nielsen, Carl (1865–1931). Tr. from the Danish by Reginald Spink. *My Childhood* (Hutchinson, 1953).

Composers | Denmark

Rainer, Yvonne (1934–). *Feelings Are Facts: A Life* (MIT, 2006).

This award-winning dancer, choreographer, and filmmaker was born and grew up in the San Francisco area. Interspersing her memoir's text are diary entries and dozens of black-and-white photographs. Also, a "Name Index" is included. The first 5 chapters (pages 1–113) focus on her first 21 years.

Dancers ✧ Diaries and Journals ✧ Motion Picture Producers and Directors ✧ Screenwriters | CA (Northern)

Raynor, John (1909–1970). *A Westminster Childhood* (Cassell, 1973).

Musicians | England

Reeves, Martha (1941–), and Mark Bego. *Dancing in the Street: Confessions of a Motown Diva* (Hyperion, 1994).

Pages 13–99 (chs. 1–4).

African Americans ✧ Singers | AL ✧ MI

Rorem, Ned (1923–). *Knowing When to Stop: A Memoir* (Simon and Schuster, 1994).

Pages 32 to about 217. Describes his early life in the Chicago area.

City Life ✧ Composers ✧ Gays ✧ Growing Up Between WWI and WWII | IL

Rubinstein, Artur (1887–1982). *My Young Years* (Knopf, 1973).

Covers him to about age 30. Contains descriptions of many great musicians whom he knew.

Musicians | Poland ✧ England

Salerno-Sonnenberg, Nadja (1961–). *Nadja, On My Way* (Crown, 1989).

Written in the first person, this work was expanded several times by the author, although the original manuscript was by David Allender. Marketed for a young audience, this 84-page memoir is on the violinist's early life and includes worldwide concert tours.

Italian Americans ✧ Musicians | Italy ✧ NJ ✧ NYC ✧ PA (Philadelphia)

Schnabel, Artur (1882–1951). *My Life and Music* (St. Martin's, 1963).

Pages 6 to about 56.

Composers ✧ Musicians | Austria

Slenczynska, Ruth (1925–), and Louis Biancolli. *Forbidden Childhood* (Doubleday, 1957).

Pages 12 to about 230. She was a talented pianist whose father beat her when she made mistakes in her playing.

Family Violence ✧ Growing Up Between WWI and WWII ✧ Musicians | CA (Northern)

Slick, Grace (b. Grace Wing) (1939–), with Andrea Cagan. *Somebody to Love? A Rock-and-Roll Memoir* (Warner Books, 1998).

Pages 4–71 (chs. 1–12).

Singers | CA

Smith, James Todd (aka L.L. Cool J) (1968–), with Karen Hunter. *I Make My Own Rules* (St. Martin's, 1997).

Pages 10 to about 134.

African Americans ✧ Generation X ✧ Singers | NY (Long Island)

Spector, Ronnie (1943–) (b. Veronica Bennett), with Vince Waldron. *Be My Baby: How I Survived Mascara, Miniskirts, and Madness, Or My Life as a Fabulous Ronette* (Harmony Books, 1990).

Pages 1–102 (chs. 1–9).

City Life ✧ Singers | NYC (Spanish Harlem)

Sting (b. Gordon Matthew Sumner) (1951–). *Broken Music: A Memoir* (Dial, 2003).

Covers this famous musician's life from his childhood through his adolescence.

Baby Boomers ✧ Composers ✧ Musicians | England

Szigeti, Joseph (1892–1973). *With Strings Attached: Reminiscences and Reflections* (Cassell, 1949) (First published by Knopf, 1947).

Pages 15 to about 96. He was a master violinist.

Musicians | Hungary ✧ Europe

Tallchief, Maria (1925–), with Larry Kaplan. *Maria Tallchief: America's Prima Ballerina* (H. Holt, 1997).

Pages 4 to about 90 (chs. 1–nearly all of 5). She was a famous ballerina and married ballet master George Balanchine.

Dancers ✧ Growing Up Between WWI and WWII ✧ Native Americans | OK

Tharp, Twyla (1941–). *Push Comes to Shove: An Autobiography* (Bantam Books, 1992).

Pages 6 to about 65 focus on her childhood and youth.

Choreographers ✧ Dancers | IN (?) ✧ CA (Southern) ✧ NYC

Tucker, Tanya (1958–). *Nickel Dreams: My Life* (Hyperion, 1997).

Pages 11–142 (chs. 1–29).

Baby Boomers ✧ Singers | TX (West)

Comedians, Humorists, and Vaudevillians

Anderson, Louie (1953–). *Dear Dad: Letters from an Adult Child* (Viking, 1989).

Baby Boomers ✧ Children of Alcoholics ✧ Comedians ✧ Fathers and Sons ✧ Letters | MN

Brenner, David (1945–). *Nobody Sees You Eat Tuna Fish* (Arbor House, 1986).
Pages 9–93 are on his childhood and adolescence. This period of Brenner's youth is also covered by the following entry.
Comedians I PA

Brenner, David (1945–). *Soft Pretzels with Mustard* (Arbor House, 1983).
About the first 200 pages are on his childhood and adolescence.
Comedians I PA

Buchwald, Art (1925–2007). *Leaving Home: A Memoir* (Putnam, 1993).
To 23 years.
Child Institutional Care ✧ Growing Up Between WWI and WWII ✧ Humorists ✧ Journalists ✧ Marines, U.S. WWII I NYC (Queens) ✧ Marshall Islands

Burnett, Carol (1933–). *One More Time: A Memoir by Carol Burnett* (Random House, 1986).
Pages 3–238 (about chs. 1–24).
Children of Alcoholics ✧ Christian Scientists ✧ Comedians ✧ Grandmothers I CA (Southern: Hollywood)

Butler, Brett (1958–). *Knee Deep in Paradise* (Hyperion, 1996).
More than 140 pages on her first 20 years. Her mother left her father when she was 4 years old.
Actresses ✧ Baby Boomers ✧ Comedians I GA

Chace, Rebecca (1960–). *Chautauqua Summer: Adventures of a Late-Twentieth-Century Vaudevillian* (Harcourt, Brace, 1993).
Describes a summer in her childhood.
Baby Boomers ✧ Summer ✧ Vaudevillians I U.S. (Northwest) ✧ Canada

Chaplin, (Sir) Charlie (1889–1977). *My Autobiography* (Simon and Schuster, 1964).
Pages 4 to about 130. Includes his worldwide tours. See also his son's memoir (ch. 17).
Actors ✧ Comedians ✧ Motion Picture Actors and Actresses ✧ Vaudevillians ✧ Victorian Era British Memoirists ✧ Worldwide Travel I England

Cosby, Bill (1937–). *Childhood* (Putnam, 1991).
Comedians I PA

Cox, Wally (1924–1973). *My Life as a Small Boy* (Simon and Schuster, 1961).
Actors ✧ Children's Authors ✧ Comedians ✧ Dramatists ✧ Growing Up Between WWI and WWII ✧ Short Story Writers I MI

Crystal, Billy (c.1947–). *700 Sundays* (Warner Books, 2005).
With wit and humor, Crystal lovingly recalls his early years, before his father passed away when the future comedian was only 15. For a similar memoir, see "Lidz, Franz" (ch. 7).
Baby Boomers ✧ Baseball ✧ Comedians ✧ Family Memoirs ✧ Fathers and Sons ✧ Motion Picture Actors and Actresses ✧ Motion Picture Producers and Directors ✧ Screenwriters ✧ Uncles I NY (Long Island)

Feig, Paul (1962–). *Kick Me: Adventures in Adolescence* (Three Rivers, 2002).
This is a collection of humorous essays. He created the 1990s TV situation comedy *Freaks and Geeks*. The following memoir covers this same general period of Feig's youth.
Baby Boomers ✧ Essayists ✧ Humorists ✧ School Bullying I MI

Feig, Paul (1962–). *Superstud: Or How I Became a 24-Year-Old Virgin* (Three Rivers, 2005).

Covering his adolescence and young adulthood into the early 1980s, this humorous memoir focuses on Feig's misadventures with the opposite sex.

Baby Boomers ✧ Essayists ✧ Humorists ✧ Sexuality | MI

Fry, Stephen (1957–). *Moab Is My Washpot: An Autobiography* (Hutchinson, 1997).

Covers his first 20 years.

Baby Boomers ✧ Comedians ✧ Gays ✧ Motion Picture Actors and Actresses | England

Grizzard, Lewis (1946–1994). *I Haven't Understood Anything Since 1962: And Other Nekkid Truths* (Villard, 1992).

The following memoir covers the same general period of Grizzard's youth.

Humorists ✧ Journalists | GA

Grizzard, Lewis (1946–1994). *My Daddy Was a Pistol, and I'm a Son of a Gun* (Villard, 1986).

Humorists ✧ Journalists | GA

Havoc, June (b. Ellen Hovick) (1916–living 2007). *Early Havoc* (Simon and Schuster, 1959).

Her sister was Gypsy Rose Lee (see entry in this chapter). Covers her first 14 years.

Growing Up Between WWI and WWII ✧ Motion Picture Actors and Actresses ✧ Vaudevillians | WA (?) ✧ NYC (?)

Keillor, Garrison (b. Gary Keillor) (1942–). *Lake Wobegon Days* (Viking, 1985).

These anecdotes are based on his early years in Anoka, MN. About 160 scattered pages.

Country Life ✧ Humorists | MN

Kornbluth, Josh (1959?–). *Red Diaper Baby: 3 Comic Monologues* (Mercury House, 1996).

Pages 3–122 (the first 2 pieces) focus on his youth.

Baby Boomers ✧ Communists ✧ Humorists ✧ Princeton University | NYC ✧ NJ

Lauder, (Sir) Harry (1870–). *Roamin' in the Gloamin* (Lippincott, 1928).

Pages 24 to about 100.

Comedians | Scotland

Leacock, Stephen (1869–1944). *The Boy I Left Behind Me: Unfinished Autobiography* (Doubleday, 1946).

Covers up to his 20th year. Published posthumously, these represent the first 4 chapters Leacock had written of the memoir he intended to title *My Memories and What I Think.*

Humorists ✧ Victorian Era British Memoirists | Canada (Ontario)

Levenson, Sam(uel) (1911–1980). *Everything But Money* (Simon and Schuster, 1966).

He grew up with 7 siblings, becoming a teacher and then a comedian.

City Life ✧ Family Memoirs ✧ Humorists ✧ Jews ✧ Slums ✧ Teachers | NYC (East Harlem)

Marx, Harpo (b. Adolph; later called Arthur) (1888–1964). *Harpo Speaks . . . About New York* (Little Bookroom, 2001).

About 55 pages. From a chapter in *Harpo Speaks* (B. Geis Associates, 1961).

City Life ✧ Comedians ✧ Motion Picture Actors and Actresses ✧ Musicians ✧ Pantomime ✧ Vaudevillians | NYC

McManus, Patrick F. (1933–), and Patricia "The Troll" McManus Gass. *Whatchagot Stew: A Memoir of an Idaho Childhood with Recipes and Commentaries* (H. Holt, 1989).

Memoirs take up about 60 pages, followed by a longer section of recipes from his childhood. For another memoir on this period of McManus's youth, see the entry in chapter 2.

Cookery ✧ Humorists | ID

Rose Marie (1923–living 2007). *Hold the Roses* (University Press of Kentucky, 2002).

About the first 60 pages. This memoir contains much re-created dialogue, and follows her through assorted show business tours (e.g., Cleveland and Atlantic City, NJ). Her career has spanned the entertainment media of vaudeville, radio, film, and television.

Actresses ✧ Comedians ✧ Entertainers ✧ Growing Up Between WWI and WWII ✧ Singers ✧ Vaudevillians | NYC ✧ CA (Southern: Los Angeles)

Sedaris, David (1957–). *Naked* (Little, Brown, 1997).

For another memoir on his youth, see the entry in ch. 9.

Baby Boomers ✧ Essayists ✧ Gays ✧ Humorists ✧ Radio Broadcasters ✧ Short Story Writers | NC

Shepherd, Jean (1923–1999). *In God We Trust: All Others Pay Cash* (Doubleday, 1966).

For a similar light memoir, see "Morris, Willie" (ch. 8) for *Good Old Boy: A Delta Boyhood* (1971). Note: Shepherd adopts the autobiographical persona "Ralph Parker" in his written memoirs, as well as in his popular 1983 film *A Christmas Story*. According to biographer Eugene Bergmann, Shepherd's memoirs combine fact and fiction.

Growing Up Between WWI and WWII ✧ Humorists | IN

Shepherd, Jean (1923–1999). *Wanda Hickey's Night of Golden Memories and Other Disasters* (Doubleday, 1971).

Growing Up Between WWI and WWII ✧ Humorists | IN

Twain, Mark (pseud. of Samuel Langhorne Clemens) (1835–1910). *Life on the Mississippi* (J.R. Osgood, 1883).

A classic re-creation of the riverboat age. See also "Morris, Willie" (ch. 8) for *Good Old Boy: A Delta Boyhood*. A related—although mainly adult—light memoir set on this river is *My Life on the Mississippi: Or, Why I Am Not Mark Twain* (Little, Brown, 1973), by Richard Bissell.

Boats ✧ Critics (Literary) ✧ Essayists ✧ Humorists ✧ Journalists ✧ Nineteenth-Century Pre-Industrial Age Memoirists ✧ Novelists ✧ Short Story Writers ✧ Mississippi River | MO

Twain, Mark (pseud. of Samuel Langhorne Clemens) (1835–1910). Ed. by Walter Blair. *Mark Twain's West: The Author's Memoirs About His Boyhood, Riverboats and Western Adventures* (Lakeside, 1983).

Boats ✧ Critics (Literary) ✧ Essayists ✧ Humorists ✧ Journalists ✧ Nineteenth-Century Pre-Industrial Age Memoirists ✧ Novelists | MO

Ward, Andrew (1946–). *Fits and Starts: The Premature Memoirs of Andrew Ward* (Little, Brown, 1978).

Humorists ✧ Photographers ✧ Radio Broadcasters | IL ✧ India ✧ CT

Ziegfeld, Patricia (1916–). *The Ziegfelds' Girl: Confessions of an Abnormally Happy Childhood* (Little, Brown, 1964).
Florenz Ziegfeld and Billie Burke were her parents.
Animal Eccentrics ✧ Entertainers ✧ Growing Up Between WWI and WWII ✧ Vaudevillians | NY ✧ CA (Southern: Hollywood)

Talk Show Hosts and Broadcast Media Commentators and Interviewers

Brudnoy, David (1940–2004). *Life Is Not a Rehearsal: A Memoir* (Doubleday, 1997).
Pages 4 to about 85.
AIDS Virus ✧ College Teachers ✧ Gays ✧ Journalists ✧ Radio Broadcasters ✧ Talk Show Hosts ✧ Yale University | MN ✧ CT

King, Larry (b. Lawrence Harvey Zeiger) (1933–), with Marty Appel. *When You're from Brooklyn, Everything Else Is Tokyo* (Little, Brown, 1992).
Broadcasters ✧ City Life ✧ Jews ✧ Talk Show Hosts | NYC (Brooklyn)

Simon, Scott (1952–). *Home and Away: Memoir of a Fan* (Hyperion, 2000).
About 114 scattered pages (1–138).
Baby Boomers ✧ Baseball ✧ City Life ✧ Quakers ✧ Radio Journalists | IL (Chicago)

Chapter 12

The Play's the Thing: Sports, Recreation, and Athletes

Lives involving sports and recreation are the common focus of the memoirs presented within this chapter. These memoirs about such pursuits have been divided here into two sections—those involving team athletic activity and those participating in solo athletic activities.

In the first part of this chapter, memoirs by team sports enthusiasts include those by such players and coaches as professional basketball star "Magic" Johnson, college basketball champ Rebecca Lobo, and New York Yankees Manager Joe Torre. Nonathletes having unique insights into certain team sports are also represented in this section, specifically by sports journalist Robert Mayer and by Jennifer Allen, daughter of former Washington Redskins coach George Allen.

The second part of chapter 12 lists coming-of-age memoirs by solo sports participants who have engaged in such widely ranging pursuits as tennis, running, boxing, hunting, fishing, wrestling, diving, and gymnastics. Among the nearly 2 dozen titles in the second section are recent memoirs by snowboarder Tina Basich, skater Kathryn Bertine, and surfer Thad Ziolkowski.

Given the concentrated focus on youth culture in the U.S., the number of coming-of-age memoirs produced by athletes is less than one might anticipate. Perhaps this is best accounted for by the fact that, in this country, sports records and outstanding performances from the arenas of professional baseball, football, basketball, and hockey—whose participants are most often in their twenties or thirties—occupy the national media spotlight more often than the superlative athletic efforts recorded by younger individuals. (Exceptions include skateboarding and such Olympic events as track and field.)

Team Sports

Baseball, Basketball, Football, and Hockey

Allen, Jennifer (1961–). *Fifth Quarter: The Scrimmage of a Football Coach's Daughter* (Random House, 2000).

Focuses on her from about 7 to about 18 years.

Baby Boomers ✦ Fathers and Daughters ✦ Football | CA (Southern) ✦ Washington, DC

Clayton, Bruce (1939–). *Praying for Base Hits: An American Boyhood* (University of Missouri, 1998).

He evokes his youth in Kansas City during the 1950s.

Baseball ✧ College Teachers ✧ Fathers and Sons ✧ Grandmothers ✧ Suicide and Suicide Victims I MO

Feller, Bob (1918–living 2007), with Bill Gilbert. *Now Pitching, Bob Feller: A Baseball Memoir* (Birch Lane Press, 1990).

Pages 16–93. Feller entered the Baseball Hall of Fame after many years of pitching for the Cleveland Indians.

Baseball ✧ Farm Life ✧ Growing Up Between WWI and WWII I IA ✧ OH

Hayes, Bob (1942–2002), with Robert Pack. *Run, Bullet, Run: The Rise, Fall, and Recovery of Bob Hayes* (Harper & Row, 1990).

Some 70 pages.

African Americans ✧ Drug Abuse ✧ Football ✧ Running I FL

Higgins, George V. (1939–1999). *The Progress of the Seasons: Forty Years of Baseball in Our Town* (H. Holt, 1989).

About 56 scattered pages.

Baseball ✧ Essayists ✧ Journalists ✧ Novelists ✧ Short Story Writers I MA

Hill, Grant (1972–). *Change the Game: One Athlete's Thoughts on Sports, Dreams, and Growing Up* (Warner Books, 1996).

About 110 pages (3–11, 17–18, 20 to about 118).

Basketball ✧ Generation X I VA

Johnson, Earvin ("Magic") (1959–). *My Life* (Random House, 1992).

Pages 3 to about 116. This memoir, with more of a focus on Johnson's MI roots, is continued by the following entry.

AIDS Virus ✧ Baby Boomers ✧ Basketball I MI ✧ CA (Southern)

Johnson, Earvin ("Magic") (1959–), and Richard Levin. *Magic* (Viking, 1983).

About 104 scattered pages, 31–202.

AIDS Virus ✧ Baby Boomers ✧ Basketball I MI ✧ CA (Southern)

Jordan, Pat (1941–). *A False Spring* (Dodd, Mead, 1975) (1998 rpt., Simon and Schuster).

The focus here is on him from about 17 to 20 years, including his travels to major and minor league baseball cities across North America. It is continued by the following entry.

Baseball I CT

Jordan, Pat (1941–). *A Nice Tuesday: A Memoir* (Golden, 1999).

Some 60 scattered pages.

Baseball I CT

Lobo, Ruthann, and Rebecca Lobo (1974?–). *The Home Team: Of Mothers, Daughters, and American Champions* (Kodansha International, 1996).

The chapters alternate, with half written by Rebecca (RuthAnn's daughter); about 85 pages written by Rebecca focus on her first 21 years.

Basketball ✧ Generation X ✧ Mothers and Daughters I MA ✧ CT

Mayer, Robert (1939–). *Baseball and Men's Lives: The True Confessions of a Skinny-Marink* (Delta, 1994) (2003 rpt., Houghton Mifflin, *Notes of a Baseball Dreamer*).

Pages 5–108 are substantially on his first 21 years.

Anti-Communist Movements ✧ Baseball ✧ City Life ✧ Journalists ✧ Novelists | NYC

McGough, Matthew (c. 1976–). *Bat Boy: My True Life Adventures Coming of Age with the New York Yankees* (Doubleday, 2005).

A lawyer reminiscences about his 2 years (1992–1993) as a Yankees bat boy while a high school student.

Baseball ✧ Generation X ✧ Lawyers | NYC (Bronx)

Oliphant, Thomas (1945?–). *Praying for Gil Hodges: A Memoir of the 1955 World Series and One Family's Love of the Brooklyn Dodgers* (St. Martin's, 2005).

He tells how his family's love for the Dodgers sustained them through his father's years of illness and other difficult times.

Baseball ✧ City Life ✧ Family Memoirs ✧ Journalists | NYC (Manhattan)

Torre, Joe (1940–), with Tom Verducci. *Chasing the Dream: My Lifelong Journey to the World Series: An Autobiography* (Bantam Books, 1997).

Pages 1 to about 89.

Baseball ✧ Italian Americans | NYC (Brooklyn)

Walker, Chet (1940–), with Chris Messenger. *Long Time Coming: A Black Athlete's Coming of Age in America* (Grove, 1995).

African Americans ✧ Basketball | MI

Solo Sports

Billiards, Boxing, Cycling, Diving, Exercise Gurus, Fishing, Golf and Caddying, Gymnastics, Hunting, Running, Skateboarding, Skating, Snowboarding, Surfing, Table Tennis, Tennis, and Wrestling

Austin, Tracy (1962–), with Christine Brennan. *Beyond Center Court: My Story* (W. Morrow, 1992).

About 110 pages focus on her first 21 years, including worldwide tennis matches. She won her first national tennis title at age 11.

Baby Boomers ✧ Sciatica ✧ Tennis | CA (Southern)

Bannister, (Sir) Roger (1929–). *The Four Minute Mile* (Dodd, Mead, 1955).

Pages 11, 28–118.

Growing Up Between WWI and WWII ✧ Oxford University ✧ Running | England

Basich, Tina (1969–), with Kathleen Gasperini. *Pretty Good for a Girl: The Autobiography of a Snowboarding Pioneer* (HarperEntertainment, 2003).

Generation X ✧ Snowboarding | CA (Northern)

Bertine, Kathryn (1975–). *All the Sundays Yet to Come: A Skater's Journey* (Little, Brown, 2003).

She details her past life of international show tours with "Hollywood on Ice."

Generation X ✧ Skating | U.S.

Browning, Kurt (1966–), with Neil Stevens. *Kurt: Forcing the Edge* (HarperCollins, 1991).

About 53 of this memoir's first 58 pages cover his first 21 years, including his world travels in skating competitions. He was a 3-time World Figure Skating champion.

Generation X ✧ Skating | Canada (Alberta)

Carter, Rubin "Hurricane" (1937–). *The Sixteenth Round: From Number 1 Contender to # 45472* (Viking, 1974).

On page 122, he's only about 17 years old.

African Americans ✧ Boxing ✧ Crime | NJ

Dempsey, Jack (1895–1983), and Myron M. Stearns. *Round by Round: An Autobiography* (Whittlesey House, McGraw-Hill, 1940).

Pages 3 to about 106. Includes 16 illustrations depicting boxing stances.

Boxing | CO ✧ UT

Evert, Chris (1954–), with Neil Amdur. *Chrissie: My Own Story* (Simon and Schuster, 1982).

About the first 100 pages (chs. 1–7) cover her first 21 years, including international tennis matches in England and France.

Baby Boomers ✧ Tennis | FL

Gish, Robert (1940–). *Songs of My Hunter Heart: A Western Kinship* (Iowa State University, 1992).

About 122 scattered pages.

Hunting | NM ✧ OK

Hawk, Tony (1968–), with Sean Mortimer. *Hawk: Occupation, Skateboarder* (Regan Books, 2000).

Generation X ✧ Skateboarding | CA (Southern)

Heywood, Leslie. *Pretty Good for a Girl* (Free Press, 1998).

Runners | AZ

Holder, Charles (1851–1915). *Along the Florida Reef* (D. Appleton and Company, 1892).

Fishing ✧ Island Life ✧ Nineteenth Century Pre-Industrial Age Memoirists | FL

Jelinek, Henry, Jr. (1944–), and Ann Pinchot. *On Thin Ice* (Prentice-Hall, 1965).

Skating | Czechoslovakia (?)

Joyner-Kersee, Jacqueline (1962–), with Sonja Steptoe. *A Kind of Grace: The Autobiography of the World's Greatest Female Athlete* (Warner Books, 1997).

Pages 12 to about 121 (chs. 1–12).

African Americans ✧ Baby Boomers ✧ Running | IL ✧ CA (Southern)

Lewin, Ted (1935–). *I Was a Teenage Professional Wrestler* (Orchard Books, 1993).

He wrestled professionally, 1952–1965.

Wrestling | NY

Lipinski, Tara (1982–), as told to Emily Costello. *Triumph on Ice* (Bantam Books, 1997).
Covers her through her early adolescence, including worldwide ice skating competitions.
Generation Y ✧ Skating | MI ✧ TX ✧ DE

Louganis, Greg (1960–), with Eric Marcus. *Breaking the Surface* (Random House, 1995).
The first 100 pages.
Baby Boomers ✧ Diving ✧ Gays | CA (Southern)

Manley, Elizabeth (1965–), as told to Elva Oglanby. *Thumbs Up! The Elizabeth Manley Story* (Macmillan of Canada, 1990).
Pages 1 to about 137. As an Olympic athlete, she suffered from depression.
Generation X ✧ Mental Health ✧ Skating | Canada (Ontario)

Mosconi, Willie (1913–1993), and Stanley Cohen. *Willie's Game: An Autobiography* (Macmillan, 1993).
Pages 1–65.
Billiards ✧ Growing Up Between WWI and WWII | PA

Orser, Brian (1961–), with Steve Milton. *Orser: A Skater's Life* (Key Porter Books, 1988).
Baby Boomers ✧ Skating | Canada (Ontario)

Simmons, Richard (1948–). *Still Hungry After All These Years: My Story* (GT, 1999).
Pages 10 to about 137.
Baby Boomers ✧ Exercise ✧ Gurus | LA (?)

Strug, Kerri (c. 1977–), with John P. Lopez. *Landing on My Feet: A Diary of Dreams* (Andrews McMeel Publishing, 1997).
Generation X ✧ Gymnastics | AZ

Waitzkin, Fred (1945?–). *The Last Marlin: The Story of a Family at Sea* (Viking, 2000).
Pages 3 to about 136.
Fishing ✧ Jews | NY ✧ Bahamas

Zaharias, Mildred ("Babe") Didrikson (1914–1956), as told to Harry Paxton. *This Life I've Led; My Autobiography* (Barnes, 1955).
About the first 70 pages. She was a leading woman golfer and Olympic gold medalist.
Athletes ✧ Growing Up Between WWI and WWII | TX

Ziolkowski, Thad (1960–). *On a Wave: A Surfer Boyhood* (Atlantic Monthly, 2002).
The author reflects on the role surfing played in bringing him peace while growing up in a troubled family.
Baby Boomers ✧ College Teachers ✧ Divorce ✧ Family Memoirs ✧ Poets ✧ Stepchildren ✧ Surfing ✧ Teachers | FL

Chapter 13

Lives of Care, Creation, and Calculation: Health Professionals, Scientists, and Mathematicians

Individuals whose lives became intertwined with everything from stethoscopes to psychiatry and apothecaries are represented in this chapter, which showcases more than 50 memoirs. Nineteenth-century "horse doctors" (medical practitioners who made their house calls in their horse and buggies), pioneering nurses, sex therapists, and psychotherapists are all catalogued here.

The first part of this chapter focuses on the recollections of doctors, nurses, and medical students. This last category is exemplified by Carol North's striking 1987 memoir, *Welcome, Silence: My Triumph Over Schizophrenia.* North overcame a diagnosis of catatonic schizophrenia on the way to graduating from medical school. Other recollections found in this section include a memoir by Clara Barton (who founded the American Red Cross), and one by Arthur Schnitzer, an Austrian whose unusual career was a melding of practicing medicine and writing fiction.

The second part of this chapter lists and describes more than a dozen coming-of-age works by persons who, as adults, entered a mental health profession. Among the more colorful of these are the volumes by psychoanalyst Elisaveta Fen (who grew up in Russia) and Judy Lewis, a clinical psychologist who was for years the unacknowledged daughter of Clark Gable and Loretta Young.

The chapter continues with 4 memoirs that tell what it was like to grow up around an American pharmacy during the 20th century. One of these, by Gildiner, is rooted in the Niagara Falls region during the 1950s and 1960s. The remaining 3 reminiscences—by Richard Armour, Virgil Lagomarcino, and Will Campbell—are set between 1915 and 1945.

Unlike the volumes contributed by his more lighthearted companions in this chapter, Campbell's tone is serious, as he poignantly re-creates his formative years dealing with his mentally ill brother. (This latter autobiographical theme is also developed in Jay Neugeboren's affecting 1997 memoir, *Imagining Robert,* which is about life with a bipolar brother.)

The memoirs in this chapter also examine the early years of a dozen scientists—persons who became expert in the application of the tools of science to the world and to our place within it. Three of them are by NASA aeronautical engineer Homer Hickam, whose memoirs tell of his modest beginnings in West Virginia. (The story of his hardscrabble boyhood and adolescence also forms the basis of the prize-winning 1999 film *October Sky*.)

Moving from rockets to rocks, this chapter also contains works by Louis A. Bibler and Carl Grunsky. Although born a half-century and a half-continent apart, these memoirists are united by their common pursuit, that of the geologist.

Autobiographical writings by a mathematical duo are also found here. The disparate cultural backgrounds of Russian Sofiia Kovalevskaia and American Norbert Wiener are bound together by their subjects' superior abilities and aptitudes involving numerical operations and theories.

Other scientists represented here include anthropologist J. J. Bones, archeologist Luther Cressman, surveyor Henry M. Lyman, civil engineer Henry Petroski, and inventor Charles Francis Jenkins. Of these, perhaps Petroski's story is the most unusual and engaging: His formative years are shown against the foil of his youthful experiences as a newspaper carrier.

The second section of chapter 2 lists memoirs by naturalists—experts in the natural sciences.

Doctors, Nurses, and Medical Students

Barton, Clara (1821–1912). *The Story of My Childhood* (Baker & Taylor, 1907).
As a teenager she taught at nearby schools. As an adult she founded the American Red Cross.
Nineteenth-Century Pre-Industrial Age Memoirists ✧ Nurses ✧ Teachers I MA

Bridie, James (pseud. of Osborne Henry Mavor) (1888–1951). *One Way of Living* (Constable, 1939).
Pages 16 to about 125. In middle age he ended his career as a surgeon and college professor to write more than 40 plays, becoming Scotland's first major playwright of the 20th century.
College Teachers ✧ Country Life ✧ Dramatists ✧ Physicians I Scotland

Carossa, Hans (1878–1956). *A Childhood* (Secker & Warburg, 1930) (First published in German, 1922).
Continued by the following entry, this is the 1st vol. of Carossa's classic autobiographical tetralogy. In addition to practicing medicine as a civilian, Carossa served as a German medical officer during WWI.
Novelists ✧ Physicians ✧ Poets I Germany

Carossa, Hans (1878–1956). *Boyhood and Youth* (Putnam, 1932) (First published in German, 1928).
This is the 2nd vol. of his memoirs.
Novelists ✧ Physicians ✧ Poets I Germany

Cunningham, John Henry (1877–1960). *As the Twig Is Bent: Being Chronicles and Anecdotes of Juvenile and Medical Memories* (Plimpton Press, 1936).
Pages 14–116 focus on his first 15 years.
Physicians I MA

Doyle, Helen MacKnight (1873–1957). *A Child Went Forth: The Autobiography of Dr. Helen MacKnight Doyle* (Gotham House, 1934).
Frontier and Pioneer Life ✧ Physicians I SD

Drake, Daniel (1785–1852). Ed. By Charles D. Drake. *Pioneer Life in Kentucky: A Series of Reminiscental Letters from Daniel Drake . . . to His Children* (Robert Clarke, 1870).

Eighteenth-Century Memoirists ✧ Frontier and Pioneer Life ✧ Letters ✧ Physicians | KY

Gonzalez-Crussi, F(rank) (1936–). *There Is a World Elsewhere: Autobiographical Pages* (Riverhead Books, 1998).
Pages 11 to beyond 111.

Mexican Americans ✧ Physicians | Mexico

Han, Suyin (pseud. of Elizabeth Chou) (1917–). *A Mortal Flower: China, Autobiography, History* (J. Cape, 1966).
Covers 1927–1938.

Growing Up Between WWI and WWII ✧ Novelists ✧ Physicians | China

Hawkins, Cora (1886?–). *Buggies, Blizzards, and Babies* (Iowa State University, 1971).
Pages 9–144 (chs. 2–14).

Physicians | IA

Lewis, Faye Cashatt (1896–). *Nothing to Make a Shadow* (Iowa State University, 1971).
Her medical practice lasted from 1943 to 1969.

Frontier and Pioneer Life ✧ Physicians | SD

Mah, Adeline Yen (1937–). *Falling Leaves: The True Story of an Unwanted Chinese Daughter* (Wiley, 1997) (Title sometimes appears as *Falling Leaves Return to Their Roots*).
Pages 34–137.

Chinese Americans ✧ Mothers and Daughters ✧ Physicians ✧ Stepchildren | China

Mullin, James (1846–1920). *The Story of a Toiler's Life* (Maunsel & Roberts, 1921; University College Dublin Press ed., ed. by Patrick Maume, 2000).
About the first 80 pages (chs. 1–4) focus on him from 11 to 21 years. Struggling against difficult conditions in post-famine Ireland, as well as against prejudices against the Irish in England, he persevered to become a physician.

Nineteenth-Century Pre-Industrial Age Memoirists ✧ Physicians ✧ Poets | Ireland

Nasrin, Taslima (1962–). *Meyebela: My Bengali Girlhood* (Steerforth, 1998).
Covers her from her early childhood until about 14 years. She depicts a world of injustice and violence against women in particular.

Journalists ✧ Muslims ✧ Physicians ✧ Poets | East Pakistan (i.e., Bangladesh)

North, Carol (1954–). *Welcome, Silence: My Triumph Over Schizophrenia* (Simon and Schuster, 1987).
Pages 27 to about 150.

Baby Boomers ✧ Medical Students ✧ Physicians ✧ Schizophrenia | IA

Pacheco, Ferdie (1927–living 2007). *Ybor City Chronicles: A Memoir* (University Press of Florida, 1994).
Covers him from 8 to 18 years. He was Muhammad Ali's physician.

Boxing ✧ Growing Up Between WWI and WWII ✧ Painters ✧ Physicians | FL

Ramon y Cajal, Santiago (1852–1934). Tr. by E(dward) Horne Craigie with the assistance of Juan Cano. *Recollections of My Life* (American Philosophical Library, 1937) (First published in Spanish, 1917).

Pages 6, 7, 14, to about 202.

Nineteenth-Century Pre-Industrial Age Memoirists ✧ Physicians I Spain

Sacks, Oliver (1933–). *Uncle Tungsten: Memories of a Chemical Boyhood* (Knopf, 2001).

The author of *The Man Who Mistook His Wife for a Hat and Other Clinical Tales* (Summit Books, 1985) and *Awakenings* (E.P. Dutton, 1983) describes the intellectual curiosity that was instilled in him at an early age by his science-minded parents and uncle.

Abuse (Physical) ✧ Brothers ✧ Intellectual Life ✧ Jews ✧ Neurologists ✧ Uncles ✧ WWII I England

Schnitzler, Arthur (1862–1931). Tr. by Catherine Hutter. *My Youth in Vienna* (Holt, Rinehart and Winston, 1970) (First published in German, 1968).

Dramatists ✧ Novelists ✧ Physicians ✧ Short Story Writers I Austria

Schweitzer, Albert (1875–1965). Tr. from the German by C. T. Campion. *My Childhood and Youth* (Allen and Unwin, 1924). (1960 rpt., Unwin) (American title, *Memoirs of Childhood and Youth* [Macmillan, 1949]).

This is a 78-page work.

Clergy ✧ Humanitarians ✧ Lecturers ✧ Missionaries ✧ Musicians ✧ Physicians ✧ Theologians I Germany

Selzer, Richard (1928–). *Down from Troy: A Doctor Comes of Age* (W. Morrow, 1992).

Essayists ✧ Growing Up Between WWI and WWII ✧ Hudson River ✧ Physicians ✧ Short Story Writers I NY

Thomajan, Puzant (1879–). *Worcester Memories: Sentimental Recollections of a Native Son* (Cultural and Library Organizations of the Armenian Church of Our Saviour, 1983).

About 70–90 pages. He was born in Armenia.

Armenian Americans ✧ Immigrants ✧ Physicians I MA

Van Devanter, Lynda (1947–), with Christopher Morgan. *Home Before Morning: The Story of an Army Nurse in Vietnam* (Beaufort Books, 1983).

Starting on page 21, about the first 50 pages focus on her from about 20 to about 21 years. Set in the Southern U.S., this memoir takes place mainly in Virginia.

Baby Boomers ✧ Nurses ✧ Vietnam Conflict I VA

Mental Health Professions

Bepko, Claudia (1949?–). *The Heart's Progress: A Lesbian Memoir* (Viking, 1997).

About the first 100 pages focus on her high school and college years.

Baby Boomers ✧ Catholics ✧ Divorce ✧ Lesbians ✧ Psychotherapists I ME

Cournos, Francine (1945–). *City of One: A Memoir* (W.W. Norton, 1999).

Pages 22 to about 150.

Bereavement ✧ Child Institutional Care ✧ College Teachers ✧ Jews ✧ Mental Health ✧ Orphans ✧ Psychiatrists I NYC (Bronx)

Fen, Elisaveta (pseud. of Lydia Jackson) (1900?–1983). *A Russian Childhood* (Methuen, 1961).

This, the 1st vol. of her 4-vol. autobiography, is continued by the following entry.

Psychoanalysts ✧ Translators I Russia

Fen, Elisaveta (pseud. of Lydia Jackson) (1900?–1983). *A Girl Grew Up in Russia* (Andre Deutsch, 1970).

Psychoanalysts ✧ Translators I Russia

Fen, Elisaveta (pseud. of Lydia Jackson) (1900?–1983). *Remember Russia* (Hamilton, 1973).

The first 200–300 pages.

Psychoanalysts ✧ Translators I Russia

Horney, Karen (1885–1952). *The Adolescent Diaries of Karen Horney* (Basic Books, 1980).

The first 4 of these 5 diaries cover her first 18 years; also included are some letters she wrote at age 20.

Diaries and Journals ✧ Psychoanalysts I Germany

Jung, C(arl) G(ustav) (1875–1961). Tr. from the German by Richard Winston and Clara Winston. *Memories, Dreams, Reflections* (Pantheon Books, 1963).

About the first 93 pages.

Psychoanalysts I Switzerland

Kalellis, Peter (1926?–). *One More Spring: A Story of Hope and Friendship* (Crossroad Publishing, 1995).

Covers a youthful period of his life, starting in 1941, when he was 15.

Psychotherapists ✧ WWII I Greece

Lewis, Judy (1935–). *Uncommon Knowledge* (Pocket Books, 1994).

About 200 scattered pages; her parents were Clark Gable and Loretta Young (ch. 11). As an adult, she was a clinical psychologist and actress. For a similar memoir, see "Dahlinger, John" (ch. 17).

City Life ✧ Gable, Clark ✧ Motion Picture Actors and Actresses ✧ Young, Loretta I CA (Southern) ✧ NYC

Manning, Martha (1952–). *Chasing Grace: Reflections of a Catholic Girl, Grown Up* (HarperSanFrancisco, 1996).

About 102 scattered pages. This is a very life-affirming memoir of her years growing up in Chicago, with descriptions of trips to visit relatives in Boston and NYC.

Baby Boomers ✧ Catholics ✧ Psychotherapists I IL ✧ MA ✧ NYC

Palmer, E. Hoyt (1897–1985). *Country Boy Grown Old: His Story of the Early Days* (Vantage, 1985).

Pages 1–88.

Clergy ✧ Country Life ✧ Grandfathers ✧ Mountain Life ✧ Psychologists ✧ Summer I NJ ✧ PA

Reich, Wilhelm (1897–1957). Ed. by Mary Boyd Higgins and Chester Raphael. Tr. by Philip Schmitz and Jerri Tompkins. *Passion of Youth: An Autobiography, 1897–1922* (Farrar, Straus, and Giroux, 1988).

Diaries and Journals ✧ Letters ✧ Psychoanalysts I Austria

Skinner, B(urrhus) F(rederic) (1904–1990). *Particulars of My Life* (Knopf, 1976).

He was the famous behaviorist who wrote such works as *Walden Two* (1948).

College Teachers ✧ Psychologists | PA

Sperber, Manes (1905–1984). Tr. from the German by Joachim Neugroschel. *God's Water Carriers* (Holmes & Meier, 1987).

Pages 4–156 focus on his first 13 years; this memoir is continued by the following entry. He was an associate of Alfred Adler, founder of a new branch of psychology. This is the first title in Sperber's autobiographical trilogy All Our Yesterdays (Holmes & Meier, 1987–1994).

Essayists ✧ Novelists ✧ Prisoners ✧ Psychologists ✧ WWI | Austria-Hungary

Sperber, Manes (1905–1984). Tr. from the German by Harry Zohn. *The Unheeded Warning, 1918–1933* (Holmes & Meier, 1991).

Pages 3 to about 81 cover him from 13 to 21 years.

Essayists ✧ Novelists ✧ Prisoners ✧ Psychologists ✧ WWI | Austria-Hungary ✧ Austria ✧ Germany

Viscott, David (1938–1996). *Dorchester Boy: Portrait of a Psychiatrist as a Very Young Man* (Arbor House, 1973).

Memoir examines only his boyhood and adolescence.

Psychiatrists ✧ Radio Broadcasters | MA

Westheimer, Ruth (1928–). *All in a Lifetime: An Autobiography of Dr. Ruth K. Westheimer* (Warner Books, 1987).

Pages 6 to about 110. As an adult, she became the world's most famous sex therapist.

Growing Up Between WWI and WWII ✧ Psychologists | Germany

Pharmacists and Drug Store Life

Armour, Richard (1906–1989). *Drug Store Days: My Youth Among the Pills & Potions* (McGraw-Hill, 1959).

Entire book is on his childhood and adolescence. Author was a satirist who wrote such parodies of history as *It All Started with Columbus* (McGraw-Hill, 1953).

College Teachers ✧ Drug Stores and Pharmacists ✧ Humorists ✧ Philologists | CA (Southern)

Campbell, Will (1924–). *Brother to a Dragonfly* (Seabury, 1977).

Pages 11 to about 100. During the author's youth, his brother was confined to a psychiatric ward. (For a similar work, see Jay Neugeboren's memoir *Imagining Robert* [W. Morrow, 1997].)

Brothers ✧ Civil Rights Workers ✧ Drug Stores and Pharmacists ✧ Growing Up Between WWI and WWII ✧ Mental Health | MS

Gildiner, Catherine (1948–). *Too Close to the Falls* (ECW Press, 1999).

Covers her first 13 years.

Baby Boomers ✧ Catholics ✧ Drug Stores and Pharmacists ✧ Eccentrics ✧ Humorists ✧ Psychologists | NY

Lagomarcino, Virgil (1921–). *A Window on Main Street, or, Life Above the Corner Drug* (Iowa State University, 1994).

Depressions (Economic) ✧ Drug Stores and Pharmacists ✧ Growing Up Between WWI and WWII ✧ Intellectual Life | IA

Scientists, Mathematicians, Inventors, and Engineers

Bennahum, David S. (1968–). *Extra Life: Coming of Age in Cyberspace* (Basic Books, 1998).

In a lively manner, the author describes his total immersion in the culture of early personal computer technology, including programming and hacking.

Computer Hacking ✧ Education ✧ Generation X | France (Paris) ✧ NYC (Manhattan)

Bibler, Louis A. (1914–). *Back Home Again* (Guild Press of Indiana, 1993).

Farm Life ✧ Geologists ✧ Growing Up Between WWI and WWII | IN

Bone, J(ay) J(asper). *The Pygmy Press Presents J. J. Bone's Going Native: A Young Man's Quest for His Identity Leads Him to an African Forest and Its People* (Pygmy Press, 1990).

This memoir is set when its author was 19 years old.

Anthropologists | Africa

Cressman, Luther (1897–1994). *A Golden Journey: Memoirs of an Archaeologist* (University of Utah, 1988).

The first half of this memoir is on his childhood. As an adult, he was briefly married to cultural anthropologist Margaret Mead.

Archaeologists | PA

Grunsky, Carl (1855–1934). Ed. by Clotilde Grunsky Taylor. *Stockton Boyhood: Being the Reminiscences of Carl Ewald Grunsky Which Cover the Years from 1855 to 1877* (Friends of the Bancroft Library, University of California, Berkeley, 1959).

Geologists ✧ Nineteenth-Century Pre-Industrial Age Memoirists | CA (Northern)

Hall, Edward T(witchell), Jr. (1914–). *An Anthropology of Everyday Life: An Autobiography* (Doubleday, 1992).

Pages 3–beyond 134.

Divorce ✧ Ethnologists ✧ Growing Up Between WWI and WWII | MO ✧ NM ✧ CA ✧ Germany ✧ MA ✧ CO ✧ AZ

Hickam, Homer (1943–). *Rocket Boys* (Delacorte, 1998).

This memoir is continued by the following 2 entries. *Rocket Boys* was adapted as the 1999 film *October Sky*, which won the 2000 Broadcast Film Critics Association Award as Best Family Film.

Aerospace Industries ✧ Engineers (Aeronautical) | WV

Hickam, Homer (1943–). *The Coalwood Way* (Delacorte, 2000).

Focuses on him at 16 years, as a high school senior.

Aerospace Industries ✧ Engineers (Aeronautical) | WV

Hickam, Homer (1943–). *Sky of Stone* (Delacorte, 2001).

Hickam's 3rd memoir takes place in 1961, with him returning home from college to help his father defend himself against accusations of involvement in a coal miner's accidental death.

Aerospace Industries ✧ Engineers (Aeronautical) ✧ Fathers and Sons ✧ Mountain Life ✧ Summer | WV

Jenkins, Charles Francis (1869?–1934). *The Boyhood of an Inventor* (National Capital Press, 1931).

Inventors | IN

Kovalevskaia, Sofiia (1850–1891). Ed. and tr. by Beatrice Stillman. *A Russian Childhood* (Springer-Verlag, 1978).

Mathematicians ✧ Nineteenth-Century Pre-Industrial Age Memoirists | Russia

Lyman, Henry M. (1835–1904). *Hawaiian Yesterdays: Chapters from a Boy's Life in the Islands in the Early Days* (A.C. McClurg, 1906).

Island Life ✧ Missionaries ✧ Nineteenth-Century Pre-Industrial Age Memoirists ✧ Surveyors | HI

Petroski, Henry (1942–). *Paperboy: Confessions of a Future Engineer* (Knopf, 2002).

Focuses on 1954–1958. The author affectingly shows how his boyhood experiences as a newspaper carrier helped prepare him for his career in engineering.

Catholics ✧ City Life ✧ College Teachers ✧ Engineers (Civil) ✧ Paperboys | NYC (Queens)

Ward, Lester (1841–1913). Ed. by Bernhard J. Stern. *Young Ward's Diary: A Human and Eager Record of the Years Between 1860 and 1870* (Putnam, 1935).

The 1st section, "Youth in Rural Pennsylvania," focuses on him from about 19 to 21 years. He was a pioneer in the field of sociology.

College Life ✧ College Teachers ✧ Diaries and Journals ✧ Fatherless Families ✧ Geologists ✧ Nineteenth-Century Pre-Industrial Age Memoirists ✧ Paleontologists ✧ Sociologists | PA

Wiener, Norbert (1894–1964). *Ex-Prodigy: My Childhood and Youth* (Simon and Schuster, 1953).

Fathers and Sons ✧ Mathematicians | MA

Chapter 14

Worlds of Commerce and Government: Business, Finance, Politicians, and the Rich

The autobiographical accounts in this chapter reveal young minds that typically possessed qualities of leadership and powers of abstract analysis, which usually led to careers in business, finance, or politics. Individuals born into lives of wealth and influence also contributed other coming-of-age memoirs gathered in this chapter.

The first section lists recollections by individuals who, as adults, found a calling in various occupations involving money or commerce. Several economists are represented here, such as the late, internationally renowned Harvard economist John Kenneth Galbraith, who describes his early years in Canada. The cultural diversity of these backgrounds is remarkable. For example, at almost the same time that future banker R. H. Mottram was coming of age in Victorian England, future banker John Quincy Wolf was growing up in the wilds of Arkansas.

This chapter's second part focuses on the young lives of politicians or other members of political families. Diplomats, statesmen, ambassadors, and other government officials tell their stories here. Although most of the works here are by American authors (such as Maureen Reagan and Jimmy Carter), the voices we hear in this section cross international boundaries, as evidenced by the recollections included here by Italian Susanna Agnelli, German Theodor Heuss, and Israeli Yigal Allon.

The chapter closes with autobiographical writings by persons whose birth into great affluence assured them of lives of material comfort. Memoirs by such persons as high society philanthropist Brooke Astor are offered here, as well as those by the late Countess Marion Donhoff and India's Princess Devi.

Business and Finance

Businesspersons, Bankers, Economists, and Advertising (e.g., Copywriters)

Donohue, Lynn (1957–), with Pamela Hunt. *Brick by Brick: A Woman's Journey* (Spinner Publications, 2000).

Baby Boomers ✧ Businesspersons ✧ Construction Industry ✧ Hippies ✧ Labor Leaders and Unions ✧ Masons | MA

Eisner, Jack (b. Jacek Zlatka) (1926–2003). Ed. by Irving A. Leitner. *The Survivor* (W. Morrow, 1980).

Covers him from 13 to 19 years.

Businesspersons ✧ Holocaust Survivors ✧ Jews | Poland

Galbraith, John Kenneth (1908–2006). *The Scotch: A Wryly Affectionate Account of Growing Up in Canada* (Houghton Mifflin, 1964).

College Teachers ✧ Economists | Canada (Ontario)

Gordy, Berry, Sr. (1888–1978). *Movin' Up: Pop Gordy Tells His Story* (Harper & Row, 1979).

Pages 3 to about 60. His son, Berry Gordy Jr., founded Motown Records.

African Americans ✧ Country Life ✧ Gordy, Berry, Jr. ✧ Racism | GA

Grove, Andrew S. (b. Andris Gros) (1936–). *Swimming Across* (Warner Books, 2001).

Covers his first 20 years. He achieved fame as chairman and co-founder of Intel Corporation.

Businesspersons ✧ Holocaust Survivors ✧ Hungarian Americans ✧ Immigrants ✧ Jews ✧ Scarlet Fever | Hungary

Lundborg, Louis B(illings). (1906–1981). *Up to Now* (W.W. Norton, 1978).

More than 160 scattered pages.

Bankers ✧ Stanford University | CA (Northern) ✧ MT

Mandel, Edmund, as told to Lynn Egerman. *The Right Path: The Autobiography of a Survivor* (KTAV Publishing House, 1994).

As an adult, he worked in the commercial food business.

Businesspersons ✧ Holocaust Survivors ✧ Hungarian Americans ✧ Jews | Hungary

Mellon, Thomas (1813–1908). Ed. by Mary Louise Briscoe. *Thomas Mellon and His Times* (University of Pittsburgh, 1994) (First published, W.G. Johnston, 1885).

Pages 9–82.

Bankers ✧ Nineteenth-Century Pre-Industrial Age Memoirists | Ireland ✧ MD ✧ PA

Mill, John Stuart (1806–1873). *Autobiography of John Stuart Mill* (Columbia University, 1924).

Pages 5 to about 148 focus on his first 21 years; the following entry is a companion volume that chronicles about a 1-year period, when Mill was a teenager visiting France. (Written 1853–1856.)

Economists ✧ Nineteenth-Century Pre-Industrial Age Memoirists ✧ Mental Health ✧ Philosophers | England

Mill, John Stuart (1806–1873). Ed. by Anna Jean Mill. *John Mill's Boyhood Visit to France: Being a Journal and Notebook Written by John Stuart Mill in France, 1820–21* (University of Toronto, 1960).

Diaries and Journals ✧ Economists ✧ Mental Health ✧ Nineteenth-Century Memoirists ✧ Philosophers | France

Mottram, R(alph) H(ale) (1883–1971). *The Window Seat or Life Observed* (Hutchinson, 1954).

About page 18 to about page 163 (chs. 2–22). This is a classic memoir, whose first volume covers Mottram's first 35 years. (Vol. 2 is titled *Another Window Seat, or Life Observed*.)

Bankers ✧ Historians (Cultural) ✧ Journalists ✧ Novelists ✧ Short Story Writers ✧ Victorian Era British Memoirists ✧ WWI | England

Robbins, (Baron) Lionel Charles (1898–1984). *Autobiography of an Economist* (Macmillan, 1971).

Pages 11–71 (chs. 1–3).

Economists | England

Sowell, Thomas (1930–). *A Personal Odyssey* (Free Press, 2000).

Pages 2 to about 74.

African Americans ✧ Economists ✧ College Teachers ✧ Growing Up Between WWI and WWII ✧ Intellectual Life ✧ Photographers ✧ Racism | NC ✧ NYC (Harlem) ✧ Washington, DC

Taulbert, Clifton (1945–). *Watching Our Crops Come In* (Viking, 1997).

Pages 7 to about 64 (chs. 1–3) focus on him from 18 to 21 years. See ch. 5 for his 2 prequels.

African Americans ✧ Bankers ✧ Racism | Washington, DC ✧ MS

Tugwell, Rexford Guy (1891–1979). *The Light of Other Days* (Doubleday, 1962).

Asthma ✧ Economists | NY

Wolf, John Quincy (1864–1949). *Life in the Leatherwoods: An Ozark Boyhood Remembered* (Memphis State University, 1974; rev. ed., Memphis State University, 1980).

Bankers ✧ Farm Life ✧ Mountain Life | AR

Zimmer, Jill (pseud. of Jill Robinson) (1936–). *With a Cast of Thousands: A Hollywood Childhood* (Stein and Day, 1963).

See also "Schary, Dore" (ch. 11; her father).

Advertising Copywriters ✧ Journalists ✧ Radio Journalists ✧ Teachers | CA (Southern: Hollywood)

Politicians, Diplomats, Statesmen, Ambassadors, and Other Government Officials; Leaders (U.S. Presidents); and Political Families

Agnelli, Susanna (1922–). *We Always Wore Sailor Suits* (Viking, 1975).

She grew up in Italy, during Mussolini's regime. She was the first woman in Italy to serve as Minister of Foreign Affairs. Granddaughter of the founder of the Fiat automobile company, as an adult she was elected mayor of Monte Argentario.

Feminists ✧ Growing Up Between WWI and WWII ✧ High Society ✧ Politicians | Italy

Allon, Yigal (born Yigal Paicovitch) (1918–1980). Tr. from the Hebrew by Reuven Ben-Yosef. *My Father's House* (W.W. Norton, 1976).

Pages 16–179. He was Israel's foreign minister.

Fathers and Sons ✧ Government Officials ✧ Growing Up Between WWI and WWII ✧ Homes and Haunts | Jews ✧ Palestine (i.e., Israel)

Bellmon, Henry (1921–), with Pat Copeland. *The Life and Times of Henry Bellmon* (Council Oak Books, 1992).

Pages 19 to about 70. He was an OK governor and U.S. senator, as well as a Silver Star recipient for his actions during WWII.

Farm Life ✧ Government Officials | OK

Black, Shirley Temple (1928–). *Child Star: An Autobiography* (McGraw-Hill, 1988).
  Her first 25 years are focused on here. She worked for the United Nations and the U.S. State Department, championing environmental and children's rights. See also "Temple, Shirley" (ch. 11).
    Ambassadors and Diplomats ✧ Government Officials ✧ Growing Up Between WWI and WWII ✧ Motion Picture Actors and Actresses I CA (Southern: Hollywood)

Bumpers, Dale (1925–). *The Best Lawyer in a One-Lawyer Town: A Memoir* (Random House, 2003).
  A drunken driver killed his parents when he was 24. He served as governor and senator from Arkansas and helped defend President Clinton during his impeachment trial.
    Depressions (Economic) ✧ Farm Life ✧ Government Officials ✧ Growing Up Between WWI and WWII ✧ Lawyers ✧ Politicians I AR

Carter, Jimmy (1924–). *An Hour Before Daylight: Memories of a Rural Boyhood* (Simon and Schuster, 2001).
  Pages 28–256 focus on him from 4 to 21 years. He writes of relationships with 5 people who changed his life.
    Depressions (Economic) ✧ Farm Life ✧ Fathers and Sons ✧ Growing Up Between WWI and WWII ✧ Presidents, U.S. I GA

Churchill, (Sir) Winston S. (1874–1965). *A Roving Commission: My Early Life* (Scribner's Sons, 1930) (British variant, *My Early Life: A Roving Commission* [T. Butterworth, 1930]).
  To page 88 (chs. 1–5). Churchill was British prime minister during WWII.
    Historians (Military) ✧ Journalists ✧ Military Life ✧ Statesmen I England

Clinton, Bill (1946–). *My Life* (Knopf, 2004).
  About the first 100 pages.
    Country Life ✧ Family Violence ✧ Fatherless Families ✧ Presidents, U.S. ✧ Stepfathers I AR

Cole, Cyrenus (1863–1939). *I Remember, I Remember: A Book of Recollections* (State Historical Society of Iowa, 1936).
  About 86 scattered pages (17 to about 114).
    Journalists ✧ Politicians I IA

Daniel, Clifton Truman (1957–). *Growing Up with My Grandfather: Memories of Harry S Truman* (Carol Publishing Group, 1995).
  About 125 scattered pages (pages 3 to about 143).
    Baby Boomers ✧ Grandfathers ✧ Truman, Harry I NYC (Manhattan) ✧ MO ✧ NC

Eisenhower, Dwight D. (1890–1969). *At Ease: Stories I Tell to Friends* (Doubleday, 1967).
  About 65 scattered pages (throughout "Book One: The Abilene Years") .
    Eisenhower, Dwight D. ✧ Military Life ✧ Presidents, U.S. I TX ✧ KS

Felton, Rebecca (1835–1930). *Country Life in Georgia in the Days of My Youth* (Index Printing Company, 1919).
  Pages 9–76 focus on her girlhood and youth. She was a U.S. senator.
    Country Life ✧ Politicians I GA

Heuss, Theodor (1884–1963). Tr. from the German by Michael Bullock. *Preludes to Life: Early Memoirs* (Citadel, 1955).
He was president of the Federal German Republic (1949–1959). (Note: The sequel to this memoir is not available in English translation.)
Journalists ✧ Politicians | Germany

Jenkins, Michael (1936–). *A House in Flanders: A Memoir* (Souvenir Press, 1992).
Set in 1951.
Ambassadors and Diplomats ✧ Homes and Haunts ✧ Summer | France

Kerrey, Bob (1943–). *When I Was a Young Man: A Memoir* (Harcourt, Inc., 2002).
About 60 pages.
Military Life ✧ Politicians ✧ Uncles ✧ Vietnam Conflict | NE ✧ Vietnam

Lodge, Henry Cabot (1850–1924). *Early Memories* (Scribner's Sons, 1913) (1975 rpt., Arno).
Pages 3–199.
Historians ✧ Nineteenth-Century Pre-Industrial Age Memoirists Politicians | MA ✧ Europe

Long, Mary Alves (1864–). *High Time to Tell It* (Duke University, 1950).
As an adult, she worked for the League of Nations.
Plantation Life | NC

Mellon, Paul (1907–1999), with John Baskett. *Reflections in a Silver Spoon: A Memoir* (W. Morrow, 1992).
Pages 62 to about 115.
Ambassadors and Diplomats ✧ Arts Patrons ✧ Choate School ✧ Government Officials ✧ Wealth ✧ Yale University | PA ✧ MA ✧ CT

Mfume, Kweisi (1948–), with Ron Stodghill II. *No Free Ride: From the Mean Streets to the Mainstream* (One World, 1996).
Pages 9–167 (chs. 1–6).
African Americans ✧ Baby Boomers ✧ Civil Rights Workers ✧ Politicians | MD

O'Meara, Walter (1897–1989). *We Made It Through the Winter: A Memoir of a Northern Minnesota Boyhood* (Minnesota Historical Society, 1974).
The entire body of the main text (pages 1–113) is on his boyhood in a sawmill town. O'Meara conducted classified work for the U.S. during WWII, and was a publicist for presidential candidate Adlai Stevenson in 1956.
Advertising Copywriters ✧ Government Officials ✧ Journalists ✧ Lumber Camps ✧ Novelists ✧ Short Story Writers | MN

Reagan, Maureen (1941–2001). *First Father, First Daughter: A Memoir* (Little, Brown, 1989).
The first 134 pages cover her girlhood and young adulthood.
Cancer ✧ Reagan, Ronald | CA (Southern) ✧ NY ✧ VA ✧ Washington, DC

Ritchie, Charles (1906–1995). *My Grandfather's House: Scenes of Childhood and Youth* (Macmillan of Canada, 1987).
Pages xiii–xv, 1 to about 125.
Ambassadors and Diplomats ✧ Grandfathers ✧ Harvard University | Canada (Nova Scotia) ✧ England ✧ MA

Roosevelt, Theodore (1858–1919). *Theodore Roosevelt's Diaries of Boyhood and Youth* (Scribner's Sons, 1928).
Covers him from 9 to 18 or 19 years
Diaries and Journals ✧ Hunting ✧ Natural History ✧ Nineteenth-Century Pre-Industrial Age Memoirists ✧ Presidents, U.S. | Belgium ✧ France ✧ England

Roosevelt, Theodore (1858–1919). *All in the Family* (Putnam, 1929).
Hunting ✧ Natural History ✧ Nineteenth-Century Pre-Industrial Age Memoirists ✧ Presidents, U.S. | NY (Long Island)

Tallents, (Sir) Stephen George (1884–1958). *Man and Boy* (Faber & Faber, 1943).
Pages 1–20, 37 to about 139. As an adult, he served in such capacities as secretary of the Empire Marketing Board.
Government Officials ✧ Harrow ✧ Oxford University | England

Truman, (Mary) Margaret (1924–), with Margaret Cousins. *Souvenir: Margaret Truman's Own Story* (McGraw-Hill, 1956) (British variant, *My Own Story* [Eyre & Spottiswoode, 1956]).
Pages 1–82. She was the daughter of Harry S. Truman.
Growing Up Between WWI and WWII ✧ Novelists ✧ Radio Broadcasters ✧ Singers ✧ Truman, Harry | MO ✧ Washington, DC

Visconti, Giovanni Venosta (1829–1914). Tr. from the 3rd ed. by William Prall. *Memoirs of Youth: Things Seen and Known, 1847–1860* (Houghton Mifflin, 1914).
Pages 1–154 (chs. 1–12).
Ambassadors and Diplomats ✧ Nineteenth-Century Pre-Industrial Age Memoirists ✧ Politicians | Italy

Wealthy and Royal Families

See entries in the section "Patrons of the Arts" in chapter 10 for memoirs involving wealthy supporters of the arts.

Astor, Brooke (1902–living 2007). *Patchwork Child* (Harper & Row, 1962).
She served in editorial capacities for *House and Garden* magazine, 1946–1992.
Arts Patrons ✧ Centenarians ✧ Debutantes ✧ Editors ✧ High Society ✧ Philanthropists ✧ Wealth | China (Peking) ✧ WA ✧ HI ✧ Panama

Bailey, Margaret Emerson (1880–1949). *Good-bye Proud World* (Scribner, 1945).
More than 200 pages. Written from a third-person perspective, this memoir retains actual names of persons from her early years.
Books and Reading ✧ Bryn Mawr ✧ Family Memoirs ✧ Grandmothers ✧ High Society ✧ Wealth | RI ✧ PA

Bingham, Madeleine (aka Lady Clanmorris) (1912–1988). *Cheapest in the End* (Dodd, Mead, 1963).
Starting on page 20, more than 100 scattered pages; she was the mother of Charlotte Bingham (see ch. 3 entry).
Dramatists ✧ High Society ✧ Novelists ✧ Short Story Writers ✧ Wealth | England

Bowne, Eliza Southgate (1783–1809). *A Girl's Life Eighty Years Ago: Selections from the Letters of Eliza Southgate Bowne* (Scribner's Sons, 1887) (1980 rpt., Corner House).

She rejected the idea of arranged marriages. Bowne grew up in ME before attending school in Medford, MA. Pages 3 to about 196 contain letters written by her from 13 to 21 years.

Eighteenth-Century Memoirists ✧ Feminists ✧ Letters ✧ Wealth I MA

Cabot, Elizabeth Rogers Mason (1834–1920). Ed. by P.A.M. Taylor. *More Than Common Powers of Perception: The Diary of Elizabeth Rogers Mason Cabot* (Beacon, 1991).

Pages 42–147 focus on her from 9 to 21 years

Diaries and Journals ✧ High Society ✧ Nineteenth-Century Pre-Industrial Age Memoirists ✧ Wealth I MA

Cantwell, Mary (1931?–2000). *American Girl: Scenes from a Small-Town Childhood* (Random House, 1992).

She grew up in a privileged environment; as an adult, she served on the *New York Times* editorial board. She was also a *New York Times* columnist.

Catholics ✧ Country Life ✧ Grandmothers ✧ Journalists ✧ Wealth I RI

Cooper, (Lady) Diana (1892–1986). *The Rainbow Comes and Goes* (R. Hart-Davis, 1958).

Pages 11 to about 112 (chs. 1–6).

Actresses ✧ Eccentrics ✧ High Society ✧ Victorian Era British Memoirists ✧ Wealth I England

Devi (of Jaipur), Gayatri (1919–), and Santha Rama Rav. *A Princess Remembers: The Memoirs of The Mararani of Jaipur* (Lippincott, 1976).

Pages 41–130.

Growing Up Between WWI and WWII ✧ Princesses I England ✧ India

Donhoff, (Countess) Marion (1909–2002). Tr. from the German by Jean Steinberg. *Before the Storm: Memories of My Youth in Old Prussia* (Knopf, 1990) (First published in German, 1988).

Royalty I East Prussia (i.e., Lithuania)

Gilman, Susan Jane (1965–). *Hypocrite in a Pouffy White Dress: Tales of Growing Up Groovy and Clueless* (Warner Books, 2005).

Gilman tells of her adventures and misadventures growing up on Manhattan's Upper West Side.

Divorce ✧ Eccentrics ✧ Generation X ✧ Hippies ✧ Jews ✧ Journalists ✧ Wealth I NYC (Manhattan)

Hermione, Countess of Ranfurly (1913–2001). *The Ugly One: The Childhood Memoirs of Hermione, Countess of Ranfurly, 1913–39* (M. Joseph, 1998).

Pages 1–4, and about pages 40 to about 149.

Growing Up Between WWI and WWII ✧ Royalty I Wales ✧ England

Hohenzollern, Friedrich Willhelm (King William II) (1859–1941). *My Early Life* (George H. Doran, 1926).

Covers the first 30 years of his life.

Nineteenth-Century Pre-Industrial Age Memoirists ✧ Royalty I Germany

Ishimoto, (Baroness) Shidzue (1897–2001). *East Way, West Way: A Modern Japanese Girlhood* (Farrar & Rinehart, 1936).

Covers her life to about a week after her marriage, at about 16 or 17 years. Influenced by Margaret Sanger of the U.S., she was the first influential woman to promote birth control in Japan. She was also active in labor reform.

Centenarians ✧ Reformers ✧ Royalty | Japan

Kean, Robert Winthrop (1893–1980). *Fourscore Years, My First Twenty-Four* (Privately printed, 1974).

He served in Congress for 20 years.

Harvard University ✧ Politicians ✧ Resorts ✧ Wealth | NYC (Manhattan) ✧ NJ ✧ MA ✧ AK (?)

Keyes, Frances Parkinson (1885–1970). *Roses in December* (Doubleday, 1960).

Covers her to about 19 years

Fatherless Families ✧ Novelists ✧ Wealth | VT ✧ MA

Klein, Patsy. *Growing Up Spoiled in Beverly Hills* (Lyle Stuart, 1986).

She is not to be confused with singer Patsy Cline (1932–1963).

Anorexia Nervosa ✧ City Life ✧ Wealth | CA (Southern: Beverly Hills)

Loelia, Duchess of Westminster (b. Loelia Ponsonby) (1902–1993). Foreword by Sir Noel Coward. *Grace and Favour: The Memoirs of Loelia Duchess of Westminster* (Weidenfeld & Nicolson, 1961).

Starting with ch. 2, about 100 pages. Includes 23 black-and-white illustrations and a 7-page index. Noel Coward was her grandson.

Debutantes ✧ Editors ✧ Royalty | England ✧ Scotland

Lubbock, (Lady) Sybil (1879–1943). *The Child in the Crystal* (J. Cape, 1939).

Covers about her first 20 years.

High Society ✧ Victorian Era British Memoirists | England

Marie, Grand Duchess of Russia (1890–1948). Tr. from the French and Russian under the editorial supervision of Russell Lord. *Education of a Princess: A Memoir* (Viking, 1930).

Pages 10 to about 138.

Princesses | Russia

Matthau, Carol (1932–). *Among the Porcupines: A Memoir* (Turtle Bay Books, 1992).

About 50–60 pages seem to be on her first 21 years. She was married to writer William Saroyan (see ch. 5 entry) and actor Walter Matthau.

Actresses ✧ Child Institutional Care ✧ Matthau, Walter ✧ Saroyan, William ✧ Wealth | TX (?) ✧ NYC (?)

Mernissi, Fatima (or Fatema) (1940–). *Dreams of Trespass: Tales of a Harem Girlhood* (Addison-Wesley, 1994).

As an adult, she became a published sociologist.

Harems ✧ Muslims ✧ Sociologists | Morocco

Moats, Alice-Leone (1909?–1989). *Violent Innocence* (Duell, Sloan and Pearce, 1951).

Covers about her first 12 years. She enjoyed a privileged childhood.

Foreign Correspondents ✧ Journalists ✧ Wealth | Mexico

Peabody, Marian Lawrence (1875–). *To Be Young Was Very Heaven* (Houghton Mifflin, 1967).
About 103 scattered pages (3–133). The title is derived from a poem by William Wordsworth.
Diaries and Journals ✧ High Society ✧ Wealth | MA ✧ IL ✧ Washington, DC ✧ Italy ✧ England ✧ Switzerland ✧ France

Princess Alice, Duchess of Gloucester (1901–2004). *Memories of Ninety Years* (Collins & Brown, 1991).
Pages 10 to about 85. At the time of her death, she had been the longest-lived member of England's royal family.
Centenarians ✧ Princesses | England

Satrapi, Marjane (1969–). *Persepolis: The Story of a Childhood* (Pantheon Books, 2003).
Focusing on her from 10 to 14 years, this account details Satrapi's tumultuous life during the Islamic Revolution. This is written in the form of a graphic novel, and was adapted as a film in 2007.
Cartoonists ✧ Generation X ✧ Graphic Novels ✧ Iran–Iraq War ✧ Royalty | Iran

Sedgwick, Henry Dwight (1861–1956). *Memoirs of an Epicurean* (Bobbs-Merrill, 1942).
Pages 15–101.
Biographers ✧ Essayists ✧ High Society ✧ Historians ✧ Wealth | NY ✧ NYC ✧ MA

Setsuko, Princess Chichibu (1909–1995). Tr. by Dorothy Britton. *The Silver Drum: A Japanese Imperial Memoir* (Global Oriental, 1996) (First published in Japanese, 1991).
Pages 1–118 (ch. 1–first page of ch. 7).
Princesses | England ✧ Washington, DC ✧ Japan

Sultana (1956–), with Jean Sasson. *Princess: A True Story of Life Behind the Veil in Saudi Arabia* (W. Morrow, 1992).
Pages 19, 25, to about 209 focus on Sultana from 4 to about 21 years.
Princesses | Saudi Arabia ✧ Egypt

Torregrosa, Luisita Lopez. *The Noise of Infinite Longing: A Memoir of a Family—and an Island* (Rayo/HarperCollins, 2004).
She grew up in Puerto Rico during the 1950s, in a privileged but dysfunctional family. Torregrosa later worked as an editor at the *New York Times*.
Baby Boomers (?) ✧ Bereavement ✧ Divorce ✧ Family Memoirs ✧ Fatherless Families ✧ High Society ✧ Island Life ✧ Journalists ✧ Wealth | Puerto Rico

Van de Water, Virginia Terhune (1865–1945). *The Heart of a Child: Some Reminiscences of a Reticent Childhood* (W.A. Wilde, 1927).
This is an account of her travels with her parents.
Etiquette ✧ Home Economics ✧ Novelists ✧ Wealth | NYC ✧ Europe

Victoria, Queen (1819–1901). Ed. by Viscount Escher. *Girlhood of Queen Victoria: A Selection from Her Majesty's Diaries Between the Years 1832 and 1840: 2 Volumes* (Longmans, Green, 1912).
Diaries and Journals ✧ Royalty | England

Von Rezzori, Gregor (1914–1998). Tr. from the German by H. F. Broch de Rothermann. *The Snows of Yesteryear: Portraits for an Autobiography* (Knopf, 1989).

This reminiscence is set during the final years of the Austro-Hungarian Empire.

Growing Up Between WWI and WWII ✧ High Society ✧ Novelists ✧ Radio Broadcasters ✧ Screenwriters | Romania

Chapter 15

Inside and Outside the Law: Lawyers, Judges, Police, Criminals, and Prisoners

This chapter's 2 sections highlight memoirs penned by more than 3 dozen persons who have devoted their lives to the law—whether serving it, seeking to change it from within, or circumventing and breaking it. The first section contains a dozen reminiscences by persons of no less legal and social influence than former Supreme Court Justices William O. Douglas and Sandra Day O'Connor. Their accounts of their early years in Washington State and Arizona—far removed from the corridors of power of their nation's capital—prefigure the course of their adult years, which were spent adjudicating rulings that would affect the course of an entire country.

This part of chapter 15 also surveys works by such high-profile lawyers as Gerry Spence (who represented Karen Silkwood), Harold Krents (whose legal work fighting for rights for disabled individuals inspired the play and film *Butterflies Are Free*), and Joseph Choate (who prosecuted the corrupt "Tweed Ring" of New York City). Also surveyed here are autobiographical writings by policeman David Hunter and politician Barack Obama.

The second section of chapter 15 is devoted to the memoirs of those who have acted outside of the law. The 1st-person stories of persons convicted of sensational crimes of violence, such as those by Manson family member Susan Atkins and "Long Island Lolita" Amy Fisher, are contained here, as well as those by international con artist Frank Abagnale Jr. Susan Berman, Kim Rich, and Antoinette Giancana provide insider views of growing up in families enmeshed in the culture of organized crime. Stories of innocent victims of wartime incarceration are also found here, such as those told by Helen Colijn and Ernest W. Michel.

Lawyers, Judges, and Police

Blackiston, Henry C(urtis) (1909–2001). *Those Happy Years: Childhood, Boyhood and Youth* (Princeton University, 1986).
He practiced law in NYC for more than 35 years.
Lawyers

Choate, Joseph (1832–1917). *The Boyhood and Youth of Joseph Hodges Choate* (Scribner, 1917).

This account is also found in the 2-volume work *The Life of Joseph Hodges Choate: As Gathered Chiefly from His Letters* (Scribner, 1920). Pages 35–96 focus on his first 21 years, although a significant number discuss historical events outside his everyday life. As a lawyer in NYC, he was retained as a prosecutor in such high-profile cases as those involving the Tweed Ring and Standard Oil.

> Ambassadors and Diplomats ✧ Lawyers ✧ Nineteenth-Century Pre-Industrial Age Memoirists | MA

Douglas, William O. (1898–1980). *Go East, Young Man: The Early Years* (Random House, 1974).

> Pages 1–113 (chs. 1–8).

> Judges | WA

Douglas, William O. (1898–1980). *Of Men and Mountains* (Chronicle Books, 1950).

> About 54 scattered pages.

> Camps ✧ Cascade Mountains ✧ Fishing ✧ Hikers ✧ Hunters ✧ Infantile Paralysis ✧ Judges ✧ Mountain Life ✧ Outdoor Life | WA ✧ OR

Hunter, David (1947–). *Trailer Trash from Tennessee* (Rutledge Hill, 1995).

> Baby Boomers ✧ Journalists ✧ Police ✧ Working Class Whites | TN

Hupalo, Kathleen Fixsen (1945–). *Family Farm: A Compilation of Short Stories* (HCM, 2000).

> About growing up in rural MN in the 1940s, 1950s, and 1960s.

> Civil Rights Workers ✧ Country Life ✧ Lawyers | MN

Krents, Harold (1944–1987). *To Race the Wind: An Autobiography* (Putnam, 1972).

His life inspired the Broadway play and 1972 film *Butterflies Are Free*. As an adult, he fought for justice for disabled individuals.

> Blindness ✧ City Life ✧ Government Officials ✧ Lawyers | NYC

Newbolt, (Sir) Henry (1862–1938). *My World as in My Time: Memoirs of Sir Henry Newbolt, 1862–1932* (Faber & Faber, 1932).

Pages 2 to about 138 (about chs. 1–11). Includes 15 plates. He was an acquaintance of novelist Joseph Conrad.

> Critics (Literary) ✧ Lawyers ✧ Novelists ✧ Oxford University ✧ Poets ✧ Victorian Era British Memoirists | England

Obama, Barack (1961–). *Dreams from My Father: A Story of Race and Inheritance* (Times Books, 1995).

About 100 pages. He was president of *Harvard Law Review*. He also campaigned for the 2008 Democratic Party nomination for the presidency.

> Baby Boomers ✧ Civil Rights Workers ✧ Intellectual Life ✧ Lawyers ✧ Politicians ✧ Racially Mixed Children ✧ Racism | HI

O'Connor, Sandra Day (1930–), and H. Alan Day. *Lazy B: Growing Up on a Cattle Ranch in the American Southwest* (Random House, 2002).

This is a collaboration between the 1st woman to serve as a U.S. Supreme Court judge (1981–2005) and her brother.

> Brothers ✧ Collaborations by Relatives ✧ Growing Up Between WWI and WWII ✧ Ranch Life ✧ Sisters ✧ Summer ✧ Supreme Court Justices | AZ

Spence, Gerry (1929–). *The Making of a Country Lawyer* (St. Martin's, 1996).

He achieved national prominence when Karen Silkwood's children hired him as their lawyer, after their mother died.

Growing Up Between WWI and WWII ✧ Lawyers I WY

Townsend, William Henry (1890–1964). *Hundred Proof: Salt River Sketches & Memoirs of the Blue-Grass* (University of Kentucky, 1964).

A lawyer by profession, he also wrote books on Lincoln and for years was a close friend of Carl Sandburg (see entries in ch. 9).

Lincoln, Abraham ✧ Lawyers ✧ Sandburg, Carl I KY

Underwood, Francis Henry (1825–1894). *Quabbin: The Story of a Small Town: With Outlooks Upon Puritan Life* (Lee and Shepard, 1893).

Country Living ✧ Lawyers ✧ Nineteenth-Century Pre-Industrial Age Memoirists I MA

Crime, Criminals, and Prisoners

Including Accounts of Concentration and Internment Camp Captivity

Abagnale, Frank W., Jr. (1948–), with Stan Redding and Frank W. Abagnale. *Catch Me If You Can: The Amazing True Story of the Most Extraordinary Liar in the History of Fun and Profit* (Grosset & Dunlap, 1980).

He's only 20 on page 216. Adapted into a 2002 film starring Leonardo DiCaprio.

Baby Boomers ✧ Catholics ✧ College Teachers ✧ Crime ✧ Lawyers ✧ Physicians ✧ Pilots ✧ Prisoners I NYC (Bronx) ✧ NY ✧ FL ✧ GA ✧ UT ✧ CA (Northern) ✧ NV ✧ IL ✧ Mexico ✧ England ✧ France ✧ MA ✧ Turkey ✧ AZ ✧ CA (Southern) ✧ Italy ✧ VT ✧ Sweden ✧ Canada (Quebec: Montreal)

Allan, Sheila (1924–). *Diary of a Girl in Changi, 1941–1945* (Kangaroo, 1994).

She was held captive in Changi Prison, after Singapore fell to the Japanese in WWII.

Diaries and Journals ✧ Growing Up Between WWI and WWII ✧ Prisoners ✧ WWII I Singapore

Atkins, Susan (1948–), with Bob Slosser. *Child of Satan, Child of God* (Logos International, 1977).

About the first 100 pages.

Baby Boomers ✧ Christian Converts ✧ Crime ✧ Cults I CA

Berman, Susan (1945–2000). *Easy Street* (Dial, 1981).

About 89 scattered pages. During her youth, her father ran hotels for mob bosses in Las Vegas. He died a natural death when she was 12. Susan's murder in 2000 remains unsolved. For similar memoirs, see "Rich, Kim" and "DeMeo, Albert" (this section).

Crime ✧ Fatherless Families ✧ Journalists ✧ Wealth I NV ✧ CA (Southern) ✧ ID ✧ OR

Bunker, Edward (1933–2005). Introduction by William Styron. *Education of a Felon: A Memoir* (St. Martin's, 2000).

About the first 120 pages. At age 17, he was the youngest inmate in San Quentin's history. He wrote screenplays for 3 films, including the Oscar-nominated *Runaway Train* (1985).

Books and Reading ✧ Child Institutional Care ✧ Crime ✧ Divorce ✧ Prisoners ✧ Runaways ✧ Screenwriters I CA (Southern)

Colijn, Helen (1921?–). *Song of Survival: Women Interned* (White Cloud, 1995).
Covers her during her internment (1942–1945), when she was about 20–23 years old. This memoir was adapted into the 1997 film *Paradise Road*.

Camps (Internment) ✧ WWII I Indonesia

DeMeo, Albert (1966–). *For the Sins of My Father: A Mafia Killer, His Son, and the Legacy of a Mob Life* (Broadway Books, 2002).
About the first 240 pages. His father was murdered shortly before Albert turned 17. For a similar memoir, see "Berman, Susan" (this section).

Crime ✧ Murder ✧ Fathers and Sons ✧ Generation X I NY (Long Island)

Devlin, Mark (1948–). *Stubborn Child* (Atheneum, 1985).
Pages 21 to about 176 cover from 7 to 21 years.

Baby Boomers ✧ Child Institutional Care ✧ Crime ✧ Prisoners I MA ✧ VA

Fisher, Amy (1974–), and Sheila Weller. *Amy Fisher: My Story* (Pocket Books, 1993).

Crime ✧ Generation X I NY (Long Island)

Giancana, Antoinette (1935–), and Thomas C. Renner. *Mafia Princess: Growing Up in Sam Giancana's Family* (W. Morrow, 1984).
Pages 12–80 focus on her first 21 years.

City Life ✧ Crime ✧ Fathers and Daughters ✧ Italian Americans I IL (Chicago)

Gifford, Barry (1946–). *The Phantom Father: A Memoir* (Harcourt, Brace, 1997).

Crime ✧ Fatherless Families ✧ Fathers and Sons ✧ Grandfathers ✧ Novelists ✧ Poets ✧ Uncles I IL

Hearst, Patricia (1954–), with Alvin Moscow. *Every Secret Thing* (Doubleday, 1982).
About the first 400 pages. See also "Holman, Virginia" (ch. 7).

Baby Boomers ✧ Crime ✧ Cults I CA (Northern)

Hoard, G. Richard (1952/1953–). *Alone Among the Living* (University of Georgia, 1994).
Much re-created dialogue; focuses on him from 14 to 18 years.

Baby Boomers ✧ Bereavement ✧ Fatherless Families ✧ Methodists ✧ Murder ✧ Radio Journalists I GA

Klasner, Lily (1862–1946). Ed. by Eve Ball. *My Girlhood Among Outlaws* (University of Arizona, 1972).

Crime ✧ Frontier and Pioneer Life I NM ✧ TX

Lessard, Suzannah (1944–). *The Architecture of Desire: Beauty and Danger in the Stanford White Family* (Dial, 1996).
About 104 scattered pages. She is White's great-granddaughter; his life inspired E. L. Doctorow's novel *Ragtime* (Random House, 1975) and the film *The Girl in the Red Velvet Swing* (1955).

Abuse (Sexual) ✧ Architects ✧ Homes and Haunts ✧ Incest ✧ Journalists ✧ Murder ✧ White, Stanford I NY (Long Island) ✧ Italy

McCall, Nathan (1955–). *Makes Me Wanna Holler: A Young Black Man in America* (Random House, 1994).

African Americans ✧ Baby Boomers ✧ Journalists ✧ Prisoners I FL ✧ Morocco ✧ VA

McMullen, Richie (1943–). *Enchanted Youth* (Gay Men's Press, 1990) (Originally published as *Enchanted Boy* [Gay Men's Press, 1989]).

Focuses on him at age 15.

Gays ✧ Prostitution ✧ Sexuality | England

Michel, Ernest W. (1923–). Foreword by Leon Uris. *Promises to Keep* (Publishers Group West, 1993).

Pages 1–99 (Prologue–ch. 12) focus on him from 15 to 21 years. His parents died at Auschwitz; he was imprisoned there and at other labor camps.

Auschwitz ✧ Bereavement ✧ Holocaust Survivors ✧ Jews ✧ Philanthropists | Germany ✧ Poland

Nuwere, Ejovi (1981–), and David Chanoff. *Hacker Cracker: A Journey from the Mean Streets of Brooklyn to the Frontiers of Cyberspace* (W. Morrow, 2002).

Includes a glossary of computer terms. Growing up on the streets of Brooklyn, Nuwere details his involvement with computer hacking, starting at age 14.

AIDS Virus ✧ Bereavement ✧ Computer Hacking ✧ Generation X ✧ Grandmothers ✧ Security Specialists | NYC (Brooklyn)

Rich, Kim (1958–). *Johnny's Girl: A Daughter's Memoir of Growing Up in Alaska's Underworld* (W. Morrow, 1993).

Pages 45–292. For a similar memoir, see "Berman, Susan" (this section).

Baby Boomers ✧ Crime ✧ Fathers and Daughters ✧ Journalists ✧ Mental Health ✧ Murder ✧ Strippers | AK

Rodriguez, Luis J. (1954–). *Always Running: A Memoir of La Vida Loca Gang Days in L.A.* (Curbstone, 1993).

Baby Boomers ✧ Gangs ✧ Hispanic Americans ✧ Publishers ✧ Slums | CA (Southern)

Shakur, Sanyika (aka Monster Kody Scott) (1963–). *Monster: The Autobiography of an L.A. Gang Member* (Atlantic Monthly, 1993).

Gangs | CA (Southern: Los Angeles)

Shaw, Clifford Robe (1896–). *The Jack-Roller; A Delinquent Boy's Own Story* (University of Chicago, 1930).

Pages 47–163 consist of an autobiographical account by a boy whose name is given only as "Stanley."

Reformatories | IL (Chicago)

Slovo, Gillian (1952–). *Every Secret Thing: My Family, My Country* (Little, Brown, 1997).

About 80 pages (11, 15–18, 39–113).

Civil Rights Workers ✧ Communists ✧ Murder ✧ Novelists ✧ Orphans | South Africa ✧ England

Sterry, David Henry (1957–). *Chicken: Self-Portrait of a Young Man for Rent* (Regan Books, 2002).

Set during his college freshman year in the 1970s, when he worked as a teenage prostitute.

Actors ✧ Baby Boomers ✧ Catholics ✧ Children of Immigrants ✧ Prostitution ✧ Sexuality | CA (Southern)

Weller, Sheila (1945–). *Dancing at Ciro's: A Family's Love, Loss, and Scandal on the Sunset Strip* (St. Martin's, 2003).

Focusing on her youth in 1950s Hollywood, Weller describes a subculture of violence and hollow American dreams. For a similar memoir, see "Berman, Susan" (this section).

Crime ✧ Entertainment Industry ✧ Family Memoirs ✧ Family Violence ✧ Fathers and Daughters ✧ Jews ✧ Journalists ✧ Uncles I CA (Southern: Hollywood)

Wolff, Geoffrey (1937–). *The Duke of Deception: Memories of My Father* (Random House, 1979).

See also "Wolff, Tobias" (ch. 17).

Aerospace Industries ✧ College Teachers ✧ Crime ✧ Essayists ✧ Fathers and Sons ✧ Jews ✧ Novelists I CA (Southern) (?)

Yakir, Pyotr (1923?–). Ed. by Robert Conquest. *A Childhood in Prison* (Macmillan, 1972).

He describes his teenage years, spent in Soviet prisons.

Growing Up Between WWI and WWII ✧ Prisoners I Soviet Union

Chapter 16

The Darker Side of Childhood: Outcasts, Violence, Abuse, Poverty, and Other Traumas

This chapter is composed of 5 parts: "Outcasts," "Family Violence and Other Family Abuse," "Poverty and Times of Economic Depression," "Substance Abuse," and "Other Family Dysfunctions and Trauma." The reminiscences shared here reflect life experiences that, for the more than 150 profiled authors, were difficult both to endure and later to revisit in the writing of their memoirs.

The first 2 sections list autobiographical works that convey the trauma of childhood rejection, stemming from forces that are essentially political, social, or familial. Jewish immigrants whose experiences were not a direct outgrowth of the Holocaust also tell their stories here. (See the second parts of chapters 6 and 15 for memoirs of Holocaust victims.) Years of emotional struggle in difficult adoptive environments are described by some of these writers. Still other memoirists recount comings-of-age that were plagued by various forms of physical abuse at home, school, or elsewhere. (For further thematically related memoirs, see "Family Violence" in the subject index.)

The third section relates to other entries in this volume that may be found in the subject index under "Country Life," "Crime," and "Slums," but in these books the poverty is a crushing reality that leaves emotional scars on the writer. Some 40 works are listed here, ranging from accounts of hardscrabble farm life in Maine, to re-creations of lives of abject poverty in Dublin, Ireland, to evocations of youth lived in the American heartland during the Dust Bowl years of the Great Depression. One of the more poignant titles listed here is *King of the Hill*, a childhood memoir by A. E. Hotchner (himself a biographer and acquaintance of Ernest Hemingway), who survived painful years growing up in St. Louis.

Substance abuse provides the focus of the fourth section of the chapter. Autobiographical writings by children of alcoholics are included here, such as those by actresses Suzanne Sommers and Mariette Hartley. Contained here as well are works by persons whose recreational use of alcohol or other drug dependence impaired their well-being and in some instances jeopardized their lives.

The final part of this chapter gives voice to young lives in torment from a host of other sources, often in tandem. Jill Christman paints a bleak picture of a young life afflicted by one trauma after another, including abuse at the hands of a neighbor and the death of her fiancé. Other memoirs in this section also speak of the debilitating effects of bereavement, such as *Name All the Animals*, by Alison Smith, whose brother died in an accident while she was a teenager. Works by Signe Hammer and Linda Sexton are affecting reminiscences by women whose mothers committed suicide. Other memoirs represented in this chapter relate formative years that were interrupted by such traumatic events as a sibling's running away or living in a chemically toxic environment.

Outcasts

Refugees, Immigrants, and Emigrants; Divorce and Orphan Trauma; Rape and Bullying Victims; Adoptive Family Abuse; and Abusive Psychiatric Treatment

Aciman, André (1951–). *False Papers* (Farrar, Straus, and Giroux, 2000).
About 50 scattered pages (between pages 3 and 156).
Aunts ✧ Immigrants ✧ Jews | Egypt ✧ France (Paris) ✧ NYC

Adamic, Louis (1899–1951). *Laughing in the Jungle: The Autobiography of an Immigrant* (Harper & Brothers, 1932).
Adamic is almost 21 on page 186.
Immigrants ✧ Military Life ✧ WWI | Yugoslavia ✧ NYC ✧ Panama ✧ LA ✧ France

Antin, Mary (b. Mary Antin Grabau) (1881–1949). *From Plotzk to Boston* (W.B. Clarke, 1899).
Pages 12–15, 17–80. This work has long been regarded as a classic immigrant memoir. It was later incorporated in the memoir in the following entry.
Hale, Edward Everett ✧ Immigrants ✧ Jews ✧ Lecturers ✧ Reformers ✧ Slums | Russia ✧ MA

Antin, Mary (b. Mary Antin Grabau) (1881–1949). *The Promised Land* (Houghton Mifflin, 1969) (First published in English, Houghton Mifflin, 1912).
Pages 1–363 are on her childhood and adolescence. Antin's is one of the most detailed of immigrant memoirs. This is an expanded composite of her shorter works *From Plotzk to Boston* (W.B. Clarke, 1899) and its sequel *At School in the Promised Land: Or, the Story of a Little Immigrant* (Houghton Mifflin, 1912).
Immigrants ✧ Jews ✧ Lecturers ✧ Reformers ✧ Slums | Russia ✧ NYC ✧ MA

Asayesh, Gelareh (1962–). *Saffron Sky: A Life Between Iran and America* (Beacon, 1999).
Some 50–55 scattered pages.
Immigrants ✧ Journalists | Iran ✧ NC

Asgedom, Mawi (1976–). *Of Beetles and Angels: A Boy's Remarkable Journey from a Refugee Camp to Harvard* (Megadee Books, 2001).
Covers his youth up to graduation from Harvard University.
Generation X ✧ Harvard University ✧ Immigrants ✧ Racism ✧ Refugees | Ethiopia ✧ IL (Chicago) ✧ MA

Bevington, Helen (1906–2001). *Charley Smith's Girl: A Memoir* (Simon and Schuster, 1965).
Describes how she became separated from her divorced parents.
Divorce ✧ Poets | NY

Blanco, Jodee (1964–). *Please Stop Laughing at Me: One Woman's Inspirational Story* (Adams Media, 2003).

Blanco describes the various humiliations she suffered from bullies throughout her school years.

Abuse (Psychiatric) ✧ Baby Boomers ✧ Catholics ✧ Public Relations ✧ School Bullying | IL

Blend, Martha (1930–). *A Child Alone* (Vallentine Mitchell, 1995).

Pages 1 to about 146 (chs. 1–9). At age 9 she was moved to England by Kindertransport.

Holocaust Survivors ✧ Jews ✧ Refugees | Austria ✧ England

Bonin, Adelyn I. (1920–). *Allegiances: A Memoir* (Fithian, 1993).

Pages 9 to about 137. Describes her years as a Berlin schoolgirl, then her immigration to Palestine.

College Teachers ✧ Growing Up Between WWI and WWII ✧ Immigrants ✧ Jews ✧ WWII | Germany ✧ Palestine (i.e., Israel)

Brady, Katherine. *Father's Days: A True Story of Incest* (Seaview Books, 1979).

Covers her from 8 to 18 years.

Baby Boomers (?) ✧ Fathers and Daughters ✧ Incest | MN

Brown, John (1792?–1829). *Memoir of Robert Blincoe, An Orphan Boy: Sent from the Workhouse of St. Pancras, London, at Seven Years of Age, to Endure the Horrors of a Cotton Mill, Through His Infancy and Youth, with a Minute Detail of His Sufferings. Being the First Memoir of the Kind Published . . .* (J. Doherty, 1832).

About 64 pages of orally transmitted reminiscences, which Blincoe provided to John Brown in interviews from 1820 to 1824.

City Life ✧ Nineteenth Century Pre-Industrial Age Memoirists ✧ Orphans | England

Burch, Jennings (1941–). *They Cage the Animals at Night* (New American Library, 1984).

From 8 to 11 years. Within a 3-year period he lived in several institutions and foster homes.

Catholics ✧ Child Institutional Care ✧ Family Violence ✧ Orphans | NYC (Brooklyn)

Caley, Kate Young. *The House Where the Hardest Things Happened: A Spiritual Memoir About Belonging* (Doubleday, 2002).

Set in the mid-1960s, this memoir describes the progressive ostracism of her family by the townspeople she had grown up among.

Baby Boomers (?) ✧ Hippies ✧ Poets ✧ Spiritual Life | NH

Chotzinoff, Samuel (1889–1964). *A Lost Paradise: Early Reminiscences* (Knopf, 1955).

A memorable anecdote in this work tells about the author's mother randomly wading through New York City crowds for months to find a relative. The author was a noted pianist.

City Life ✧ Critics (Music) ✧ Immigrants ✧ Musicians | England ✧ NYC (Lower East Side)

Cohen, Rose (1880–1925). *Out of the Shadow: A Russian Jewish Childhood on the Lower East Side* (George H. Doran, 1918) (1995 rpt., Cornell University).

City Life ✧ Immigrants ✧ Jews | NYC (Lower East Side)

Craft, Phil (1927–), and Stan Friedland. *An Orphan Has Many Parents* (KTAV Publishing House, 1998).

Depressions (Economic) ✧ Growing Up Between WWI and WWII ✧ Orphans | NYC (Brooklyn)

Czerniawski, Adam (1934–) *Scenes from a Disturbed Childhood* (Serpent's Tail, 1991).

He and his family fled from both Nazi and communist forces.

Family Memoirs ✧ Poets ✧ Refugees ✧ Translators ✧ WWII I England

Denes, Magda (1934–1996). *Castles Burning: A Child's Life in War* (W.W. Norton, 1997).

Holocaust Survivors ✧ Jews ✧ Refugees I Hungary ✧ Germany ✧ France ✧ Cuba

Dobie, Kathy. *The Only Girl in the Car: A Memoir* (Dial, 2003).

She describes events that preceded and followed being gang raped during the 1960s, when she was 14.

Abuse (Sexual) ✧ Baby Boomers (?) ✧ Books and Reading ✧ Catholics I CT

Fisher, Antwone Quenton (1959–), with Mim Eichler Rivas. *Finding Fish: A Memoir* (W. Morrow, 2001).

Pages 27 to about 273. This memoir was adapted in 2002 into the film *Antwone Fisher*.

Abuse (Sexual) ✧ Adoptees ✧ African Americans ✧ Baby Boomers ✧ Military Life ✧ Motion Picture Producers and Directors ✧ Screenwriters I OH

Fleming, Keith (1959–). *The Boy with the Thorn in His Side: A Memoir* (W. Morrow, 2000).

His uncle was writer Edmund White (1940–).

Baby Boomers ✧ City Life ✧ Divorce ✧ Family Violence ✧ Gays ✧ Mental Health ✧ Stepchildren ✧ Uncles I NYC (Upper West Side)

Fox, Anne L. (1926–). *My Heart in a Suitcase* (Vallentine Mitchell, 1996).

Pages 1 to about 141 (chs. 1–7).

Holocaust Survivors ✧ Jews ✧ Refugees I Germany ✧ England

Gissing, Vera (1928–). *Pearls of Childhood: The Poignant True Wartime Story of a Young Girl Growing Up in an Adopted Land* (St. Martin's, 1988).

Jews ✧ Refugees I Czechoslovakia (?) ✧ England

Hamilton, Sharon Jean (b. Karen Agnes Fleming) (1944–). *My Name's Not Susie: A Life Transformed by Literacy* (Heinemann, 1995).

About 59 scattered pages.

Adoptees ✧ College Teachers ✧ Illiteracy I Canada (Manitoba: Winnipeg)

Hayslip, Le Ly (1949–). *When Heaven and Earth Changed Places: A Vietnam Woman's Journey from War to Peace* (Doubleday, 1989).

Buddhists ✧ Refugees ✧ Vietnam Conflict I Vietnam

Heppner, Ernest G. (1921–). *Shanghai Refuge: A Memoir of the World War II Jewish Ghetto* (University of Nebraska, 1993).

Pages 4 to about 108.

Jews ✧ Refugees ✧ WWII I Germany ✧ China

Hilton, Ella E. Schneider (1936–), Angela K. Hilton, Ella S. Hilton, and Karl A. Roider. *Displaced Person: A Girl's Life in Russia, Germany, and America* (Louisiana State University, 2004).

This is Hilton's account of the displacements she and her mother endured during WWII.

Fatherless Families ✧ Mothers and Daughters ✧ Refugees ✧ WWII ✧ Russia I Germany ✧ MS

Him, Chanrithy (1965–). *When Broken Glass Floats: Growing Up Under the Khmer Rouge: A Memoir* (W.W. Norton, 2000).

Generation X ✧ Refugees | Cambodia

Hitchman, Janet (b. Elsie May Fields) (1916–1980). *The King of the Barbareens: The Autobiography of an Orphan* (Putnam, 1960).

All but the last few pages.

Dramatists ✧ Growing Up Between WWI and WWII ✧ Mental Health ✧ Orphans ✧ Short Story Writers | England

Hoffman, Eva (1945–). *Lost in Translation: A Life in a New Language* (E.P. Dutton, 1989).

About the first 160 pages.

Cold War ✧ College Teachers ✧ Editors ✧ Holocaust Survivors ✧ Immigrants ✧ Jews | Poland ✧ Canada (British Columbia)

Hoggart, Richard (1918–living 2007). *A Local Habitation: Life and Times, 1918–1940* (Chatto & Windus, 1988).

This is the first of an autobiographical trilogy, collected in A Measured Life: The Times and Places of an Orphaned Intellectual (Transaction, 1994). In the 1988 edition, about pages 9 to about 195 of *A Local Habitation* focus on his first 21 years.

Aunts ✧ College Teachers ✧ Grandmothers ✧ Growing Up Between WWI and WWII ✧ Historians (Cultural) ✧ Orphans ✧ Uncles | England

Horne, Alistair (1925–). *A Bundle from Britain* (Macmillan, 1993).

Pages 1–6, 62–320 (part of ch. 1, chs. 3–11).

Bereavement ✧ Growing Up Between WWI and WWII ✧ Immigrants ✧ Millbrook School ✧ WWII | England ✧ NY

Jadhav, Narendra. *Untouchables: One Family's Triumph Over the Caste System in Modern India* (Scribner, 2005).

The difficult formative years of the respective childhoods of the author (an economist) and his parents are related through diary entries and other autobiographical narratives. Members of this family were born outcasts in the lowest Hindu caste level, the Dalits (sometimes referred to as "Untouchables").

Collaborations by Relatives ✧ Dalits ✧ Diaries and Journals ✧ Economists ✧ Family Memoirs | India

Johnson, Axel P. (1886–). *Smuggled into Paradise: Saga of an Immigrant Youth* (Dorrance, 1958).

About 75–80 pages.

College Teachers ✧ Immigrants ✧ Journalists ✧ Lawyers ✧ Politicians ✧ Telegraph Operators | Sweden ✧ LA ✧ IL

Kopelnitsky, Raimonda (1977–), and Kelli Pryor ("First two sections tr. by William Spiegelberger"). *No Words to Say Goodbye: A Young Jewish Woman's Journey from the Soviet Union into America: The Extraordinary Diaries of Raimonda Kopelnitsky* (Hyperion, 1994).

Pages 37–272 are diary entries covering September 2, 1989, through June 7, 1992.

Diaries and Journals ✧ Generation X ✧ Immigrants ✧ Jews | Soviet Union (i.e., Ukraine) ✧ NYC (Brooklyn)

Krutein, Eva (?–living 1994). *Eva's War: A True Story of Survival* (Amador, 1990).
A memoir written in the form of a novel.

Bereavement ✧ Holocaust Survivors ✧ Refugees ✧ Suicide and Suicide Victims ✧ WWII | Germany ✧ Chile (?) CA (?)

Laqueur, Walter (Ze'ev) (1921–). *Thursday's Child Has Far to Go: A Memoir of the Journeying Years* (Scribner's Sons, 1992).
Pages 23 to about 203.

Growing Up Between WWI and WWII ✧ Historians ✧ Intellectual Life ✧ Jews | Germany ✧ Israel

Lauck, Jennifer (1964–). *Blackbird: A Childhood Lost and Found* (Pocket Books, 2000).
Covers her first 11 years; this memoir is continued by *Still Waters* (this ch.).

Adoptees ✧ Baby Boomers ✧ Bereavement ✧ Caregiving ✧ Family Violence ✧ Journalists ✧ Mothers and Daughters | NV ✧ CA (Southern)

Lewis, Mindy (1952?–). *Life Inside: Surviving a Difficult Adolescence: A Memoir* (Atria Books, 2002).
The first part of this work focuses on her from 15 to 18 years, while she was living in a psychiatric hospital.

Abuse (Psychiatric) ✧ Artists ✧ Baby Boomers ✧ Essayists ✧ Fatherless Families ✧ Schizophrenia ✧ Suicide and Suicide Victims | NYC (Manhattan)

Lopez, Charlotte (1976–), and Susan Dworkin, contr. *Lost in the System* (Simon and Schuster, 1996).

Adoptees ✧ Child Institutional Care ✧ Children of the Mentally Ill ✧ Generation X | Puerto Rico (?) ✧ VT

Louise, Regina. *Somebody's Someone: A Memoir* (Warner Books, 2003).
Focuses on her from 10 to 15 years. After being neglected, shuttled about, and abused by relatives until she was 13, Regina lived in a series of foster and group homes, despite which she maintained an optimistic outlook.

Abuse (Emotional) ✧ African Americans ✧ Child Institutional Care ✧ Family Violence ✧ Hair Stylists | TX ✧ NC ✧ CA

McKenzie, Richard B. (c. 1942–). *The Home: A Memoir of Growing Up in an Orphanage* (Basic Books, 1996).
His mother killed herself when he was 10.

Child Institutional Care ✧ Children of Alcoholics ✧ College Teachers ✧ Historians (Cultural) ✧ Orphans ✧ Suicide and Suicide Victims | NC

Meckler, Brenda (1900–). *Papa Was a Farmer* (Algonquin Books of Chapel Hill, 1988).
Focuses almost exclusively on her first 17 years. Born in Russia, she moved with her family to the U.S. in 1904.

Farm Life ✧ Immigrants ✧ Jews | Russia ✧ OH

Norling, Donna Scott (1932– or 1933–). *Patty's Journey: From Orphanage to Adoption and Reunion* (University of Minnesota, 1996).
Pages 1 to about 140 (chs. 1–12).

Adoptees ✧ Child Institutional Care ✧ Depressions (Economic) | MN

Oufkir, Malika (1953–), and Michele Fitoussi. Tr. by Ros Schwartz. *Stolen Lives: Twenty Years in a Desert Jail* (Wheeler, 2001).

About the first 80–100 pages. Once a wealthy young heiress, Oufkir tells of her family's sudden separation and imprisonment following a failed coup attempt by her father against King Hassan II.

Fatherless Families ✧ Harems ✧ Prisoners ✧ Royalty | Morocco

Pejovich, Ted (1945–). *The State of California: Growing Up Foreign in the Backyards of Eden* (Knopf, 1989).

Set in the 1950s.

Immigrants | CA (Central)

Percival, Nora Lourie (1914–). *Weather of the Heart: A Child's Journey Out of Revolutionary Russia* (High Country, 2001).

Focusing on her from 3 to 8 years, this memoir describes her escape from Communist Russia with her mother.

Communists ✧ Fatherless Families ✧ Grandparents ✧ Growing Up Between WWI and WWII ✧ Immigrants ✧ Jews ✧ Mothers and Daughters | Russia

Razor, Peter (1929–). *While the Locust Slept: A Memoir* (Minnesota Historical Society, 2001).

Before becoming a journeyman electrician, Razor endured a painful childhood that included mistreatment by his parents and at a school for orphans.

Abuse (Physical) ✧ Child Institutional Care ✧ Children of Alcoholics ✧ Children of the Mentally Ill ✧ Electricians ✧ Family Violence ✧ Farm Life ✧ Growing Up Between WWI and WWII ✧ Native Americans ✧ Orphans ✧ Racism | MN

Rhodes, Richard (1937–). *A Hole in the World: An American Boyhood* (Simon and Schuster, 1990).

This memoir is continued by the following entry.

Bereavement ✧ Child Institutional Care ✧ Family Violence ✧ Farm Life ✧ Journalists ✧ Stepmothers ✧ Suicide and Suicide Victims | MO

Rhodes, Richard (1937–). *Making Love: An Erotic Odyssey* (Simon and Schuster, 1992).

About 60 pages focus on his first 21 years.

Child Institutional Care ✧ Journalists ✧ Sexuality | MO ✧ NYC

Segal, Lore (1928–). *Other Peoples' Houses* (Harcourt, Brace & World, 1964).

The first 158 pages focus on her before she entered college. A native Austrian, she fled to Holland at age 10 to avoid the Nazis, and then moved to England.

College Teachers ✧ Growing Up Between WWI and WWII ✧ Immigrants ✧ Short Story Writers ✧ Translators | Austria ✧ Holland ✧ England

Tobias, Sigmund (1932–). *Strange Haven: A Jewish Childhood in Wartime Shanghai* (University of Illinois, 1999)

College Teachers ✧ Jews ✧ Refugees ✧ WWII | Germany ✧ China

Ung, Loung (1970–). *First They Killed My Father: A Daughter of Cambodia Remembers* (HarperCollins, 2000).

Focus is on her from 5 to 9 years, during Pol Pot's cruel regime. For a similar memoir from a different culture, see "Frank, Anne" (ch. 6).

Fatherless Families ✧ Generation X ✧ Immigrants ✧ Khmer Rouge ✧ Orphans ✧ Prisoners | Cambodia

Vlasopolos, Anca (1948–). *No Return Address: A Memoir of Displacement* (Columbia University, 2000).

Pages 13 to about 194.

College Teachers ✧ Critics (Literary) ✧ Immigrants ✧ Jews | Romania ✧ France ✧ Belgium ✧ Germany ✧ MI

Walter, Elizabeth Barbara (1940–). *Barefoot in the Rubble* (Pannonia, 1997).

Covers 1945–1950. Following 2 years in communist concentration camps, she and her family fled to Germany and then the U.S., in 1950.

Camps (Internment) ✧ Prisoners ✧ Refugees ✧ WWII | Yugoslavia ✧ Germany ✧ U.S.

Wasilewska, Eugenia (b. Eugenia Laessig) (1922–). *The Silver Madonna; or, The Odyssey of Eugenia Wasilewska* (Allen & Unwin, 1970).

Covers her from 17 to 18 or 19 years.

Prisoners ✧ Refugees ✧ WWII | Siberia

Weinstein, Frida Scheps (1935?–). Tr. by Barbara Loeb Kennedy. *A Hidden Childhood, 1942–1945* (Hill and Wang, 1985) (First published in French, 1983).

She hid from the Nazis for 3 years in a French convent. After living in Jerusalem with her father, at about age 20 she served for 2 years in the Israeli Army, before coming to the U.S.

Holocaust Survivors ✧ Jews ✧ Journalists ✧ Refugees | France

Wermuth, Henry (1923–). *Breathe Deeply, My Son* (Vallentine Mitchell, 1993).

Pages 5 to about 156. In 1938 he and his family were deported from Germany to Poland.

Holocaust Survivors ✧ Jews ✧ Refugees | Germany ✧ Poland

Wojciechowska, Maia (1927–). *Till the Break of Day: Memories, 1939–1942* (Harcourt Brace Jovanovich, 1972).

She and her family left Poland when the Nazis occupied it.

Refugees ✧ WWII | Poland ✧ France

Wolf, Hannie (1925–). *Child of Two Worlds* (Purcells, 1979).

Covers her first 15 years. She and her family fled through Europe and Asia from Nazi persecution, finally settling in CO.

Refugees | Germany ✧ Russia ✧ Korea ✧ Japan ✧ CO

Zuker-Bujanowska, Liliana (1928–). *Liliana's Journal: Warsaw 1939–1945* (Dial, 1980).

Diaries and Journals ✧ Holocaust Survivors ✧ Jews ✧ Refugees ✧ Slums | Poland

Family Violence and Other Family Abuse

Allen, Charlotte Vale (1941–). *Daddy's Girl* (Wyndham Books, 1980).

Pages 7 to about 115 are on her first 22 years.

Fathers and Daughters ✧ Incest | Canada (Ontario: Toronto)

Ashworth, Andrea (1969–). *Once in a House on Fire* (Metropolitan Books, 1998).

Covers her from 5 to 18 years. After her father's drowning death when she was 5, she suffered physical and emotional abuse from 2 stepfathers. Most of her youth was spent in northern England.

College Teachers ✧ Drowning Victims ✧ Family Violence ✧ Fatherless Families ✧ Generation X ✧ Racially Mixed Children ✧ Stepfathers | England ✧ Canada

Cameron, Marcia (1941–). *Broken Child* (Kensington Books, 1994).

Abuse (Sexual) ✧ Family Violence ✧ Multiple Personality Disorder

Foveaux, Jessie Lee Brown (1899–1999). *Any Given Day: The Life and Times of Jessie Lee Foveaux* (Warner Books, 1997).

Pages 8 to about 177. (This memoir was written in 1979.)

Alcoholism ✧ Centenarians (?) ✧ Divorce ✧ Abuse (Spousal) | KS ✧ MO

Fowler, Connie May (1959?–). *When Katie Wakes: A Memoir* (Doubleday, 2002).

During her childhood her mother beat her.

Baby Boomers ✧ Children of Alcoholics ✧ Dogs ✧ Family Violence ✧ Fatherless Families ✧ Novelists | FL

Fraser, Sylvia (1935–). *My Father's House: A Memoir of Incest and of Healing* (Doubleday Canada, 1987).

Pages 3 to about 119 (chs. 1–7).

Fathers and Daughters ✧ Incest ✧ Novelists | Canada (Ontario)

Hayward, Brooke (1937–). *Haywire* (Knopf, 1977).

Perhaps the first mass-published memoir of a dysfunctional Hollywood childhood, preceding Christina Crawford's *Mommie Dearest* (ch. 11) by a year; see also "Hyman, B. D." (this section).

Actresses ✧ Divorce ✧ Mental Health ✧ Models | CA (Southern: Hollywood)

Helget, Nicole Lea. *The Summer of Ordinary Ways* (Borealis Books, 2005).

Covers her first 19 years. She re-creates a childhood filled with parental abuse.

Children of Alcoholics ✧ Family Violence ✧ Farm Life ✧ Generation X | MN

Hoffman, Richard (1949–). *Half the House* (Harcourt, Brace, 1995).

Abuse (Sexual) ✧ Baby Boomers | PA

Hyman B(arbara) D(avis) (1947–). *My Mother's Keeper* (W. Morrow, 1985).

Pages 12 to about 180 (ch. 1 of Part I–ch. 2 of Part II). Her mother was Bette Davis. Covers her youth on the West coast as well as her private school education on the East Coast. See similar memoirs: "Crawford, Christina" (ch. 11) and "Hayward, Brooke" (this section).

Baby Boomers ✧ Children of Alcoholics ✧ Davis, Bette ✧ Family Violence ✧ Motion Picture Actors and Actresses | CA (Southern: Hollywood) ✧ PA

McCourt, Frank (1930–). *Angela's Ashes: A Memoir* (Scribner, 1996).

Covers him to age 19.

Children of Alcoholics ✧ Depressions (Economic) ✧ Family Violence ✧ Growing Up Between WWI and WWII ✧ Irish Americans ✧ Slums ✧ Teachers | NYC ✧ Ireland

McKuen, Rod (1933–). *Finding My Father: One Man's Search for Identity* (Cheval Books, 1976).

Abuse (Sexual) ✧ Composers ✧ Depressions (Economic) ✧ Family Violence ✧ Fatherless Families ✧ Fathers and Sons ✧ Poets ✧ Singers ✧ Stepchildren | U.S. (West)

Michener, Anna J. (1977–). *Becoming Anna: The Autobiography of a Sixteen-Year-Old* (University of Chicago, 1998).

Covers her first 16 years.

Abuse (Psychiatric) ✧ Child Institutional Care ✧ Family Violence ✧ Generation X ✧ Grandmothers ✧ Psychiatrists | U.S. (Midwest)

Morris, Debbie (b. Debbie Cuevas) (1964–), with Gregg Lewis. *Forgiving the Dead Man Walking: Only One Woman Can Tell the Entire Story* (Zondervan Publishing House, 1998).

Pages 11 to about 185 cover her from 16 to 21 years. Her experiences inspired the 1995 Oscar-winning film *Dead Man Walking*.

Abuse (Sexual) ✧ Baby Boomers ✧ Forgiveness ✧ Murder I LA ✧ AL

Moss, Barbara Robinette. *Change Me into Zeus' Daughter* (Loess Hills Books, 1999).

Set in the 1960s. In its depiction of family violence spawned by alcoholism, this memoir has been compared to *Angela's Ashes* (see "McCourt, Frank," this section).

Baby Boomers ✧ Children of Alcoholics ✧ Facial Abnormalities ✧ Family Violence ✧ Racism I AL

Ramsey, Martha (1954–). *Where I Stopped: Remembering Rape at Thirteen* (Putnam, 1995).

Abuse (Sexual) ✧ Baby Boomers I NJ

Ryan, Michael (1946–). *A Secret Life: An Autobiography* (Pantheon Books, 1995).

Pages 11 to about 297. After being molested as a boy, he became addicted to sex.

Abuse (Sexual) ✧ Children of Alcoholics ✧ Poets ✧ Sexuality I WI ✧ FL ✧ NJ ✧ IN

S., Tina (1969?–), and Jamie Pastor Bolnick. *Living at the Edge of the World: A Teenager's Survival in the Tunnels of Grand Central Station* (St. Martin's, 2000) (Variant title, *Living at the Edge of the World: How I Survived the Tunnels of Grand Central Station* [St. Martin's Griffin, 2001]).

Almost entire book chronicles her from 16 to 20 years.

City Life ✧ Generation X ✧ Runaways I NYC

Scholinski, Daphne (1966?–), and Jane Meredith Adams. *Last Time I Wore a Dress* (Riverhead Books, 1998).

Covers her from about 15 to 18 years.

Abuse (Psychiatric) ✧ Artists ✧ Family Violence ✧ Gender Identity ✧ Generation X ✧ Sexuality I IL

Sebold, Alice (1963?–). *Lucky* (Scribner, 1999).

Focuses on her at age 18.

Abuse (Sexual) ✧ Baby Boomers ✧ Crime I NY

Slaughter, Carolyn (1946–). *Before the Knife: Memories of an African Childhood* (Doubleday, 2002).

This popular British novelist tells of the trauma she endured as the chronic victim of sexual abuse by her father.

Desert Life ✧ Incest ✧ Novelists ✧ Psychotherapists I England ✧ Botswana (Kalahari Desert)

Tarbox, Katherine (1982?–). *Katie.com: My Story* (E.P. Dutton, 2000).

She was the victim of a sexual predator whom she met through the Internet.

Abuse (Sexual) ✧ Generation Y (?) I CT

Zanichkowsky, Stephen (1952–). *Fourteen: Growing Up Alone in a Crowd* (Basic Books, 2002).

He was the 8th of 14 children and was the victim of brutality and neglect at the hands of his parents.

Baby Boomers ✧ Catholics ✧ Family Memoirs ✧ Family Violence ✧ Lithuanian Americans I NYC (Brooklyn)

Poverty and Times of Economic Depression

Bragg, Rick (1959–). *All Over But the Shoutin'* (Pantheon Books, 1997).
He is a Pulitzer Prize–winning reporter for the *New York Times*.
Baby Boomers ✧ Journalists ✧ Working Class Whites | AL

Bray, Rosemary (1955–). *Unafraid of the Dark: A Memoir* (Anchor Books, 1998).
She's only in the 8th grade on page 87.
African Americans ✧ Baby Boomers ✧ Slums | IL (Chicago)

Burton, Ben (1929–). *The Chicken That Won a Dogfight* (August House, 1993).
Country Life ✧ Depressions (Economic) ✧ Growing Up Between WWI and WWII | AR

Buyukmihci, Hope Sawyer (1913–2001). *Hoofmarks* (J.N. Townsend, 1994).
She wrote numerous magazine articles on wildlife topics and cofounded the Unexpected Wildlife Refuge in Newfield, NJ.
Birders ✧ Farm Life ✧ Grandfathers ✧ Growing Up Between WWI and WWII ✧ Painters ✧ Photographers ✧ Sketchers ✧ Wildlife | NY

Canfield, Patrick. *Growing Up With Bootleggers, Gamblers & Pigeons* (Interlude Enterprises, 1992).
Crime ✧ Depressions (Economic) ✧ Growing Up Between WWI and WWII ✧ Miners ✧ Pigeons | PA

Childers, Mary (1952–). *Welfare Brat: A Memoir* (Bloomsbury USA, 2005).
This is an inspirational account of a woman who overcame an early life of extreme poverty. Covers her from 10 to 16 years.
Baby Boomers ✧ Catholics ✧ Children of Alcoholics ✧ Family Memoirs ✧ School Bullying ✧ Slums ✧ Working Class Whites | NYC (Bronx)

Cowan, Evelyn (1924–). *Spring Remembered: A Scottish Jewish Childhood* (Southside, 1974).
The first 14 chapters are set in 1929; the final 4 chapters bring her Glasgow childhood up to 1932.
Fatherless Families ✧ Growing Up Between WWI and WWII ✧ Jews ✧ Slums | Scotland

Crosbie, Paddy (1913–). *"Your Dinner's Poured Out!": Boyhood in the Twenties in a Dublin That Has Disappeared* (O'Brien, 1981).
His first 17 years. Includes a glossary of Dublin slang.
Growing Up Between WWI and WWII | Ireland (Northern)

Crowley, Elaine (1927–). *A Dublin Girl: Growing Up in the 1930s* (Soho, 1998) (First published as *Cowslips and Chainies* [Lilliput, 1996]).
Growing Up Between WWI and WWII ✧ Novelists | Ireland (Northern)

Cullen, Bill (1942–). *It's a Long Way from Penny Apples* (Forge, 2003).
One of 12 siblings, Cullen recounts his incredible rags-to-riches story. Told from a third-person perspective.
Businesspersons ✧ Catholics ✧ Grandmothers ✧ Homes and Haunts ✧ Slums ✧ Wealth | Ireland (Northern)

Forrester, Helen (1919–) (pseud. of Jamunadevi Bhatia). *Twopence to Cross the Mersey* (Jonathan Cape, 1974).
Covers her from 12 to 14 years. This memoir is continued by the 3 following entries, which also focus on the author's early years.
Depressions (Economic) ✧ Growing Up Between WWI and WWII ✧ Novelists | England

Forrester, Helen (1919–) (pseud. of Jamunadevi Bhatia). *Minerva's Stepchild* (Bodley Head, 1979).
Later published with *Twopence to Cross the Mersey* as *Liverpool Miss* (Fontana/Collins, 1982).
Depressions (Economic) ✧ Growing Up Between WWI and WWII ✧ Novelists | England

Forrester, Helen (1919–) (pseud. of Jamunadevi Bhatia). *By the Waters of Liverpool* (Bodley Head, 1981).
Depressions (Economic) ✧ Growing Up Between WWI and WWII ✧ Novelists | England

Forrester, Helen (1919–) (pseud. of Jamunadevi Bhatia). *Lime Street at Two* (Bodley Head, 1985).
Depressions (Economic) ✧ Growing Up Between WWI and WWII ✧ Novelists | England

Glasser, Ralph (1916–2002). *Growing Up in the Gorbals* (Chatto & Windus, 1986).
This memoir is continued by the following entry.
Depressions (Economic) ✧ Growing up Between WWI and WWII ✧ Slums | Scotland

Glasser, Ralph (1916–2002). *Gorbals Boy at Oxford* (Chatto & Windus, 1988).
Growing Up Between WWI and WWII ✧ Oxford University | England

Hall, Floriana (1927–). *Small Change: A Story of a Young Child's Life During the Depression Years* (Hobblebush Books, 1997).
Depressions (Economic) ✧ Growing Up Between WWI and WWII | PA ✧ OH

Hanners, LaVerne (1921–). *Girl on a Pony* (University of Oklahoma, 1994).
College Teachers ✧ Country Life ✧ Depressions (Economic) ✧ Dust Bowl ✧ Growing Up Between WWI and WWII ✧ Poets | CO ✧ NM ✧ OK

Harnack, Curtis (1927–). *The Attic: A Memoir* (Iowa State University, 1993).
His early years are also focused on by the following entry. See also "Onerheim, Margaret Ott" (ch. 4) and "Twedt, Jerry L." (ch. 3) for other titles in the Iowa Heritage Collection series.
Farm Life ✧ Growing Up Between WWI and WWII | IA

Harnack, Curtis (1927–). *We Have All Gone Away* (Doubleday, 1973) (1998 rpt., Iowa State University).
Farm Life ✧ Growing Up Between WWI and WWII | IA

Harper, Beth C. (1898–). *Childhood to Womanhood: A Memoir—Seattle and Juneau, with Stops Along the Way* (REP, 2006).
This reminiscence focuses on her impoverished first 19 years, growing up in WA and AK. She wrote this account in 1980.
Child Labor ✧ Slums | WA ✧ AK

Hastings, Robert J. (1924–). *A Nickel's Worth of Skim Milk: A Boy's View of the Great Depression* (Southern Illinois University, 1972).
Covers him 1930–1938.
Depressions (Economic) ✧ Growing Up Between WWI and WWII | IL

Hastings, Robert J. (1924–). *A Penny's Worth of Minced Ham: Another Look at the Great Depression* (Shawnee Books, 1986).
Focuses on his memories of neighborhood grocery stores during the Great Depression.
Depressions (Economic) ✧ Growing Up Between WWI and WWII | IL

Heren, Louis (1919–1995). *Growing Up Poor in London* (Hamilton, 1973).
The following entry is a companion volume.
Depressions (Economic) ✧ Growing Up Between WWI and WWII | England

Heren, Louis (1919–1995). *Growing Up on the Times* (Hamilton, 1978).
Depressions (Economic) ✧ Growing Up Between WWI and WWII | England

Holden, Adele V. (1919–). *Down on the Shore: The Family and Place That Forged a Poet's Voice* (Tidewater, 1999).
African Americans ✧ Depressions (Economic) ✧ Growing Up Between WWI and WWII ✧ Poets ✧ Teachers | MD

Hotchner, A(aron) E(dward) (1921–living 2007). *King of the Hill: A Memoir* (Harper & Row, 1972).
A classic memoir with a hotel setting, adapted as the fine 1993 film of the same title. This memoir is continued by the following entry. As an adult, Hotchner was a friend and biographer of Ernest Hemingway. For a similar memoir, see "Lewis, Stephen Lewis" (ch. 4).
Biographers ✧ Depressions (Economic) ✧ Growing Up Between WWI and WWII | MO (St. Louis)

Hotchner, A(aron) E(dward) (1921–living 2007). *Looking for Miracles: A Memoir About Loving* (Harper & Row, 1975).
Focuses on him at age 16.
Biographers ✧ Camps ✧ Growing Up Between WWI and WWII ✧ Summer | MO (?)

Hynes, Samuel Lynn (1924–). *The Growing Seasons: An American Boyhood Before the War* (Viking, 2003).
Without overstating his emotions, Hynes movingly depicts life as a youth during the Depression. He also wrote a sequel (ch. 1).
Bereavement ✧ College Teachers ✧ Critics (Literary) ✧ Depressions (Economic) ✧ Farm Life ✧ Growing Up Between WWI and WWII ✧ Stepchildren | MN

Jacobs, Harvey (1915–1997). *We Came Rejoicing: A Personal Memoir of the Years of Peace* (Rand McNally, 1967).
College Teachers ✧ Country Life ✧ Growing Up Between WWI and WWII | IN

James, Marie (1926–1996), as told to Jane Hertenstein. *Orphan Girl: The Memoir of a Chicago Bag Lady* (Cornerstone, 1998).
Pages 5 to about 80.
Growing Up Between WWI and WWII ✧ Homeless Children ✧ Slums | NE ✧ CA (Southern)

Jamison, Dirk (196?–). *Perishable: A Memoir* (Chicago Review Press, 2006).
Covering 7 years in the 1960s–1970s, this gritty account tells about the author and his dysfunctional family subsisting on garbage. For a similar memoir also devoid of self-pity, see "Wolff, Tobias" (ch. 17).
Abuse (Sexual) ✧ Baby Boomers ✧ Divorce ✧ Family Violence ✧ Mormons I CA ✧ OR

Kemp, James Malcolm (1923–). *The Golden, Olden Days: Growing Up Poor and Not Knowing It: An Autobiographical Family Biography* (Kemp, 1991).
Covers him from 3 to 14 years.
Depressions (Economic) ✧ Family Memoirs ✧ Growing Up Between WWI and WWII I MA

Kirkup, James (1918–living 2007). *The Only Child* (Collins, 1957).
Covers his first 6 years. Continued by the following entry.
Depressions (Economic) ✧ Dramatists ✧ Gays ✧ Growing Up Between WWI and WWII ✧ Poets ✧ Slums ✧ Translators I England

Kirkup, James (1918–living 2007). *Sorrows, Passions and Alarms: An Autobiography of Childhood* (Collins, 1959).
Covers him from 6 to 18 years.
Depressions (Economic) ✧ Dramatists ✧ Gays ✧ Growing Up Between WWI and WWII ✧ Poets ✧ Slums ✧ Translators I England

Ladd, Jerrold (1970–). *Out of the Madness: From the Projects to a Life of Hope* (Warner Books, 1994).
More than 100 pages.
African Americans ✧ Generation X ✧ Journalists ✧ Slums I TX

Lopez-Stafford, Gloria (1937–). *A Place in El Paso: A Mexican-American Childhood* (University of New Mexico, 1996).
Mexican Americans ✧ Slums I TX

McKain, David (1937–). *Spellbound: Growing Up in God's Country* (University of Georgia, 1988).
Pages 10–236 (basically chs. 2–22) focus on his first 18 years. This memoir reflects the raw living of his blue collar youth. He grew up in the Allegheny Mountains.
Allegheny Mountains ✧ Mountain Life ✧ Poets I PA

Mebane, Mary (1933–). *Mary* (Viking, 1981) (1997 rpt., University of North Carolina, *Mary: An Autobiography*).
About the first 225 pages.
African Americans I NC

Metz, Myrtle (1924–). *Of Haviland and Honey: A Colorado Girlhood* (Pruett, 1992).
Set in a small western CO town during the Depression.
Depressions (Economic) ✧ Growing Up Between WWI and WWII I CO

Monroe, Sylvester (1951–), and Peter Goldman. *Brothers: Black and Poor: A True Story of Courage and Survival* (W. Morrow, 1988).
He grew up on Chicago's South Side.
African Americans ✧ Baby Boomers ✧ College Teachers ✧ Journalists I IL (Chicago)

Nash, Sunny (1949–) *Bigmama Didn't Shop at Woolworth's* (Texas A & M University, 1996).

Includes a 6-page index.

African Americans ✧ Baby Boomers ✧ Grandmothers ✧ Racism | TX

Nexo, Martin Andersen (1869–1954). Tr. from the Danish by J. B. C. Watkins. *Under the Open Sky: My Early Years* (Vanguard, 1938).

Pages 10–330 focus on his childhood. This proletarian novelist grew up in extreme poverty.

Communists ✧ Novelists ✧ Short Story Writers | Denmark

Nicholson, "Lord Chief Baron" (given name: Renton) (1809–1861). Ed. by John L. Bradley. *Rogue's Progress: The Autobiography of "Lord Chief Baron" Nicholson* (Houghton Mifflin, 1965) (Originally published in 1860, *The Lord Chief Baron Nicholson*).

Pages 4 to about 65.

Nineteenth Century Pre-Industrial Age Memoirists ✧ Slums | England

O'Connor, Frank (1903–1966) (pseud. of Michael O'Donovan). *An Only Child* (Knopf, 1961).

Catholics ✧ Critics (Literary) ✧ Dramatists ✧ Librarians ✧ Novelists ✧ Short Story Writers ✧ Translators | Ireland

Roberts, Robert (1905–1974). *A Ragged Schooling: Growing Up in the Classic Slum* (University Press, 1976).

Depressions (Economic) ✧ Slums | England

Rutland, Robert (1922–). *A Boyhood in the Dust Bowl, 1926–1934* (University Press of Colorado, 1995).

Depressions (Economic) ✧ Dust Bowl ✧ Growing Up Between WWI and WWII | OK

Sheklow, Edna. *So Talently My Children* (World, 1966).

Reminiscent of *Cheaper by the Dozen*, by Frank Gilbreth Jr. (see ch. 17), Sheklow's early 20th-century memoir differs in that it does not rely on re-created dialogue.

Depressions (Economic) ✧ Immigrants ✧ Jews | NYC (Brooklyn)

Shrout, Bill (1926–). *From Mud Pies and Lilac Leaves* (Honeybil, 1997).

Depressions (Economic) ✧ Farm Life ✧ Growing Up Between WWI and WWII | IN

Smith, Emma (pseud.) (1895–). Foreword by A. L. Rowse. *A Cornish Waif's Story: An Autobiography* (E.P. Dutton, 1956).

Pages 15 to about 161 focus on her first 21 years. The author wrote this memoir when in her early sixties. She was the daughter of a miner blinded in an accident; she spent much of her girlhood traveling with an organ-grinder and his wife through rural England.

Children's Authors ✧ Country Life ✧ Grandparents ✧ Novelists ✧ Slums ✧ Stepfathers ✧ Victorian Era British Memoirists | England

Smoot, Ken(neth Eugene) (1931–). *A Penny's Worth of Candy: Sketches from a Rural Childhood During and After the Great Depression* (Privately printed, 1999).

Depressions (Economic) | MO

Sonnenfeld, Kelly. *Memories of Clason Point* (E.P. Dutton, 1998).

City Life ✧ Depressions (Economic) ✧ Growing Up Between WWI and WWII ✧ Immigrants ✧ Jews ✧ Prohibition I NYC (Bronx)

Start, Clarissa (1917–). *I'm Glad I'm Not Young Anymore* (Patrice, 1990).

Pages 20 to about 164. She was a columnist for the *St. Louis Post-Dispatch*; she was also an antique dealer.

Antique Dealers ✧ Depressions (Economic) ✧ Growing Up Between WWI and WWII ✧ Journalists I MO

Summer, Lauralee (1976–). *Learning Joy from Dogs Without Collars: A Memoir* (Simon and Schuster, 2003).

Raised in poverty by her eccentric mother, Summer's rags-to-riches memoir covers her first 22 years.

Books and Reading ✧ Depressions (Mental) ✧ Eccentrics ✧ Fatherless Families ✧ Generation X ✧ Harvard University ✧ Homeless Children ✧ Lesbians I OR ✧ CA ✧ MA

Tea, Michelle (1971–). *Chelsea Whistle* (Seal, 2002).

Tea describes bleak years growing up in a working-class suburb of Boston during the 1970s–1980s.

Bisexuals ✧ Catholics ✧ Children of Alcoholics ✧ Divorce ✧ Fatherless Families ✧ Generation X ✧ Racism ✧ Slums ✧ Working Class WhitesI MA

Walker, Mark (1919–). *Maine Roots: Growing Up Poor in the Kennebec Valley* (Picton, 1994).

Covers his first 18 years.

Farm Life ✧ Growing Up Between WWI and WWII I ME

Zacharias, Karen Spears. *Hero Mama* (W. Morrow, 2005).

Zacharias wrote this memoir to her father, who died while serving in Vietnam, and to her mother, who then raised Karen and her two siblings with few financial resources. The author is an award-winning journalist.

Baby Boomers (?) ✧ Fatherless Families ✧ Journalists ✧ Mothers and Daughters ✧ Slums ✧ Vietnam Conflict I TN

Substance Abuse

Hamill, Pete (1935–). *A Drinking Life: A Memoir* (Little, Brown, 1994).

About the first 200 pages.

Catholics ✧ Children of Alcoholics ✧ City Life ✧ Journalists ✧ Liquor I NYC

Hartley, Mariette (1940–). *Breaking the Silence* (Putnam, 1988).

About 90–100 scattered pages.

Abuse (Spousal) ✧ Alcoholism ✧ Children of Alcoholics ✧ Motion Picture Actors and Actresses I CT ✧ CA (Southern: Hollywood)

Hemingway, Lorian (1951–). *Walk on Water: A Memoir* (Simon and Schuster, 1998).

About 50–60 pages. Ernest Hemingway was her grandfather.

Alcoholism ✧ Baby Boomers ✧ Editors ✧ Fishing I MS ✧ FL

Judge, Mark (1964–). *Wasted: Tales of a Gen-X Drunk* (Hazelden, 1997).

Alcoholism ✧ Catholics ✧ Generation X I Washington, DC

King, Marian (1900?–1986). *The Recovery of Myself: A Patient's Experience in a Hospital for Mental Illness* (Yale University, 1931).

Drug Abuse ✧ Mental Health | Washington, DC

Marino, Carmine Vincent (1938–). *Journey from Hell* (Habilitat, 1996).

Drug Abuse | HI

McLaurin, Tim (1953–2002). *The Keeper of the Moon: A Southern Boyhood* (W.W. Norton, 1991).

Alcoholism ✧ Cancer ✧ Children of Alcoholics ✧ Family Memoirs ✧ Farm Life ✧ Novelists ✧ Storytellers | NC

Paterson, Judith (1936–). *Sweet Mystery: A Book of Remembering* (Farrar, Straus, and Giroux, 1996).

Children of Alcoholics ✧ Children of Drug Abusers ✧ College Teachers ✧ Family Violence ✧ Mental Health | AL

Smith, Lynn Marie. *Rolling Away: My Agony with Ecstasy* (Atria Books, 2005).

An aspiring actress in NYC who had just graduated from a high school in PA, Smith experimented with Ecstasy, cocaine, and LSD. Nearly destroying her life, she finally turned it around and now is an eloquent spokeswoman against drug abuse.

Actresses ✧ Drug Abuse | NYC

Somers, Suzanne (1946–). *Keeping Secrets* (Warner Books, 1988).

Actresses ✧ Children of Alcoholics ✧ Entertainers ✧ Family Violence ✧ Models | CA (Northern)

Zailckas, Koren (1980–). *Smashed: Story of a Drunken Girlhood* (Viking Adult, 2005).

This memoir, which covers the author's life from 14 to 23 years, traces the devastating wake left in her life by alcohol abuse. The text is divided into 4 sections: "Initiation," "Usual," "Excess," and "Abuse."

Alcoholism ✧ Catholics ✧ College Life ✧ Generation X ✧ Liquor ✧ Rape ✧ Suicide and Suicide Victims ✧ Syracuse University | MA (Boston) ✧ NY

Other Family Dysfunctions and Trauma

Bereavement, Suicide, Self-Mutilation, Teen Pregnancy/Motherhood, Runaways, Homelessness, Etc.

General Dysfunctions and Trauma

Balter, Marie (1930–), and Richard Katz. *Nobody's Child* (Addison-Wesley, 1987).

Pages 3–65. After living in a mental hospital for 20 years, she finished high school, then college, and earned a master's degree at Harvard. Marlo Thomas portrayed Balter in the film *Nobody's Child*.

Children of Alcoholics ✧ Growing Up Between WWI and WWII ✧ Mental Health ✧ Mental Health Activists | MA

Christman, Jill (1969–). *Darkroom: A Family Exposure* (University of Georgia, 2002).

The author overcame years of family and personal tragedies, including abuse by a neighbor and the death of her fiancé.

Abuse (Sexual) ✧ Anorexia Nervosa/Bulimia ✧ Artists ✧ Bereavement ✧ Brothers ✧ College Teachers ✧ Counterculture Childhoods ✧ Generation X ✧ Mental Health ✧ Self-Mutilation | RI ✧ WA

Diehl, Margaret (1955–). *The Boy on the Green Bicycle: A Memoir* (Soho, 1999).

This memoir describes how, as a girl, she tried to cope with her brother's accidental death and her father's suicide. See also "Smith, Alison" (this ch.).

Baby Boomers ✧ Bereavement ✧ Brothers ✧ Fatherless Families ✧ Suicide and Suicide Victims | NJ ✧ NYC

Diski, Jennifer (1947–). *Skating to Antarctica: A Journey to the End of the World* (Ecco, 1997).

About 74 scattered pages. She traces the roots of her depression.

Abuse (Sexual) ✧ Baby Boomers ✧ Children of Alcoholics ✧ Family Violence ✧ Mental Health Novelists | England

Glaser, Sherry (1960–). *Family Secrets: One Woman's Affectionate Look at a Relatively Painful Subject* (Simon and Schuster, 1997).

Pages 5–83.

Anorexia Nervosa/Bulimia ✧ Baby Boomers ✧ Bisexuals ✧ City Life ✧ Dramatists ✧ Drug Abuse ✧ Grandmothers ✧ Jews ✧ Manic-Depression ✧ Mothers and Daughters ✧ New Age | NYC (Bronx)

Holiday, Billie (1915–1959), with William Duffy. *Lady Sings the Blues* (Viking Penguin, 1956).

Pages 5–62. Adapted as a film.

Abuse (Sexual) ✧ African Americans ✧ Drug Abuse ✧ Prostitution ✧ Racism ✧ Singers | Maryland ✧ NYC

Silverman, Sue William. *Because I Remember Terror, Father, I Remember You* (University of Georgia, 1996).

Covers her from 4 to 18 years.

Anorexia Nervosa/Bulimia ✧ Bankers ✧ Family Violence ✧ Fathers and Daughters ✧ Generation X (?) ✧ Government Officials ✧ Incest

Bereavement

Barrington, Judith (1944–). *Lifesaving: A Memoir* (Eighth Mountain, 2000).

More than 80 pages (at least pages 13–38, 42–96). Covers her from 19 to 22 years. Describes her coming to terms with the deaths of her parents (as a result of a cruise ship fire), when she was 19.

Lesbians ✧ Poets | England ✧ Spain

Bordewich, Fergus M. (1948–). *My Mother's Ghost* (Doubleday, 2000).

Pages 3 to about 33, 203–278. The author tells of coping with guilt feelings as a result of unintentionally bringing about his mother's death. (For a memoir on a brother's accidental death, see "Smith, Alison," this section.)

Baby Boomers ✧ Bereavement ✧ Forgiveness ✧ Journalists ✧ Matricide ✧ Mothers and Sons | NY

Humphrey, William (1924–1997). *Farther Off From Heaven* (Knopf, 1977).

Covers his first 13 years. Includes this disclaimer: "The names of some of the people who figure in this account have been changed to spare them or their survivors pain or embarrassment." This is a powerful and articulate memoir, often considered a classic.

Bereavement ✧ Depressions (Economic) ✧ Fatherless Families ✧ Growing Up Between WWI and WWII ✧ Novelists ✧ Ranch Life ✧ Short Story Writers | TX

Smith, Alison (1968–). *Name All the Animals: A Memoir* (Scribner, 2004).
Describes how, over time, she and her family tried to cope with her older brother's accidental death when she was 15 to18 years old. See also "Diehl, Margaret" (this ch.). (For a memoir on a mother's accidental death, see "Bordewich, Fergus," this section.)

Anorexia Nervosa/Bulimia ✧ Bereavement ✧ Brothers ✧ Catholics ✧ Family Memoirs ✧ Generation X I NY

Suicide

Ditlevsen, Tove (1918–1976). Tr. from the Danish by Tiina Nunnally. *Early Spring* (Seal, 1985).
Combines her first 2 memoirs, both published in 1967: *Childhood* (pages 3–97) and *Youth* (pages 101–222). Together they cover her first 18 years. She grew up in a working-class neighborhood in Copenhagen. She took her own life. This work is widely considered a classic.

City Life ✧ Growing Up Between WWI and WWII ✧ Suicide and Suicide Victims ✧ Working Class Whites I Denmark

Gary, Romain (b. Romain Kacew) (1914–1980). *Promise at Dawn* (Harper & Brothers, 1961).

Growing Up Between WWI and WWII ✧ Novelists ✧ Suicide and Suicide Victims I Poland

Gray, Spalding (1941–2004). *Sex and Death to the Age 14* (Random House, 1986).
Pages 3 to about 71.

Actors ✧ Humorists ✧ Suicides and Suicide Victims I RI ✧ MA

Hammer, Signe (1940–). *By Her Own Hand: Memoirs of a Suicide's Daughter* (Soho, 1991).
About 118 scattered pages (pages 3 to about 188).

Mothers and Daughters ✧ Suicide and Suicide Victims I IN ✧ PA

Kofman, Sarah (1934–1994). *Rue Ordener, Rue Labat* (University of Nebraska, 1996).
Pages 5–85 focus on her from 8 to about 18 years.

Auschwitz ✧ Holocaust Survivors ✧ Jews ✧ Suicide and Suicide Victims I France (Paris) ✧ Poland

Layton, Deborah (1953–). *Seductive Poison: A Jonestown Survivor's Story of Life and Death in the People's Temple* (Doubleday/Anchor, 1998).
About 51 pages (between pages 9 and 63).

Baby Boomers ✧ Cults ✧ Suicide and Suicide Victims I UT ✧ CA (Southern) ✧ CA (Northern) ✧ England

Mann, Klaus (1906–1949). *Turning Point: Thirty-five Years in This Century* (L.B. Fischer, 1942).
The first half focuses on his childhood and adolescence. He was the eldest son of novelist Thomas Mann, nephew of novelist Heinrich Mann, and brother of Golo Mann (see ch. 8).

Dramatists ✧ Essayists ✧ Mann, Heinrich ✧ Mann, Thomas ✧ Revolutionaries ✧ Suicide and Suicide Victims I Germany

Mittelholzer, Edgar (1909–1965). *A Swarthy Boy* (Putnam, 1963).

Hotel Receptionists ✧ Journalists ✧ Novelists ✧ Suicide and Suicide Victims I Guyana

Sexton, Linda (1953–). *Searching for Mercy Street: My Journey Back to My Mother, Anne Sexton* (Little, Brown, 1994).
About pages 11–188; she is the daughter of the famous poet.

Baby Boomers ✧ Mothers and Daughters ✧ Sexton, Anne ✧ Suicide and Suicide Victims I MA

Treadway, David C. (1946?–). *Dead Reckoning: A Therapist Confronts His Own Grief* (Basic Books/HarperCollins, 1996).

About 51 scattered pages.

Bereavement ✧ Children of Alcoholics ✧ Psychologists ✧ Sailing ✧ Suicide and Suicide Victims

Wickham, DeWayne (1946–). *Woodholme: A Black Man's Story of Growing Up Alone* (Farrar, Straus, and Giroux, 1995).

He grew up traumatized by his parents' murder-suicide.

African Americans ✧ Caddies ✧ Murder ✧ Suicide and Suicide Victims | MD

Wilsey, Sean (1970–). *Oh the Glory of It All* (Penguin, 2005).

In this amusing memoir, the founding editor of the literary journal *McSweeney's* shares tales of his early life, which was a whirlwind involving celebrities, private schools, and travel; his father was an entrepreneur, his mother a society columnist, and his stepmother an eccentric who asked him to join her in a suicide pact.

Divorce ✧ Eccentrics ✧ Editors ✧ Entertainers ✧ Family Memoirs ✧ Generation X ✧ Journalists ✧ Stepmothers ✧ Suicide and Suicide Victims ✧ Wealth ✧ Worldwide Travel | CA (Northern: San Francisco)

Woolf, Virginia (1882–1941). Ed. by Mitchell A. Leaska. *A Passionate Apprentice: The Early Journals, 1897–1909: Virginia* (Harcourt Brace Jovanovich, 1990).

Covers her from 14 to 27 years. She was married to Leonard Woolf (see ch. 9). See also "Kennedy, Richard" (ch. 9); he worked for the Woolfs.

Bereavement ✧ Bisexuals ✧ Bloomsbury Group ✧ Critics (Literary) ✧ Diaries and Journals ✧ Essayists ✧ Incest ✧ Journalists ✧ Mental Health ✧ Novelists ✧ Publishers ✧ Short Story Writers ✧ Suicide and Suicide Victims ✧ Victorian Era British Memoirists | England

Miscellaneous Dysfunctions

Including Self-Mutilation, Teenage Pregnancy/Motherhood, Missing Persons, Runaways, the Homeless, the Child Porn Industry, and Toxic Waste Environments

Antonetta, Susanne (1956–). *Body Toxic: An Environmental Memoir* (Counterpoint, 2001).

She grew up in a polluted part of suburban America.

African-Caribbean Americans ✧ Baby Boomers ✧ Cancer ✧ Environmentally Induced Diseases | NJ

Ciment, Jill (1953–). *Half a Life* (Crown, 1996).

From 14 to 17 years.

Baby Boomers ✧ Children of the Mentally Ill ✧ Crime ✧ Gangs ✧ Runaways ✧ Strippers | CA (Southern)

Donofrio, Beverly (1953?–). *Riding in Cars with Boys: Confessions of a Bad Girl Who Makes Good* (W. Morrow, 1990).

Baby Boomers ✧ Journalists ✧ Pregnancy (Teen) | CT

Erlbaum, Janice. *Girlbomb: A Halfway Homeless Memoir* (Villard, 2006).

Set during Erlbaum's teenage years in the 1980s, this reminiscence includes a considerable amount of re-created dialogue.

Alcoholism ✧ Child Institutional Care ✧ Divorce ✧ Drug Abuse ✧ Fatherless Families ✧ Generation X ✧ Homeless Children ✧ Journalists ✧ Racism ✧ Runaways ✧ Stepfathers | NYC (Manhattan)

Flook, Maria (1952–). *My Sister Life: The Story of My Sister's Disappearance* (Pantheon Books, 1997).

Baby Boomers ✧ Mental Health ✧ Missing Persons ✧ Runaways | DE

Fox, Paula (1923–). *Borrowed Finery: A Memoir* (H. Holt, 2001).
She describes her nomadic childhood and adolescence, raised by neglectful parents.

Child Institutional Care ✧ Children of Alcoholics ✧ Children's Authors ✧ Growing Up Between WWI and WWII ✧ Novelists ✧ Pregnancy (Teen) ✧ Uncles | NY ✧ CA (Southern) ✧ Cuba ✧ Canada (Montreal)

Green, Melissa. *Color Is the Suffering of Light: A Memoir* (W.W. Norton, 1995).
She was born in the 1950s; covers her to about age 12.

Abuse (Sexual) ✧ Baby Boomers ✧ Children of Alcoholics ✧ Family Violence ✧ Farm Life ✧ Poets ✧ Self-Mutilation ✧ Translators | MA

Hein, Teri (1950s–). *Atomic Farmgirl: The Betrayal of Chief Qualchan, the Appaloosa, and Me* (Fulcrum, 2000) (pbk. ed., *Atomic Farmgirl: Growing Up Right in the Wrong Place* [Houghton Mifflin, 2003]).

Baby Boomers ✧ Farm Life ✧ Teachers ✧ Toxic Waste Sites | WA

Irvine, Lucy (1956–). *Runaway* (Random House, 1987).
Pages 3 to about 242.

Abuse (Sexual) ✧ Baby Boomers ✧ Runaways | England ✧ Scotland ✧ Israel ✧ Greece ✧ Yugoslavia ✧ Austria ✧ Germany

Kettlewell, Caroline. *Skin Game: A Cutter's Memoir* (St. Martin's, 1999).
Pages 3 to about 145; set in 1960s–1970s.

Baby Boomers ✧ Self-Mutilation | VA ✧ NY

Kingsland, Rosemary (1941–). *The Secret Life of a Schoolgirl* (Crown, 2003) (Published in England as *Hold Back the Night: Memoirs of a Lost Childhood, a Warring Family, and a Secret Affair with Richard Burton* [Century, 2003]).
Focuses on her life from 14 to 15 years, especially her relationship with Richard Burton.

Burton, Richard ✧ Scandals (Sexual) ✧ WWII | England

Lau, Evelyn (1970–). *Runaway: Diary of a Street Kid* (International Village Book Store, 1994).

Diaries and Journals ✧ Drug Abuse ✧ Generation X ✧ Prostitution ✧ Runaways | Canada (BR COL)

Lauck, Jennifer (1964–). *Still Waters* (Pocket Books, 2001).
Resuming where her memoir *Blackbird* ended (when she was 12; see entry in this chapter), this volume carries her through her traumatic teenage years.

Adoptees ✧ Baby Boomers ✧ Brothers ✧ Family Violence ✧ Journalists ✧ Suicide and Suicide Victims | NV ✧ WA (?) ✧ OR (?)

Lords, Traci (b. Nora Louise Kuzma) (1968–) *Traci Lords: Underneath It All* (HarperEntertainment, 2003).
More than 100 pages. After being raped at age 10, she moved with her mother to CA, where she appeared in X-rated films. She later renounced her involvement in the sex industry.

Abuse (Sexual) ✧ Actresses ✧ Drug Abuse ✧ Entertainers ✧ Fatherless Families ✧ Generation X ✧ Singers | OH ✧ CA (Southern: Hollywood)

Matousek, Mark (195?–). *Sex, Death, Enlightenment: A True Story* (Riverhead Books, 1996).

Baby Boomers ✧ Editors ✧ Fatherless Families ✧ Gays ✧ CA (Southern)

Miller, Susan J. (1949–). *Never Let Me Down: A Memoir* (H. Holt, 1998).

About 200 pages (pages 3–10, 25–211).

Baby Boomers ✧ Children of Drug Abusers ✧ Fathers and Daughters ✧ Incest I NJ

Moorman, Margaret (1949–). *Waiting to Forget* (W.W. Norton, 1996).

See also her companion memoir (ch. 7).

Baby Boomers ✧ Bereavement ✧ Manic-Depression ✧ Pregnancy (Teen) I VA

Pelzer, David (1960–). *A Child Called "It": An Abused Child's Journey from Victim to Victor* (Omaha Press Publishing Company, 1993).

This memoir is continued by the following 3 entries.

Baby Boomers ✧ Child Institutional Care ✧ Children of Alcoholics ✧ Family Violence I CA (Northern)

Pelzer, David (1960–). *The Lost Boy: A Foster Child's Search for the Love of a Family* (Omaha Press Publishing Company, 1994).

Baby Boomers ✧ Child Institutional Care ✧ Children of Alcoholics ✧ Family Violence I CA (Northern)

Pelzer, David (1960–). *A Man Named Dave: A Story of Triumph and Forgiveness* (E.P. Dutton, 1999).

About the first 100 pages focus on him from about 12 to about 21 years.

Baby Boomers ✧ Child Institutional Care ✧ Children of Alcoholics ✧ Family Violence I CA (Northern)

Pelzer, David (1960–). *The Privilege of Youth: A Teenager's Story of Longing for Acceptance and Friendship* (E.P. Dutton, 2004).

Focuses on his late high school years.

Baby Boomers ✧ Child Institutional Care ✧ Children of Alcoholics ✧ Family Violence I CA (Northern)

Reynolds, Rick (1951–). *Only the Truth Is Funny: My Family, and How I Survived It* (Hyperion, 1992).

Baby Boomers ✧ Children of Alcoholics ✧ Comedians ✧ Family Memoirs ✧ Manic-Depression

Sparks, Beatrice, ed. *Annie's Baby: The Diary of Anonymous, a Pregnant Teenager* (Avon Books, 1998).

Diaries and Journals ✧ Generation X (?) ✧ Pregnancy (Teen)

Stapinski, Helene (1965–). *Five-Finger Discount: A Crooked Family History* (Random House, 2001).

Set in the 1970s–1980s; the author recounts her youth in a family of criminals, growing up in a toxic section of NJ.

City Life ✧ Crime ✧ Eccentrics ✧ Generation X ✧ Italian Americans ✧ Journalists ✧ Polish Americans ✧ Toxic Waste Sites I NJ ✧ NYC (Manhattan)

Thompson, Jean (pseud.). *The House of Tomorrow* (Harper & Row, 1967).

Focus is on her at 20 years.

Baby Boomers (?) ✧ Pregnancy (Teen)

Chapter 17

Spanning the Generations: Mothers, Daughters, Fathers, Sons, and Extended Family

As in chapter 16, the memoirs gathered here are arranged in 5 categories. Family life is again the focus. Generally, however, the periods of childhood and adolescence recalled in the present chapter are less emotionally turbulent than those desribed elsewhere.

The 54 memoirs in the first section illuminate relationships between the authors (while in their youth) and their parents. (Additional coming-of-age memoirs involving this theme may be found by consulting the subject index under any of these topics: "Fathers and Daughters," "Fathers and Sons," "Mothers and Daughters," and "Mothers and Sons.") Some of the finest of these are reminiscences by sons or daughters of famous authors (e.g., the works by Ianthe Brautigan, Margaret Salinger, and Rosalind Baker Wilson). In some cases, the son or daughter memoirist has also gained a considerable measure of fame as a writer (e.g., Martin Amis, Michael J. Arlen, Christopher Dickey, and Auberon Waugh). Memoirs involving parental caregiving are also found in this section.

The second part of this chapter contains a dozen memoirs that describe what it was like to grow up in (oftentimes quirky) extended families, amid such relatives as grandparents, aunts, and uncles. Some of the families we meet here will be familiar to some readers (e.g., the memoir involving the family of Dolly Parton).

Like some of the memoirs described in the preceding chapter, the autobiographical writings in the third section of this chapter re-create early stages of life spent in orphanages or in foster homes. The works surveyed here, however, re-create experiences that were relatively less painful than those presented in the other chapter. For example, *The Autobiography of a Happy Orphan* is the subtitle of the volume here by Leslie Thomas.

Autobiographical writings that focus on comings-of-age with a sibling define the fourth section. Two of these may be termed epistolary memoirs (i.e., the volumes edited by Carol Bleser and Diane DeManbey Duebber), in that they contain verbatim correspondence that passed between the siblings. Two of the more recognizable authors included here are Edgar Eisenhower (brother of President Dwight Eisenhower) and Mikal Gilmore (brother of convicted murderer Gary).

The final section is concerned with general family memoirs of the type that we sometimes associate with American films produced in the 1940s and 1950s (e.g., *I Remember Mama, How Green Was My Valley*). The fact that at least one of them, *The Prize*

Winner of Defiance, Ohio, is the basis for a well-received film released in 2005 is an indication, however, that a well-told family memoir has retained its appeal in our popular culture.

Parents

Fathers and Sons, Fathers and Daughters, Mothers and Sons, Mothers and Daughters, and Parental Caregiving

Ackerley, J(oe) R(andolph) (1896–1967). *My Father and Myself* (Penguin, 1971).
Regarded by many as a classic coming-of-age memoir.

Dramatists ✧ Editors ✧ Fathers and Sons ✧ Gays ✧ Novelists ✧ Poets | England

Acland, Eleanor (1879?–1933). *Goodbye for the Present: The Story of Two Childhoods, Milly, 1878–88 & Ellen, 1913–24* (Macmillan, 1935).
Mothers and Daughters ✧ Novelists | England

Amis, Martin (1949–). *Experience: A Memoir* (Talk Miramax Books, 2000).
About 110 scattered pages (from pages 3 to 369). His father was comic novelist Kingsley Amis. For a similar memoir, see "Arlen, Michael J." (this section).

Baby Boomers ✧ Fathers and Sons ✧ Novelists ✧ Short Story Writers | England

Arlen, Michael J. (1930–). *Exiles* (Farrar, Straus, and Giroux, 1970).
About 140 scattered pages (pages 27–226). His father was novelist Michael Arlen, who wrote *The Green Hat* (1924). For a similar memoir, see "Amis, Martin" (previous entry).

Fathers and Sons ✧ Growing Up Between WWI and WWII | France ✧ England ✧ NYC (Manhattan) ✧ CA (Southern) ✧ NH ✧ MA (Martha's Vineyard) ✧ VA

Bair, Bruce (1944–). *Good Land: My Life as a Farm Boy* (Steerforth, 1997).
He tells of his strained relationship with his atheistic father, who wanted to pass the family farm on to him.

Farm Life ✧ Fathers and Sons | KS

Birger, Trudi (1927–), with Jeffrey M. Green. *A Daughter's Gift of Love: A Holocaust Memoir* (Jewish Publication Society, 1992) (First published in German, 1990).
Pages 15–192 (ch. 1–6). She refused to leave her mother in a death camp.

Camps (Internment) ✧ Holocaust Survivors ✧ Jews ✧ Mothers and Daughters | Germany

Bolles, Joshua K. (1898–). *Father Was an Editor* (W.W. Norton, 1940).
Includes much re-created dialogue.

Editors ✧ Fathers and Sons | CT

Brautigan, Ianthe (1960–). *You Can't Catch Death: A Daughter's Memoir* (St. Martin's, 2000).
About 111 scattered pages (between pages 4–172). Her father, a counterculture writer, killed himself when she was in her early twenties.

Baby Boomers ✧ Brautigan, Richard ✧ Fathers and Daughters ✧ Suicide and Suicide Victims | CA (Northern) ✧ MT

Campbell, Bebe (1950–2006). *Sweet Summer: Growing Up with and Without My Dad* (Putnam, 1989).
Campbell is only 12 or 13 on page 203.
African Americans ✧ Baby Boomers ✧ Fatherless Families ✧ Fathers and Daughters ✧ Summer I NC ✧ PA

Carcaterra, Lorenzo (1954–). *A Safe Place: The Story of a Father, a Son, a Murder* (Villard, 1993).
At age 14 the author discovered that his father was a murderer.
Baby Boomers ✧ Family Violence ✧ Fathers and Sons ✧ Italian Americans ✧ Murder I NYC (Hell's Kitchen)

Carrighar, Sally (1898–1985). *Home to the Wilderness* (Houghton Mifflin, 1973).
Tells of her difficult relationship with her mother during the memoirist's early years.
Mothers and Daughters ✧ Natural History ✧ Zoologists I MA

Carroll, James (1943–). *An American Requiem: God, My Father, and the War That Came Between Us* (Houghton Mifflin, 1996).
About 116 pages (page 2 to about page 152). Carroll was born in Washington, DC.
Catholics ✧ Cold War ✧ Fathers and Sons ✧ Novelists ✧ Vietnam Conflict

Chambers, Veronica (1971–). *Mama's Girl* (Riverhead Books, 1996).
Her mother and stepmother were emotionally abusive to her.
African Americans ✧ Divorce ✧ Editors ✧ Family Violence ✧ Generation X ✧ Journalists ✧ Mothers and Daughters ✧ Panamanian Americans ✧ Photographers ✧ Stepmothers I NYC (Brooklyn) ✧ CA (Southern)

Chaplin, Michael (1946–). *I Couldn't Smoke the Grass on My Father's Lawn* (Putnam, 1966).
Covers his first 18 years; he is (Sir) Charlie Chaplin's son. See also his father's memoir (ch. 11).
Chaplin, (Sir) Charlie ✧ Fathers and Sons ✧ Motion Picture Actors and Actresses I CA (Southern) England ✧ France ✧ Switzerland

Chernin, Kim (1940–). *In My Mother's House: A Daughter's Story* (Perennial, 1994) (First published by Ticknor & Fields, 1983).
Pages 206–288.
Communists ✧ Jews ✧ Mothers and Daughters I NYC ✧ Soviet Union ✧ CA (Southern)

Cheuse, Alan (1940–). *Fall Out of Heaven: An Autobiographical Journey* (G.M. Smith, 1987).
About 83 scattered pages. For a similar memoir set in NJ, see "Kunhardt, Philip, Jr." (this section).
Fathers and Sons ✧ Novelists I NJ

Conlon-McIvor, Maura. *FBI Girl: How I Learned to Crack My Father's Code* (Warner Books, 2004).
The author tells how, while growing up in the 1960s–1970s, she came to understand and respect her father's quiet demeanor; her brother was a Downs Syndrome baby.
Brothers ✧ Catholics ✧ Downs Syndrome ✧ Fathers and Daughters ✧ Irish Americans I CA (Southern)

Cooper, Wyatt (1927–1978). *Families: A Memoir and a Celebration* (Harper & Row, 1975).

Fathers and Sons ✧ Growing Up Between WWI and WWII

Dahlinger, John (1923–1984), as told to Frances Spatz Leighton. *The Secret Life of Henry Ford* (Bobbs-Merrill, 1978).

About 97 scattered pages. Dahlinger claims to be the illegitimate son of Henry Ford. For a similar memoir, see "Lewis, Judy" (ch. 13).

Businesspersons ✧ Fathers and Sons ✧ Ford, Henry ✧ Growing Up Between WWI and WWII I MI

Davis, Tracey (1961–), with Dolores A. Barclay. *Sammy Davis Jr., My Father* (General Pub. Group, 1996).

Pages 35–140.

Baby Boomers ✧ Davis, Sammy, Jr. ✧ Fathers and Daughters I CA (Southern: (Hollywood) ✧ NYC ✧ NV ✧ HI

Day, Ingeborg (1941–). *Ghost Waltz: A Memoir* (Viking, 1980).

After coming to the U.S. as an exchange student, she researched her father's past activities as a Nazi.

Fathers and Daughters ✧ Nazis and Neo-Nazis I Austria

Dayan, Yael (1939–). *My Father, His Daughter* (Farrar, Straus, and Giroux, 1985).

Pages 42 to about 155.

Fathers and Daughters ✧ Statesmen I Palestine (i.e., Israel)

Dickey, Christopher (1951–). *Summer of Deliverance: A Memoir of Father and Son* (Simon and Schuster, 1998).

About 122 scattered pages.

Baby Boomers ✧ Children of Alcoholics ✧ Dickey, James ✧ Fathers and Sons ✧ Journalists I TX ✧ France ✧ FL ✧ GA ✧ Italy ✧ OR ✧ CA ✧ MA ✧ VA

Edmonds, Walter Dumaux (1903–1998). *Tales My Father Never Told* (Syracuse University, 1995).

Fathers and Sons ✧ Novelists I NYC ✧ NY

Froncek, Thomas (1942–). *Home Again, Home Again: A Son's Memoir* (Arcade, 1996).

Pages 11 to about 201 cover him from 7 to 21 years.

Caregiving ✧ Parents (Aging or Infirm) I WI

Gebler, Carlo (1954–). *Father and I: A Memoir* (Little, Brown, 2000).

Pages 31 to about 268 (chs. 4–48).

His mother was novelist Edna O'Brien.

Baby Boomers ✧ Fathers and Sons ✧ Novelists ✧ O'Brien, Edna I Ireland (North) ✧ England

Gilbreth, Frank B., Jr. (1911–2001). *Time Out for Happiness* (Crowell, 1970).

About 67 scattered pages. See also entries by him in this chapter for *Cheaper by the Dozen* and *Belles on Their Toes*, which are companion memoirs to this volume.

Foreign Correspondents ✧ Journalists ✧ Military Life ✧ Mothers and Sons ✧ Photographers I NJ

Gosse, (Sir) Edmund (1849–1928). *Father and Son: A Study of Two Temperaments* (Scribner's Sons, 1907) (1973 rpt., Hammondsworth, *Biographical Recollections*).

Bereavement ✧ Critics (Literary) ✧ Fathers and Sons ✧ Librarians ✧ Natural History ✧ Nineteenth-Century Pre-Industrial Age Memoirists ✧ Poets ✧ Translators | England

Haslam, Gerald (1937–). *Coming of Age in California: Personal Essays.* **2nd ed.** (Devil Mountain Books, 2000).

About 74 scattered pages. (The first edition of this work was published in 1990.)

Catholics ✧ Fathers and Sons ✧ Football ✧ Hispanic Americans ✧ Homes and Haunts | CA (Central)

Henderson, Bill (1941–). *His Son: A Memoir* **(Pushcart, 2000).**

More than 100 pages focus on his first 21 years. This is an updated version of *His Son: A Child of the Fifties* (W.W. Norton, 1981).

College Life ✧ Editors ✧ Fathers and Sons ✧ Publishers ✧ Spiritual Life | PA

Holtz, William (1932–). *Gathering the Family* (University of Missouri, 1997).

Family Memoirs | MI

Howey, Noelle. *Dress Codes: Of Three Girlhoods—My Mother's, My Father's, and Mine* (Picador USA, 2002).

Howey tells what it was like to grow up in suburban OH with a father whose gender identity issues resulted in his having transsexual surgery.

Children of Transsexuals ✧ Fathers and Daughters ✧ Gender Identity ✧ Sexuality | OH

Jordan, Teresa (1955–). *Riding the White Horse Home: A Western Family Album* (Pantheon Books, 1993).

About 62 scattered pages.

Baby Boomers ✧ Bereavement ✧ Fathers and Daughters ✧ Folklorists ✧ Journalists ✧ Natural History ✧ Radio Producers ✧ Ranch Life ✧ Yale University | WY ✧ CT

Kunhardt, Philip, Jr. (1928–2006). *My Father's House* (Random House, 1970).

Some 141 pages (pages 24–227). For a similar memoir set in NJ, see "Cheuse, Alan" (this section).

Biographers ✧ Editors ✧ Fathers and Sons ✧ Homes and Haunts | NJ

Levendel, Isaac (1936–). *Not the Germans Alone: A Son's Search for the Truth of Vichy* (Northwestern University, 1999).

About 186 scattered pages (between pages 3–229). Exposed by Nazi collaborators in France, his mother was sent to Auschwitz when he was 7.

Bereavement ✧ Holocaust Survivors ✧ Jews ✧ Missing Persons ✧ Mothers and Sons ✧ Teachers ✧ WWII | France

Lichtenberg, Greg. *Playing Catch with My Mother: Coming to Manhood When All the Rules Have Changed* (Bantam Books, 1999).

Focuses on him from infancy through high school, during the 1970s–1980s.

Baby Boomers ✧ City Life ✧ Divorce ✧ Feminists ✧ Mothers and Sons | NYC (Manhattan)

MacLeish, William H. (1928–). *Uphill with Archie: A Son's Journey* (Simon and Schuster, 2001).

About page 21 to about page 178. He's the son of poet Archibald MacLeish.

Fathers and Sons ✧ Growing Up Between WWI and WWII ✧ MacLeish, Archibald | MA

Malcolm, Andrew (1943–). *Huddle: Fathers, Sons, and Football* (Simon and Schuster, 1992).

More than 100 pages focus on his first 21 years. See also his companion memoir *Someday* (ch. 7).

Fathers and Sons ✧ Football ✧ Historians (Cultural) ✧ Journalists | OH

Martin, Lee (1955–). *From Our House: A Memoir* (E.P. Dutton, 2000).

Accidents (Agricultural) ✧ Baby Boomers ✧ Family Violence ✧ Farm Life ✧ Fathers and Sons ✧ Homes and Haunts | IL

Mason, Bobbie Ann (1940–). *Clear Springs: A Memoir* (Random House, 1999).

Farm Life ✧ Grandmothers ✧ Mothers and Daughters ✧ Novelists ✧ Short Story Writers | KY

McFadden, Cyra (1937–). *Rain or Shine: A Family Memoir* (University of Nebraska, 1988) (First published, Knopf, 1986).

About 85 pages, between pages 16 and 114.

Eccentrics ✧ Family Memoirs ✧ Fathers and Daughters ✧ Journalists ✧ Rodeo Life | MT ✧ CA (Northern)

Murphy, Dervla (1931–). *Wheels Within Wheels* (Ticknor & Fields, 1980).

On page 96, she's only 10 years old; by the end of this 236-page memoir, she's 31 or 32.

Country Life ✧ Cycling ✧ Parents (Aging or Infirm) ✧ Travel Writers | Ireland

Nichols, Beverley (1899–1983). *Father Figure* (Simon and Schuster, 1972).

By page 93 he's only 15. This memoir relies on much reconstituted dialogue.

Cats ✧ Children of Alcoholics ✧ Children's Authors ✧ Composers ✧ Dramatists ✧ Family Violence ✧ Fathers and Sons ✧ Foreign Correspondents ✧ Gardeners ✧ Journalists ✧ Novelists ✧ Oxford University ✧ Patricide | England

Nuland, Sherwin B. (1930–). *Lost in America: A Journey with My Father* (Knopf, 2003).

Pages 9 to about 192 (last part of ch. 1–ch. 11). The author, a physician, has written an ode to his father through this memoir of his early years growing up in the Bronx.

Bereavement ✧ City Life ✧ Depressions (Economic) ✧ Depressions (Mental) ✧ Fathers and Sons ✧ Growing Up Between WWI and WWII ✧ Immigrants ✧ Jews ✧ Physicians ✧ Syphilis ✧ Yale University | NYC (Bronx) ✧ CT

Ostransky, Leroy (1918–1993). *Sharkey's Kid: A Memoir* (W. Morrow, 1991).

Focuses on his first 15 years.

Books and Reading ✧ Boxing ✧ City Life ✧ College Teachers ✧ Crime ✧ Fathers and Sons ✧ Grandfathers ✧ Growing Up Between WWI and WWII ✧ Immigrants ✧ Intellectual Life ✧ Jews ✧ Musicians ✧ Prohibition | NYC (Lower East Side)

Peck, Scott (1968–). *All-American Boy: A Gay Son's Search for His Father* (Scribner, 1995).

Fathers and Sons ✧ Gays ✧ Generation X ✧ Journalists ✧ Sexuality | MD (?)

Phillips, Mark (1952–). *My Father's Cabin: A Tale of Life, Loss, and Land* (Lyons, 2001).

More than 100 pages (chapters 2–9).

Baby Boomers ✧ Beekeeping ✧ Country Life ✧ Fathers and Sons ✧ Journalists ✧ Working Class Whites | NY

Previn, Dory (1929–). *Midnight Baby: An Autobiography* (Macmillan, 1976).
Covers her first 10 years.

Actresses ✧ Catholics ✧ Children of Alcoholics ✧ Composers ✧ Depressions (Economic) ✧ Drug Abuse ✧ Entertainers ✧ Fathers and Daughters ✧ Growing Up Between WWI and WWII ✧ Librettists ✧ Mental Health ✧ Models ✧ Musicians ✧ Singers | NJ

Salinger, Margaret A. (1956–). *Dream Catcher: A Memoir* (Washington Square, 2000).
Pages 117 to about 382. Her father is J. D. Salinger.

Baby Boomers ✧ Fathers and Daughters ✧ Salinger, J. D. | NH

Sayer, Mandy (1963–). *Dreamtime Alice: A Memoir* (Ballantine Books, 1998).
Focuses on her at 20–21 years. She was born in Australia.

Dancers ✧ Fathers and Daughters ✧ Novelists | NYC ✧ LA (New Orleans)

Seabrook, Jeremy (1939–). *Mother and Son* (Pantheon Books, 1980).
Covers his first 15 years.

Country Life ✧ Dramatists ✧ Gays ✧ Mothers and Sons ✧ Social Workers ✧ Sociologists | England

Shyer, Marlene, and Christopher Shyer (1961–). *Not Like Other Boys: Growing Up Gay: A Mother and Son Look Back* (Houghton Mifflin, 1996).
About 103 scattered pages.

Baby Boomers ✧ Collaborations by Relatives ✧ Gays ✧ Mothers and Sons ✧ Sexuality | NY ✧ CT ✧ VT

Sinatra, Tina (1948–), with Jeff Coplon. *My Father's Daughter: A Memoir* (Simon and Schuster, 2000).
Pages 24–124. Frank Sinatra was her father.

Baby Boomers ✧ City Life ✧ Fathers and Daughters ✧ Sinatra, Frank ✧ Singers | CA (Southern: Hollywood)

Sledge, Michael (1962–). *Mother and Son: A Memoir* (Simon and Schuster, 1995).
He was born in Houston.

Baby Boomers ✧ Bereavement ✧ Gays ✧ Mothers and Sons ✧ Oil Fields ✧ Stepchildren | TX

Solotaroff, Ted (1928–). *Truth Comes in Blows* (W.W. Norton, 1998).

College Teachers ✧ Critics (Literary) ✧ Depressions (Economic) ✧ Editors ✧ Family Violence ✧ Fathers and Sons ✧ Growing Up Between WWI and WWII ✧ Intellectual Life ✧ Jews | NJ

Tait, Katharine (1923–). *My Father, Bertrand Russell* (Harcourt Brace Jovanovich, 1975).
Pages 61 to about 152.

Editors ✧ Fathers and Daughters ✧ Growing Up Between WWI and WWII ✧ Russell, (Sir) Bertrand ✧ Teachers ✧ Translators | England

Thayer, Charles W. (1910–1969). *Muzzy* (Harper & Row, 1966).

Mothers and Sons | PA

Trussoni, Danielle. *Falling Through the Earth* (H. Holt, 2006).
With some humor, Trussoni describes growing up in the 1980s as the daughter of a divorced Vietnam veteran who frequented a neighborhood bar.

Bars ✧ Children of Alcoholics ✧ Crime ✧ Divorce ✧ Fathers and Daughters ✧ Generation X ✧ Vietnam Conflict ✧ Working Class Whites | WI

Waugh, Auberon (1939–2001). *Will This Do? The First Fifty Years of Auberon Waugh: An Autobiography* (Century, 1991).

Pages 16–145. See also entries for Evelyn Waugh (his father) and Alec Waugh (his uncle) (both ch. 9).

Fathers and Sons ✧ Journalists ✧ Novelists | England

Wilson, Rosalind Baker (1923–). *Near the Magician: A Memoir of My Father, Edmund Wilson* (Grove Weidenfeld, 1989).

About 111 scattered pages. Her father was the renowned literary critic Edmund Wilson.

Critics (Literary) ✧ Fathers and Daughters ✧ Growing Up Between WWI and WWII ✧ Wilson, Edmund | NJ

Wolff, Tobias (1945–). *This Boy's Life: A Memoir* (Atlantic Monthly, 1989).

This was adapted as a film in 1993. See also the entry for his brother, Geoffrey Wolff (ch. 15). For a similar memoir also devoid of self-pity, see "Jamison, Dirk" (ch.16).

Aerospace Industries ✧ College Teachers ✧ Divorce ✧ Editors ✧ Family Violence ✧ Journalists ✧ Mothers and Sons ✧ Novelists ✧ Short Story Writers ✧ Stepfathers | WA

Extended Families

Grandparents, Aunts, and Uncles

Bates, Kenneth F(rancis) (1904–1994). *Salome's Heritage* (Vantage, 1977).

His strong-willed Aunt Salome is the central figure of this memoir.

Aunts | MA

Holman-Hunt, Diana (1913–1993). *My Grandmothers and I* (W.W. Norton, 1960).

Growing Up Between WWI and WWII ✧ Needlepoint | England

Homans, Abigail Adams (1879–1974). *Education by Uncles* (Houghton Mifflin, 1966).

At least pages 1–98.

Adams (Presidential) Family ✧ Uncles | MA

Narayan (b. Narayanswami), R(asipuram) K(rishnaswami) (1906–2001). *My Days: A Memoir* (Chatto & Windus, 1975).

About 68 pages.

Essayists ✧ Grandmothers ✧ Novelists ✧ Short Story Writers | India

Nekola, Charlotte (1952–). *Dream House: A Memoir* (W.W. Norton, 1993).

Between pages 4 and 158, about 137 pages.

Aunts ✧ Baby Boomers ✧ Bereavement ✧ Cancer ✧ Children of Alcoholics ✧ College Teachers ✧ Family Memoirs ✧ Grandmothers ✧ Poets ✧ Uncles | MO

Njeri, Itabari (aka Jill Stacey Moreland) (b. 1940s or 1950s). *Every Good-bye Ain't Gone: Family Portraits and Personal Escapades* (Times Books, 1990).

Various chapters focus on assorted family members. As an adult, she was a reporter for the *Los Angeles Times.*

Actresses ✧ African Americans ✧ City Life ✧ Essayists ✧ Radio Journalists ✧ Singers | NYC (Harlem)

O'Connor, Philip (1916–1998). *Memoirs of a Public Baby* (British Book Centre, 1958).
Pages 32–134 cover his first 16 years. He worked as a reporter and editor for the *Los Angeles Times.*
Editors ✧ Growing Up Between WWI and WWII ✧ Librarians ✧ Poets | England

(Parton), Willadeene (1941?–). *In the Shadow of a Song: The Story of the Parton Family* (Bantam Books, 1985).
About 80–90 scattered pages (from 35 to 132). Parts of this were adapted for inclusion in her 1996 memoir *Smoky Mountain Memories: Stories from the Hearts of Dolly Parton's Family* (see entry in Appendix A, "Bibliography of Collective Works").
Country Life ✧ Family Memoirs ✧ Singers | TN

Partridge, Bellamy (1878–1960). *Big Family* (Whittlesey House, 1941).
The following 2 entries also focus on Partridge's early years.
Family Memoirs | NY

Partridge, Bellamy (1878–1960). *Excuse My Dust* (McGraw-Hill, 1943).
Family Memoirs | NY

Partridge, Bellamy (1878–1960). *Salad Days* (Crowell, 1951).
Family Memoirs | NY (?)

Raverat, Gwen (1885–1957). *Period Piece: A Cambridge Childhood* (W.W. Norton, 1952).
Charles Darwin was her grandfather.
Aunts ✧ Darwin, Charles ✧ Eccentrics ✧ Engravers (Wood) ✧ Uncles ✧ Victorian Era British Memoirists | England

Ruark, Robert (1915–1965). *The Old Man and the Boy* (H. Holt, 1957).
Recounts his youthful life of outdoor sports and recreation with his grandfather.
Accountants ✧ Dogs ✧ Grandfathers ✧ Growing Up Between WWI and WWII ✧ Hunting ✧ Journalists ✧ Merchant Marines ✧ Novelists ✧ Sportswriters | NC

Ruark, Robert (1915–1965). *The Old Man's Boy Grows Older* (Holt, Rinehart and Winston, 1961).
The newspaperman continues to explore the influence his grandfather had on him, as Ruark transitions into adulthood.
Accountants ✧ Dogs ✧ Grandfathers ✧ Growing Up Between WWI and WWII ✧ Hunting ✧ Journalists ✧ Merchant Marines ✧ Novelists ✧ Sportswriters | NC

Sperry, Willard (1882–1954). *Summer Yesterdays in Maine: Memories of Boyhood Vacation Days* (Harper & Brothers, 1941).
Focuses on him from about 3 to 18 years. Contains pencil drawings by Charles H. Woodbury. He was dean of the Divinity School of Harvard University.
Clergy ✧ Essayists ✧ Grandfathers ✧ Harvard University ✧ Summer | ME

Blended Families

Adoptive and Other Surrogate Family Life, Including Nonabusive Orphanage Experience

See entries in the section "Outcasts" in chapter 16 for memoirs involving abusive orphanage experiences.

Bolton, Isabel (pseud. of Mary Britton Miller) (1883–1975). *Under Gemini: A Memoir* (Harcourt, Brace & World, 1966).

After their parents drowned, the author and her twin sister were raised by their grandmother and then by a governess.

Drowning Victims ✧ Grandmothers ✧ Orphans ✧ Twins | CT

Choy, Wayson (1939–). *Paper Shadows: A Chinatown Childhood* (Viking, 1999).

Parts One and Two (pages 6–274) focus on his first 11 years.

Adoptees ✧ Chinese Canadians ✧ Novelists | Canada (BR COL: Vancouver)

Cunningham, Laura (1947–). *Sleeping Arrangements* (Knopf, 1989).

See the sequel, *A Place in the Country* (ch. 9).

Baby Boomers ✧ City Life ✧ Dramatists ✧ Eccentrics ✧ Novelists ✧ Orphans ✧ Uncles | NYC (Bronx)

Farrington, Harry (1880–1930). *Kilts to Togs; Orphan Adventures* (Macmillan, 1930).

MD

Simpson, Eileen (1918–2002). *Orphans, Real and Imaginary* (Weidenfeld & Nicolson, 1987).

In addition to recounting her own experiences as an orphan, Simpson explores the literature and history of orphanhood. She was married to poet John Berryman.

City Life ✧ Orphans ✧ Psychotherapists | NYC

Thomas, Leslie (John) (1931–). *This Time Next Week: The Autobiography of a Happy Orphan* (Constable, 1964).

Orphans | England

Wilson, Rex L. (1927?–). *Out East of Aline: An Adoption Memoir* (Uncommon Buffalo, 2000).

Focuses on him from 4 to about 12 years.

Adoptees ✧ Archaeologists ✧ Depressions (Economic) ✧ Dust Bowl ✧ Farm Life ✧ Growing Up Between WWI and WWII | OK

Siblings

Ashley, Edwin (1909–), and Cliff Ashley (1913–). Ed. by Diane deManbey Duebber. *The Ed Letters: Memories of a New England Boyhood* (Spinner Publications, 2001).

This volume compiles letters from Cliff to Ed, which (years later) inspired related recollections by Ed, which are also included. These brothers grew up in coastal MA during the 1920s.

Brothers ✧ Letters | MA

Connell, Maria Bryan Harford, and Julia Bryan Cumming. Ed. by Carol Bleser. *Tokens of Affection: The Letters of a Planter's Daughter in the Old South* (University of Georgia, 1996).

Pages 3–109 contain letters written by Maria Bryan Harford Connell when she was between 16 and 21 years old to her sister, Julia Bryan Cumming (her elder by 5 years).

Letters ✧ Nineteenth-Century Pre-Industrial Age Memoirists ✧ Plantation Life | GA

Delany, Sarah (1889–1999) and A(nnie) Elizabeth (1891–1995). *Having Our Say: The Delany Sisters' First 100 Years* (Kodansha International, 1993).
>Pages 9 to about 84 (chs. 2–13) focus on their childhood and adolescence.
>African Americans ✧ Centenarians ✧ Collaborations by Relatives ✧ Dentists ✧ Racism ✧ Reformers ✧ Sisters ✧ Teachers | NC

Eisenhower, Edgar (1889–1971). *Six Roads from Abilene: Some Personal Recollections of Edgar Eisenhower* (Wood & Reber, 1960).
>Eisenhower, Dwight D. ✧ Presidents (U.S.) | KS

Gelissen, Rena (1920–), with Heather Dune Macadam. *Rena's Promise: A Story of Sisters in Auschwitz* (Beacon, 1995).
>Focuses on her later teenage years, starting at about age 17.
>Auschwitz ✧ Holocaust Survivors ✧ Jews ✧ Sisters | Poland ✧ Germany

Gilmore, Mikal (b. Michael) (1951–). *Shot in the Heart* (Doubleday, 1994).
>About 18 pages scattered among pages ix–47, and all of pages 121–307. His older brother, Gary, was executed by a UT firing squad in 1977; this memoir focuses on both brothers' formative years.
>Baby Boomers ✧ Brothers ✧ Crime ✧ Murder ✧ Working Class Whites | OR ✧ UT

Godden, Jon (1906–1984), and (Margaret) Rumer Godden (1907–1998). *Two Under the Indian Sun* (Knopf, 1966).
>Covers 1914–1919. See also following entry.
>Children's Authors ✧ Collaborations by Relatives ✧ Dramatists ✧ Novelists ✧ Sisters | India

Godden, (Margaret) Rumer (1907–1998). *A Time to Dance, No Time to Weep* (Beech Tree Books, 1987).
>About 93 scattered pages are on her first 20 years. Her sister was Jon Godden (previous entry).
>Children's Authors ✧ Dramatists ✧ Novelists ✧ Sisters | India

Salas, Floyd (1931–). *Buffalo Nickel: A Memoir* (Arte Publico, 1992).
>He shared his early years with a drug-addicted brother who was involved with crime and a brother who was a genius. This memoir is structured like a novel.
>Bereavement ✧ Boxing ✧ Brothers ✧ College Teachers ✧ Novelists ✧ Suicides and Suicide Victims | CO ✧ CA

Thompson, Anne Hall Whitt. *See* Whitt, Anne Hall

Van der Heidl, Dirk. Tr. by Mrs. Anton Deventer. *My Sister and I: The Diary of a Dutch Boy Refugee* (Faber & Faber, 1941).
>Diaries and Journals ✧ Refugees ✧ Sisters ✧ WWII | Netherlands

Whitt, Anne Hall (1930–1996) (maiden name of Anne Hall Whitt Thompson). *The Suitcases: Three Orphaned Sisters in the Great Depression in the South* (Acropolis Books, 1982).
>Adoptees ✧ Bereavement ✧ Depressions (Economic) ✧ Fathers and Daughters ✧ Growing Up Between WWI and WWII ✧ Orphans ✧ Sisters | NC

Family Memoirs

Including Church Families

See the second section in chapter 14 for memoirs involving political families; see the last 2 subsections in chapter 6 for memoirs involving military families.

Aldrich, Margaret Chanler (1870–). *Family Vista: The Memoirs of Margaret Chanler Aldrich* (William-Frederick Press, 1958).
   About 50 scattered pages.
   Family Memoirs I NY

Bell, Mary Hayley (1911–2005). *What Shall We Do Tomorrow? The Story of My Families* (Cassell, 1968).
   Starting with page 16, more than 100 pages. She was the mother of British actress Hayley Mills.
   Actresses ✧ Dramatists ✧ Family Memoirs ✧ Growing Up Between WWI and WWII ✧ Justices of the Peace ✧ Poets I China ✧ England

Blais, Madeleine (1947–). *Uphill Walkers: A Memoir of a Family* (Atlantic Monthly, 2001).
   Her father died when she was 5. She had 5 siblings, including a brother with psychological problems. (For a similar memoir, see *Imagining Robert*, by Jay Neugeboren [W. Morrow, 1997].)
   Baby Boomers ✧ Brothers ✧ Catholics ✧ Family Memoirs ✧ Fatherless Families ✧ Irish Americans ✧ Journalists ✧ Mental Health I MA

Buckley, Carol (1938–). *At the Still Point: A Memoir* (Simon and Schuster, 1996).
   Pages 13–116 (chs. 2–15). She is the sister of William F. Buckley and Senator James Buckley. She was editor of *National Review*.
   Catholics ✧ Editors ✧ Family Memoirs ✧ High Society ✧ Mental Health ✧ Wealth I CT

Carter, John Franklin (1897–1967). *The Rectory Family* (Coward-McCann, 1937).
   Pages 4 to about 270.
   Clergy ✧ Episcopalians ✧ Family Memoirs I MA

Chagall, Bella (1895–1944). Tr. from the Yiddish by Norbert Guterman. *Burning Lights* (Schocken Books, 1946).
   To about her first 12–15 years. She was the youngest of 7 siblings. Includes line drawings by Marc Chagall (her husband). Glossary of terms on pages 265–268.
   Chagall, Marc ✧ Family Memoirs ✧ Jews ✧ Journalists I Russia

Chase, Justine (1906–). *A World Remembered* (Yankee Publications, 1988) (First published as *Document of a Child* [W.L. Bauhan, 1980]).
   Focuses on her youth at her family's 2 winter homes. Her mother provided still-lifes and portraits for this memoir.
   Actresses ✧ Collaborations by Relatives ✧ Dramatists ✧ Family Memoirs ✧ High Society ✧ Poets ✧ Wealth I CT

Coe, Wilbur (1893–). *Ranch on the Ruidoso: The Story of a Pioneer Family in New Mexico, 1871–1968* (Knopf, 1968).
   Pages 74–168 cover him to age 20.
   Family Memoirs ✧ Frontier and Pioneer Life ✧ Ranch Life I NM

Conaway, James (1941–). *Memphis Afternoons: A Memoir* (Houghton Mifflin, 1993).
    The onset of Alzheimer's disease in his father provided the impetus for this work, set in the 1950s.
    Alzheimer's Disease ✧ Family Memoirs ✧ Grandfathers ✧ Intellectual Life ✧ Journalists ✧ Novelists ✧ Uncles | TN

Cooper, Mireille (1893–). *The Happy Season* (Pellegrini & Cudahy, 1952) (First published as *Swiss Family Burnand* [Eyre & Spottiswoode, 1951]).
    She grew up in a family of 10.
    Family Memoirs | Switzerland

Cullerton, Brenda. *The Nearly Departed; Or, My Family and Other Foreigners* (Little, Brown, 2003).
    The author re-creates her youth growing up in a family of eccentrics in conservative Ridgefield, CT. For another memoir set in Ridgefield, CT, see "Salzman, Mark" (ch. 9).
    Advertising Copywriters ✧ Children of Alcoholics ✧ Eccentrics ✧ Family Memoirs ✧ Humorists | CT

Day, Clarence (1874–1935). *God and My Father* (Knopf, 1931).
    The following two entries also focus on Day's early years.
    City Life ✧ Family Memoirs | NYC

Day, Clarence (1874–1935). *Life with Father* (Knopf, 1935).
    City Life ✧ Family Memoirs | NYC

Day, Clarence (1874–1935). *Life with Mother* (Knopf, 1937).
    City Life ✧ Family Memoirs | NYC

Dell, Diana J. (1946–). *Memories Are Like Clouds* (Xlibris, 1996).
    Set in the 1950s–1960s. She re-creates the bucolic world of her childhood that existed prior to losing her brother in Vietnam.
    Bereavement ✧ Brothers ✧ College Teachers ✧ Disc Jockeys ✧ Family Memoirs ✧ Immigrants ✧ Journalists ✧ Photographers ✧ Social Workers ✧ Teachers ✧ Vietnam Conflict | PA

Dixon, Madeline Cutler. *With Halo Atilt* (Beacon, 1965).
    Her father was a Unitarian minister.
    Clergy ✧ Family Memoirs ✧ Unitarians | MA (?)

Durst, Paul (1921–1986). *Roomful of Shadows* (Dobson, 1975).
    Family Memoirs ✧ Fatherless Families ✧ Growing Up Between WWI and WWII ✧ Novelists ✧ Uncles | MO

Earley, Tony (1961–). *Somehow Form a Family: Stories That Are Mostly True* (Algonquin Books of Chapel Hill, 2001).
    This is a collection of autobiographical essays.
    Baby Boomers ✧ Bereavement ✧ Family Memoirs ✧ Mountain Life ✧ Novelists ✧ Sisters | NC

Ely, Stanley (1932–). *In Jewish Texas: A Family Memoir* (Texas Christian University, 1998).
    Pages 3–213 (about chs. 1–23).
    Family Memoirs ✧ Gays ✧ Jews | TX

Eyster, Virginia (1924–). *Journey of the Heart: A Loving Family Memoir* (Walker, 1986).

Family Memoirs ✧ Growing Up Between WWI and WWII I OH ✧ MO (?)

Farjeon, Eleanor (1881–1965). *Portrait of a Family* (Frederick A. Stokes, 1935) (Variant title, *A Nursery in the Nineties* [Gollancz, 1935]).

Pages 189 to about 442.

Children's Authors ✧ Family Memoirs ✧ Victorian Era British Memoirists I England

Fletcher, Grace Nies (1895–). *Preacher's Kids* (E.P. Dutton, 1958).

Clergy ✧ Family Memoirs I MA

Frothingham, Eugenia (1874–). *Youth and I* (Houghton Mifflin, 1938).

Covers her first 30 years.

Debutantes ✧ Family Memoirs ✧ High Society I MA ✧ France ✧ Italy

Gifford, Edward S(tewart), Jr. (1907–). *Father Against the Devil* (Doubleday, 1966).

About the first 140 pages (chs. 1–12) cover his childhood and adolescence.

Family Memoirs ✧ Fathers and Sons ✧ Spiritual Life I PA

Gilbreth, Frank B., Jr. (1911–2001), and Ernestine Gilbreth Carey (1908–2006). *Cheaper by the Dozen* (Crowell, 1948).

This was adapted into a 1950 film, which was remade as a Steve Martin movie in 2003. The following entry is this memoir's sequel; see also the entry by Gilbreth in this chapter for *Time Out for Happiness*. For a similar memoir, see "Sheklow, Edna" (ch. 16).

Collaborations by Relatives ✧ Family Memoirs I NJ

Gilbreth, Frank B., Jr. (1911–2001). *Belles on Their Toes* (Crowell, 1950).

Family Memoirs I NJ

Goyer, Jane (1894–1992?). *So Dear to My Heart: Memories of a Gentler Time* (Harper & Row, 1990).

Family Memoirs I MA

Green, Anne (1899–1979?). *With Much Love* (Harper, 1948).

About pages 66–276 focus on her first 15 years. Her brother is Julian Green (see entries in chs. 4 and 6).

Family Memoirs I France

Haaglund, Lois (1929–). *Tough, Willing, and Able: Tales of a Montana Family* (Mountain Press, 1997).

Family Memoirs ✧ Growing Up Between WWI and WWII ✧ Ranch Life I MT

Harding, Bertita (1902–). *Mosaic in the Fountain* (Lippincott, 1949).

By book's end, Harding is still in her mid-to-late adolescence.

Catholics ✧ Family Memoirs ✧ Grandparents ✧ Historians I Germany ✧ Mexico

Haygood, Wil. (1954–). *The Haygoods of Columbus: A Love Story* (Houghton Mifflin, 1997).

Pages 15–197 cover his first 21 years.

African Americans ✧ Baby Boomers ✧ Family Memoirs I OH

Hunt, Rockwell (1868–1966). *Boyhood Days of "Mr. California": Rockwell Hunt and Four Brothers in the 1870s* (Caxton, 1965).

Family Memoirs ✧ Ranch Life | CA (Northern)

Irvine, Lyn (pseud.) (1901–1973). *So Much Love, So Little Money* (Faber & Faber, 1957).

She grew up in a theatrical family.

Bloomsbury Group ✧ Family Memoirs ✧ Publishers | England

Kip, Herbert Zabriskie (1874–). *The Boy I Knew the Best* (R.G. Badger, 1932).

Dutch Reformed Church ✧ Family Memoirs | NY

Lee, Eliza (1794–1864). *Sketches of a New England Village, in the Last Century* (J. Munroe, 1838).

Clergy ✧ Country Life ✧ Family Memoirs ✧ Nineteenth-Century Pre-Industrial Age Memoirists | NH

MacDonald, Michael Patrick (1966–). *All Souls: A Family Story from Southie* (Beacon, 1999).

This gritty memoir is set in South Boston and tells of the struggles faced by his single mother and 10 siblings. MacDonald's life story is continued by the following entry.

Brothers ✧ Crime ✧ Drug Abuse ✧ Family Memoirs ✧ Fatherless Families ✧ Generation X ✧ Irish Americans ✧ Murder ✧ Racism ✧ Suicide and Suicide Victims ✧ Working Class Whites | MA (South Boston)

MacDonald, Michael Patrick (1966–). *Easter Rising: An Irish American Coming Up From Under* (Houghton Mifflin, 2006).

Starting with his teenage years, MacDonald describes a life immersed in punk rock, as he tries to survive the mean streets of Boston and NYC.

Brothers ✧ Crime ✧ Drug Abuse ✧ Family Memoirs ✧ Fatherless Families ✧ Generation X ✧ Irish Americans ✧ Murder ✧ Racism ✧ Suicide and Suicide Victims ✧ Working Class Whites | MA (South Boston) ✧ NYC (Lower East Side)

Matthews, Sallie (1861–1938). *Interwoven: A Pioneer Chronicle* (Anson Jones, 1936).

Pages 8–154. Western historian J. Frank Dobie wrote that this memoir, "more than any other ranch chronicle that I know, reveals the family life of old-time ranches."

Family Memoirs ✧ Frontier and Pioneer Life ✧ Ranch Life | TX (West)

McGratty, Arthur (1909–1975). *I'd Gladly Go Back* (Newman, 1951).

Clergy ✧ Family Memoirs | NYC (Brooklyn)

McKenney, Ruth (1911–1972). *The McKenneys Carry On* (Harcourt, Brace, 1940).

Entire memoir is on her girlhood and employs much re-created dialogue. *My Sister Eileen* (Harcourt, Brace, 1938) is primarily biographical rather than autobiographical, but contains further anecdotes on family life during Ruth's youth.

Family Memoirs | OH

Meyer, Edith Patterson (1895–1993). *For Goodness' Sake! Growing Up in a New England Parsonage* (Abingdon, 1973).

She was one of 5 children.

Clergy ✧ Family Memoirs ✧ Methodists | MA ✧ CT

Miller, Christian (1920–). *A Childhood in Scotland* (John Murray, 1981).
Focuses on her first 10 years. In her fifties, she bicycled from VA to OR and wrote about it in *Daisy, Daisy: A Journey Across America on a Bicycle* (Doubleday, 1981).

Cycling ✧ Family Memoirs ✧ Family Violence ✧ Growing Up Between WWI and WWII ✧ Travel Writers I Scotland

Mitford, Jessica (1917–1996). *Daughters and Rebels: The Autobiography of Jessica Mitford* (Houghton Mifflin, 1960) (British title, *Hons and Rebels* [Gollancz, 1960]) .
Pages 1–183 (chs. 1–20) focus on her first 20 years. This is a classic family memoir, which employs some re-created dialogue. She became famous as the author of the 1963 exposé *The American Way of Death* (Simon and Schuster, 1963). See "Sitwell, Osbert" (ch. 8) for a memoir of another British family that had similarly gifted and eccentric members.

Civil War (Spanish) ✧ Communists ✧ Eccentrics ✧ Family Memoirs ✧ Journalists I England

Morehead, Don (193?–), Ann Morehead, and Donald M. Morehead. *A Short Season: Story of a Montana Childhood* (University of Nebraska, 1998).
Set in the 1940s. He had to assume adult responsibilities when his father died of a burst appendix.

Appendicitis ✧ Bereavement ✧ Collaborations by Relatives ✧ Family Memoirs ✧ Fathers and Sons ✧ Native Americans ✧ Ranch Life I MT

Patrick, Sean (1937–). Patrick's Corner (Pelican, 1992).

Catholics ✧ Family Memoirs ✧ Irish Americans I OH

Pifer, Drury (1933–). *Innocents in Africa: An American Family's Story* (Harcourt, Brace, 1994).
Covers 1932–1945.

Depressions (Economic) ✧ Dramatists ✧ Family Memoirs ✧ Miners ✧ Nazis ✧ Pilots ✧ Racism I South Africa

Porter, Alyene. *Papa Was a Preacher* (Abingdon-Cokesbury, 1944).
Probably set in the 1920s.

Clergy ✧ Family Memoirs I TX

Robbins, Sarah (1817–1910). *Old Andover Days: Memories of a Puritan Childhood* (Pilgrim, 1908).

Clergy ✧ Family Memoirs ✧ Nineteenth-Century Pre-Industrial Age Memoirists I MA

Ryan, Terry (1946?–2007). *The Prize Winner of Defiance, Ohio: How My Mother Raised 10 Kids on 25 Words or Less* (Simon and Schuster, 2001).
Ryan lovingly describes growing up with 9 siblings and a tireless mother, who sustained the family economically by winning contests. This was adapted into a film in 2005, starring Julianne Moore and Woody Harrelson.

Baby Boomers (?) ✧ Children of Alcoholics ✧ Contests ✧ Family Memoirs ✧ Family Violence ✧ Humorists ✧ Mothers and Daughters ✧ Poets I OH

Simpson, Jeffrey. *American Elegy: A Family Memoir* (E.P. Dutton, 1996).

Family Memoirs ✧ Gays ✧ Sexuality I PA

Sousa, John Philip, III (1913–1993?). *My Family Right or Wrong* (Doubleday, Doran, 1943).

Entire light memoir focuses on his pre-adult years. His grandfather was bandleader John Philip Sousa.

Composers ✧ Family Memoirs ✧ Grandfathers ✧ Growing Up Between WWI and WWII ✧ Music and Musicians | CA

Spence, Hartzell (1908–). *Get Thee Behind Me: My Life as a Preacher's Son* (McGraw-Hill, 1942).

He was the son of a minister.

Clergy ✧ Family Memoirs ✧ Methodists | IA

Streatfeild, Noel (1895?–1986). *A Vicarage Family: An Autobiographical Story* (F. Watts, 1963).

Focusing on herself from 12 to 16 years, this memoirist was also the author of about 70 other books. In the preface she admits to having changed the names of some family members and refers to herself in this reminiscence as "Vicky." A 2-page bibliography of Streatfeild's works follows the text. A dozen illustrations by Charles Mozley are scattered throughout.

Actresses ✧ Children's Authors ✧ Clergy ✧ Critics (Literary) ✧ Editors ✧ Family Memoirs ✧ Grandparents ✧ Novelists ✧ Victorian Era British Memoirists | England

Swados, Elizabeth (1951–). *The Four of Us: The Story of a Family* (Farrar, Straus, and Giroux, 1991).

Baby Boomers ✧ Family Memoirs ✧ Schizophrenia | NY

Welles, Winifred (1893–1939). *The Lost Landscape: Some Memories of a Family and a Town in Connecticut, 1659–1906* (H. Holt, 1946).

Pages 1–79 focus on her youth.

Children's Authors ✧ Family Memoirs ✧ Poets | CT

Woollcott, Barbara. None But a Mule (Viking, 1944).

The author was a niece of literary critic Alexander Woollcott. This is a lighthearted memoir.

Family Memoirs ✧ Humorists ✧ Island Life | MD ✧ MA (Martha's Vineyard)

Appendix A

Bibliography of Collective Works

The titles in this bibliography gather early-life autobiographical writings (essays, vignettes, and so forth) by various groups of individuals, according a commonality shared by members of these groups, such as gender, ethnicity, race, or religion.

Because some categories (such as "Americans," "Multicultural," "Women," "Writers," and "Teen") are very broad or diffuse, they do not appear as subject terms for the entries in this appendix. Also, unlike works by individual memoirists, these books often are anthologies that cover diverse subjects. Therefore, not all entries have subject terms.

Those works listed here that do center on a sufficiently localized setting have been appropriately indexed by the place-name terms at the end of their entries. These geographic terms are included in the index at the end of this appendix. Not all entries have settings/geographic terms.

Abbott, Franklin, ed. *Boyhood, Growing Up Male: A Multicultural Anthology* (Crossing, 1993).

More than 40 accounts.

Alexander, Rae Pace, comp. *Young and Black in America* (Random House, 1970).

Excerpts from memoirs by Richard Wright, Daisy Bates, Malcolm X, Jimmy Brown, Anne Moody, Harry Edwards, and David Parks.

African Americans | U.S.

Anderson, Chester G., ed. *Growing Up in Minnesota: Ten Writers Remember Their Childhoods* (University of Minnesota, 1976).

Contributors include Harrison Salisbury and Robert Bly.

MN

Andrews, Clarence, ed. *Growing Up in Iowa* (Iowa State University, 1978).

IA

Andrews, Clarence, ed. *Growing Up in the Midwest* (Iowa State University, 1981).

U.S. (Midwest)

Anthony, Carolyn, ed. *Family Portraits: Remembrances by Twenty Distinguished Writers* (Doubleday, 1989).

Contributors include Margaret Atwood, Louis Auchincloss, Daniel J. Boorstin, Mary Higgins Clark, Clyde Edgerton, Gail Godwin, Alfred Kazin, Joyce Carol Oates, Walker Percy, Sara Paretsky, May Sarton, Isaac Bashevis Singer, Wallace Stegner, Gloria Steinem, Susan Allen Toth, and Jonathan Yardley.

Armstrong, Louise. *Kiss Daddy Goodnight: A Speak-out on Incest* (Hawthorn Books, 1978).
Contains about 20 first-person accounts, extracted from 183 interviews conducted by the author.
Incest

Arnold, Eleanor, ed. *Voices of American Homemakers* (Indiana University, 1985).
Under the heading "The Homemaker and Her Life," pages 15–95 consist of the following sections, which have many direct quotations from some of more than 200 interviewed women: "Growing Up," "Education," and "Courtship and Marriage."
Homemakers | U.S.

Atkins, Jacqueline. *Memories of Childhood* (E.P. Dutton in association with the Museum of American Folk Art, 1989).
Photos of award-winning quilts are accompanied by explications regarding the childhood imagery displayed in each one.
Quilts

Augenbraum, Harold, and Ilan Stavans, eds. *Growing Up Latino: Memoirs and Stories* (Houghton Mifflin, 1993).
The 25 contributors include Richard Rodriguez, Gary Soto, Piri Thomas, Edward Rivera, Nicholasa Mohr, and Oscar "Zeta" Acosta.
Latinos

Avery, Gillian, ed. *The Echoing Green: Memories of Victorian Youth* (Viking, 1975) (British title, *The Echoing Green: Memories of Regency and Victorian Youth*).
Victorian Era British Memoirists

Avery, Gillian, ed. *Unforgettable Journeys: An Anthology . . .* (F. Watts, 1965).
Some of the 35 extracts are from longer memoirs, while others are from novels.
Travel Writers

Bachelder, Louise, comp. *How Dear to My Heart, Are the Scenes of My Childhood* (Peter Pauper, 1970).
A 62-page collection of quotations.
Quotations

Backes, Clarus, ed. *Growing Up Western: Recollections* (Knopf, 1989).
Contributors: Dee Brown, A. B. Guthrie Jr., David Lavender, Wright Morris, Clyde Rice, Wallace Stegner, and Frank Waters.
U.S. (Western)

Baker, Mark. *Women: American Women in Their Own Words* (Simon and Schuster, 1990).
This book's second section ("Sugar, Spice, Things Not So Nice," pages 59–103) consists of about 3 dozen recollections of unnamed women describing events from their formative years.
U.S.

Bar-On, Dan. *Legacy of Silence: Encounters with Children of the Third Reich* (Harvard University, 1989).
Interviews with 13 post–middle-aged survivors of Nazi Germany.
Nazi Germany

Bass, Ellen, and Louise Thornton, et al., eds. *I Never Told Anyone: Writings by Women Survivors of Child Sexual Abuse* (Harper & Row, 1983).
Contains about 20 prose memoirs.
Abuse (Sexual)

Berger, Larry, and Dahlia Lithwick, eds. *I Will Sing Life: Voices from the Hole in the Wall Gang* (Little, Brown, 1992).
Inspirational writings from 7 children with terminal illnesses.
Illnesses (Terminal)

Berger, Maurice (1956–). *White Lies: Race and the Myths of Whiteness* (Farrar, Straus, and Giroux, 1999).
Besides including 47 scattered pages on the author's youthful recollections of NYC, this book contains vignettes (generally set in the NYC area) from 14 other individuals.
City Life ✧ Racism | NYC

Berlin, Ira, et al., eds. *Remembering Slavery: African Americans Talk About Their Personal Experiences of Slavery and Freedom* (New Press, 1998).
Slavery

Berry, Carmen Renee, and Tamara Traeder. *Girlfriends: Invisible Bonds, Enduring Ties* (Wildcat Canyon, 1995).
Sections include "Sharing Girlhood Adventures," "Remembering Friends," and "Women's Rites."
Female Friendships

Berry, J. Bill, ed. *Home Ground: Southern Autobiography* (University of Missouri, 1991).
U.S. (Southern)

Blewett, Mary H. *The Last Generation: Work and Life in the Textile Mills of Lowell, Massachusetts, 1910–1960* (University of Massachusetts, 1990).
Oral histories of 30 former textile workers.
Mill Girls | MA

Board, John C., ed. *A Special Relationship: Our Teachers and How We Learned* (Pushcart, 1991).
Recalling their youth, 68 notables honor an influential teacher in their lives. Contributors include Benjamin Rush, George McGovern, Eleanor Roosevelt, Aaron Copland, Bruce Catton, Angela Davis, May Sarton, and Martin Luther King Sr.
Teachers

Boas, Jacob, ed. *We Are Witnesses: The Diaries of Five Teenagers Who Died in the Holocaust* (H. Holt, 1995).
Writings are by David Rubinowicz (age 13, Poland), Yitzhak Rudashevski (age 13, Lithuania), Moshe Flinker (age 19, Poland), Eva Heyman (age 13, Hungary), and Anne Frank.
Diaries and Journals ✧ Holocaust Survivors

Bowman, Carol. *Children's Past Life Memories: How Past Life Experiences Can Affect Your Child Today* (Bantam Books, 1997).
Contains numerous accounts of childhood and youth.

Brannum, Mary, and the Editors. *When I Was 16* (Platt & Munk, 1967).
Contains memoirs by 18 women (e.g., Eileen Ford, Margaret Mead, Bette Davis, Marisa Berenson, Frances Scott Fitzgerald Lanahan, Marianne Moore, Mrs. Lyndon Baines Johnson).

Braybrooke, Neville, ed. *Seeds in the Wind: Early Signs of Genius, Virginia Woolf to Graham Greene* (Mercury House, 1989).
Writings by famous 20th-century authors, when they were 5–17 years old.

Brody, Leslie, ed. *Daughters of Kings: Growing Up as a Jewish Woman in America* (Faber & Faber, 1997).
Consists of essays by 13 women (including Brody), most of whom are Jewish, and many of whom have current or recent ties to Boston or NYC universities.
City Life ✧ Jews ✧ Spiritual Life I U.S.

Brostoff, Anita, with Sheila Chamovitz. *Flares of Memory: Stories of Childhood During the Holocaust* (Oxford University, 2001).
Collects vignettes from more than 40 European Jews.
Holocaust Survivors

Brough, James, with Annete, Cecile, Marie, and Yvonne Dionne. *The Dionne Quintuplets' Story: From Birth Through Girlhood to Womanhood: "We Were Five"* (Simon and Schuster, 1963).
About the first 200 pages of this memoir by 4 of the Canadian quintuplets focuses on their first 21 years (1934–1955).
Births (Multiple) ✧ Collaborations by Relatives I Canada

Burnett, John, ed. *Destiny Obscure: Autobiographies of Childhood, Education and Family from the 1820s to the 1920s* (John Allen, 1982; 1994 rpt., Routledge).
Growing Up Between WWI and WWII ✧ Nineteenth-Century Pre-Industrial Age Memoirists

Burnett, Whit(ney), ed. *Time to Be Young: Great Stories of the Growing Years* (Lippincott, 1945).
A potpourri of short autobiographical and fictional selections.

Burningham, John, ed. *When We Were Young: A Compendium of Childhood* (Bloomsbury, 2005).
Contains recollections by both famous and obscure persons.

Byrne, Robert and Teresa Skelton, selectors. *Every Day Is Father's Day: The Best Things Ever Said About Dear Old Dad* (Ballantine Books, 1989).
Contributors include Art Linkletter, Clarence Day, Richard Feynman, John Mortimer, John Osborne, Alice Walker, Lewis Grizzard, Signe Hammer, Mark Twain, Edmund Gosse, G. B. Shaw.
Fathers and Daughters ✧ Fathers and Sons ✧ Quotations

Cahill, Susan, ed. *Mothers: Memories, Dreams and Reflections by Literary Daughters* (New American Library, 1988).
Mothers and Daughters

Cain, Chelsea, ed. Foreword by Moon Unit Zappa. *Wild Child: Girlhoods in the Counterculture* (Seal, 1999).
Reminiscences of daughters of hippies.
Generation Y ✧ Hippies

Canadian Childhoods: A Tundra Anthology in Words and Art Showing Children of Many Backgrounds Growing Up in Many Parts of Canada (Tundra Books, 1989).
Canada

Canfield, Jack, et al., eds. *Chicken Soup for the Kid's Soul: 101 Stories of Courage, Hope and Laughter* (Health Communications, 1998).
Based on 42 interviews.

Canfield, Jack, et al., eds. *Chicken Soup for the Preteen Soul: 101 Stories of Changes, Choices and Growing Up for Kids, Ages 10–13* (Health Communications, 2000).

Canfield, Jack, et al., eds. *Chicken Soup for the Teenage Soul: 101 Stories of Life, Love and Learning* (Health Communications, 1997).

Canfield, Jack, et al., eds. *Chicken Soup for the Teenage Soul II: 101 More Stories of Life, Love and Learning* (HCI Teens, 1998).

Canfield, Jack, et al., eds. *Chicken Soup for the Teenage Soul III: 101 More Stories of Life, Love and Learning* (HCI Teens, 2000).

Canfield, Jack, et al., eds. *Chicken Soup for the Teenage Soul Letters: Letters of Life, Love, and Learning* (HCI Teens, 2001).
Letters

Canfield, Jack, et al., eds. *A Little Spoonful of Chicken Soup for the Teenage Soul* (Garborg's Heart'n'Home, 1998).
A short collection of only 64 pages.

Carroll, Rebecca. *Sugar in the Raw: Voices of Young Black Girls in America* (Crown, 1997).
Interviews with 15 girls, from 11 to about 20 years old.
African Americans I U.S.

Cassidy, Carol, ed. *Girls in America: Their Stories, Their Words—: Beauty Queens, Synchronized Swimmers, Double Dutchers, Rugby Players, Cheerleaders, and Teenage Moms* (TV Books, 1999).
Contains more than 2 dozen interviews with teenage girls.
U.S.

Cateura, Linda Brandi, ed. *Growing Up Italian* (W. Morrow, 1987).
Some of the 24 profiled subjects are Mario Cuomo, Gay Talese, and Francis Ford Coppola.
Italian Americans

Chyet, Stanley F., ed. *Lives and Voices; A Collection of American Jewish Memoirs with Drawings of the Times* (Jewish Publication Society, 1972).
Consists of 9 contributions by men who achieved career greatness.
Jews I U.S.

Coan, Peter Morton. *Ellis Island Interviews: In Their Own Words* (Facts on File, 1997).
Immigrants

Colman, Penny. *Girls: A History of Growing Up Female in America* (Scholastic Trade, 2000).
Diaries, memoirs, and letters from girls are included in this collection.
Diaries and Journals ✧ Letters | U.S.

Conant, Martha Pike, et al. *A Girl of the Eighties: At College and at Home* (Houghton Mifflin, 1931).
Focusing primarily on the early years of her sister Charlotte Howard Conant, this unusual book combines sections of biographical analysis by Martha with 72 pages of childhood letters by Charlotte.
Collaborations by Relatives ✧ Letters | MA

Conway, Jill Kerr, ed. *Written by Herself: Autobiographies of American Women, an Anthology* (Vintage Books, 1992).
Contains 25 reminiscences by such women as Harriet Ann Jacobs, Marian Anderson, S. Josephine Baker, Louise Bogan, Margaret Bourke-White, and Gloria Steinem.
U.S.

Conway, Jill Kerr, ed. *Written by Herself: Women's Memoirs from Britain, Africa, Asia, and the United States* (Vintage Books, 1996).
Contains 14 reminiscences by such women as Margery Perham, Mary Benson, Emma Mashinini, Vijaya, Lakshmi Pandit, and Gloria Wade-Gayles.
Africa ✧ Asia ✧ Britain ✧ U.S.

Conway, Jill Kerr, ed. *In Her Own Words: Women's Memoirs from Australia, New Zealand, Canada and the United States* (Vintage Books, 1999).
Some of these 12 women's recorded memories are on their youth.
Australia ✧ Canada ✧ New Zealand ✧ U.S.

Cooper, Paulette, ed. *Growing Up Puerto Rican* (Arbor House, 1972).
Contains 17 first-person accounts by Puerto Rican youth; introduction of book is by Cooper, who saw her parents murdered in Belgium during the Holocaust.
Puerto Rican Americans

Cordier, Mary Hurlbut. *Schoolwomen of the Prairies and Plains: Personal Narratives From Iowa, Kansas, and Nebraska, 1860s–1920s* (University of New Mexico, 1992).
Some of the excerpted accounts are by women under 22 years old.
Growing Up Between WWI and WWII ✧ Nineteenth-Century Pre-Industrial Age Memoirists ✧ Teachers | U.S. (Prairies and Plains)

Cox, L. Norma, ed. *Dear Dad: Famous People's Loving Letters to Their Father* (Saybrook, 1987).
Only some letters refer to childhood memories.
Fathers and Daughters ✧ Fathers and Sons ✧ Letters

Critchfield, Richard. *Those Days: An American Album* (Anchor Press/Doubleday, 1986).
Covering 1774–1944, this work comprises nearly 40 chapters, each of which is an oral account by a different living or deceased relative of the author.
U.S.

Cronkite, Kathy. *On the Edge of the Spotlight* (W. Morrow, 1981).
Each chapter is by the child of a celebrity (e.g., Arlo Guthrie, son of Woody Guthrie).
Children of Celebrities

Curwen, Henry Darcy, ed. *Exeter Remembered* (Phillips Exeter Academy, 1965).
Recollections of their student days at Phillips Exeter Academy are presented in essays by 47 individuals (e.g., Donald Ogden Stewart, Sloan Wilson, Nathaniel Benchley, Richard S. Salant, Arthur M. Schlesinger Jr., and Richard P. Bissell).
Phillips Exeter Academy | NH

Dargan, Amanda, and Steven Zeitlin. *City Play* (Rutgers University, 1990).
More than 100 present and former residents of NYC, most of whom grew up between WWI and WWII, recount their memories of playing childhood games.
City Life ✧ Games ✧ Growing Up Between WWI and WWII | NYC

David, Jay (pseud. of William Adler), ed. *Growing Up Black* (W. Morrow, 1968).
Consists of 25 contributions. (Avon Books issued a revised ed. in 1992.)
African Americans

David, Jay (pseud. of William Adler), ed. *Growing Up Jewish* (W. Morrow, 1969).
(William Morrow also issued a 1996 ed. of this title.)
Jews

David, Jay (pseud. of William Adler), and Helise Harrington, eds. *Growing Up African* (W. Morrow, 1971).
Africans

David, Kati. *A Child's War: World War II Through the Eyes of Children* (Avon Books, 1989).
This expanded version of a Dutch work contains accounts by 15 individuals.
WWII

Davis, Clyde Brion, ed. *Eyes of Boyhood* (Lippincott, 1953).
An anthology of autobiographical material, as well as poems and stories.

De Jesus, Joy L., ed. *Growing Up Puerto Rican: An Anthology* (W. Morrow, 1997).
The coming of age of 20 modern writers is profiled in as many essays.
Puerto Rican Americans

De La Mare, Walter. *Early One Morning in the Spring: Chapters on Children and on Childhood As It Is Revealed in Particular and in Early Writings* (Faber & Faber, 1949).
In this 600-page anthology, the famous British poet here has gathered quotations by children.
Quotations

DePaul, Kim, ed. *Children of Cambodia's Killing Fields: Memoirs by Survivors* (Yale University, 1997).
Memoirs by 29 children (5–17 years), during Cambodia's domination by the Communist Khmer Rouge.
Cambodian Americans

Desetta, Al, ed. *The Heart Knows Something Different: Teenage Voices from the Foster Care System* (Persea Books, 1996).
Nearly 40 young writers talk about their past personal experiences with foster care.
Child Institutional Care

Dickson, Brenton H. *Once Upon a Pung* (Privately printed, 1963).
Collects the reminiscences of youth of 19 senior citizens who grew up in Weston, MA.
MA

Dillard, Annie, and Cort Conley, selectors and eds. *Modern American Memoirs* (HarperCollins, 1995).
Several entries focus on the memoirists' youthful years. Among the 35 autobiographical profiles are pieces by such writers as Harry Crews, Wallace Stegner, Richard Wright, Anne Moody, and John Edgar Wideman.
U.S.

Dobie, Bertha McKee, et al. *Growing Up in Texas: Recollections of Childhood by Bertha McKee Dobie, Terrell Maverick Webb, and Numerous Others* (Encino Press, 1972).
Gathers vignettes by 13 notable Texans.
TX

Dorris, Michael, and Emilie Buchwald, eds. *The Most Wonderful Books: Writers on Discovering the Pleasures of Reading* (Milkweed Editions, 1997).
Contains 57 vignettes by such writers as Kathleen Norris, Scott Spencer, and Nicholson Baker.

Drimmer, Frederick, ed. *Scalps and Tomahawks: Narratives of Indian Captivity* (Coward McCann, 1961) (1985 rpt., Dover Publications, *Captured by Indians: 15 Firsthand Accounts, 1750–1870*).
Seven of the narratives are from persons who were children or adolescents during at least part of their captivities: James Smith, Thomas Brown, John Slover, John Tanner, Charles Johnston, John Rodgers Jewitt, and Fanny Kelly.
Eighteenth-Century Memoirists ✧ Indian Captivity ✧ Nineteenth-Century Pre-Industrial Age Memoirists

Dunn, Brad. *When They Were 22: 100 Famous People at the Turning Point in Their Lives* (Andrews McMeel Publishing, 2006).
The profiled celebrities include Sean Connery, Robert Altman, Brad Pitt, Ernest Hemingway, and Steven Hawking.

Dwork, Deborah. *Children with a Star: Jewish Youth in Nazi Europe* (Yale University, 1991).
Contains diaries, letters, and oral histories.
Diaries and Journals ✧ Jews ✧ Letters ✧ Nazi Germany

Dyja, Thomas, ed. *Life-changing Stories of Coming of Age* (Marlowe, 2001).
Among the 13 vignettes contained here are selections by Rick Moody, Russell Banks, Gregor von Rezzori, and Jacki Lyden.

Edelman, Bernard, ed. *Dear America: Letters Home from Vietnam* (W.W. Norton, 1985).
Many of these letters are by men under age 22.
Baby Boomers ✧ Letters ✧ Vietnam Conflict

Ehrlich, Amy, ed. *When I Was Your Age: Original Stories About Growing Up, Volume 1* (Candlewick, 1996).

Among the 10 writers represented are Laurence Yep, Walter Dean Myers, Susan Cooper, Reeve Lindbergh, and Avi. Each essay is preceded by a black-and-white photo of that person as a child and is followed by a note from the contributor.

Ehrlich, Amy, ed. *When I Was Your Age: Volume 2* (Candlewick, 2002).

This collection gathers pieces by 10 more writers (e.g., Norma Fox Mazer, Jane Yolen, Paul Fleischman, E. L. Konigsburg, and Joseph Bruchac). Each essay is preceded by a black-and-white photo of that person as a child and is followed by a note from the contributor.

Eidse, Faith, and Nina Sichel, eds. *Unrooted Childhoods: Memories of Growing Up Global* (Intercultural, 2004).

Consists of narratives by 20 individuals (e.g., Pat Conroy, Isabel Allende, and Pico Iyer) who grew up outside their native lands.

Immigrants

Ellison, Elaine Krasnow, and Elaine Mark Jaffe. *Voices from Marshall Street, Jewish Life in a Philadelphia Neighborhood, 1920–1960* (Camino Books, 1994).

Anecdotes are sprinkled throughout 9 chapters with titles such as "Daughters and Sons Speak," "Street Characters," and "Rites of Passage."

Baby Boomers ✧ City Life ✧ Growing Up Between WWI and WWII ✧ Jews | Philadelphia

Evasdaughter, Elizabeth N. *Catholic Girlhood Narratives: The Church and Self-Denial* (Northeastern University, 1996).

Catholic Girlhoods

Faulkner, Audrey Olsen, et al., comps. *When I Was Comin' Up: An Oral History of Aged Blacks* (Archon Books, 1982).

Thirteen African American residents of Newark, NJ describe their youthful years in such chapters as "Work Made Me a Lady," "Scared of Everything When I Grew Up," and "Going to Live Like My Father Lived." These are followed by a 13-page essay ("Background for Our Historians' Lives") that provides a sociological overview of the factors that affected these profiled persons.

African Americans | NJ

Fellows, Will, collector and ed. *Farm Boys: Lives of Gay Men from the Rural Midwest* (University of Wisconsin, 1996).

Contains 37 accounts, spanning "before the mid-1960s" through the "mid-1980s."

Baby Boomers ✧ Farm Life ✧ Gays ✧ Generation X | U.S. (Midwest)

Fernea, Elizabeth Warnock, ed. *Remembering Childhood in the Middle East, Memoirs from a Century of Change* (University of Texas, 2002).

Fernea here has assembled autobiographical accounts of the Middle Eastern childhoods of 3 dozen men and women.

Middle East

Fiffer, Sharon, and Steve Fiffer, eds. *Family: American Writers Remember Their Own* (Pantheon Books, 1996).

Youthful times are recalled by 19 contributors (e.g., Deborah Tannen, bell hooks, Stuart Dybek, Marion Wink, Edward Hoagland, Edwidge Danticat, and Brent Staples).

Family Memoirs | U.S.

Filopovic, Zlata, and Melanie Challenger, eds. *Stolen Voices: Young People's War Diaries, from World War I to Iraq* (Penguin, 2007).

Co-editor Filopovic wrote her own wartime diary during the Bosnian War (see ch. 6). This collection contains 14 chronologically arranged diaries.

Diaries ✧ Military Life

Fimrite, Ron, ed. *Birth of a Fan* (Macmillan, 1993).

Common theme of these 15 reminiscences is baseball; contributors include Roger Angell, Robert Creamer, Anne Lamott, and Frank DeFord.

Baseball

Firestone, Ross, ed. *A Book of Men: Visions of the Male Experience* (Stonehill, 1975).

See also "Levin, Martin" (this appendix).

Flynn, Robert, and Susan Russell, comps. *When I Was Just Your Age* (University of North Texas, 1992).

Collects interviews on the Texas childhoods of 13 old-timers.

TX

French, Susan Ashley. *Toys in the Sand: Recovering Childhood Memories in Lakeville, Massachusetts* (Privately printed, 1989).

Interviews with town residents who were born around the turn of the century.

MA

Frommer, Harvey. *Growing Up at Bat: 50 Years of Little League Baseball* (Pharos, 1989).

The section titled "Alumni Voices: Reminiscences" (pages 132–87) collects reminiscences of 43 men, such as Bill Bradley, Brent Musburger, Nolan Ryan, Steve Garvey, Eddie Murray, George Brett, Mike Ditka, Doug Flutie, Kareem Abdul-Jabbar, Kurt Russell, Tom Selleck, Bruce Springsteen, Joseph Campanella, Henry Winkler, William Cohen, and Michael Smith (pilot of the doomed shuttle *Challenger*).

Little League Baseball

Frommer, Myrna Katz. *It Happened in Brooklyn: An Oral History of Growing Up in the Borough in the 1940s, 1950s, and 1960s* (Harcourt, Brace, 1993).

Noted contributors include Robert Merrill, Mel Allen, Al Lewis, and Pat Cooper.

City Life ✧ NYC (Brooklyn)

Frommer, Myrna Katz, and Harvey Frommer. *Growing Up Jewish in America: An Oral History* (Harcourt, Brace, 1995).

Consists of about 100 accounts by men and women (from their early twenties to their late nineties) who grew up across the U.S.

Jews I U.S.

Garrod, Andrew, and Colleen Larrimore, eds. *First Person, First Peoples: Native American College Graduates Tell Their Life Stories* (Cornell University, 1997).

Autobiographical narratives of 13 Native Americans, all of whom graduated from Dartmouth College.

College Life ✧ Dartmouth College ✧ Native Americans I U.S.

Garrod, Andrew, et al., eds. *Souls Looking Back: Life Stories of Growing Up Black* (Routledge, 1999).
Contains 16 accounts by students (who studied at Dartmouth College, Simmons, and McGill University) who are African American and biracial (all have African American fathers).

African Americans ✦ College Life ✦ Dartmouth College ✦ McGill University ✦ Simmons College

Gesensway, Deborah, and Mindy Roseman. *Beyond Words: Images from America's Concentration Camps* (Cornell University, 1987).
Consists of 25 accounts of camp survivors.

Internment Camps

Gilbar, Steven, selector. *The Open Door: When Writers First Learned to Read* (David R. Godine, 1989).
Accounts by 7 women and 22 men are included; except for the entry by Harper Lee, each reminiscence is accompanied by a black-and-white photo or other rendering of the contributor, followed by a short prefatory essay by Gilbar and the autobiographical narrative (by such writers as William Cobbett, Winston Churchill, Jean Rhys, and Paule Marshall). The volume concludes with an "Afterword," by John Y. Cole, director of The Center for the Book at the Library of Congress.

Books and Reading

Gilbert, Martin. *The Boys: The Untold Story of 732 Young Concentration Camp Survivors* (H. Holt, 1997).
Holocaust Survivors ✦ Jews

Gordon, Alice, and Vincent Virga, eds. *Summer* (Addison-Wesley, 1990).
In this mixture of nonfiction and fiction pieces, memoirs of youth are included by such persons as Daniel Okrent, Anatole Broyard, Michael Dorris, Verlyn Klinkenborg, Roy Blount Jr., James McCourt, and Donald Hall.

Summer

Gottlieb, Sherry Gershon. *Hell No, We Won't Go! Resisting the Draft During the Vietnam War* (Viking, 1991).
Contains remembrances by expatriates, conscientious objectors, resisters, the physically unfit, and others.

Baby Boomers ✦ Pacifists ✦ Vietnam Conflict

Gray, Mary L. *In Your Face: Stories from the Lives of Queer Youth* (Haworth, 1999).
Contains essays by 15 gay, lesbian, and bisexual teenagers.

Bisexuals ✦ Gays ✦ Lesbians

Haining, Peter, ed. *Great Irish Short Stories of Childhood* (Souvenir Press, 1997).
An anthology of reminiscences and short stories.

Ireland

Hamilton, Carl, ed. *Pure Nostalgia* (Iowa State University, 1979).

Hampstead, Elizabeth. *Settlers' Children: Growing Up on the Great Plains* (University of Oklahoma, 1991).
Interspersed throughout the text are diary and journal extracts focusing on the youth of about 17 boys and girls from pioneer families in the late 1800s and early 1900s.

Diaries and Journals ✦ Frontier and Pioneer Life | North Dakota (and, to a less extent, adjacent regions)

Handley, Helen, and Andrea Samelson, eds. *Child: A Literary Companion* (Pushcart, 1988).
This is a compilation of more than 400 quotations (from unknown as well as renowned persons) that bear on childhood.
Quotations

Hareven, Tamara K., and Randolph Langenbach. *Amoskeag: Life and Work in an American Factory-City* (Pantheon Books, 1978).
Of the some 45 transcribed oral histories contained in this work, 33 contain accounts of the subject's childhood or adolescence.
Textile Factories I NH

Harris, Alex, ed. *A World Unsuspected: Portraits of Southern Childhood* (University of North Carolina, 1987).
Has 11 chapter-length entries by such contributors as Bobbie Ann Mason, Padgett Powell, and Sheila Bosworth.
U.S. (Southern)

Harris, Mark Jonathan, and Deborah Oppenheimer, eds. *Into the Arms of Strangers, Stories of the Kindertransport* (Bloomsbury, 2000).
Contains Holocaust recollections by 13 individuals.
Holocaust Survivors

Harvey, Harriet. *Stories Parents Seldom Hear: College Students Write About Their Lives and Families* (Delacorte, 1982).
Accounts of youth by various Yale students.
College Life ◇ Family Memoirs ◇ Yale University

Hastings, Scott E., Jr., and Elsie Hastings. *Up in the Morning Early: Vermont Farm Families in the Thirties* (University Press of New England, 1992).
Consists of dozens of interviews conducted during the 1970s, about Vermont farm life during the 1930s.
Depressions (Economic) ◇ Farm Life I VT

Hauser, Stuart T., Joseph P. Allen, and Eve Golden. *Out of the Woods: Tales of Resilient Teens* (Harvard University, 2006).
Crime ◇ Drug Abuse ◇ Mental Health ◇ Suicide and Suicide Victims

Hayes, E. Nelson, ed. *Adult Children of Alcoholics Remember: True Stories of Abuse and Recovery by ACOAS* (Harmony Books, 1989).
The editor has selected 17 accounts, including 1 from his own youth. All but 1 of these are from a first-person perspective.
Children of Alcoholics

Hegi, Ursula. *Tearing the Silence: On Being German in America* (Simon and Schuster, 1997).
Contains edited transcripts of interviews she conducted with 15 persons who lived some or all of their formative years in postwar Germany before immigrating to the U.S.
German Americans IU.S.

Heller, David. *Growing Up Isn't Hard to Do If You Start Out as a Kid* (Villard, 1991).
Assembles quotations by children.
Quotations

Heron, Ann, ed. *Two Teenagers in Twenty: Writings by Gay and Lesbian* Youth (Alyson, 1994).
An expansion and revision of *One Teenager in Ten* (Alyson, 1983), this is a collection of 43 personal narratives, some of which are autobiographical, focusing on issues involving homosexuality.
Gays ✧ Lesbians

Hochberg-Marianska, Maria, and Noe Gruss, eds. Tr. by Bill Johnston. *The Children Accuse* (Vallentine Mitchell, 1996).
Verbatim accounts by dozens of Holocaust survivors, grouped under the headings "The Ghettos," "The Camps," "On the Aryan Side," "In Hiding," "The Resistance," "Prison," and "Adults on Children."
Holocaust Survivors

Holbrook, Sabre. *Growing Up in France* (Antheum, 1980).
Has interviews with several children who grew up in diverse regions of that country.
France

Hong, Maria, ed. *Growing Up Asian American: An Anthology* (W. Morrow, 1993).
Essays and fiction by 32 contributors, such as Amy Tan, Maxine Hong Kingston, and Gus Lee. These are organized under the categories "First Memories," "The Beginnings of Identity," and "Growing Up," and are set in CA, NYS, and Hawaii.
Asian Americans I U.S.

Hoobler, Dorothy, and Thomas Hoobler, eds. *Real American Girls Tell Their Own Stories* (Atheneum Books for Young Readers, 1999).
Six first-person accounts (including writings by Louisa May Alcott and Martha Carey Thomas, a founder of Bryn Mawr) cover the period 1756–1950.
Baby Boomers ✧ Diaries and Journals ✧ Eighteenth-Century Memoirists ✧ Growing Up Between WWI and WWII I U.S.

Hoover, Herbert. *On Growing Up: His Letters from and to American Children* (W. Morrow, 1949) (1962 rpt., Morrow).
Letters ✧ Presidents, U.S. I U.S.

Howe, Florence, and Jean Casella, eds. *Almost Touching the Skies: Women's Coming of Age Stories* (Feminist Press at the City University of New York, 2000).
Contains 22 narratives—some of which are fictional—by writers who have been previously published by the Feminist Press, such as Zora Neale Hurston, Kate Chopin, Edith Konecky, and Louise Meriwether.

Howey, Noelle, and Ellen Samuels, eds. *Out of the Ordinary: Essays on Growing Up with Gay, Lesbian, and Transgender Parents* (St. Martin's, 2000).
Collects 21 essays.
Children of Gays ✧ Children of Lesbians ✧ Children of Transsexuals

Hoyland, John, ed. *Fathers and Sons* (Serpent's Tail, 1992).
Consists of 8 pieces by these (largely British) writers: David Simon, John Fowles, David Epstein, Christopher Rawlence, John McVicar, John Hoyland, Paul Atkinson, and Francis King. These reminiscences and essays pertain to the relationships between fathers and sons, as well as how boys grow into men.
Fathers and Sons | England

Hurmence, Belinda, ed. *Before Freedom, When I Just Can Remember: Twenty-seven Oral Histories of Former South Carolina Slaves* (J.F. Blair, 1989).
All but a few accounts contain memories from their subjects' first 21 years.
African Americans Slavery | SC

Hurmence, Belinda, ed. *My Folks Don't Want Me to Talk About Slavery: Twenty-One Oral Histories of Former North Carolina Slaves* (J.F. Blair, 1984).
All accounts but those from Ann Parker and Thomas Hall focus significantly on their first 21 years.
African Americans ✧ Slavery | NC

Hurmence, Belinda, ed. *Slavery Time When I Was Chillun* (Philomel Books, 1997).
Contains 12 oral histories.
African Americans ✧ Slavery

Hyslop, Donald, Alastair Forsyth, and Sheila Jemima, eds. Titanic *Voices, Memories from the Fateful Voyage* (St. Martin's, 1997).
Contains a good number of survivors' youthful memories of their time aboard the doomed ship (April, 1912).
Titanic

Isaacs, Neil D. *Innocence & Wonder: Baseball Through the Eyes of Batboys* (Masters Press, 1994).
Vignettes told by 135 batboys of their on-field and off-field interactions with professional baseball players and managers, from the 1920s to the 1980s.
Baseball

Jemison, Marie S., and Ellen Sullivan, eds. *An Alabama Scrapbook* (Privately printed, 1988).
Contains 32 memoirs of growing up in AL.
AL

Jones, LeAlan, and Lloyd Newman, with David Ismay. *Our America: Life and Death on the South Side of Chicago* (Scribner, 1997).
Oral accounts from dozens of inner-city Chicago youth.
City Life | Chicago

Jones, Louis C(lark), ed. *Growing Up in the Cooper Country: Boyhood Recollections of the New York Frontier* (Syracuse University, 1965).
Pages 27–86 cover the youth (3–21 years) of Levi Beardsley (1785–1857), as extracted from his memoir *Reminiscences* (1852); pages 93–187 cover the youth (4–20 or 21 years) of Henry Clark Wright (1797–1870), as extracted from his memoir *Human Life* (1849).
Eighteenth-Century Memoirists ✧ Frontier and Pioneer Life ✧ Nineteenth-Century Pre-Industrial Age Memoirists | NY

Jones, Suzanne, ed. *Growing Up in the South: An Anthology of Modern Southern Literature* (Mentor, 1991).
Contributions of 25 excerpts from works of fiction and nonfiction, including pieces by Maya Angelou, Lee Smith, and Bobbie Ann Mason.
U.S. (Southern)

Jordan, Terry, comp. *Growing Up in the Fifties* (MacDonald, 1990).
Collects pieces by 7 British women. See "Landau, Cecile" (this appendix) for companion volume.
Baby Boomers | England

Joseph, Stephen M., ed. *The Me Nobody Knows: Children's Voices from the Ghetto* (Discus, 1969).
City Life ✧ Slums

Kahn, Laurie Susan. *Sleepaway: The Girls of Summer and the Camps They Love* (Workman, 2003).
Kahn has assembled dozens of childhood reminiscences from American women who attended summer camps throughout the 20th century. Photographs, letters, songs, and other camp memorabilia are included.
Summer

Kaplan, Judy, and Lynn Shapiro, eds. *Red Diapers: Growing Up in the Communist Left* (University of Illinois, 1998).
Contains 41 prose reminiscences, nearly all of which are original to this collection; followed by a 4-page glossary.
Communists

Katz, Eileen, et al. *Deaf Women's Lives: Three Self-Portraits* (Gallaudet University, 2005).
Deafness

Kaufman, Polly Welts. *Women Teachers on the Frontier* (Yale University, 1984).
Some of the extended accounts are from women under 22 years old.
Female Teachers ✧ Frontier and Pioneer Life

Keller, Charles, comp. *Growing Up Laughing: Humorists Look at American Youth* (Prentice-Hall, 1981).
Humorists | U.S.

Keyes, Ralph, ed. *Sons on Fathers: A Book of Men's Writing* (Prentice-Hall, 1992).
Nearly 80 contributions, arranged by life stage, are from such men as Robert Bly, John Cheever, Bob Greene, Edmund Gosse, Anatole Broyard, Harry Crews, Stanley Elkin, James Dickey, Bill Moyers, and Lewis Grizzard.

Khu, Josephine M. T., ed. *Cultural Curiosity: Thirteen Stories About the Search for Chinese Roots* (University of California, 2001).
Chinese Americans

King, Alan. *Matzo Balls for Breakfast: And Other Memories of Growing Up Jewish* (Free Press, 2004).

Includes pieces from more than 75 contributors.

Entertainers ✧ Jews

Kirchheimer, Gloria and Manfred. *We Were So Beloved: Autobiography of a German Jewish Community* (University of Pittsburgh, 1997).

Contains 21 recollections by 11 individuals whose formative years were lived around the time of the Holocaust.

Holocaust Survivors | Germany

Kisseloff, Jeff. *You Must Remember This: An Oral History of Manhattan from the 1890s to World War II* (Harcourt Brace Jovanovich, 1989).

City Life ✧ Growing Up Between WWI and WWII | Manhattan

Lamar, Jay, and Jeanie Thompson, eds. *The Remembered Gate: Memoirs by Alabama Writers* (University of Alabama, 2002).

Some of the 19 contributors' pieces focus on their youth.

AL

Landau, Cecile, comp. *Growing Up in the Sixties* (MacDonald, 1991).

Collects pieces by 7 British women. See "Jordan, Terry" (this appendix) for companion volume.

Baby Boomers | England

Leibovitz, Maury, and Linda Solomon, eds. *Legacies* (HarperCollins, 1993).

Jews

Levin, Martin, ed. *Five Boyhoods* (Doubleday, 1962).

Focuses on the childhoods of these men: Howard Lindsay, Harry Golden, Walt Kelly, William Knowlton Zinsser, and John Updike. See also "Firestone, Ross" (this appendix).

Levine, Ellen. *Freedom's Shadow: Young Civil Rights Activists Tell Their Own Stories* (Putnam, 1993).

Accounts by 30 African Americans whose youths were spent in MI, AL, and AR during the 1950s and 1960s.

African Americans ✧ Baby Boomers ✧ Civil Rights Workers ✧ Racism | U.S. (Southern)

Lewis, Linda Rannells. *Birthdays: Their Delights, Disappointments, Past and Present, Worldly, Astrological, and Infamous* (Little, Brown, 1976).

Chapters 1 and 2 (pages 3–58) contain memories of childhood birthdays.

Birthdays

Lewis, Sydney. *"A Totally Alien Life-Form": Teenagers* (New Press, 1996).

Adolescents tell about their lives.

Generation X (?) ✧ Generation Y (?)

Linkletter, Art. *Kids Say the Darndest Things* (Prentice-Hall, 1957).

This classic work is illustrated by *Peanuts* cartoonist Charles M. Schulz and introduced by Walt Disney.

Quotations

Lipper, Joanna. *Growing Up Fast* (Picador, 2003).

In this unusual combination of collective memoir and sociological analysis, the author devotes a chapter apiece to the lives of 6 teenage mothers living in the economically depressed city of Pittsfield, MA.

City Life ✧ Generation Y ✧ Pregnancy (Teen) ✧ Slums ✧ Working Class Whites | MA

Litoff, Judy Barrett, and David C. Smith, eds. *Since You Went Away: World War II Letters from American Women on the Home Front* (Oxford University, 1991).

Correspondence from the daughters, girlfriends, and wives of servicemen appear in such chapters as "Courtship by Mail," "War Brides," and "I Took a War Job."

Letters WWII | U.S.

Longmore, Jane, comp. *When I Was a Child: Childhood Memories of the Famous* (Crocodile, 1986).

Celebrities

Lopez, Tiffany Ana, ed. *Growing Up Chicana/o* (Avon Books, 1993).

Contains 20 pieces by such writers as Patricia Preciado Martin, Gerald Haslam, Sandra Cisneros, and Ron Arias.

Mexican Americans

Loughmiller, Campbell, and Lynn Loughmiller, comps. and eds. *Big Thicket Legacy* (University of Texas, 1977).

Contains 20 chapter-length oral histories by elderly individuals who recall growing up in the densely grown area of southeastern TX known as Big Thicket.

Country Life | TX

Loundon, Sumi D., ed. *Blue Jean Buddha: Voices of Young Buddhists* (Wisdom Publications, 2001).

Essays by 16 of this work's 28 contributors focus on their first 21 years.

Buddhists

Lund, Candida, collector. *Coming of Age* (Thomas More, 1982).

Incorporates 28 coming-of-age tales, some fictional, while others are memoirs from such persons as Jade Snow Wong, Ingrid Bergman, Ben Hecht, and Shirley MacLaine.

Lyons, Mary E. *Keeping Secrets: The Girlhood Diaries of Seven Women Writers* (H. Holt, 1995).

Includes portions of the teenage diaries of Louisa May Alcott, Kate Chopin, Alice Dunbar-Nelson, Ida Wells-Barnett, Sarah Jane Foster, Charlotte Forten, and Charlotte Perkins Gilman.

Diaries and Journals

Manning, Diane. *Hill Country Teacher: Oral Histories from the One-Room School and Beyond* (Twayne, 1990).

At least 6 of this work's 7 sections contain extensive recollections by 6 women who taught in rural TX locales, beginning when they were 17–20 years old.

Female Teachers | TX

Marks, Marlene Adler, ed. *Nice Jewish Girls: Growing Up in America* (Plume, 1996).

Female Jews | U.S.

Martin, Patricia Preciado. *Songs My Mother Sang to Me: An Oral History of Mexican American Women* (University of Arizona, 1992).

Gathers 10 recollections from southern AZ towns, ranches, and mining camps from the late 1800s and early 1900s.

Female Mexican Americans ✧ Frontier and Pioneer Life ✧ Miners ✧ Mountain Life ✧ Ranch Life I AZ ✧ U.S.

Martone, Michael, ed. *Townships* (University of Iowa, 1992).

Some 24 essayists recall their Midwestern youth.

U.S. (Midwest)

Mathieson, William D. (1941–). *My Grandfather's War; Canadians Remember the First World War, 1914–1918* (Macmillan of Canada, 1981).

Many recollections are included, although the ages of the memoirists are seldom specified; see also "Reid, Gordon" (this appendix)

Canadians ✧ WWI

Mazer, Anne, ed. *Going Where I'm Coming From: Memoirs of American Youth* (Persea Books, 1995).

Fourteen narratives by such multicultural writers as Graham Salisbury, Susan Power, Lee A. Daniels, and Tracy Marx.

U.S.

McClanahan, Alexandra J. *Growing Up Native in Alaska* (CIRI Foundation, 2000).

In 13 geographically arranged chapters, 13 men and 12 women, born mostly between 1962 and 1972, discuss their youth.

Baby Boomers ✧ Generation X I AK

McCullough, David Willis, ed. *American Childhoods: An Anthology* (Little, Brown, 1987).

Collects recollections from the childhoods of 40 prominent persons, most of whom are 20th-century writers (e.g., Eudora Welty, Jean Fritz, Mark Twain, Edith Wharton, Harry Crews, and Ai Ling Ai), as well as such figures as U. S. Grant and John Adams.

U.S.

McEwan, Christian, ed. *Jo's Girls: Tomboy Tales of High Adventure, True Grit, and Real Life* (Beacon, 1997).

Tomboys

McNaron, Toni A. H., and Yarrow Morgan, eds. *Voices in the Night: Women Speaking About Incest* (Cleis, 1982).

About 10 of this collection's 42 pieces are prose memoirs.

Incest

Merriam, Eve, ed. *Growing Up Female in America; Ten Lives* (Doubleday, 1971).
U.S.

Monti, Ralph, ed. *I Remember Brooklyn: Memories of Famous Sons and Daughters* (Carol Publishing Group, 1991).
Includes memories by such celebrities as Alan King, Vincent Gardenia, Jane Brody, and Rudolph Giuliani.
Celebrities ✧ City Life | NYC (Brooklyn)

Morgan, Jill. *Fathers and Daughters: A Celebration in Memoirs, Stories, and Photographs* (Signet, 1999).
A mix of autobiographical vignettes and fictional pieces.
Fathers and Daughters

Murphy, Jim. *The Boys' War: Confederate and Union Soldiers Talk About the Civil War* (Clarion Books, 1990).
Includes diary entries and letters of boys who were under 17 when they fought in the Civil War.
Civil War (U.S.) ✧ Diaries and Journals ✧ Nineteenth-Century Pre-Industrial Age Memoirists

Mussey, Barrows, ed. *We Were New England: Yankee Life by Those Who Lived It* (Stackpole Sons, 1937).
Pages 9–100 offer accounts covering the New England childhood, adolescence, and college years of such individuals as Anna Green Winslow, Lyman Beecher, J. T. Buckingham, S. G. Goodrich, Julia Cowles, and John Neal.
New England

Nelson, G(eoffrey) K(enneth). *Countrywomen on the Land: Memories of Rural Life in the 1920s and 1930s* (Alan Sutton, 1992).
Each of the first 14 chapters focuses on the rural British youth of a woman; the 15th chapter provides shorter accounts by 6 other British women.
Country Life ✧ Growing Up Between WWI and WWII | England

Nelson, G(eoffrey) K(enneth). *Seen and Not Heard: Memories of Childhood in the Early 20th Century* (Alan Sutton, 1993).
Contains 14 accounts from youths spent in rural England.
Country Life | England

New York Historical Society and Trinity School. *Centuries of Childhood in New York: A Celebration on the Occasion of the 275th Anniversary of Trinity School* (New-York Historical Society, 1984).
Chapters: "Colonial Children, 1709–1776," "Children of the Republic, 1776–1865," "Children of the Industrial Era, 1865– 1920," "The Twentieth Century Child, 1920–1945," and "Euphemia Mason Olcott, A Child's View of Childhood in New York."
City Life ✧ Eighteenth-Century Memoirists ✧ Growing Up Between WWI and WWII ✧ Nineteenth-Century Pre-Industrial Age Memoirists | NYC

Nguyen-Hong-Nhiem, Lucy, and Joel Martin Halpern, eds. *The Far East Comes Near: Autobiographical Accounts of Southeastern Asian Students in America* (University of Massachusetts, 1989).
Asian Americans | U.S.

Nikkah, John, with Leah Furman. *Our Boys Speak: Adolescent Boys Write About Their Inner Lives* (St. Martin's Griffin, 2000).
Includes about 50 signed essays by boys (12–18 years) from all over the U.S., focusing on such immediately personal issues as trust, friendship, love, alienation, self-identity, and self-esteem.

O'Hearn, Claudine Chiawei, ed. *Half and Half: Writers on Growing Up Biracial and Bicultural* (Pantheon Books, 1998).
Contains 18 essays, of which some are nonfiction recollections.
Racially Mixed Children

Ohle, David, et al., eds. *Cows Are Freaky When They Look at You: An Oral History of the Kaw Valley Hemp Pickers* (Watermark, 1991).
Focuses on hippies living in Lawrence, KS, during the 1960s.
Baby Boomers ✧ Farm Life | KS

Orchard, Imbert. *Growing Up in the Valley: Pioneer Childhood in the Lower Fraser Valley* (Sound and Moving Image Division, 1983).
Interviews of 23 men and women who lived some or all of their early years in southern British Columbia during the late 1800s or early 1900s.
Frontier and Pioneer Life | Canada (BR COL)

Owings, Alison. *Frauen: German Women Recall the Third Reich* (Rutgers University, 1993).
Six of the 29 women quoted recount living in Germany under the Third Reich during their first 21 years: Mathilde Mundt, Verena Groth, Irene Burchert, Ursula Kretzschmar, Anna Maier, and Rita Kuhn.
Nazi Germany ✧ WWII

Owings, Alison. *Hey, Waitress! The USA from the Other Side of the Tray* (University of California, 2002).
About 17 of the 35 interviewed waitresses began working tables as teenagers; about 5 others began at age 20 or 21.
Waitresses ✧ U.S.

Ozment, Steven, ed. and narrator. *Three Behaim Boys: Growing Up in Early Modern Germany* (Yale University, 1990).
Collects letters from 3 boys who represent 3 generations of the same Nuremberg family, during the 1500s and 1600s.
Letters | Germany

Parton, Willadeene (1941?–). *Smoky Mountain Memories: Stories from the Hearts of Dolly Parton's Family* (Rutledge Hill, 1996).
Much of the material here has been adapted from her book, *In the Shadow of a Song: The Story of the Parton Family* (1985).
Mountain Life ✧ Singers

Patterson, Robert, et al., comps. *On Our Way; Young Pages from American Autobiography* (Holiday House, 1952).
These 27 pieces are culled from the writings of such notable Americans as Sherwood Anderson, P. T. Barnum, William O. Douglas, Frederick Douglass, Bob Feller, Langston Hughes, Burl Ives, Helen Keller, Emily Kimbrough, Mary Roberts Rinehart, and Mark Twain.
U.S.

Pearlman, Mickey, ed. *A Place Called Home: Twenty Writing Women Remember* (St. Martin's, 1996).
Erica Jung, Arlene Hirschfield, and others recall happy and traumatic aspects of their youth.

Perata, David D. *Those Pullman Blues: An Oral History of the African American Railroad Attendant* (Twayne, 1996).
Except for the fourth chapter (pages 66–81), parts of all the other chapters contain reminiscences by 7 men of times before they were 21 years old.
African Americans ✧ Railroad Travel I U.S.

Perdue, Charles L., Jr., Thomas E. Barden, and Robert K. Phillips, eds. *Weevils in the Wheat: Interviews with Virginia Ex-Slaves* (University Press of Virginia, 1976).
Compilation of more than 150 reminiscences of ex-slaves conducted by 20 Virginia Writers' Project personnel, 1936–1940; many of these oral accounts include details of slaves' childhood and adolescence.
African Americans ✧ Plantation Life ✧ Slavery I VA

Pran, Dith, and Kim DePaul, eds. *Children of Cambodia's Killing Fields: Memoirs by Survivors* (Yale University, 1997).
Cambodian Americans

Preston, John, ed. *Hometowns: Gay Men Write About Where They Belong* (E.P. Dutton, 1991).
These 29 essays describe what growing up was like in such settings as Medfield, MA; Greenfield, WI; Okemos, MI; and Miami, FL.
Gays

Pryce-Jones, Alan, ed. *Little Innocents: Childhood Reminiscences* (Cobden- Sanderson, 1932).
Contains reminiscences by 30 British contributors, such as John Betjeman, Rose Macaulay, Lord Alfred Douglas, Dorothy Wellesley, and Harold Nicolson.
England

Rafkin, Louise, ed. *Different Mothers: Sons and Daughters of Lesbians Talk About Their Lives* (Cleis, 1990).
Children of Lesbians

Reed, Gwendolyn, comp. *Beginnings* (Atheneum, 1971).

Reid, Gordon, ed. *Poor Bloody Murder* (Mosaic, 1980).
Contains first-person accounts by Canadians of combat in WWI; see also entry "Mathieson, William D." (this appendix).
Canadians ✧ WWI

Riley, Patricia, ed. Growing Up Native American: *An Anthology* (W. Morrow, 1993).
Essays and excerpts from the fiction of 22 writers, arranged under the sections "Going Forward, Looking Back," "The Nineteenth Century," "Schooldays," and "Twentieth Century."
Native Americans I U.S.

Robinson, Lennox. *Three Homes* (M. Joseph, 1938).
His siblings, Tom and Dora, have assisted in the writing of this unusual collective memoir of an Irish childhood. (Note: "Esmé Stuart" are his first 2 names, but they are usually dropped.).
Siblings | Ireland

Romilly, Esmond. *Out of Bounds* (Hamilton, 1935).
Includes an account of the early lives of Giles and Esmond, brothers whose uncle was Winston Churchill.
Brothers ✧ Churchill, (Sir) Winston | England

Root, Esther Sayles, and Marjorie Crocker. *Over Periscope Pond: Letters from Two American Girls in Paris: October 1916–January 1918* (Houghton Mifflin, 1918).
They assisted refugees.
Letters ✧ Refugees ✧ WWI | France

Rosenberg, Maxine B. *Hiding to Survive: Stories of Jewish Children Rescued from the Holocaust* (Clarion Books, 1998).
Fourteen individuals relate their memories of being protected by Gentiles in Poland, France, Belgium, Lithuania, Germany, and Holland.
Holocaust Survivors ✧ Jews ✧ WWII

Samuel, Wolfgang W. E. *The War of Our Childhood: Memories of World War II* (University Press of Mississippi, 2002).
Accounts of Germany by 16 men and 11 women, born between 1933 and 1942. The book is divided into 3 parts: "War from the Sky," "War on the Ground," and "Other Dimensions of War."
WWII | Germany

Sander, Joelle. *Before Their Time: Four Generations of Teenage Mothers* (Harcourt Brace Jovanovich, 1991).
Oral accounts by 4 African American women from 4 successive generations.
Female African Americans

Sanders, Tobi Gillian, and Joan Frances Bennett. *Members of the Class Will Keep Daily Journals: The Barnard College Journals of Tobi Gillian Sanders and Joan Frances Bennett: Spring 1968* (Winter House, 1970).
Diary entries were recorded when the authors were about 18–19.
Baby Boomers ✧ College Life ✧ Diaries and Journals | NYC

Santiago, Esmeralda, and Joie Davidow, eds. *Las Christmas: Favorite Latino Authors Share Their Holiday Memories* (Knopf, 1998).
Contains contributions from more than 20 writers.
Christmas ✧ Latinos

Santiago, Esmeralda, and Joie Davidow, eds. *Las Mamis: Favorite Latino Authors Remember Their Mothers* (Knopf, 2000).
Compilation of 14 essays by such writers as Piri Thomas, Ilan Stavans, Francisco Goldman, Junot Diaz, and Gioconda Belli.
Latinos ✧ Mothers and Daughters ✧ Mothers and Sons

Schlissel, Lillian. *Women's Diaries of the Westward Journey* (Schocken Books, 1992).
 Among its 6 selections are writings by Barsina Rogers French and Rebecca Nutting Woodson, who were teenagers when crossing the country with their families.
 Diaries and Journals ✧ Female Pioneers ✧ Frontier and Pioneer Life

Schneider, Bart, ed. *Race: An Anthology in the First Person* (Crown Trade Paperbacks, 1997).
 The first section of this work, "Homeplace," contains 7 essays by such writers as Henry Louis Gates Jr., Michael Dorris, and Richard Rodriguez.
 Racism

Schneider, Gertrude, ed. *The Unfinished Road: Jewish Survivors of Latvia Look Back* (Praeger, 1991).
 Remembrances of 13 individuals who survived the Holocaust.
 Holocaust Survivors ✧ Jews | Lithuania

Schwartz, Alvin, collector and ed. *When I Grew Up Long Ago: Family Living, Going to School, Games and Parties, Cures and Death, A Comet, A War, Falling in Love, and Other Things I Remember* (Lippincott, 1978).
 Vignettes from 156 interviewees who were growing up in the U.S. during 1890–1914.
 Quotations

Sebbar, Leila, ed. *An Algerian Childhood: A Collection of Autobiographical Narratives* (Ruminator Books, 2001).
 Includes pieces from 16 Arab, Jewish, and Kabyle male and female contributors.
 Algerians | Algeria

Sellar, Deborah, ed. *When I Was a Child: Reminiscences of Childhood in New Zealand* (Shoal Bay, 1998).
 Consists of recollections by 22 noted New Zealanders.
 New Zealand

Sewell, Marilyn, ed. *Resurrecting Grace: Remembering Catholic Girlhoods* (Beacon, 2001).
 Contributors include such noted contemporary writers as Anna Quindlen, Tobias Wolff, Frank McCourt, Patricia Hampl, and Sandra Cisneros.
 Catholic Girlhoods

Seybold, David, ed. *Fathers and Sons: An Anthology* (Weidenfeld, 1992).
 Collects essays.
 Fathers and Sons

Shain, Charles, and Samuella Shain, eds. *Growing Up in Maine* (Down East Books, 1991).
 Excerpts from 22 writers' nonfiction works; among the contributors are Kate Douglas Wiggin, Mary Ellen Chase, Robert P. Tristram Coffin, and John Gould.
 ME

Shandler, Sara. *Ophelia Speaks: Adolescent Girls Write About Their Search for Self* (HarperPerennial, 1999).
 Subjects discussed in this frank collection include eating disorders, friendship, sexuality, family dynamics, and feminism.

Shreve, Susan Richards, and Porter Shreve. *Tales Out of School: Contemporary Writers on Their Student Years* (Beacon, 2001).

Seventeen contributors (e.g., David Sedaris, Michael Patrick MacDonald) recollect their experiences in American classrooms.

Education Teachers

Sichrovsky, Peter, comp. Tr. by Jean Steinberg. *Born Guilty: Children of Nazi Families* (Basic Books, 1988).

This work contains interviews.

Children of Nazis

Simonoff, Eric, ed. *Sleepaway: Writings on Summer Camp* (Riverhead Books, 2005).

The editor has collected 20 short pieces by noted writers that include such forms as memoir, essay, short story, poem, and cartoon. Contributors include James Atlas, David Sedaris, Margaret Atwood, and Ursula K. LeGuin.

Camps ✧ Summer

Singer, Bennett, ed. *Growing Up Gay: An Anthology for Young People* (New Press, 1993).

Potpourri of fiction and nonfiction selections, some of the latter contributed by such persons as Audre Lord, Quentin Crisp, and Martina Navratilova.

Gays

Sliwowska, Wiktoria, ed. Tr. by Julian Bussgang and Fay Bussgang. *The Last Eyewitnesses, Children of the Holocaust Speak* (Northwestern University, 1998) (First published in Polish, 1993).

Some 65 Polish survivors tell their stories.

Holocaust Survivors

Smallwood, James, ed. *And Gladly Teach: Reminiscences of Teachers from Frontier Dugout to Modern Module* (University of Oklahoma, 1976).

Has dozens of recollections of both teachers' childhood recollections as pupils themselves, as well as of their fledgling experiences as teachers; vignettes principally focus on the late 1800s through the Great Depression, with a smaller number focusing on the 1940s–1960s.

Baby Boomers ✧ Growing Up Between WWI and WWII ✧ Students ✧ Teachers

Somers, Suzanne. *Wednesday's Children: Adult Survivors of Abuse Speak Out* (Putnam, 1992).

Accounts of emotional, physical, or sexual abuse are related by such famous people as Cindy Williams, Desi Arnaz Jr., Angie Dickinson, Gary Crosby, Patti Davis, former Dallas Cowboy "Hollywood" Henderson, and Dee Wallace Stone.

Abuse

Soto, Gary. *California Childhood: Recollections and Stories of the Golden State* (Creative Arts Books, 1988).

Authors ✧ Baby Boomers ✧ Mexican Americans ✧ Poets | CA

Stavsky, Lois, and I. E. Mozeson. *The Place I Call Home: Voices and Faces of Homeless Teens* (Shapolsky, 1990).

Descriptions of homelessness by 31 NYC adolescents.

City Life ✧ Homeless | NYC

Stickland, Irina, comp. *The Voices of Children: 1700–1914* (Blackwell, 1973).
This unusual work collects extracts from published and unpublished books, letters, and diaries; about 10 of these relate to British childhoods from a first-person perspective.

Diaries and Journals ✧ Eighteenth-Century Memoirists England ✧ Growing Up Between WWI and WWII ✧ Letters Nineteenth-Century Pre-Industrial Age Memoirists ✧ Victorian Era British Memoirists

Stone, Laurie, ed. *Close to the Bone: Memoirs of Hurt, Rage, and Desire* (Grove, 1998).
The 8 pieces contained herein focus on painful memories from such writers as Lois Gould, Catherine Texier, Peter Trachtenberg, and Jerry Stahl.

Pain (Emotional)

Stratton, Joanna L. *Pioneer Women, Voices from the Kansas Frontier* (Simon and Schuster, 1981).
Includes dozens of extended quotations by women, some of whom are under age 21 years according to the table in the backmatter, which provides women's ages during their emigrations ("Guide to the Lilla Day Monroe Collection of Pioneer Stories") .

Female Pioneers ✧ Frontier and Pioneer Life I KS

Stratton, Royal B. *Captivity of the Oatman Girls* (Carlton & Porter, 1859) (1970 rpt., Saddle River).
Pages 40, 42, 61–265 contain direct quotations by siblings Lorenzo and Olive Oatman during the period 1851–1856, when they were held captive by Apache Indians, following their capture and their parents' murder. Lorenzo was 14 when this occurred.

Indian Captivity ✧ Nineteenth-Century Pre-Industrial Age Memoirists I NM

Strickland, Dorothy, ed. *Listen Children: An Anthology of Black Literature* (Bantam Books, 1982).
Contributors to this anthology's 22 selections (recollections, stories, poems, a speech, and a play) by African Americans include Stevie Wonder, Langston Hughes, Wilma Rudolph, and Lucille Clifton.

African Americans

Sturgis, Ingrid, ed. *Aunties: Thirty-five Writers Celebrate Their Other Mother* (Ballantine Books, 2004).
Primarily contributed by women, these recollections—many including memories from childhood or adolescence—even include some poems and recipes.

Aunts I U.S.

Sumrall, Amber Coverdale, and Patrice Vecchione, eds. *Catholic Girls: Stories, Poems, and Memoirs . . .* (Penguin U.S.A., 1992).
Some of the 52 writers here include Mary Gordon, Louise Erdrich, Mary McCarthy, Francine Prose, and Audre Lorde.

Catholic Girlhoods

Thibodeau, Lynn, ed. *Remember, Remember* (Carillon Books, 1978).
The 58 pieces are arranged under the headings "Do You Remember?," "The Times—The Places—The People," "It's History Now," and "The End of an Era."

Toth, Susan Allen, and John Coughlan, eds. *Reading Rooms* (Doubleday, 1991).
Among the 68 late-20th-century American writers toasting public libraries are Eudora Welty, Isaac Asimov, James Baldwin, E. B. White, and Nikki Giovanni.

Libraries

Truscott, Mary R., ed. *Brats* (E.P. Dutton, 1989).

Spread through a dozen thematically arranged chapters are extended quotations from 40 former "military brats."

Military Brats

Tunnell, Michael O., and George W. Chilcoat. *The Children of Topaz: The Story of a Japanese-American Internment Camp* (Holiday House, 1996).

This is a diary kept in 1943 at a UT camp by a third-grade class.

Camps (Internment) ✧ Diaries and Journals ✧ WWII | U.S.

Uys, Errol Lincoln. *Riding the Rails: Teenagers on the Move During the Great Depression* (TV Books, 1999).

Has more than 500 interviews with people who, as teenagers, crisscrossed the U.S. on railroads between 1929 and 1941.

Depressions (Economic) ✧ Growing Up Between WWI and WWII ✧ Railroad Travel

Van Buren, Abigail. *Where Were You When President Kennedy Was Shot? Memories and Tributes to a Slain President* (Andrews and McMeel, 1993).

The famous columnist culled a few hundred responses from the 300,000 she received from her readers; they are arranged in 12 chapters.

Assassinations ✧ Baby Boomers ✧ Bereavement ✧ Presidents, U.S.

Vegh, Claudine. Tr. by Ros Schwartz. *I Didn't Say Goodbye* (E.P. Dutton, 1984) (First published in French, 1979).

Consists of interviews with 17 adults who survived the Holocaust.

Holocaust Survivors

Verny, Thomas R., ed. *Gifts of Our Fathers: Heartfelt Remembrances of Fathers and Grandfathers* (Crossing, 1994).

Includes youthful memoirs by 16 (primarily Canadian) writers (5 men and 11 women), such as Mike Lipstock, Elisavietta Ritchie, William J. Smart, Joan Hoekstra, and Janice Levy.

Fathers and Daughters ✧ Fathers and Sons ✧ Grandfathers

Wade-Gayles, Gloria, ed. *Father Songs: Testimonies by African-American Sons and Daughters* (Beacon, 1997).

Includes selections from 62 contributors, such as Marcia Dyson, Dorothy Perry Thompson, Charles R. Braxton, Katie Lee Crane, Theodore Jennings, Mirriam DeCosta-Willis, and Don Belton.

African Americans ✧ Fathers and Daughters ✧ Fathers and Sons | U.S.

Wagenknecht, Edward, ed. *When I Was a Child: An Anthology* (E.P. Dutton, 1946).

In 9 chapters, collects vignettes from 39 British and American authors.

Waxman, Maron L., ed. *Christmas Memories with Recipes* (Farrar, Straus, and Giroux, 1988).

Consists of 25 chapters, each by a different writer (e.g., Craig Claiborne, Lee Bailey, Martha Kostyra Stewart), with such diverse childhood Christmas settings as Freetown, VA; Riverside, CA; Nutley, NJ; Cesenatico, Italy; suburban Boston, MA; Lima, Peru; northern MN; Quebec; and PA.

Christmas ✧ Cookery

Webb, Sheyann, and Rachel West Nelson (as told to Frank Sikora). *Selma, Lord, Selma: Girlhood Memories of the Civil-Rights Days* (University of Alabama, 1980).

Set in the 1960s.

African Americans ✧ Baby Boomers ✧ Civil Rights Workers | AL

Weiss, M(orton) Jerry, and Helen S. Weiss, eds. *From One Experience to Another, Award-Winning Authors Share Real-Life Experiences Through Fiction* (Tor/Forge, 1997).

Contains 15 autobiographical vignettes by such writers as Richard Peck, Joan Lowery Nixon, Avi, Jay Bennett, Joan Bauer, and Susan Beth Pfeffer.

Werner, Emmy E. *Pioneer Children on the Journey West* (Westview, 1995).

Frontier and Pioneer Life

West, Elliott. *Growing Up with the Country: Childhood on the Far Western Frontier* (University of New Mexico, 1989).

Collects excerpts from 9 persons' accounts of growing up in the U.S. West.

Frontier and Pioneer Life | U.S. (Western)

Westall, Robert, comp. *Children of the Blitz: Memories of Wartime Childhood* (Viking, 1985).

WWII | England

Wigginton, Eliot, ed. *A Foxfire Christmas: Appalachian Memories and Traditions* (Doubleday, 1990).

Written and edited by high school English students in GA, this work includes taped interviews recounting Christmases during the 1930s.

Christmas ✧ Depressions (Economic) ✧ Growing Up Between WWI and WWII ✧ Mountain Life | GA

Wilber, Cynthia J. *For the Love of the Game: Baseball Memories from the Men Who Were There* (W. Morrow, 1992).

Reminiscences from 39 major league players who took the field during the 1940s and 1950s, many of which go back to their childhoods; some contributors are Yogi Berra, Bobby Doerr, and Monte Irvin.

Baseball

Wilkes, Corinne, ed. *Dear Diary, I'm Pregnant: Teenagers Talk About Their Pregnancy* (Annick, 1997).

Generation X (?) ✧ Generation Y (?) ✧ Pregnancy (Teen)

Winokur, Jon, comp. and ed. *Fathers* (E.P. Dutton, 1993).

Vignettes are arranged under such headings as "Heroes," "Lost Fathers," and "Legacies."

Celebrities ✧ Fathers and Daughters ✧ Fathers and Sons

Wolin, Jeffrey A. *Written in Memory: Portraits of the Holocaust* (Chronicle Books, 1997).

Through oral history, documentary narrative, and art photography, 43 Holocaust survivors are profiled.

Holocaust Survivors

Wormser, Richard. *Growing Up in the Great Depression* (Atheneum, 1994).

Contains personal accounts, interviews, letters, and photographs.

Depressions (Economic) ✧ Growing Up Between WWI and WWII

Yetman, Norman R., ed. *When I Was a Slave: Memoirs from the Slave Narrative Collection* (Dover, 2002).

Drawn from Yetman's *Voices from Slavery* (Holt, Rinehart and Winston, 1970), these 34 verbatim accounts detail the childhood, adolescent, and adult years of African American slaves of the 19th century.

Nineteenth-Century Pre-Industrial Age Memoirists ✧ Racism ✧ Slavery | U.S (Southern)

Index

Insofar as possible, entries here are compatible with the terms in the indexes to the main body of this volume. Works that are classifiable by subject term only as collections of reminiscences by Americans, teenagers, women, or men are not indexed here, due to the broadness of these categories. (However, a few gender-related categories are included, such as "Fathers and Daughters," "Mill Girls.") Excluded as well are works that collect memoirs by individuals who can only be categorized by such generic labels as "writers" or "memoirists."

Works that are classifiable by geographic association (e.g., Growing Up in Minnesota) are indexed here by place-name (state, region, country, etc.). Only those memoirs whose titles contain variations of "America" or "United States" are indexed under the term "United States." However, titles that obviously focus on a specific part of the U.S. are indexed under that more specific location only, for example, U.S. (Southern). If the name of a work's author is undetermined, the volume's title has been substituted for it.

Only primary authors', editors', and compilers' names have been indexed in the case of collaborative works. Numerals in parentheses appearing after an author's name indicate that the volume contains citations to multiple titles on that subject by that author. Also, please note that editorial and compiler attributions have been dropped from authors' names in this index. A question mark enclosed in parentheses (?) after a name indicates uncertainty about that memoirist's birth year, which could affect whether he or she should be included within a generational subject term such as "Generation X."

In order to conserve space, entries that are in close alphabetical and thematic proximity to each other here usually are not cross-referenced to one another.

Chicago. Jones, LeAlan. *See also* **City Life; Slums**

Chicano Americans. *See* **Mexican Americans**

Child Institutional Care. Desetta, Al

Children of Alcoholics. Hayes, E. Nelson

Children of Celebrities. Cronkite, Kathy. *See also* **Celebrities**

Children of Lesbians. Rafkin, Louise. *See also* **Lesbians**

Children of Nazis. Sichrovsky, Peter. *See also* **Germany; Nazi Germany**

Children of Transsexuals. Howey, Noelle. *See also* **Bisexuals; Gays; Lesbians**

Chinese Americans. Khu, Josephine M. T. *See also* **Asian Americans; Racially Mixed Children**

Christmas. Santiago, Esmeralda; Waxman, Maron L.; Wigginton, Eliot

Churchill, (Sir) Winston. Romilly, Esmond. *See also* **England**

City Life. Berger, Maurice; Brody, Leslie; Dargan, Amanda; Ellison, Elaine Krasnow; Frommer, Myrna Katz; Jones, LeAlan; Joseph, Stephen M.; Kisseloff, Jeff; Lipper, Joanna; Monti, Ralph; New York Historical Society and Trinity School; Stavsky, Lois. *See also* **Chicago; Manhattan; New York City; NYC (Brooklyn); Philadelphia; Slums**

Civil Rights Workers. Levine, Ellen; Webb, Sheyann. *See also* **African Americans; Alabama; Politicians; Racism**

Civil War (U.S.). Murphy, Jim. *See also* **Military Life; Plantation Life; Slavery**

Collaborations by Relatives. Brough, James, et al.; Conant, Martha Pike, et al. *See also* **Family Memoirs**

College Life. Garrod, Andrew (2); Harvey, Harriet; Sanders, Tobi Gillian. *See also* **Books and Reading; Dartmouth College; Education; Libraries; McGill University; Schools; Simmons College; Students; Teachers; Yale University**

Comedians. *See* **Humorists**

Communists. Kaplan, Judy

Cookery. Waxman, Maron L.

Country Life. Loughmiller, Campbell; Nelson, G(eoffrey) K(enneth) (2). *See also* **Camps; Farm Life; Frontier and Pioneer Life; Ranch Life; U.S. (Midwest)**

Crime. Hauser, Stuart T., et al.

Dartmouth College. Garrod, Andrew (2). *See also* **College Life; Education**

Deafness. Katz, Eileen

Depressions (Economic). Hastings, Scott E., Jr.; Uys, Errol Lincoln; Wigginton, Eliot; Wormser, Richard. *See also* **Growing Up Between WWI and WWII; Slums**

Diaries and Journals. Boas, Jacob; Colman, Penny; Dwork, Deborah; Filopovic, Zlata; Hampstead, Elizabeth; Hoobler, Dorothy; Lyons, Mary E.; Murphy, Jim; Sanders, Tobi Gillian; Schlissel, Lillian; Stickland, Irina; Tunnell, Michael O.

Diseases (Terminal). *See* **Illnesses (Terminal)**

Drug Abuse. Hauser, Stuart T., et al.

Education. Shreve, Susan Richards. *See also* **Books and Reading; College Life; Dartmouth College; Libraries; McGill University; Phillips Exeter Academy; Schools; Simmons College; Teachers**

Eighteenth-Century Memoirists (1695–1789 Births). Drimmer, Frederick; Hoobler, Dorothy; Jones, Louis C(lark); New York Historical Society and Trinity School; Stickland, Irina. *See also* **Frontier and Pioneer Life**

Ellis Island. *See* **New York City; Immigrants**

Emotion, Painful. *See* **Abuse; Painful Emotion**

England. Conway, Jill Kerr; Esmond, Romilly; Hoyland, John; Jordan, Terry; Landau, Cecile; Nelson, G(eoffrey) K(enneth) (2); Pryce-Jones, Alan; Stickland, Irina; Westall, Robert. *See also* **Churchill, (Sir) Winston**

Growing Up Between WWI and WWII. Burnett, John; Cordier, Mary Hurlbut; Dargan, Amanda; Ellison, Elaine Krasnow; Hoobler, Dorothy; Kisseloff, Jeff; Nelson, G(eoffrey) K(enneth); New York Historical Society and Trinity School; Smallwood, James; Stickland, Irina; Uys, Errol Lincoln; Wigginton, Eliot; Wormser, Richard. *See also* **Depressions (Economic)**

Hearing Loss. *See* **Deafness**

Hippies. Cain, Chelsea

Holocaust Survivors (some of the cited memoirists did not survive the Holocaust). Boas, Jacob; Brostoff, Anita; Gilbert, Martin; Harris, Mark Jonathan; Hochberg-Marianska, Maria; Kirchheimer, Gloria; Rosenberg, Maxine B.; Schneider, Gertrude; Sliwowska, Wiktoria; Vegh, Claudine; Wolin, Jeffrey A. *See also* **Immigrants; Jews; Lithuania; Nazi Germany; Refugees**

Homeless. Stavsky, Lois

Homemakers. Arnold, Eleanor

Humorists. Keller, Charles

Illnesses (Terminal). Berger, Larry

Immigrants. Coan, Peter Morton; Eidse, Faith. *See also* **Holocaust Survivors; Refugees**

Incest. Armstrong, Louise; McNaron, Toni A. H. *See also* **Abuse; Abuse (Sexual)**

Indian Captivity. Drimmer, Frederick; Stratton, Royal B. *See also* **Native Americans**

Internment Camps. Gesensway, Deborah

Iowa. Andrews, Clarence. *See also* **Country Life; Farm Life; U.S. (Midwest)**

Ireland. Haining, Peter; Robinson, Lennox

Italian Americans. Cateura, Linda Brandi. *See also* **Racially Mixed Children**

Jews. Brody, Leslie; Chyet, Stanley F.; David, Jay; Dwork, Deborah; Ellison, Elaine Krasnow; Frommer, Myrna Katz; Gilbert, Martin; King, Alan; Leibovitz, Maury; Rosenberg, Maxine B.; Schneider, Gertrude. *See also* **Algerians; Female Jews; Holocaust Survivors**

Kansas. Ohle, David; Stratton, Joanna L. *See also* **Country Life; Farm Life; Frontier and Pioneer Life; U.S. (Midwest); U.S. (Prairies and Plains)**

Latinos. Augenbraum, Harold; Santiago, Esmeralda (2). *See also* **Mexican Americans; Racially Mixed Children**

Lesbians. Gray, Mary L.; Heron, Ann. *See also* **Bisexuals; Children of Lesbians; Children of Transsexuals; Gays**

Letters. Canfield, Jack; Colman, Penny; Conant, Martha Pike; Cox, L. Norma; Dwork, Deborah; Edelman, Bernard; Hoover, Herbert; Litoff, Judy Barrett; Ozment, Steven; Root, Esther Sayles; Stickland, Irina

Libraries. Toth, Susan Allen. *See also* **Books and Reading; College Life; Education; Teachers**

Lithuania. Schneider, Gertrude. *See also* **Holocaust Survivors**

Little League Baseball. Frommer, Harvey. *See also* **Baseball; Sports**

Maine. Shain, Charles. *See also* **New England**

Manhattan. Kisseloff, Jeff. *See also* **City Life; New York City**

Massachusetts. Blewett, Mary H.; Conant, Martha Pike; Dickson, Brenton H.; French, Susan Ashley; Lipper, Joanna. *See also* **New England**

McGill University. Garrod, Andrew. *See also* **College Life; Education**

Men. *See* **Baseball; Bisexuals; Fathers and Sons; Gays**

Mental Health. Hauser, Stuart T., et al. *See also* **Suicide and Suicide Victims**

Mexican Americans. Lopez, Tiffany Ana; Soto, Gary. *See also* **Female Mexican Americans; Latinos; Racially Mixed Children**

Middle East. Fernea, Elizabeth Warnock

Midwest U.S. *See* **U.S. (Midwest)**

Military Brats. Truscott, Mary R.

Military Life. Filopovic, Zlata. *See also* **Civil War (U.S.); Vietnam Conflict; WWI; WWII**

Mill Girls. Blewett, Mary H. *See also* **Textile Factories**

Miners. Martin, Patricia Preciado. *See also* **Mountain Life; U.S. (Western)**

Minnesota. Anderson, Chester G.

Mothers and Daughters. Cahill, Susan; Santiago, Esmeralda. *See also* **Family Memoirs; Fathers and Daughters; Fathers and Sons**

Mothers and Sons. Santiago, Esmeralda. *See also* **Family Memoirs; Fathers and Daughters; Fathers and Sons**

Mountain Life. Martin, Patricia Preciado; Parton, Willadeene; Wigginton, Eliot. *See also* **Frontier and Pioneer Life; Miners; U.S. (Western)**

Native Americans. Garrod, Andrew; Riley, Patricia. *See also* **Frontier and Pioneer Life; Indian Captivity; Racially Mixed Children**

Nazi Germany. Bar-On, Dan; Dwork, Deborah; Owings, Alison. *See also* **Children of Nazis; Holocaust Survivors; Jews**

New England. Mussey, Barrows. *See also* **Maine; Massachusetts; New Hampshire; United States; Vermont**

New Hampshire. Curwen, Henry Darcy; Hareven, Tamara K. *See also* **New England**

New Jersey. Faulkner, Audrey Olsen

New Mexico. Stratton, Royal B. *See also* **U.S. (Western)**

New York City. Berger, Maurice; Dargan, Amanda; New York Historical Society and Trinity School; Sanders, Tobi Gillian; Stavsky, Lois. *See also* **Ellis Island; Manhattan; NYC (Brooklyn)**

New York State. Jones, Louis C(lark)

New Zealand. Conway, Jill Kerr; Sellar, Deborah. *See also* **Australia**

Nineteenth-Century Pre-Industrial Age Memoirists (1790–1859 Births). Burnett, John; Cordier, Mary Hurlbut; Drimmer, Frederick; Jones, Louis C(lark); Murphy, Jim; New York Historical Society and Trinity School; Stickland, Irina; Stratton, Royal B.; Yetman, Norman R. *See also* **Frontier and Pioneer Life; Plantation Life; Slavery**

North Carolina. Hurmence, Belinda. *See also* **U.S. (Southern)**

North Dakota. Hampstead, Elizabeth. *See also* **Country Life; Farm Life; Frontier and Pioneer Life; U.S. (Prairies and Plains)**

NYC (Brooklyn). Frommer, Myrna Katz; Monti, Ralph. *See also* **City Life; New York City; Slums**

Pacifists. Gottlieb, Sherry Gershon. *See also* **Vietnam Conflict**

Painful Emotion. Stone, Laurie

Philadelphia. Ellison, Elaine Krasnow

Phillips Exeter Academy. Curwen, Henry Darcy. *See also* **Education; New Hampshire; Schools**

Plantation Life. *See also* **Civil War (U.S.); Nineteenth-Century Pre-Industrial Age Memoirists; Slavery.** Perdue, Charles L., Jr.

Poets. Soto, Gary

Politicians. *See* **Civil Rights Workers; Presidents, U.S.; Statesmen**

Poverty. *See* **Slums; Working Class Whites**

Prairies and Plains (U.S.). *See* **U.S. (Prairies and Plains)**

Appendix B

Disputed Titles

The following are titles of works whose general fidelity to fact as memoirs of childhood and/or adolescence has been challenged; a fertile source of titles of memoirs that mostly focus on their subjects' adult years is the body of work contributed by the meticulous historian of the American West, Ramon F(rederick) Adams (1889–1976). In particular, see *Burs Under the Saddle: A Second Look at Books and Histories of the West* (1964) and *More Burs Under the Saddle: Books and Histories of the West* (1979).

Alhadeff, Gini (1951–). *The Sun at Midday: Tales of a Mediterranean Family* (1997).
According to some scholars, this autobiographical work, set in Egypt, abounds with outright errors and assertions of dubious authenticity.

Anonymous. *Go Ask Alice* (1971).
Since its publication, persistent questions have been raised concerning the factuality of this work (set in the 1960s), causing publishers to market the title as a work of fiction. Aileen Pace Nilsen, a psychologist and youth counselor, initially claimed the book was based on the diary of one of her patients. In the late 1970s, however, she admitted that the work is a composite of some of her clients' experiences.

Behrman, S(amuel) N(athaniel) (1893–1973). *The Worcester Account* (1954).
The author describes visiting anarchist Emma Goldman's ice cream parlor; however, he would have been either unborn or an infant at that time.

Burroughs, Augusten (b. Christopher Robison) (1965–). *Running with Scissors: A Memoir* (2002).
The family of Dr. Rodolph H. Turcotte filed a lawsuit against Burroughs, claiming this is a largely fictional work. This purported memoir, set in the 1980s, describes the author's relationship with his mentally ill mother's dysfunctional psychiatrist. The book was adapted as a movie in 2006.

Carcaterra, Lorenzo (1954–). *Sleepers* (1995).
Names have been changed, and events herein recounted may have been altered significantly or manufactured.

Carr, Emily (1871–1945). (Especially) *The Book of Small* (1942) and *Growing Pains: The Autobiography of Emily Carr* (1946).
The subject of these works is the artist's girlhood in Victoria, British Columbia, and her subsequent struggles as a painter. Eleanor Munro of the *Los Angeles Times Book Review* cites Carr's claim to have run away to San Francisco at age 16 as one of her distortions. Scholar Peter Sanger (in an essay in a 1987 issue of the *Antigonish Review*) also took Carr to task, citing examples of her

misrepresenting details of both her inner and outer life. Carr also wrote 2 or 3 other autobiographical works. She died soon after completing *Growing Pains.*

Carter, Forrest (1927?–1979). *The Education of Little Tree: A True Story* (1976).
Purporting to recount the author's Cherokee boyhood during the 1930s, this work was discovered in 1991 to have been the fabrication of Asa Carter, a militant segregationist who was a speech writer for Governor George Wallace.

Chase, Truddi (1937?–). *When Rabbit Howls: By the Troops for Truddi Chase* (1987).
The veracity of this alleged memoir has been challenged by many; its author claims to have had 92 personalities, after having suffered sexual abuse at the age 2.

Curtiss, Huston (1922–). *Sins of the Seventh Sister: A Memoir of the Gothic South* (2003).
Purporting to be a memoir of his childhood in WV, this book includes claims that are difficult or impossible to verify regarding a number of violent attacks; his aunt's supposed extended affair with a senator; and other claims involving an opera star, whose identity is implied to be Stella Roman.

Damon, Bertha. *Grandma Called It Carnal* (1938).
This is an example of a self-confessed work of considerable prevarication. It humorously describes her early years being raised by her grandmother in New England.

Drannan, Captain William F. (1832–). *Thirty-one Years on the Plains and in the Mountains; or, The Last Voice from the Plains: An Authentic Record of a Life Time of Hunting, Trapping, Scouting and Indian Fighting in the Far West* (1910).
Ramon Adams disputes the factuality of much of this narrative.

Frey, James (1970?–). *A Million Little Pieces* (2003).
In 2006, police reports and other sources disputed the veracity of many claims made in this, a memoir (set in MI and OH) that had initially been endorsed by Oprah Winfrey (who later retracted her endorsement of this work). Frey has admitted embellishing his narrative with falsehoods.

Hale, Nancy (1908–1988). *A New England Girlhood* (1938).
Although some sources list this as a memoir, Hale freely admitted that, when writing this book, she fictionalized her childhood experiences in order to enhance their interest to the reader.

Haley, Alex (1921–1992). *Roots: The Saga of an American Family* (1976).
Some scholars assert that Haley blended fiction and fact in a disingenuous (or otherwise irresponsible) manner, in this best-selling volume (which was the basis of television's first "mini-series" in 1977). Also, 2 plagiarism suits were brought against him, first, by Margaret Walker Alexander, author of *Jubilee* (1966), and second by Harold Courlander, author of *The African* (1968). Alexander's charges were eventually dropped, but Haley admitted to plagiarism of at least 3 paragraphs in the Courlander suit and paid $500,000 in out-of-court settlement fees.

Johnson, Anthony Godby (1977–). *A Rock and a Hard Place: One Boy's Triumphant Story* (1993).
During the late 1990s, *New Yorker* writer Tad Friend and other literary sleuths cast doubt on the veracity of this account of sexual abuse because of its supposed author's refusal to appear in public and the similarity of Johnson's voice on the telephone to that of his supposed foster mother, Vicki Fraginals.

Knox, Cleone (1744–). Ed. by "her Kinsman Alexander Blacker Kerr." *The Diary of a Young Lady of Fashion: In the Year 1764–1765* (1926).

This was a clear fraud, written by Magdalen King-Hall.

Koolmatrie, Wanda (1949–). *My Own Sweet Time* (1994).

This was a hoax perpetrated by Leon Carmen.

Leroy, J. T. *The Heart Is Deceitful Above All Things* (2001) and *Sarah* (2000).

According to *New York Times* reporter Warren St. John, the male author of these works is actually the woman Savannah Knoop.

Menchu Tum, Rigoberta (1960?–). *I, Rigoberta Menchu* (1984).

According to a book by American anthropologist David Stoll, *Rigoberta Menchu and the Story of All Poor Guatemalans* (1999), key details presented in this purported memoir of the early life of the 1992 Nobel Peace Prize are fabrications.

Miller, Joaquin (1839–1913). Ed. by Sidney G. Firman. *Overland in a Covered Wagon: An Autobiography* (1930).

Much skepticism has been expressed regarding the authenticity of Miller's purported reminiscences here.

Modupe, Prince (1901–). *I Was a Savage* (1957).

Accusations have appeared (see 1958 *Book Review Digest*) that some of the details of the African youth culture described herein are fraudulent. Covering his first 21 years, this work tells of his early years in French West Africa, as well as his Westernized education and Christian indoctrination there.

Monroe, Marilyn (1926–1962), and Ben Hecht. *My Story* (1974).

This work was published a dozen years after her death. It was cobbled together by Ben Hecht, and is thought by some to be of dubious scholarship.

Nasdijj (1950–). *Geronimo's Bones: A Memoir of My Brother and Me* (2004).

The factuality of a number of events and circumstances described in this volume has come into question since its publication.

Whiteley, Opal Stanley (1899–). *Opal Whiteley: The Unsolved Mystery: Together with Opal Whiteley's Diary, "The Journal of an Understanding Heart"* (1962) (from writings originally published in 1920).

Believing she was a descendent of French royalty, she claimed to have written about her childhood when she was only 6.

Wilkomirski, Binjamin (1941?–). Tr. from the German by Carol Brown. *Fragments: Memories of a Wartime Childhood, 1939–1948* (1996) (Published in German by Schocken Books, 1995).

This supposed re-creation of a man who in fact became a noted Swiss classical musician has generated a storm of controversy about its veracity (see, e.g., article in October 20, 1998 issue of the *Boston Globe*).

Appendix C

Coming-of-Age Movies Based on Autobiographical or Semiautobiographical Writings: A Selective Filmography

All That Jazz: 1979 film, based on memories of youth of Bob Fosse

Almost Famous: 2000 Oscar-winning film based on memories of youth of Cameron Crowe

Amarcord: 1974 Oscar-winning film based on memories of youth of Federico Fellini. See also *Four Hundred Blows*

Angel at My Table: 1984 film based on memoir titled *To the Is-Land*, by Janet Frame

Angela's Ashes: 1999 Oscar-nominated film based on same-titled, Pulitzer Prize–winning memoir by Frank McCourt

Antwone Fisher: 2002 film based on memoir titled *Finding Fish*, by Antwone Fisher

Au Revoir, Les Enfants: 1987 film based on memories of youth of Louis Malle

Auntie Mame: 1958 Oscar-nominated film (remade as 1974 film *Mame*) based on memoir *Auntie Mame*, by Patrick Dennis

Basketball Diaries: 1995 film based on same-titled memoir by Jim Carroll

Bell Jar: 1979 film based on same-titled novel by Sylvia Plath

Biloxi Blues: 1988 film based on same-titled play by Neil Simon; preceded by *Brighton Beach Memoirs*

Brighton Beach Memoirs: 1986 film based on same-titled play by Neil Simon; followed by *Biloxi Blues*

Butterflies Are Free: 1972 Oscar-winning film based on memoir titled *To Race the Wind*, by Harold Krents

Catch Me If You Can: 2002 Oscar-nominated film based on same-titled memoir by Frank W. Abagnale Jr.

Cheaper by the Dozen: 1950 film (loosely remade in 2003) based on same-titled memoir by Frank B. Gilbreth Jr.

Childhood of Maxim Gorky: 1938 film based on same-titled memoir

Child's Christmas in Wales: 1986 film based on same-titled poem by Dylan Thomas

Christmas Story: 1983 film partly based on memoir titled *Wanda Hickey's Night of Golden Memories and Other Disasters*, by Jean Shepherd

Coal Miner's Daughter: 1980 Oscar-winning film based on same-titled memoir by Loretta Lynn

Corn Is Green: 1945 film based on memoir titled *George: An Early Autobiography*, by George Emlyn Williams

Crooklyn: 1994 film based on memories of director Spike Lee, his brother, and his sister, growing up in 1970s Brooklyn, NY

Dead Man Walking: 1995 Oscar-winning film based on memoir titled *Forgiving the Dead Man Walking*, by Debbie Morris

Europa Europa: 1990 film based on memories of Solomon Perel

Four Hundred Blows: 1959 film based on memories of Federico Fellini; followed by *Love at Twenty* (see entry). (See also *Amarcord*.)

Girl, Interrupted: 1999 Oscar-winning film based on same-titled memoir by Susanna Kaysen

Goldbergs: 1951 film (retitled *Molly*) based on memoir titled *Molly and Me*, by Gertrude Berg

Good Old Boy: A Delta Boyhood: 1988 film based on same-titled memoir by Willie Morris; see also *My Dog Skip*

Goodfellas: 1990 Oscar-winning film based on memoir titled *Wiseguy*, by Nicholas Pileggi

Grass Harp: 1996 film based on memories of Truman Capote

Guide to Recognizing Your Saints: 2006 film based on same-titled memoir by Dito Montiel

Haywire: 1980 Emmy-nominated television film based on same-titled memoir by Brooke Hayward

Heavenly Creatures: 1994 film based on diaries of Pauline Parker

Horse of Pride: 1980 film based on memoir titled *Horse of Pride: Life in a Breton Village*, by Pierre-Jakez Helias

How Green Was My Valley: 1941 Oscar-winning film based on same-titled memoir by Richard Llewellyn

Hurricane: 1999 Oscar-nominated film based on memoir titled *Sixteenth Round . . .*, by Rubin "Hurricane" Carter

I Know Why the Caged Bird Sings: 1979 television film based on same-titled memoir by Maya Angelou

I Never Promised You a Rose Garden: 1977 film based on same-titled memoir by Hannah Green

I Remember Mama: 1948 Oscar-nominated film based on memoir titled *Mama's Bank Account*, by Kathryn Forbes

If You Could See What I Hear: 1982 film based on same-titled memoir by Tom Sullivan

King of the Hill: 1993 film based on same-titled memoir by A(aron) E(dward) Hotchner

Lady Sings the Blues: 1972 Oscar-nominated film based on same-titled memoir by Billie Holiday

Lakota Woman: Siege at Wounded Knee: 1994 television film based on memoir titled *Lakota Woman*, by Mary Crow Dog

Learning Tree: 1969 film based on same-titled novel by Gordon Parks

Life with Father: 1947 Oscar-nominated film based on same-titled memoir by Clarence Day

Lost in Yonkers: 1993 film based on same-titled play by Neil Simon

Love at Twenty: 1962 film based on memories of Federico Fellini; preceded by *Four Hundred Blows* (see entry). (See also *Amarcord*.)

Molly. See *Goldbergs*

Mommie Dearest: 1981 film based on same-titled memoir by Christina Crawford

My Childhood: 1938 film based on same-titled memoir by Maxim Gorky

My Dog Skip: 2000 film based on same-titled memoir by Willie Morris; see also *Good Old Boy: A Delta Boyhood*

My Father's Glory: 1990 film (followed by 1990 film *My Mother's Castle*) based on memoir titled *The Days Were Too Short* (rpt. as *My Father's Glory and My Mother's Castle*), by Marcel Pagnol

My Left Foot: 1989 Oscar-winning film based on same-titled memoir by Christy Brown

My Life as a Dog: 1985 Oscar-nominated 1985 film based on same-titled memoir by Reidar Jonsson

My Life So Far: 1999 film based on same-titled memoir by Denis Forman

My Mother's Castle. See *My Father's Glory*

Nowhere in Africa: 2001 Oscar-winning 2001 film based on same-titled novel by Stefanie Zweig

October Sky: 1999 film based on same-titled memoir by Homer H. Hickam Jr.

Once Upon a Time When We Were Colored: 1996 film based on same-titled memoir by Clifton Taulbert

Our Hearts Were Young and Gay: 1944 film based on same-titled memoir by Cornelia Otis Skinner

Padre Padrone: 1977 film based on same-titled memoir by Gavino Ledda

Paradise Road: 1997 film based on memoir titled *Song of Survival: Women Interned*, by Helen Colijn

Persepolis: 2007 award-winning film, based on same-titled memoir by Marjane Satrapi

Prize Winner of Defiance, Ohio: 2005 film based on same-titled memoir by Terry Ryan

Prozac Nation: 2004 straight-to-video film based on same-titled memoir by Elizabeth Wurzel

Radio Days: 1987 film based on memories of Woody Allen

Rascal: 1969 film based on same-titled memoir by Sterling North

Riding in Cars with Boys: 2001 film based on same-titled novel by Beverly D'Onofrio

A River Runs Through It: 1992 film based on Norman MacLean's same-titled autobiographical novel

Running with Scissors: 2006 film based on same-titled book by Augusten Burroughs

Sleepers: 1996 Oscar-nominated 1996 film based on same-titled purported memoir by Lorenzo Carcaterra

Strawberry Statement: 1970 film based on same-titled journal by James Simon Kunen

Swimming to Cambodia: 1987 film based on same-titled short memoir by Spalding Gray

This Boy's Life: 1993 film based on same-titled memoir by Tobias Wolff

A Tree Grows in Brooklyn: 1945 Oscar-winning film based on same-titled novel by Betty Smith

Unstrung Heroes: 1995 Oscar-nominated film based on same-titled memoir by Franz Lidz

Appendix D

Resources

Adams, Timothy Dow. *Telling Lies in Modern American Autobiography* (University of North Carolina, 1990).

Adamson, Lynda G. *Notable Women in American History: A Guide to Recommended Biographies and Autobiographies* (Greenwood, 1999).

Andrews, William L. *Classic American Autobiographies* (Penguin USA, 1992).

Arch, Stephen Carl. *After Franklin: The Emergence of Autobiography in Post-Revolutionary America, 1780–1830* (University Press of New England, 2001).

Augenbraum, Harold, and Margarite F. Olmos, eds. *The Latino Reader: An American Literary Tradition from 1542 to the Present* (Houghton Mifflin, 1997).

Barman, Jean. *Growing Up British in British Columbia: Boys in Private School* (University of British Columbia, 1984). See bibliography (pp. 223–244).

Barrington, Judith. *Writing the Memoir: From Truth to Art* (Eighth Mountain, 1997).

Barros, Carolyn A., and Johanna M. Smith, eds. *Life-writings by British Women, 1660–1815: An Anthology* (Northeastern University, 2000).

Bates, E. Stuart. *Inside Out: An Introduction to Autobiography* (Sheridan House, 1937). See especially "Index to Recollections of Childhood," pp. 715–716.

Baum, Willa K., and David K. Dunaway, eds. *Oral History: An Interdisciplinary Anthology* 2nd ed. (American Association for State and Local History, 1996).

Baur, John. *Growing Up with California: A History of California's Children* (Kramer, 1978).

Baxter, Charles, ed. *The Business of Memory: The Art of Remembering in an Age of Forgetting* (Consortium Book Sales, 1999).

Bel Geddes, Joan. *Childhood and Children: A Compendium of Customs, Superstitions, Theories, Profiles, and Facts* (Oryx, 1997).

Bell, Susan Groag, and Marilyn Yalom, eds. *Revealing Lives: Autobiography, Biography, and Gender* (State University of New York, 1990).

Bjorklund, Diane. *Interpreting the Self: Two Hundred Years of American Autobiography* (University of Chicago, 1998).

Bontemps, Arna, sel. *Great Slave Narratives* (Beacon, 1969).

351

Bowen, Catherine Drinker. *Adventures of a Biographer* (Little, Brown, 1958).

————. *Biography: The Craft and the Calling* (Little, Brown, 1968).

Bowen, Elizabeth. *The Mulberry Tree: Writings of Elizabeth Bowen* (Virago, 1986). See the eponymous essay on pp. 13–21.

Boyd, Herb, ed. *Autobiography of a People: Three Centuries of African American History Told by Those Who Lived It* (Doubleday, 2000).

Breines, Wini. *Young, White, and Miserable: Growing Up Female in the Fifties* (Beacon, 1992).

Brett, Simon, ed. *The Faber Book of Diaries* (Faber & Faber, 1987).

Brian, Denis. *What Biographers Don't Tell You* (Prometheus Books, 1994).

Brignano, Russell C. *Black Americans in Autobiography: An Annotated Bibliography of Autobiographies and Autobiographical Books Written Since the Civil War.* rev. and expanded ed. (Duke University, 1984).

Briscoe, Mary Louise, et al., eds. *American Autobiography, 1945–1980: A Bibliography* (University of Wisconsin, 1982).

Brown, Carrie. *Rosie's Mom: Forgotten Women Workers of the First World War* (Northeastern University, 2002).

Brumble, H. David, III. *Annotated Bibliography of American Indian and Eskimo Autobiographies* (University of Nebraska, 1981).

Busch, Akiko. *Geography of Home: Writings About Where We Live* (Princeton Architectural, 1999).

Buss, Helen M. *Mapping Our Selves: Canadian Women's Autobiography* (McGill-Queen's University, 1993).

Calvert, Karin. *Children in the House: The Material Culture of Early Childhood, 1600–1900* (Northeastern University, 1992).

Clement, Priscilla Ferguson. *Growing Pains: Children in the Industrial Age, 1850–1890* (Twayne, 1997).

Clifford, James L. *From Puzzles to Portraits: Problems of a Literary Biographer* (University of North Carolina, 1970).

Cline, Cheryl. *Women's Diaries, Journals, and Letters: An Annotated Bibliography* (Garland, 1989).

Clyman, Toby W., and Judith Vowles. *Russia Through Women's Eyes: Autobiographies from Tsarist Russia* (Yale University, 1996).

Cobb, Edith. *The Ecology of Imagination in Childhood* (Columbia University, 1977). Introduction by Margaret Mead.

Coe, Richard N. *When the Grass Was Taller: Autobiography and the Experience of Childhood* (Yale University, 1984).

Conway, Jill Ker. *When Memory Speaks: Reflections on Autobiography* (Knopf, 1998).

Cooley, Thomas. *Educated Lives: The Rise of Modern Autobiography in America* (Ohio State University, 1976).

Cox, Joseph T. *The Written Wars: American War Prose Through the Civil War* (Archon Books, 1996).

Culley, Margo, ed. *American Women's Autobiography: Fea(s)ts of Memory* (University of Wisconsin, 1992).

———. *A Day at a Time: The Diary Literature of American Women from 1764 to the Present* (Feminist Press at the City University of New York, 1985).

Derounian-Stodola, Kathryn Zabelle, and James Arthur Levernier. *The Indian Captivity Narrative, 1550–1900* (Twayne, 1993).

Diner, Hasia R. *Lower East Side Memories: A Jewish Place in America* (Princeton University, 2000).

Eakin, John Paul. *American Autobiography: Retrospect and Prospect* (University of Wisconsin, 1991).

———, ed. *Fictions in Autobiography: Studies in the Art of Self-Invention* (Princeton University, 1985).

Edel, Leon. *Writing Lives: Principia Biographica* (W.W. Norton, 1984). This is a reworking and expansion of Edel's *Literary Biography* (Indiana University, 1959).

Eisen, George. *Children and Play in the Holocaust* (University of Massachusetts, 1988).

Engel, Susan. *Context Is Everything: The Nature of Memory* (W.H. Freeman, 1999).

Eskin, Blake. *A Life in Pieces: The Making and Unmaking of Binjamin Wilkomirski* (W.W. Norton, 2002).

Evasdaughter, Elizabeth N. *Catholic Girlhood Narratives: The Church and Self-Denial* (Northeastern University, 1996).

Finney, Brian. *The Inner I: British Literary Autobiography of the Twentieth Century* (Oxford University, 1985).

Folkenflik, Robert, ed. *The Culture of Autobiography: Constructions of Self-Representation* (Stanford University, 1993).

Forman-Brunell, Miriam, ed. *Girlhood in America: An Encyclopedia.* 2 vols. (ABC-CLIO, 2001). See particularly "Mill Girls" entry (pp. 451–457) and "Coming-of-Age Narratives" section (pp. 411–413) of "Latina Girls" entry.

Freedman, Russell. *Children of the Wild West* (Clarion Books, 1983).

Galbraith, Gretchen R. *Reading Lives: Reconstructing Childhood, Books, and Schools in Britain, 1870–1920* (St. Martin's, 1997). See especially pp. 25–37, 170–172.

Garis, Robert. *Writing About Oneself: Selected Writing* (Heath, 1965).

Gates, Henry Louis, Jr., ed. *Bearing Witness: Selections from African-American Autobiography in the Twentieth Century* (Pantheon Books, 1990).

Goertzel, Victor, and Mildred G. Goertzel. *Cradles of Eminence* (Little, Brown, 1962).

Good, Howard. *The Journalist as Autobiographer* (Scarecrow, 1993).

Graff, Harvey J., ed. *Growing Up in America: Historical Experiences* (Wayne State, 1987).

Grubgeld, Elizabeth. *Anglo-Irish Autobiography: Class, Gender, and the Forms of Narrative* (Syracuse University, 2004).

Hampl, Patricia. *I Could Tell You Stories: Sojourns in the Land of Memory* (W.W. Norton, 1999).

Hannabuss, Stuart, Rita Marcella, et al. *Biography and Children: A Study of Biography for Children and Childhood in Biography* (Library Association Publications, 1993).

Harjo, Joy, and Gloria Bird, eds. *Reinventing the Enemy's Language: North American Native Women's Writing* (W.W. Norton, 1997).

Hoff, Benjamin. *The Singing Creek Where the Willows Grow: The Mystical Nature Diary of Opal Whiteley* (Ticknor & Fields, 1986).

Holmes, Richard. *Footsteps: Adventures of a Romantic Biographer* (Viking, 1985).

Holroyd, Michael. *Works on Paper: The Craft of Biography and Autobiography Writing* (Counterpoint, 2002).

Hooton, Joy. *Stories of Herself When Young: Autobiographies of Childhood by Australian Women* (Oxford University, 1990).

Hynes, Samuel. *The Soldiers' Tale: Bearing Witness to Modern War* (Viking, 1997).

Jacobson, Marcia Ann. *Being a Boy Again; Autobiography and the American Boy Book* (University of Alabama, 1994).

Jampolsky, Gerald G. M. D., and Lee L. Jampolsky. *Listen to Me: A Book for Men and Women About Fathers and Sons* (Celestial Arts, 1996).

Johnson, Alexandra. *The Hidden Writer: Diaries and the Creative Life* (Doubleday, 1997).

Jolly, Margaretta, ed. *Encyclopedia of Life Writing: Autobiographical and Biographical Forms.* 2 vols. (Fitzroy Dearborn, 2001).

Kaplan, Louis, comp. *Bibliography of American Autobiographies* (University of Wisconsin, 1961).

Kater, Michael H. *Hitler Youth* (Harvard University, 2004).

Kearns, Kevin C. *Dublin Pub Life and Lore: An Oral History* (Gill & Macmillan, 1996).

———. *Dublin Street Life and Lore: An Oral History* (Dun Laoghaire, 1991).

———. *Dublin Tenement Life: An Oral History* (Gill & Macmillan, 1994).

Kestenberg, Judith S., and Ira Brenner. *The Last Witness: The Child Survivors of the Holocaust* (American Psychiatric Press, 1996).

Kett, Joseph F. *Rites of Passage: Adolescence in America 1790 to the Present* (Basic Books, 1977).

King, Wilma. *Stolen Childhood: Slave Youth in Nineteenth-Century America* (Indiana University, 1995).

Krupat, Arnold, ed. *Native American Autobiography: An Anthology* (University of Wisconsin, 1994).

Lappin, Elena, ed. *Jewish Voices, German Words: Growing Up Jewish in Postwar Germany and Austria* (Catbird, 1994).

Lejeune, Philippe, and John Paul Eakin. *On Autobiography* (University of Minnesota, 1988).

Leonard, Elizabeth. *All the Daring of the Soldier: Women of the Civil War Armies* (W.W. Norton, 1999). Details the lives of such individuals as Maria Isabella ("Belle") Boyd, Antonia Ford, and Virginia Moon.

Levi, Giovanni, and Jean-Claude Schmitt, eds. *A History of Young People in the West. Volume 1: Ancient and Medieval Rites of Passage.* Translated by Camille Naish (Harvard University, 1997).

———. *A History of Young People in the West. Volume 2: Stormy Evolution to Modern Times.* Translated by Carol Volk. (Harvard University, 1997).

Lifschutz, E., comp. *Bibliography of American and Canadian Jewish Memoirs and Autobiographies in Yiddish, Hebrew and English* (Yivo Institute for Jewish Research, 1970).

Lochhead, Marion Cleland. *Their First Ten Years: Victorian Childhood* (John Murray, 1956).

Lukas, Richard C. *Did the Children Cry?: Hitler's War Against Jewish and Polish Children, 1939–1945* (Hippocrene, 1994).

MacLeod, Anne Scott. *American Childhood: Essays on Children's Literature of the Nineteenth and Twentieth Centuries* (University of Georgia, 1994). See especially pp. 5, 6, 9, 100, 101.

Madigan, Carol Orsag, and Ann Elwood. *When They Were Kids: Over 400 Sketches of Famous Childhoods* (Random House, 1998).

Matthews, William, comp., with the assistance of Roy Harvey Pearce. *American Diaries: An Annotated Bibliography of American Diaries Written Prior to the Year 1861* (J.S. Canner, 1959).

May, Henry F. *The End of American Innocence: A Study of the First Years of Our Own Time, 1912–1917* (Knopf, 1964).

Miller, Alice. *Prisoners of Childhood.* Translated by Ruth Ward (Basic Books, 1981).

Miller, Russell. *Behind the Lines: The Oral History of Special Operations in World War II* (St. Martin's, 2002).

Mintz, Alan. *"Banished from Their Father's Table": Loss of Faith in Hebrew Autobiography* (Indiana University, 1989).

Mintz, Steven. *Huck's Raft: A History of American Childhood* (Belknap Press, 2004).

Moran, William. *The Belles of New England: The Women of the Textile Mills and the Families Whose Wealth They Wove* (Thomas Dunne/St. Martin's, 2002).

Moynihan, Ruth B., et al. *So Much to Be Done: Women Settlers on the Mining and Ranching Frontier.* 2nd ed. (University of Nebraska, 1998).

Nelson, Emmanuel S., ed. *African American Autobiographers: A Sourcebook* (Greenwood, 2002).

Neuman, Shirley, ed. *Autobiography and Questions of Gender* (F. Cass, 1991).

Olney, James. *Memory & Narrative: The Weave of Life-Writing* (University of Chicago, 1999).

Osherson, Samuel. *Finding Our Fathers: The Unfinished Business of Manhood* (Free Press, 1986).

Padilla, Genaro M. *My History, Not Yours: The Formation of Mexican American Autobiography* (University of Wisconsin, 1993).

Parini, Jay. *The Norton Book of American Autobiography* (W.W. Norton, 1999). Writings of 62 memoirists are included.

Pascal, Roy. *Design and Truth in Autobiography* (Harvard University, 1960).

Patterson, David. *Along the Edge of Annihilation: The Collapse and Recovery of Life in the Holocaust Diary* (University of Washington, 1999).

Patterson, Robert, Mildred Mebel, and Lawrence Hill, sels. *On Our Way: Young Pages from American Autobiography* (Holiday House, 1952).

Ponsonby, Arthur. *English Diaries: A Review of English Diaries from the Sixteenth to the Twentieth Century* (Methuen, 1923).

Pugh, Deborah, and Jeanie Tietjen. *"I Have Arrived Before My Words": The Autobiographical Writings of Homeless Women* (Charles River Press, 1997).

Raphael, Ray. *The Men from the Boys: Rites of Passage in Male America* (University of Nebraska, 1988).

Reid, B(enjamin). L(awrence). *Necessary Lives: Biographical Reflections* (University of Missouri, 1990).

Rhodes, Carolyn H., ed. *First Person Female American: A Selected and Annotated Bibliography of the Autobiographies of American Women Living After 1950* (Whitston, 1980).

Rideing, W. H. *The Boyhood of Living Authors* (Crowell, 1887).

Robinson, Paul. *Gay Lives: Homosexual Autobiography from John Addington Symonds to Paul Monette* (University of Chicago, 1999).

Rose, Lionel. *The Erosion of Childhood: Childhood Oppression in Britain, 1860–1918* (Routledge, 1991).

Rose, Phyllis, ed. *The Norton Book of Women's Lives* (W.W. Norton, 1993).

Sayre, Robert F., ed. *American Lives: An Anthology of Autobiographical Writing* (University of Wisconsin, 1994).

Schwartz, Marie Jenkins. *Born in Bondage: Growing Up Enslaved in the Antebellum South* (Harvard University, 2000).

Schwarz, Daniel R. *Imagining the Holocaust* (St. Martin's, 1999). Includes a section on memoirs.

Sinyard, Neil. *Children in the Movies* (St. Martin's, 1992). See the chapter "Artistry and Autobiography."

Slide, Anthony. *Silent Players: A Biographical and Autobiographical Study of 100 Silent Film Actors and Actresses* (University Press of Kentucky, 2002).

Smith, Allen. *Directory of Oral History Collections* (Oryx, 1988).

Stearns, Peter N. *Be a Man! Males in Modern Society* (Holmes & Meier, 1990).

Stuhr-Rommereim, Rebecca. *Autobiographies by Americans of Color, 1980–1994: An Annotated Bibliography* (Whitston, 1997).

Sturrock, John. *The Language of Autobiography* (Cambridge University, 1993).

Suleiman, Susan Rubin. *Crises of Memory and the Second World War* (Harvard University, 2006).

Sweeney, Patricia E. *Biographies of British Women: An Annotated Bibliography* (ABC-CLIO, 1993).

Trowbridge, J. T. "The American Boy." *North American Review* (February 1889): 217–225.

Tuska, Jon, and Vicki Piekarski. *The Frontier Experience: A Reader's Guide to the Life and Literature of the American West* (McFarland, 1984).

Valent, Paul. *Child Survivors of the Holocaust* (Brunner-Routledge, 2002).

Wachtel, Andrew. *The Battle for Childhood: Creation of a Russian Myth* (Stanford University, 1990).

Wachtel, Andrew. "The Russian Pseudo-autobiography and the Creation of Russian Childhood." Ph.D. thesis, University of CA Berkeley, 1987.

Ward, Colin. *The Child in the City* (Pantheon Books, 1978).

Watkins, James H., ed. *Southern Selves: From Mark Twain and Eudora Welty to Maya Angelou and Kaye Gibbons* (Random House/Vintage, 1998).

West, Elliott. *Growing Up with the Country: Childhood on the Far-Western Frontier* (University of New Mexico, 1989).

West, Elliott, and Paula Petrik, eds. *Small Worlds: Children and Adolescents in America, 1850–1950* (University Press of Kansas, 1992).

Wiedmer, Caroline. *The Claims of Memory: Representations of the Holocaust in Contemporary Germany and France* (Cornell University, 1999).

Wishy, Bernard. *The Child and the Republic: The Dawn of Modern American Child Nurture* (University of Pennsylvania, 1968).

Zall, P. M. *Becoming American: Young People in the American Revolution* (Linnet Books, 1993).

Zanjani, Sally. *A Mine of Her Own: Women Prospectors in the American West, 1850–1950* (University of Nebraska, 1997).

Subject Index

The entries in this index focus principally on ethnic identity; vocation; avocation; intellectual, spiritual, and sexual orientations; and physical and emotional infirmities. Unless otherwise noted, avocational subject entries apply to the memoirist rather than to a parent of the memoirist. (However, unless otherwise noted, the term "Clergy" has been assigned to memoirs that focus on an author's experiences as the son or daughter of a member of the clergy.)

Place-names, which are provided for nearly all main entries, are not included here, with the exception of such specific and general locales as "Eton College," "Auschwitz," "High School Life," "Worldwide Travel," and "Homes and Haunts." Consult the Settings Index for further geographical access to the memoirs.

Certain terms (e.g., "Christianity," "Elementary Schools," "Emotional Abuse," "Employment," "Friendship," "Hobbies," "Love," "Poverty," and "Rock'n'Roll") are not included in this index because they refer to rites of passage and other life experiences that pervade nearly all the memoirs listed in this work. However, selective memoirs incorporating these elements as significant themes may be found by turning to such terms as "Spiritual Life," "School Life," "Abuse," "Slums," or "Musicians."

Other widely encompassing subject categories, such as "Businesspersons," "Country Life," "Critics (Social)," "Fathers and Sons," "Grandparents," "Intellectual Life," and "Pregnancy (Teen)," are included here and refer the user to a representative cross-section of relevant memoirs.

It should be noted that, despite being included in the category "Holocaust Survivors," a (small) number of titles in that category are by persons who did not survive the Holocaust (e.g., David Sierakowiak); their writings typically include references to persons who did survive the Nazi horror. Also, some of the memoirists listed under "Holocaust Survivors" in fact died during the Holocaust.

The category "Africans" differs from "African Americans" in that the former designates persons of African ethnicity whose formative years were not spent in the U.S. (or the colonies that preceded the formation of the country). The memoirs under the entry "Seafaring Life" differ from those under "Voyages" in that they do not necessarily contain accounts of lengthy excursions on an ocean or sea. The entry "Suicide Victims" refers to relatives and other loved ones depicted in memoirs as affected by the suicidal behavior or thoughts of the memoirist or other individual significant to the memoir.

A numeral following a name entry indicates that multiple coming-of-age memoirs by that author are included in this work, with each memoir bearing on the associated subject. (Typical subjects include such intrinsic or deeply rooted elements of personal identity as racial or ethnic identity; intellectual proclivities or aptitudes; vocational bents; medical conditions; and state of mind due to effects of abuse [physical, emotional, sexual, psychiatric]—the roots of which are commonly traceable to a person's birth or early youth, and which subsequently continue to resonate throughout one's adult years.) Within this index, a question mark enclosed in parentheses (?) indicates that the accuracy of the term preceding it is unconfirmed.

Persons whose most notable acting has occurred not in films (i.e., on stage, radio, or television) are indexed under "Actors" or "Actresses"; those whose most notable acting has occurred in films are indexed under "Motion Picture Actors and Actresses." Although cross-referencing between thematically related entries is abundant, to conserve space, it usually has not been used with related entries that are close to each other in the alphabetical listing.

Critics (Social). Benjamin, Walter; Broun, Heywood Hale; hooks, bell (2); Ruskin, John. *See also* **Historians (Cultural); Intellectual Life; Philosophers; Reformers**

Critics (Television). James, Clive

Critics (Theater). Hamilton, Iain; Rich, Frank; Young, Stark

Crowley, Aleister. Calder-Marshall, Arthur. *See also* **Occult**

Cuban Americans. Anders, Gigi; Bejel, Emilio; Fernandez Barrios, Flor; Suarez, Vergil. *See also* **Hispanic Americans; Mexican Americans; Racially Mixed Children**

Cults. Atkins, Susan; Hearst, Patricia; Noyes, Pierrepont; Ross, Marie. *See also* **Counterculture Childhoods; Hippies; Religious Persons; Revolutionaries**

Cultural Revolution (China). *See* **China's Cultural Revolution (1966–1977)**

Curators. Chamson, André (2). *See also* **Librarians**

Cycling. Miller, Christian; Murphy, Dervla. *See also* **Country Life; Outdoor Recreation**

Dalits. Jadhav, Narendra. *See also* **Indian Americans**

Dancers. De Mille, Agnes (2); Dunham, Katherine; Enters, Angna; Farrell, Suzanne; Karsavina, Tamara; Kent, Allegra; Kirkland, Gelsey; Kirstein, Lincoln; Li Cunxin; Rainer, Yvonne; Sayer, Mandy; Tallchief, Maria; Tharp, Twyla. *See also* **Anorexia Nervosa/Bulimia; Ballet Directors; Burlesque; Choreographers; Critics (Dance); Entertainers; Models; Singers; Theater**

Danesi, Natalia. Murray, William. *See also* **Actresses; Singers**

Danish Americans. Favrholdt, Visti. *See also* **Racially Mixed Children**

Darwin, Charles. Raverat, Gwen

Davis, Bette. Hyman, B(ette) D(avis). *See also* **Family Violence; Motion Picture Actors and Actresses**

Davis, Sammy, Jr. Davis, Tracey. *See also* **Entertainers**

Deafness. Abrams, Charlotte; Carstens, Grace; Davis, Lennard; Golan, Lew; Heppner, Cheryl M.; Keller, Helen; Kisor, Henry; Laborit, Emmanuelle; Martineau, Harriet; Miller, R(obert) H(enry); Sidransky, Ruth; Walker, Lou Ann; Whitestone, Heather; Wright, David

Death. *See* **Bereavement; Cancer; Drowning Victims; Fratricide; Matricide; Murder; Paralysis; Right to Die; Suicide and Suicide Victims**

Debutantes. Astor, Brooke; Frothingham, Eugenia; Hale, Nancy; Loelia, Duchess of Westminster. *See also* **High Society**

Decorative Arts. Langseth-Christensen, Lillian; Marokvia, Mireille. *See also* **Fashion Designers; Needlepoint**

Dentists. Delaney, Sarah; Nguyen, Kien. *See also* **Physicians**

Depressions (Clinical). *See* **Manic-Depression; Mental Health**

Depressions (Economic). Abrams, Charlotte; Arnett, Marvin V.; Belvin, Ed; Bennett, Kay; Bumpers, Dale; Burton, Ben; Canfield, Patrick; Carter, Jimmy; Cleary, Beverly; Craft, Phil; Craig, John; Foote, Horton; Forrester, Helen (4); Gallant, John; Giscard, John; Glasser, Ralph; Hall, Floriana; Gutkin, Harry and Mildred; Hall, Donald; Hall, Floriana; Hanners, LaVerne; Hastings, Robert J. (2); Hillerman, Tony; Heren, Louis (2); Hofvendahl, Russ; Holden, Adele V.; Hotchner, A(aron) E(dward); Humphrey, William; Hynes, Samuel Lynn; Jones, G(reen) C.; Kemp, James Malcolm; Kirkup, James (2); Kloefkorn, William (3); Lagomarcino, Virgil; Lewis, Stephen; Love, Edmund G.; McCourt, Frank; Mathias, Frank F(urlong); McKuen, Rod; Metz, Myrtle; Moskowitz, Faye (2); Murray, Nina Chandler; Myrdal, Jan (3); Noble, Christina; Norling, Donna Scott; Nuland, Sherwin B.; Peters, Robert; Petrakis, Harry; Pifer, Drury; Porterfield, Bill; Previn, Dory; Reid, B(enjamin) L(awrence); Roberts, Robert; Rutland, Robert; Sandberg, Sara; Schroeder, Walter; Scully, Julia; Sheklow, Edna; Shrout, Bill; Smoot, Ken(neth) Eugene; Solotaroff, Ted; Sonnenfeld, Kelly; Start, Clarissa; Talese, Gay; Thomas, Gwyn; Weil, Dorothy; Whitt, Anne Hall; Wilson, Rex L. *See also* **Dust Bowl; Growing Up Between WWI and WWII; Homeless Children; Prohibition; Slums**

Depressions (Mental). Harris, E. Lynn; Nuland, Sherwin B.; Summer, Lauralee. *See also* **Mental Health; Suicide and Suicide Victims**

Desert Life. Slaughter, Carolyn. *See also* **Jungle Life**

Designers (Costume). Beaton, Cecil; Enters, Angna. *See also* **Theater**

Designers (Set). Beaton, Cecil; Bemelmans, Ludwig. *See also* **Theater**

Diabetes. Dominick, Andie; Roney, Lisa

Diaries and Journals. Allan, Sheila; Anonymous (2 authors); Bashkirtseff, Marie; Bassett,

Editors (*Cont.*)
Mumford, Lewis; Murray, William; Nesbit; Edith; O'Connor, Philip; Patai, Joseph; Peterkiewicz, Jerzy; Phillips, Margaret Mann; Sangster, Margaret; Sender, Ramon (Jose); Sobol, Louis; Solotaroff, Ted; Staples, Brent; Steffens, (Joseph) Lincoln; Streatfeild, Noel; Sullivan, Mark; Surmelian, Leon; Tait, Katharine; Thomas, Lowell; Van Doren, Carl; Van Wyck, Chris; Wagenknecht, Edward; Wakefield, Dan; Warner, Charles Dudley; Warren, Robert Penn; Watkins, Mel; Weeks, Edward; White, Claire Nicolas; White, William Allen; Wilsey, Jean; Windham, Kathryn Tucker; Winfrey, Carey; Winterich, John Tracy; Wolff, Tobias; Woodcock, George. *See also* **Fashion Editors; Journalists; Publishers**

Education. Bennahum, David S.; Burton, Warren; Buscaglia, Leo; Canby, Henry Seidel; Cary, Lorene; Chamoiseau, Patrick; Cole, Margaret; Fitzgerald, Robert; Gonzalez, Ray; Jeune, Margaret; Keller, Helen; Kingdon, Frank; Love, Edmund G. (2); MacCracken, Henry; Mehta, Ved (3); Miller, Hugh; Neill, A(lexander) S(utherland); Raphael, Frederic; Richmond, (Sir) Arthur; Rodriguez, Richard; Tagore, (Sir) Rabindranath (2); Webb, Ruth Cameron; Wiggin, Kate Douglas; Windom, Jane Hutcheson. *See also* **Amherst College; Bates College; Books and Reading; Boston University; Bryn Mawr; Cambridge University; Choate School; Clemson University; College Life; College Teachers; Columbia College; Columbia University; Cornell University; Eton College; Exeter Academy; Guidance Counselors; Harrow; Harvard University; High School Life; Home Schooling; Illiteracy; Intellectual Life; King's College; Knox College; Lafayette College; Lawrenceville Academy; Learning Disabled Youth; Lecturers; Librarians; Millbrook School; Oxford University; Phillips-Exeter Academy; Philosophers; Pomona College; Princeton University; School Integration; School Superintendents; St. John's Military Academy; Shanghai American School; Stanford University; Syracuse University; Teachers; University of Florida; University of Virginia; University of Wisconsin; Vassar College; Wellesley College; Westminster School; Yale University**

Educators. *See* **Books and Reading; College Presidents; Civil Rights Workers; College Teachers; Intellectual Life; Librarians; School Superintendents; Teachers**

Eighteenth-Century Memoirists (1695-1789 Births). Bamford, Samuel; Bewick, Thomas; Bowne, Eliza Southgate; Burney, Frances; Casanova, Giacomo; Cowles, Julia; De Mist, Augusta; De Quincey, Thomas; Drake, Daniel; Farnham, Eliza; Gilman, Caroline; Goethe, Johann Wolfgang von; Greenman, Jeremiah; Johnston, Charles; Kelly, Michael; Knox, Cleone; Martin, Joseph Plumb; Shaw, Robert; Sherburne, Andrew; Sibbald, Susan; Smith, James; Tanner, John; Walter, Jakob; Winslow, Anna Green; Wister, Sarah (Sally); Wynne, Elizabeth. *See also* **Frontier and Pioneer Life**

Eisenhower, Dwight D. Eisenhower, Dwight D.; Eisenhower, Edgar. *See also* **Presidents, U.S.**

Electricians. Razor, Peter

Elephants. Poole, Joyce

Emigrants. *See* **Immigrants**

Engineers (Aeronautical). Hickam, Homer

Engineers (Civil). Beard, Daniel Carter; Mallonee, Richard C(arvel); Manea, Norman; Mezlekia, Nega; Petroski, Henry. *See also* **Builders; Cartographers; Surveyors**

Engravers (Wood). Bewick, Thomas; Raverat, Gwen

Entertainers. Lady Chablis; Lords, Traci; Previn, Dory; Rose Marie; Somers, Suzanne; Wilsey, Jean. *See also* **Actors; Actresses; Burke, Billie; Comedians; Dancers; Davis, Sammy, Jr.; Disc Jockeys; Mime Artists; Motion Picture Actors and Actresses; Musicians; Pantomine; Singers; Theater; Vaudevillians; Ziegfeld, Florenz**

Entertainment Industry. Weller, Sheila. *See also* **Crime; Motion Picture Actors and Actresses; Motion Picture Producers and Directors; Movies; Resorts**

Environmentally Induced Diseases. Antonetta, Susanne. *See also* **Cancer; Natural History; Toxic Waste Sites**

Episcopalians. Canby, Henry Seidel (2); Carter, John Franklin; Dana, Nathalie. *See also* **Clergy; Religious Persons; Spiritual Life**

Eskimos. Chisholm, Colin; Pinson, Elizabeth Bernhardt. *See also* **Inuits; Native Americans**

Essayists. Alvarez, A(lfred); Alvarez, Julia; Baring, Maurice; Beard, Jo Ann; Birkerts, Sven; Blunt, Judy; Boll, Heinrich; Brookes, Tim; Buckley, Christopher; Buechner, Frederick; Burroughs, John; Canby, Henry

Seidel (2); Carr, Emily; Chamson, André (2); Church, Richard (2); Cloete, Stuart; Coffin, Robert; Dahlberg, Edward; Dall, Caroline; Dawson, Fielding; De Quincey, Thomas; Dillard, Annie; Doolittle, Hilda; Elliott, George P(aul); Feig, Paul (2); Fries, Kenny; Gide, Andre; Ginzburg, Natalia; Green, Julian (4); Grierson, Francis; Hale, Janet Campbell; Hall, Donald; Harris, Trudier; Hawthorne, Julian; Higgins, George V.; Jordan, June; Karr, Mary (2); Kato, Shuichi; Kipling, Rudyard; Leonard, Hugh (2); Lewis, Mindy; Lindbergh, Anne Morrow; Lopate, Phillip; Manea, Norman; Mann, Klaus; Masefield, John (4); Medina, Pablo; Mehta, Ved (7); Morris, Wright; Moskowitz, Faye (2); Mphahlele, Ezekiel; Myrdal, Jan (3); Nabokov, Vladimir; Narayan, R(asipuram) K(rishnaswami); Njeri, Itabari; Ortiz Cofer, Judith; Perera, Victor; Peterkiewicz, Jerzy; Price, Reynolds; Priestley, J(oseph) B(oynton); Quennell, (Sir) Peter; Quiller-Couch, (Sir) Arthur; Raphael, Frederic; Raymond, Ernest; Reese, Lizette Woodworth; Rexroth, Kenneth; Richler, Mordecai; Rodriguez, Richard; Sangster, Margaret; Saroyan, William (2); Sarraute, Nathalie; Schumann, Willy; Sedaris, David (2); Sedgwick, Henry Dwight; Selzer, Richard; Servid, Carolyn; Sheed, Wilfrid; Sitwell, (Sir) Osbert (2); Sperber, Manes (2); Sperry, Willard; Spragg, Mark; Stuart, Jesse (2); Suckow, Ruth; Sutin, Lawrence; Tolstoy, (Count) Leo; Twain, Mark (2); Van Druten, John; Vidal, Gore; Warner, Charles Dudley; Warren, Robert Penn; Waugh, Evelyn; Wells, H(erbert) G(eorge); Welty, Eudora; West, Paul; Williamson, Henry (2); Wolff, Geoffrey; Woodcock, George; Woolf, Leonard S.; Woolf, Virginia; Young, Stark. *See also* **Humorists**

Ethnicities. *See* **Racially Mixed Children**

Ethnologists. Hall, Edward T(witchell), Jr.; Van Den Berghe, Pierre. *See also* **Anthropologists; Archaeologists; Paleontologists; Sociologists**

Etiquette. Van de Water, Virginia Terhune. *See also* **Home Economics**

Eton College. Baring, Maurice; Brinsley-Richards, James; Connolly, Cyril; Green, Henry; James, M(ontague) R(hodes); Jones, L(awrence) E(velyn); Lancaster, (Sir) Osbert; Lubbock, Percy; MacCarthy, Mary; Paul, C(harles) Kegan; Sitwell, (Sir) Osbert (2). *See also* **College Life; Education; High School Life; Teachers**

Euthanasia. *See* **Right to Die**

Exercise Gurus. Simmons, Richard. *See also* **Anorexia Nervosa/Bulimia; Outdoor Recreation; Sports**

Exeter Academy. Vidal, Gore. *See also* **Education; High School Life**

Explorers. *See* **Adventurers; Boats; Peary, Robert; Road Trips; Seafaring Life; Travel Writers; Voyages**

Facial Abnormalities. Fox, Debbie; Grealy, Lucy; Kusz, Natalie; Moss, Barbara Robinette. *See also* **Accidents (Agricultural); Amputees**

Falconers. Ford, Emma. *See also* **Birders**

Family Memoirs. Agle, Nan Hayden; Alberti, Rafael; Aldrich, Margaret Chanler; Alexander, Shana; Allan, Elizabeth Randolph; Archer, Chalmers, Jr.; Armstrong, Martin Donisthorpe; Bailey, Margaret Emerson; Bechdel, Alison; Bell, Mary Hayley; Benson, E(dward) F(rederic); Berg, Gertrude; Bernstein, Carl; Blais, Madeleine; Bolster, Alice; Bowen, Catherine Drinker; Brace, Gerald Warner; Braithwaite, Max; Brautigan, Ianthe; Brown, Cecil; Buckley, Carol; Caldwell, Gail; Carlson, Avis; Carter, John Franklin; Cascone, Gina; Chagall, Bella; Chase, Justine; Childers, Mary; Chotzinoff, Samuel; Coe, Wilbur; Conaway, James; Cooper, Mireille; Crystal, Billy; Cullerton, Brenda; Czerniawski, Adam; Day, Clarence (3); Dell, Diana J.; Dixon, Madeline Cutler; Durst, Paul; Earley, Tony; Ely, Stanley; Eyster, Virginia; Farjeon, Eleanor; Fletcher, Grace Nies; Frothingham, Eugenia; Gage, Nicholas; Gallagher, Dorothy; Gifford, Edward S(tewart), Jr.; Gilbreth, Frank, Jr. (2); Goyer, Jane; Green, Anne; Haaglund, Lois; Hagen, Lois; Harding, Bertita; Hatsumi, Reiko; Hautzig, Esther; Haygood, Wil; Holman, Virginia; Holtz, William; Hudson, W(illiam) H(enry); Hunt, Rockwell; Iacuzzo, Terry; Irvine, Lyn; Jadhav, Narendra; Janes, E(dward) C.; Jaramillo, Cleofas M.; Kemp, James Malcolm; Khaing, Mi Mi; Kip, Herbert Zabriskie; Lancaster, Robert S.; Lee, Eliza; Levensen, Sam(uel); Lidz, Franz; Loti, Pierre (2); Low, Lema; Luft, Lorna; Mabie, Janet; MacCracken, Henry; MacDonald, Michael Patrick (2); Mangione, Jerre. Geraldo); Márquez, Gabriel García; Marshall, Audrey; Matthews, Sallie; May, Someth; Mayer, Edith Patterson; McFadden, Cyra; McGratty, Arthur; McKenney, Ruth; McLaurin, Tim; Miller, Arthur; Miller, Christian; Mitford, Jessica; Moody, Ralph; Morehead, Don, et al.; Murray, Nina Chan-

Family Memoirs (*Cont.*)
dler; Nekola, Charlotte; Oliphant, Thomas; O'Neill, Molly; Pamuk, Orhan;. Parton), Willadeene; Patrick, Sean; Patridge, Bellamy (3); Pifer, Drury; Porter, Alyene; Rekdal, Paisley; Reynolds, Rick; Robbins, Sarah; Roberts, Steven; Ryan, Terry; Santiago, Esmeralda (2); Sendyk, Helen; Shields, Karena; Simon, Clea; Simpson, Jeffrey; Skinner, Cornelia Otis; Slezak, Walter; Smith, Alison; Sousa, John Philip, III; Spence, Hartzell; Stanforth, Willa Bare; Stryker, Charlotte; Swados, Elizabeth; Taber, Gladys (2); Talese, Gay; Taulbert, Clifton; Thornton, Yvonne S.; Topp, Mildred (2); Torregrosa, Luisita Lopez; Uchida, Yoshiko (2); Van Nuys, Laura Bower; Von Staden, Wendegard; Walls, Jeannette; Weller, Sheila; Welles, Winifred; Wilder, Laura Ingalls (7); Wilsey, Jean; Wollaston, Percy; Woollcott, Barbara; Zanichkowsky, Stephen; Ziolkowski, Thad. *See also* **Aunts; Brothers; Collaborations by Relatives; Fatherless Families; Immigrants; Sisters; Uncles;** religious and ethnic subjects, such as **Catholics; Irish Americans; Italian Americans; Jews**

Family Violence. Aman; Ashworth, Andrea; Burch, Jennings; Cameron, Marcia; Carcaterra, Lorenzo; Chambers, Veronica; Clinton, Bill; Crawford, Christina; Fleming, Keith; Fowler, Connie May; Green, Melissa; Gregory, Julie; Hare, Augustus John; Harris, E. Lynn; Helget, Nicole Lea; Herrick, William; Holley, Tara; Hyman, B(arbara) D(avis); Jackson, La Toya; Jamison, Dirk; Jordan, June; Karr, Mary (2); Kipling, Rudyard; Lauck, Jennifer (2); Lichtenberg, Greg; Louise, Regina; Martin, Lee; McCall, Bruce; McCourt, Frank; McGahern, John; McKuen, Rod; Michener, Anna J.; Miller, Christian; Moore, Judith; Moss, Barbara Robinette; Nasdijj; Nichols, Beverley; Noble, Christina; Paterson, Judith; Pelzer, David (4); Razor, Peter; Rhodes, Richard; Ryan, Terry; St. Aubin de Teran, Lisa; Scheeres, Julia; Scholinski, Daphne; Silverman, Sue William; Slenczynska, Ruth; Solotaroff, Ted; Somers, Suzanne; Weller, Sheila; Williams, Donna; Wolff, Tobias; Zanichkowsky, Stephen. *See also* **Abuse (Emotional); Abuse (Physical); Abuse (Spousal); Alcoholism; Children of Alcoholics; Crime; Divorce; Incest; Murder; Patricide; Schizophrenia**

Farm Life. Abbott, Shirley; Archer, Fred (2); Artley, Bob; Babb, Sonora; Bair, Bruce; Barnard, Ellsworth; Bartel, Irene Brown;

Bellmon, Henry; Bibler, Louis A.; Binns, Archie; Bodwell, Dorothy; Bolster, Alice; Bonebright, Mrs. Sarah; Boyle, Harry (3); Britt, Albert; Brooks, Sara; Brown, Cecil; Brown, Harriet. Maria D. Brown); Bumpers, Dale; Burroughs, John; Buyukmihci, Hope Sawyer; Carter, Jimmy; Coffey, Marilyn; Coffin, Robert; Collins, Louisa; Crews, Harry; Crowell, Evelyn; Croy, Homer (2); Dabney, Virginia Bell; DeLuca, Sara; Driscoll, Charles B(enedict 2); Eastman, E(dward) R(oe); Eleazer, J(ames) M.; Engle, Paul E.; Erdman, Loula Grace; Feller, Bob; Fields, Mamie; Fish, Charles; Fuller, Alexandra; Gallant, John; Good, Howard E.; Gould, Franklin Farrar; Gould, R(alph) E(rnest); Green, Melissa; Hancock, George; Harnack, Curtis (2); Hall, Donald; Hein, Teri; Helget, Nicole Lea; Hill, James Langdon; Hillerman, Tony; Huston, Paul Griswold; Hutchison, Nell; Hynes, Samuel Lynn; Jackson, Jacqueline Dougan; Jager, Ronald; Jones, Bryan L.; Kavanagh-Priest, Anne; Kittredge, William; Ladd, Carl E(dwin); Lancaster, Robert S.; Lark, Fred A.; Love, Marianne; Marquart, Debra; Martin, Lee; Mason, Bobbie Ann; Mason, Harry Morgan; May, Jim; McLaurin, Tim; Meckler, Brenda; Meyers, Kent; Miller, R(obert) H(enry); Moody, Ralph (4); Morgan, Elizabeth; Muir, Edwin; Nordyke, Lewis; O'Callaghan, Sean; Olmstead, Robert; Pattee, Fred Lewis; Pearson, Haydn; Peters, Robert; Pinti, Pietro; Quarton, Marjorie; Randolph, Buckner; Razor, Peter; Rhodes, Richard; Roberts, (Dean) Isaac Phillips; Scheeres, Julia; Shatraw, Milton; Shrout, Bill; Smith, Ethel Sabin; Sneller, Anne Gertrude; Snyder, Grace Yost and Nellie; Steel, Samuel Augustus; Trenka, Jane Jeong; Tressler, Irving D.; Turner, William H(enry); Twedt, Jerry L.; Wakeman, Sarah Rosetta; Walker, Mark; Warner, Charles Dudley; Weitzman, David; Wilson, Rex L.; Wolf, John Quincy; Wollaston, Percy; Woodcock, George; Xan, Erna Oleson; Watson, Jo Anna Holt; Wysor, Rufus Johnston. *See also* **Accidents (Agricultural); Bog Farming; Country Life; Frontier and Pioneer Life; Homes and Haunts; Hunters; Jungle Life; Ranch Life**

Fascism. Loy, Rosetta. *See also* **Communists; Nazis and Neo-Nazis**

Fashion Designers. Gould, Lois; Vanderbilt, Gloria (2). *See also* **Decorative Arts; Models**

Fashion Editors. Kimbrough, Emily (2). *See also* **Editors**

Fatherless Families. Accomando, Claire Hsu; Adams, Elizabeth; Alford, Thomas Wildcat; Bejel, Emilio; Benjamin, David; Berman, Susan; Blais, Madeleine; Campbell, Bebe; Clinton, Bill; Cowan, Evelyn; Dahl, Roald; Datcher, Michael; Diehl, Margaret; Durst, Paul; Erlbaum, Janice; Fowler, Connie May; Fowler, Gene; Fraser, Joelle; Gifford, Barry; Hilton, Ella E. Schneider; Hoard, G. Richard; Humphrey, William; Jennings, Kevin; Keyes, Frances Parkinson; King, Dexter Scott; Latifi, Afschineh; Lewis, Mindy; Lords, Traci; Lucie-Smith, Edward; MacDonald, Michael Patrick (2); Matousek, Mark; McKuen, Rod; Moehringer, J. R.; Moody, Ralph; Oakes, Philip (2); Oufkir, Malika; Percival, Nora Lourie; Sartre, Jean-Paul; Segun, Mabel; Siringo, Charles A(ngelo); Skoyles, John; Smith, Dennis; Summer, Lauralee; Tea, Michelle; Torregrosa, Luisita Lopez; Ung, Loung; Ward, Lester; Wiesel, Elie; Williams, Rita; Wray, Fay; Zacharias, Karen Spears. *See also* **Adoptees; Bereavement; Divorce; Family Memoirs; Homeless Children; Orphans; Poverty; Pregnancy (Teen); Stepfathers**

Fathers and Daughters. Abbott, Shirley; Allen, Charlotte Vale; Allen, Jennifer; Anderson, Hesper; Bechdel, Alison; Bergen, Candice; Brady, Katherine; Campbell, Bebe; Chukovskaia, Lidiia; Conlon-McIvor, Maura; Davis, Tracey; Day, Ingeborg; Dayan, Yael; De Mist, Augusta; Diallo, Nafissatou; Fraser, Sylvia; Giancana, Antoinette; Jordan, Teresa; Maynard, Fredelle; McFadden, Cyra; Miller, Susan J.; Peary, Marie; Previn, Dory; Rich, Kim; St. Johns, Adela Rogers; Salinger, Margaret A.; Sayer, Mandy; Segun, Mabel; Silverman, Sue William; Simon, Kate (2); Sinatra, Tina; Tait, Katharine; Thornton, Yvonne S.; Trussoni, Danielle; Weller, Sheila; Whitt, Anne Hall; Wilson, Rosalind Baker. *See also* **Caregiving; Grandfathers; Grandparents; Incest; Mothers and Daughters; Mothers and Sons; Parents (Aging or Infirm); Patricide**

Fathers and Sons. Ackerley, J(oe) R(andolph); Amis, Martin; Anderson, Louie; Arlen, Michael J.; Bair, Bruce; Bakker, Jay; Bolles, Joshua K.; Bowles, Paul; Carcaterra, Lorenzo; Carroll, James; Carter, Jimmy; Cheuse, Alan; Clayton, Bruce; Cohen, Rich; Cooper, Wyatt; Corbett, William; Crosby, Gary; Crystal, Billy; Dahlinger, John; DeMeo, Albert; Dickey, Christopher; Driscoll, Charles B(enedict); Edmonds, Walter Dumaux; Gifford, Barry; Gifford, Edward S(tewart), Jr.; Gosse, Edmund; Haslam, Gerald; Henderson, Bill; Hickam, Homer; Keith, Michael C.; King, Dexter Scott; Kunhardt, Philip, Jr.; Kwan, Michael David; Ledda, Gavino; MacLeish, William H.; Malcolm, Andrew; Martin, Lee; May, Lee; McKuen, Rod; Mehta, Ved; Milne, Christopher; Morehead, Don, et al.; Nichols, Beverley; Nuland, Sherwin B.; Ostransky, Leroy; Peck, Scott; Phillips, Mark; Roberts, Steven; Runyon, Damon, Jr.; Sawyer, Scott; Schildkraut, Joseph; Sheed, Wilfrid; Solotaroff, Ted; Soucheray, Joe; Tompkins, Ptolemy (Christian); Warren, Robert Penn; Waugh, Auberon; Wiener, Norbert; Wolff, Geoffrey. *See also* **Caregiving; Grandfathers; Grandmothers; Grandparents; Mothers and Daughters; Mothers and Sons; Parents (Aging or Infirm); Patricide; Stepfathers**

Faulkner, William. Falkner, Murry. *See also* **Novelists; Short Story Writers**

Feminists. Agnelli, Susanna; Ahmed, Leila; Alexander, Shana; Bell, Susan Groag; Blackwell, Alice; Bottome, Phyllis; Bowne, Eliza Southgate; Brittain, Vera; Brown, Rita Mae; Conway, Jill Ker; Dall, Caroline; De Beauvoir, Simone; El Saadawi, Nawal; Faderman, Lillian; Goldman, Emma; Gornick, Vivian; hooks, bell (2); Johnston, Jill; Lichtenberg, Greg; Lutyens, Emily; Martineau, Harriet; McCarthy, Mary (2); McNaron, Toni; O'Brien, Edna; Piercy, Marge; Roiphe, Anne; Sand, George; Smith, Lillian; Spewack, Bella; Ugwu-Oju, Dympna; Warner, Sylvia Townsend; Wolf, Naomi; Xie, Bingying. *See also* **Reformers; Revolutionaries**

Fiction Writers. *See* **Novelists; Short Story Writers**

Fighter Pilots. Hynes, Samuel Lynn; Kittredge, William; Koger, Fred; Salter, James. *See also* **Aerospace Industries; Air Force, U.S.; Pilots; WWII**

Filipino Americans. Reyes, Norman. *See also* **Racially Mixed Children**

Film Personalities. *See* **Motion Picture** entries; **Movies**

Financiers. *See* **Bankers; Businesspersons**

Finnish Americans. Engelmann, Ruth. *See also* **Racially Mixed Children**

Firearms. *See* **Crime; Hunters**

Firefighters. Smith, Dennis. *See also* **Police**

Fishing. Douglas, William O.; Hemingway, Lorian; Holder, Charles; Janes, E(dward) C.; Middleton, Harry; Ruhen, Olaf;

Grandfathers (*Cont.*)
Waciuma, Charity; Wallace, Mary. *See also*
**Fathers and Daughters; Fathers and
Sons; Stepchildren**

Grandmothers. Bailey, Margaret Emerson;
Balakian, Peter; Bolton, Isabel; Brando,
Marlon; Burnett, Carol; Cantwell, Mary;
Clayton, Bruce; Cullen, Bill; Diallo,
Nafissatou; Doolittle, Hilda; Giovanni,
Nikki; Greenfield, Eloise; Hoggart, Rich-
ard; Lin, Alice; Mabry, Marcus; Mason,
Bobbie Ann; Meeropol, Robert; Michener,
Anna J.; Miss Read; Moore, Judith;
Narayan, R(asipuram); Nash, Sunny;
Nekola, Charlotte; Nuwere, Ejovi; Swan,
Madonna; Weir, Molly. *See also* **Mothers
and Daughters; Mothers and Sons;
Stepchildren**

Grandparents. Accomando, Claire Hsu; Berg,
Gertrude; Birkerts, Sven; Briggs, Wallace;
Bruchac, Joseph; Davis-Goff, Annabel;
Harding, Bertita; Holley, Tara; Masters,
Hilary; Miller, R(obert) H(enry); Myrdal,
Jan; Niu-Niu; Origo, Iris; Percival, Nora
Lourie; Pinson, Elizabeth Bernhardt; Sage,
Lorna; Sartre, Jean-Paul; Smith, Emma;
Streatfeild, Noel; Teale, Edwin Way. *See
also* **Fathers and Daughters; Fathers and
Sons; Mothers and Daughters; Mothers
and Sons; Stepfathers; Stepchildren**

Graphic Novels. Bechdel, Alison; Eisenstein,
Bernice; Gallant, John; Karasik, Paul and
Judy; Satrapi, Marjane. *See also* **Cartoon-
ists; Illustrators**

Greek Americans. Gage, Nicholas; Petrakis,
Harry; Thompson, Ariadne. *See also* **Racially Mixed Children**

Grief. *See* **Bereavement**

Gropius, Walter. Mahler-Werfel, Alma. *See also*
Architects

Groupies. Des Barres, Pamela; Johnson, Joyce;
Sullivan, Caroline. *See also* **Hippies; Musicians**

**Growing Up Between WWI and WWII
(1912–1930 Births).** Abrahams, Peter;
Abrams, Charlotte; Adam-Smith, Patsy;
Adams, Richard; Agnelli, Susanna; Alexan-
der, Shana; Allan, Sheila; Allen, Robert
Thomas; Allon, Yigal; Altick Richard D.;
Alvarez, A(lfred); Anderson, Daphne; An-
derson, Elizabeth Callaway; Angell, Roger;
Angelou, Maya (2); Archer, Chalmers, Jr.;
Archer, Fred; Arlen, Michael J.; Arnett,
Marvin V.; Arney, Ivy V.; Asher, Don;
Auchincloss, Louis; Baines, Frank; Baker,
Russell; Baldwin, Michael; Bannister, (Sir)
Roger; Barltrop, Robert; Bates, Daisy;
Behan, Brendan (2); Bell, Mary Hayley;

Bell, Susan Groag; Belvin, Ed; Bennett,
Kay; Berger, Clyde; Bergman, Ingmar;
Bibler, Louis A.; Birmingham, Frederic;
Black, Shirley Temple; Bogarde, Dirk;
Boll, Heinrich; Bond, Tommy ("Butch") ;
Bonin, Adelyn I.; Bonner, Elena; Bose,
Pradip; Boyd, Harry; Boyle, Harry (3);
Brando, Marlon; Bresee, Clyde; Briggs,
Wallace; Broun, Heywood Hale; Buchwald,
Art; Buechner, Frederick; Bumpers, Dale;
Burgess, Anthony; Burton, Ben; Buscaglia,
Leo; Buyukmihci, Hope Sawyer; Cameron,
Donald Angus; Campbell, Will; Canfield,
Patrick; Carlisle, Olga; Carter, Jimmy;
Cary, Diana; Champlin, Charles;
Chandruang, Kumat; Church, John L.;
Cleary, Beverly (2); Clooney, Rosemary;
Cobb, Richard; Coghlin, Frank "Junior";
Colebrook, Joan; Collier, Richard; Collins,
Robert; Connor, Lawrence S(tanton); Coo-
per, Jackie; Cooper, Wyatt; Corder,
Jim(my) W(ayne); Cowan, Evelyn; Cow-
per, Richard; Cox, Wally; Craft, Phil;
Craig, John; Cronkite, Walter; Crosbie,
Paddy; Cross, John Keir; Crowley, Elaine;
Crume, Paul; Dabney, Virginia Bell; Dahl,
Roald; Dahlinger, John; Daiches, David;
Davis, Paxton; Davison, Peter; Dawson,
Fielding; Delderfield, R(onald) F(rederick);
De Rachewiltz, Mary; Devi (of Jaipur),
Gayatri; Ditlevsen, Tove; Dodge, Ernest;
Donoghue, Denis; Drake, Mary; Durrell,
Gerald; Durst, Paul; Dyment, Clifford;
Earle, Virginia; Eddy, Roger; Elliott,
George P(aul); Engelmann, Ruth; Espey,
John (4); Eyster, Virginia; Fairbanks,
Evelyn; Farmaian, Sattareh; Favrholdt,
Visti; Feller, Bob; Fermor, (Sir) Patrick
Leigh (2); Foley, Winifred; Fontaine, Joan;
Foote, Horton; Forman, (Sir John) Denis;
Forrester, Helen (4); Fox, Paula; Frame,
Janet; Fraser, Eugenie; Fraser, Ronald;
Fritz, Jean; Fussell, Paul; Gallagher,
Charles; Gallant, John; Gary, Romain;
Gatheru, R. Mugo; Gay, Peter. Jack); Gay,
Ruth; Gillespie, Janet (2); Ginsbourg, Sam;
Ginzburg, Natalia; Girodias, Maurice;
Giscard, John; Glasser, Ralph (2); Goff,
Beth; Gray, John; Greene, A(lvin) C(arl);
Greenfield, Eloise; Gutkin, Harry and Mil-
dred; Haaglund, Lois; Hall, Donald; Hall,
Edward T(witchell), Jr.; Hall, Floriana;
Hall, Monty; Hamilton, Iain; Hannam,
Charles; Hanners, LaVerne; Harbinson,
Robert; Hardy, Barbara; Harnack, Curtis
(2); Hastings, Robert J. (2); Hastings, Scott,
Jr.; Hautzig, Esther; Havoc, June; Hayes,
Maurice (2); Hazelton, Nika Standen;

Spufford, Francis; Starkie, Walter; Venable, Richard Henry; Weitzman, David; Worcester, Donald; Wright, Louis. *See also* **Critics (Art); Folklorists; Intellectual Life; Journalists; Philosophers; Sociologists; Travel Writers**

Historians (Literary). *See* **Critics (Literary)**

Historians (Military). Catton, Bruce; Churchill, (Sir) Winston S.; Collier, Richard; Love, Edmund G. (2). *See also* **Military Life**

Historians (Religious). Eliade, Mircea; Friesel, Evyatar; Halivni, David. *See also* **Theological Writers**

Historians (Social). *See* **Historians; Historians (Cultural)**

Hitchhiking. Brookes, Tim; Conover, Ted; Kaufman, Kenn; Keith, Michael C. *See also* **Gypsies; Hoboes; Railroad Travel; Road Trips; Runaways; Travel Writers**

Hitler, Adolf. O'Toole, Peter

Hitler Youth Movement. Durlacher, Gerhard; Hunt, Irmgard; Koehn, Ilse; Schroeder, Walter; Schumann, Willy; Von der Grun, Max; Von Staden, Wendegard. *See also* **Holocaust; Nazis and Neo-Nazis; WWII**

Hoboes. Conover, Ted; Herrick, William; London, Jack; Roskolenko, Harry. *See also* **Gypsies; Hitchhiking; Homeless Children; Railroad Travel; Road Trips**

Hockey. Roy, Travis

Holocaust Survivors. Appleman-Jurman, Alicia; Auerbacher, Inge; Birenbaum, Halina; Birger, Trudi; Bitton-Jackson, Livia (2); Blatt, Thomas Toivi; Blend, Martha; Breznitz, Shlomo; Darvas, Miriam; Defonseca, Misha; de Gaulle-Anthonioz, Genevieve; Denes, Magda; Deutschkron, Inge; Edvardson, Cordelia; Eisner, Jack; Fleuk, Toby; Fox, Anne L.; Friedlander, Saul; Friesel, Evyatar; Gelissen, Rena; Geve, Thomas; Gold, Ruth; Graf, Malvina; Grove, Andrew S.; Halivni, David; Heller, Fanya; Hoffman, Eva; Horn, Joseph; Isaacson, Judith; Isacovici, Salomon; Jackson, Livia; Joffo, Joseph; Kalib, Goldie; Kent, Evelyn Julia; Kimmelman, Mira; Kluger, Ruth; Kofman, Sarah; Korn, Abram; Kroh, Aleksandra; Krutein, Eva; Lang, George; Laver, Betty; Leitner, Isabella (2); Levendel, Isaac; Levi, Trude; Ligocka, Roma; Loy, Rosetta; Mandel, Edmund; Meyers, Odette; Michel, Ernest W.; Morhange-Begue, Claude; Nir, Yehuda; Opdyke, Irene; Perel, Shlomo; Perl, Lila; Reiss, Johanna; Rosen, Sara; Schulman, Faye; Semprun, Jorge; Sender, Ruth; Sendyk, Helen; Siegal, Aranka; Sierakowiak, David; Steinberg, Paul; Stern, Edgar; Ten Boom, Corrie; Toll, Nelly S.; Trahan, Elizabeth; Turgel, Gina; Velmas, Edith; Weinstein, Frida Scheps; Weisman, Murray; Wermuth, Henry; Wieck, Michael; Wiesel, Elie; Winter, Miriam; Zamoyska-Panek; Zuker-Bujanowska, Liliana. *See also* **Anti-Semitism; Armenian Americans; Camps (Internment); Children of Holocaust Survivors; Hitler Youth Movement; Jews; Khmer Rouge; Missing Persons; Nazis and Neo-Nazis; Prisoners; Refugees; Russian Purges (1934–1938); Slums; WWII**

Home Economics. Van de Water, Virginia Terhune. *See also* **Etiquette**

Homeless Children. Erlbaum, Janice; James, Marie; Summer, Lauralee. *See also* **Depressions (Economic); Fatherless Families; Hoboes; Orphans; Runaways; Slums**

Homes and Haunts. Allon, Yigal; Arnow, Harriette; Briggs, Wallace; Collier, Richard; Corbett, Elizabeth Frances; Crews, Harry; Earle, Virginia; Fraser, Ronald; Haslam, Gerald; Jenkins, Michael; Johnson, Josephine Winslow; Karr, Mary (2); Kirk, Mary Wallace; Kunhardt, Philip, Jr.; Lessard, Suzannah; Lubbock, Percy; Martin, Lee; Maxwell, Gavin; Mitchell, John; Murray, Albert; Neilson, Elisabeth; Noyes, Pierrepont; O'Hara, Lucy Hudgins; Pulsifer, Susan; Thirkell, Angela; Welfare, Mary. *See also* **Castles; Child Institutional Care; College Life; Country Life; Drug Stores and Pharmacists; Farm Life; Frontier and Pioneer Life; High School Life; Island Life; Jungle Life; Lakes; Mountain Life; Plantation Life; Ranch Life; Resorts; Riverboats; Seafaring Life**

Home Schooling. Murray, Nina Chandler. *See also* **Education**

Horses. Buyukmihci, Hope Sawyer; Quarton, Marjorie; Winfrey, Carey; Worcester, Donald

Horticulturalists. Standifer, Leon C. *See also* **Gardeners; Natural History**

Hotel Receptionists. Mittelholzer, Edgar. *See also* **Resorts**

Hotels and Motels. *See* **Resorts**

Houses. *See* **Homes and Haunts; Resorts**

Hudson River. Black, Jennie; Edey, Marion; Goff, Beth; Hamlin, Huybertie; Lamont, Miller, Christopher; Thomas; Selzer, Richard. *See also* **Connecticut River Valley; Irving, Washington; Mississippi River**

Lawrenceville Academy. Buechner, Frederick; Laflin, Louis Ellsworth; Mabry, Marcus. *See also* **College Life; Education; High School Life; Teachers**

Lawyers. Abagnale, Frank W., Jr.; Blackiston, Henry C(urtis); Bumpers, Dale; Choate, Joseph Hodges; Follain, Jean; Goethe, Johann Wolfgang von; Hulton, Edward; Hupalo, Kathleen Fixsen; Johnson, Axel P.; Krents, Harold; Lancaster, Robert S.; Latifi, Afschineh; McGough, Matthew; Mortimer, John; Newbolt, (Sir) Henry; Obama, Barack; Saraute, Nathalie; Spence, Gerry; Townsend, William Henry; Underwood, Francis Henry; Warner, Charles Dudley; Wechsberg, Joseph (2). *See also* **Civil Rights Workers; Crime; Judges; Policemen; Supreme Court Justices**

Learning Disabilities. Miranda, James. *See also* **Education; Mental Health**

Lecturers. Acton, Harold; Altick, Richard D.; Alvarez, A(lfred); Antin, Mary (2); Arnett, Marvin V.; Boll, Heinrich; Bottome, Phyllis; Bowen, Catherine Drinker; Bresee, Clyde; Brittain, Vera; Buscaglia, Leo; Cameron, Donald Angus; Chace, James; Chase, Mary Ellen (2); Coffin, Robert; Cole, Margaret; Conway, Jill Ker; Dall, Caroline; Davison, Peter; Day-Lewis, C(ecil); Giovanni, Nikki; Gough, John B.; Harbinson, Robert; Maurois, André; Russell, (Sir) Bertrand; Schweitzer, Albert; Seton, Ernest Thompson; Tagore, (Sir) Rabindranath (2); Thomas, Lowell; Wiesel, Elie. *See also* **Education**

Lee, Harper. Moates, Marianne. *See also* **Novelists**

Leg Abnormalities. Fries, Kenny. *See also* **Paralysis**

Lesbians. Barrington, Judith; Bechdel, Alison; Bepko, Claudia; Brown, Rita Mae; Faderman, Lillian; Johnston, Jill; Leduc, Violette; Lorde, Audre; McNaron; Toni; Morris, Bonnie J.; Murray, William (Janet Flanner); Smith, Lillian; Summer, Lauralee; Warner, Sylvia Townsend. *See also* **Bisexuals; Children of Transsexuals; Flanner, Janet; Gays; Transsexuals; Transvestites**

Letters. Anderson, Louie; Anonymous; Ashley, Edwin and Cliff; Bleser, Carol; Bonham Carter, (Lady) Violet; Bowne, Eliza Southgate; Cooke, Chauncey H(erbert); Drake, Daniel; Durstewitz, Jeff; Faulkner, William; Keller, Helen; Lindbergh, Anne Morrow; Lindbergh, Charles A(ugustus); Lutyens, Emily; Ondaatje, Michael; Reich, Wilhelm; Upson, Theodore F.; Wakeman, Sarah Rosetta. *See also* **Collaborations by Relatives; Diaries and Journals**

Lewis, C(live) S(taples). Gresham, Douglas. *See also* **Religious Persons; Theological Writers**

Lexicographers. Mistral, Frederic. *See also* **Books and Reading; Linguists; Philologists**

Librarians. Abish, Walter; Brown, Dee; Casanova, Giacomo; Cleary, Beverly; Gosse, (Sir) Edmund; Liverani, Mary Rose; Lorde, Audre; Lubbock, Percy (2); Mowat, Farley (3); O'Connor, Frank; O'Connor, Philip; Powell, Lawrence Clark; Wright, Louis. *See also* **Books and Reading; Curators; Education; Intellectual Life; Teachers**

Librettists. Loos, Anita; Plomer, William; Previn, Dory; Rexroth, Kenneth; West, Jessamyn; Zweig, Stefan. *See also* **Composers; Musicians**

Lincoln, Abraham. Townsend, William Henry. *See also* **Presidents, U.S.**

Lindbergh, Charles A(ugustus). Lindbergh, Anne Morrow; Lindbergh, Reeve. *See also* **Pilots**

Linguists. De Rachewiltz, Mary; Helias, Pierre-Jakez. *See also* **Lexicographers; Philologists; Translators**

Liquor. Hamill, Pete; Zailckas, Koran. *See also* **Alcoholism**

Literary Critics and Literary Historians. *See* **Critics (Literary)Lithuanian Americans.** Zanichkowsky, Stephen. *See also* **Racially Mixed Children**

Longfellow, Henry Wadsworth. Skinner, Henrietta. *See also* **Poets Lumber Camps.** Churchill, Samuel; Hawley, Robert; O'Meara, Walter. *See also* **Forests Lutyens, (Sir) Edwin.** Lutyens, Emily. *See also* **Architects**

Lutyens, (Sir) Edwin. Lutyens, Emily. *See also* **Architects**

MacLean Hospital. Kaysen, Susanna. *See also* **Mental Health**

MacLeish, Archibald. MacLeish, William H. *See also* **Poets**

Magicians. Brown, Cecil

Malaria. Fuller, Alexandra; Seton, Ernest Thompson

Manic-Depression. Moorman, Margaret (2); Reynolds, Rick. *See also* **Children of the Mentally Ill; Eccentrics; Mental Health**

Manicurists. Henrey, Madeleine (2)

Mann, Heinrich. Mann, Golo; Mann, Klaus. *See also* **Novelists**

Mann, Thomas. Mann, Golo; Mann, Klaus. *See also* **Novelists**

Marines, U.S. Ball, Phil; Buchwald, Art; Ehrhart, W(illiam) D(aniel); Lince, George; Mackin, Eltin; Ogden, Richard E.; Spiller, Harry;

Swofford, Anthony; Winfrey, Carey. *See also* **Military Life; WWI; WWII**

Maritime Life. *See* **Seafaring Life; Voyages**

Maryland Institution for the Blind. Arms, Mrs. Mary L. (Day). *See also* **Blindness**

Masons. *See* **Construction Industry**

Massacres. *See* **War**

Masters, Edgar Lee. Masters, Hilary. *See also* **Poets**

Mathematicians. Kovalevskaia, Sofiia; Russell, (Sir) Bertrand; Wiener, Norbert. *See also* **Scientists**

Matricide. Bordewich, Fergus M. *See also* **Bereavement; Mothers and Sons; Murder; Patricide**

Matthau, Walter. Matthau, Carol. *See also* **Actors**

McCarthyism. *See* **Anti-Communist Movements; Cold War**

McCubbin, Frederick. Mangan, Kathleen. *See also* **Artists**

Medical Students. North, Carol. *See also* **Nurses; Physicians**

Meningitis. Heppner, Cheryl M. *See also* **Paralysis**

Mennonites. Eby, Kermit; Smith, Charles Henry. *See also* **Clergy; Religious Persons; Spiritual Life**

Mental Health. Bechdel, Alison; Blais, Madeleine; Buckley, Carol; Campbell, Will; Christman, Jill; Cournos, Francine; Daniels, Lucy; Duke, Patty; Fleming, Keith; Flook, Maria; Foster, Patricia; Gordon, Emily Fox; Hayward, Brooke; Heller, Fanya; Helms, Alan; Hitchman, Janet; Jackson, Anne; Karr, Mary (2); Kaysen, Susanna; Kehoe, Louise; King, Marian; Kipling, Rudyard; Mairs, Nancy; Manley, Elizabeth; Mill, John Stuart (2); Noble, Christina; Paterson, Judith; Previn, Dory; Rich, Kim; St. Aubin de Teran, Lisa; Schrank, Robert; Smith, Bob; Tierney, Gene; Vilar, Irene; Woolf, Virginia. *See also* **Abuse (Emotional); Abuse (Psychiatric); Bereavement; Caregiving; Children of the Mentally Ill; Counselors; Depressions (Mental); Diseases ; Eccentrics; Gender Identity; Learning Disabled Youth; MacLean Hospital; Manic-Depression; Multiple Personality Disorder; Munchausen Syndrome by Proxy; Neurologists; Physicians; Psychiatrists; Psychologists; Psychotherapists; Schizophrenia; Stuttering; Suicide and Suicide Victims**

Mental Health Personnel. Lin, Alice

Merchant Marines. Ruark, Robert (2)

Methodists. Hayward, Helen Harry; Hoard, G. Richard; Meyer, Edith Patterson; Spence,

Hartzell; Tempe, Gertrude. *See also* **Clergy; Religious Persons; Spiritual Life**

Mexican Americans. Galarza, Ernesto; Garcia, Lionel G.; Gonzalez, Ray; Gonzalez-Crussi, F(rank); Lopez-Stafford, Gloria; Lucas, Maria; Navarrette, Ruben, Jr.; Ponce, Mary; Rodriguez, Richard; Ruben; Soto, Gary (5); Taylor, Sheila Ortiz and Sandra O.; Urrea, Luis Alberto.

Military Life. Adamic, Louis; Bode, E(mil) A(dolph); Bowley, F(reeman) S(parks); Boyd, Maria Isabella ("Belle") ; Churchill, (Sir) Winston S.; Cooke, Chauncey H(erbert); Cropton, John; Davis, Paxton; Edmonds, Sarah Emma; Eisenhower, Dwight D.; Fisher, Antwone Quenton; Ford, William Wallace; Gilbreth, Frank B., Jr.; Greenman, Jeremiah; Hamilton, (Sir) Ian; Heller, Joseph; Hillerman, Tony; Jamison, Matthew; Kahn, Sy; Knef, Hildegard; Jorgensen, Christine; Kerrey, Bob; Kotlowitz, Robert; Kropotkin, Peter; Lee, Agnes; Liebling, A(bbott) J(oseph); Livermore, Thomas L(eonard); Lynch, Jessica; Martin, Joseph Plumb; Massey, Raymond; Masters, John; Mauldin, Bill (2); Maurois, André; Milne, Christopher; Morgan, Elizabeth; Murray, Albert; Paulsen, Gary (2); Perel, Shlomo; Peters, Robert; Putnam, George Haven; Raymond, Ernest; Salter, James; Schroeder, Walter; Shaw, John Robert; Sitwell, (Sir) Osbert (2); Starkie, Walter; Steel, Samuel Augustus; Stillwell, Leander; Swofford, Anthony; Triplet, William S.; Upson, Theodore F.; Wakeman, Sarah Rosetta; Walter, Jakob; Wister, Sarah (Sally); Xie, Bingying. *See also* **Air Force, U.S.; American Indian Wars; Army, U.S.; Bosnian War; Civil War (Spanish); Civil War (U.S.); Confederate States of America; Historians (Military); Iran–Iraq War; Korean War; Marines, U.S.; Merchant Marines; Napoleonic Wars; Naval Life; Paraplegia; Persian Gulf War; POWs; Prisoners; Revolutionaries; Sailors; Sino-Japanese Conflict; Vietnam Conflict; War; War of Independence; West Point; WWI; WWII**

Millbrook School. Horne, Alistair. *See also* **College Life; Education; High School Life; Teachers**

Mills (Textile). *See* **Textile Mills**

Milne, A. A. Milne, Christopher (2). *See also* **Children's Authors**

Mime Artists. Enters, Angna. *See also* **Theater**

Miners. Bennett, Edwin; Bullock, Jim; Canfield, Patrick; Jones, G(reen) C.; McKell, Kather-

Erna Oleson. *See also* **Racially Mixed Children**

Novelists. Abrahams, Peter; Ackerley, J(oe) R(andolph); Adams, Richard; Alvarez, A(lfred); Alvarez, Julia; Amis, Martin; Andrews, Raymond; Armstrong, Martin Donisthorpe; Asquith, (Lady) Cynthia; Auchincloss, Louis; Babb, Sonora; Bagnold, Enid; Bailey, Paul; Barea, Arturo; Baring, Maurice; Baring-Gould, Sabine; Bates, H(erbert) E(rnest); Benson, E(dward) F(rederic); Berners, (Lord) Gerald (2); Bingham, Charlotte; Bingham, Madeleine; Binns, Archie; Blackwood, Algernon; Boll, Heinrich; Booth, Martin; Bottome, Phyllis; Boyce, Neith; Brittain, Vera; Brown, Dee; Brown, Rita Mae; Bryher; Buechner, Frederick; Burgess, Anthony; Burnett, Frances Hodgson; Butts, Mary; Calder-Marshall, Arthur; Caldwell, Taylor; Calisher, Hortense (2); Candlin, Enid Saunders; Canetti, Elias; Carossa, Hans (2); Carroll, Gladys Hasty (2); Carroll, James; Chace, James; Carstens, Grace; Caspary, Vera; Chamson, André (2); Charyn, Jerome (2); Chase, Mary Ellen (2); Cheuse, Alan; Choy, Wayson; Chukovskaia, Lidiia; Church, Richard (2); Clarke, Austin (2); Cloete, Stuart; Cole, Margaret; Colette; Conaway, James; Conde, Maryse; Corbett, Elizabeth Frances; Cowper, Richard; Crews, Harry; Croft-Cooke, Rupert (3); Crowley, Elaine; Croy, Homer (2); Cunningham, Laura (2); Curwood, James Oliver; Dahl, Roald; Dahlberg, Edward; Davenport, Marcia; Davis, Rebecca Harding; Day-Lewis, C(ecil); De Blasis, Celeste; Deland, Margaret (2); Delderfield, R(onald) F(rederick); Djilas, Milovan; Doig, Ivan (2); Doolittle, Hilda; Doucet, Clive; Douglas, Lloyd C(assel); Dovlatov, Sergei; Dreiser, Theodore; Drewe, Robert; DuMaurier, Daphne; Duncan, Lois; Durst, Paul; Earley, Tony; Edmonds, Walter Dumaux; Eliade, Mircea; Elliott, George P(aul); Ellis, Alice Marie; Ernaux, Annie; Espey, John (4); Falkner, Murry (William Faulkner); Faulkner, William; Ferber, Edna; Fergusson, Harvey; Figes, Eva; Forester, C(ecil) S(cott); Forrester, Helen (4); Fowler, Connie May; Fox, Paula; Frame, Janet; France, Anatole (3); Franzen, Jonathan; Fraser, Christine (2); Fraser, Sylvia; Gale, Zona; Garcia, Lionel G.; Garland, Hamlin (2); Garnett, David; Gary, Romain; Gebler, Carlo; Gide, Andre; Gifford, Barry; Giles, Janice; Ginzburg, Natalia; Glynne-Jones, William; Godden, Jon;

Godden, (Margaret) Rumer (2); Goethe, Johann Wolfgang von; Gorky, Maxim; Gould, Lois; Goytisolo, Juan; Graves, Robert; Grayson, David; Green, Henry; Green, Julian (4); Greene, Graham; Hackett, Francis; Hale, Janet Campbell; Hale, Nancy; Hamilton, Hugo; Han, Suyin; Harris, E. Lynn; Hawthorne, Julian; Haymon, S(ylvia) T(heresa 2); Healy, Dermot; Hecht, Ben; Heller, Joseph; Herrick, William; Higgins, Aidan; Higgins, George V.; Hillerman, Tony; Holmes, Marjorie; Hong Ying; Howard, Maureen; Howells, William Dean; Hudson, W(illiam) H(enry); Humphrey, William; Hurst, Fannie; Husayn, Taha (2); Huxley, Elspeth (3); Isherwood, Christopher; James, Clive; James, Henry (2); Johnston, Wayne; Kantor, MacKinlay; Kastner, Erich; Kataev, Valentin; Kavanagh, P(atrick) J(oseph); Kaye, M(ary) M(argaret) (2); Kazantzakis, Nikos; Kerr, M. E.; Keyes, Frances Parkinson; Kim, Richard E.; Kipling, Rudyard; Kittredge, William; Lagerlof, Selma (4); Lawrence, Kathleen Rockwell; Laye, Camara; Leduc, Violette; Lehrer, Jim (2); Lewis, C(live) S(taples); Lindbergh, Anne Morrow; Lindbergh, Reeve; Lindsay, Jack; Lisicky, Paul; Lively, Penelope; London, Jack; Longstreet, Stephen; Loos, Anita; Loti, Pierre (2); Lowndes, Bessie Belloc; Loy, Rosetta; Lucie-Smith, Edward; Lutyens, Mary; Lynch, Hannah; Machen, Arthur; MacKenzie, Compton (3); Mamet, David; Márquez, Gabriel García; Marsh, Ngaio; Martineau, Harriet; Masefield, John (4); Mason, Bobbie Ann; Masters, John; Maurois, André; Maxwell, Gavin; Mayer, Robert; McCarthy, Mary (2); McGahern, John; McInnes, Graham (3); McLaurin, Tim; Mittelholzer, Edgar; Moates, Marianne; Monette, Paul; Morris, Edita; Morris, Wright; Mortimer, John; Mortimer, Penelope; Mottram, R(alph) H(ale); Murray, Albert; Murray, William; Myrdal, Jan (3); Nabokov, Vladimir; Narayan, R(asipuram) K(rishnaswami); Nasrin, Taslima; Nathan, Daniel; Naughton, Bill (4); Neihardt, John; Newbolt, Sir Henry; Nexo, Martin Andersen; Nichols, Beverley; Nordan, Lewis; Oakes, Philip (2); O'Brien, Edna; O'Brien, Tim; O'Connor, Frank; O'Connor, Jack; O'Flynn, Criostoir; Olmstead, Robert; O'Meara, Walter; Ondaatje, Michael; Ortiz Cofer, Judith; Pagnol, Marcel; Pamuk, Orhan; Paul, Elliot (4); Paustovsky, Konstantin (2); Peterkiewicz, Jerzy; Petry, Ann; Picano,

ward; Meyerstein, Edward Harry William; Mortimer, John; Newbolt, (Sir) Henry; Nichols, Beverley; Paul, C(harles) Kegan; Potter, Stephen; Quennell, (Sir) Peter; Rees, Coronwy; Rowse, A(lfred) L(eslie); Ruskin, John; Sitwell, (Sir) Sacheverell; Tallents, (Sir) Stephen George; Waugh, Evelyn. *See also* **Cambridge University; College Life; Education; High School Life; Teachers**

Ozarks. *See* **Mountain Life**

Pacifists. Baker, Adelaide; Bergen, Candice; Boll, Heinrich; Brittain, Vera; Brody, Leslie; King, Dexter Scott; Kovic, Ron; Nagel, Charles; Naughton, Bill (4); Partridge, Frances; Reid, B(enjamin) L(awrence); Zweig, Stefan. *See also* **Beat Generation; Buddhists; Civil Rights Workers; Counterculture Childhoods; Hippies; Intellectual Life; King, Martin Luther, Jr.; Philosophers; Reformers; Revolutionaries; Socialists; Vietnam Conflict**

Painters. Alberti, Rafael; Andrews, Marietta Minnigerode; Bashkirtseff, Marie; Beaux, Cecilia; Bemelmans, Ludwig; Boston, L(ucy) M(aria); Brainard, Joe; Buyukmihci, Hope Sawyer; Carr, Emily; Dawson, Fielding; Enters, Angna; Juta, Jan; Longstreet, Stephen; Markino, Yoshio; Marsh, Ngaio; Maxwell, Gavin; Min, Anchee; Pacheco, Ferdie; Rexroth, Kenneth; Richmond, Sir Arthur; Rothenstein, (Sir) William; Schlesinger, Marian; Smith, Bob; Soskice, Juliet M. (Ford Madox Brown, Dante Gabriel Rosetti); Strindberg, August; Strong, George Templeton; Tagore, (Sir) Rabindranath (2); Wollheim, Richard; Young, Stark. *See also* **Artists; Cartoonists; Chagall, Marc; Critics (Art); Sketchers**

Pakistani Americans. *See* **Asian Americans**

Paleontologists. Ward, Lester. *See also* **Anthropologists; Archaeologists; Ethnologists**

Panamanian Americans. Chambers, Veronica. *See also* **Hispanic Americans; Mexican Americans; Racially Mixed Children**

Pantomime. *See also* **Entertainers** Marx, Harpo

Paperboys. Kloeflorn, William (2); Petroski, Henry

Paralysis. *See* **Accidents (Agricultural); Arthritis; Infantile Paralysis; Meningitis; Multiple Sclerosis; Paraplegia; Polio; Quadriplegia; Stroke**

Paraplegia. Fraser, Christine (2); Hockenberry, John; Kovic, Ron; Lagerlof, Selma (3). *See also* **Cerebral Palsy; Military Life; Quadriplegia; Stroke**

Parents (Aging or Infirm). Froncek, Thomas; Kittredge, William; Murphy, Dervla. *See also* **Caregiving; Fathers and Daughters; Fathers and Sons; Mothers and Daughters; Mothers and Sons; Patricide; Right to Die**

Pasternak, Boris. Pasternak, Alexander. *See also* **Novelists; Poets**

Patricide. Nichols, Beverley. *See also* **Fathers and Daughters; Fathers and Sons; Matricide; Murder; Parents**

Patrons, Art. *See* **Arts Patrons**

Peary, Robert. Peary, Marie. *See also* **Adventurers**

Peddlers and Peddling. Holmes, Frank Lincoln Duane. *See also* **Businesspersons; Gypsies; Hoboes**

Pedophilia. *See* **Abuse (Sexual); Family Violence; Incest**

Pentecostalism. Barnes, Kim. *See also* **Religious Persons**

Persian Gulf War (1991). Swofford, Anthony. *See also* **Military Life; War**

Persian Gulf War (2003). Lynch, Jessica. *See also* **Military Life; War**

Petroleum Industries. Hill, Margaret Hunt. *See also* **Oil Fields**

Pharmacists. *See* **Drug Stores and Pharmacists**

Philanthropists. Astor, Brooke; Michel, Ernest W. *See also* **Arts Patrons; Wealth**

Phillips-Exeter Academy. Lamont, Thomas. *See also* **College Life; Education; High School Life; Teachers**

Philologists. Armour, Richard; MacNeil, Robert; Renan, Ernest. *See also* **Books and Reading; Lexicographers; Linguists**

Philosophers. Boll, Heinrich; Eliade, Mircea; Koestler, Arthur; Kropotkin, Peter; Mill, John Stuart (2); Russell, (Sir) Bertrand; Santayana, George; Sartre, Jean-Paul; Tagore, (Sir) Rabindranath (2); Tolstoy, (Count) Leo; Wollheim, Richard. *See also* **Ayer, A. J.; Historians (Cultural); Intellectual Life; Pacifists; Reformers; Religious Persons; Russell, (Sir) Bertrand; Spiritual Life**

Photographers. Beaton, Cecil; Blue, Carroll Parrott; Buyukmihci, Hope Sawyer; Chambers, Veronica; Dell, Diana J.; Gilbreth, Frank B., Jr.; Jorgensen, Christine; Masters, Hilary; Min, Anchee; Morris, Wright; Murray, Albert; Sartor, Margaret; Scully, Julia; Sowell, Thomas; Topp, Mildred (2); Villiard, Paul; Ward, Andrew; Wechsberg, Joseph (2)

Radio Journalists. Adler, Margot; Couturie, Sylvia; Hoard, G. Richard; Kern, Janet; Lyden, Jacki; Njeri, Itabari; Simon, Scott; Thomas, Lowell; Wicks, Ben; Zimmer, Jill

Radio Producers. Jordan, Teresa. *See also* **Broadcast Journalists; Foreign Correspondents; Journalists; Talk Show Hosts**

Railroad Travel. Hofvendahl, Russ; London, Jack; Love, Edmund G.; Porter, Barton. *See also* **Hitchhiking; Hoboes; Road Trips; Travel Writers**

Rain Forests. Apple, Arnold; Sari, Riska Orpa. *See also* **Forests**

Ranch Life. Baker, Pearl Biddlecome; Beasley, Gertrude; Blunt, Judy; Church, John L.; Coe, Wilbur; Collins, Hubert; Cook, Harold; De Blasis, Celeste; Doig, Ivan (2); Dobie, J(ames) Frank; Farris, Frances Bramlette; Fergusson, Harvey; Gilbert, Fabiola Cabeza de Baca; Goodwyn, Frank; Greene, A(lvin) C(arl); Haaglund, Lois; Hall, Monty; Hammock, Robert; Howard, Dorothy Gray; Humphrey, William; Hunt, Rockwell; Huntley, Chet; Jackson, Ralph Semmes; Jordan, Teresa; Keys, Willis; Kittredge, William; Lewis, William J.; Lewis, Willie J.; MacConnell, C(harles) E(dward); Matthews, Sallie; Moody, Ralph (3); Morehead, Don, et al.; Myrdal, Jan; Nichols, Dave; O'Connor, Sandra Day; Olson, Ted; Patterson, Paul; Payne, Stephen; Rather, Dan; Siringo, Charles A(ngelo); Smith, Sarah Bixby; Spragg, Mark; Von Tempski, Armine; Winniford, Lee. *See also* **Country Life; Farm Life; Frontier and Pioneer Life; Homes and Haunts; Hunters; Mountain Life; Oil Fields; Rodeo Life**

Rangers. Bennett, Edwin. *See also* **Mountain Life; Outdoor Recreation**

Rape. Zailckas, Koran. *See also* **Abuse (Sexual); Incest**

Reagan, Ronald. Reagan, Maureen. *See also* **Presidents, U.S.**

Recreation. *See* **Exercise Gurus; Natural History; Outdoor Recreation; Sports**

Reformatories. Shaw, Clifford Robe. *See also* **Child Institutional Care; Crime**

Reformers. Antin, Mary (2); Baez, Joan; Bamford, Samuel; Blackwell, Alice; Bonner, Elena; Delaney, Sarah; Douglass, Frederick (4); Farnham, Eliza; Ishimoto, Baroness Shidzue; Jordan, June; Mowat, Farley (3); Mumford, Lewis; Myrdal, Jan (3); Neill, A(lexander) S(utherland); Noble, Christina; Ratushinskaya, Irina; Ross, Marie; Russell, (Sir) Bertrand; Salbi, Zainab; Sinclair,

Upton; Snow, Wilbert; Souljah, Sister; Steffens, (Joseph) Lincoln; Tagore, (Sir) Rabindranath (2); Webb, Beatrice; Wiesel, Elie. *See also* **Abolitionists; Activists; Anarchists; Anti-Communist Movements; Civil Rights Workers; Communists; Feminists; Hale, Edward Everett; Humanitarians; Intellectual Life; Labor Leaders and Unions; Pacifists; Philosophers; Politicians; Racism; Revolutionaries; Socialists; Strikes and Lockouts; Teachers; Tiananmen Square Incident**

Refugees. Abish, Walter; Alvarez, Julia; Aman; Asgedom, Mawi; Blend, Martha; Bok, Francis; Brombert, Victor; Czerniawski, Adam; Denes, Magda; Eire, Carlos; Fernandez Barrios, Flor; Figes, Eva; Fox, Anne L.; Friesel, Evyatar; Gissing, Vera; Hakakian, Roya; Hayslip, Le Ly; Heppner, Ernest G.; Hilton, Ella E. Schneider; Him, Chanrithy; Huynh, Quang Nhuong; Krutein, Eva; Latifi, Afschineh; May, Someth; Salbi, Zainab; Samuel, Wolfgang W. E.; Tobias, Sigmund; Van der Heidl, Dirk; Walter, Elizabeth Barbara; Wasilewska, Eugenia; Weinstein, Frida Scheps; Wermuth, Henry; Wojciechowska, Maia; Wolf, Hannie; Zuker-Bujanowska, Liliana. *See also* **Boat People; Holocaust Victims; Immigrants; Jews**

Religious Leaders. Ten Boom, Corrie

Religious Persons. *See* **Baptists; Black Muslims; Buddhists; Camps (Revivalist); Catholics; Christian Converts; Christian Scientists; Clergy; Cults; Dutch Reformed Church; Episcopalians; Fundamentalism (Christian); Historians (Religious); Jehovah's Witnesses; Lamas; Lewis, C(live) S(taples); Mennonites; Methodists; Missionaries; Mormons; Muslims; Nuns; Pentecostalism; Philosophers; Presbyterians; Quakers; Seminaries; Shakers; Spiritual Life; Televangelism; Theologians; Theological Writers; True Believers; Unitarians**

Rescue Workers. *See* **Firefighters**

Resorts. Grossinger, Tania; Harriman, Margaret; Kean, Robert Winthrop; Lewis, Stephen; Vance, Joel M.; Wollheim, Richard. *See also* **Bars; Catskill Mountains; Entertainment Industry; Homes and Haunts; Hotel Receptionists; Island Life; Playboy Mansion; Seaside Resorts**

Restaurateurs. Bemelmans, Ludwig; Lang, George. *See also* **Cookery; Food Writers; Waitresses**

Kimbrough, Emily (2); Kurosawa, Akira; Leonard, Hugh (2); Longstreet, Stephen; Loos, Anita; Mamet, David; Montagu, Ivor; Mortimer, John; O'Brien, Edna; Pagnol, Marcel; Paul, Elliot (4); Rainer, Yvonne; Richler, Mordecai; Salter, James; Salzman, Mark; Schary, Dore; Schickel, Richard; Semprun, Jorge; Spewack, Bella; Spragg, Mark; Surmelian, Leon; Van Druten, John; Vaughan, Richard; Von Rezzori, Gregor; Wakefield, Dan; West, Jessamyn; Wynn, Ned. *See also* **Dramatists; Motion Picture Producers and Directors**

Sculptors. Enters, Angna; Pinkwater, Daniel; Trevor (Cox), William. *See also* **Artists; French, Daniel Chester**

Seafaring Life. Cogill, Burgess; Dana Jr., Richard Henry; Doane, Benjamin; Masefield, John (4); Morison, Samuel Eliot; Rawson, Kennett; Tyng, Charles; Watkins, Bill. *See also* **Boats; Homes and Haunts; Island Life; Sailors; Voyages; Whaling**

Seaside Resorts. Mahoney, Rosemary; Wallace, Mary. *See also* **Resorts; Summer**

Secretaries. Undset, Sigrid

Security Specialists. Nuwere, Ejovi

Self-Cultured/Self-Educated. *See* **Intellectual Life**

Self-Mutilation. Christman, Jill; Green, Melissa; Kettlewell, Caroline. *See also* **Abuse (Physical); Anorexia Nervosa/Bulimia; Suicide and Suicide Victims**

Seminaries. Cornwell, John. *See also* **Spiritual Life**

Servants. Tucker, Margaret. *See also* **Wealth**

Sexton, Anne. Sexton, Linda. *See also* **Poets**

Sexuality. Abbott, Shirley; Bechdel, Alison; Feig, Paul; Howey, Noelle; Jennings, Kevin; Mairs, Nancy; McMullen, Richie; Peck, Scott; Picano, Felice; Rhodes, Richard; Ryan, Michael; Scholinski, Daphne; Sears, James T.; Shyer, Marlene and Christopher; Simpson, Jeffrey; Sterry, David Henry. *See also* **Dominatrixes; Gays; Lesbians; Prostitution; Strippers; Transsexuals; Transvestites**

Sexual Scandals. Bakker, Jay; Kingsland, Rosemary. *See also* **Crime**

Shakers. Sprigg, June. *See also* **Religious Persons; Spiritual Life**

Shakespeare, William. Smith, Bob; Wright, Louis. *See also* **Dramatists; Theatrical Producers and Directors**

Shanghai American School. Espey, John. *See also* **Education; High School Life**

Sheep. Smith, Sarah Bixby

Shepherds. Cameron, Donald Angus; Conway, Jill Ker; Harbinson, Robert; Irigaray, Louis; Ledda, Gavino. *See also* **Country Life; Natural History**

Ships. *See* **Boats; Riverboats; Seafaring Life**

Short Story Writers. Abrahams, Peter; Amis, Martin; Anderson, Sherwood (2); Angell, Roger; Armstrong, Martin Donisthorpe; Auchincloss, Louis; Barea, Arturo; Baring, Maurice; Baring-Gould, Sabine; Bates, H(erbert) E(rnest); Benson, E(dward) F(rederic); Bingham, Madeleine; Blackwood, Algernon; Boll, Heinrich; Bottome, Phyllis; Buechner, Frederick; Butts, Mary; Calisher, Hortense (2); Cameron, Donald Angus; Clarke, Austin (2); Cloete, Stuart; Colette; Cox, Wally; Dahl, Roald; Davis, Rebecca Harding; Dawson, Fielding; Djilas, Milovan; Doolittle, Hilda; Faulkner, William; Ferber, Edna; Forester, C(ecil) S(cott); Gide, Andre; Green, Henry; Hale, Greene, Graham; Hale, Edward Everett; Hall, Donald; Harbinson, Robert; Hawthorne, Julian; Higgins, George V.; Hitchman, Janet; Hong Ying; Hoyt, Murray; Humphrey, William; Hurst, Fannie; Husayn, Taha (2); Isherwood, Christopher; James, Henry (2); James, M(ontague) R(hodes); Kantor, MacKinlay; Kataev, Valentin; Kipling, Rudyard; Lively, Penelope; Lodi, Edward; London, Jack; Loti, Pierre (2); Lowndes, Bessie Belloc; MacDonagh, Tom; Machen, Arthur; Manea, Norman; Márquez, Gabriel García; Marshall, Alan; Martineau, Harriet; Masefield, John (4); Mason, Bobbie Ann; Maurois, André; McCarthy, Mary (2); McGahern, John; Morris, Edita; Morris, Wright; Mortimer, John; Moskowitz, Faye (2); Mottram, R(alph) H(ale); Mphahlele, Ezekiel; Nabokov, Vladimir; Narayan, R(asipuram) K(rishnaswami); Nathan, Daniel; Neihardt, John; Nesbit, Edith; Nexo, Martin Andersen; O'Brien, Edna; O'Connor, Frank; Olmstead, Robert; O'Meara, Walter; Paustovsky (2), Konstantin; Payne, Stephen; Perera, Victor; Plomer, William; Pohl, Frederik; Porter, Hal; Price, Reynolds; Pritchett, (Sir) V(ictor) S(awdon); Quiller-Couch, (Sir) Arthur; Ramakrishnan, Prema; Rhys, Jean; Rowse, A(lfred) L(eslie) (2); Roy, Gabrielle; Salter, James; Saroyan, William (2); Schnitzler, Arthur; Sedaris, David (2); Segal, Lore; Selzer, Richard; Singer, Isaac Bashevis (3); Singer, I(srael) J(oseph); Sitwell, (Sir) Osbert (2); Spewack, Bella; St. Johns, Adela Rogers; Stuart, Jesse (2);

Wilson, Edmund. Wilson, Rosalind Baker. *See also* **Writers**

Working Class Whites. Bailey, Paul; Bragg, Rick; Childers, Mary; Clemens, Paul; Dittersen, Tove; Gilmore, Mikal; Hunter, David; Davis, Jennings, Kevin; Lennard; MacDonald, Michael Patrick (2); Moehringer, J. R.; Phillips, Mark; Tea, Michelle; Trussoni, Danielle. *See also* **Slums**

Worldwide Travel. Anderson, George K(umler); Chaplin, (Sir) Charlie; Wilsey, Jean. *See also* **Road Trips; Voyages**

Wrestling. Lewin, Ted

Writers. *See* **Advertising Copywriters; Architectural Writers; Beat Generation; Berenson, Bernard; Biographers; Bloomsbury Group; Books and Reading; Business Writers; Children's Authors; College Teachers; Comedians; Conrad, Joseph; Critics (Film); Critics (Literary); Critics (Music); Diaries and Journals; Dramatists; Editors; Education; Essayists; Folklorists; Food Writers; Ginsberg, Allen; Historians; Historians (Cultural); Humorists; Intellectual Life; Irving, Washington; Journalists; Kipling, Rudyard; Lecturers; Lee, Harper; Letters; Lewis, C(live) S(taples); Lexicographers; Librarians; Librettists; Linguists; Novelists; Philologists; Poets; Publishers; Radio Journalists; Salinger, J. D.; Screenwriters; Sexton, Anne; Shakespeare, William; Short Story Writers; Sportswriters; Storytellers; Strachey, Lytton; Technical Writers; Theological Writers; Translators; Travel Writers; Twain, Mark; Wilson, Edmund**

WWI. Adamic, Louis; Bemelmans, Ludwig; Birmingham, Frederic; Brittain, Vera; Cloete, Stuart; Cropton, John; Ettinger, Albert and A. Churchill; Graves, Robert; Gray, James H(enry); Helias, Pierre-Jakez; Mackin, Eltin; Massey, Raymond; Mottram, R(alph) H(ale); Nelson, Ozzie; Raymond, Ernest; Seaton, Grace Mary; Sperber, Manes (2); Triplet, William S.; Waugh, Alec. *See also* **Gallipoli Campaign; Growing Up Between WWI and WWII; Military Life**

WWII. Abish, Walter; Accomando, Claire Hsu; Agee, Joel; Allan, Sheila; Arnett, Marvin V.; Bailey, Anthony; Bailey, Paul; Bassett, John T.; Bernhard, Thomas; Bidermann, Gottlob Herbert; Bonin, Adelyn I.; Brombert, Victor; Buchwald, Art; Carlisle, Olga; Charyn, Jerome; Church, John L.; Colijn, Helen; Cornwell, John; Couturie, Sylvia; Czerniawski, Adam; David, Janina

(2); de Gaulle-Anthonioz, Genevieve; Foreman, Michael; Frank, Anne; Fussell, Paul; Heppner, Ernest G.; Higa, Tomika; Hillen, Ernest (2); Hillerman, Tony; Hilton, Ella E. Schneider; Hokett, Norene; Horne, Alistair; Houston, Jeanne Wakatsuki and James D.; Hunt, Irmgard; Hynes, Samuel Lynn; Idrac, Armand; Kahn, Sy; Kalellis, Peter; Kelly, Clara Olink; Kent, Evelyn Julia; Kernan, Alvin; Kingsland, Rosemary; Koger, Fred; Kotlowitz, Robert; Krutein, Eva; Kwan, Michael David; Lambert, Derek; Lauer, Betty; Levendel, Isaac; Liebster, Simone Arnold; Lince, George; Lively, Penelope; Mallonee, Richard C(arvel); Manea, Norman; Markovna, Nina; Mathias, Frank F(urlong); Miller, R(obert) H(enry); Morgan, Elizabeth; Opdyke, Irene; Pasquarello, Tony; Patent, Gregory; Perel, Shlomo; Peters, Robert; Sacks, Oliver; Schickel, Richard; Schloss, Eva; Schroeder, Walter; Schumann, Willy; Scully, Julia; Skriabina, Elana; Standifer, Leon C.; Surayya, Kamala; Taylor, Sheila Ortiz and Sandra O.; Tobias, Sigmund; Trahan, Elizabeth; Uchida, Yoshiko (2); Van Den Berghe, Pierre; Van der Heidl, Dirk; Varney, Joyce; Von der Grun, Max; Von Staden, Wendegard; Walter, Elizabeth Barbara; Wasilewska, Eugenia; West, Paul; Wheal, Donald James; Wicks, Ben; Winter, Miriam; Wojciechowska, Maia; Wolf, Hannie; Zamoyska-Panek. *See also* **Atomic Bomb Victims; Camps (Internment); Fighter Pilots; Growing Up Between WWI and WWII; Hitler Youth Movement; Holocaust Survivors; Marines, U.S.; Military Life; Nazis and Neo-Nazis; Russian Purges (1934–1938); Sino-Japanese Conflict**

Wynn, Ed. Wynn, Ned. *See also* **Comedians**

Wynn, Keenan. Wynn, Ned. *See also* **Motion Picture Actors and Actresses**

Yale University. Brudnoy, David; Canby, Henry Seidel; Jordan, Teresa; Massey, Raymond; Mellon, Paul; Moehringer, J. R.; Nuland, Sherwin B.; Tobias, Andrew. *See also* **College Life; Education**

Young, Brigham. Spencer, Clarissa. *See also* **Religious Persons; Spiritual Life**

Young, Loretta. Lewis, Judy. *See also* **Motion Picture Actors and Actresses**

Ziegfeld, Florenz. Ziegfeld, Patricia. *See also* **Burke, Billie; Entertainers**

Zoologists. Carrighar, Sally; Montagu, Ivor; Wilder, Hawthorne. *See also* **Natural History**

Settings Index

This index covers the predominant settings of the memoirs in the main body of this book. Included here are some 85 nations, past and present, as well as all 50 U.S. states and Washington, DC. Also represented here are such locales as "Puerto Rico," "Kalahari Desert," and "Ottoman Empire." The preponderance of authors found here fall under entries associated with England and the U.S.

Because such a large number of memoirs are set in New York City, that city has its own entry. (Also, it is to be confessed that a disproportionately large number of entries fall under "Massachusetts" because in the course of compiling and researching potential entries, the author examined hundreds of autobiographies found on the shelves of bookstores in his home state, the Bay State.)

To find the titles of memoirs by these authors, refer to the author's name in the Author/Title Index, where the page numbers have been included. (In this index only primary authors' names are given for collaborative memoirs.)

For additional guidance in identifying memoirs by setting, consult Chapters 1 through 5, which are broken into sections by settings. Some institutions and other specific locales (e.g., "Harvard University," "Auschwitz") and some prominent natural features of the world (e.g., "Appalachian Mountains," "Mississippi River") are included in the Subject Index and the index section of Appendix A rather than here. Those indexes also include such terms as "Island Life," "Mountain Life," and "City Life."

For entries appearing under "United States," either the setting of the memoir covers an indeterminate number of states (such as memoirs about flying or hitchhiking), or it is unclear in which state(s) a memoir was principally set. Similarly, for entries appearing under "California," either the memoir's setting shifts about in that state, or it is unclear whether the memoir is mainly set in northern, central, or southern California.

Most of the entries in this index are names of nations; occasionally they are the names of smaller areas, such as regions—"United States (Midwest)," "California (North)"—or cities (e.g., "New York City," "Washington, DC") . Terms in parentheses that do not designate a compass point, such as "(North)" or other direction (e.g., "Midwest") are more modern place-name equivalents of the term they accompany, for example, "Northwest Territory (i.e., Ohio)."

In some instances, it is probable but not certain that a memoirist visited or resided in a given setting; in these cases that memoirist's bibliographical entry has a "(?)" next to the setting(s) in question.

For clarity, place-names have not been abbreviated in this index, although they are abbreviated in the bibliographical entries.

Horne, Alistair; Hughes, Mary Vivian; Hulton, Edward; Huxley, Elspeth; Irvine, Lucy; Irvine, Lyn; Isherwood, Christopher; Jackson, Annabel; James, M(ontague) R(hodes); Johnston, Jill; Jones, L(awrence) E(velyn); Kavanagh, P(atrick) J(oseph); Kehoe, Louise; Kelly, Michael; Kemble, Fanny; Kendon, Frank; Kennedy, Richard; Keppel, Sonia; Kimberley, Ken; Kingdon, Frank; Kingsland, Rosemary; Kipling, Rudyard; Kirkup, James; Kirstein, Lincoln; Knox, Cleone; Lambert, Derek; Lancaster, (Sir) Osbert; Layton, Deborah; Lee, Laurie; Lehmann, (Rudolph) John (Frederick); Lessing, Doris; Lewis, C(live) S(taples); Lewis, Edith Nicholl; Loelia, Duchess of Westminster; Lubbock, Percy; Lubbock, (Lady) Sybil; Lucie-Smith, Edward; Lutyens, Emily; Lutyens, Mary; MacCarthy, Mary; MacDonagh, Tom; Machen, Arthur; MacKenzie, Compton; Maclaren-Ross, Julian; Markham, Captain F.; Marshall, Audrey; Martineau, Harriet; Masefield, John; Massey, Raymond; May, James Lewis; McCowen, Alec; McInnes, Graham; McMullen, Richie; Meyerstein, Edward Harry William; Mill, John Stuart; Mills, Heather; Milne, A(lan) A(lexander); Milne, Christopher; Miss Read; Mitford, Jessica; Montagu, Ivor; Mortimer, John; Mortimer, Penelope; Mottram, R(alph) H(ale); Muggeridge, Malcolm; Nabokov, Vladimir; Naughton, Bill; Nelson, Ozzie; Nesbit, Edith; Newbolt, (Sir) Henry; Nichols, Beverley; Nicholson, "Lord Chief Baron"; Noble, Christina; Oakes, Philip; O'Brien, George; O'Connor, Philip; Origo, Iris; Osborne, John; O'Toole, Peter; Palmer, Herbert E.; Partridge, Frances; Paul, C(harles) Kegan; Paul, Leslie Allen; Peabody, Marian Lawrence; Phillips, Margaret Mann; Plomer, William; Pollock, Alice Wykeham-Martin; Potter, Stephen; Powell, Anthony; Powell, (Lady) Violet; Priestley, J(oseph) B(oynton); Princess Alice, Duchess of Gloucester; Pritchett, (Sir) V(ictor) S(awdon); Quennell, (Sir) Peter; Quiller-Couch, (Sir) Arthur; Raine, Kathleen; Raphael, Frederic; Raverat, Gwen; Raymond, Ernest; Raynor, John; Read, (Sir) Herbert; Reid, Forrest; Rhys, Jean; Richards, Laura E.; Richardson, H(enry) H(andel); Richmond, (Sir) Arthur; Ritchie, Charles; Robbins, (Baron) Lionel Charles; Roberts, Cecil; Roberts, Robert; Rodaway, Angela; Roosevelt, Theodore; Rothenstein, (Sir) William; Rowse, A(lfred)

L(eslie); Rubinstein, Artur; Ruskin, John; Russell, (Sir) Bertrand; Sacks, Oliver; Sage, Lorna; Salusbury, Hilda Ann; Sassoon, Siegfried; Scannell, Dorothy; Seabrook, Jeremy; Segal, Lore; Setsuko, Princess Chichibu; Shaw, Charles; Shears, Sarah; Sheed, Wilfrid; Shepard, Ernest; Sibbald, Susan; Simpson, John; Sitwell, (Sir) Osbert; Sitwell, Sacheverell; Slaughter, Carolyn; Slovo, Gillian; Smith, Emma; Soskice, Juliet M.; Spufford, Francis; Sting; Strachey, Richard; Streatfeild, Noel; Sturt, George; Sutcliff, Rosemary; Sykes, John; Tait, Katharine; Tallents, (Sir) Stephen George; Thirkell, Angela; Thomas, (Philip) Edward; Thomas, Leslie (John); Thompson, Flora; Trelawny, Edward John; Treneer, Anne; Uttley, Alison; Van Druten, John; Victoria, Queen; Wagstaff, Patty; Wakefield, Tom; Warner, Sylvia Townsend; Warren C(larence) Henry; Watkins, Bill; Watkins, Paul; Waugh, Alec; Waugh, Auberon; Waugh, Evelyn; Webb, Beatrice; Wells, H(erbert) G(eorge); West, Paul; Wheal, Donald James; Whipple, Dorothy; Williamson, Henry; Wingfield, Sheila; Wollheim, Richard; Woolf, Leonard Sidney; Woolf, Virginia; York, Michael

Ethiopia. Asgedom, Mawi; Mezlekia, Nega
Europe. Armstrong, Hamilton Fish; Baring-Gould, Sabine; Berlioz, Hector; Brody, Leslie; Brombert, Victor; Brooks, Van Wyck; Cushman, Mary; Fermor, (Sir) Patrick Leigh; Green, Julian; Hare, Augustus John; James, Henry; Kelly, Michael; Kirstein, Lincoln; Lodge, Henry Cabot; Lowndes, Bessie Belloc; Milne, Christopher; Peary, Marie; Powell, (Lady) Violet; Schildkraut, Joseph; Skinner, Cornelia Otis; Szigeti, Joseph; Van de Water, Virginia Terhune; Watson, Hildegarde Lasell; Wharton, Edith; Windom, Jane Hutcheson; Wynne, Elizabeth

Fiji. Low, Lema
Finland. Pekkanen, Toivo
Florida. Abagnale, Frank W., Jr.; Anders, Gigi; Barber, Lylah; Bejel, Emilio; Brown, Rita Mae; Conroy, Frank; Dickey, Christopher; Duncan, Lois; Eire, Carlos; Evert, Chris; Fowler, Connie May; Grammer, Kelsey; Hamilton, (Muriel) Elizabeth; Hayes, Bob; Heller, Michael; Herrick, William; Holder, Charles; Kercheval, Jesse Lee; Lady Chablis; McCall, Nathan; Morgan, Elizabeth Oliver, Kitty; Pacheco, Ferdie; Rosen, Christine; Ryan, Michael; Smith, Lillian; Winfrey, Carey; Ziolkowski, Thad

Author/Title Index

Alphabetization is letter-by-letter, and punctuation and parentheses are ignored; for example, "Osborne, John" precedes "Osborn, Vera"; *"New England Boyhood and Other . . ."* precedes *"New England Boyhood* (Hitchcock)"; and *"Maudie"* precedes *"Maud* (Rittenhouse)."

When a title begins with an article ("A," "An," "The"), the article has been dropped. Articles within a title, however, have not been skipped when alphabetizing. Also in alphabetical sequence are names of authors in parentheses and bracketed expressions (such as "[series]"). Personal titles and forms of address—such as "Sir," "Mrs.," "Lady," "Jr.," "Sr.," "Dr.," "Rev.," "King," "Lord," "Baron," "Dame," "Count," and "Countess"—have been skipped in alphabetizing, unless such a title or form of address is customarily included as part of the person's name (e.g., "The Lady Chablis" and "Madame Judith").

Titles that begin with numbers precede the alphabetical sequence in this index. Each title entry is followed by the surname of its author in parentheses, to help reduce confusion between or among memoirs with similar or identical titles.

For a small percentage of titles, authorship was a collaborative effort between the subject and an amanuensis, often a descendant of the subject, who shaped, distilled, or otherwise completed the memoir by gathering, organizing, or transcribing some or all of the reminiscence, working from notes, partial drafts, oral history interviews, or miscellaneous recollected utterances of the subject. These are often colloquially known as "As Told To" memoirs. Such writings typically retain a first-person perspective. In these instances, annotations to author entries and "See" entries clarify the identities of amanuenses involved in such collaborations.

"See" entries are included for pseudonyms and other name variants, such as women authors' maiden and married names. Many title variants—as in the instances of reprints or American versus British editions—are cross-indexed here also. Titles in a given author's autobiographical series (whether 3 or more discrete volumes or 1 volume that includes 3 or more memoirs) have been cross-referenced to that author.

In the rare instance of 2 authors sharing both the same surname and given name, birth year and death year information has been included to distinguish between them.

Due to space limitations, names of collaborators, translators, editors, abridgers, and annotators rarely appear in this index. (One exception is editor Carol Bleser, who assembled a memoir consisting of letters that passed between two sisters. Similarly, Harriet Brown completed a memoir of her grandmother's life from the latter's dictated transcriptions. A third example is John Brown, the amanuensis who constructed Robert Blincoe's memoir from a series of oral interviews conducted over a 4-year period.)

Asterisks following an author's name indicate the number of memoirs he or she has authored or co-authored in English that focus significantly on his or her youth. Series are identified in this index even if the name of the series does not appear on the individual entries.

Mama's Girl (Chambers), 291
Mamet, David, 226
Man and Boy (Tallents), 256
Manchild in the Promised Land (Brown), 93
Mandel, Edmund, 252
Manea, Norman, 120
Mangan, Kathleen, 88
Mangione, Jerre (Geraldo), 150
Manley, Elizabeth, 241
Manley, Seon, 97
*Man Named Dave: A Story of Triumph and For-
    giveness* (Pelzer), 288
*Manners and Customs of Several Indian Tribes. See
    Memoirs of a Captivity Among the Indians
    of North America* (Hunter)
Mann, Golo, 151
Manning, Martha, 247
Mann, Klaus, 285
Man of Ashes (Isacovici), 110
Man of the Family (Moody), 172
*Man of the Plains: Recollections of Luther North:
    1856–1882* (North), 29
Mao's Last Dancer (Li Cunxin), 230
Maple, Maude, 61
Marbacka (Lagerlof), 175
Marble Foot: An Autobiography: 1905–1938
    (Quennell), 205
March, Ann. *See* Woolson, Constance
*March Past: Reminiscences of Elizabeth Randolph
    Preston Allan* (Allan), 114
*Margin Released: A Writer's Reminiscences and
    Reflections* (Priestley), 197
Maria Tallchief: America's Prima Ballerina
    (Tallchief), 232
Marie, Grand Duchess of Russia, 258
Marilyn and Me: Sisters, Rivals, Friends
    (Strasberg), 224
Marino, Carmine Vincent, 283
Markham, Captain F., 43
Markino, Yoshio, 214
*Mark It with a Stone: A Moving Account of a
    Young Boy's Struggle to Survive the Nazi
    Death Camps* (Horn), 110
Markovna, Nina, 120
*Mark Twain Made Me Do It & Other Plains Adven-
    tures* (Jones), 53
*Mark Twain's West: The Author's Memoirs About
    His Boyhood, Riverboats and Western Ad-
    ventures* (Twain), 235
Mar, M. Elaine, 99
Marokvia, Mirelle, 73
Marquart, Debra, 230
Márquez, Gabriel García. *See* García Márquez, Ga-
    briel
Marshall, Alan, 131

Marshall, Audrey, 222
Marsh, Ngaio, 181
Martin, Carolyn, 131
Martineau, Harriet, 138
Martin, Joseph Plumb, 116
Martin, Lee, 294
Marx, Adolph. *See* Marx, Harpo
Marx, Harpo, 235
Mary Emma & Company (Moody), 172
Mary (Mebane), 280
Masefield, John****, 191
Mason, Bobbie Ann, 294
Mason, Harry Morgan, 28
Massaquoi, Hans J., 120
Massey, Raymond, 223
Masson, Jeffrey Moussaieff, 147
Masters, Hilary, 166
Masters, John, 10
Matane, Paulias, 35
Mathers, Jerry, 223
Mathias, Frank F(urlong), 57
Matousek, Mark, 288
Mattera, Don, 162
Matthau, Carol, 258
Matthews, Sallie, 303
Maudie: An Oregon Trail Childhood (Maple), 61
Maud (Rittenhouse), 205
Mauldin, Bill**, 215, 216
Maurice, Edward Beauclerk, 10
Maurois, André, 138
Maverick's Progress: An Autobiography (Flexner),
    198
Mavor, Osborne Henry. *See* Bridie, James
Maxwell, Gavin, 14
Mayer, Edwin, 195
Mayer, Robert, 239
May, James Lewis, 209
May, Jim, 53
May, Lee, 154
Maynard, Fredelle, 66
Maynard, Isabelle, 145
Maynard, Joyce**, 154
Mayne, Isabella. *See* Rittenhouse, Isabella Maud
May, Someth, 82
M'Baye, Marietou. *See* Bugal, Ken
McBride, James, 103
McBride, Mary Margaret, 57
McCall, Bruce, 216
McCall, Nathan, 264
McCarthy, Mary**, 162
McCaskey, Townsend, 43
McCloskey, Eunice, 191
McClure, S(amuel) S(idney), 210
McCourt, Frank, 275
McCowen, Alec, 223

About the Author

JEFFREY E. LONG, former associate editor of and longtime reviewer for *American Reference Books Annual,* currently works at the Lamar Soutter Library, University of Massachusetts Medical School, Worcester, MA, and is co-editor of *SoutteReview*.